Corliss K. Slack
Nov 09

Crusades
Volume 8, 2009

Crusades

Edited by
Benjamin Z. Kedar, Jonathan S.C. Riley-Smith
and Jonathan Phillips with William J. Purkis

Editorial Board
Benjamin Z. Kedar (*Editor; Hebrew University, Jerusalem, Israel*)
Jonathan Riley-Smith (*Editor; University of Cambridge, U.K.*)
Jonathan Phillips (*Editor; Royal Holloway, University of London, U.K.*)
William J. Purkis (*Associate Editor; University of Birmingham, U.K.*)
Christoph T. Maier (*Reviews Editor; University of Zurich, Switzerland*)
Denys Pringle (*Archaeology Editor; University of Cardiff, U.K.*)
François-Olivier Touati (*Bulletin Editor; Université François-Rabelais de Tours, France*)
Michel Balard (*University of Paris I, France*)
James A. Brundage (*University of Kansas, U.S.A.*)
Robert Cook (*University of Virginia, U.S.A.*)
Jaroslav Folda (*University of North Carolina, U.S.A.*)
Robert B.C. Huygens (*University of Leiden, The Netherlands*)
David Jacoby (*Hebrew University, Jerusalem, Israel*)
Catherine Otten (*University of Strasbourg, France*)
Jean Richard (*Institut de France*)

Crusades is published annually for the Society for the Study of the Crusades and the Latin East by Ashgate. A statement of the aims of the Society and details of membership can be found following the Bulletin at the end of the volume.

Manuscripts should be sent to either of the Editors in accordance with the guidelines for submission of papers on p. 333.

Subscriptions: Crusades (ISSN 1476–5276) is published annually.

Subscriptions are available on an annual basis and are £65 for institutions and non-members, and £25 for members of the Society. Prices include postage by surface mail. Enquiries concerning members' subscriptions should be addressed to the Treasurer, Professor James D. Ryan (see p. 264). All orders and enquiries should be addressed to: Subscription Department, Ashgate Publishing Ltd, Wey Court East, Union Road, Farnham, Surrey, GU9 7PT, U.K.; tel.: +44 (0)1252 331600; fax: +44 (0)1252 736736; email: journals@ashgatepublishing.com

Requests for Permissions and Copying: requests should be addressed to the Publishers: Permissions Department, Ashgate Publishing Ltd, Wey Court East, Union Road, Farnham, Surrey, GU9 7PT, U.K.; tel.: +44 (0)1252 331600; fax: +44 (0)1252 736736; email: journals@ashgatepublishing.com. The journal is also registered in the U.S.A. with the Copyright Clearance Center, 222 Rosewood Drive, Danvers MA 01923, U.S.A.; tel.: +1 (978) 750 8400; fax: +1 (978) 750 4470; email: rreader@copyright.com and in the U.K. with the Copyright Licensing Agency, 90 Tottenham Court Road, London, W1P 9HE; tel.: +44 (0)207 436 5931; fax: +44 (0)207 631 5500.

Crusades

Volume 8, 2009

Published by ASHGATE *for the
Society for the Study of the Crusades
and the Latin East*

© 2009 by the Society for the Study of the Crusades and the Latin East

All rights reserved. No part of this publication may be reproduced, stored in a retrieval system or transmitted in any form or by any means, electronic, mechanical, photocopying, recording or otherwise without the prior permission of the publisher.

Published by
Ashgate Publishing Limited
Wey Court East
Union Road
Farnham
Surrey GU9 7PT
England

Ashgate Publishing Company
Suite 420
101 Cherry Street
Burlington, VT 05401–4405
USA

Ashgate website: http://ashgate.com

ISBN: 978-0-7546-6709-4

ISSN 1476–5276

Typeset by N²productions

The paper used in this publication meets the minimum requirements of the American National Standard for Information Sciences – Permanence of Paper for Printed Library Materials, ANSI Z39.48-1984

Printed and bound in Great Britain by
MPG Books Group, UK

CONTENTS

Abbreviations ix

ARTICLES

The Frankish Castle of Blanche Garde and the Medieval and Modern Village
of Tell es-Safi in the Light of Recent Discoveries 1
Adrian J. Boas and Aren M. Maeir

Penthesilea on the Second Crusade: Is Eleanor of Aquitaine the Amazon
Queen of Niketas Choniates? 23
Michael Evans

"Like Purest Gold Resplendent": The Fiftieth Anniversary of the Liberation
of Jerusalem 31
Amnon Linder

The Debate on Twelfth-Century Frankish Feudalism: Additional Evidence
from William of Tyre's *Chronicon* 53
Jonathan Rubin

Anglo-Norman Intervention in the Conquest and Settlement of Tortosa,
1148–1180 63
Lucas Villegas-Aristizábal

Die Kreuzzugsmotivation Friedrichs II. 131
Volker Caumanns

A Neglected Quarrel over a House in Cyprus in 1299: The Nicosia
Franciscans vs. the Chapter of Nicosia Cathedral 173
Chris Schabel

Animal Bones from an Industrial Quarter at Malbork, Poland: Towards an
Ecology of a Castle Built in Prussia by the Teutonic Order 191
Mark Maltby, Aleks Pluskowski and Krish Seetah

REVIEWS

Elena Bellomo, *The Templar Order in North-West Italy (1143–c.1330)*
(Anne Gilmour-Bryson) 213

Jochen Burgtorf, *The Central Convent of Hospitallers and Templars: History, Organization, and Personnel* (Jonathan Riley-Smith)   216

Griechische Briefe und Urkunden aus dem Zypern der Kreuzfahrerzeit: Die Formularsammlung eines königlichen Sekretärs im Vaticanus Palatinus graecus 367, ed. and trans. Alexander Beihammer (Peter Edbury)   218

Byzantines and Crusaders in Non-Greek Sources, 1025–1204, ed. Mary Whitby (Susan B. Edgington)   219

Simonetta Cerrini, *La révolution des Templiers: Une histoire perdue du XIIe siècle* (Karl Borchardt)   221

Paul M. Cobb, *Usama ibn Munqidh: Warrior-Poet of the Age of the Crusades* (Niall Christie)   223

Gary Dickson, *The Children's Crusade: Medieval History, Modern Mythistory* (Christoph T. Maier)   225

George Akropolites, *The History*, trans. with an introduction and commentary by Ruth Macrides (Paul Stephenson)   227

Norman Housley, *Fighting for the Cross: Crusading to the Holy Land*; *Competing Voices from the Crusades*, ed. Andrew Holt and James Muldoon (Susan B. Edgington)   229

International Mobility in the Military Orders (Twelfth to Fifteenth Centuries): Travelling on Christ's Business, ed. Jochen Burgtorf and Helen Nicholson (Paul F. Crawford)   233

Conor Kostick, *The Social Structure of the First Crusade* (Jonathan Riley-Smith)   235

Christopher MacEvitt, *The Crusades and the Christian World of the East: Rough Tolerance* (Jonathan Phillips)   237

Hannes Möhring, *Saladin: The Sultan and His Times, 1138–1193*, trans. David S. Bachrach with an introduction by Paul M. Cobb (John V. Tolan)   239

Gli ordini ospedalieri tra centro e periferia. Giornata di studio Roma, Istituto Storico Germanico, 16 giugna 2005, ed. Anna Esposito and Andreas Rehberg (Karl Borchardt)   240

Jacques Paviot, *Les ducs de Bourgogne, la croisade et l'Orient (fin XIVe siècle – XVe siècle)* (Claudius Sieber-Lehmann)   242

Philippe de Mézières, *Une epistre lamentable et consolatoire addressée en 1397 à Philippe le Hardi, duc de Bourgogne, sur la défaite de Nicopolis (1396)*, ed. Philippe Contamine and Jacques Paviot, with Céline Van Hoorebeeck (Norman Housley)   244

Jonathan Phillips, *The Second Crusade: Extending the Frontiers of Christendom* (Deborah Gerish)   246

Religiones Militares. Contributi all storia degli Ordini religiosi-militari nel medioevo, ed. Anthony Luttrell and Francesco Tommasi (Jonathan Riley-Smith)   249

Jonathan Riley-Smith, *The Crusades, Christianity, and Islam* (James M. Powell)   250

Alexios G. C. Savvides, *Byzantino-Normannica: The Norman Capture of Italy and the First Two Norman Invasions in Byzantium (A.D. 1081–1085 and 1107–1108)* (Ralph-Johannes Lilie)   251

The Seventh Crusade, 1244–1254: Sources and Documents, ed. and trans. Peter Jackson (Michael Lower)   252

Alessandro Vanoli, *La Spagna delle tre culture. Ebrei, cristiani e musulmani tra storia e mito* (Nikolas Jaspert)   254

SHORT NOTICES

Diplomatics in the Eastern Mediterranean 1000–1500: Aspects of Cross-Cultural Communication, ed. Alexander D. Beihammer, Maria G. Parani and Christopher D. Schabel   256

The Fourth Crusade: Event, Aftermath, and Perceptions: Papers from the Sixth Conference of the Society for the Study of the Crusades and the Latin East, Istanbul, Turkey, 25–29 August 2004, ed. Thomas F. Madden   257

The Military Orders. Volume 3: History and Heritage, ed. Victor Mallia-Milanes   257

The Military Orders. Volume 4: On Land and by Sea, ed. Judi Upton-Ward   258

Jonathan Riley-Smith, *Crusaders and Settlers in the Latin East*   259

Bulletin No. 29 of the SSCLE   261

Guidelines for the Submission of Papers   333

Membership Information   335

Abbreviations

AA	Albert of Aachen, *Historia Ierosolimitana. History of the Journey to Jerusalem*, ed. and trans. Susan B. Edgington. Oxford, 2007
AOL	*Archives de l'Orient latin*
Autour	*Autour de la Première Croisade. Actes du colloque de la Society for the Study of the Crusades and the Latin East: Clermont-Ferrand, 22–25 juin 1995*, ed. Michel Balard. Paris, 1996
Cart Hosp	*Cartulaire général de l'ordre des Hospitaliers de Saint-Jean de Jérusalem, 1100–1310*, ed. Joseph Delaville Le Roulx. 4 vols. Paris, 1884–1906
Cart St Sép	*Le Cartulaire du chapitre du Saint-Sépulcre de Jérusalem*, ed. Geneviève Bresc-Bautier, Documents relatifs à l'histoire des croisades 15. Paris, 1984
Cart Tem	*Cartulaire général de l'ordre du Temple 1119?–1150. Recueil des chartes et des bulles relatives à l'ordre du Temple*, ed. Guigue A.M.J.A., (marquis) d'Albon. Paris, 1913
CCCM	Corpus Christianorum. Continuatio Mediaevalis
Chartes Josaphat	*Chartes de la Terre Sainte provenant de l'abbaye de Notre-Dame de Josaphat*, ed. Henri F. Delaborde, Bibliothèque des Écoles françaises d'Athènes et de Rome 19. Paris, 1880
Clermont	*From Clermont to Jerusalem: The Crusades and Crusader Societies 1095–1500. Selected Proceedings of the International Medieval Congress, University of Leeds, 10–13 July 1995*, ed. Alan V. Murray. International Medieval Research 3. Turnhout, 1998
Crusade Sources	*The Crusades and their Sources: Essays Presented to Bernard Hamilton*, ed. John France and William G. Zajac. Aldershot, 1998
CS	*Crusade and Settlement: Papers read at the First Conference of the Society for the Study of the Crusades and the Latin East and Presented to R.C. Smail*, ed. Peter W. Edbury. Cardiff, 1985
CSEL	Corpus Scriptorum Ecclesiasticorum Latinorum
EC, 1	*The Experience of Crusading 1: Western Approaches*, ed. Marcus G. Bull and Norman J. Housley. Cambridge, 2003
EC, 2	*The Experience of Crusading 2: Defining the Crusader Kingdom*, ed. Peter W. Edbury and Jonathan P. Phillips. Cambridge, 2003

FC	Fulcher of Chartres, *Historia Hierosolymitana (1095–1127)*, ed. Heinrich Hagenmeyer. Heidelberg, 1913
GF	*Gesta Francorum et aliorum Hierosolimitanorum*, ed. and trans. Rosalind M.T. Hill and Roger Mynors. London, 1962
GN	Guibert of Nogent, *Dei gesta per Francos*, ed. Robert B.C. Huygens CCCM 127A. Turnhout, 1996
Horns	*The Horns of Hattin*, ed. Benjamin Z. Kedar. Jerusalem and London, 1992
Kreuzfahrerstaaten	*Die Kreuzfahrerstaaten als multikulturelle Gesellschaft. Einwanderer und Minderheiten im 12. und 13. Jahrhundert*, ed. Hans Eberhard Mayer with Elisabeth Müller-Luckner. Schriften des Historischen Kollegs, Kolloquien 37. Munich, 1997
Mansi. *Concilia*	Giovanni D. Mansi, *Sacrorum conciliorum nova et amplissima collectio*
MGH	Monumenta Germaniae Historica
MO, 1	*The Military Orders: Fighting for the Faith and Caring for the Sick*, ed. Malcolm Barber. Aldershot, 1994
MO, 2	*The Military Orders, vol. 2: Welfare and Warfare*, ed. Helen Nicholson. Aldershot, 1998
MO, 3	*The Military Orders, vol. 3: History and Heritage*, ed. Victor Mallia-Milanes. Aldershot, 2008
Montjoie	*Montjoie: Studies in Crusade History in Honour of Hans Eberhard Mayer*, ed. Benjamin Z. Kedar, Jonathan Riley-Smith and Rudolf Hiestand. Aldershot, 1997
Outremer	*Outremer. Studies in the History of the Crusading Kingdom of Jerusalem Presented to Joshua Prawer*, ed. Benjamin Z. Kedar, Hans E. Mayer and Raymond C. Smail. Jerusalem, 1982
PG	Patrologia Graeca
PL	Patrologia Latina
PPTS	Palestine Pilgrims' Text Society Library
RHC	*Recueil des Historiens des Croisades*
Darm	*Documents arméniens*
Lois	*Les assises de Jérusalem*
Oc	*Historiens occidentaux*
Or	*Historiens orientaux*
RHGF	Recueil des Historiens des Gaules et de la France
RIS	Rerum Italicarum Scriptores
NS	New Series
ROL	*Revue de l'Orient latin*
RRH	Reinhold Röhricht, comp., *Regesta regni hierosolymitani*. Innsbruck, 1893

RRH Add	Reinhold Röhricht, comp., *Additamentum*. Innsbruck, 1904
RS	Rolls Series
Setton, *Crusades*	*A History of the Crusades*, general editor Kenneth M. Setton, 2nd edn., 6 vols. Madison, 1969–89
SRG	Scriptores Rerum Germanicarum
WT	William of Tyre, *Chronicon*, ed. Robert B.C. Huygens, with Hans E. Mayer and Gerhard Rösch, CCCM 63–63A. Turnhout, 1986

The Frankish Castle of Blanche Garde and the Medieval and Modern Village of Tell es-Safi in the Light of Recent Discoveries

Adrian J. Boas (University of Haifa)
and *Aren M. Maeir* (Bar Ilan University)

Introduction

Medieval castles were built to carry out a variety of defensive and administrative functions.[1] In many cases, when they had outlived their original purpose they continued to provide protection and supervision for towns and villages that grew up outside their walls and further afield. This was frequently true in the West, where the *faubourg* became a common feature of the medieval landscape. Likewise, in the Frankish East, quasi-urban and rural settlements developed outside the walls of castles like Bethgibelin (Beit Govrin/Bayt Jibrin) and Château Pèlerin ('Atlit), to name just two examples. Frankish castles also became kernels of post-Frankish settlements. Many a village in the Near East has at its centre the ruins of a Frankish castle, and this is the case at Tell es-Safi, located 30 kilometres east of the coastal city of Ascalon in the southern coastal plain of Israel (Grid ref. 135/123; see Fig. 1).

The Tell es-Safi/Gat archaeological project has been investigating this site since a surface survey was carried out in 1996, followed by full-scale excavations since 1997.[2] The original aim of the project had been to carry out a multi-season investigation of the site combining a study of the Bronze and Iron Age periods with one of the medieval and post-medieval remains, including the Frankish

---

[1] A recent important addition to the ongoing debate on the purpose, design and functions of castles is Ronnie Ellenblum's *Crusader Castles and Modern Histories* (Cambridge, 2007).

[2] The survey of 1996 was carried out by Adrian J. Boas (then of the Hebrew University of Jerusalem), Aren M. Maeir (Bar Ilan University), Martin Szusz (Department of Land of Israel Studies) and Tami Schneider (Claremont Graduate School). The first excavation season of 1997 was directed by Adrian J. Boas and Aren M. Maeir. Since 1998 (up until the present) the excavation has continued under the direction of Aren M. Maeir (during 1999–2000, co-directed by Carl Ehrlich of York University). Publications on these excavations include Aren M. Maeir and Adrian J. Boas, "Archaeology in Israel: Tell e-Safi," *American Journal of Archaeology* 102 (1998), pp. 785–86; Aren M. Maeir, "Canaanites and Philistines: Recent Excavations at Tell es-Safi/Gath, Israel (1996–2001)," in *The Proceedings of the 3rd International Conference on the Archaeology of the Ancient Near East, Paris, 2002*, ed. Pierre de-Miroschedji, Jean-Claude Margueron and J. P. Thalmann (Winona Lake, in Press); Aren M. Maeir and Carl Ehrlich, "Excavating Philistine Gath: Have We Found Goliath's Hometown?," *Biblical Archaeology Review* 27/6 (2001), pp. 22–31. For an aerial photograph of the Gath excavation, see Duby Tal, Moni Haramati and Shimon Gibson, *Flights into Biblical Archaeology* (Jerusalem-Herzlia, 2007), p. 45.

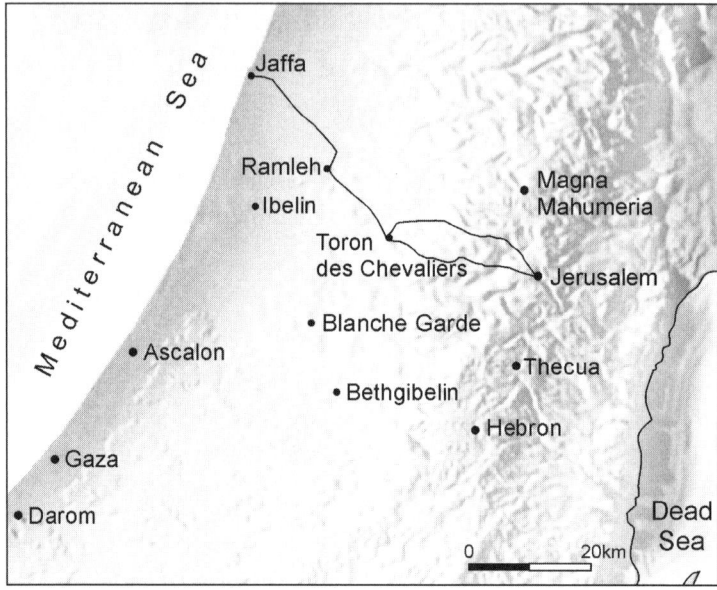

Fig. 1 Map of Blanche Garde and sites mentioned in the text.

castle, Blanche Garde (Fig. 2).[3] Whereas the first of our aims met with success in a preliminary season (1997) followed by additional seasons (1998–2001), the excavation of the medieval and post-medieval remains did not come to fruition due to the opposition of local villagers because the castle and other medieval structures lie within the area of the former village cemeteries.[4] In order to salvage something from this situation, we decided to re-examine the available archaeological and historical evidence. The following is a discussion of Blanche Garde Castle and the village from the medieval period to the present day.

Medieval and Modern History of the Site

In the first years following the establishment of the kingdom of Jerusalem in 1099, the Franks occupied all the coastal towns except Tyre, which held out until 1124,

---

[3] The ancient tell is now generally identified with the Iron Age city of Philistine Gath: see Anson F. Rainey, "The Identification of Philistine Gath. A Problem in Source Analysis for Historical Geography," *Eretz Israel* 12 (Jerusalem, 1975), pp. 63–76; William Schniedewind, "The Geopolitical History of Philistine Gath," *Bulletin of the American Schools of Oriental Research* 309 (1998), pp. 69–77; Maeir and Ehrlich, "Excavating Philistine Gath."

[4] Incidentally, the archaeologists Bliss and Macalister ran into exactly the same opposition in 1899 when they attempted to excavate an Iron Age city gate directly below the castle to the south. See Frederick J. Bliss and Robert A. S. Macalister, *Excavations in Palestine During the Years 1898–1900* (London, 1902), pp. 30, 36.

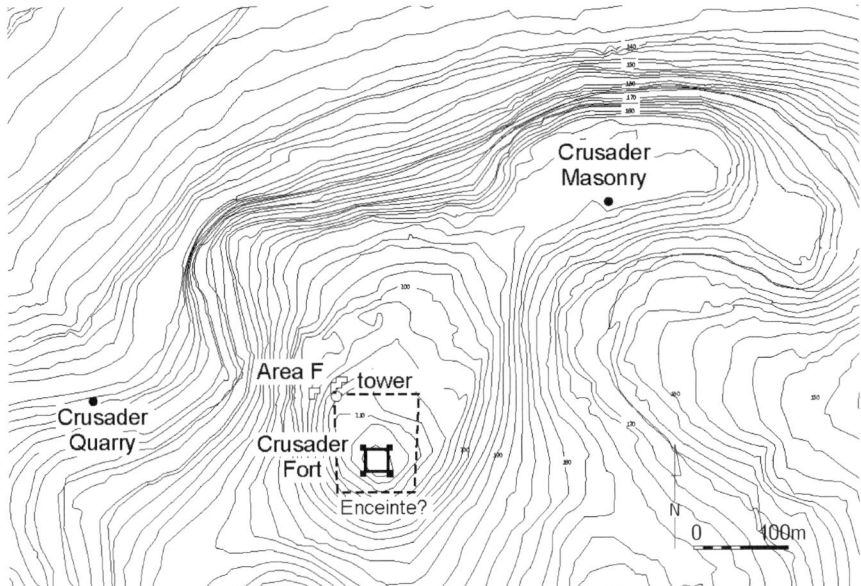

Fig 2   Plan of Tell es-Safi.

and Ascalon, which was not taken until 1153. For much of this period, Ascalon remained an outpost of Fatimid opposition to the Franks and served as a base from which raiding parties carried out sorties into the hinterland of the kingdom of Jerusalem. These raids were mostly aimed towards the region of Ramleh (1107) and the road to Jerusalem (1109) and on occasion (1109, 1113, 1124, and 1152) even reached the neighbourhood of the capital.[5] The Franks sought to end these attacks, but with little success. In the 1130s and 1140s a more serious attempt was made to halt these episodes by the construction of a group of fortified outposts around Ascalon (see Fig. 1). William of Tyre relates that these castles were constructed in order to contain and threaten the people of Ascalon: by increasing the number of

---

[5] In the attack near Ramleh 500 people were killed (AA, p. 727). In 1109, the road from Jaffa to Jerusalem was attacked (FC, pp. 514–18). In the same year a Fatimid sortie from Ascalon reached the capital (AA, pp. 646–47). In 1113, they attacked Jerusalem while the king was in the north (WT, p. 525). In 1115, raiders from Ascalon attacked Jaffa (WT, p. 531). In 1124, they reached Magna Mahumeria (al-Bira) north of Jerusalem (FC, pp. 731–32; WT, p. 595). In 1132, Arsuf was attacked (WT, p. 653) and in 1139, after the construction of the castle at Bethgibelin, a raid reached Thecua (Tekoʿa) located about 8 kilometres south of Bethlehem (WT, p. 681). By the 1140s, following the construction of the castles at Bethgibelin, Ibelin (Yavne), Blanche Garde (Tell es-Safi) and Toron des Chevaliers (Latrun), there seem to have been fewer raids, although both Bethgibelin and Ibelin were subject to attack from Ascalon around 1150 (see Usama Ibn-Munqidh, *The Book of Contemplation: Islam and the Crusades*, trans. Paul M. Cobb (London, 2008), p. 25); and the fear of attack from the Ascalonites was still felt by travellers on the Jerusalem–Hebron road. This was recorded in Ranieri of Pisa's biography written by his disciple Benincasa and discussed by Benjamin Z. Kedar, "A Second Incarnation in Frankish Jerusalem," in *EC, 2*, p. 83.

fortified places in the vicinity of the city the Franks could harass and terrorize the inhabitants of Ascalon.[6] In 1136, King Fulk built a castle at Beit Govrin, known as Bethgibelin. In 1141 he erected a castle at Yavne called Ibelin, erroneously identified by William of Tyre as the biblical city of Gath, and in 1142 he constructed the castle of Blanche Garde on Tell es-Safi. The latter was the best placed of the three to locate and oppose Muslim sorties. The castle was known by the Latin name *Alba Specula* or *Alba Custodia*.[7] It appears as *Alba Specula* on the fourteenth-century map of the Holy Land drawn by a Genoese mapmaker, Pietro Vesconte.[8] It is also called *Candida Custodia*,[9] but is most often referred to by its French name *Blanche Garde* (the White Fortress), which takes various forms including *Blanchegarda*[10] and *Blanchewarda*.[11] The name is clearly a reference to the white chalk cliffs of Tell es-Safi, which rise as a landmark above the plain east of Ascalon (Fig. 3). The Arabic name Tell es-Safi means "clear (pure) hill."

William of Tyre records that the site for the castle was chosen because, although it was low in comparison with the mountainous countryside to the east, it was high in contrast to more level land towards the coast and was conveniently near to the other strongholds built around Ascalon and overlooked the city itself. As a result it was effective in preventing raids carried out by the Ascalonites. He referred to Blanche Garde as being well fortified by nature and noted that it had four suitably high towers.

The castles around Ascalon appear to have been an effective curb on the raids into the Frankish hinterland. They also had an additional effect: their presence provided a sense of safety, encouraging people to leave the protection of the city walls and settle in the countryside. William of Tyre states that after the castle was

---

[6] WT, pp. 707–8. As Kedar notes, based on the biography of Ranieri of Pisa and William of Tyre's statements regarding Bethgibelin, Ronnie Ellenblum's view that these castles were built not to oppose Fatimid Ascalon but for some other purpose needs to be modified. See Ronnie Ellenblum, "Three Generations of Frankish Castle-Building in the Latin Kingdom of Jerusalem," in *Autour*, p. 538; Kedar, "A Second Incarnation," n. 25; WT, pp. 640, 660, 706–7. Ellenblum himself recently referred to the continuation of raids from Ascalon but comments that scholars tend to ignore similar Frankish raids on Muslims and that the threat of Muslim attack continued in spite of the construction of new castles. See Ellenblum, *Crusader Castles*, pp. 155–61. Steven Tibble sees the construction of Blanche Garde and the other castles in the region, together with the establishment of the southern lordships of Bethgibelin and Ibelin, the separation from the county of Jaffa, of the fief of Ramleh, and of the seigneurie of Mirabel, as part of the aftermath of the failed revolt by Hugh II of Jaffa against Fulk in 1134. See Steven Tibble, *Monarchy and Lordships in the Latin Kingdom of Jerusalem* (Oxford, 1989), pp. 50–55.

[7] *RRH*, no. 512, p. 135; *Itinerarium Peregrinorum et Gesta Regis Ricardi*, ed. William Stubbs, in *RS*, vol. 38.1 (London, 1864), pp. 299, 346; WT, p. 708; *AOL*, vol. 2B (Paris, 1884), p. 145, no. 28.

[8] Vesconte's map along with others was attached to the first edition of the work *Liber secretorum fidelium crucis super Terrae Sanctae recuperatione et conservatione* by the Venetian, Marino Sanudo, which was presented to the pope in 1321. On this see Evelyn Edson, "Reviving the Crusade: Sanudo's schemes and Vesconte's maps," in *Eastward Bound: Travel and Travellers*, ed. Rosamund Allen (Manchester, 2004), pp. 131–55.

[9] *Itinerarium*, pp. 344, 345, 366, 367.

[10] *RRH*, no. 331, p. 85.

[11] *Itinerarium*, p. 280.

Fig. 3   Photograph (ca. 1920s) of Arab village of Tell es-Safi facing south. Note Antillyah Well in right foreground (Israel Antiquities Authority, Mandatory Archives)

constructed many settlements grew up around it and the whole district became much more secure.[12]

It was not only security that these castles provided. Similar to the fortified and unfortified estate centres found throughout the Frankish territory they served as centres of rural administration, residences of local landlords or their representatives and places where taxes and tithes were collected and stored. The desire of Frankish burgesses to settle in the countryside is a phenomenon worthy of lengthy discussion elsewhere. It is worth noting, however, that William of Tyre saw the attraction, in the case of the settlement at Darum (Deir al-Balah, south of Gaza), as being related to the fact that it was easier for men of limited means to make a living in these settlements than in the towns.[13] It is also probable that, by becoming peasants, some of the Frankish burgesses were returning to a way of life that was familiar to them as former free inhabitants of rural *burgi* or *villes neuves* before they came to the East.

The evidence for settlements around the castle found in charters is limited. There are only clear references to two villages in the lordship of Blanche Garde; an unnamed village (*casal*) belonging to the Church of St. Mary of the Latins noted in a royal charter of 1158–9 and another *casal* called Danube mentioned in 1166.[14] The territory directly under Blanche Garde's authority may have been quite limited.

---

[12]   WT, p. 708.
[13]   WT, p. 937.
[14]   *RRH*, no. 331, p. 85; *RRH Add*, no. 422a, p. 25. On the map of Cedric N. Johns "Palestine of the Crusades" published in 1944/1946 (reprinted 1964) and on the map of the Crusader Kingdom of Jerusalem, published by Joshua Prawer and Meron Benvenisti in *Atlas of Israel* (Jerusalem and Amsterdam, 1970),

Bayer refers to a site named Khirbat Deir el-Butm possibly to be identified with Casale Bothme located two and a half kilometres east-south-east of Tell es-Safi which was not in the lordship of Blanche Garde but in that of Bethgibelin (formerly in the lordship of Hebron).[15]

Blanche Garde was joined to the county of Jaffa in 1151 when Amalric, future king and brother of Baldwin III, received Jaffa as an apanage.[16] Its custodian, Arnulf (*Arnulfus castellanus de Blanchagarda*), became one of the richest and most powerful barons of the realm. With the occupation of Ascalon by the Franks in 1153, the original function of Blanche Garde and the other castles built around the city was no longer relevant. From 1166 Blanche Garde was in an independent seigneurie held by the impoverished Walter of Beirut of the Brisbarre family who, because of heavy ransom payments, had been forced to cede to the king his more lucrative lordship of Beirut.[17] In the *Assises de Jerusalem* compiled by Jean d'Ibelin, which date to the mid-thirteenth century but reflect the situation in the twelfth century, Blanche Garde appears in a list of lesser fiefs having the right of coinage (although no coins minted there have yet been identified).[18] In 1187, after defeating the Franks at Hattin, Saladin took Ascalon and, in 1191, after suffering a crushing defeat at Arsuf, he destroyed Blanche Garde, together with the defences of Ascalon, Gaza, Jaffa and a number of other castles. In December 1191, on his way south from Ramleh, Richard Coeur de Lion was ambushed in the vicinity of Blanche Garde and barely escaped being taken prisoner by the Ayyubid army.[19] In the following April Richard captured and killed some Muslims between Blanche Garde and Gaza.[20] He was again briefly at Blanche Garde in June 1192 and in the same year signed a three-year truce which returned Ascalon and the surrounding fortresses to the Egyptians.[21]

IX/10, Danube (*Danuba*) is identified with the village of Idhnibba (grid ref. 1364/1322) located a few kilometres north-east of Blanche Garde.

[15] Gustav Bayer, "Die Kreuzfahrergebiete von Jerusalem und Hebron," *Zeitschrift der Deutschen Palästina-Vereins* 65 (1942), p. 183. Cedric N. Johns placed it on his map within the seigneurie of Blanche Garde but he does not indicate territory under control of Bethgibelin. Some additional properties in the territory of Blanche Garde are mentioned in Baldwin V's charter to St. Samuel: Mayer, "Sankt Samuel auf dem Freudenberge," *Quellen und Forschungen aus italienischen Archiven und Bibliotheken* 44 (1964), 35–71; reprinted in *Kreuzzüge und lateinischer Osten* (London, 1983), chapter 8. The small size of the lordship is commented on by Denys Pringle, in Alan V. Murray, ed., *The Crusades: An Encyclopedia*, I, p. 169. Pringle suggests that the lordship's income may have been supplemented by unrecorded income from the royal domain of Acre.

[16] A charter of 1158 records Blanche Garde as being held by Amalric who was still the count of Jaffa (*RRH*, no. 331, p. 85).

[17] See Tibble, *Monarchy and Lordships*, p. 62.

[18] John of Ibelin, *Le livre des Assises*, ed. Peter W. Edbury (Leiden, 2003), p. 604.

[19] *Itinerarium*, p. 299.

[20] Ibid., p. 346.

[21] Ibid., pp. 424–30; Bahāʾ al-Dīn Ibn Shaddād, *The Rare and Excellent History of Saladin or al-Nawādir al-Sulṭāniyya waʾl-Maḥāsin al-Yūsufiyya*, trans. Donald S. Richards (Aldershot, 2002), pp. 228–30.

Little is known of the castle in the thirteenth century. The Arab geographer Yaqut al-Hamawi (d. 1228), describes it simply as a fortress near Bayt Jibrin in the Ramleh district.[22] It is not specifically mentioned by Matthew Paris in his detailed account of the treaty between the Egyptian Sultan, as-Salih Najm ad-Din Ayyub, and Richard of Cornwall in 1241.[23] In 1244, Blanche Garde was recaptured by the Muslims and dismantled.

After the Crusader period, the earliest direct reference to a village on the tell itself is found in the last census taken in the sixteenth century where it is referred to as having a population of around 500.[24] It paid taxes on wheat, barley, fruit, sesame, goats, beehives and other produce.[25] In the mid-nineteenth century, according to Edward Robinson, the village lay near the middle of the tell, stretching down the slope.[26] The sheikh of the village, Muhammad Sellim, was of the Azazeh family, hereditary lords of Bayt Jibrin, who had been forced to take up residence on the tell after participating in the rebellion of 1834 against Ibrahim Pasha.[27] They are probably the same family now known as al-Azi, originally from Egypt, who served as tax collectors in the village under Turkish rule. By the twentieth century the village had spread from the centre of the tell down the northern and western slopes (see Fig. 3). This expansion had probably already occurred in the later part of the nineteenth century.[28] The village continued a slow increase in population well into the twentieth century. In the census of 1922 the population had hardly increased since the sixteenth century; it is given as 644.[29] The census of 1945 gives a figure of 1290.[30] The village survived another three years. In 1948 its population numbered 1,547 villagers.[31] The Israel Defence Forces captured the village in July of that year and the inhabitants were expelled.[32] After 1949 the al-Azi family resettled nearby

---

[22] Guy Le Strange, *Palestine under the Moslems* (Boston and New York, 1890), p. 544.

[23] For Matthew Paris's list of territories regained by the truce of 1241, see Matthew Paris, *Chronica Majora*, ed. Henry R. Luard, RS 57/4 (London, 1877), pp. 142–43.

[24] Wolf D. Hütteroth and Kamal Abdulfattah, *Historical Geography of Palestine, Transjordan and Southern Syria in the Late 16th Century*, Erlanger Geographische Arbeiten, Sonderband 5 (Erlangen, 1977), map – Settlements and Population 1005 H./1596 A.D.

[25] Ibid., p. 150.

[26] Edward Robinson (and Eli Smith), *Biblical Researches in Palestine, Mount Sinai and Arabia Petraea*, vol. 2 (London, 1841), p. 363.

[27] According to Robinson, the sheikh's uncle and brother were beheaded for their part in the rebellion (*Biblical Researches*, p. 364).

[28] Most of the remains from the ruined houses that cover the central part of the tell consist of rubble and mortar. There is very little cement and there are none of the iron beams that were used in building in the early twentieth century.

[29] John Bernard Barron, *Report and General Abstracts of the Census of 1922* (Jerusalem, 1922), p. 10.

[30] Government of Palestine, Office of Statistics, *Village Statistics, April 1945* (Jerusalem, 1945), p. 23.

[31] Issa Nakleh, ed., *Encyclopedia of the Palestine Problem* (New York, 1991), p. 363.

[32] See Benny Morris, *The Birth of the Palestinian Refugee Problem Revisited* (Cambridge, 2004), pp. 436–37, 443.

to the west of the ruined village and still graze their cattle and flocks on the tell and its vicinity.

Earlier Accounts and Archaeological Research

William of Tyre's description of the castle of Blanche Garde as *opidum cum turribus quattuor congrue altitudinis*[33] is that of a typical enclosure castle with a central courtyard and projecting corner towers, the form which is found in the Late Iron Age, as well as the Hellenistic, Roman, Byzantine and Umayyad periods, and which was adopted by the Franks in the twelfth century.[34] In the mid-nineteenth century when Edward Robinson described the ruins, he called them "merely the indistinct foundations apparently of a castle on the highest part, constructed of large hewn stones."[35] The plan drawn by Emmanuel G. Rey a few years later followed the description of William of Tyre with the addition of a keep in the centre of the courtyard (A), and outworks to the north (B) (Fig. 4).[36] In the century and a half since Rey drew his plan, the ruins have deteriorated even more. No trace of the outworks or the keep can be seen today, except perhaps for a small section of wall just below the southern side of the castle. There is no mention of either feature in 1874, when the British Survey of Western Palestine visited the site,[37] and they are described as having disappeared by 1899, when Frederick Bliss and Robert Macalister excavated at Tell es-Safi.[38] These structures were perhaps dismantled by the villagers for building stone, subsequent to Rey's visit (which took place between 1857 and 1864). The small size of the enclosed area within the castle makes unlikely the existence of an internal keep.[39] In any case, Rey's reconstruction of it is based on very fragmentary remains. On the other hand, the existence of outworks seems better founded and was confirmed by the excavations of Bliss and Macalister in 1899–1900 which revealed in an area to the north of the castle, and in line with Rey's outer enclosure, "ruins of a tower" built of both roughly dressed and marginally drafted ashlars and measuring approximately 6.5 × 7.5 metres. The

---

[33] WT, p. 708.

[34] This type is sometimes referred to by the Latin *quadriburgium* or simply *castrum*. Other Frankish examples include Giblet (at ancient Byblos, north of Beirut), Coliath, north of Tripoli, *Castellum Regis* (M'iliya) in the Western Galilee and Burj Bardawil, south of Nablus.

[35] Robinson, *Biblical Researches*, p. 363.

[36] Emmanuel G. Rey, *Etude sur les monuments de l'architecture militaire des croisés en Syrie*, Collection des documents inédits sur l'histoire de France, Série 1, Histoire politique (Paris, 1871), fig. 39. Note that Rey's map is oriented to the south.

[37] Claude R. Conder and Horatio H. Kitchener, *Survey of Western Palestine*, vol. 2 (London, 1882), p. 440.

[38] Bliss and Macalister, *Excavations in Palestine*, p. 37.

[39] Judging by Rey's plan, the keep would have measured about 4.5 × 6 metres, smaller even than the smallest keeps built by the Templars on the road between Jerusalem and the Jordan River: see Denys Pringle, "Templar Castles on the Road to the Jordan," in *MO, 1*, pp. 148–66. Kennedy refers to Rey's "A" as "possibly a cistern." See Hugh Kennedy, *Crusader Castles* (Cambridge, 1994), p. 32.

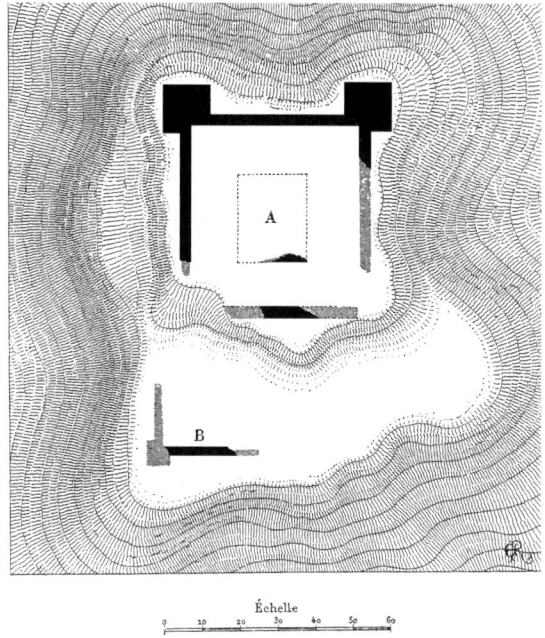

Fig. 4   Rey's plan of Blanche Garde Castle (Rey 1871, fig. 39)

tower had a gate about 3 metres wide.[40] If we add the sections of the outworks noted by Rey and excavated by Bliss and Macalister to our plan, together with the small section of a wall still visible below the castle to the south, the castle takes on a concentric form with the original four-towered castle (or *quadriburgium*) forming its inner core surrounded by the towered outworks, which perhaps contained within them additional structures.

Current Research

Subsequent to the preliminary 1996 season, an architectural survey of the exposed remains of the castle and its immediate environs was carried out in 1997.[41]

A: Remains of the Castle

The castle was situated on the highest part of Tell es-Safi on the southern spur 214 metres above sea level and 100 metres above Nahal Elah, a perennial stream

---

[40] Bliss and Macalister, *Excavations in Palestine*, p. 37.
[41] See note 2.

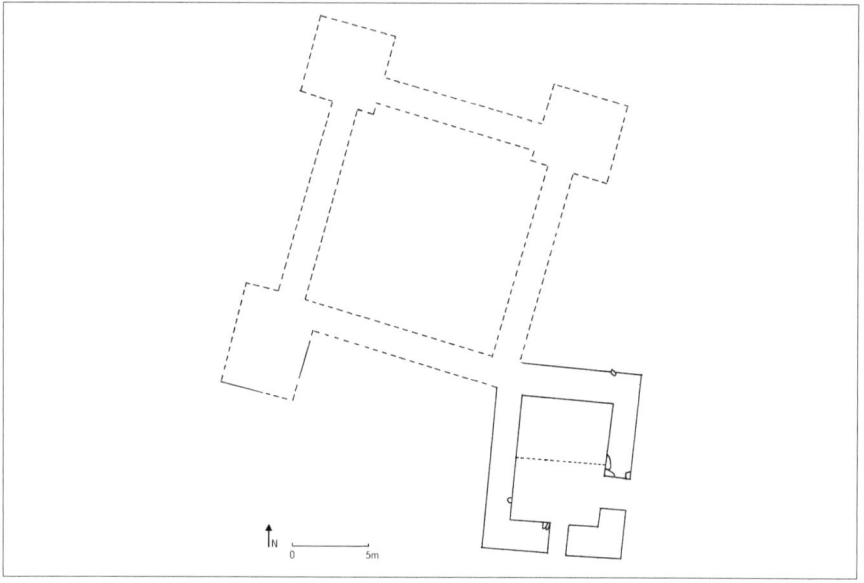

Fig. 5 Plan of Blanche Garde Castle (1996 survey)

to the north which is fed for much of the year by two springs. It overlooks a vast area stretching from Ramleh and Latrun in the north, the Hebron hills and Judean foothills in the east, the northern Negev in the south, and west across the plain to the coast from Ibelin (Yavne) or even Jaffa on a clear day, to Gaza.

Two of the four towers of the castle can still be traced (one of them largely rebuilt as a *maqam* – Muslim shrine – in the nineteenth century) and the hillocks formed by the remnants of the other two are easily discernible (Fig. 5).[42] The ruins consist of a courtyard structure measuring roughly 16 × 16 metres (as it is only vaguely traceable on the surface, the width of the walls as shown on our plan is an estimation). From the scanty surface evidence it would seem that the small, salient corner towers were each no more than 4 or 5 metres square. The south-west tower displays typical Frankish masonry. Of the outworks, only the vaguest remains of an outer wall can be seen on the surface to the south of the inner castle; nothing

---

[42] It is important to emphasize here that the plan we have prepared is based on very meagre surface remains. Archaeological work sometimes reveals that the plan of a building differs considerably from the theoretical reconstructions based on pre-excavation observations. See for example T. E. Lawrence's analysis of Chastel Pèlerin ('Atlit Castle) written prior to the excavations carried out in the 1930s – see: T. E. Lawrence, *Crusader Castles* (Oxford, 1936; reissued with an introduction by Denys Pringle, 1988), p. 71; and the plans of Belvoir Castle drawn by the Survey of Western Palestine (Conder and Kitchener, *Survey of Western Palestine*, p. 117) and those published by R. C. "Otto" Smail in *Crusading Warfare* (Cambridge, 1956), p. 249, compared to those drawn after the excavations carried out by Ben-Dov in 1963–68. See: Meir Ben-Dov, "Belvoir (Kokhav Ha-Yarden)," in *New Encyclopedia of Archaeological Excavations in the Holy Land*, ed. Ephraim Stern, vol. 1 (Jerusalem, 1999), p. 183.

Fig. 6 Frankish ashlars (south-west tower)

can be seen of Rey's inner keep or of the walls and tower that appear on his plan.[43] However, the ongoing excavations on the tell have recently exposed part of a tower with horn-work to the north-east of the castle (F on Fig. 2).

The stonework consists of marginally dressed ashlars and rubble and mortar fill (Fig. 6), although few of the stones display the typically Frankish diagonal tooling and there were no observable mason's marks.[44]

B: The Quarry

A quarried outcropping of hard limestone (*nari*) lying atop very soft chalk was discovered in the survey of 1997 about 300 metres south-west of the castle near the base of the tell (see Fig. 2). Within the area of the quarry there are at least four worked stones with marginal drafting similar to those found in the castle remains. These ashlars were prepared at the quarry, apparently for construction of the castle, but were never used, perhaps because they were partly damaged. The technique by which the rock was separated from the outcropping can clearly be seen. In order to separate a stone, "V"-shaped channels were cut around it down to the soft limestone layer. Once it was freed on all sides, the stone could easily be prised loose from the chalk layer beneath it (Fig. 7a and b).

---

[43] See Rey, *Etude*, fig. 39.
[44] On Frankish stonework see Adrian J. Boas, *Crusader Archaeology. The Material Culture of the Latin East* (London, 1999), pp. 219–20.

Fig. 7a and b   The quarry at Tell es-Safi showing worked stones left in situ (Photo: author)

At Vadum Jacob Castle (Metzad ʿAteret) north of the Sea of Galilee, where a similar but considerably larger quarry was found, the limestone strata overlie a layer of basalt. At Blanche Garde, as at Vadum Jacob, oxen were probably used to haul carts carrying the heavy ashlars up to the top of the hill. The drafted stones found in the quarry at Tell es-Safi are the same size as a section of stone that had not yet been freed: 80 × 40 × 40 cm. The distance and steep incline of the tell give some cause for speculation as to why the Franks chose to quarry rocks from so low on the hillside when a very large area higher up and nearer the castle was available. However, there are numerous signs of quarrying in the upper expanse of rock and it is possible that at some stage, after having worked the upper sections, the Franks moved down the hill in search of additional stones.[45]

C: The Village of Tell es-Safi

As mentioned above, according to William of Tyre, the security afforded by the building of the castle enabled villagers to settle the surrounding area. The surface survey carried out in 1996 over the entire area of the tell did not produce any evidence of a twelfth-century village on the tell itself. However, the excavations by Bliss and Macalister may be enlightening in this regard. They opened a large trench on the plateau to the north of the castle and uncovered there "a series of large rudely-constructed chambers, with walls consisting chiefly of rubble laid in mortar, but containing some dressed stones, which showed the unmistakable fine diagonal chiselling of the crusader era. Several *voussoirs* scattered about had the same chiselling."[46] This area is some distance from the castle and, while the stones could have been carried here at a later date, the typically Frankish diagonal tooling is not present on any of the visible stones in the area of the castle, which are mostly marginally drafted. They may well have come from some other contemporary structure, such as a church. The presence on the tell of some other architectural elements of medieval date, such as a Romanesque, Corinthian-style capital, also seems to suggest that there was indeed a settlement on the tell.

D: The Maqam of El-Khadr

Over the eastern tower of the castle are the remains of a *maqam* devoted to *el-Khadr*.[47] Members of the British Survey who visited the site in 1874 mention this as a "sacred building called el-Khudr, possibly on the site of a chapel of St. George."[48] In 1899, Bliss and Macalister noted that the villagers said that this building was constructed about thirty years previously.[49] Therefore, when the British saw it in 1874 it must have been fairly new, an assumption supported by the fact that it was not recorded by Rey when he visited Blanche Garde a decade earlier.[50]

---

[45] Ronnie Ellenblum et al., *Vadum Jacob. Final Report*, forthcoming.
[46] Bliss and Macalister, *Excavations in Palestine*, p. 31.
[47] El Khadr is identified as either St. Elias/Elijah or as St. George. See Agostino Augustinović, *"El Khadr" and the Prophet Elijah* (Jerusalem, 1972), pp. 9–10.
[48] Conder and Kitchener, *Survey of Western Palestine*, p. 440.
[49] Bliss and Macalister, *Excavations in Palestine*, p. 37.
[50] The existence of a shrine to El Khadr at Tell es-Safi is mentioned by Augustinović, 1972, p. 13, as well.

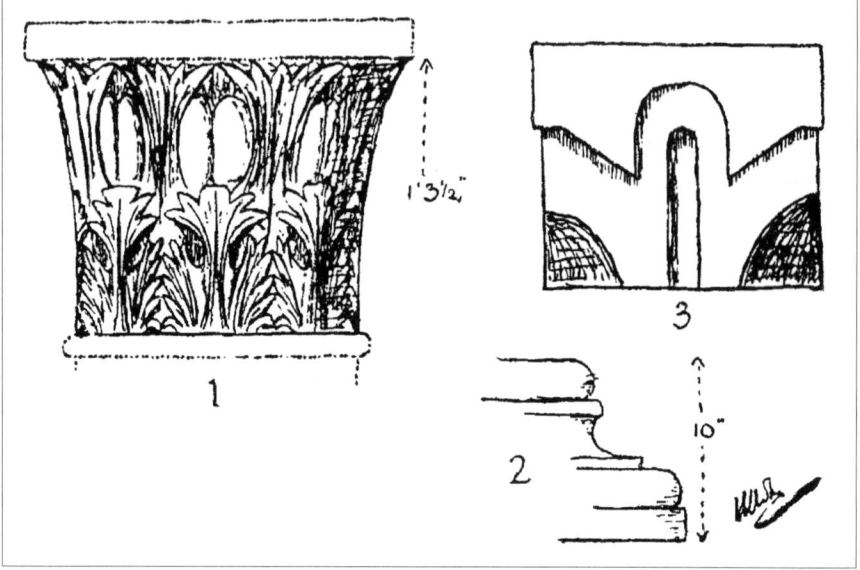

Fig. 8 Architectural fragments observed by Bliss and Macalister (1902, p. 38)

Remains of the *maqam* consist of a rectangular building measuring approximately 10 × 12 metres, with a barrel-vault and two entrances, one on the east and the other on the south (see Fig. 5). It is not exactly aligned with the curtain walls and the Frankish towers. The eastern entrance has a doorpost from the original structure with a bolt-hole and a second doorpost lies on the slope further east.

Finds from the Crusader Period

Only a small number of finds dating to the Crusader period have so far been recorded. The Regional Museum at nearby Kibbutz Kfar Menahem possesses a Corinthian-style marble capital, possibly that mentioned above, which was found in the area of the castle.[51] However, Moshe Yisrael, the curator of the Kfar Menahem Museum, recalls that it was taken from the vicinity of the castle. Bliss and Macalister mention and give rather crude drawings of an early Romanesque capital and a debased Corinthian capital as well as two Attic bases (Fig. 8).[52] An interesting, possibly medieval, column of white marble with twisted fluting at the base and vertical fluting above, now lying outside the entrance to the museum is said by the curator to have also been found in the area of the castle (Fig. 9). However, Conder and

---

[51] Bliss and Macalister, *Excavations*, p. 38, referred to it as "lying beside the wely on the north-east plateau."

[52] Ibid.

Fig. 9   Fluted column observed by Conder and Kitchener (1874, p. 440)

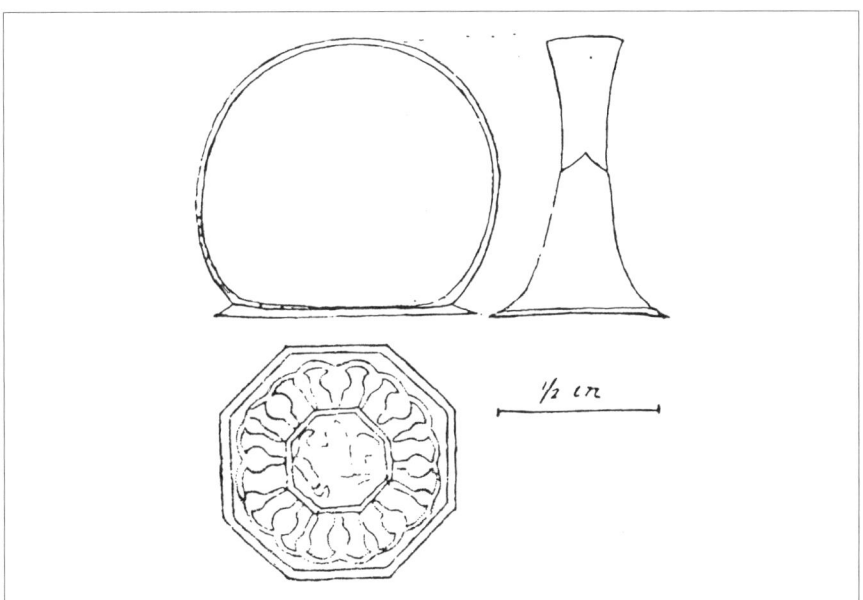

Fig. 10   Signet ring found by Bliss and Macalister (1902, p. 38)

Kitchener record having seen it in 1874 built into the side of a trough by the Bir el-Wad (Well in the Valley).[53] Bliss and Macalister also found two silver coins and a rather unusual signet ring (Fig. 10).[54]

---

[53]   Conder and Kitchener, *Survey of Western Palestine*, vol. 2, p. 440.
[54]   Bliss and Macalister, *Excavations in Palestine*, p. 38. Its present location is unknown.

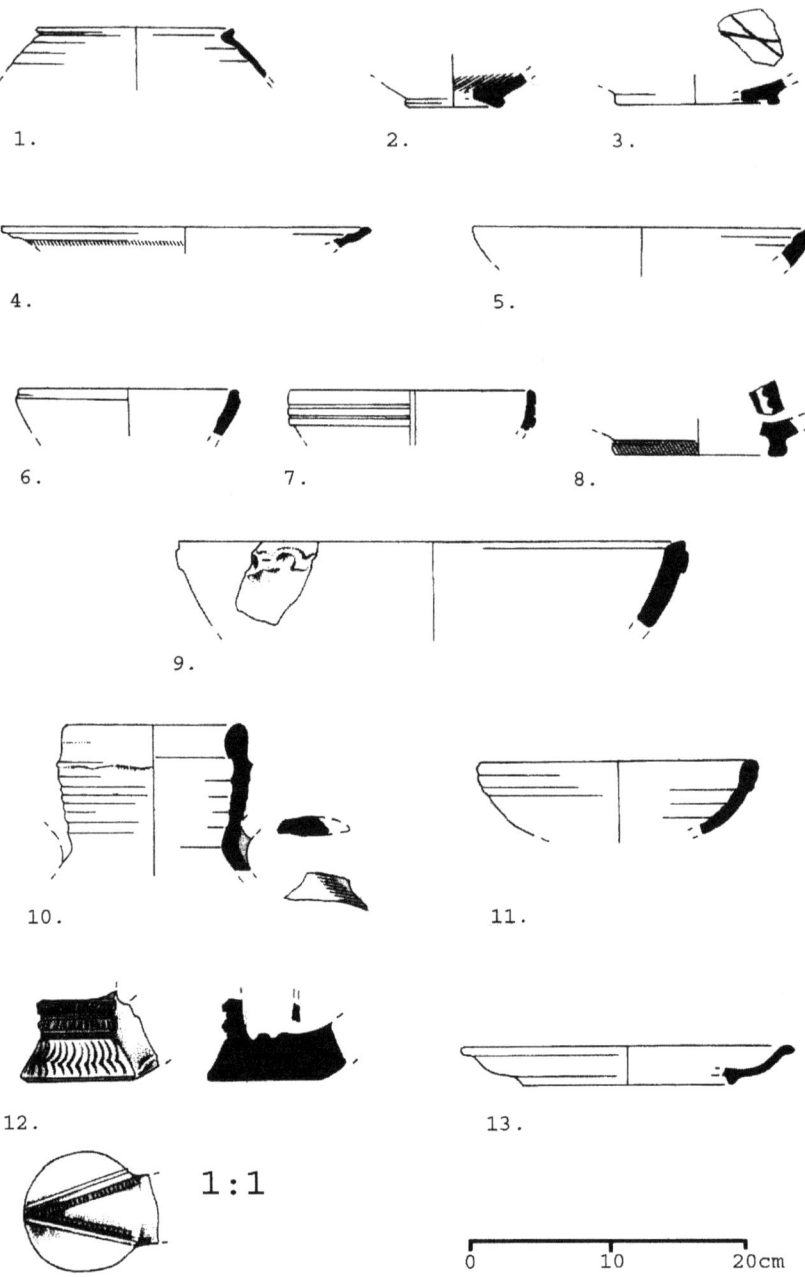

Fig. 11 Ceramics found at Tell es-Safi during the 1996 survey.

Ceramic Finds

Only a comparatively small quantity of medieval and post-medieval ceramics was found in the 1996 survey. Figure 11 shows a sampling of the ceramics found in the survey.

Abbasid/Fatimid-Crusader Period Pottery (Fig. 11:1–2)

1. *Lead-Glazed Globular Cooking Pot* (19/111). Everted rim. Diameter: 14 cm. Typical coarse, red-brown cooking ware. Spatters of glaze are on the interior and rim. This is the common cooking pot form from the ninth century on. The everted rim is typical of the later Frankish phase (twelfth to thirteenth centuries, Avissar Type 7).[55]

2. *Alkaline-Glazed Bowl* (5/153). Ring-base. Diameter: ca. 7 cm. Well levigated buff coloured fabric with some silt-size inclusions. On the interior is a discoloured (dark purple-grey) vitrified glaze. This piece dates to the Abbasid-Fatimid period (ninth to eleventh centuries).[56] Very little pottery from these periods was recovered in the survey.

Crusader-Ayyubid Period Pottery (Fig. 11:3–5)

3. *Lead-Glazed Sgraffito Decorated Bowl* (19/149). Ring-base. Diameter: 10 cm. Coarse red-brown fabric with silt-size inclusions. The interior has a dark-green lead glaze over white slip with fine sgraffito. This is a typical Crusader period bowl of local manufacture.[57]

4. *Lead-Glazed Manganese Painted Bowl* (53/3). Sloping ledge-rim. Diameter: 27 cm. Coarse red-brown fabric with silt-size inclusions. It has a yellow lead glaze over white slip with decoration painted in manganese-coloured glaze. Like the previous piece, this is a typical Crusader period bowl of local manufacture. However, the manganese painted decoration is comparatively uncommon, most vessels in this class being decorated with either sgraffito or slip-painting.[58]

5. *Crusader Period Imported Lead-Glazed Bowl* (48/225). Rim. Diameter: 25 cm. Coarse orange fabric with sand-size inclusions and voids. The interior has a cream-coloured lead glaze over white slip and there is a thin slip-wash on the exterior.

---

[55] Miriam Avissar, "The Medieval Pottery," in Amnon Ben-Tor, Miriam Avissar and Yuval Portugali, *Yoqneʿam I: The Late Periods*, Qedem Reports 3 (Jerusalem, 1996), pp. 135–36.
[56] Ibid., pp. 84–85, type 11.
[57] Ibid., pp. 91–92, type 36.
[58] See Denys Pringle, "Medieval Pottery from Caesarea: The Crusader Period," *Levant* 17 (1985), fig. 9:52, which has manganese painted decoration together with sgraffito.

This is Megaw's "Early Thirteenth-Century Aegean Ware."[59] Neutron Activation Analysis has shown that many of these vessels found in the kingdom of Jerusalem were manufactured in Cyprus.[60]

Mamluk Period Ceramics (Fig. 11:6–8)

6. *Monochrome Lead-Glazed Bowl* (174). Rim. Diameter: 16 cm. Coarse light-brown fabric with inclusions. The interior has a spotty dark-green lead glaze over thin white slip. This probably dates to the thirteenth or fourteenth century. In the Mamluk period the colour of the local table ware is generally lighter than that of the Crusader period.

7. *Fine Metallic Lead-Glazed Bowl* (19/88). Vertical rim with rilling on the exterior. Estimated diameter: 17 cm. Thin, hard-fired metallic fabric, brown in colour with silt-size inclusions. The interior and upper exterior has a spotty dark-green lead glaze over thin slip. According to Pringle, this may be similar to the "Metallic" and "Roulette" wares of Corinth that date to the late thirteenth and fourteenth centuries.[61]

8. *Yellow and Green Gouged Ware Bowl* (19/109). Ring-base. Diameter: 14 cm. Thickly potted very hard pinkish coloured fabric. The interior has a green lead glaze over white slip. A gouged decoration is cut in the slip.[62] This type dates to the late thirteenth and fourteenth centuries.

Ottoman Period Pottery (Fig. 11:9–13)

9. *Hand-Made Basin* (51/2). Rim. Diameter: 39 cm. Thick, coarse fabric. Finger-impressed band around the rim on the exterior. This type of ware first appears in the medieval period in the twelfth or thirteenth century[63] and this example could in fact date prior to the Ottoman period. It is, however, very common in the later period and much of the hand-made pottery at Tell es-Safi clearly came from the late Ottoman village.

10. *Storage Jar* (34/3). Rim and neck to shoulder with part of a handle. Diameter: 12.5 cm. Well levigated yellow-orange fabric. There is a twisted band just below the rim on the exterior. This is a typical late Ottoman storage jug, usually in the grey "Gaza Ware" fabric.

---

[59] Ann H. S. Megaw, "An Early Thirteenth Century Aegean Glazed Ware," in *Studies in Memory of D.T. Rice*, ed. Giles Robertson and George Henderson (Edinburgh, 1975), pp. 34–45.

[60] See Adrian J. Boas, "Import of Western Ceramics to the Latin Kingdom of Jerusalem," *Israel Exploration Journal* 44 (1994), pp. 102–22.

[61] Denys Pringle, "Thirteenth Century Pottery from the Monastery of St. Mary of Carmel," *Levant* 16 (1984), p. 103, fig. 656.

[62] Ibid., pp. 106–7, fig. 8:69–71.

[63] Ibid., p. 95.

11. *Gaza Ware Bowl* (15/13). Rim and wall. Diameter: 20 cm. Well levigated grey fabric. Gaza ware is very common throughout Israel and north as far as southern Syria. It dates to the Ottoman period and becomes very common in the nineteenth and early twentieth centuries.

12. *Tobacco Pipe (chibouk)* (46/402). Lower bowl with disc-shaped keel, part of the shaft. Fabric: Hard-fired reddish-yellow fabric with dark red burnished slip on the exterior and rouletted and incised decoration. Tobacco pipes are common finds in the Ottoman period. This type is typical of the nineteenth century and, according to St John Simpson, may have been manufactured in Jerusalem.[64]

13. *Undecorated Porcelain Bowl* (52/32). Complete profile except for lower base. Diameter: 24 cm. Fabric: Hard white porcelain. Probably an import from Western Europe and dating to the last phase of the village in the late nineteenth or early twentieth century.

Interpretation of the Castle, Its Development and Function

Judging from William of Tyre's description, in its earliest phase the castle of Blanche Garde consisted of only the enclosure castle. This structure measures a mere 16 × 16 metres – tiny when compared to other Frankish castles of this type (Fig. 12). Indeed, it is small when compared to most Frankish fortresses except for the simple tower keeps, some of which are considerably larger and most of which have outworks as well.[65]

The small size of Blanche Garde has consistently been overlooked or misinterpreted. According to the description of the Survey of Western Palestine, the castle appeared to be "about 50 yards square."[66] Bliss and Macalister wrote that according to Rey it was "about 60 metres square."[67] Kennedy describes it as "about 50 metres across" and Pringle wrote that it was "about 50–60 m square."[68] Quoting Rey, the *New Encyclopedia of Archaeological Excavations in the Holy Land* noted that "each side was 60 m long"[69] and most recently Ellenblum gave similar erroneous measurements in a comparative chart of twelfth-century castles.[70]

---

[64] St. John Simpson, "The Clay Pipes," in *Belmont Castle*, ed. Richard Harper and Denys Pringle, British Academic Monographs 10 (Oxford, 2000), p. 165.

[65] The smallest towers in the kingdom of Jerusalem were those built by the Templars on the road to the Jordan; Cisterna Rubea (Maldoim), which measures 9.3 × 8.5 metres but had outworks expanding its overall size to 59–62 × 47–50 metres (not including the moat), and the tower at Bait Jubr at-Tahtani, which measures 9.5 × 6.6–8.1 metres. See Pringle, "Templar Castles on the Road to Jordan," pp. 159, 165.

[66] Conder and Kitchener, *Survey of Western Palestine*, p. 440.

[67] Bliss and Macalister, *Excavations in Palestine*, pp. 36–37. This appears to be an erroneous reading of Rey's scale of 60 feet as 60 metres.

[68] Kennedy, *Crusader Castles*, p. 32; Denys Pringle, *Secular Buildings in the Crusader Kingdom of Jerusalem* (Cambridge, 1997), p. 93.

[69] *New Encyclopedia*, ed. Stern, vol. 4, p. 1523.

[70] Ellenblum, *Crusader Castles*, p. 183, fig. II.I.

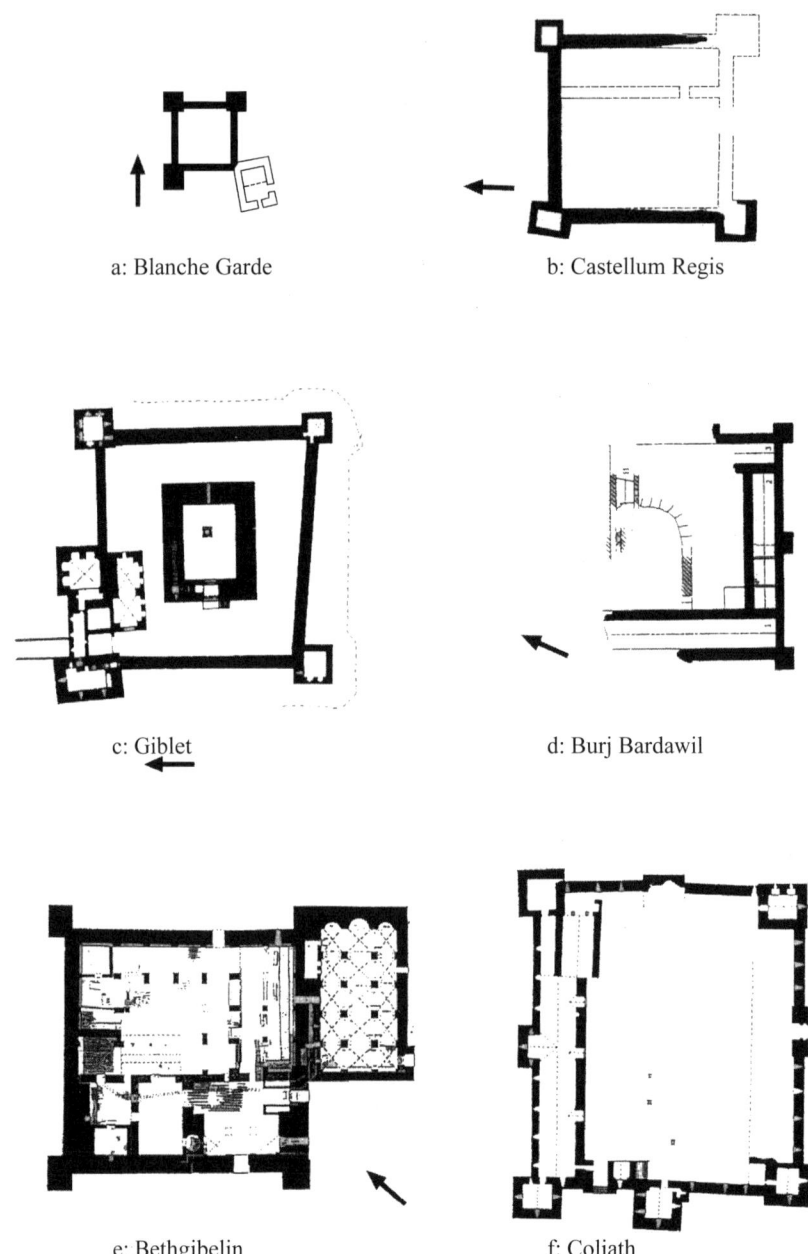

Fig 12 Comparative plans of Frankish castles

Sources: b, after Denys Pringle, *Secular Buildings in the Frankish Kingdom of Jerusalem* (Cambridge, 1997), fig. 36; c, after W. Müller-Wiener, *Castles of the Crusaders* (London, 1966), p. 64; d, after Pringle, *Secular Buildings*, fig. 24; e, after A. Kloner and M. Cohen, "The Crusader Fortress at Bet Govrin," *Qadmoniot*, 33.1 (Hebrew, 2000), p. 33; f, after Paul Deschamps, *Châteaux des Croisés en Terre Sainte*, vol. 3 (Paris, 1973), p. 311.

The small dimensions are notable when Blanche Garde is compared to other Frankish enclosure castles. Castellum Regis, for example, measures ca. 45 × 45 metres (including the towers; see Fig. 12b); Giblet, north of Beirut, measures ca. 50 × 50 metres (see Fig. 12c), and Coliath, north of Tripoli, is 63 × 56 metres (see Fig. 12f). Blanche Garde is a quarter the size of the inner castle of Bethgibelin, which measures 46 × 48 metres (see Fig. 12e). Even the castle which formed the earlier stage of the farmhouse at Burj Bardawil, south of Nablus, is ca. 50 × 50 metres (see Fig 12d).

The size of Blanche Garde raises the question of the function of this building. William of Tyre was very clear on this matter – he wrote that the purpose of the castle was to curb the attacks of Ascalon into the hinterland of the kingdom. However, we have to ask how large a garrison such a small castle could support. The small size of the towers or turrets makes it likely that they were of solid construction.[71] If so, and as there is no evidence for vaults in the interior of the curtain, or for Rey's central keep, the number of knights in residence would have been distinctly limited, unless the structure was vaulted internally and functioned as a turreted keep.[72] Would a handful of knights have sufficed to fulfil the castle's function as a policing post against raids from Ascalon? Taking into account its admirable location, it is possible that the castle was primarily intended to serve as a lookout from which warning of a raid could be relayed to the larger castle at Bethgibelin, or perhaps to Ibelin and Ramleh.[73]

With regard to the outworks – without excavation it is impossible to date this addition and we can only estimate its extent. It is certainly reasonable to consider the construction of these outworks as a later enhancement of the original castle, similar to those added to the castle of Darum. According to William of Tyre, when Darum was built in 1141 it was a small enclosure castle with neither moat nor barbican.[74] However, by the 1190s it had considerable outworks.[75] It is also probable that the outer fortification line at Bethgibelin, with as many as twenty

---

[71] The tower to the south-west, which is the only one of the three that can be seen today on the surface, appears to be of solid construction. The towers of the inner castle of Bethgibelin are only slightly larger and may have been solid as well.

[72] The Byzantine quadriburgia at 'En Boqeq and Upper Zohar are of comparable size and have hollow turrets; see *Levant* 30 (1998), pp. 203–8.

[73] This is perhaps why William of Tyre stated that the garrison from Blanche Garde attacked Ascalon more often in company with men from the other fortresses (WT, p. 708).

[74] WT, p. 937.

[75] *Itinerarium*, p. 353. By the time of the Third Crusade Darum is described as having "seventeen towers, strong and well-placed, one of which rose above the others. On the outside, it was surrounded by a deep ditch, revetted with stone on one side and with the natural rock on the other" (ibid.). This, as Denys Pringle points out, suggests that the castle developed from a small four-towered quadriburgium into a larger castle with outworks including corner and interval towers (Pringle [Introduction], in Lawrence, *Crusader Castles*, p. xxxvi).

towers, was added at the same time; Blanche Garde too appears to have undergone similar enhancement.[76] The question remains as to when this occurred.

The answer may lie in the changing strategic importance of this region during the second half of the twelfth century. We may have here evidence for two distinct stages of castle building in the south of the kingdom, aimed at answering two different political developments. During the late 1130s and early 1140s the kingdom faced a threat from Fatimid Ascalon. In answer to this, the Franks built a ring of simple, small enclosure castles intended to encircle the city and isolate it, thus removing the danger of Fatimid raids into the interior of Frankish territory. Once Fatimid Ascalon fell to the Franks in 1153, these castles were no longer required to fulfil their original task. From that time they probably served only the needs of local administration. In the early 1170s, however, a new threat faced the kingdom, once again from the south, and this time from Saladin and Ayyubid Egypt. In December 1170 Saladin opened his *jihad* against the Franks by attacking Darum. In preparation for this assault, or perhaps in its aftermath, the Franks may have decided to strengthen their castles in the south, adding additional lines of fortification and thereby turning the small simple enclosure castles into larger, better fortified concentric castles. These could hold large garrisons and their supplies and were intended to play an important role in the defence of the southern frontier. In this manner the castles at Darum, Blanche Garde and Bethgibelin, perhaps also those at Gaza and Ibelin, which had previously housed limited garrisons, were now enlarged and enhanced with concentric fortifications.[77] A similar process occurred in the centre of the kingdom and also further north where small castles such as Toron des Chevaliers (Latrun), Belmont (Suba, originally an unfortified rural estate centre), Belvoir and Safed, amongst others, were rebuilt by the Military Orders into larger, better-defended castles to help fortify the hinterland of the kingdom and its north-eastern frontier against the nascent danger of the unified Ayyubid army led by Saladin.[78]

---

[76] For Ibelin we have no comparative evidence for outworks, but this castle probably had a similar history to the others. This is indeed suggested by the fact that here, as in the other *castra*, a Frankish settlement grew up around the castle which had a Court of Burgesses (*Lois*, p. 419).

[77] Darum was built considerably later (ca. 1169), well after the occupation of Ascalon. Thus it did not form part of the defensive ring of castles around Fatimid Ascalon. However, it was a similar castle to those at Yavne, Tell es-Safi and Beit Govrin and perhaps to the castle at Gaza (constructed in 1149), which William of Tyre did not describe other than making a brief reference to its walls and towers (WT, p. 776). He described Darum (ibid., p. 937) as being of moderate dimensions, barely covering more than a stone's throw of ground, square in form with a tower at each corner, one of which was more massively constructed and better fortified than the others. There was neither a moat nor a barbican. But cf. note 75 above.

[78] For an expansive discussion on castle development in the Latin East and the use of concentric defences see Ellenblum, *Crusader Castles*.

Penthesilea on the Second Crusade: Is Eleanor of Aquitaine the Amazon Queen of Niketas Choniates?

Michael Evans

Central Michigan University

The Second Crusade (1145–49) was a pivotal event in the formation of Eleanor of Aquitaine's reputation. It was during the crusade that her marriage to Louis VII, king of France, reached crisis point, and she was accused of the most outrageous behaviour. The most notorious incident involving Eleanor on the crusade was her alleged incestuous affair with her uncle, Raymond, prince of Antioch. This charge was levelled against her by a contemporary, the English writer John of Salisbury, and subsequently developed by other chroniclers.[1] However, many aspects of the legend of Eleanor's scandalous behaviour on crusade derive less from contemporary accusations than from misinterpretations by later historians. Influenced by Eleanor's existing bad reputation, they were predisposed to believe the worst of her. She also neatly fitted the stereotype of the scandalous queen (which she shared with the likes of Isabella, "the She-wolf of France"). Indeed, later medieval legend condemned her as the murderer of Rosamund Clifford, her rival for the affections of her second husband Henry II, and even of having an affair with Saladin. Later, a combination of misogyny and Victorian morality condemned her as a woman who stepped beyond the bounds of seemly female behaviour. Even today, Eleanor is frequently treated in a stereotypically "female" manner; a recent biography informs us that she and her ladies would have enjoyed their stay in Constantinople for the opportunities it afforded them to go shopping.[2] This paper is concerned with just one of the tales about Eleanor; namely the claim that during the crusade she and her ladies dressed up as Penthesilea and the Amazons.

This legend derives ultimately from a reference in the *Historia* of Niketas Choniates, a Byzantine courtier who wrote at the beginning of the thirteenth century, in other words, more than half a century after Louis and Eleanor's visit to Constantinople en route to Syria in 1147, which occurred several years before his own birth. Niketas describes a remarkable woman among the crusader army:

---

[1] For a reassessment of Eleanor's conduct at Antioch, see Jean Flori, *Aliénor d'Aquitaine: la reine insoumise* (Paris, 2004), pp. 295–335; translated as *Eleanor of Aquitaine: Queen and Rebel*, trans. Olive Casse (Edinburgh, 2007). See also Natasha R. Hodgson, *Women, Crusading and the Holy Land in Historical Narrative* (Woodbridge, 2007), pp. 131–34; Jonathan P. Phillips, *The Second Crusade: Extending the Frontiers of Christendom* (London, 2007), pp. 210–12.

[2] Douglas Boyd, *Eleanor, April Queen of Aquitaine* (Stroud, 2004), p. 89.

A cloud of enemies, a dreadful and death-dealing pestilence, fell upon the Roman borders: I speak of the campaign of the Germans, joined by other kindred nations. Females were numbered among them, riding horseback in the manner of men, not on coverlets sidesaddle but unashamedly astride, and bearing lances and weapons as men do; dressed in masculine garb, they conveyed a wholly martial appearance, more mannish than the Amazons. One stood out from the rest as another Penthesilea and from the embroidered gold which ran around the hem and fringes of her garment was called Goldfoot [Χρυσόπους].[3]

The woman was not named Eleanor, nor was she referred to as a queen. Neither she nor her companions were explicitly said to have dressed as Amazons; they dressed in a masculine fashion, carried arms, and were compared to Penthesilea and her Amazons. They were not, however, said to have deliberately dressed in such a way as to imitate these mythological figures. Nor was the leading actress French: Niketas uses the term 'Αλεμανοι, which applies to the German people of the western Empire.[4] It seems unlikely that Niketas could have employed 'Αλεμανοι to refer to the crusaders as a whole, because he favoured the word Latins (Λατινοι) when describing westerners in general.[5] The potentially ambiguous term Γερμανοι, which means French not Germans, is not used by Niketas. On occasion, he may have confused the Germans and French, as when he attributed a German crusade victory to Louis's Frenchmen.[6] Furthermore, Χρυσόπους may belong to the "kindred nations" of the Germans, which could include their French crusader allies. Beyond that, however, there is no compelling evidence to link Eleanor to this "Penthesilea." The woman and her companions are compared to Amazons because they are masculine, and armed, not because they are in fancy dress. From these bare bones, many have concluded that this Amazonian woman was Eleanor, and historians have subsequently cited one another in circular fashion to support this identification. For example, Harry Magoulias, the modern editor and English translator of Choniates, refers the reader to Steven Runciman for the identification of "Goldfoot" with Eleanor, warning the reader that "Runciman, however, does not cite his sources."[7] Runciman did not actually make this identification, except to refer in a footnote to the "legend that Queen Eleanor came at the head of a company of Amazons," and stating that this story is "based on a remark by Nicetas ... that

---

[3] Niketas Choniates, *"O City of Byzantium": Annals of Niketas Choniates*, ed. and trans. Harry J. Magoulias (Detroit, 1984), p. 35; Niketas Choniates, *Historia*, ed. Jan-Louis Van Dieten, 2 vols. (Berlin and New York, 1975), 2:60. The appellation "Chrysópous" is mysterious. In light of it being applied to a mounted person, it may be relevant that George Akropolites (1217–82) gives this as a name for Manuel Laskaris's horse. *The History*, trans. Ruth Macrides (Oxford, 2007), p. 301.

[4] Steven Runciman, *A History of the Crusades*, 3 vols. (Cambridge, 1951–54), 2:262, n. 4. Niketas's contemporary John Kinnamos used Γερμανοι to mean French, but 'Αλεμανοι to mean Germans.

[5] Alexander Kazhdan, "Latins and Franks in Byzantium: Perception and Reality from the Eleventh to the Twelfth Century," in *The Crusades from the Perspective of Byzantium and the Muslim World*, ed. Angeliki E. Laiou and Roy Parviz Mottadeh (Washington, D.C., 2001), p. 84.

[6] Choniates, *Historia*, ed. Van Dieten, p. xvii.

[7] Ibid., p. 376, n. 153.

the German army contained a number of fully armed women."[8] Van Dieten, in his edition of Niketas's chronicle, published in 1975 identified Chrysópous with Eleanor, in a terse note in the index: "sc. Eleanora Franciae regina."[9] In turn, Roy Owen, in his 1992 biography of Eleanor, repeated the identification, yet acknowledged that Eleanor's Amazonian performance was a legend, as he traced back its gradual evolution. He rightly attributed the story to Niketas, but then asserted that the Byzantine historian "surely had Eleanor herself in mind when he described the arrival of the crusaders at Constantinople."[10] But why must he "surely" have done so? Had he been thinking of Eleanor, why would he not have said so? If no less a figure than the queen of France had behaved in such a way, why would Niketas have omitted identifying her as such? Even Jean Flori, in a commendably critical approach to this incident in his 2004 biography of Eleanor, writes that "la reine à laquelle il [Niketas] fait allusion semble bien être Aliénor, dont la présence ne passait évidement pas inaperçue."[11] A self-fulfilling process seems to have built up by which historians have reinforced one another by citing the identification of Chrysópous with Eleanor without backing up the assertion with a careful reading of the evidence. In the words of F. M. Chambers, the legend has thereby "gained a certain respectability from the company it has kept."[12]

The account in Niketas's chronicle should be treated with great care. Firstly, it refers to events over half a century before the time that Niketas was writing. Magoulias refers to the "Eleanor" story as an example of material collected by Niketas from "popular accounts."[13] Furthermore, it is part of a hostile view of the crusaders – Niketas's pestilential "cloud of enemies." The portrayal of enemy women as "unnaturally" masculine and warlike was a common topos in medieval chronicles, often using classical imagery in the way Niketas did with his reference to the Amazons. Guibert of Nogent's account of the First Crusade described Muslim women going into battle carrying bows and quivers "like a new Diana," and demonstrating their unnatural and unfeminine nature by callously abandoning their children as they fled before the crusader army.[14] The Persian-Arabic historian ʿImad ad-Din al-Isfahani described crusader women going into battle in full armour, their true sex only being discovered when they were stripped of their armour in death. This topos also had been employed previously by the Byzantine historian John Zonaras, who described Persian women warriors in this way. Clearly the image of a woman dressed and armed as a man was one used against the enemy "Other" to discredit him (or her) and to emphasize the alterity of

---

[8] Runciman, *History of the Crusades*, 2:262, n. 1.
[9] Choniates, *Historia*, ed. Van Dieten, 2:87.
[10] D. D. Roy Owen, *Eleanor of Aquitaine: Queen and Legend* (Oxford, 1992), p. 149.
[11] Flori, *Aliénor d'Aquitaine*, pp. 65–66.
[12] Frank McMinn Chambers, "Some Legends of Eleanor of Aquitaine," *Speculum* 16 (1941), p. 460.
[13] Choniates, *Historia*, ed. Van Dieten, p. xvii.
[14] GN, p. 225.

his (or her) culture.¹⁵ Niketas's description of "Goldfoot" should surely be viewed as part of this tradition. She was unnatural, as a woman who carries arms like a man, and was therefore symptomatic of the "pestilential" nature of the westerners, who are described in non-human terms as vermin or a miasmic cloud. "Goldfoot" is also sexualised, reflecting a Byzantine view of the westerners as more bestial than the more refined peoples of Byzantium. Goldfoot riding astride her horse is portrayed as an act that is unfeminine but also "shameless." The depiction of westerners as more animal and sexual was also used by Byzantine writers to represent western men. For example, it has been noted that Anna Komnene's description of the first crusaders in Constantinople used such language of their leaders. Matthew Bennett has called her description of Bohemund that "of a fine horse ... a mere animal with human intelligence," as she emphasized his large stature, strong body, and broad, flaring nostrils.¹⁶ This view of western Christians was shared by the Muslims, as can be seen in Usama ibn Munqidh's view of the Franks "as mere beasts possessing no other virtues but courage and fighting."¹⁷ The "Franks," for their part, chose to insult the "Greeks" in a different way, repeatedly questioning their fighting abilities and often labelling them as effeminate.

How, then, do we "know" that this woman was Eleanor? The identification in the modern imagination – in the English-speaking world, at least – would seem to be based not on any medieval account, but on the nineteenth-century presentation of Eleanor by Agnes Strickland, and her sister Elizabeth, the biographers of England's queens. A number of medieval chroniclers denounced Eleanor's supposed scandalous behaviour on the crusade, but they chose to dwell on rumours of her incestuous adultery with her uncle, Raymond, prince of Antioch; they made no mention of her Amazonian exploits in Constantinople.¹⁸ The Stricklands, however, took up the theme of Eleanor's masculine behaviour which was so clearly contrary to the Victorian view of how a decent woman should behave. In Elizabeth's biography of Eleanor, published in 1840, the queen's fancy dress appearance as Penthesilea occured when Louis and his lords took the cross at Vézelay in 1147:

> When queen Eleanora received the cross ... she directly put on the dress of the Amazons; and her ladies, all actuated by the same frenzy, mounted on horseback, and forming a light squadron, surrounded the queen when she appeared in public, calling themselves queen Eleanora's bodyguard. They practised Amazonian exercises, and performed a thousand follies in public, to animate their zeal as practical crusaders. By the suggestion of their

---

[15] Carole Hillenbrand, *The Crusades: Islamic Perspectives* (Edinburgh, 1999), p. 348; *Ioannis Zonaras*, ed. B. G. Nieburg, 2 vols. (Bonn, 1841–45), 2:595.

[16] Matthew Bennett, "Virile Latins, Effeminate Greeks and Strong Women: Gender Definitions on Crusade?," in *Gendering the Crusades*, ed. Susan B. Edgington and Sarah Lambert (Cardiff, 2001), p. 17.

[17] 'Usama ibn-Munqidh, *The Book of Contemplation: Islam and the Crusades*, trans. Paul M. Cobb (London, 2008), p. 144.

[18] Penny McCracken, "Scandalizing Desire: Eleanor of Aquitaine and the Chroniclers," in *Eleanor of Aquitaine: Lord and Lady*, ed. Bonnie Wheeler and John Carmi Parsons (New York and Basingstoke, 2002), pp. 247–63.

young queen, this band of mad-women sent their useless distaffs, as presents, to all the knights and nobles who had the good sense to keep out of the crusading expedition.[19]

Agnes Strickland, the senior and more celebrated partner in the team, saw herself as an objective historian who wished to record "facts, not opinions."[20] The above passage however, betrays her and her sister's prejudice against women who took on unseemly, "masculine" roles, and also their disapproval of Catholic crusades from which it was "good sense" to be absent. Agnes was a great supporter of the Anglican establishment as well as anti-feminist, refusing to lend her support to a petition for women's property rights.[21] Moreover, the reference that she cited for Eleanor's Amazonian performance is post-medieval, although in the first edition, she refers – erroneously – to Suger and "contemporary historians." In the 1889 condensed edition, she refers the reader to *La Vie de Suger*, an eighteenth-century history written by M. d'Aubigny in 1739.[22] Suger himself did not record the events of the Second Crusade. His successor as the chronicler (and later abbot) of Saint-Denis, Odo of Deuil, makes no mention of Eleanor behaving in this manner, and presents Louis's crusading exploits in flattering terms. He would scarcely draw attention to scandalous behaviour on the part of Louis's queen. However, by the nineteenth century, Eleanor's scandalous reputation was so firmly implanted that even "objective" historians' opinions of her were coloured by the legend.

In fairness to the Stricklands, it must be noted that their account of Eleanor's Amazonian exploits was shared by the pioneering crusade historian Joseph Michaud. In his *Histoire des Croisades* of 1829, he stated that "[a] great number of women, attracted by the example of Eleanor of Guienne, took up the cross, and armed themselves with sword and lance ... History relates that distaffs and spindles were sent to those who would not take up arms, as an appropriate reproach for their cowardice."[23] Unlike the Stricklands, Michaud did not say that Eleanor and her ladies were responsible for the sending of distaffs, and his view of the crusade was more positive, even romantic, as Eleanor and Louis departed in the company of the inevitable troubadours. Michaud, from Catholic, royalist France, identified with the crusaders, and was even dubbed a "Knight of the Holy Sepulchre" in Jerusalem after he retraced the route of the First Crusade.[24] The distaff incident seems to be based on an account of such behaviour by the author of the *Itinerarium* of Richard I on the Third Crusade, and in this instance it was men who sent distaffs

---

[19] Agnes Strickland, *Lives of the Queens of England*, 12 vols. (London, 1840–47), 1:313.

[20] Mary Delorme, "'Facts not Opinions' – Agnes Strickland," *History Today* 38:2 (1988), p. 46.

[21] Ibid., p. 49.

[22] Strickland, *Lives of the Queens of England*, 1:313; and *Lives of the Queens of England*, condensed ed., 6 vols. (London, 1889) 1:297–98, citing M. d'Aubigny, *Vie de Suger* (Paris, 1739).

[23] Cited in Owen, *Eleanor of Aquitaine*, p. 150.

[24] Elizabeth Siberry, "Images of the Crusades in the Nineteenth and Twentieth Centuries," in *The Oxford History of the Crusades*, ed. Jonathan Riley-Smith (Oxford, 1999), p. 373.

to one another.[25] Michaud's account was dependent upon those of seventeenth- and eighteenth-century historians. De Larrey's 1691 *Histoire d'Eléonor d'Aquitaine* seems to mark the earliest appearance of the story that Eleanor and her ladies dressed as Amazons at Vézelay.[26] The tale was repeated in Dom François Armand Gervaise's 1721 *Histoire de Suger*,[27] and thence by D'Aubigny in his *Vie de Suger* cited by the Stricklands.

Twentieth-century biographers of Eleanor have been more sceptical about her Amazonian exploits, recognizing the Vézelay incident as a legend, yet still have been inclined to give it too much credence. Amy Kelly's 1950 biography called it "a legend" but went on to say, "[t]he tale is in character, and later allusions to Amazons en route, found in Greek historians, give substance to it."[28] The Greek "historians" [*sic*] turns out to be Niketas, whose account, as we have seen, is itself legendary. Kelly also stated that Eleanor maintained "her role as Penthesilea, which, as it is said, had been such a success and inspiration at Vézelay," and made herself doubly reliant on Niketas to support her portrayal of the Amazonian Eleanor.[29] Kelly has been described as "a biographer with a colorful imagination."[30]

Alison Weir's popular biography of 1997, which is heavily dependent on Kelly's at this point, sows further confusion. Referring to the Vézelay incident she argued, "[m]ost historians dismiss the tale as pure legend, because there are no contemporary accounts of it, but it is in keeping with what we know of Eleanor's character ... The tale may have originated from the eye-witness account of a Greek observer ..."[31] The Greek "eye-witness" is of course Niketas, who was not even born at the time. To make matters worse, Weir erroneously cited Gervase of Canterbury, a twelfth-century English chronicler, as her source, surely a mistaken reading of the "Gervaise" (meaning F. A. Gervaise's 1721 work) in Kelly's footnotes. Referring to Eleanor's appearance in Constantinople, Weir again puts forward Niketas's account as "probably an eye-witness description," adding "[t]his was almost certainly Eleanor ... and it may be that the so-called legends of her dressing up as an Amazon are really based on fact."[32] Both Kelly and Weir refer the reader to a "similar story" in Orderic Vitalis as proof that women really did dress as Amazons. However, Orderic's description of the warlike Isabel of Conches (dubbed "Isabella of Anjou"

---

[25] *Das* Itinerarium peregrinorum: *Eine zeitgenössische englishe Chronik zum dritten Kreuzzug in ursprünglicher Gestalt*, ed. Hans Eberhard Mayer (Stuttgart, 1962), p. 277.

[26] Isaac de Larrey, *Histoire d'Eléonor de Guienne* (Paris, 1691), p. 37; cited in Chambers, "Some Legends," p. 460.

[27] François A. Gervaise, *Histoire de Suger*, 3 vols. (Paris, 1721), 3:118; cited in Amy Kelly, *Eleanor of Aquitaine and the Four Kings* (Cambridge, MA, 1950), p. 35.

[28] Kelly, *Eleanor of Aquitaine*, p. 35.

[29] Ibid., p. 38.

[30] Ralph V. Turner, cited by Elizabeth A. R. Brown, "Eleanor of Aquitaine Reconsidered: The Woman and her Seasons," in *Eleanor of Aquitaine: Lord and Lady*, p. 30, n. 3.

[31] Alison Weir, *Eleanor of Aquitaine, by the Wrath of God, Queen of England* (London, 1999), p. 51.

[32] Ibid., p. 58.

by Weir), does not say that Isabel was (or acted or dressed like) an Amazon, merely that "she deserved comparison with" the Amazon queens of legend.[33]

To see how other Eleanor myths might develop, we can consider Curtis Walker's article of 1949.[34] The defeat of the French crusader army at Mount Cadmus was widely blamed on Eleanor who supposedly took command of part of the army and interfered with the tactics of Louis and his generals. Inappropriate female behaviour was therefore held responsible for military disaster, as Eleanor, like Niketas's "Goldfoot," scandalously usurped the male prerogative of making war. Walker cites how Victorian historians such as Bishop Stubbs were influenced by the Eleanor myth, decrying how "her undisguised flirtations had spread confusion and dismay and discord in the noblest host that ever went to the East."[35] To this I would add the Stricklands again, who railed against "the freaks of queen Eleanor and her female warriors [which] were the cause of all the misfortunes that befell king Louis and his army, especially the defeat at Laodicea."[36] She interfered with Louis's strategy for no better reason than that she wished to make camp "in a lovely romantic valley, full of verdant grass and gushing fountains," while the army was encumbered by having to carry the outlandish "array of the lady warriors." Walker points out that the accounts of Odo of Deuil (who accompanied the army) and of William of Tyre make no mention of Eleanor having a role in the battle. The notion that Eleanor intervened in the battle "riding at the head of a column" emerged in the work of the French historian Alfred Richard, writing in 1903, and (like the Vézelay story) is dependent on a seventeenth-century source, the historian Maimbourg.[37] Odo and William's accounts blamed the defeat on the rash actions of Geoffrey of Rancon, but later accounts shifted the blame to Eleanor.[38] Comments such as Stubbs's "noblest army," betray the emotional engagement of many nineteenth- and early twentieth-century historians with crusades. They identified with the crusaders, lamented their defeats, and looked for someone to blame, with Eleanor proving a useful scapegoat. The Stricklands, in contrast, did not identify with the crusade, and regarded it as a ridiculous exercise. It was, therefore, wholly appropriate that it should be sabotaged by Eleanor's outrageous behaviour.

Jean Flori, in his 2004 biography of Eleanor, cautions us to be wary of the accounts of her during the crusade reminding us, for example, that the reference to her taking the cross in 1146 was written by the continuator of Suger some thirty years after the event.[39] He urges prudence in assessing tales of Eleanor's

---

[33] Orderic Vitalis, *The Ecclesiastical History*, ed. and trans. Marjorie Chibnall, 6 vols. (Oxford, 1969–80), 4:212–15.

[34] Curtis H. Walker, "Eleanor of Aquitaine and the Disaster at Cadmos Mountain on the Second Crusade," *American Historical Review* 55 (1949–50), pp. 857–61.

[35] Walter of Coventry, *Memoriale Fratris Walteri de Coventria*, ed. William Stubbs, RS 58, 2 vols. (London, 1873), 2:xxix, n. 1; Walker, "Eleanor of Aquitaine," p. 857.

[36] Strickland (1840–47), 1:314.

[37] Walker, "Eleanor of Aquitaine," p. 857, n. 1.

[38] Ibid., pp. 859–60.

[39] Flori, *Aliénor d'Aquitaine*, p. 65.

Amazonian behaviour, arguing that a combination of Niketas's account, and medieval Amazon literature such as Benoît de Sainte-Maure's *Roman de Troie*, "a excité l'imagination de plusieurs historiens, qui les relient un peu trop rapidement aux jugements des chroniqueurs imputant l'échec de la deuxième croisade à la présence de trop nombreuses femmes au sein des armées chrétiennes."[40] He credits de Larrey and Gervaise with the creation of Eleanor's Amazonian myth, before pointedly reminding us that "[a]u XXe siècle encore, certains auteurs accréditent cette version romancée."[41]

In conclusion, it would appear that the legend of Eleanor dressing as Penthesilea developed in the following way. De Larrey must have known of the "Chrysópous" incident in Niketas's chronicle, and applied it to the ceremony at Vézelay. It would seem that he misunderstood contemporary accounts of Eleanor and her ladies taking the cross to imply that they were assuming a martial role as crusaders. In fact, the crusade was a form of pilgrimage, and wearing the cross did not necessarily commit a person to fight. Many accounts attest to the large numbers of non-combatants, both male and female, who accompanied the crusades. Later historians took de Larrey's story uncritically, and embroidered it with their own misconceptions, such as the Stricklands' attributing to Eleanor's ladies the act of handing out distaffs to stay-at-homes. They were happy to assign outrageous behaviour to Eleanor on the basis of what they believed they "knew" of her character from the very legends that they themselves were helping to propagate. Finally, twentieth-century historians, both popular and academic, have unwittingly given further life to these stories by simply citing one another without critically examining the sources, and allowing themselves to be influenced by an image of Eleanor based on legend. The image of Eleanor and her ladies as Amazons owes more to the prejudices of later generations than to the historical Eleanor, or to the character created by Niketas Choniates.

---

[40] Ibid., p. 66.
[41] Ibid., p. 67.

"Like Purest Gold Resplendent": The Fiftieth Anniversary of the Liberation of Jerusalem

Amnon Linder

The Hebrew University, Jerusalem

On 15 July 1149, Frankish Jerusalem celebrated the fiftieth anniversary of its liberation in 1099 with the dedication of the new church of the Holy Sepulchre. A commemorative inscription in verse was painted in gold letters above one of the arches leading to the Golgotha chapel, to the right of those entering through the main twin-gates from the south. It has been partially preserved in three copies: those made by John of Würzburg[1] and Theoderic[2] within two decades of the dedication, and by Quaresmius in 1626, though by that time its text had already become "almost obliterated, and what remains is unintelligible."[3] Quaresmius's copy, although inferior to those made by John of Würzburg and Theoderic, is nonetheless useful by way of a control for the two earlier copies and as a basis for the reconstruction of the inscription's final part, omitted by his two forerunners. Textual reconstructions are, by definition, somewhat speculative, but Quaresmius's readings have significantly reduced the purely speculative element in the reconstructions proposed by students of this inscription.[4]

The inscription reads as follows (reconstructed elements in italics):

1. Est locus iste sacer sacratus sanguine Christi
2. Per nostrum sacrare sacro nichil addimus[5] isti
3. Sed domus huic sacro circum superedificata
4. Est quinta decima Quintilis luce sacrata
5. Cum reliquis patribus a Fulcherio[6] patriarcha
6. Cuius tunc quartus patriarchatus *annus erat*
7. *Septem septies* semel unus ab urbe

---

[1] *Peregrinationes tres*, ed. Robert B. C. Huygens, CCCM 139 (Turnhout, 1994), hereafter cited as John.

[2] Ibid., hereafter cited as Theoderic.

[3] Franciscus Quaresmius, *Elucidatio Terrae Sanctae*, 2 (Antwerp, 1630), p. 483, hereafter cited as Quaresmius.

[4] Among the more frequently cited reconstructions: Melchior De Vogüé, *Les églises de la Terre Sainte* (Paris, 1860), p. 217; Peter Thomsen, "Die lateinischen und griechischen Inschriften des Stadt Jerusalem," *Zeitschrift des Deutschen Palästina-Vereins* 44 (1921), pp. 33–34; Sabino de Sandoli, *Corpus inscriptionum Crucesignatorum Terrae Sanctae* (Jerusalem, 1974), pp. 49–50; Martin Biddle, *The Tomb of Christ* (Stroud, 1999), pp. 93–94, hereafter cited as Biddle.

[5] *Sic* Theoderic, Quaresmius; "additur" John.

[6] *Sic* Theoderic; "alvicherico" Quaresmius.

8. Quae similis puri*ssimo auro*[7] *claru*erat[8]
9. Ex ortu Domini numerabantur simul ann*i* ...[9]
10. Undecies *centum et quadraginta novemque*
11. ... iudices ...[10]

The text commemorates, consequently, a dedication solemnized by Patriarch Fulcher with other prelates on 15 July 1149, on the fiftieth anniversary of the liberation of Jerusalem. Opinions have varied, however, as to the identity of the edifice consecrated. While the *opinio communis* has identified it with the entire Holy Sepulchre church as reconstructed by the Franks,[11] another interpretation restricts it to the Calvary/Golgotha structure alone: this was originally advanced by Thomsen in 1921 and more recently by Biddle.[12] It consists, essentially, of two complementary arguments: a) denying the traditional thesis that the 1149 dedication applied to the complete church and arguing that only the Calvary/Golgotha structure was consecrated in its course, and b) claiming that the complete church was consecrated sometime between 1163 and 1167/9, fifteen to twenty years later. As Biddle's advocacy of this thesis has been particularly articulate and straightforward, it offers a valuable platform for appraising the traditional dating anew.

Biddle opens his refutation of the traditional thesis with the observation that "It is notorious ... that William of Tyre makes no mention of such a dedication."[13] An *argumentum ex silentio* is a notoriously weak argument – unless the whys and wherefores of that silence are convincingly demonstrated – and it is particularly deficient in this instance, because Biddle goes on to concede that the putative later dedication is not mentioned by William of Tyre either, suggesting "perhaps because it took place before his return from Europe to the kingdom in 1165."[14] Yet, as William was absent from the kingdom between 1146 and 1165,[15] a period

---

[7] "similis" should be construed here with the dative rather than the genitive for this is the more common form in echoing biblical usage, and, furthermore, because it is used here as an adjective rather than substantive and demands, therefore, the dative.

[8] "erant" Quaresmius.

[9] Quaresmius signals a considerable lacuna between "ann*i*" and "u<i>ndecies."

[10] *Sic* Quaresmius – introducing, possibly, the Indiction date.

[11] To cite just few of the many – René Grousset, *L'histoire des croisades et du royaume franc de Jérusalem*, vol. 2 (Paris, 1935), p. 314; Raymond C. Smail, *The Crusaders in Syria and the Holy Land* (London, 1973), pp. 129–30; Joshua Prawer, *The Latin Kingdom of Jerusalem: European Colonialism in the Middle Ages* (London, 1972), p. 208; Bernard Hamilton, "Rebuilding Zion: The Holy Places of Jerusalem in the Twelfth Century," *Studies in Church History* 14 (1977), pp. 106–7; Jaroslav Folda, "The South Transept Façade of the Church of the Holy Sepulchre in Jerusalem: An Aspect of 'Rebuilding Zion'," *Crusade Sources*, p. 239.

[12] Martin Biddle developed this thesis in several publications. See Biddle, passim, and "The History of the Church of the Holy Sepulchre," in *The Church of the Holy Sepulchre*, ed. Martin Biddle et al. (New York, 2000), pp. 23–69. See also Colin Morris, *The Sepulchre of Christ and the Medieval West from the Beginning to 1600* (Oxford, 2005), p. 193.

[13] Biddle, p. 92.

[14] Ibid., p. 96.

[15] See Huygens' introduction to his edition of William of Tyre's *Chronicon*, CCCM 63 (1986), p. 1.

covering 1149 and the period between 1163 and 1165, his silence about both dates should be considered as equally "notorious"; in fact, as completely inconsequential in either proving or disproving the one or the other. A second argument against the traditional thesis consists of the claim that "it has become increasingly obvious that parts of the church and some of its sculpture belong not to the 1130s and 1140s but to the 1150s and later"[16] – an observation that confuses dedication and the end of construction. Quite apart from the fact that the precise dates of the completion of both the fabric and the decoration of the Holy Sepulchre are largely unknown, all estimates based on stylistic and iconographic criteria are just that, estimates and no more, some more plausible than the others, but all manifestly unreliable for the purpose of precise dating, especially when such estimates are being used to distinguish between short time-spans such as single decades. Differentiating between art produced in the 1140s and in the 1150s, for example, is more apparent than real, because the actual creation of such art extended, not infrequently, over and beyond single decades.

Another challenge to the traditional interpretation of this inscription resulted from a strictly literal reading of its text. Biddle concluded, on these grounds, that the inscription "is not a record of the dedication of the whole church,"[17] and that "if [it] ... means what it says"[18] it commemorates the dedication of the "complex of chapels ... that still surround the Rock of Calvary."[19] "The text is quite explicit," he argues: only the Calvary Hill is meant by "locus iste sacer" in line 1 – "the place where [Jesus'] blood was shed. Nothing is said about the tomb, the place of his resurrection"[20] – and the reference in line 3 to the "domus huic sacro circum superedificata," "is in reality a precise and accurate description"[21] of the Calvary complex of chapels.

The notion that Calvary could be distinguished from the Tomb, the site of the Resurrection, on the grounds that the consecration through Jesus' blood applies to the first but not to the second, seems unwarranted, especially as it runs counter to the theological tenet that Christ's Passion and Resurrection should be perceived as a successive unfolding in time and space of what was, essentially, a cohesive whole. Peter the Venerable, notably, explicated this belief – in his sermon *De laude Dominici Sepulchri*[22] – in terms of closely interconnected cause and effect, payment and reward, victory and triumph.[23] This stimulated, from the very beginnings of the

---

[16] Biddle, p. 92.
[17] Ibid., p. 95.
[18] Ibid., p. 96.
[19] Ibid., p. 95.
[20] Ibid.
[21] Ibid.
[22] "Petri Venerabilis sermones tres," ed. Giles Constable, *Revue bénédictine* 64 (1954), pp. 224–72; text, pp. 232–72.
[23] "Mors enim Christi resurrectionis et ascensionis causa est, resurrectio vel ascensio ipsius causae effectus est. Mors Christi praelii victoria est, resurrectio et ascensio triumphus victoriae est. Mors Christi precium est, resurrectio et ascensio praemium est." Ibid., p. 251.

Holy Sepulchre, a powerful drive to achieve spatial unification in the concentration of the relevant *loca sancta* (mainly the Calvary Hill and the Anastasis, although other *loca* were successively added to them) in one determined area. It also opened up a complementary and centripetal process of gathering-in of relics, traditions and rituals from other sites in Jerusalem and the vicinity. That migration encompassed prefigurative Old Testament relics such as Adam's skull, Abraham's and Melchisedec's altar, David's horn of anointment and Solomon's seal. Furthermore, it also included Christian relics associated with various episodes in Jesus' Passion and Resurrection, as well as New Testament figures such as John the Baptist, Mary and the Apostles, along with saints and Christian emperors – Mary the Egyptian, Constantine, Helena and Heraclius. Under the Latins this unifying drive finally achieved its object with the comprehensive integration of the numerous churches and chapels in that area into one church, presided over by one patriarch and served by one chapter. That sense of a comprehensive unity inspired Pope Innocent II's address to the canons of the Holy Sepulchre in 1138 as those who "apud gloriosum Sepulcrum ejus ... et alia sacratissima loca in quibus Redemptor mundi ... vincula, flagella, crucis ignominiam, vulnera mortemque sustinuit, regulariter militatis ... sacrosanctam ecclesiam Sancti Sepulcri in qua, divinis obsequiis insistentes, passionem dominicam et victoriossime crucis triumphum assidue oculata fide recolitis ...".[24] The idea was expressed again in the title given to the church in a document issued by King Fulk of Jerusalem in the same year: "gloriosa dominicae Passionis ac Resurrectionis ecclesia."[25] Recourse to the idea of an archetypal consecration with the blood of Christ reinforced it even further. The notion that the entire church of the Holy Sepulchre had originally been consecrated with the blood of Jesus, as well as the glory of the Ascension, was articulated in a deed of gift made by Rodrigo, count of Traba, to the Holy Sepulchre – in the presence of Patriarch William – during his pilgrimage to Jerusalem in 1137/8. The deed's preamble – most probably drafted by the chapter's draftsman – solemnly declares: "patres nostri narraverunt nobis sanctam Dominicae Resurrectionis aecclesiam a quibusque fidelibus caeteris excellentius venerandam, quia eam idem Dominus noster Iesus Christus non prophetarum [verbis] non martyrum sanguine consecravit, sed sua presentia et proprii respersione cruoris Resurrectionisque et Ascensionis gloria quasi firmis et coherentibus privilegiis ac supervenienti prerogativa specialem sibi ac propriam dedicavit ..."[26] In consequence, the 1149 inscription's reference to "Est locus iste sacer sacratus sanguine Christi," far from being new, or spatially restricted and exclusive, was inspired by a notion already documented among the canons of the Holy Sepulchre in 1138, and reflecting a decidedly comprehensive sense.

The integration of all these separate *loca* in one church did not involve the abrogation of the specific physiognomy of any of them, or of its unique role in the Sacred History, as commemorated and celebrated throughout that area: Calvary, the

---

[24] *Cart St Sép*, no. 7, p. 45.
[25] Ibid., no. 34, p. 99.
[26] Ibid., no. 72, pp. 170–71.

Tomb, the Crypt of the Invention and the other *loca* have retained their individuality within the overarching whole. Their integration resulted, however, in a different perspective, in a much clearer view of their cohesion in a church, as an "ecclesia," generating in the process that rich cluster of feelings, beliefs and activities that the very concept of "ecclesia" – with the far more compelling concept of "Ecclesia" it adumbrated – so easily and readily evoked in the twelfth century. An excessively literal and restrictive interpretation of the inscription runs the risk of reducing it into a mere signpost, even though its elaborate literary style – poetical[27] as well as rhetorical[28] – sustains, precisely, that rich conception of "ecclesia"/"Ecclesia" through evocations appropriate to a church dedication-service in general and to that of the Holy Sepulchre in particular. The inscription's original audience decoded its allusions and comprehended its meanings beyond the text's immediate, literal level, thanks to their familiarity with the relevant codes; above all the Scriptures with their commentaries and with the dedication-liturgy. The same decoding should be undertaken by the modern historian.

Once this approach is adopted it becomes clear that the inscription evokes, in the first place, one particular biblical narrative of dedication – Jacob's dedication of the altar in Bethel (=Domus Dei) following his dream-vision: "Cumque evigilasset Iacob ... ait: Vere Dominus est in loco isto et ego nesciebam ... quam terribilis, inquit, est locus iste; non est hic aliud nisi domus Dei et porta caeli ... Et lapis iste ... vocabitur Domus Dei ..."[29] A typical prefigurative plot of dedication, this was integrated into the liturgy of dedication together with its distinct terminology, mainly through the terms/concepts "locus iste sanctus" and "domus dei." The twelfth-century dedication service of the Roman Pontifical in the version of the Pontifical of Apamea – possibly employed in Jerusalem in the 1149 dedication – drew from this passage its Magnificat antiphon,[30] a consecration antiphon,[31] the Benedictus antiphon,[32] and the Introit[33] as well as the Gradual[34] of the Dedication Mass. The anniversary commemoration of the Holy Sepulchre's dedication, as instituted by Patriarch Fulcher in 1150 at the earliest and documented in the manuscript tradition,[35]

---

[27] Its first part, at least, consists of rhymed hexameters; our partial knowledge of the rest precludes any definite judgement.

[28] See the diastole of the syllable "sac" in lines 1–4: "sacer sacratus ... sacrare sacro ... sacro ... sacrata" and Sandoli's remark there (*Corpus inscriptionum*, p. 50). A similar stylistic approach appears in the inscription "intus ad depositionem Domini: 'A caris caro cara dei lacrimata levatur / A cruce ... [etc.]'," as copied by John of Würzburg (John, p. 141).

[29] Gn 28.16–17, 22.

[30] *Le Pontifical Romain du XIIe siècle*, ed. Michel Andrieu (Città del Vaticano, 1938), xvii, no. 21, p. 181: "O quam metuendum est locus iste; vere non est hic aliud nisi domus dei ... [etc.]."

[31] Ibid., no. 55, p. 189: "Erexit Iacob lapidem in titulum, fundens oleum desuper."

[32] Ibid., no. 56, p. 189: "Mane surgens ... Vere locus iste sanctus est et ego nesciebam."

[33] Ibid., no. 71, p. 193: "Terribilis est locus iste: hic domus Dei est ... [etc.]."

[34] Ibid., no. 75, p. 193: "Locus iste a Deo factus est inestimabile sacramentum."

[35] Vatican City, MS. Barb. lat. 659, the Barletta Ordinary – Barletta, Archivio della Chiesa del Santo Sepolcro, MS s.n. and Wrocław, Biblioteka Uniwersitecka we Wrocławiu [olim Breslau, Kgl. und Universitätsbibliothek], MS. I.Q.175.

borrowed several items from the same source; namely the Magnificat antiphon in the Vespers Office,[36] two antiphons[37] and a responsory[38] in the Second Nocturn, two responsories[39] in the Third Nocturn, the Benedictus antiphon[40] in Lauds, the Introit[41] and the Gradual[42] in the High Mass of the Dedication Anniversary, and two responsories[43] in the Second Vespers. Another antiphon taken from the Jacob narrative is signaled in the First Nocturn (attached to the second psalm) in the Wroclaw manuscript.[44] Once it is realized that the inscription's "domus" is much more than a mere structure, or even a "complex of chapels," the adjective "superedificata" should be appreciated against a dedicatory background; in fact, as a clear allusion to 1 Cor 3.10–13, which reads: "Unusquisque autem videat quomodo superaedificet, fundamentum enim aliud nemo potest ponere preter id quod positum est qui est Christus Iesus; si quis autem superaedificat supra fundamentum hoc … [etc.]." It appears, indeed, as the Terce Chapter in Patriarch Fulcher's Anniversary Office of the Dedication of the Holy Sepulchre, duly preceded by the dedication-antiphon "Domus mea domus orationis vocabitur."[45]

The prominence of Jacob's story as a prefigurative dedication-narrative in a liturgical context was not limited to the Holy Sepulchre alone; in the nearby church of the Templum Domini, John of Würzburg recorded an inscription reading "Vere Dominus est in loco isto et ego nesciebam … [etc.]."[46] A survey of the relevant data in Hesbert's *Corpus Antiphonalium Officii* proves, furthermore, that this was a longstanding European phenomenon with a constant, as well as an evolving relevance, common to all the dedication rites, secular as well as monastic.[47] Thus it was easily recognizable to the Latin population of the Holy Land and to the crusaders and pilgrims who visited the kingdom. A Second Nocturn responsory,[48] for example, consists of the respond "O quam metuendus est locus iste. Vere non est hic aliud nisi domus Dei et porta coeli," attached to five different verses, all but one borrowed from Jacob's tale in Genesis. This is attested in six important ecclesiastical centers, namely Saint-Denis (monastic cursus, thirteenth century) and

---

[36] "O quam metuendus est locus iste … [etc.]."

[37] "Vidit Jacob scalam … et dixit: Vere locus iste sanctus est" and "Erexit Iacob lapidem."

[38] "O quam metuendus est locus iste; V. Vere Dominus est in loco isto … [etc.]."

[39] "Mane surgens Iacob … votum vovit Domino: Vere locus iste sanctus est … [etc.]; V. Cumque mane surgens …" and "Terribilis est locus iste: non est hic aliud nisi domus dei … V. Cumque evigilasset Iacob … ait: Vere locus iste sanctus est …."

[40] "Mane surgens Iacob … votum vovit Domino: Vere locus iste sanctus est … [etc.]."

[41] "Terribilis est locus iste."

[42] "Locus iste a Deo."

[43] "Terribilis est locus iste: non est aliud nisi domus dei… Vere etenim Dominus est in loco isto… [etc.]" and "Mane surgens Iacob … votum vovit Domino: Vere locus iste sanctus est … [etc.]."

[44] "Erit mihi Dominus in deum, et lapis iste vocabitur domus dei."

[45] Documented in all three manuscripts – Vatican, Barb. lat. 659, MS Barletta and Wroclaw, I.Q.175.

[46] John, p. 94.

[47] *Corpus Antiphonalium Officii*, ed. Renatus-Joannes Hesbert (Rome, 1968), nos. 2665, 3691, 4065, 5415, 7126, 7286, 7763.

[48] Ibid., no. 7286.

Saint-Maur-les-Fossés (monastic cursus, twelfth century),[49] Silos (monastic cursus, eleventh century) and Ivrea (Roman cursus, eleventh century),[50] Rheinau (monastic cursus, thirteenth century),[51] Saint-Loup in Benevent (monastic cursus, twelfth century),[52] and Ivrea again (Roman cursus, eleventh century).[53]

The second volet in the revisionist thesis advances four arguments for dating the consecration of the "Crusader church ... between the accession of Amaury in 1163 and the years 1167/9."[54] None of them, however, relate explicitly to the church's consecration, unless one assimilates "completion" with "consecration," and even in regard to the proposed late date of completion the evidence adduced is far from conclusive. Let us consider these arguments in detail.

The first argument concerns the number and arrangement of the *loca sancta*, the foci of devotion and liturgy in and around the Anastasis. This was most forcefully put forward by De Vogüé, who argued that between 1102 and 1167 the Holy Sepulchre cartulary consistently enumerated only four "sanctuaires."[55] He signaled a sudden change in 1169: from that date, he believed, the cartulary testified to an augmented list (nine *loca* are in fact enumerated in the 1168/9 document, as dated by its most recent editor[56]) that included all the *loca* comprised in the various structures integrated into the new overarching church. He deduced from this that the new church was "inaugurated" between 1167 and 1169.[57]

This argument is flawed in several respects. First, the two documents cited do not open and close a series of documents on this subject; in fact, they are the only documents in the cartulary between 1102/3 and 1168/9 that refer to the Holy Sepulchre foci of devotion, thus, the claim that the cartulary "consistently enumerates" only these four *loca* between these dates is not sustainable. The alleged "new" situation in 1167 could have been brought about much earlier in theory, at any time between 1102 and 1168/9. Nor does the 1168/9 document open up a

---

[49] "V. Surgens ergo mane Jacob, tulit lapidem quem supposuerat capiti suo et erexit in titulum, fundensque oleum desuper, dixit. Vere."

[50] "V. Vere Dominus est in loco isto, et ego nesciebam. Non est (=Ivrea). Et porta (=Silos)."

[51] "V. Domum istam protege, Domine, et angeli tui custodiant muros ejus. Vere" (not from Jacob's narrative).

[52] "V. Mane surgens Jacob, erigebat lapidem in titulum; fundens oleum desuper, votum vovit Domino, dicens. Vere."

[53] "V. Mane surgens Jacob, votum vovit Domino deo et dixit. Vere."

[54] Biddle, p. xi.

[55] The Sepulchre, the Cross, and two altars in the Anastasis – the Principal Altar and the Parochial Altar (*Cart St Sép*, no. 19 [dated Nov. 1102 – 24 March 1103], p. 73).

[56] The Sepulchre, the Cross, the Great Altar in the choir, the Prison with its altar, the Altar of SS Peter and Stephen, the Invention of the Cross "with all its altars," the Parochial Altar by the chevet of the Sepulchre, the Cathedra behind the Great Altar, and the Compass (*Cart St Sép*, no. 150 [dated 25 Dec. 1168 – 24 Dec. 1169], p. 294).

[57] "... depuis 1102 jusqu'à 1167, cette énumération est toujours la même ... A partir de 1169 ... elle s'augmente, et comprend, outre les sanctuaires précédentes, tous ceux qui se sont trouvés réunis à l'église primitive par les constructions des Croisés. Ce changement subit de rédaction semble placer entre ... 1167 et 1169 l'inauguration des nouveaux edifices" (De Vogüé, *Les églises de la Terre Sainte*, p. 218). Biddle followed his lead (Biddle, p. 96).

new series of similar documents. With the exception of a single confirmation[58] by Pope Alexander III in 1170 – which merely repeats the tenor of Patriarch Amaury's document from 1168/69 – it remains unique. The real cause of this "sudden" interest in the enumeration of Holy Sepulchre's *loca sancta* did not arise, however, from any hypothetical architectural transformation of the church at that time, but from the well-documented conflict that broke out between the patriarch and the chapter concerning the lawful extent of the patriarch's intervention in the chapter's affairs and the rights of both sides over the revenues derived – among other sources – from these *loca*. A series of four papal bulls[59] issued in February and March 1168 testify to the active intervention of Pope Alexander III, in response to an appeal lodged before him by a delegation that the chapter had sent to the curia. In effect, Amaury's detailed document represents a conciliatory step towards the chapter by recognizing its pecuniary rights over certain *loca*, specifically enumerated for this purpose.[60]

Furthermore, as the two documents from 1102 and 1168/9 deal with the particular issue of the chapter's properties and its rights in the church's *loca sancta* and, more specifically, with the partition of the revenues derived from them between the patriarch and the chapter, they cannot be regarded as complete, exhaustive inventories of all the Holy Sepulchre altars and places of devotion. The overall number of these places at any given time certainly exceeded the four enumerated in 1102/3, even the nine specified in 1168/69. Saewulf's account, practically contemporaneous with the 1102/3 document, noted twelve *loca sancta* in the Anastasis and in its immediate vicinity,[61] the Russian pilgrim Abbot Daniel enumerated thirteen in 1106/7,[62] John of Würzburg recorded twelve after 1150,[63]

---

[58] *Cart St Sép*, no.151, pp. 297–301.

[59] Ibid., nos. 143–46, pp. 278–87.

[60] See the recent discussion in Klaus-Peter Kirstein, *Die lateinischen Patriarchen von Jerusalem* (Berlin, 2002), pp. 305–7.

[61] The Sepulchre, the Prison, the Invention of the Cross, the Column of Flagellation, the Stripping of clothes, the Dressing with the scarlet robe – Crowning with the crown of thorns – and Partition of garments, the Place of Crucifixion, Golgotha, the Chapel of St. Mary – the Embalming and robing of Christ's body, the *Compas* – Apparition to Mary Magdalen, Chapel of St. Mary, Chapel of St. John (Huygens, *Peregrinationes* [above, note 1], pp. 65–66).

[62] The Great Altar in the Anastasis, the Sepulchre, the Omphalos, the Place of Crucifixion, Chapel of the Calvary, the Partition of garments – Crowning with the crown of thorns – Dressing with the scarlet robe, Altar of Abraham, Place of the Striking of Christ's face, the Prison, the Invention of the Cross, the place of the Virgin's Fervor, the Gate of St. Mary the Egyptian, and the Verification of the True Cross (*Enchiridion locorum sanctorum*, ed. Donatus Baldi (Jerusalem, 1982), no. 946, pp. 656–61).

[63] The Calvary altar ("altare ... in honore dominicae passionis consecratum"), the Prison ("'Carcer domini' appellatur"), under Calvary "altare ... vocatur 'Ad Sanctum Sanguinem'," the Omphalos – the Apparition to Mary Magdalen – where Joseph washed and clothed Jesus' corpse, the Sepulchre, the western altar "Ad Sanctum Sepulchrum," the Great Altar ("in honore anastasios"), the altar in the Invention crypt ("Helenae honorem ... consecratum"), a particle of the Cross reserved in the part of the church opposite Calvary, the Great Altar in the choir, the St. Stephen Altar and the St. Peter Altar (John, pp. 117, 119–24).

and Theoderic visited more than twenty-one[64] in ca. 1169,[65] roughly simultaneously with the lower time-limit of the supposed inauguration of the new edifice – with nine "sanctuaires" in all – in 1167/69.

Moreover, De Vogüé's survey of the Holy Sepulchre "sanctuaires" – especially altars – completely ignores the numerous foci of devotion possessed and served by the non-Latin Churches, places of no practical interest to the property administrators of the patriarch and the chapter but clearly significant for any reconstruction of the architectural and liturgical history of the Holy Sepulchre. The true extent of this phenomenon can be appreciated from the fleeting references given in Theoderic's account: apart from the Armenian and Syrian chapels and the altar already mentioned, Theoderic specified that once the Latin daily Office in the Holy Sepulchre was terminated the Syrians were accustomed to hold their service either by that altar or in any of the church's apses, for "plura in ipsa ecclesia habent altariola nullorumque nisi suis usibus apta vel concessa."[66] Furthermore, the Greek Orthodox Typikon of the Anastasis, dated to 1122, strongly points to a routine liturgical activity of the Greek Orthodox clergy in the Holy Sepulchre by that date.[67]

The claim that no new altars were consecrated between 1102/3 and 1168/9 is refuted by John of Würzburg's statement that four altars were consecrated on the very same day on which the church was dedicated – on 15 July 1149: the Great Altar in the choir, the Altar on the summit of Calvary, the St. Peter's Altar and the St. Stephen's Altar.[68] All four were most probably located in the eastern part of the new edifice. If John's information is accurate about the last two altars, it reflects the first stage in the evolution of the altar designated in the 1168/9 document as "the SS. Peter and Stephen altar" – resulting, probably, from the transfer and unification

---

[64] The Sepulchre, the Altar of the Laying ("altare quidam parvum sed reverendum ... ubi corpus dominicum antequam sepulture daretur positum fuisse a Ioseph et Nycodemo" in the Anastasis), the Altar behind the entrance to the Grave, the Altar by the Sepulchre's chevet (=Parochial), the Principal Altar ("Principale altare nomini et honori domini Salvatoris attitulaum" in the Choir), the Patriarchal Cathedra (in the Choir), the Altar of Deposition (in the Choir), the Altar of the Syrians ("ante ostium vero ipsius chori altare non mediocre quod ad Surianorum tantummodo spectat officium"), the Armenian Chapel of St. Mary, the Syrian Chapel of the Holy Cross, the Chapel of the Holy Cross with an altar ("capella in qua altare reverendum honori sancte crucis attitulatum"), the Prison with an altar, the Altar of St. Nicholas, the Chapel of St. Helen – Invention of the Cross with an altar – Altar of St. James, the relic of the Column of Flagellation within an altar, the Chapel under the belfry, the Chapel of St. John the Baptist – Baptistery, a third chapel in the courtyard, Calvary – the Place where the Cross was fixed with an altar, the Chapel of Golgotha, the Chapel of the Three Marys (Huygens, pp. 147–49, 151, 153–57).

[65] See ibid., p. 28.

[66] Ibid., pp. 151–52.

[67] See Bernard Hamilton, *The Latin Church in the Crusader States: The Secular Church* (London, 1980), pp. 170–71, and Johannes Pahlitzsch, "The Greek Orthodox Church in the First Kingdom of Jerusalem (1099–1187)," in *Patterns of the Past, Prospects of the Future. The Christian Heritage in the Holy Land*, ed. Thomas Hummel, Kervork Hintlian and Ulf Carmesund (London, 1999), pp. 204–5.

[68] "Nam ea die quatuor etiam altaria in eadem aecclesiae sunt consecrata, scilicet altare maius et illud superius in Calvaria et duo in latere aecclesia ex opposita parte, unum scilicet in honore sancti Petri et aliud in honore sancti Stephani protomartyris" (John, p. 124).

of the two saints' relics in one altar between 1149 and 1168/9.[69] If, on the other hand, he mistook one altar dedicated to the two saints for two separate altars, the consecration of that twin-titled altar should be backdated to 1149. It still existed by 1255, though under the title of St. Peter's alone, for on that date St. John's Hospital obligated itself to pay annually a priest who will celebrate the divine service "quando civitas Jerosolimitana erit in manus Christianorum ... in ecclesia Sepulcri Dominici ad altare S. Petri."[70]

The second argument adduced for dating the dedication of the entire church to 1167–69 refers, in effect, to its completion rather than dedication. Biddle believes that John of Würzburg emphasized the newness of the recently-built Frankish choir: "adjectionem novae ecclsiae ... illud novum et de novo additum aedificium"[71] and comments that "these words might refer to a building finished twenty years before, but their reiterated emphasis reflects better a completion in the decade before his visit."[72] The date Biddle assigns to John's pilgrimage – ca. 1170 – would fit well, therefore, with a presumed completion/dedication in 1167/69.

Three difficulties render this dating of John's pilgrimage to ca. 1170 highly speculative. First, it is not supported by any proof whatsoever: it simply homes in on the lower end of the approximate dating originally proposed by Tobler and subsequently adopted by Manitius[73] – between 1160 and 1170. Second, that dating depends on the assumption that the expression "novum et de novo" refers to the immediate rather than the more distant past; the previous decade rather than the past two decades, or even earlier. This typically modern perception of time was not shared, apparently, by John of Würzburg, for he employed the same expression – "venerabilia loca nova et de novo exstructa"[74] – in his final survey of thirteen churches and chapels in Jerusalem that were not directly commemorative of the main events in Christ's life, some of them positively pre-Frankish and others documented as functioning since the early part of the century.[75] Among them he lists the Sepultures of the Pilgrims at Haceldama, St. John the Baptist with its hospital, St. Mary the Latin, the Armenian Church of St. Sabas, the Armenian Church of James the Major, St. Mary of the Germans with its hospital, St. Peter in Chains,

---

[69] *Cart St Sép*, no. 150, p. 294.

[70] *Cart Hosp*, vol. 2 (1897), no. 2732, pp. 779–80. Röhricht's *Regesta* failed to transmit faithfully the Hospitaller's tranquil confidence in future events, replacing "quando civitas Jerosolimitana erit in manus Christianorum" with a sceptical "si urbs Hierosolimitana recepta fuerit" (*RRH*, no. 1234, pp. 324–25).

[71] John, p. 122.

[72] Biddle, p. 97.

[73] Max Manitius, *Geschichte der lateinischen Literatur des Mittelalters*, 3 (Munich, 1931), p. 620.

[74] John, p. 130.

[75] The pre-Frankish Syrian church of Haceldama was given in 1143 to the Hospital, the pre-Frankish St. John the Baptist is mentioned by Saewulf in 1102/3, St. Mary the Latin was constructed already in the ninth century, the Armenian Church of St. Sabas was pre-Frankish as it was mentioned by Saewulf in 1102/3, St. Anne was already functioning in 1104 when Queen Erda was forced to join its monastic community, and the Jacobite St. Mary Magdalene was constructed in the ninth century and renovated in 1092.

the Templars' Church, St. Anne, the Jacobite St. Mary Magdalene and others.[76] All or some of these churches could have been undergoing construction or decoration during the 1160s, but to deduce from the expression "novum et de novo" alone the completion or dedication during that decade of all the thirteen churches in this category is simply wrong. This expression might refer to the "new" Frankish era, more than half a century old by 1150 and recognized as "new" in reference to the "old" pre-Frankish Christian past of Jerusalem, or it might simply indicate a slower perception of time, quite unlike the modern sense of "new" as against "old" and covering more than one decade.

The third difficulty concerns the attempt to assign exact dates to either John's pilgrimage or the text that narrates its course. The problem touches, essentially, all medieval literary texts: exact dates depend on the "author's version," on the text as actually written by the author, but most efforts to search for such an "authentic version" are destined to fail, for very few medieval texts have survived in such a form.[77] More often than not the author's version(s) underwent a progressive process of editing – intentional and otherwise – by editors, copyists, commentators and readers. Travel and pilgrimage accounts are even more problematic in this context, for the rules that governed this genre emphasized the narrative's practical as well as spiritual value – as a useful guidebook, an exhortation to pilgrimage or a virtual substitute offering meditation in place of the actual journey – at the expense of real personal experience.[78] Their professed commitment, at the same time, to faithfully documenting a given reality (places, people, events, objects, times) involved a method of composition that was far more complex and difficult to realize than that employed in other types of literary creation – fiction, for example. In the best case it began with the actual gathering and recording of information, moved through an interim rough draft while still on the journey,[79] and ended with a polished version

---

[76] John, pp. 131–37.

[77] And not a few authors published more than one "final version." Fulcher of Chartres, for example, produced two versions of his *Historia Hierosolymitana*: in the first he narrated events up to 1124, and in the second he rewrote substantial parts of the first edition and carried the narrative down to 1127. A careful comparison between the two editions discloses the intellectual evolution of this first-generation crusader. See Verena Epp, "Die Entstehung eines 'Nationalbewusstseins' in den Kreuzfahrerstaaten," *Deutsches Archiv* 45 (1989), pp. 596–604, esp. pp. 597–601. Gerald of Wales published four versions of his *Topographia Hibernica* and two each of the *Itinerarium Kambriae* and the *Descriptio Kambriae* (Manitius, *Geschichte*, pp. 625, 632–34).

[78] See Jean Richard, *Les récits de voyages et de pèlerinages*, Typologie des sources du Moyen Âge occidental 38 (Turnhout, 1981), esp. pp. 15–23, and Ora Limor, "Pilgrims and Authors: Adomnan's *De locis sanctis* and Hugeburc's *Hodoeporicon sancti Willibaldis*," *Revue bénédictine* 114 (2004) pp. 253–75.

[79] For example Egeria's *Itinerarium* – written down and terminated in Constantinople from where it was sent back home while the author was still on her journey, planning to go on and visit other places (XXIII.10: "De quo loco ... iam propositi erat ... ad Asiam accedendi ...," ed. Otto Prinz, Heidelberg 1960, p. 30), and Magister Gregorius during his Roman visit, sending his draft to his colleagues back home and promising to supply the missing information once he were able to do some serious research at leisure after his return ("At cum favente deo in [corrupt reading] ex hac peregrinatione rediero, denuo que nunc ambigua sunt et que penitus latent adhuc maiori mora et exercitatiori indagacione perscrutabor,

produced at leisure at home.[80] Other cases testify to a less rigorous method, omitting the laborious primary recording or avoiding the intermediate rough draft and relying upon memory alone, supplemented by information garnered from authoritative guide-books and previous travel accounts. Any attempt to extract chronological indicators from this type of literature should be grounded, therefore, on a correct distinction between three major levels of composition – a) primary recording, b) the author's rough draft and "final" version(s), and c) the consecutive editing process. The value of such indicators will depend, obviously, on the level from which they derive, depreciating progressively down the authorial/editorial stemma, from the most useful at the primary level of personal recording to, potentially, the least credible on the level of the latest version in circulation.

John's text displays these difficulties. There is no mistaking his pious, spiritual motivation: the text was meant to serve Dietrich – the dedicatee – as a useful introduction and guide-book if and when he made the Jerusalem pilgrimage. Alternatively, it could offer him the means to contemplate the holy places in Jerusalem spiritually and thus increase his devotion to their sanctifying quality.[81] Both pilgrimage and text are organized, consequently, according to two interlocking schemes: the first follows the earthly manifestations of the major events in the history of salvation with Christ at its center, each event perceived as "sacramentum"; the second scheme emphasizes the progressively unfolding character of this series of events by assimilating them to the Seven Seals of the Revelation.[82] John's personal circumstances become rather insignificant in this perspective, and he is practically absent (as a living individual person) from the scenes he describes (with one notable exception – a patriotic German outburst; see below). That self-effacement eliminated almost all datable personal information of the sort that renders Abbot Daniel's travel account so valuable for our knowledge of the early Frankish rule in the Holy Land. The same perspective induced John to supplement his knowledge with information received from authoritative written sources, but the combination

---

et perscrutata gratanter amicis partibor," ed. G. Rushforth, "Magister Gregorius De Mirabilibus Urbis Romae: A New Description of Rome in the Twelfth Century," *Journal of Roman Studies* 9 (1919), c. 25, p. 55, also Robert B. C. Huygens, ed., *Narracio de mirabilibus Urbis Rome* (Leiden, 1970), c. 25, p. 26, and Cristina Nardella, *Il fascino di Roma nel Medioevo: Le "Meraviglie di Roma" di maestro Gregorio* (Rome, 1997), c. 27, p.166.

[80] The extant text of the *Itinerarium* of Antoninus Placentinus was composed after his return, as it refers to Jericho dates which he brought back home ("in provincia," ed. Paul Geyer, *Itinera Hierosolymitana* CSEL 39, c. 14, p. 169).

[81] "Quam descriptionem tibi acceptam fore estimo, ideo scilicet, quia evidenter singula per eam notata tibi, quandoque ... huc venienti, sponte et sine inquisitionis mora et difficultate tanquam nota tuis sese ingerunt oculis, vel, si forte non veniendo haec intuitu non videbis corporeo, tamen ex tali noticia et contemplatione eorum ampliorem quoad sanctificationem ipsorum devotionem habebis" (John, p. 79).

[82] "Computantur ... haec septem sigilla, videlicet nativitas domini seu incarnatio, baptismus, passio, ad inferos descensio, resurrectio, ascensio, futuri iudicii representatio ..." (ibid., p. 89). Six of the seven are located in Jerusalem, and John hesitates as to the place where the Last Judgement will take place, although he quotes the Prophet Joel in regard to the Valley of Josaphat. The first Seal comprises three "Sacraments" – the Incarnation in Nazareth, the Nativity in Bethlehem, and the Presentation in the Temple (John, p. 88).

of directly observed data with received information can only undermine the veracity of what seem to be datable observations. A telling example of this was pointed out by Huygens: John's reference to the church being built "now" at Jacob's Well – "ubi nunc aecclesia constituitur" – seems to indicate the time of his visit there as well as that of the construction, but he "may never have seen the church himself, because he took the mention from his source for the passage: Fretellus …: 'ubi nunc … ecclesia constituitur.' "[83] Huygens found, indeed, that "nearly 45% of … [John's] narrative have been taken straight from Fretellus" and that John's "dependence on Fretellus is more often than not literal."[84] Extracting chronological indications from John's text, consequently, is far less simple than it might appear at first sight.

Two definite chronological indications can nevertheless be extracted from his text. Both are first-level data – personally observed and recorded in place by the author, who prided himself, and rightly so, on his meticulous information-gathering, especially in Jerusalem.[85] The first is his transcription of the dedication-inscription with its date – 15 July [1149], and the other his account of the combined annual service on 15 July of the Liberation Festivity with the Anniversary of the Holy Sepulchre Dedication as instituted by Patriarch Fulcher between 1150 and 1157 (Fulcher died on 20 November 1157).[86] These indications provide the exact date of 15 July 1149 and the approximate date of 1150–57 for the *terminus a quo* of John's visit to Jerusalem. A third indication – his reference to the siege of Damascus in 1148[87] – does not contribute much, for it is already subsumed in the reference to 1149 and, furthermore, John could have acquired this piece of knowledge anywhere and anytime – say in Würzburg and prior to his pilgrimage.

A fourth chronological indication, one of a much more speculative nature, concerns the paean to the superior prowess of the Germans as against the French, a patriotic outburst motivated by what John believed to be the deliberate suppression of the record of the German crusaders' true role in the liberation of Jerusalem, and his stated belief that were the Germans fully mobilized (and "fully" is the key-word here, practically absolving the German crusaders from the fiasco before Damascus), they would have long ago extended the frontiers of Christendom beyond the Nile to the south and Damascus to the east.[88] He attached to this diatribe his own contribution for keeping the record straight – a poetical epitaph celebrating Wigger, the first crusader to enter Jerusalem, who was German rather than French:

---

[83] Ibid., Introduction, p. 28.
[84] Ibid., Introduction, pp. 18–19.
[85] "loca venerabilia … precipue in civitate sancta Hierusalem, quanto expressius et studiosius potui denotando, in eis facta et epygrammata sive prosaice sive metrice stili officio colligere laboravi" (Ibid., p. 79).
[86] Ibid., pp. 123–24.
[87] "… factum illud apud Damascum cum rege Cunrado" (ibid., p. 135).
[88] "Quae utique Christianitatis provincia iam dudum terminos suos ultra Nilum versus meridiem et ultra Damascum versus orientem extendisset, si tanta copia Alemanorum, quanta est istorum, adesset" (ibid., p. 126).

"Franco, non Francus, Wigger."[89] It is quite possible – to adopt a suggestion made originally by Graboïs[90] – that the references to "beyond the Nile and Damascus" allude to concrete historical events – to the Damascus siege and to the first Egyptian campaign of King Amaury in 1163 (only one campaign was obviously necessary for John to be cognizant of the military drive towards the Nile, and it is reasonable to assume that that was the first in that series of campaigns). It should probably be attributed to a later stage in the text's composition – to the draft that John composed in Jerusalem during his stay in the city: in the prologue he refers to Jerusalem with the word "huc" (hither),[91] and unless we are dealing here with a literary convention, Jerusalem appears to be the place where this text was written down for the first time. If this is the case, 1163–64 should be seen as the *terminus a quo* for the edited version.

The only certain and exact *terminus a quo* for John's pilgrimage consists, therefore, of 15 July 1149; a more extended *terminus a quo* is spread over seven years, from 1150 to 1157; the contribution of 1163 for this purpose is more hypothetical, but it should perhaps be accepted as the *terminus a quo* of the edited text. These chronological indications do not warrant more than that: they are manifestly inadequate for an exact – or even an approximate – dating of the completion or dedication of the Holy Sepulchre.

A third argument for a later dating of the dedication/completion, to between 1163 and 1167/69, derives from the observation that shortly after the beginning of Amaury's reign in 1163 "a new type of denier was issued showing ... the distinctive shape of the conical 'dome' over the Rotunda of the Holy Sepulchre."[92] This is somewhat puzzling, for the appearance of this distinctive shape could have been motivated by several reasons other than the commemoration of the completion/ dedication, just as the appearance of the Tower of David and the Templum Domini on the Frankish coinage did not necessarily commemorate specific events in the history of these edifices. On closer examination,[93] furthermore, the premise of the argument – the dating of the "Amalricus" coins with the Holy Sepulchre type to "shortly after 1163" – falls apart. As these coins bear no identification marks concerning either mint or date, all attempts to date them depend on the name "Amalricus" and on the presumed dates of hoards in which they were included. Scholars have accordingly identified this type with either King Amaury (1163–74) or with King Aimery (1197–1205). The recent preference for the former rests on the

---

[89] Ibid., p. 125.

[90] Aryeh Graboïs, "Le pèlerin occidental en Terre Sainte à l'époque des croisades et ses réalités: la relation de pèlerinage de Jean de Wurtzbourg," *Études de civilisation médiévale (IXe–XIIe siècles), Mélanges E.-R. Labande* (Poitiers, 1974), pp. 367–76.

[91] Addressing Dietrich, John states: "quandoque divina inspiratione et tuitione huc venienti ..." (John, p. 79).

[92] Biddle, p. 96.

[93] Roberto Pesant, "The 'Amalricus' Coins of the Kingdom of Jerusalem," in *Coinage in the Latin East*, ed. Peter W. Edbury and David M. Metcalf (Oxford, 1980), pp. 105–21. See also John Porteous, "Crusader Coinage with Greek and Latin Inscriptions," in: Setton, *Crusades*, 6:374.

fact that specimens of this type were found in the Samos hoard, believed to have been buried between ca. 1170 and ca. 1185.[94] Assuming that the identification of "Amalricus" with Amaury is correct, one is still in the dark as to the date when that type was introduced: it could have happened at any time between 1163 and 1174.[95] An argument put together on the premise that this coinage was introduced shortly after 1163 is founded, therefore, on shaky ground indeed, and becomes clearly circular when numismatists rely on the dedication/completion's date suggested by historians and diplomatists,[96] who adopt the "numismatic data" in their turn in support of their own dating.

The fourth – and final argument in this series – concerns the "Genoese Golden Inscription" that was allegedly placed in the Rotunda in 1105, reproducing the tenor of a putative charter of privileges granted to the Genoese in recognition of their participation in the conquest of the Holy Land. Biddle argues that it was destroyed in the time of Amaury (1163–74), "certainly no later than 1169 and possibly by 1167… it can only have taken place when the Byzantine apse was demolished to open up the Rotunda to the new east end."[97] The very existence of that inscription and the authenticity of the document it purports to reproduce, however, have been challenged in 1976 and are still the subject of a lively scholarly debate, notably between M.-L. Favreau-Lilie and H. E. Mayer[98] – on the prosecution's bench – and B. Z. Kedar and A. Rovere[99] for the defense. In the absence of a decisive proof one way or the other the discussion turns around probabilities (historical, philological

---

[94] "Difficult as the Samos hoard is to date precisely, it seems to fall in the period 1170–1185" (Pesant, "The 'Amalricus' Coins," p. 116).

[95] Pesant is quite clear about this: "The series may have commenced shortly after Amaury's succession, ca. 1165 (although we have no way of knowing how promptly the new type was introduced) … We do not know that the coinage reform took place after the accession of Amaury in 1163, for changes of type in the twelfth century were often delayed or deferred" (ibid., pp. 114, 116). Metcalf – in the discussion that followed Pesant's paper – was equally cautious: "the 'Amalricus' coins were struck before 1174, and perhaps even as early as 1163" (ibid., p. 116).

[96] Metcalf concludes, on grounds of De Vogüé's thesis on the completion of the new crusaders' church as "a single legal entity, the basilica of the Holy Sepulchre" between 1167 and 1169, that "It would be understandable if the new coinage type, which must post-date 1163, were in fact post-1167" (David M. Metcalf, *Coinage of the Crusades and the Latin East in the Ashmolean Museum, Oxford*, 2nd ed. (London, 1995), pp. 57–58; detailed discussion of this type in pp. 57–71).

[97] Biddle, p. 95.

[98] Hans Eberhard Mayer and Marie-Luise Favreau, "Das Diplom Balduins I. für Genua und Genuas Goldene Inschrift in der Grabeskirche," *Quellen und Forschungen aus italienischen Archiven und Bibliotheken* 55/56 (1976), pp. 22–95; Hans Eberhard Mayer, "Genuas gefälschte Goldene Inschrift in der Grabeskirche," *Zeitschrift des Deutschen Palästina-Vereins* 116 (2000), pp. 63–75.

[99] Benjamin Z. Kedar, "Genoa's Golden Inscription in the Church of the Holy Sepulchre: A Case for the Defence," in *I Comuni Italiani nel Regno Crociato di Gerusalemme*, ed. Gabriella Airaldi and Benjamin Z. Kedar (Genoa, 1986), pp. 317–35; Antonella Rovere, "'Rex Balduinus Ianuensibus privilegia firmavit et fecit': Sulla presunta falsità del diploma di Baldovino I in favore dei Genovesi," *Studi medievali*, 3e s. 37 (1996), pp. 95–133; Benjamin Z. Kedar, "Again: Genoa's Golden Inscription and King Baldwin I's Privilege of 1104," in *Chemins d'Outre-Mer; Études d'histoire sur la Mediterranée médiévale offertes à Michel Balard*, ed. Damien Coulon, Catherine Otten-Froux and Paule Pagès (Paris, 2004), pp. 495–502.

and architectural-archeological): the jury, consequently, is still out. But, even if one accepts the premise that the Golden Inscription existed and that it was wilfully demolished, it does not necessarily follow that its destruction was in any way linked with the final stage of the church's construction, especially in light of the fact that the exact location of that inscription in the Rotunda is still a matter of dispute: the eastern Byzantine apse is not the only location suggested in recent literature. The entire argument bears only on the edifice's completion and is largely irrelevant to the issue of the putative later dedication of the entire church.

A crucial corroboration of the thesis that the 1149 dedication applied to the entire church rather than Calvary alone can be found in the liturgy of the Anniversary of that dedication. Practiced in the Holy Sepulchre from ca. 1150 until 1187, it was subsequently preserved and commemorated by the institutions that followed the Holy Sepulchre liturgy, wholly or partially, among them the three military orders of the Temple, the Hospital and the Teutonic Knights. For almost fifty years after 1099 the Day of the Liberation of Jerusalem, also called the Feast of Jerusalem,[100] was annually celebrated in Jerusalem on 15 July with an elaborate liturgical programme.[101] It was performed mainly in the Holy Sepulchre but extended also to the Templum Domini church and to the city at large, in a stational pattern that combined Office, festive Mass and Processions, and assembled together the Holy Sepulchre clergy with the general public, inhabitants of the city as well as pilgrims and crusaders. Gerhoh of Reichersberg observed rightly that "quae dies [=15 July] adhuc Hierosolimae ita celebris habetur, ut in ea cum summa diligentia officium tantae victoriae congruum celebretur ...."[102] The celebrations on that day consisted of a full proper Office that commenced on the Vespers of 14 July and continued throughout the night with Matins, Lauds and Prime. After Prime a festive procession led by the patriarch made its way to the Templum Domini, held a *statio* at the gate of the church, went out through the southern gate of the Temple enclosure, proceeded along the city walls and held another *statio* by the monumental golden cross that marked the place where the first crusaders scaled the wall and entered the city in 1099. The patriarch preached to the assembly there and gave it his blessing, and then the procession made its way back to the Holy Sepulchre and held another *statio* in front of the Sepulchre. After the Office of Terce, a solemn Liberation Mass ("Laetare Hierusalem") was celebrated, followed, throughout the day, by the proper Office of the later Lesser Hours – Sext and None. A Second proper Vespers closed the festivities.

---

[100] Variously designated as "Dies liberationis Hierusalem," "Festivitas Hierusalem."

[101] Amnon Linder, "The Liturgy of the Liberation of Jerusalem," *Mediaeval Studies* 55 (1990), pp. 110–31; idem, "A New Day, New Joy: The Liberation of Jerusalem on 15 July 1099," in *L'idea di Gerusalemme nella spiritualità Cristiana del medioevo*, ed. Walther Brandmüller (Città del Vaticano, 2003), pp. 46–64.

[102] *Gerhohi Praepositi Reichersbergensis Commentarius in Psalmos*, In Ps. XXXIII, ed. Ernst Sackur, MGH LdL 3 (1897), p. 431.

That twenty-four hours long programme was held for the last time in 1148: the dedication solemnized on 15 July 1149 practically signaled its demise. The rubric of the new service of the Dedication Anniversary service, inserted next to the old Liberation service in four liturgical books (the Holy Sepulchre's Ordinary of Barletta, a Templars' Breviary, a Teutonic Order's Ordinary and a Hospitallers' Breviary), reads as follows: "Eodem die dedicatio ecclesie dominici sepulchri quam sollempniter celebramus, iuxta voluntatem et preceptum domini Fulcherii patriarche, missa matutinalis de captione tantum canitur, sed processio nunquam dimittitur, sed festive peragitur, ut prescriptum est."[103] The regulation referred to was made, therefore, between 1150 – the first time that the annual Anniversary of the dedication was due – and Fulcher's death in 1157. The rubric itself seems to have been entered at that time, while Fulcher was still alive, for it quotes his name without the usual epithets for the deceased, such as "bonae/sanctae/piae memoriae." A date closer to 1150 is suggested by the fact that Fulcher was certainly called upon to settle the problem of these two liturgical programs falling on the same day already towards 1150, the first anniversary of the dedication: his directive on that matter ("nova institutio," "preceptum," "mandatum") should not have been issued, therefore, much later than that date.

Fulcher solved the problem posed by the two concurrent programmes by eliminating the Office part of the old Liberation service from the main celebration of the day and integrating its Mass and stational processions – in a decidedly subsidiary position (the Liberation Mass was downgraded from High to Morrow Mass) – into the new Dedication Anniversary programme. The fact that the old Liberation Office was still copied into the liturgical directories produced after 1149 suggests that it was not entirely abolished but relegated to the margins and still observed in some way – say, in a side chapel and probably only partially. The reformed festivity of that day consisted, however, of an Office that focused entirely on the Dedication – from the First Vespers on 14 July to the closing Second Vespers on the 15th, a Liberation Morning Mass ("Laetare Hierusalem") after Prime followed by the traditional Procession from the Holy Sepulchre and back again, and the Dedication High Mass ("Terribilis est locus") with the Dedication Office of Sext, None and Vespers. The terminology employed in both the general rubric ("dedicatio ecclesie

---

[103] This is the rubric transmitted in the two earliest manuscripts – the Templars' Breviary (Vatican, Barb. lat. 659, fol. 102, written in Jerusalem, 1153–57; I have emended "nonquam" to "nunquam," as in the two other manuscripts) and the Holy Sepulchre Ordinary (Barletta, Archivio della Chiesa del Santo Sepolcro, s.n., copied 1202–28, fol. 120v, with the following two variants: "cantatur," *om.* "ut prescriptum est"). The Templars' Breviary refers to that reform earlier: "De hac liberatione secundum nova institutione nichil facimus preter processionem et missam matutinalem, propter dedicationem ecclesie." The Teutonic Order's Ordinary, in a fourteenth-century copy (Wrocław, I.Q.175, fol. 115), presents several variants but no substantial changes: "Eodem die dedicatio ecclesie dominici sepulchri. Quam agimus sollempniter iuxta mandatum domini Fulcherii patriarche. [Item] Missa matutinalis tantum de captione cantatur. Sed processio numquam obmittitur. Sed festive peragatur." The Hospital's Breviary, in a fifteenth-century copy (Vienna, ÖNB, Cod. Palat. 1928, fol. 79), preserved only the rubric's first phrase: "Eodem die dedicatio dominici sepulchri, quam sollempniter celebramus." It omitted the entire Anniversary section as well, while retaining the Liberation service.

dominici sepulchri") and the rubric to the First Vespers ("In dedicatione ecclesie dominici sepulchri") is unequivocal as to the identification of the church involved. It recurs, indeed, in the Calendars of the Frankish liturgical books composed after 1150, relegating, again, the Liberation to a second place, behind the Dedication.[104] It also appears in Calendars of liturgical books produced in several European churches, a clear evidence to the spread abroad of this information from Jerusalem and of a certain liturgical practice linked to it.[105] The church dedicated by Fulcher on 15 July 1149, whose Dedication Anniversary was established by him in ca. 1150 (and at any rate before 1157) as an integrated service commemorating both Dedication and Liberation in a radical reform of a long-established liturgical tradition, was, consequently, the new Frankish church of the Holy Sepulchre in its entirety.

The real significance of that event can be appreciated only when that Dedication is put in context, the particular context of the Frankish church and the general context of Frankish society as a whole on its fiftieth anniversary.

The new Frankish Holy Sepulchre should be seen, in the first place, as an example of the general drive to validate the Christian possession of the Holy Land through Christian ritual, and to bring out the spiritual essence of the Frankish political and societal enterprise in the rites that created and manifested that essence. Church-building was essential to this, for churches were not only indispensable for the performance of ritual, they served also as permanent, visual and exhortatory tokens of the sanctifying presence of the holy in the *loca sancta*, and the Holy Land was practically covered by such *loca*.[106] Hence the drive to build churches, financed with local and European resources, initiated on the very morrow of the liberation and continued – with an even greater force and stamina – until 1187 and, to some extent, even later. Pringle estimated the total number of the churches which were built, rebuilt or restored in the Frankish kingdom of Jerusalem to exceed 400.[107] This is a staggering figure, especially when one considers the limited area and time-span involved: it highlights the centrality of ritual and the concomitant church-building in the crusading/pilgrimage experience. The list includes a number of non-Latin churches, a telling example of the actual collaboration of non-Latins in what is usually considered to be a purely Latin enterprise.

This energetic church-building was stimulated, on a more prosaic, day-to-day basis, by the ever-growing needs of an expanding population. The demographic

---

[104] Under the entry for 15 July the Psalter written in Acre ca. 1223–25 (Florence, Biblioteca Riccardiana, Ms. 323, fol. 4) signals "Dedicatio ecclesie S. Sepulchri et festivitas Jerusalem quando capta fuit a Christianis," the Holy Sepulchre Sacramentary written in Acre ca. 1225–28 (London, BL, Ms. Egerton 2902, fol. 4) refers to "Dedicatio ecclesie dominici sepulchri et liberatio Ierusalem," and a Jerusalem Breviary produced in the fourteenth century by the Premonstratensians of Bellapaïs, Cyprus (St. Wandrille, Bibl. de l'Abbaye, ms. P.12), indicates "Dedicatio s. Sepulchri" and adds: "et quando capta fuit I[erusalem]."

[105] Among them Beauvais, Fontevrault, Nantes, Naples, Orleans, and Soissons.

[106] See Hamilton, *Latin Church*, pp. 361–62.

[107] Denys Pringle, "Churches in the Crusader Kingdom of Jerusalem (1099–1291)," in *Ancient Churches Revealed*, ed. Yoram Tsafrir (Jerusalem, 1993), p. 29.

growth of the Frankish population in the kingdom and in the principalities in the north during the first three quarters of the twelfth century was, indeed, unprecedented: the insignificant remnants of the First Crusade expanded in only three generations to about half a million – half of them in the kingdom and half in the north – as a result, mainly, of immigration from Europe.[108] The numerical predominance of immigrants over native-born Franks was only to be expected in the first generation, of course, but it was maintained in some sectors and groups for quite a long time, for example among settlers in the new township of La Mahomerie or in the new settlement of Bethgibelin,[109] the personnel of the Royal Chancery and Court[110] and the Latin clergy from top to bottom.[111] The ongoing immigration of European nobles, furthermore, caused severe strains between new-comers and the old nobility right up to Hattin and well beyond.[112] Yet the actual number of Latins present in the kingdom and the principalities in any given time was much larger than the sum total of natives plus immigrants, for the permanent population was augmented, in an almost steady rhythm, by a movement of temporary residents. This encompassed pilgrims, crusaders and para-crusaders,[113] mercenaries, members of the military

---

[108] This estimate is given by Rudolf Hiestand, "Der lateinische Klerus der Kreuzfahrerstaaten: geographische Herkunft und politische Rolle," *Kreuzfahrerstaaten*, p. 50. Joshua Prawer was much more conservative: he calculated the kingdom's population in the 1180s to be no more than 100,000–120,000 (*Histoire du royaume latin de Jérusalem*, trans. Gérard Nahon, 1 (Paris, 1969), pp. 568–69), an enormous increase, nevertheless, from the population of several thousands at the utmost in 1100, an estimate based on 200 knights and 1,000 infantry. This fantastic growth (even according to Prawer's estimate, let alone Hiestand's) dwarfs by far the exceptionally strong demographic expansion during the same century in Western Europe: Josiah Cox Russell calculated an increase of 66 per cent for France and the Low Countries, 75 per cent for Germany and Scandinavia, 65 per cent for Britain, 56 per cent for Italy and 14 per cent for Iberia ("The Population of the Crusader States," in: Setton, *Crusades*, 5:298); one need not subscribe entirely to Russell's method or figures in order to acknowledge, nevertheless, the real demographic growth that took place in these countries during the period under discussion.

[109] Joshua Prawer, "Colonization Activities in the Latin Kingdom of Jerusalem," *Revue belge de philologie et d'histoire* 29 (1951), pp. 1063–118, and Ronnie Ellenblum, *Frankish Rural Settlement in the Latin Kingdom of Jerusalem* (Cambridge, 1998), esp. pp. 75–78. While their interpretations of this phenomenon diverge, Prawer and Ellenblum practically agree that the non-natives predominated among the settlers (Ellenblum demonstrates that some 60 per cent of the settlers in Mahomeria with known place of origin came from Europe as against 40 per cent from various places in the Latin East; and the proportion was even higher in Bethgibelin, where most of the identifiable 74 per cent hailed from southern France and northern Spain; it is only reasonable to assume, furthermore, that a considerable number of the settlers who had come from localities in the Latin kingdom and principalities were European-born immigrants as well). The names of the La Mahomerie burgesses are listed in *Cart St Sép*, no. 117, pp. 238–39.

[110] Hans Eberhard Mayer, "Einwanderer in der Kanzlei und am Hof der Kreuzfahrerkönige von Jerusalem," in *Kreuzfahrerstaaten*, pp. 25–42.

[111] Hiestand, "Der lateinische Klerus," pp. 43–68.

[112] Such tensions came to the fore especially under King Fulk and Queen Melisende. See Hans Eberhard Mayer, "Studies in the History of Queen Melisende of Jerusalem," *Dumbarton Oaks Papers* 26 (1972), pp. 95–182, and "Angevins versus Normans: The New Men of King Fulk of Jerusalem," *Proceedings of the American Philosophical Society* 133 (1989), pp. 1–25.

[113] The different sources of military manpower and their demographic implications are clearly defined in Raymond C. Smail, *Crusading Warfare 1097–1193*, 2nd ed. (Cambridge, 1995), esp. pp.

orders on tours of duty, fortune-hunters, merchants and artisans (such as the Italian seasonal population in the coastal cities),[114] whose stay varied according to the personal circumstances of each individual and the nature of his business. This might range from a hasty, breathless visit to a more leisurely, extended stay that lasted for several months or even years. The religious needs of large segments of that temporary population – pilgrims and crusaders – far exceeded, of course, the religious needs of any "normal" population, in the Holy Land or elsewhere: for they had to participate in as many services and visit as many Holy Places as they could possibly manage in the short time at their disposal. Some of these needs were catered for by the clerics they brought with them – a phenomenon well documented in organized crusades and in less formally organized groups of pilgrims; but there is no mistaking the additional burden put on the local ecclesiastical resources by this additional demand, over and above the growth in the routine needs of the Christian population of the land. Hence the accrued need for liturgy, clergy and churches; hence the seemingly top-heavy hierarchy (2 patriarchs, 11 archbishops, at least 22 bishops) and an enlarged diocesan organization (35 dioceses, 17 in the south and 18 in the north);[115] top-heavy and hypertrophied for the needs of the relatively small population of the land they might be, but reasonably adequate, all the same, to the demands presented by the actual population in need of ecclesiastical ministration, not to mention other factors that determined ecclesiastical status and organization.

Jerusalem occupies a particularly privileged position on the church-building map of the kingdom: of the 200 churches for which there is archaeological evidence, 62 were constructed in Jerusalem alone.[116] Hamilton's appraisal of how the Franks "rebuilt Zion" outlined an almost permanent building campaign throughout the city and in its vicinity, a project that was of the very essence of the crusading enterprise. The 1130s and the 1140s seem to have witnessed particularly vigorous building activity: the dated inscriptions in the Church of the Nativity in Bethlehem – published by Kühnel – indicate construction and decoration work between 1130 and 1169,[117] the Templum Domini was solemnly dedicated in 1141,[118] the Armenian church of St James was completed in the 1140s, and Bethany was rebuilt during the 1140s as a convent by Queen Melisende.

88–96. More recently in Jonathan Riley-Smith, "Families, Crusades and Settlement in the Latin East, 1102–1131," in *Kreuzfahrerstaaten*, pp. 1–12.

[114] Marie-Luise Favreau-Lilie, "Durchreisende und Zuwanderer. Zur Rolle der Italiener in den Kreuzfahrerstaaten," in: *Die Kreuzfahrerstaaten*, pp 69–86.

[115] Rudolf Hiestand, "Der lateinische Klerus."

[116] Denys Pringle, "Les édifices ecclésiastiques du royaume latin de Jérusalem: une liste provisoire," *Revue biblique* 89 (1982), pp. 92–98. See also Bernard Hamilton, "Rebuilding Zion: The Holy Places of Jerusalem in the Twelfth Century," *Studies in Church History* 14 (1977), pp. 105–16, and "The Latin Church in the Crusader States," in *East and West in the Crusader States*, ed. Kriinie Ciggaar and Herman Teule, 1 (Leuven, 1996), pp. 1–20.

[117] Gustav Kühnel, *Wall Painting in the Latin Kingdom of Jerusalem* (Berlin, 1988), pp. 4–5, 18–19.

[118] WT, p. 699.

One should note, however, that the process of church-building was not confined to the masons' construction-sites and the decorators' workshops: it involved also production of liturgical manuscripts, vessels and vestments. William of Tyre – who certainly knew what he was talking about in this regard – described those aspects of the foundation and endowment of the convent and church of Bethany as follows: "Contulit etiam [Melisanda] eidem monasterio sacra utensilia ex auro, et gemmis et argento ad multam quantitatem simul et oloserica ... sed et indumenta tam sacerdotalia quam levitica ... adiecit plura in calicibus, libris et ceteris que ad ecclesiasticos respiciunt usus ornamenta ...."[119] Some of these were probably imported from abroad, but a large proportion was undoubtedly produced in place by local artists. The unmistakably Byzantine inspiration of much of the Frankish art strongly suggests local ateliers and local production, and the large scale of the church-building campaign in the kingdom in general, and in Jerusalem in particular, indicates a comparable scale of artistic creation in all these types of art from the 1130s to the 1150s. The new church of the Holy Sepulchre, revealed in all its new glory in the dedication ceremony on 15 July 1149, could indeed be imaged as Urbs Beata Hierusalem, "like purest gold resplendent."

---

[119] Ibid., p. 710.

The Debate on Twelfth-Century Frankish Feudalism: Additional Evidence from William of Tyre's *Chronicon*

Jonathan Rubin

The Hebrew University, Jerusalem

In 1994 Susan Reynolds published a book in which she argued against many of the basic conceptions of historians relating to the term "feudalism." In the first issue of *Crusades* she tried to apply her ideas to the twelfth-century Latin kingdom of Jerusalem.[1] In that same issue an article by Peter Edbury appeared that may be considered a response to Reynolds's arguments.[2] Both historians have used evidence taken from William of Tyre's *Chronicon* to prove their cases. In this article I intend to show that using additional evidence from the *Chronicon* can shed further light on feudalism in the Latin East in the twelfth century.[3]

What are the positions taken by Reynolds and Edbury? Reynolds argues that before the twelfth century there was, in general, no connection between the grant of a fief to an individual and military services owed by him;[4] there was also no connection between such services and some special status, be it vassalage or tenancy.[5] The same holds, she believes, for the twelfth-century kingdom of Jerusalem. As evidence supporting this claim, she argues that "the word vassal seems to be rare in contemporary sources."[6] She claims that when that word is found, its use does not have to imply the grant of a fief or the creation of a strong bond "envisaged by post-romantic historians."[7]

Edbury sees the reality of feudalism in the kingdom differently. He argues that Frankish society in the twelfth century still lacked neat social and legal categories and customs. According to him, it was only gradually that "a recognizable and orderly system of land tenure and military obligation ... began to emerge."[8] He is, however, prepared to sketch some characteristics of that system. He argues that

---

[1] Susan Reynolds, "Fiefs and Vassals in Twelfth-Century Jerusalem: A View from the West," *Crusades* 1 (2002), pp. 29–48.

[2] Peter W. Edbury, "Fiefs and Vassals in the Kingdom of Jerusalem: From the Twelfth Century to the Thirteenth," *Crusades* 1 (2002), pp. 49–62.

[3] The examples discussed below are related to various parts of the Latin East. However, they all reflect the viewpoint and attitudes of an author strongly linked to the kingdom of Jerusalem.

[4] Susan Reynolds, *Fiefs and Vassals: The Medieval Evidence Reinterpreted* (Oxford, 1994), p. 477.

[5] Reynolds, "Fiefs," p. 30; Reynolds, *Fiefs*, p. 477.

[6] Reynolds, "Fiefs," p. 34.

[7] Ibid., pp. 34–35.

[8] Edbury, "Fiefs," p. 53.

the idea of service owed for fiefs existed in the kingdom before 1187 but is not reflected in all the charters of that period. For example, service is not specified in those of the charters dealing with grants to the "lordship of Joscelin." It is possible, he suggests, that "the great lords did not have a formal obligation to produce a stipulated number of knights."[9] The reason, he surmises, might have been that "landed men of moderate wealth would have been more susceptible to pressure from above and so more likely to accept closely defined obligations than would the nobles."[10] In other words, Edbury recognizes in the Frankish society of the twelfth century a partial connection between a grant of land and service owed.

In the debate concerning feudalism in the Latin East during the twelfth century, William of Tyre's *Chronicon* takes, of course, a very prominent place as the most important source for the history of the kingdom of Jerusalem for most of that period. Both Edbury and Reynolds use this text in their attempts to reveal the legal and social realities of the twelfth-century kingdom. The main argument of both historians regarding William is that he hardly uses what might be called "feudal vocabulary."[11] They differ, however, in their interpretation of this fact. For Reynolds, this fact supports the argument that the use of "feudo-vassalic" vocabulary was rare during the twelfth century and, consequently, that much of what has been attributed to the societies of that time derives from a later period. Edbury, on the other hand, argues – very convincingly, in my opinion – that William's avoidance of such words as *feudum* and *vassallus* was more for stylistic reasons than because of the way in which he perceived the social – or legal – realities of the kingdom.[12]

The main problem with both these arguments is that these historians focused on "feudal vocabulary" in a very narrow sense and thus overlooked some important evidence in the *Chronicon* touching on this issue. In the *Chronicon*, Reynolds looked for use of the words *vassallus* and *feudum* (although she also mentions *vassassor* in a footnote).[13] Edbury took into account also the term *beneficium* but still remained very much focused on the same two terms.

However, by widening our search in the *Chronicon*, it is possible to find further evidence relating to the question of feudalism in the Latin East during the twelfth century. My discussion is divided into three parts. In the first section I consider the meaning of the term *ligius* as used in the *Chronicon*. In the second, I deal with the term *hominium*, and analyze a phrase in which this term appears. In the third, I examine two short sections from the *Chronicon* which show that for William a

---

[9] Ibid., p. 49. The evidence provided by the *Tractatus de locis et statu sancte terre ierosolimitane* may weaken this argument: it is said there, concerning the great barons of the kingdom, that "omnes isti certum habent numerum militum, quos semper oportet esse paratos armis et equis, ut cotidie Saracenis insultantibus resistant." For the text, see Benjamin Z. Kedar, "The *Tractatus de locis et statu sancte terre ierosolimitane*," in *Crusade Sources*, p. 130.

[10] Edbury, "Fiefs," p. 53.

[11] Reynolds, "Fiefs," pp. 34–35; Edbury, "Fiefs," pp. 51–52.

[12] Edbury, "Fiefs," p. 52.

[13] Reynolds, "Fiefs," p. 35, n. 21.

connection existed between swearing an oath of fealty and being granted a piece of land.

It should be pointed out that the issue of the reliability of the information provided by William is irrelevant to our inquiry. I am interested here only in the way he described social and legal relations. That he described a legal transaction in a certain way does not necessarily mean that it was perceived that way by the parties involved. It does, however, mean that at the time he was writing – that is, between 1167 and 1184[14] – William thought this was how such transactions were done, or were supposed to be done. That is already an indication as to the legal and social realities of his time.

Homo ligius, fidelitas ligia

One term usually seen as connected with the feudal system, and not discussed by either Reynolds or Edbury, is *ligius*. Ganshof defined the system of liegeancy as one in which "it was recognized that there was one among the lords of a vassal who must be served with the full strictness that was characteristic of primitive vassalage: *integre*, entirely, without reserve; *contra omnes*, against all men."[15] According to Reynolds, on the other hand, *ligiam fidelitatem* meant allegiance "in the broadest twentieth-century sense of the word,"[16] and "all free inhabitants of the kingdom could, at least in some contexts, be considered *homes liges* and *femes liges*, who were bound to the king just as the king was bound to them."[17] The question is whether, by looking at the *Chronicon*, we can learn anything new regarding the way these terms were understood in the twelfth century.

The term *ligius* (in its different grammatical forms) is found four times in the *Chronicon*.[18] In three of them, the term *fidelitas ligia* is discussed: twice in connection with the oaths of Raymond of Antioch (1137) and Thoros (1159) to the Byzantine emperor,[19] and the third time in describing the oath of the "proceres et magnates regionis" to Bohemond II when he came to inherit Antioch (1126).[20] It is difficult to understand what exactly William meant by this term, as the circumstances in which it was used vary: in the first and second instances the oath is personal, connected to some physical deed (once described using the word *manualiter*[21] and once using

---

[14] Peter W. Edbury and John G. Rowe, *William of Tyre: Historian of the Latin East* (Cambridge, 1988), pp. 26, 30.
[15] François L. Ganshof, *Feudalism*, trans. Philip Grierson (New York, 1961), p. 103.
[16] Reynolds, *Fiefs*, p. 214.
[17] Reynolds, "Fiefs," p. 38.
[18] WT, p. 510 (*ligius*); pp. 613, 671, 847 (*ligiam*).
[19] WT, pp. 671 and 847 respectively.
[20] WT, p. 613.
[21] WT, p. 847.

*corporaliter*²²) and having to do with the ruling of a piece of land.²³ In the third case, the oath is collective; it is not described as connected to any physical act and its relation to a grant of land is possible but not essential.

We may be able, however, to learn something regarding this term from the analysis of two related phrases, which appear one chapter apart in the *Chronicon*. Both phrases describe relations between Bertram, the son of Raymond of Toulouse, and Baldwin I, king of Jerusalem. The first phrase concerns a compromise that was supposed to put an end to a dispute between Bertram and Guillaume Jourdain. In the *Chronicon*, the description of this agreement precedes the description of Tripoli's seizure by the Franks (July 1109). The second phrase directly follows the description of the fall of Tripoli and recounts Bertram's becoming a *domini regis homo ligius* – the only occasion where the expression *homo ligius* appears in William's chronicle. Following are the contexts of the two phrases:

> **11.9** Unde Willelmus pro parte sibi designata factus est homo principis Antiocheni, fidelitate ei manualiter exhibita, Bertramus vero partis sibi designate a domino rege Ierosolimorum investituram suscepit, ei sollempniter exhibens fidelitatem.²⁴

> **11.10** Factus est autem ibidem comes Bertramus, fidelitate manualiter exhibita, domini regis homo ligius, unde et eius successores usque in presentem diem regi Ierosolimorum idipsum tenentur exhibere.²⁵

Thus we see that the creation of a bond between Bertram and the king is mentioned twice. But there are some clear differences between the two instances. In the first, Bertram receives investiture and exhibits fidelity while Guillaume Jourdain becomes a "homo principis Antiocheni, fidelitate ei manualiter exhibita." In the second, Bertram becomes a *homo ligius* of the king, having exhibited fidelity *manualiter*.

The relation between these two phrases can be interpreted in one of two ways: either as portraying two different events or as referring to a single incident. I would like to suggest that William meant to describe two different events. The main argument in favor of this opinion is that William says Bertram "became a *homo ligius* in that same place." The expression *ibidem* here, just one sentence after the words *capta est predicta civitas*, should mean that this event took place in Tripoli. As it is impossible to connect the first bond between Bertram and the king to the

---

²² WT, p. 671.

²³ In Thoros's case, the connection between the oath and the ruling of land is not explicit. However, as it seems that the *fidelitas ligia* was linked, in some manner, to Manuel's preparedness to let Thoros retain his prior status ("resignatis presidiis que dominus imperator reposcebat, in gratiam eum restituit pleniorem, ita ut fidelitatem ligiam ... antequam ad propria reverteretur, manualiter eidem exhiberet"), it is probable that there was, in this case, a connection between the oath and the ruling of a certain territory.

²⁴ WT, p. 508.

²⁵ WT, p. 510.

city, since it was created before the Franks had access to that city, it seems the two phrases describe two different events.

Another piece of evidence pointing in the same direction is based on information supplied by one of William's sources: Albert of Aachen's *Historia Ierosolimitana*. Albert describes the dispute between Bertram and Guillaume, as well as the reconciliation between them, before mentioning the capture of Tripoli.[26] While describing these events, Albert writes that "Bertrannus ... homo eius ibidem iureiurando factus est."[27] Having described the capture of Tripoli, Albert describes Baldwin's decision to besiege Beirut. In this context he says of Bertram: "quem prefecerat eidem civitati ..."[28] This seems to imply that Albert thought Bertram's status in relation to Baldwin had changed following the capture of Tripoli. If, as seems likely, William's second phrase is, at least partially, founded upon this comment, it would follow that the two phrases were probably meant to describe two different events.[29]

It follows further that William thought that in the first instance a certain kind of bond was created between Bertram and the king, and a while later a stronger bond was forged between the two. Accordingly, an oath of fidelity did not necessarily result in becoming a *homo ligius*; otherwise, Bertram would have already become a *homo ligius* after his first oath. This analysis makes it rather difficult to accept Reynolds's above-mentioned argument regarding this term. This does not necessarily mean that the traditional interpretation is correct, but it seems we can conclude that the term *ligius* was used to indicate a particularly strong bond created by a specific kind of oath. The use of this term also implies what may be called a "hierarchy of oaths," the existence of which strengthens, to some extent, the more conservative perceptions of feudalism: if different oaths created different levels of bond between two men, that would draw us one step closer to accepting the idea of a society based on dyadic bonds rather than one based on collective oaths given to a leader.

Hominium and the Connection between Fidelity and Service

Hominium is, in its basic meaning, taken to be a synonym of *homagium*.[30] As such it can surely be seen as a part of the "feudal vocabulary." This term appears three

---

[26] AA, pp. 780 and 782 respectively.

[27] AA, p. 782.

[28] AA, p. 786.

[29] It should be noted that the *Chronicon*'s adapter/translator believed that Bertram had already become a *home liges* in the first passage: "Bertrans de ce qu'il devoit avoir fu revestuz du Roi et en devint ses hom liges." Translating the second phrase he wrote: "Li cuens Bertrans receut la ville du Roi et l'en fist homage lige de ses mains." His interpretation, however, does not make sense, as it does not explain why the second phrase was at all necessary. *Guillaume de Tyr et ses continuateurs: texte français du XIIIe siècle*, ed. Paulin Paris, 2 vols. (Paris, 1879–80), 1:392 and 395 respectively.

[30] See, for example, Jan F. Niermeyer, *Mediae Latinitatis lexicon minus*, 2nd revised ed. (Leiden, 2002), s.v. hominium.

times in the *Chronicon*.[31] In the nineteenth chapter of Book II, as well as in the *Cathalogi*, it is mentioned in relation to the oaths of the crusading leaders to the Byzantine emperor during the First Crusade. Later it is also mentioned in relation to the oath taken by all the barons of the kingdom of Jerusalem to Baldwin V. But the most interesting phrase, for our discussion, in which this term appears is the following:

> 12.17 Pontius enim, Tripolitanorum comes secundus, nescimus cuius instinctu regi Ierosolimorum suum denegabat hominium et servicium, quod de iure fidelitatis tenebatur impendere, impudenter negabat.[32]

Hominium does not have to mean here anything substantially different than fidelity. Such an interpretation of the term would also fit the other instances in which it appears in the *Chronicon*. But looking at the phrase in which the term appears may be worthwhile: we have here a clear indication of a connection between an oath of fidelity and a service promised. As the service that was promised is not performed, the king collects his men and marches to meet the rebellious count. This phrase makes it difficult to argue that such people as William of Tyre did not think there existed, at least in certain cases, a connection between giving an oath of fidelity and owing a certain service.[33]

The Relation between an Oath of Fidelity and the Grant of Land

In some cases William offers descriptions of what may be considered a "feudo-vassalic" relationship without using such words as *vassallus* or *feudum*:

> 14.20 Exigitur ergo a domino Raimundo ut, iuramento corporaliter prestito, domino patriarche fidelitatem exhibeat, versa vice suscepturus sine difficultate puellam in uxorem et cum omni quiete principatum.[34]

> 15.12 Domino igitur Raimundo primum Antiochiam, ut premisimus, accedente, antequam uxorem destinatam haberet domino Radulfo, qui tunc ecclesie preerat Antiochene, ut facilius ad optatum pertingeret fidelitatem manualiter exhibuit, spondens fide interposita quod ab ea die inantea non esset in consilio vel in facto, quod honorem, vitam aut membrum perderet aut caperetur mala captione, sicut in forma exhibende fidelitatis

---

[31] WT, pp. 186, 566, 1058; this term also appears once in the *Cathalogi quorundam magnatum de quibus mencio habita est superius*, which is included as an appendix to Robert B. C. Huygens' edition of the *Chronicon*. See WT, p. 1068.

[32] WT, p. 566.

[33] It is interesting to note that in the Old French adaptation this phrase has more of a "feudo-vassalic" connotation: "Car li cuens Poinces de Triple, ne sai par quel conseil ne par quel raison, manda au roi Baudoin qu'il ne se tenoit pas à son home, n'il ne connoissoit mie qu'il li deust servise ne amor" (*Guillaume de Tyr*, 1:458).

[34] WT, p. 658.

continetur. In qua fidelitate nec modico quidem tempore perseveravit: statim enim uxore ducta et tota regione recepta per eius studium et operam, adiunctus est eius adversariis, opem conferens et omne consilium, contra fidelitatis debitum, in eius lesionem.[35]

Here we seem to encounter some elements of the "feudo-vassalic" system: in return for an oath of fidelity, by which he is obligated not to do anything that may harm his lord, a nobleman receives the right to rule over some territory, and – not a usual part of a feudal contract – a wife. This description means that William thought that, at least in some cases, an oath and the demonstration of fidelity resulted in a grant of land. The words *versa vice* seem to imply that the young girl, as well as the right to rule over some territory, were granted specifically in return for the oath and the fidelity expressed. It is true that no positive service is mentioned here; but, on the other hand, the cited oath does show that a negative obligation – to refrain from doing rather than to do – was undertaken by the receiver of the land. It is worth mentioning, in this context, that the idea of negative obligation is central in oath formulas such as the ones presented in the *Libri feudorum*.[36]

Significantly, in the Old French adaptation these events are described in terms of *feeuté et aide* (regarding what was demanded from Raymond)[37] and *homage lige* (regarding Raymond's commitment to the Patriarch).[38] The fact that, in the *Chronicon*'s Old French adaptation, these relations are described using "feudal vocabulary" and mention the obligation of service indicates that they were understood, quite soon after William wrote his chronicle, as "feudo-vassalic" relations.[39] It may not be far-fetched to suggest that such transactions were similarly understood already in the twelfth century.

This example does not totally contradict Reynolds's ideas, since we have here a case of a fief given by the Church, and Reynolds argues that "in so far as some of the obligations and terminology that historians associate with fiefs are to be found in earlier sources, they are found chiefly in documents that record the relations of great churches with their tenants."[40] The above-mentioned phrases seem to fit this argument.

---

[35] WT, p. 691.

[36] *Das langobardische Lehnrecht*, ed. Karl Lehmann (Göttingen, 1896), pp. 120–23. It should be mentioned here that the exact wording of the oath described here by William cannot be ascribed exclusively to the influence of the *Libri feudorum*. It is possible that his version drew some elements, directly or indirectly, from a formula that appears in one of Gregory VII's *epistolae*: see *The Epistolae Vagantes of Pope Gregory VII*, ed. and trans. H. E. J. Cowdrey (Oxford, 1972), no. 69, pp. 152–53.

[37] *Guillaume de Tyr*, 2:27.

[38] Ibid., p. 64.

[39] For a discussion of the date of the translation's composition, see John Pryor, "The *Eracles* and William of Tyre: An Interim Report," in *Horns*, pp. 288–89. Regarding the translation, see also Bernard Hamilton, "The Old French Translation of William of Tyre as an Historical Source," in *EC*, 2, pp. 93–112.

[40] Reynolds, "Fiefs," p. 30.

However, another oath described by William appears to denote a connection between an oath and the grant of land, and does not have to do with the Church. Let us take another look at a citation discussed above in a different context:

11.9 Unde Willelmus pro parte sibi designata factus est homo principis Antiocheni, fidelitate ei manualiter exhibita, Bertramus vero partis sibi designate a domino rege Ierosolimorum investituram suscepit, ei sollempniter exhibens fidelitatem.[41]

Again, neither *feudum* nor *vassallus* are used here but, in my opinion, both phrases can tell us something about "feudo-vassalic" connections. The phrase concerning Bertram shows that, for William, people received the investiture for a piece of land upon showing fidelity. Thus the connection between exhibiting fidelity and receiving land is apparent in this case. The first phrase (the one concerning Guillaume) is, however, even more telling. It shows that for William of Tyre there was a connection, at least in some cases, between showing fealty, becoming someone's *homo*, and receiving land. In other words, at least in some cases a man became someone's *homo* after being given a specific piece of land, in return for his oath of fealty. We do not hear here about services owed to the lord; and we should avoid the pitfall, of which Reynolds justly warns us, of automatically understanding *homo* as a synonym of *vassallus*. It is, however, rather probable that the word *homo* here means that some kind of a special bond was created between Guillaume and the prince of Antioch, a bond that was strongly linked to a piece of land (*pro parte designata*). As it is difficult to envisage fidelity without any duties – even though these do not have to be formally stipulated – this bond probably included some type of obligations. The analogy of this phrase to the one discussed above regarding Bertram ("Factus est autem ibidem comes Bertramus, fidelitate manualiter exhibita, domini regis homo ligius")[42] suggests that *homo* may, in this case, stand for *homo ligius*. Whether or not this suggestion is accepted, the use of the term *homo principis* surely means that Guillaume's status had changed. Accepting this interpretation, we would have to conclude that we have here evidence for a case in which a bond – probably entailing some kind of obligation – was created between two nobles in return for a piece of land that was given by one of them to the other for which the latter had to exhibit fealty and whose status changed following the creation of the bond. The fact that the *Chronicon*'s adapter uses "feudal vocabulary" in the description of this event, as in the translation of the twentieth chapter of Book XIV and the twelfth chapter of Book XV (writing: "Guillaumes por la seue part fist homage de ses deus mains au prince d'Antioche" where William wrote: "factus est homo principis"), supports the suggestion that such transactions were understood by William's near contemporaries as "feudo-vassalic."[43]

---

[41] WT, p. 508.
[42] WT, p. 510.
[43] *Guillaume de Tyr*, 1:392.

The last two cases show that William believed there was a connection between giving an oath of fidelity and receiving a piece of land. In some cases that kind of transaction resulted in a promise made by the land receiver not to harm the land-granting party. Sometimes such a transaction could result in the creation of some special connection between the two parties, as the land-receiving party became a *homo* of the other party. These two descriptions weaken the assertion that there was, in the twelfth century, no connection between the grant of land and the owing of services, because it is difficult to imagine what fidelity could mean if not committing the participating parties to do certain deeds or to refrain from doing others, even in cases where such a commitment is not explicitly stated.

Conclusion

To sum up: first, we have seen that William's use of "feudal vocabulary" was not limited to the single mention of the word *vassalli* and to the use, in two cases, of the word *feudum*. The analysis of the usage of the term *ligius* shows that for William there probably existed different levels of oaths. To a certain extent this strengthens the more traditional perceptions of feudalism, as it may imply a pyramid-like structure of society. More importantly, the above examination has shown that William thought there existed, at least in some cases, connections between:

1. An oath of fidelity and some owed service
2. An oath of fidelity and the rule over a piece of land.

Although this does not make for a neat, textbook model of feudal society, and although it does not fully contradict Reynolds's arguments, it does make it rather difficult to accept them. If a person is described as receiving land in return for a personal oath, and another is described as owing service because of an oath he took earlier, it becomes improbable to think that there was, in that society, no connection between service and a grant of land, or between service and a special status. That the *Chronicon*'s adapter used "feudal vocabulary" in cases where William describes such transactions, implies that quite shortly after William completed his chronicle, such relations were understood as "feudo-vassalic." It seems likely, then, that at least some of the characteristics of feudalism existed in the Latin kingdom of Jerusalem at the time William was writing his *magnum opus*.

This argument may possibly be strengthened by evidence derived from non-Frankish sources which attests to the presence of a "feudal vocabulary," and perhaps "feudal perceptions" as well, in the twelfth-century kingdom of Jerusalem. Moshe Sharon has shown that the word *fasal* (فصل), denoting a fixed sum received by an amir in return for some service he had to render to his Ayyubid superior, appears in an Arabic inscription of 1210, which was found in a village north-west of Jerusalem. If Sharon is correct in arguing that this term is based on the term "vassal," its appearance in the inscription would indicate that the term "vassal" was widely used in the Latin kingdom before 1187. Otherwise it would be difficult to explain how the term made its way into an Arabic inscription in a village that came under Ayyubid rule after the battle of Hattin.[44] Similarly, the appearance of the word *lizios*, denoting liege, in the text of the Treaty of Devol (1108), as cited in Anna Comnena's *Alexiad*, suggests that the term was sufficiently salient among Westerners to make its way into a Greek account of a Norman-Byzantine treaty.[45]

---

[44] Moshe Sharon, "Vassal and Fasal: The Evidence of the Farkhah Inscription from 608/1210," *Crusades* 4 (2005), pp. 117–30.

[45] Anna Comnena, *Alexias*, ed. Diether R. Reinsch and Athanasios Kambylis, Corpus fontium historiae Byzantinae 40, 2 vols. (Berlin, 2001), 1:414, 415, 416, 420, 421. In the index to the work (2:90), the editors maintain that in some cases in the *Alexiad* the word *anthropos* itself means *vasallus ligius*. It is outside the scope of this paper to examine this argument. I would like to thank Professor John H. Pryor for his kind help regarding this matter.

Anglo-Norman Intervention in the Conquest and Settlement of Tortosa, 1148–1180

Lucas Villegas-Aristizábal

University of Nottingham

The conquest of Tortosa is the least well-known of the three large campaigns of the Second Crusade in Iberia, at least among English-speaking historians, although Giles Constable provided a substantial account of it in his article on the Second Crusade half a century ago and in recent years Nikolas Jaspert has also written on the subject.[1] Apart from the conquest of Lisbon (1147), the conquest of Tortosa is the only other expedition of the Second Crusade in Iberia for which there are references in the narrative sources to the specific involvement of *Anglici*.[2] Other contemporary narrative sources in England and elsewhere in Europe (except for Iberia and Italy) were relatively silent about it.[3] Although Caffaro's *De captione Almerie et Tortuose* is the only narrative source containing a reference to the English participation, there are abundant references in archival records. Some of these documents, especially those contained in the *Llibre Blanch de Santes Creus*, were exploited by Ramon Miravall in his short work on the English migration to Tortosa.[4] Other documents have been more recently uncovered by Antoni Virgili, which show that the number of English settlers was substantial in comparison to other areas of Norman and Anglo-Norman contributions in Iberia.[5]

The conquest of Tortosa had full papal support and brought the frontier of the Catalan counties fully to the Ebro valley, opening the way for the later conquests of the thirteenth century. How the Anglo-Normans came upon Tortosa is not clear from the documentary sources. It has been assumed, moreover, that the English in Tortosa were the same as, or at least a detachment of, those involved in the expedition that had captured Lisbon. If this is so, it raises the question why did so many of them not stay in Lisbon? And why did they decide to continue on their way to the Holy Land after the conquest of Lisbon and end up in the siege of Tortosa

---

[1] Giles Constable, "The Second Crusade as Seen by Contemporaries," *Traditio* 9 (1953), pp. 225–28; Nikolas Jaspert, "*Capta est Dertosa clavis Christianorum*: Tortosa and the Crusades," in *The Second Crusade: Scope and Consequences*, ed. Jonathan Phillips and Martin Hoch (Manchester, 2001), pp. 90–100.

[2] Caffaro di Rustico, *De captione Almerie et Tortuose*, ed. Antonio Ubieto Arteta (Valencia, 1973), p. 32.

[3] *Gesta Stephani*, ed. and trans. K. R. Potter (Oxford, 1976), p. 127; Henry of Huntingdon, *Historia Anglorum: The History of the English People*, ed. and trans. Diana Greenway (Oxford, 1996), pp. 750–52. Neither text mentions anything to do with the siege and conquest.

[4] Ramon Miravall, *Immigració Britànica a Tortosa* (Barcelona, 1972), pp. 7–47.

[5] *Diplomatari de la catedral de Tortosa (1062–1193)*, ed. Antoni Virgili (Barcelona, 1997), pp. 130–218; *El "Llibre Blanch" de Santes Creus*, ed. Frederic Udina Martorell (Barcelona, 1948), p. 50.

and settle there?[6] It is therefore the purpose of this article to explore this evidence and to show how this participation came to be and its consequence in relation to the resettlement of Tortosa after its Christian conquest.

The Unification of the County of Barcelona and the Kingdom of Aragon

To understand the origins of the conquest of Tortosa in 1148, one must look at the political developments preceding it in the eastern part of the peninsula. In 1134 Alfonso I of Aragon-Navarre died of wounds received in battle outside Fraga.[7] Being childless, he left his kingdom to the religious orders of the Temple, the Hospital of St. John and the canons of the Holy Sepulchre. However, this testament was too idealistic to be accepted by the nobility of his two kingdoms so the nobles decided to look for a monarch of their own.[8] The Navarrese chose Garcia while the Aragonese chose Ramiro, brother of Alfonso I, who was a monk.[9] This ended the personal union of the two kingdoms. The Aragonese managed to persuade Ramiro to marry Inez de Poitiers. As soon as the royal couple had a daughter, Patronila, she was betrothed to Ramon Berenguer IV, count of Barcelona.[10] By 1137 Ramon Berenguer IV of Barcelona was fully in control of Aragon as prince regent and Ramiro II was back in a monastery, even though Patronila was still an infant.[11]

This marriage eventually unified the Crown of Aragon and helped form an important state which counter-balanced the growing power of Castile and Leon within the peninsula until the fifteenth century. However, at this stage the Crown of Aragon was still in its infancy and Catalonia was still not united under the count of Barcelona, although his growing prestige and wealth were making him the undisputed leader of the Catalan counties. The fact that Aragon and Barcelona were not contiguous made it imperative for Ramon Berenguer IV to try to conquer what is now known as New Catalonia in order to join his two realms. This would also forestall the ability for expansion of other Catalan counts, such as the count of Urgel who became his vassal in the new territories. Continuing the process of Reconquista, which his predecessors in both Catalonia and Aragon had begun in the early twelfth century, was also of great importance to maintaining the peace within his realms, since a new noble caste was rising both in the Catalan counties

---

[6] Matthew Bennett, "Military Aspects of the Conquest of Lisbon," in *The Second Crusade*, ed. Phillips and Hoch, pp. 84–85.

[7] Jose María Lacarra, *Vida de Alfonso el batallador* (Saragossa, 1971), pp. 127–28.

[8] *Crónica del Emperador Alfonso VII*, trans. Maurilio Pérez González (León, 1997), p. 82; *Chronicle of San Juan de la Peña*, trans. Lynn Harry Nelson (Philadelphia, 1991), p. 31.

[9] *Chronicle of San Juan de la Peña*, p. 32; Joseph F. O'Callaghan, *Reconquest and Crusade in Medieval Spain* (Philadelphia, 2003), pp. 40–41; *Crónica del Emperador Alfonso VII*, p. 82.

[10] *Crónica del Emperador Alfonso VII*, p. 83; *Chronicle of San Juan de la Peña*, p. 51.

[11] José Ángel Sesma Muñoz, "De la muerte de el batallador a la llegada de el primer rey de la Corona de Aragón," in *La reconquista y el proceso de diferenciación política*, ed. Miguel Ángel Ladero Quesada, Historia de España Menéndez Pidal, vol. 9 (Madrid, 1998), pp. 678–79.

and Aragon which was hungry for new territories to conquer. If he had not followed their expansionist desires, Ramon Berenguer IV might have faced rebellion and instability within his territories as had occurred in the county of Barcelona in the first half of the eleventh century.[12]

Unlike King Afonso Henriques of Portugal, Ramon Berenguer IV did not attempt to undermine the imperial claims of Alfonso VII of Leon. Instead, he paid homage as prince regent of Aragon to the Leonese emperor.[13] This nominal vassalage to the Leonese monarch allowed him to secure control of Aragon and permitted him to continue the process of reconquest.[14] His friendly diplomatic relations with the emperor of Leon allowed him to take part in the conquest of Almeria, an important naval rival in the western Mediterranean (see Fig. 1). By participating in this venture he also managed to strengthen his relations with the Genoese who would later help him to conquer Tortosa.[15] For this purpose, Ramon Berenguer IV knew from previous experience that he would need a naval blockade. With this in mind, he sought the help of the Genoese who, since 1146, had agreed to join any military expedition to take the city.[16] The Genoese were a thriving Christian sea power with growing interests in the Iberian peninsula. For the Italian city-states, the attack on Tortosa also had great economic advantages, as had that against Almeria.[17] With it, the Genoese were able to destroy another important pirate stronghold and commercial competitor in the western Mediterranean.[18] Apart from augmenting their markets and the colonial outposts in Spain, the Genoese were also inspired by a crusading zeal, clearly aroused by the popes in the decades since the First Crusade, for campaigns of reconquest in Iberia.[19]

Sources for the Conquest of Tortosa

Contemporary Iberian sources for the conquest of Tortosa do not give details concerning the events of the siege and conquest of the city. Even later Iberian chronicles do not give much information, apart from the fact that Tortosa was conquered by Ramon Berenguer IV with help from the Genoese. As for the conquest of Almeria, Caffaro wrote a relatively detailed account of the taking of Tortosa by

---

[12] Richard Fletcher, "Reconquest and Crusade in Spain, *c.* 1050–1150," *Transactions of the Royal Historical Society*, 5th series, 37 (1987), pp. 31–47.
[13] *Crónica del Emperador Alfonso VII*, p. 84.
[14] Emilio Morera y Llauradó, *Tarragona cristiana*, vol. 1 (Tarragona, 1982), pp. 397–98.
[15] Jaspert, "Tortosa and the Crusades," p. 92.
[16] *Codice diplomatico della repubblica di Genova*, ed. Cesare Imperiale di Sant' Angelo (Rome, 1936), no. 169. The Balearic Islands were conquered by Ramon Berenguer III with Pisan help in 1113–14 but they were soon reconquered by the Almoravids. See Morera y Llauradó, *Tarragona cristiana*, vol. 1, pp. 380–96.
[17] Blanca Garí, "Why Almeria? An Islamic Port in the Compass of Genoa," *Journal of Medieval History* 18 (1992), pp. 211–33.
[18] Jaspert, "Tortosa and the Crusades," p. 93.
[19] Ibid., p. 93; Garí, "Why Almeria?" pp. 211–17.

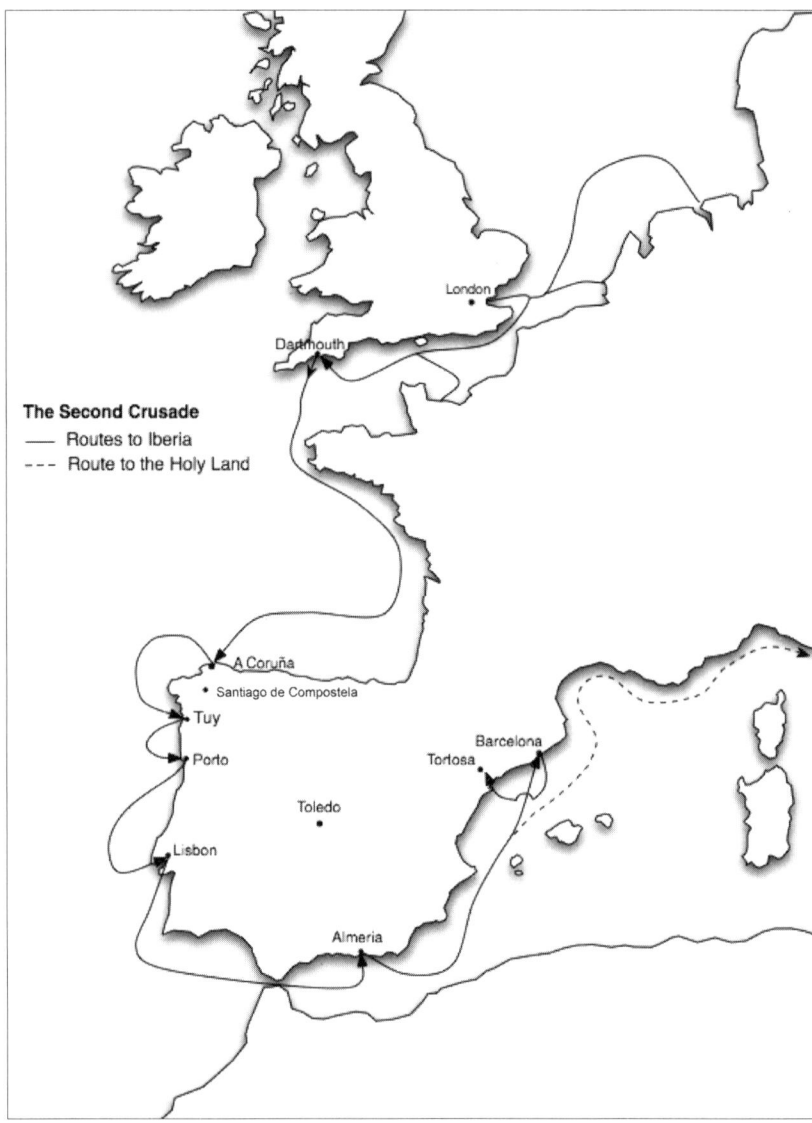

Fig. 1 Sea routes of the Second Crusade

the crusaders and it is the only narrative source to mention English involvement in the siege of the city.[20] Although Caffaro's narrative is detailed from the point of view of the Genoese at the siege, his reference to the English participation is brief.[21] Caffaro's work is, however, complemented by Genoese documents relating to the conquest of the city that were published by Cesaere Imperiale in 1936.[22]

However, the inadequacies of the narrative records can be compensated for by the relative abundance of excellent archival material.[23] Antoni Virgili, an expert on the conquest and settlement of Tortosa, has compiled a substantial collection of the records in question as part of the *Diplomatari de la catedral de Tortosa*.[24] Most of the charters are not directly about the English settlers but contain their names as witnesses. This compilation of charters is by far the largest of all the compilations of documents relating to the settlement of the city that exist in published form, but like others it suffers from the same problematic attribution of second names to English families, for example "Angles" and "Anglici." It also mentions a number of names whose Englishness is not certain, such as "Salvagnac" and "Morlans."

There are also two cartularies from the two most important monasteries of New Catalonia: Poblet and Santes Creus. These two manuscripts are kept in the municipal library of Tarragona. They were both written at the end of the twelfth century or the beginning of the thirteenth.[25] The charters and other documents from the monastery of Santes Creus were compiled in a book known as the *Llibre Blanch*, perhaps because at some point it possessed a white parchment or leather cover.[26] While the published form of the cartulary of Poblet follows the order of the charters as copied into the cartulary, in the *Llibre Blanch* Frederic Udina Martorell reordered them chronologically. This hides the fact that in the manuscript most of the charters concerning the English are placed together on folios 100–124, which suggests that the monks thought it important to keep the English community's documents close together. Agustin Altisent, a Catalan historian, has compiled another collection from the records of the monastery of Poblet, which includes documents that were

---

[20] Caffaro, *De captione Almerie et Tortuose*, pp. 30–35.

[21] Ibid., p. 32.

[22] Documentation relating to the Genoese settlement survives in many compilations in Spain and in Italy. See *Codice diplomatico*, nos. 159, 166, 168, 169, 174, 182, 190, 191, 193, 194, 196, 202, 214, 215, 216, 243 and 244.

[23] All the documents relating to the conquest and settlement of Normans and Anglo-Normans in the valley of the Ebro are listed in chronological order in the Appendix to this article. The information is set out as a table to give a clearer presentation of the content of each document. It also allows shorter footnote references to be given to the main text. The table is supplemented by an Index of Norman and Anglo-Norman names mentioned in the documents.

[24] I was unable to visit the archive of the cathedral where these documents are kept because the archive room was inaccessible after the staircase access to the room had fallen during restoration. I have used the edited versions by Virgili.

[25] *Cartulari de Poblet: edició del manuscrit de Tarragona*, ed. Joan Pons i Marqués (Barcelona, 1938), p. 9; *El "Llibre Blanch" de Santes Creus*, pp. vii–l.

[26] *El "Llibre Blanch" de Santes Creus*, pp. vii–ix.

not incorporated in the original cartulary but which are now found in the National Archive of Spain in Madrid.[27]

There are also some other very important documents which belonged to the ancient monastery of Santa Anna in Barcelona and which are now held in the Diocesan Archive of Barcelona. These have been published recently by Jesús Alturo i Perucho.[28] The two most important for this article are one relating to an early donation to the Church of the Holy Sepulchre, in which the leader of the English contingent is named as Balluini de Carona. In the other, the English cemetery is mentioned and two of the main Anglo-Normans are listed as witnesses: Gilbert Anglici and Gerald of Salvagnac.[29]

The Prelude to the Conquest of Tortosa

The siege of Tortosa had been attempted by previous counts of Barcelona, but it was not until the reign of Ramon Berenguer IV that it was possible to undertake such a venture with a realistic chance of success.[30] This is because by this date the larger cities of the Ebro valley, such as Saragossa and Tudela, were in Christian hands. In the case of Saragossa, Ramon Berenguer IV was now the prince regent of Aragon and could use his Aragonese resources and possessions as a base to hamper the Muslims in Tortosa.[31] Moreover, the approval shown by the papacy for this campaign made it possible to give this expedition the status of crusade.[32] This was an important bonus since it permitted the Barcelonese count to recruit, as Afonso Henriques had done, the help of the Anglo-Norman contingent and others from southern France, Cologne and the Low Countries. The crusader status also permitted the count to use the very great wealth of the Church to finance the expedition.[33] He was able to encourage the Genoese fleet, which scarcely required an incentive, to

---

[27] *Diplomatari de Santa Maria de Poblet*, ed. Agustín Altisent (Barcelona, 1994). See Appendix.

[28] *L'arxiu antic de Santa Anna de Barcelona del 942–1200*, ed. Jesús Alturo i Perucho (Barcelona, 1985), no. 268; Appendix, no. 31.

[29] Ibid.

[30] Antoni Virgili, *Ad detrimentum Yspanie: La conquesta de Turṭūša i la formació de la societat feudal 1148–1200* (Valencia, 2001), p. 43; Jaspert, "Tortosa and the Crusades," pp. 90–93.

[31] Virgili, *Ad detrimentum Yspanie*, pp. 46–50; José Goñi Gaztambide, *Historia de la bula de la cruzada en España* (Vitoria, 1958), pp. 85–87.

[32] A papal letter of Eugenius III gives the campaign of Ramon Berenguer IV against Tortosa the same status as that launched against the Muslims in the Holy Land: Archivo de la Corona de Aragon en Barcelona, Cancilleria, leg. 1, no. 14. Goñi Gaztambide and Constable date it to 22 June 1148 but recently Virgili has suggested it might be from 1147, which certainly gives enough time for it to have been used to attract the interest of the Anglo-Norman crusaders, since it is well accepted that the siege ended by December 1148: see Giles Constable, "A Note on the Route of the Anglo-Flemish Crusaders of 1147," *Speculum* 28 (1954), p. 526; Goñi Gaztambide, *Historia de la bula de la cruzada*, p. 86; Virgili, *Ad detrimentum Yspanie*, p. 45; I.S. Robinson, "The Papacy, 1122–1198," in *The New Cambridge Medieval History*, vol. 4.2, ed. David Luscombe and Jonathan Riley-Smith (Cambridge, 2004), p. 347.

[33] Virgili, *Ad detrimentum Yspanie*, p. 44.

accept his proposals for conquering Tortosa. The status of crusade would certainly have helped encourage this party to play a part.[34]

The Anglo-Normans' Arrival at Tortosa

How the Anglo-Norman contingent came to be involved in this expedition is not clear from the evidence. There is no surviving accord between the English and the count, nor are there Norman chronicles of the events of the expedition. Constable suggested that the Anglo-Norman crusaders were the same as those who besieged and conquered Lisbon in 1147, or at least a detachment of them.[35] This might be so, but there is no real evidence for this apart from the *Chronica Regia* of Cologne which suggests that Tortosa was conquered soon after by the Christian armies who had been involved in the Lisbon campaign.[36] However, there does not seem to be another explanation for how the English contingent became involved in this expedition apart from the possibility that they were directly invited by the count, perhaps through contacts in England and Normandy of his Norman vassal Robert Burdet.[37] This is not substantiated however, since none of the documents that show that Burdet acquired lands in Tortosa after its conquest link him in any way with the Anglo-Norman names.[38] The more likely scenario, as stated above, is that the Anglo-Norman contingent involved in the Tortosa crusade came into contact with either the count or the Genoese or both, as they passed the Straits of Gibraltar and stopped in the newly conquered city of Almeria for provisions.[39] It is also possible that they were invited by a third party or an agent working for the Genoese or the

---

[34] *Codice diplomatico*, no. 168.
[35] Constable, "A Note on the Route of the Anglo-Flemish Crusaders," pp. 525–26.
[36] *Chronica regia Coloniensis*, ed. Georg Waitz (Hanover, 1880), p. 86; Constable, "A Note on the Route of the Anglo-Flemish Crusaders," p. 526.
[37] Robert Burdet was a Norman adventurer who had arrived in Iberia in the 1120s as part of the retinue of Rotrou of Perche and who was involved in the campaigns of Alfonso the Battler in the Ebro valley. He received grants in Tudela. He was later chosen by Archbishop Olegario of Tarragona to restore the archiepiscopal see under the title of prince. Moreover, from 1130 to the 1150s he and his family administered and ruled the city and its territories. See Appendix, nos. 1, 20, 21, 26, 28, 30, 34, 35, 37, 39, 45, 49, 68. Joaquim Miret i Sans, "La familia de Robert Burdet, el restaurador de Tarragona," in *Segundo congreso de historia de la corona de Aragón: actas y memorias*, ed. Justo Martínez, vol. 1 (Huesca, 1922), pp. 53–74; Lawrence J. McCrank, "Norman Crusaders in the Catalan Reconquest: Robert Burdet and the Principality of Tarragona," *Journal of Medieval History* 7 (1981), pp. 67–82; Eloy Benito Ruano, "El principado de Tarragona," in *Estudis d'història oferts a Ramon d'Abadal i de Vinyals en el centenari del seu naixement*, ed. Jaume Sobrequés i Callicó, Sebastià Riera i Viader and Ramón de Abadal y Vinyals (Barcelona, 1994), pp. 107–19; Antonio María Jordà Fernández, "Terminologia jurídica i dret comù: a propòsit de Robert Bordet, 'Princeps' de Tarragona (s. XII)," in *El temps sota control: Homenatge a E. Xavier Ricomà Vendrell*, ed. Manuel Ruisánchez and Xavier Vendrell (Tarragona, 1997), pp. 355–62; Lucas Villegas-Aristizábal, "Norman and Anglo-Norman Participation in the Iberian Reconquista, c. 1018–c. 1248," unpublished PhD thesis (Nottingham, 2007), pp. 108–45.
[38] Appendix, nos. 60, 78, 60.
[39] Morera y Llauradó, *Tarragona cristiana*, vol. 1, p. 417.

Barcelonese count. Yet a further possibility is that the Anglo-Norman and Flemish fleets which had taken part in the siege of Lisbon decided to follow the Iberian coast round to Barcelona after they had sacked Faro in February 1148 and in this way came directly into contact with the Barcelonese either in Tarragona or Barcelona itself.[40] If this was so, the papal bull of Eugenius III would have served as an important form of encouragement for the Anglo-Norman crusaders' involvement:

> We beg, warn and exhort in the Lord to all the Christian faithful to vanquish the infidels and enemies of the cross of Christ with virility and do not doubt to join the noble man Ramon, count of Barcelona, for the defence of the Christian faith and the whole of the Holy Church. For this purpose, we confirm by our apostolic authority the same remission of sins that the blessed Pope Urban II, of whom we have happy memories, granted for the liberation of the Church.[41]

Certainly the equation of the crusade to the Holy Land with the expedition led by Ramon Berenguer IV, together with the presence of Nicholas Breakspear as a non-official papal legate, must have been reason enough for the Anglo-Normans that had been involved in the Lisbon campaign to contribute to this expedition without official encouragement from the pope himself. In the eyes of contemporaries and of the Church this proclamation made the expedition a crusade.[42] As an Englishman, Nicholas Breakspear (the future Pope Adrian IV) would have been a familiar face to those crusaders who were acquainted with him or his family. Breakspear was from Hertfordshire and probably well known in southern England where the majority of the expedition originated.[43] His reputation as abbot of Saint Ruffus and his position

---

[40] Constable, "A Note on the Route of the Anglo-Flemish Crusaders," pp. 525–26.

[41] Virgili, *Ad detrimentum Yspanie*, p. 44, n. 23: "Rogamus monemus et exhortamus in Domino quatenus ad expugnacionem infidelium et inimicorum Crucis Christi viriliter accingamini et cum nobili viro Raimundo Barchinone comite pro defensione christiane fidei et tocius sancta ecclesie cum devotione proficisci nullatenus dubitentis. Ut autem pro tanto labore dignum premium vos habituros speretis illam peccatorum remissionem que a predecessore nostro felicis memorie papa Urbano ad liberationem ecclesie tunc transeuntibus statuta est vobis auctoritate apostolica confirmamus."

[42] Jaspert, "Tortosa and the Crusades," p. 92.

[43] Details of Englishmen in the Iberian campaigns of the Second Crusade have also survived in documents relating to the granting of lands made after the conquest of Tortosa. The most notable of them, because of the abundance of documentary sources about them, are "Gilbert," "Osbert," and "Jordan." Unfortunately, because of the cryptic form of the names of these Englishmen who appear mostly with the surname Anglici or Angles, it is hard to identify exactly their place of origin in England. Nonetheless, Richard Fletcher, *Moorish Spain* (London, 2001), p. 146, suggested that Gilbert was from Devon, based on the fact that in his will he granted land to a Robert of Totnes. However, there are two groups of English in Tortosa whose surnames Savigné and Caron seem to link them directly with East Anglia, which implies that some other participants were also from this area. There is evidence from Domesday Book that members of these two families settled in East Anglia after the Norman conquest of England: see Lewis C. Loyd, *The Origins of Some Anglo-Norman Families*, ed. Charles Travis Clay and David Douglas (Leeds, 1951), pp. 25, 95. It is likely that those involved on the Lisbon campaign and the Tortosa campaign were members of the same expedition, since there is no mention of the formation of a crusading expedition in England except for those who went to Lisbon. German sources also confirm that many of the Lisbon campaign's active players continued on their way to Jerusalem after the fall

were additional incentives for the crusaders to get involved in the planned siege.[44] The involvement of Breakspear would have been of great practical importance as he could address the Anglo-Norman crusaders in their own language. This familiarity would have created a better climate of trust between the crusaders and the Iberian ruler, which had not been the case in Portugal.[45] This certainly would help to explain why so many crusaders stayed at Tortosa when they could have easily stayed at Lisbon after its conquest if part of the purpose of their expedition was to gain some wealth through the acquisition of land. Confidence in the count as overlord made it more likely for these crusaders to settle without too much hesitation.

On the other hand, as shown above, the papacy did seem to have a clear policy of crusade for Tortosa. The introduction of a papal letter of support for the expedition was certainly more convincing to the crusaders of the worthiness of their cause than the arguments mentioned in *De expugnatione Lyxbonensi*, which were placed by the author in the mouth of the bishop of Porto.[46] Not having a papal bull, the local clergy had had to resort to their own theological arguments to justify that military venture as part of the general crusade. However, Tortosa – like Almeria, Faro and Lisbon before – was not in the Holy Land and it is likely that not all the crusaders who had been involved in Lisbon were also involved in Tortosa.[47]

The conquest of Tortosa was achieved after a long siege, during which the Genoese played a vital part by blockading the river route into the Ebro. The role played during this siege by the Anglo-Normans was briefly recorded by Caffaro: "Also the English with the Templars and many other foreigners located themselves near the area of the Remolins on the river bank."[48] Here he suggests that the Anglo-Normans used their fleet to reinforce the Genoese and the Templars to attack the area of Remolins on the western side of Tortosa.[49] The Anglo-Norman contribution therefore may have been substantial but certainly not as great as that of the Genoese, who after the conquest received a great section of the city with similar conditions of

---

of this city: see Constable, "A Note on the Route of the Anglo-Flemish Crusaders," pp. 525–26; Susan Edgington, "Albert of Aachen, Saint Bernard and the Second Crusade," in *The Second Crusade*, ed. Phillips and Hoch, p. 67; Cardinal Boso, "Life of Adrian IV," in *Adrian IV: The English Pope, 1154–1159*, ed. Brenda Bolton and Anne J. Duggan (Aldershot, 2003), p. 215; Appendix, no. 34. See the Index to the Appendix for a comprehensive list of the Anglo-Norman settlers in Tortosa and the surviving evidence for their lives in the city and its territory.

[44] Damian J. Smith, "The Abbot-Crusader: Nicholas Breakspear in Catalonia," in *Adrian IV*, ed. Bolton and Duggan, pp. 30–32.

[45] Bennett, "Military Aspects of the Conquest of Lisbon," pp. 84–85.

[46] *De expugnatione Lyxbonensi*, ed. and trans. Charles W. David, with a new foreword and bibliography by Jonathan Phillips (New York, 2001), pp. 70–101.

[47] Jonathan Riley-Smith, "The Templars and the Castle of Tortosa in Syria: An Unknown Document Concerning the Acquisition of the Fortress," *English Historical Review* 84 (1969), pp. 278–84.

[48] Caffaro, *De captione Almerie et Tortuose*, p. 32: "Angli namque, una cum militibus Templi et cum multis aliis alienigenis, desuper uersus romelinum iuxta flumen steterunt."

[49] Virgili, *Ad detrimentum Yspanie*, pp. 60–67.

exemption from dues to the count for trade as seems to have been accorded to the English after the conquest of Lisbon.[50]

Apart from Caffaro's mention of the Anglo-Normans, there is another reference that helps to shed light on the makeup of the Anglo-Norman contingent. This is a charter of a donation of houses in Tortosa to the canons of the Holy Sepulchre of Jerusalem. This charter was originally in the monastery of Santa Anna in Barcelona and is now located in the diocesan archive. It is of great importance to this study not only because it is one of the first charters to survive from after the fall of Tortosa but, more importantly, because it shows in its witness list that the Anglo-Norman contingent was organized under the leadership of a *stabulari*.[51] This reference to the leader is different from the more common *constabulari*, but both clearly refer to a marshal. The name of this leader was Balluini de Carona, perhaps a Hispanicization of the name Caron or Cairon, a family originally from the Calvados region in Normandy.[52] According to Domesday Book, this family had settled in Bedfordshire after the Conquest.[53] If Balluini de Carona was a descendant of this family, it is probable that, like Harvey of Glanville (the leader of the East Anglian contingent involved in the conquest of Lisbon), he came from south-east England. It is thus possible that Balluini and some of the contingent that went to Tortosa were a detachment of Harvey of Glanville's group from East Anglia who were involved in the conquest of Lisbon. Moreover, this charter certainly confutes Morera y Llauradó's claim that Gilbert Anglici was the leader of the Anglo-Norman contingent that was involved in Tortosa.[54] As will be shown, both Gilbert Anglici and Gerald of Salvagnac were very important in the Anglo-Norman repopulation of Tortosa and perhaps after the disappearance of Balluini they became the leaders of the new community.

One of the problems concerning Balluini de Carona is that he does not appear in any other charter concerning the repopulation of Tortosa. Moreover, Gerald of Salvagnac and Gilbert Anglici, who are commonly referred to in later charters, are not mentioned in this first charter. There is a "Gilbert A." mentioned in a charter of 1149, but it is impossible to be sure that this is the Gilbert Anglici who appears so often in many of the charters of Tortosa that survive in the cartularies of Poblet and Santes Creus, and in the documents in the cathedral of Tortosa. The lack of reference in other documents to the *stabulari* of the Anglo-Norman contingent might indicate that he did not stay in Tortosa but perhaps continued on his way to the Holy Land, as many of the crusaders preferred to do after the conquest of Lisbon.[55] He might have felt inclined to fulfil his crusading vow by continuing his pilgrimage, or he might have died soon after the event. The existence of this *stabulari* as head of

---

[50] *De expugnatione*, pp. 112–15.
[51] Appendix, no. 31.
[52] Loyd, *The Origins of Some Anglo-Norman Families*, p. 25.
[53] *Domesday Book*, vol. 34, ed. John Morris (Chichester, 1986), cols. 210, 210b, 212, 212b, 214b.
[54] Morera y Llauradó, *Tarragona cristiana*, vol. 1, p. 417.
[55] *Chronica regia Coloniensis*, p. 86.

the expedition is clear from the source. It seems likely that, as *De expugnatione Lyxbonensi* explains, the appointment of leaders was done from within the ranks, based perhaps on seniority and personal prestige within the group.[56] However, as Balluini de Carona is not mentioned in *De expugnatione*, one might assume that he was chosen during the expedition's move from Lisbon to Tortosa, something which is not narrated in this chronicle or any other known source.

The Anglo-Norman Settlers

Although the details of the Anglo-Norman military input into this campaign are scarce, information regarding the post-conquest settlement compensates with abundant detail. The careers of men like Gilbert, John, Osbert and Jordan Angles, and Gerald, Stephen and William Salvagnac can be traced individually from around the first decade of the conquest of Tortosa to the last decade of the twelfth century.[57]

Of all the Norman or Anglo-Norman families the only one that can be traced back to a specific area of England is the Salvagnac or Savigné, which has usually been classified as Anglo-Norman, perhaps because of this family's very close relationship with other Anglo-Normans with the Anglici surname, such as Gilbert and Osbert, as Miravall suggested.[58] Their distinctive surname, which makes them likely to belong to at least the lower nobility, does not, however, guarantee that they were indeed of Norman origin since the name Salvagnac also exists in southern France and the southern French nobility is well documented as having contributed to the conquest of Tortosa under the leadership of Count William of Montpellier.[59] However, one important detail about Gerald of Salvagnac, who is the most frequently mentioned of the Salvagnacs in Tortosa, is that the surname appears written in an array of spellings such as *Salvaic*, *Silvanico*, *Salvinicho*, *Sovagne* and *Salvanacho*. If the surname of this family whose members (Stephen, William and Gerald) have typical Anglo-Norman names is just a misspelling by a succession of Iberian scribes who repeatedly tried to Latinize this foreign surname in the charters of Tortosa from the early 1150s to the late 1180s, it is possible that it was referring to the Anglo-Norman family of Savenie or Savigné.[60] This would be significant since, like the Glanvilles and the Carons, the Savignés were originally from Calvados in Normandy and possessed lands in East Anglia.[61] If this is the

---

[56] *De expugnatione Lyxbonensi*, pp. 54–55.
[57] See Index of the Appendix.
[58] Miravall, *Immigració britànica a Tortosa*, pp. 57–75; Virgili, *Ad detrimentum Yspanie*, p. 56. There are also a few references to some Morlans who could be Anglo-Normans, but who could also be Gascons or Bretons. See Appendix, nos. 32, 44, 125.
[59] Caffaro, *De captione Almerie et Tortuose*, p. 32: "Alia uero pars desuper a montana loca, nomine Bagnare, cum comite W(illielmo) Montispesulani tentoria poserunt."
[60] Loyd, *The Origins of Some Anglo-Norman Families*, p. 95.
[61] *Domesday Book*, vol. 34, cols. 373b, 375b, 376b.

case, it is all the more significant because, like the Glanvilles, the Savigné were also vassals of the Bigods. During the period of "the Anarchy" they were led by the troublesome Hugh Bigod, an influential figure, who changed sides on many occasions in order to expand his domains at the expense of both warring factions.[62] It is possible that his vassals did not always appreciate his political manoeuvres and were inclined to leave his service by joining a crusade.

Gerald of Savigné, as such, does not seem to appear in any English charter. Gerald is by far the best documented of the Anglo-Normans and of the Salvagnacs, with charters dating from 1151 referencing his possessions in Xerta to the late 1180s, when it appears that he was already dead.[63] He is named in 63 charters as signatory and there are references in nine surviving documents to his lands and wealth.[64] His prominence and the fact that he kept his Anglo-Norman surname may also indicate that he, together with Gilbert Anglici, was one of the main leaders of the Anglo-Norman community that settled in Tortosa after the disappearance from the historical record of Balluini de Caron after 1149.

Whilst the majority of Anglo-Norman settlers do not have a locative surname more specific than Anglici, some of their careers after they came to Tortosa can be followed in considerable detail. The most obvious examples are Gilbert Anglici, Osbert Angles and John Angles. For Gilbert Anglici there are eight charters which have direct reference to his career in Tortosa and there are twelve more documents where his possessions are mentioned, together with forty-two documents where he appears as a witness. Gilbert Anglici received lands and houses inside the city walls from the count of Barcelona and acquired a substantial group of estates growing vines and olives through his business deals with other settlers.[65]

Morera y Llauradó, Miravall and Jaspert have all suggested that Gilbert was indeed the most prominent, and perhaps the leader, of the Anglo-Norman community in Tortosa.[66] This has also been discussed by Virgili, who showed that Gilbert's influence and wealth were so great that he became an important business partner of the house of Montcada, one of the most significant noble families in the area at the time.[67] Gilbert did indeed receive enough land and fiefs from Ramon Berenguer IV to make him a very wealthy man, as is shown in charters relating to his possessions. Moreover, among the new citizens of Tortosa after its conquest, Gilbert is one of the most common witnesses to the grants by Ramon Berenguer IV and his successors.[68] Even during the reign of Alfonso II of Aragon, Gilbert received from the monarch

---

[62] Andrew Wareham, "The Motives and Politics of the Bigod Family c. 1066–1177," *Anglo-Norman Studies* 17 (1994), pp. 233–39.

[63] The first document mentioning him is a donation of some houses in the interior of Tarragona given to him by the count of Barcelona in 1151: see Appendix, no. 36.

[64] See Index of the Appendix.

[65] Appendix, nos. 141, 159, 173, 201, 209.

[66] Morera y Llauradó, *Tarragona cristiana*, vol. 1, p. 417; Miravall, *Immigració britànica a Tortosa*, p. 9; Jaspert, "Tortosa and the Crusades," p. 98.

[67] Appendix, no. 134; Virgili, *Ad detrimentum Yspanie*, p. 233.

[68] Appendix, nos. 38, 120, 133, 144, 145, 197.

himself a donation of a house inside the city walls in reward for his services and aid in helping to demarcate a street.[69] Certainly by the 1160s Gilbert had become a very wealthy and influential person in Tortosan society.

Gilbert was even able to bequeath property and money to religious institutions such as the cathedral of Tortosa, and to religious orders that had originated in the Holy Land, such as the Templars and the Hospitallers.[70] His ability to give away fiefs to these orders not only shows his power, but also suggests, as Jaspert stated, that perhaps, as a crusader, he felt obliged to support these institutions since he had not reached the Holy Land himself to fulfil his vow.[71] However, the grants of lands to the military orders in Tortosa need not necessarily mean that the Anglo-Normans felt they had not fulfilled their vows. It certainly indicates that the crusader colony became integrated with the larger land-owning institutions in the region, both for practical and ideological reasons. Nonetheless, it is apparent that Gilbert identified more with the cathedral of Tortosa, where his brother Theobald was a canon, and with the monastery of Santes Creus than with other ecclesiastical institutions of Tortosa.[72] He appears as signatory in eleven documents in the *Llibre Blanch*[73] and seven documents from the cathedral archive.[74]

Of the documents which directly relate to Gilbert, perhaps the most interesting is the testament made by Osbert Anglici when he decided to make his trip to the Holy Land in 1166.[75] This will suggests that at least some Anglo-Norman crusaders who had joined the expedition to Tortosa had originally intended to go to Jerusalem, but had been distracted on the way, settling in Tortosa. Moreover, because of their crusading vows those who died in the battle were buried in the English cemetery which was located close to the church of the Holy Sepulchre, perhaps as Jaspert suggested, to fulfil in a spiritual way their crusading vows.[76] However, in the case of Osbert Anglici, after more than a decade of living comfortably in Tortosa, he decided to fulfil his vow to go to Jerusalem and made his will in case he did not return. He appointed the most prominent Anglo-Norman settlers, Gerald of Salvagnac or Savigné and Gilbert Anglici, as guarantors of his will.

Osbert's case, however, is unique in Tortosa where he was the only one of the Anglo-Normans, about whom we know, who later specifically planned to go to Jerusalem. Yet it is likely that many from England who settled there had been under a crusading vow. Although they did not go to Jerusalem in the end, they tended to leave land and property at their new homes to the military orders, which were originally created to protect the holy places in the Holy Land and later became involved in the crusades in Iberia.

---

[69] Appendix, no. 108.
[70] Appendix, no. 156.
[71] Jaspert, "Tortosa and the Crusades," p. 99.
[72] Appendix, no. 156.
[73] Appendix, nos. 100, 106, 127, 141, 156, 157, 163, 164, 165, 180, 190.
[74] Appendix, nos. 115, 152, 159, 173, 176, 177, 201.
[75] Appendix, no. 115.
[76] Jaspert, "Tortosa and the Crusades," p. 99.

The Impact of the Anglo-Norman Crusading Colony

Certainly, the new Anglo-Norman community played an important part in the Christian settlement of this border town.[77] The settlement of Tortosa is a well-documented example of the mid-twelfth-century attempt by the Christian leaders of Iberia to extirpate the original Islamic settlements by destroying their systems of agriculture and seizing their land.[78] The documentation shows how Ramon Berenguer IV rewarded his supporters by allocating large sections of the city and its territories to them at the expense of the Saracen communities. In this the Anglo-Norman settlers played their part, as is clearly visible in earlier charters of donation where previous Muslim ownership of the land concerned is directly referred to in grants and later sales of lands or rights.[79] The formation of a Christian society in the lower valley of the Ebro was not just the result of the northern European involvement in the conquest of the city but of local realities, which existed already in this part of the peninsula.[80]

However, the formation of this social structure was certainly conducive to integrating incoming foreign Christians like the Anglo-Normans into the local communities. It is clear that, although the Anglo-Normans were a distinct minority, this factor did not stop them from interacting in business with other groups, as is shown in the documentation. Many of the members of the Anglo-Norman community appear as witnesses and active participants in transaction documents relating to local Catalans. The Anglo-Normans were clearly involved in the local agricultural economy, as many sources mention that they possessed vineyards, olive orchards and fruit trees on their lands.[81]

From the original partition of Tortosa, it is known that the city and its territory were divided among the count, the republic of Genoa and the military orders.[82] Although Ramon Berenguer IV seemed to have no objections to granting lands and properties to the newcomers, most of the evidence for the actual donations to Anglo-Normans dates to at least four to five years after the actual conquest of the city. For the most prominent Anglo-Norman settlers, like Gilbert Anglici and Gerald of Salvagnac, there are some comital donations that date from 1151.[83] Morera y Llauradó claimed that Geoffrey Anglici received a donation in 1150 from the count in Tortosa. This, however, cannot be proved, because the document he quoted does

---

[77] Virgili, *Ad detrimentum Yspanie*, p. 57.

[78] Antoni Virgili, "El monestir de Santes Creus i Tortosa (segles XII–XIII)," *Resclosa* 7 (2002), pp. 35–36; Pierre Bonnassie, *From Slavery to Feudalism in South-Western Europe*, trans. Jean Birrell (Cambridge, 1991), pp. 164–65.

[79] Appendix, nos. 72, 138, 168, 177, 189, 194.

[80] Antoni Virgili, "Conqueridors i colons a la frontera: Tortosa, 1148–1212," *Recerques: Historia, economia y cultura* 43 (2001), p. 52; Bonnassie, *From Slavery to Feudalism*, pp. 164–65, 233.

[81] See Appendix.

[82] Morera y Llauradó, *Tarragona cristiana*, vol. 1, pp. 415–16.

[83] Ibid., p. 416.

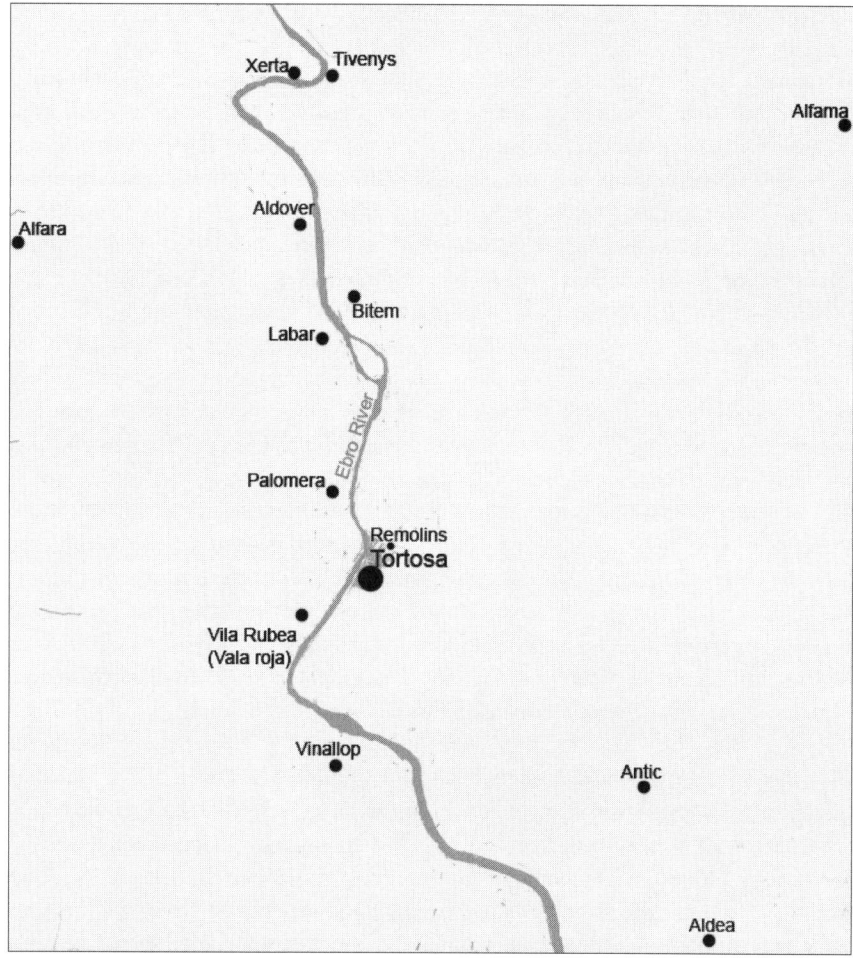

Fig. 2   The territory of Tortosa with its associated villages.

not actually indicate that it was Geoffrey Anglici, although a later charter seems to suggest that it was.[84]

The Anglo-Norman community seems to have had most of its properties north of the city. The localities of Bitem,[85] Aldover[86] and Xerta[87] saw by far the largest

---

[84] Ibid., p. 417.

[85] For documents relating to the Anglo-Norman settlers in Bitem, see Appendix, nos. 53, 54, 66, 67, 97, 107, 138, 170, 214, 215, 220, 225.

[86] For documents relating to the Anglo-Norman settlers in Aldover, see Appendix, nos. 36, 85, 141, 159, 172, 176, 177, 178, 194, 195, 206, 209.

[87] For documents relating to the Anglo-Norman settlers in Xerta, see Appendix, nos. 76, 98, 119, 128, 153, 164, 169, 173, 175, 177, 189, 193, 198, 201.

concentration of these settlers (see Fig. 2). This suggests that, although these areas were not exclusively settled by Anglo-Normans, the community was keen to maintain a relative unity around a specific zone. The reason for the choice of this specific area, however, is not clear from the evidence. On the one hand, as is demonstrated by the documents listed in the Appendix, the community was prepared to hold lands in areas like Labar and in the city of Tortosa itself, where the count granted parts of the city to these settlers. Moreover, the existence of an English cemetery ensured the attraction that the city would have for this particular foreign community, giving it a privileged position in the urban centre.[88]

The apparent lack of direct comital donations to the Anglo-Normans immediately after the conquest can be explained in several ways. First, it is likely that charters may have been lost. At the same time, it is possible that the conquest of Lleida in the following year distracted the count from producing a detailed list of donations to each individual settler of importance. Instead, he and his officials might have had some sort of previous agreement like the one he had with the Genoese and it may not have been imperative for him to produce direct donations straight away. Meanwhile, it is likely that the Anglo-Normans settled down in the area of Remolins, which Caffaro claims they were in charge of assaulting in the original conquest of the city,[89] or perhaps in Xerta or Aldover where the Anglo-Norman community managed gradually to acquire several estates.[90] However, it is hard to see how order could have been maintained in these early years if the first Anglo-Norman settlers were not given any official recognition for the lands they colonized.

It might have been the case that some kind of temporary agreement was reached with the crusading fleet that included the Anglo-Normans over the division of spoils, and for the early years their verbal or an otherwise lost agreement may have been used as a way to keep the peace. Perhaps, as leading members of the community, Gilbert Anglici and Gerald of Salvagnac were made guarantors for the Anglo-Normans while a more lasting arrangement was put in place. On the other hand, if documents relating to the original donation were awarded by the count to the early settlers in 1150 or 1151, it is possible that the settlers themselves might have kept them, and therefore the documents disappeared in this way from the historical record.[91] This, of course, would explain the puzzling lack of documents of direct donation from the count to individual settlers in Tortosa apart from the most prominent members of the Anglo-Norman community. However, this explanation is problematic since it would seem strange that no copies were made for the archives of local institutions like the cathedral and the monasteries. Certainly it is obvious that the virtual non-existence of comital donations to the Anglo-Normans was the result of one or a combination of these eventualities, since later evidence shows that

---

[88] Appendix, no. 31.
[89] Appendix, no. 31.
[90] Appendix, nos. 94, 200.
[91] Appendix, no. 33.

a vibrant Anglo-Norman community existed from the early days of the Christian conquest of Tortosa.

Yet it is hard to imagine how these settlers managed to keep their own identity within the Iberian community for more than a generation, for unlike the Genoese they did not have the support of their overlords at home in England for their venture. It is likely that as time went by they intermarried with the locals and became more Iberian and less Anglo-Norman. This is further confirmed in the historical record as the names of Anglo-Normans decrease in frequency in the first decade of the thirteenth century.[92] On the other hand, it is likely that other settlers of Iberian origin did not at first mix with the newcomers, something which might have helped to keep the distinct identity of the Anglo-Norman community for at least the life-span of the original settlers and perhaps the first generation of their children. There are some Anglo-Norman settlers like John Anglici and William Salvagnac who do not make an appearance until late in the 1170s. This may indicate that there were some English settlers who came after the original conquest at the request of family members who had made their fortune from the conquest.[93] However, apart from these two, who seem to have been related to other Anglo-Norman settlers, there is little evidence to suggest that there was a continuous influx of settlers from England into Tortosa after 1150. It seems that for the most part the original crusading venture had been the reason for their arrival and the lack of another large crusading enterprise from England until 1189 hampered any further movement of settlers. Tortosa remained a frontier town until 1238 when Jaume I of Aragon conquered Valencia.[94]

An interesting comparison can be made with the towns of the Latin East which in the second half of the twelfth century did not receive a great number of European settlers, partly as a result of the failure of the Second Crusade. However, in the case of Tortosa, although the crusade had been a success, the town's position in the second half of the twelfth century was never precarious enough to encourage the Anglo-Norman community to ask for additional help from their motherland. Except for a reference to Gerald of Hastings coming back to England to encourage Anglo-Normans to fight in Portugal, there is no reference to contacts, or indeed to calls of help, from the new communities to their compatriots in the homeland.[95]

---

[92] Appendix, nos. 216–19.

[93] See Appendix for names like William of Salvagnac and John Anglici, who seem to have arrived late and were related to prominent settlers like Gerald Salvagnac and Gilbert Anglici. It also appears that Jordan and Osbert were brothers. The number of groups of brothers who came to settle in Tortosa from England is striking. This shows the importance of kindred relationships as a form of encouragement for individuals to get involved in future crusading ventures. However, in the case of Tortosa it is impossible to know how long the tradition of each individual family was. See Jonathan Riley-Smith, "Family Traditions and Participation in the Second Crusade," in *The Second Crusade and the Cistercians*, ed. Michael Gervers (New York, 1992), pp. 101–5.

[94] Goñi Gaztambide, *Historia de la bula de la cruzada*, pp. 150–70.

[95] Symeonis Monachi, *Opera Omnia, historia regum*, vol. 2, ed. Thomas Arnold (London, 1885), p. 324: "Gilebertus episcopus Olisiponis, prædicans in Angliam, plurimos sollicitavit in Hyspaniam proficisci, Ispalim obsessuros et expugnaturos."

The most important members of the Anglo-Norman community may have acquired considerable influence in the frontier society. Despite this, their numbers were not large enough to have a lasting impact as a separate group within local society.

Conclusion

Although the Second Crusade represented a great example of the Anglo-Norman involvement in the Iberian Crusades, their subsequent involment in this theater of war was almost non-existent apart from a few expeditions to the Portuguese coast in the early thirteenth century. More strikingly, in the great conquests of the early thirteenth century in Iberia after the famous battle of Las Navas de Tolosa, there are only sporadic mentions of English soldiers or settlers.[96] On the other hand, the involvement of the Anglo-Norman contingents in the conquest of Tortosa gives a fine example of how the contribution of foreign crusaders served the Iberian rulers in their attempts to conquer Moorish territories.

---

[96] Villegas-Aristizábal, "Norman and Anglo-Norman Participation in the Iberian Reconquista," pp. 268–78.

Index of Norman and Anglo-Norman Names in Documents Table

Agnes/Inez Aguilo, wife of Robert Burdet:
  Direct reference to her: 64, 78, 83, 90, 101, 132, 136
  Witness/signatory: 28, 29, 30, 49, 68, 83, 101, 132, 136
  Reference to him or his lands: 60

Alard Anglicus:
  Reference to him or his lands: 55

Brunet Morlans, brother of Gerald Morlans:
  Direct reference to him: 55, 59, 125

Frank Anglicus:
  Direct reference to him: 75

Gales Anglicus:
  Direct reference to him: 124, 127
  Witness/signatory: 153

Gilbert Anglicus:
  Direct reference to him: 33, 108, 116, 141, 152, 156, 157
  Witness/signatory: 66, 85, 96, 100, 102, 103, 105–7, 109, 110, 113, 115, 117, 120, 123, 133, 139, 140–45, 150, 152, 156, 156, 157, 163–65, 177, 180, 197, 221
  Reference to him or his lands: 159, 176, 178, 180, 197, 209, 222

Geoffrey Anglicus:
  Direct reference to him: 159, 167, 168
  Witness/signatory: 159, 160
  Reference to him or his lands: 71, 200

Gerald Anglicus:
  Witness/signatory: 75
  Reference to him or his lands: 175

Gerald Morlans:
  Direct reference to him: 125
  Witness/signatory: 44
  Reference to him or his lands: 44

Gerald of Salvagnac:
  Direct reference to him: 48, 59, 72, 74, 76, 81, 87, 115, 138, 156, 176, 181
  Witness/signatory: 36, 40–43, 46, 47, 50–54, 56–58, 61, 66, 67, 69, 70, 73, 74, 76, 77, 80–82, 84, 87–89, 93–97, 99, 103, 104, 106, 108, 110, 112, 115, 118, 119, 122, 127, 129–31, 138, 146–50, 156, 159, 175, 181, 182, 186–88, 204, 221
  Reference to him or his lands: 98, 106, 115, 119, 167, 169, 201, 203, 216, 217, 220, 223, 224

Joan of Tortosa, daughter of Gilbert Anglicus:
  Direct reference to her: 105, 115
  Witness/signatory: 116

Jordan Anglicus, brother of Osbert Anglicus:
  Direct reference to him: 156, 169
  Witness/signatory: 63, 153, 155, 156, 169, 172, 177, 199
  Reference to him or his lands: 193, 196

John Anglicus:
  Direct reference to him: 163, 164, 166, 180, 184, 200, 206, 209, 210, 224
  Witness/signatory: 168, 172, 181, 202, 208, 213, 219

Nicholas Anglicus:
  Direct reference to him: 185, 186
  Witness/signatory: 185
  Reference to him or his lands: 194, 195

Matthew of Salvagnac:
  Reference to him or his lands: 65

Osbert Anglicus:
  Direct reference to him: 99, 115, 116, 128, 169
  Witness/signatory: 99, 105, 115
  Reference to him or his lands: 185, 215

Pagan Anglicus or Angles:
  Witness/signatory: 99, 114, 124, 127, 128,
  151, 153, 167, 172, 176
  Reference to him or his lands: 211

Peter Galeg:
  Direct reference to him: 165, 165, 224
  Witness/signatory: 111, 116, 124, 154, 159, 168, 179–81, 183, 192, 211
  Reference to him or his lands: 183

Reginald Anglicus:
  Direct reference to him: 168
  Witness/signatory: 16, 167, 168
  Reference to him or his lands: 220

Robert Burdet:
  Direct reference to him: 1, 20, 21, 26, 28, 30, 34, 35, 37, 39, 45, 49, 68
  Witness/signatory: 4, 7, 20, 28–31, 34, 49
  Reference to him or his lands: 8, 9, 11, 13, 23, 60, 64, 78, 83, 112

Robert Burdet II:
  Direct reference to him: 132, 136
  Witness/signatory: 83, 101, 132, 136

Roland Morlans:
  Direct reference to him: 32

Robert Otonis brother of William Anglicus:
  Direct reference to him: 153
  Reference to him or his lands: 35

Rotrou of Perche:
  Direct reference to him: 2, 6, 18
  Witness/signatory: 2, 25
  Reference to him or his lands: 7–13, 15, 17, 31

Theobald Anglicus, brother of Gilbert Anglicus:
  Direct reference to him: 156, 169, 172, 173, 175, 176, 177
  Witness/signatory: 153, 163–65

William Anglicus:
  Direct reference to him: 153, 166
  Reference to him or his lands: 158

William Burdet/Aquilon:
  Direct reference to him: 63, 79, 136
  Witness/signatory: 25, 28, 30, 49, 83, 101, 132

William of Salvagnac, brother of Gerald Salvaganc:
  Direct reference to him: 76, 162, 189, 198
  Witness/signatory: 76, 81, 126, 147, 148, 160–62, 189, 198, 206, 212, 214, 218
  Reference to him or his lands: 126

Appendix A: Documents relating to the conquest and settlement of Normans and Anglo-Normans in the valley of the Ebro

No.	Date	Description	Witnesses
1	1116x1118	This is the original fuero of Saragossa after its conquest by Alfonso I of Aragon. The charter does not contain the name of Rotrou, count of Perche, or Robert Burdet, which suggests that the claim that Rotrou was present at the fall of the city, made by *La Cronica de San Juan de la Peña*, is not accurate. In *Colección de fueros municipales y cartas pueblas*, ed. Tomas Muñoz y Romero, 1 (Madrid, 1847), pp. 448–49.	
2	1119	Donation by Rotrou, count of Perche, of a large amount of salt to the monks of Tiron for the salvation of his soul. It confirms that by this date Rotrou was in Normandy. In *Cartulaire de l'abbaye de la Sainte-Trinité de Tiron*, ed. Lucien Merlet, 1 (Paris, 1883), no. 22.	
3	February 1119	Fuero given to the city of Saragossa by Alfonso I and known as the Privilege of the Twenty. In *Colección de fueros municipales y cartas pueblas*, ed. Muñoz y Romero, 1, pp. 451–53.	
4	14 and 16 April 1121	Three charters of purchase of houses in Saragossa by Raol de Larrassunna. José María Lacarra, "Documentos para el estudio de la reconquista y repoblación de el valle de el Ebro," In *Estudios de la edad media de la Corona de Aragón* 2 (1946), no. 20.	A Fobert or Robert appears as witness but no surname is given
5	2 April 1121x1124, Lateran	Calixtus II proclaims war against the Moors in Spain, and offers to all bishops, princes and faithful the same kind of indulgences offered to those going to the Holy Land. In *La documentación pontificia hasta Inocencio III*, ed. Demetrio Mansilla (Rome, 1955), no. 62.	
6	April 1123	Count Rotrou donates houses to Sabinus, which used to belong to the Alcaide Aben Alimen. In José María Lacarra, "Documentos para el estudio de la reconquista y repoblación de el valle de el Ebro," *Estudios de la edad media de la Corona de Aragón* 5 (1952), no. 308.	
7	December 1124	Alfonso I gives the brothers Fruela and Pelayo three castles besides Huerva and the castle of Alcañiz. Rotrou appears as lord of Tudela. In Lacarra, "Documentos," *Estudios de la edad media de la Corona de Aragón* 5, no. 311.	
8	28 February 1125	Imes and his wife Boneta sell two tents to Sancho, bishop of Calagurritano. Rotrou appears as lord of Tudela and Robert Burdet as castellan. In Lacarra, "Documentos," *Estudios de la edad media de la Corona de Aragón* 3 (1948), no. 129.	
9	22 April 1125	Oriol Garciez buys from Salvador and his wife Maria Iñiguez some houses in Tudela that used to belong to Maomat Abenaadriz. Rotrou of Perche and Robert Burdet are mentioned with their respective positions in the city. In Lacarra, "Documentos," *Estudios de la edad media de la Corona de Aragón* 3, no. 125.	

Original	First Copy	Second Copy	Third Copy	Fourth Copy
Lost				
Lost				
Lost		Molino, *Repertorium fororum et obsevatiarum regni Aragonum*, fol. 265		
Archivo Capitular de la Seo de Zaragoza, Cartulary, fol. 46v				
Lost	Archive of the Spanish Embassy in Rome, Cod. 229, fol. 35			
Lost	*Molino, Repertorium fororum et obsevatiarum regni Aragonum*, fol. 265			
Archivo Diocesano de Zaragoza, arm. 9, cax. 1, lig. 1, no. 8				
Archivo Capitular de la Catedral de Calahorra, no. 17				
Archivo de la Catedral de Tudela, perg. no. 4				

No.	Date	Description	Witnesses
10	June 1125	Stephen, grammarian of Alfonso I and abbot of Santa Maria de Tudela, makes a donation to Sancho, scribe of Alfonso I, of a mosque besides the alhandaka, in return for the three solidos that he gave for the construction of the porch of the church. Rotrou appears as lord of Tudela. In Lacarra, "Documentos," *Estudios de la edad media de la Corona de Aragón* 5, no. 316.	
11	26 February 1126	Aimes and his wife Boneta sell two tents to the bishop of Calahorra. The charter claims that at the time Alfonso I was campaigning in Andalusia. It also mentions Rotrou as lord of Tudela and Robert in charge of the castle of Tudela. In Lacarra, "Documentos," *Estudios de la edad media de la Corona de Aragón* 3, no. 129.	
12	August 1127	Alfonso I gives to Fortun Garces Caxal houses that belonged to Iben Henderiz de Tarrazona. Rotrou appears as lord of Tudela. In Lacarra, "Documentos," *Estudios de la edad media de la Corona de Aragón* 5, no. 321.	
13	August 1127	Charter in which Alfonso I grants fueros to Tudela. Both Rotrou and Robert are mentioned. In *Colección de fueros municipales y cartas pueblas*, ed. Muñoz y Romero, 1, pp. 420–22.	
14	February 1128	Alfonso I gives to Garcia Aznar the houses that used to belong to Aben Forcagon in Ribas. Rotrou, unlike the following charter (no. 15) issued in Castilnuevo, does not appear as lord of Tudela or with any other title. In Lacarra, "Documentos," *Estudios de la edad media de la Corona de Aragón* 3, no. 140.	
15	March 1128	Alfonso I gives to Pedro Ortiz de Lizana two parcels of land in Mesones for building houses. Rotrou appears as lord of Tudela. In Lacarra, "Documentos," *Estudios de la edad media de la Corona de Aragón* 3, no. 141.	
16	1 April 1128	Will of Raimundo Mironis. In *Cartulario de Sant Cugat del Vallés*, ed. Jésus Rius Serra (Madrid, 1981), no. 898.	The scribe is Reginaldus Anglicus
17	May 1128	Alfonso I gives to Pedro Ortiz de Lizana the farm of Mesones. Rotrou appears as lord of Tudela. In Lacarra, "Documentos," *Estudios de la edad media de la Corona de Aragón* 3, no. 142.	
18	December 1128	Alfonso I gives the village and castle of Corella to Rotrou of Perche. In *Colección diplomatica medieval de la Rioja*, ed. Ildefonso Rodriquez de Lama, 2 (Logroño, 1976), no. 93.	
19	January 1129	Alfonso I gives to Fortun Iñiguez de San Celedonio land in Ribarroya. In Lacarra, "Documentos," *Estudios de la edad media de la Corona de Aragón*, 3, no. 153.	

THE CONQUEST AND SETTLEMENT OF TORTOSA, 1148–1180   87

Original	First Copy	Second Copy	Third Copy	Fourth Copy
Archivo de la Catedral de Tudela, perg. no. 8				
Archivo Capitular de la Catedral de Calahorra, no. 17				
Archivo Historico Nacional, Madrid, , Cartulary of Santa Cristiana, fol. 24r–v				
Lost				*Diccionario Geografico-Histórico de España publicado por la Real Academia de la Historia*, ed. Tómas Lopez, 2 (Madrid, 1804), p. 562.
Lost	Archivo Historico Nacional, Madrid, Documentos del Santo Sepulcro de Calatayud.			
Archivo Historico Nacional, Madrid, Cartulary of Montearagon, cod. 1067, fol. 32				
Arxiu de la Corona d'Aragó, Barcelona, Cartulary of Sant Cugat, no. 784, fol. 255				
Biblioteca Nacional de España, ms. 746, perg. 83				
Lost	Archivo municipal de Corella, copy from the 13th c., leg. 1, no. 1			
Archivo Historico Nacional, Madrid, St. John of Jerusalem Priory of Navarre, leg. 716–18				

No.	Date	Description	Witnesses
20	14 March 1129	Charter of the donation of Tarragona by Archbishop Olegario to Robert Burdet. Olegario maintains control over all the churches in the territory and Robert promises to restore the city when asked. In *Cartas de población y franquicia de Cataluña*, ed. Jose Font Rius, 1 (Barcelona, 1969), no. 51.	Robert, prince of Tarragona; Olegario, archbishop of Tarragona
21	March 1129 or later	Charter of fueros of Tarragona granted by Robert Burdet after his arrival in Tarragona. He gives the citizens exemption from taxation except for tithes and first fruits. Reference to the existence of this document is discussed in *Cartas de población y franquicia de Cataluña*, ed. Font Rius, 1, no. 52.	
22	26 October 1130, Bayona	Alfonso I grants the fueros of Tudela to the people of Corella. Rotrou appears as a witness confirming that he was back in Aragon. In *Colección diplomática medieval de la Rioja*, ed. Rodriquez de Lama, 2, no. 98.	
23	November 1131	Galin Sanz and his wife Toda exchange with his brother Gonzalo Galandiz the inherited property that they had in Tudela for the one he had in Huesca. Rotrou and Robert are still mentioned with their respective positions in Tudela. In Lacarra, "Documentos," *Estudios de la edad media de la Corona de Aragón*, 3, no. 165.	
24	March 1132	Alfonso I grants the Fuero of Asin. In *Colección de fueros municipales y cartas pueblas*, ed Muñoz y Romero, 1, pp. 505–6.	Rotrou of Perche
25	23 February 1145	Agreement made between Ramon Berenguer IV and Gerallus Alamanni over the castle of Monte Acuto, Monatclar, villa de Mager, Pontils, Sancta Perpetua. In *Colección de documentos inéditos del archivo general de la corona de Aragón*, ed. Manuel de Bofarull y de Sartorio, 4 (Barcelona, 1862), pp. 99–101.	William Aquilon, son of Robert Burdet
26	4 January 1148	Agreement proposed by Robert Burdet to Bernard Tort over the government of Tarragona. The prince agrees to maintain the norms for the designation of the local authorities, their performance in office and their fidelity. The exception of Sunday dues is extended to the new inhabitants of the city and its territory. In *Colección de fueros municipales y cartas pueblas*, ed. Muñoz y Romero, 1, no. 66.	
27	1148x1149	Charter of franchises given by Count Ramon Berenguer IV to the population of the newly conquered city of Tortosa. In *Cartas de población y franquicia de Cataluña*, ed. Font Rius, 1, no. 68.	

Original	First Copy	Second Copy	Third Copy	Fourth Copy
Lost	Arxiu Capitular de la S.I. Catedral de Tarragona, Ancient Copy, Libro de signatura 9, no. 16, fol. 17 (lost)	Arxiu de la Corona d'Aragó, Barcelona, 14th-c. transcription, Cancilleria, Registro no. 3, fol. 6	Arxiu de la Corona d'Aragó, Barcelona, 14th-c. transcription, patrimonio real Clase 4a, no. 2, fol. 2 a	
Lost				
Lost	Archivo municipal de Corella, copy from the late 12th c., Leg. 1, no. 2 a			
Archivo de la Catedral de Tudela, num. 1.059 (A) and 1.060 (B)				
Royal Archive of Barcelona (lost)				
Arxiu de la Corona d'Aragó, Barcelona, Royal Cartulary, Perg. Ramón Berenguer IV, no. 172				
Lost, it existed in the Archive of the Archdiocese of Tarragona	Transcription of the 18th c. in Mariano Mari, *Thesaurus Sanctae Metropolitanae Ecclesiae, Tarraconensis* (1783), pp. 182–84. (Ms. in the Archive of the Archdiocese of Tarragona)			
Arxiu de la Corona d'Aragó, Barcelona, Cancilleria, perg. Ramon Berenguer IV, no. 2				

No.	Date	Description	Witnesses
28	9 February 1149	Donation of the city and territory of Tarragona to Prince Robert, by Bernard Tort, archbishop of Tarragona. It confirms the previous donation by his predecessor Olegario. The archbishop will now take a fifth from all the rents. He also establishes an oven and a mill. The prince and the archbishop agree to designate together the local judges and their powers. They offer the new inhabitants exemption from Sunday dues. In *Colección de fueros municipales y cartas pueblas*, ed. Muñoz y Romero, 1, no. 69.	Robert, prince of Tarragona; Agnes, his wife; William Bordet; Bernard Tort, archbishop of Tarragona
29	9 April 1149	Donation of Mount Magons in the territory of Tarragona made by Poncius of Timor to the brothers Guillermus de Vilafranca and Ramon Arnaldo for the purpose of building a castle. In *Colección de fueros municipales y cartas pueblas*, ed. Muñoz y Romero, 1, no. 70.	Robert, prince of Tarragona; Agnes, his wife; Bernard Tort, archbishop of Tarragona
30	3 September 1149	Charter of franchises given by Prince Robert to the citizens of Tarragona. It confirms previous rights not to pay dues except for tithes and first fruits. The prince places the citizens under his jurisdiction. The archbishop approves this charter. In *Colección de fueros municipales y cartas pueblas*, ed. Muñoz y Romero, 1, no. 73.	Robert, prince of Tarragona; Agnes, his wife; William of Aquilon; Robert Burdet (II); Bernard Tort, archbishop of Tarragona
31	2 November 1149	Ramon Berenguer IV, count of Barcelona and prince of Aragon, with the common accordance of the noble consuls and the glorious people of Genoa, of Peter, Master of the Templars and his brothers, and because of the petition of the pilgrims (crusaders) that came from England and the other lands across the sea to the siege of Tortosa with the rest of the army, gives to the Order of the Holy Sepulchre of Jerusalem, to Thomas and to the other canons of the Order, houses belonging to the son of Ferri Alamin, a Saracen, citizen of Tortosa, located inside the walls in the vill of Remolins, with all rights and possessions of the land, orchards, vineyards, trees, agricultural lands and waste. In *L'arxiu antic de Santa Anna de Barcelona del 942 al 1200*, ed. Jésus Altura i Perucho (Barcelona, 1985), no. 268.	Balluini of Carona (Charone?) appears as *stabularius* of the English forces; Robert Burdet, prince of Tarragona
32	15 October 1150	Count Ramon Berenguer IV gives to Roland of Morlans houses in Tortosa that used to belong to Muhamad Algamari (Moor). In Joaquim Miret i Sans, *Les cases de Templers y Hospitalers en Catalunya* (Barcelona, 1910), no. 60.	
33	1 January 1151	The count of Barcelona grants houses in Tortosa, which had belonged to various Moors, to Gilbert Anglicus and his successors. In *El "Llibre Blanch" de Santes Creus*, ed. Frederic Udina Martorell (Barcelona, 1947), no. 50.	
34	25 January 1151	Donation of Riudoms, in the territory of Tarragona, by Prince Robert to Arnald de Palomar for the construction and maintenance of a castle to encourage the repopulation of the region. In *Cartas de población y franquicia de Cataluña*, ed. Font Rius, 1, no. 84.	Robert Burdet I

Original	First Copy	Second Copy	Third Copy	Fourth Copy
Lost	Arxiu Capitular de la S.I. Catedral de Tarragona, ancient copy of the Cathedral of Tarrragona (lost)	Arxiu de la Corona d'Aragó, Barcelona, 14th c. transcription, Cancilleria, Registro no. 3, fol. 4 a	Arxiu de la Corona d'Aragó, Barcelona, 15th c. transcription, Patrimonio Real Clase 4a, fol. 3 v. b	
Lost	Arxiu Històric municipal de Tarragona, 1235 transcription, parchment			
Lost	Reference to it in Morera y Llourado, *Tarragona cristiana*, 1, p. 441.			
Archivo Diocesano de Barcelona, Fons de Santa Anna, carp. 6, perg. 10	Archivo Diocesano de Barcelona, Santa Anna, carp. 6, perg. 11	Archivo Diocesano de Barcelona, Santa Anna, carp. 6. perg. 9		
Lost	Arxiu de la Corona d'Aragó, Barcelona, Cartulary of the Priory of the Templars of Tortosa, no. 231			
Lost	Biblioteca Pública de Tarragona, El Llibre Blanch de Santes Creus, cart. no. 168, fols. 108v–109r			
Lost	Arxiu Històric Arxidiocesà de Tarragona, copy without date made by Romeu, in the presence of Ramon de Llinas, Juan de Tortosa Guillermus de Rouric y Ferruzon (now lost)	Arxiu Històric Arxidiocesà de Tarragona, copy of B from the 14th-c. Codex A-B, Cartulary de Benet de Rocaberti, fol. 122 a		

No.	Date	Description	Witnesses
35	13 February 1151	The count of Barcelona gives houses in Tortosa, which once belonged to some Moors, to Guillelm de Trul and his wife Adalaz. In *El "Llibre Blanch" de Santes Creus*, ed. Udina Martorell, no. 52.	There is an Otonis who might be Robert Otonis, brother of William Angles
36	26 March 1151	Count Ramon Berenguer IV donates to Peter Oldegario and to his household houses in Tortosa and an orchard that used to belong to Abrahim Zegeil. He also gives him land beside the wall by a small door; also, some land which used to belong to Albedaio, and lands in Aldover. In *Diplomatari de la Catedral de Tortosa*, ed. Antoni Virgili (Barcelona, 1997), no. 27.	Gerald of Salvanech (Salvagnac)
37	August 1151	Bernard Tort returns the principality of Tarragona to Ramon Berenguer IV. The charter mentions Ramon Berenguer as prince of Tarragona. Bernard claims that this new arrangement is made with the consent of Pope Eugenius III and of the people of Tarragona. Robert Burdet and his family are not mentioned. In *Liber feudorum maior*, ed. Francisco Miquel Rosell, 1 (Barcelona, 1945), no. 247.	
38	5 August 1151	The count ratifies donations made by Archbishop Bernard of Tarragona and adds the tenth part of all the comital rents in the city to the Church of St. Mary's. In *Diplomatari de la Catedral de Tortosa*, ed. Virgili, no. 28.	Gerlald of Selvaniaco (Salvagnac), Gilbert [Anglicus]
39	7 August 1151	Dispute between Bernard Tort and Robert and his son Guillermus Aquilon. In *Colección de documentos inéditos del archivo general de la corona de Aragón*, ed. Bofarull y Sartorio 4, pp. 196–200; *Liber feudorum maior*, ed. Rosell, 1, no. 246.	
40	28 February 1153	William of Cor and his brother Berenguer sell land that had belonged to Abcegrus and his sister, to Bishop Geoffrey and the canons of St. Mary's of Tortosa. In *Diplomatari de la Catedral de Tortosa*, ed. Virgili, no. 37.	Gerald of Salviniaco (Salvagnac)
41	15 July 1153	Henricus Nigrapellis exchanges with the bishop and canons of St. Mary's of Tortosa a parcel of land which he had by the Ebro for another that they had in Villa Rubea. In *Diplomatari de la Catedral de Tortosa*, ed. Virgili, no. 40.	Gerald of Sovagne (Salvagnac)
42	6 March 1154	Peter de Ragedello for the remedy of his soul and his parents bequeaths in perpetuity to the Church of St. Mary's, Bishop Geoffrey and the canons the possessions of Avindrusc in Chalameran and in Banichalet, which is in the lands of Miravet. In *Diplomatari de la Catedral de Tortosa*, ed. Virgili, no. 54.	Gerald of Sovagnec (Salvagnac)
43	6 March 1154	Guillelm Aimeric donates to God and the the monastery of St. Mary of Poblet an orchard in Petrola on the term of Tortosa, on the other side of the Ebro. In *Diplomatari de Santa Maria de Poblet*, ed. Agustí Altisent (Barcelona, 1994), no. 161.	Gerald of Salviniacho (Salvagnac)

Original	First Copy	Second Copy	Third Copy	Fourth Copy
Lost	Biblioteca Pública de Tarragona, El Llibre Blanch de Santes Creus, cart. no. 168, fol. 102			
Arxiu Capitular de la S.I. Catedral de Tortosa, Benifallet, llaver (7: Aldover) (258,157)				
Lost	Arxiu de la Corona d'Aragó, Barcelona, Royal Cartulary, perg. Ramón Berenguer IV, no. 243			
Arxiu Capitular de la S.I. Catedral de Tortosa, Privilegis i donacions reials, 8 (505, 325)	Arxiu Capitular de la S.I. Catedral de Tortosa, Privilegis i donacions reials, fol. 18	Arxiu Capitular de la S.I. Catedral de Tortosa, Privilegis i donacions reials, fol. 21	Arxiu Capitular de la S.I. Catedral de Tortosa, Comú del capítol, 1, 16	Arxiu Capitular de la S.I. Catedral de Tortosa, Constitucions, 19
Lost	Arxiu de la Corona d'Aragó, Barcelona, Royal Cartulary, perg. Ramón Berenguer IV, no. 242			
Lost	Arxiu Capitular de la S.I. Catedral de Tortosa, Cartulary 2, Titol IV, fols. 109v–110v			
Arxiu Capitular de la S.I. Catedral de Tortosa, Genova, Vila-roja. (3: Vila-roja, 1) (130.135) ABC				
Lost	Arxiu Capitular de la S.I. Catedral de Tortosa, Cartulary 6, d, 144, fol. 53			
Lost	Biblioteca Pública de Tarragona, Cartulari de Poblet, ms. 241, fol 137r–v	Archivo Historico Nacional, Madrid, Clero secular y regular, c. 2002, fol. 16		

No.	Date	Description	Witnesses
44	13 June 1154	Andreu Lobret and his wife Breta and his son Iouan sell to Guillelm Arnall two orchards in the area of Arenal. One of the orchards is besides that of Gerald of Morlans. In *Diplomatari de Santa Maria de Poblet*, ed. Altisent, no. 163.	Gerald of Morlans
45	14/24 September 1154	Donation of Cambrils by Prince Robert to Bertrand for its repopulation. Reference in Joseph Blanch, *Arxiepiscopologi de la santa església metropolitana i primada de Tarragona*, 1, (Tarragona, 1985), p. 93.	
46	October 1154	Saurina, widow of Ademar, and her children sell to Bernard of Sancto Poncio the possessions which they had received from the count of Tortosa. In *Diplomatari de la Catedral de Tortosa*, ed. Virgili, no. 45.	Gerald of Savagne (Salvagnac)
47	19 October 1154	Count Ramon Berenguer IV grants to Peter de Sancto Poncio a house located against the wall of Tarragona and between the houses of John de Prohins and the houses that used to belong to Ademar Podio and which are by the entrance of the church of St. Mary and the river. In *Diplomatari de la Catedral de Tortosa*, ed. Virgili, no. 48.	Gerald of Sovagne (Salvagnac)
48	8 February 1155	Taboet, his wife Sancha and their children sell to Gerald of Savagne (Salvagnac) and his family orchards in Xerta which use to belong to various Moors. In *El "Llibre Blanch" de Santes Creus*, ed. Udina Martorell, no. 62.	
49	22 February 1155	Count Ramon Berenguer IV, Archbishop Bernard of Tarragona and Prince Robert of Tarragona grant to the monastery of Poblet the locality of Dol de Lop. In *Cartulari de Poblet edició del manuscrit de Tarragona*, ed. Joan Pons i Marqués (Barcelona, 1938), no. 246.	Prince Robert, his wife Agnes and his son William appear as signatories
50	5 March 1155	Peter of Rajadell grants to the monastery of Poblet orchards in Tortosa that he inherited from Avin Pedros. Conditions are attached to the donation. In *Cartulari de Poblet*, ed. Pons i Marqués, no. 195.	Gerald of Savagnec (Salvagnac)
51	13 March 1155	Grimoardus, abbot of Poblet, grants to Bernard and his family the honour which the count had given to them in the locality of Xerta. In *Cartulari de Poblet*, ed. Pons i Marqués, no. 203.	Gerald of Salvaniacho (Salvagnac)
52	14 March 1155	Berenguer Pinol and his wife Ermesend, and his son Berenguer and his wife Ermesend, for the remedy of their souls, donate an orchard located in Banifalet on the banks of the Ebro. In *Diplomatari de Santa Maria de Poblet*, ed. Altisent, no. 170.	Gerald of Salvaniacho (Salvagnac)
53	6 April 1155	Sibilla, wife of Gandolph Carbonari, with the permission of Martin Golias, grants part of the land that she had in Bitem in exchange for 70 morabis for charity. The land had been given originally by the count after the conquest from the Saracens. In *Diplomatari de la Catedral de Tortosa*, ed. Virgili, no. 56.	Gerald of Sovangnec (Salvagnac) and Martin of Sovagne (Salvagnac)
54	25 May 1156	Ramon of Cartelliaco sells to Peter Olegrario two lands that he had as concession from Ramon Berenguer IV for 4 pounds of dinars and 6 solidos. One was in Bitem and the other in Giramascor. In *Diplomatari de la Catedral de Tortosa*, ed. Virgili, no. 69.	Gerald of Salvaniaco (Salvagnac)

THE CONQUEST AND SETTLEMENT OF TORTOSA, 1148–1180

Original	First Copy	Second Copy	Third Copy	Fourth Copy
Archivo Historico Nacional, Madrid, Clero secular y regular, c. 2002, fol. 7				
Lost				
Arxiu Capitular de la S.I. Catedral de Tortosa, subtresoreria, 1, 65	Arxiu Capitular de la S.I. Catedral de Tortosa, Cartulary 2, titol III, d. XVI, fols. 68–70			
Lost	Arxiu Capitular de la S.I. Catedral de Tortosa, Cartulary 2, titol III d. II fol. 53	Arxiu Capitular de la S.I. Catedral de Tortosa, Cartulary 9, fol. 95r	Arxiu Capitular de la S.I. Catedral de Tortosa, Cartulary 9A, pergs. 243–44	
Lost	Biblioteca Pública de Tarragona, El Llibre Blanch de Santes Creus, cart. no. 168, fol. 102v			
Lost	Biblioteca Pública de Tarragona, Cartulari de Poblet, ms. 241, fol. 161r–v			
Archivo Historico Nacional, Madrid, Clero secular y regular, c. 2002, fol. 13	Biblioteca Pública de Tarragona, Cartulari de Poblet, ms. 241, fol. 129r			
Archivo Historico Nacional, Madrid, Clero secular y regular, c. 2002, fol. 18	Biblioteca Pública de Tarragona, Cartulari de Poblet, ms. 241, fol. 133r–v			
Lost	Archivo Historico Nacional, Madrid, Clero secular y regular, c. 2002, fol. 20	Biblioteca Pública de Tarragona, Cartulari de Poblet, ms. 241, fol. 134v		
Lost	Arxiu Capitular de la S.I. Catedral de Tortosa, Cartulary 6, d. 157, fol. 60r			
Arxiu Capitular de la S.I. Catedral de Tortosa, Tevizola (2: Bitem) (260.113)	Arxiu Capitular de la S.I. Catedral de Tortosa, Cartulary 6, D. 115, fol. 43	Arxiu Capitular de la S.I. Catedral de Tortosa, Cartulary 5, D. 105, fols. 52v–53r		

No.	Date	Description	Witnesses
55	29 June 1156	Brunetus and his wife Paschalia sell a land to Peter of Sancto Matrino, with the land of Alardus (Gerald?) Anglico on the west. In *El "Llibre Blanch" de Santes Creus*, ed. Udina Martorell, no. 70.	
56	6 July 1156	Gaimundus and his wife Saurina exchange with William Copons lands that they had in Penpin and in Villa Nova. In *Diplomatari de la Catedral de Tortosa*, ed. Virgili, no. 75.	Gerald of Salvaniaco (Salvagnac)
57	23 July 1155	Peter Guillemi and his wife Pereta sell to the brothers of the Temple land in Araval in the territory of Tortosa. In Laurea Pagarolas, *La comanda del Temple de Tortosa: primer periode* (Tortosa, 1984), no. 3.	Gerald Salvaneg (Salvagnac)
58	23 July 1156	Peter Guillelmus, an Aragonese knight, with his wife Pereta, sell to Americius, brother and Master of the order of the Temple in Tortosa, land on the place known as Araval by the River Ebro. In Pagarolas, *La comanda del Temple de Tortosa: primer periode*, no. 5.	Gerald of Salvaniaco (Salvagnac)
59	1 August 1156	Brunetus and his wife Paschalia sell land planted with olives in Villa Nova in the territory of Tortosa to Gerald of Salviniaco (Salvagnac). The land is contiguous to the land of Arnaldo Anglico on its western boundary. In *El "Llibre Blanch" de Santes Creus*, ed. Udina Martorell, no. 72.	
60	4 August 1155	Bartholome Gramiticus donates to St. Mary's of Tortosa lands which had been granted to him by Robert Burdet, prince of Tarragona, and his wife Agnes. In *Diplomatari de la Catedral de Tortosa*, ed. Virgili, no. 59.	
61	17 September 1156	Count Ramon Berenguer IV gives the farm of Xerta to St. Mary's Vallis Lauree. In *El "Llibre Blanch" de Santes Creus*, ed. Udina Martorell, no. 80.	Gerald of Salviniacho (Salvagnac)
62	8 February 1157	William of Aquilone and his wife Amaalit give Peter Carbonello and his wife Arsenda a land in Semoll in the county of Barcelona. In *El "Llibre Blanch" de Santes Creus*, ed. Udina Martorell, no. 74.	
63	7 April 1157	Martinus Golia and his wife Sebila sell to Aimericus and the Templars their orchard located in the place known as Palomberia which is in the territory of Tortosa. In Pagarolas, *La comanda del Temple de Tortosa: primer periode*, no. 6.	Jordan (Anglicus?)
64	18 April 1157	Donation of Burga by Ines, wife of Robert Burdet, in favour of the brothers Berenguer and Thomas Eixumus for its repopulation under the feudal over-lordship of the church of Tarragona. Reference in Blanch, *Arxiepiscopologi*, 1, p. 94.	
65	17 April 1157	Ugo de Ciger and his wife Gullelma sell to Peter of Santo Minato a parcel of land which they had on the other side of the Ebro from Tortosa. It is located south-west of the land of Matthew Salvanico (Salvagnac). In *Diplomatari de la Catedral de Tortosa*, ed. Virgili, no. 78.	

Original	First Copy	Second Copy	Third Copy	Fourth Copy
Lost	Biblioteca Pública de Tarragona, El Llibre Blanch de Santes Creus, cart. no. 168, fol. 109v			
Arxiu Capitular de la S.I. Catedral de Tortosa, Extrainventari (258,120), ABC				
Lost	Arxiu de la Corona d'Aragó, Barcelona, Sec. 5, arm. 4, v. III, doc. 116, fol. 37r			
Lost	Arxiu de la Corona d'Aragó, Barcelona, Sec. 5. arm. 4, v. III, no. 93, fol. 30v			
Lost	Biblioteca Pública de Tarragona, El Llibre Blanch de Santes Creus, cart. no. 168, fol. 110			
Lost	Arxiu Capitular de la S.I. Catedral de Tortosa, Cartulary 6, d. 215, fol. 85r			
Lost	Biblioteca Pública de Tarragona, El Llibre Blanch de Santes Creus, cart. no. 168, fol. 147			
Archivo Historico Nacional, Madrid, Santes Creus, perg. 33				
Lost	Arxiu de la Corona d'Aragó, Barcelona, Sec. 5. arm. 4, v. III, no. 189, fol. 60v			
Lost				
Arxiu Capitular de la S.I. Catedral de Tortosa, Benifassa, Refalgari, 19 (275,73)				

No.	Date	Description	Witnesses
66	29 April 1157	Peter Compan and his wife Pereta sell to St. Mary's of Tortosa and Bishop Geoffrey a land which they had in Bitem out of charity. In *Diplomatari de la Catedral de Tortosa*, ed. Virgili, no. 79.	Gilbert Anglicus and Gerald of Salvagnac (Salvagnac)
67	24 May 1157	Bertrand of Castelet sells to William Copons a farm known as Antig in the territory of Tortosa with all its buildings and everything that is part of it for 200 morabitanos. In *Diplomatari de la Catedral de Tortosa*, ed. Virgili, no. 80.	Gerald of Salvaneg (Salvagnac)
68	14 July 1157	Donation of Salou by Prince Robert, his wife Ines and his son Guillermus, with the compliance of Count Ramon Berenguer IV of Barcelona and Archbishop Bernard Tort, to Pedro Rasura for its repopulation, the construction of a castle and a village. Reference in Blanch, *Arxiepiscopologi*, 1, pp. 93–94.	Guillelmus Burdet, Agnes, Robert Burdet II
69	31 August 1157	Bernardus Mitifag and his wife Maria Balluuma exchange with Aimericus, brother and Master of the Templars in Tortosa, one of their lands for 20 Morabatins. In Pagarolas, *La comanda del Temple de Tortosa: primer periode*, no. 8.	Gerald of Salvanichao (Salvagnac)
70	24 October 1157	Poncius, scribe of the count of Barcelona, and Peter Reiadel grant to St. Mary's of Tortosa and Bishop Geoffrey land which they share by the Ebro in front of Quart Castle, which had been given to them by the count of Barcelona. In *Diplomatari de la Catedral de Tortosa*, ed. Virgili, no. 81.	Gerald of Selvaneg (Salvagnac)
71	14 December 1157	Ramon, abbot of Sant Cugat del Valles, exchanges with William Aragonese and his wife Pereta land in Labar contiguous to that of Geoffrey Angles. In *Diplomatari de la Catedral de Tortosa*, ed. Virgili, no. 82.	
72	8 February 1158	Osbert Nigrapel and his wife Boneta exchange with Gerald Salvanico land and an Alzeziram (?) close to Arenis which used to belong to Galib, a Saracen scribe, for a land in Villa Robea and 5 loads of barley. In *Diplomatari de la Catedral de Tortosa*, ed. Virgili, no. 97.	
73	9 February 1158	Peter Stephani and his wife Guia and his cousin Arnou sell to the Jew Haion of Azuz an orchard which had been owned by Avin Ezbaballa for 60 mora. In *Diplomatari de la Catedral de Tortosa*, ed. Virgili, no. 98.	Gerald of Salvanec (Salvagnac)
74	12 March 1158	Abbot Peter of St. Mary's Valle Laures gives as a fief the honour of Davus Farago Larraic and some other properties (some given to the monastery by Gerald of Selvangech) to Guillelm of Trull and his wife Adelaida. If they want to change the arrangement they must consult with the abbot as well as Gerald of Selviniacho. In *El "Llibre Blanch" de Santes Creus*, ed. Udina Martorell, no. 85.	Gerald of Selviniacho (Salvagnac)
75	27 April 1158	Fulco Rurso pledges a vineyard in Tortosa to Frank Anglicus. Gerald Anglicus appears as a witness and guarantor. In *El "Llibre Blanch" de Santes Creus*, ed. Udina Martorell, no. 77.	Gerald Anglicus
76	May 1158	Gerald of Salviniaco (Salvagnac) with his brother William and his wife Aladais gives some olive orchards in Xerta to the church of St. Mary's Vallis Lauree and Peter the abbot and the brothers there. In *El "Llibre Blanch" de Santes Creus*, ed. Udina Martorell, no. 78.	Gerald and William Silviniaco (Salvagnac)

Original	First Copy	Second Copy	Third Copy	Fourth Copy
Lost	Arxiu Capitular de la S.I. Catedral de Tortosa, Cartulary 2, titol IV, d. XXVI, fols. 108v–109			
Arxiu Capitular de la S.I. Catedral de Tortosa, Camarles 41 (267,130)	Arxiu Capitular de la S.I. Catedral de Tortosa, Camarles no number, (220,130)			
Lost				
Lost	Arxiu de la Corona d'Aragó, Barcelona, Sec. 5. arm. 4, v. III, no. 194, fol. 61v			
Arxiu Capitular de la S.I. Catedral de Tortosa, Trevizola (1: Anglerola) (223,144)				
Arxiu Capitular de la S.I. Catedral de Tortosa, Bonifallet (3: Llaver, Bercat) (210,123) ABC	Arxiu Capitular de la S.I. Catedral de Tortosa, Cartulary 6, d. 181, fol. 70r			
Arxiu Capitular de la S.I. Catedral de Tortosa, Arenes, Tivenys (4: Arenes) ABC				
Arxiu Capitular de la S.I. Catedral de Tortosa, Remolins (3: Vilanova) (234,130)				
Lost	Biblioteca Pública de Tarragona, El Llibre Blanch de Santes Creus, cart. no. 168, fol. 3			
Lost	Biblioteca Pública de Tarragona, El Llibre Blanch de Santes Creus, cart. no. 168, fol. 103v			
Lost	Biblioteca Pública de Tarragona, El Llibre Blanch de Santes Creus, cart. no. 168, fol. 104			

No.	Date	Description	Witnesses
77	May 1158	Guillelm Ramon and his brother Oto bequeath some olive orchards to St. Mary's Vallis Lauree. In *El "Llibre Blanch" de Santes Creus*, ed. Udina Martorell, no. 79.	Gerald of Selviniacho (Salvagnac)
78	6 June 1158	Agnes, formerly wife of Robert, count of Tarragona, and her son William Burdet, give to St. Mary's of Tortosa, Bishop Geoffrey and the canons, with the agreement of Bernard, archbishop of Tarragona, and Ramon Berenguer IV, count of Barcelona, a land that they have in Vilagrassa and one located at the foot of the city walls of Tarragona that had been given to Bartholomew. The tithes and first fruits of the church of Tarragona are exempted. In *Diplomatari de la Catedral de Tortosa*, ed. Virgili, no. 88	
79	6 June 1158	Bernard, archbishop of Tarragona, gives to St. Mary's of Tortosa, Bishop Geoffrey and the canons, a land that he possesses in Vilagrassa and one at the foot of the city walls of Tarragona. In *Diplomatari de la Catedral de Tortosa*, ed. Virgili, no. 89.	
80	26 August 1158	Mauricius de Muners exchange with the Templars all the lands that he had in Tortosa for land that the Templars had in Amalep. In Pagarolas, *La comanda del Temple de Tortosa: primer periode*, no. 11.	Gerald of Selvaneco (Salvagnac)
81	16 November 1158	Gerald of Salvanec grants for his soul and that of his parents orchards and other properties to St. Mary's of Vallaure. In *El "Llibre Blanch" de Santes Creus*, ed. Udina Martorell, no. 84.	Gerald of Selvanec (Salvagnac), his brother William of Selvainec (Salvagnac), and Stephanus Selvanec (Salvagnac)
82	27 December 1158	Frederic, prior of St. Mary's of Valle Clara, with the permission of the abbot of Flabonis Montis, gives to St Mary's of Tortosa and to Bishop Geoffrey the land of Valle Clara. In *Diplomatari de la Catedral de Tortosa*, ed. Virgili, no. 95.	Gerald of Salvanieco (Salvagnac)
83	30 April 1159	Agnes, wife of Robert Burdet, grants franchises to the people of Constanti, which was being founded. Reference in Joseph Blanch, *Arxiepiscopologi*, 1, p. 94.	Agnes, William Burdet, Robert Burdet II
84	6 January 1159	Peter of Bovilla and his wife Esclamunda give to the church of St. Mary's of Tortosa two orchards that they had in Andusc, so the church will be able to burn lamps, acquire books and decorate the main altar. In *Diplomatari de la Catedral de Tortosa*, ed. Virgili, no. 110.	Gerald of Silviniaco (Salvagnac)
85	26 February 1159	William de Copons and his wife Tropiana reach agreement with Peter of Tortosa, his mother Mary and his wife Ermegarda, on the division of some buildings. Guillem will have the honour of Xerta and Pere of Aldover will have the fourth part of the fruits. Guillem pays 8 solidis for the agreement and 4 dinars for the charter. In *Diplomatari de la Catedral de Tortosa*, ed. Virgili, no. 112.	Gilbert Anglicus and Gerald of Salvingac (Salvagnac)
86	29 June 1159	Carbonel of Minorissa and his wife Aidelina sell to the church of St. Nicholas of Tortosa an agricultural land in Arenis for 11 morabitins. In *Diplomatari de la Catedral de Tortosa*, ed. Virgili, no. 100.	Gerald of Silvanegco (Salvagnac)

Original	First Copy	Second Copy	Third Copy	Fourth Copy
Lost	Biblioteca Pública de Tarragona, El Llibre Blanch de Santes Creus, cart. no. 168, fol. 112			
Lost	Arxiu Capitular de la S.I. Catedral de Tortosa, Cartulary 6, d. 213, fol. 84			
Lost	Arxiu Capitular de la S.I. Catedral de Tortosa, Cartulary 6, 214, fols. 84v–85r			
Lost	Arxiu de la Corona d'Aragó, Barcelona, Sec. 5. arm. 4, v. III, no. 195, fols. 61v–62r			
Lost	Biblioteca Pública de Tarragona, El Llibre Blanch de Santes Creus, cart. no. 168, fol. 110v			
Arxiu Capitular de la S.I. Catedral de Tortosa, Bishop 1, 38 (305,175)	Arxiu Capitular de la S.I. Catedral de Tortosa, Bishop and Capitol, 2.2	Arxiu Capitular de la S.I. Catedral de Tortosa, Cartulary 6, d. 195, fol. 75v–6r	Arxiu Capitular de la S.I. Catedral de Tortosa, Cartulary 5, d. 18, fols. 7v–8r	
Lost				
Lost	Arxiu Capitular de la S.I. Catedral de Tortosa, Cartulary 4, d. 96, fols. 88v–99r			
Arxiu Capitular de la S.I. Catedral de Tortosa, Remolins (7: Xerta) (213,100), ABC				
Arxiu Capitular de la S.I. Catedral de Tortosa, Arenes, Tivenys (4: Arenes)				

No.	Date	Description	Witnesses
87	14 August 1159	Dispute between Bishop Geoffrey and Andreas Mala Domo for the oven of Sanct Jacobi. The court ruled on the side of the Bishop but Andreu was pardoned because he was too poor to pay the bishop the fine. Gerald of Salvinico was one of those involved in the decision and he was also a signatory of the document. In *Diplomatari de la Catedral de Tortosa*, ed. Virgili, no. 103.	Gerald of Salvinico (Salvagnac)
88	28 September 1159	Peter Guillelm and his wife Pereta offer to St. Mary's of Tortosa their bodies on the day of their death, with the houses and honour which they had received from the count of Barcelona. In *Diplomatari de la Catedral de Tortosa*, ed. Virgili, no. 105.	Gerald of Slaviniacho (Salvagnac)
89	November 1159	Peter Stephani, his wife Guila and his cousin Arnaldus sell to Bernard of Sanct Poncio and his wife Agnes a land in Campol, which they had received from the count of Barcelona, for 40 morabetinos. In *Diplomatari de la Catedral de Tortosa*, ed. Virgili, no. 106.	Gerald de Silviniaco (Salvagnac)
90	11 January 1160	Agnes, countess of Tarragona, and her sons William and Richard grant to the monastery of St. Mary's Valle Laura, a land in the area of Codoyn close to Franchulino. In *El "Llibre Blanch" de Santes Creus*, ed. Udina Martorell, no. 95.	
91	13 January 1160	Peter of Ente and his wife Matheua exchange with Bishop Geoffrey of Tortosa and the canons a piece of land that they had from a comital donation in Fachalfurin, for another pice of land that the bishop had in Capite Avinalup. East of this land was the land of Gerard of Silviniaco. In *Diplomatari de la Catedral de Tortosa*, ed. Virgili, no. 108.	Gerard of Silviniaco (Salvagnac)
92	16 March 1160	Pictavó and his wife Berenguera sell to Peter of Sentmenat and his wife two parcels of land that they have in Arenys for 4 good morabits, aedinos and lupinos. In *Diplomatari de la Catedral de Tortosa*, ed. Virgili, no. 113.	Glibert Anglicus
93	26 March 1160	Ramon de Puigalt grants to Ramon de Copons houses which he has in the Remolins and trees that used to belong to Avinambar, and he also bequeaths all the honours that he possessed in Xerta. In *Cartulari de Poblet*, ed. Pons i Marqués, no. 183.	Gerald of Selvaneg (Salvagnac)
94	1 April 1160	Poncius Sorularis and his wife Maria exchange with Eneg Sancio, master of the house of Tortosa, a land in the territory of Tortosa in the area known as Palomera, for a land in Faduna and some currency. In Pagarolas, *La comanda del Temple de Tortosa: primer periode*, no. 15.	Gerald of Selvaneg (Salvagnac)
95	25 October 1160	Will of Arnaldus of Martorel: he donates houses that he had in Martorel, and the rest goes to his mother. In *Diplomatari de la Catedral de Tortosa*, ed. Virgili, no. 117.	Gerald of Silvanaico (Salvagnac)
96	22 February 1161	Richard Pallipari, his wife Raimunda and his daughter Raimunda sell to Bishop Geoffrey a piece of land that they have in Vilaroja by comital donation that was property of Abochazuz, for 4 marobits, lupinos and aiadinos. In *Diplomatari de la Catedral de Tortosa*, ed. Virgili, no. 121.	Gilbert Anglicus and Gerald Salvingac (Salvagnac)
97	13 April 1162	Patronela, queen of Aragon and countess of Barcelona, gives to St. Mary's of Tortosa an orchard in Bitem that had been bought from Peter of Saragossa. In *Diplomatari de la Catedral de Tortosa*, ed. Virgili, no. 122.	Gerald of Silviniaco (Salvagnac)

Original	First Copy	Second Copy	Third Copy	Fourth Copy
Arxiu Capitular de la S.I. Catedral de Tortosa, Extrainventari (230, 285)	Arxiu Capitular de la S.I. Catedral de Tortosa, Cartulary 2, titol III, d. I, fol. 52			
Lost	Arxiu Capitular de la S.I. Catedral de Tortosa, Cartulary 6, d. 133, fol. 49			
Arxiu Capitular de la S.I. Catedral de Tortosa, Subtresoreria 2, 80 (290.88)				
Lost	Biblioteca Pública de Tarragona, El Llibre Blanch de Santes Creus, cart. no. 168, fol. 78			
Lost	Arxiu Capitular de la S.I. Catedral de Tortosa, Cartulary 2, titol IV, d. XXXVII, fol. 120			
Lost	Arxiu Capitular de la S.I. Catedral de Tortosa, Cartulary 2, titol IV, d. III, fols. 85v–86			
Archivo Historico Nacional, Madrid, Clero secular y regular, c. 2005, fol. 8	Biblioteca Pública de Tarragona, Cartulari de Poblet, no. 183			
Lost	Arxiu de la Corona d'Aragó, Barcelona, Sec. 5. arm. 4, v. III, no. 191, fol. 61r			
Lost	Arxiu Capitular de la S.I. Catedral de Tortosa, Cartulary 6, no. 103, fol. 36v			
Arxiu Capitular de la S.I. Catedral de Tortosa, Genova (5: Vila-roja), 15 (250,162)				
Lost	Arxiu Capitular de la S.I. Catedral de Tortosa, Cartulary 4, d. 99, fol. 91r	Arxiu Capitular de la S.I. Catedral de Tortosa, Cartulary 2, títol IV, d. XI, fols. 94v–5r		

No.	Date	Description	Witnesses
98	15 May 1162	Bertran of Toulouse and his wife Joradana sell to Peter John of Granada three fifths of an orchard that the children of Avigalards possessed and two fifths of the honour, in Xerta, for 16 marobits of gold. It mentions the orchards of Gerald Salvagnac. In *Diplomatari de la Catedral de Tortosa*, ed. Virgili, no. 126.	A Gerald Gasc (Gascon?)
99	22 May 1162	Gilbert Anglicus (Angles) gives to St. Mary's of Tortosa an olive plantation that belonged to Avincel and other lands that he had in Mont Rog which used to belong to Lacabat, on condition that lamps are burned day and night. In *Diplomatari de la Catedral de Tortosa*, ed. Virgili, no. 127.	Osbert Anglicus, Pagan Anglicus and Gerald of Silviniacho (Salvagnac)
100	3 June 1163	Adelendis widow of Guillem Trull sells the honour of Andusc to the monastery of St. Mary's Valle Laura. In *El "Llibre Blanch" de Santes Creus*, ed. Udina Martorell, no. 110.	Gilbert Anglicus
101	12 June 1162	Agnes, countess of Tarragona, with the counsel of her sons pledges to Bertran de Castelet a parcel of land in the territory of Tarragona, in the place known as Port Fabregad. In *Diplomatari de Santa Maria de Poblet*, ed. Altisent, no. 227.	Agnes, William Burdet, Robert Burdet II
102	5 November 1163	After falling sick, Peter of Rajadell draws up his will: he names as principal heirs his wife and the cathedral of Tortosa. In *Diplomatari de la Catedral de Tortosa*, ed. Virgili, no. 134.	Gilbert Anglicus
103	12 March 1164	Marin Monstrou and his wife Maria sell to Simon Monstrou and his wife Dominica one honour that they had by donation of the count, free from feudal obligations, in Funiana for 120 maribits of gold. In *Diplomatari de la Catedral de Tortosa*, ed. Virgili, no. 151.	Gilbert Anglicus and Gerald of Salvingac (Salvagnac)
104	27 April 1164	Bishop Geoffrey with the consent of the chapter grants land for building houses to Dominic and his wife Ermessenda. In *Diplomatari de la Catedral de Tortosa*, ed. Virgili, no. 140.	Gerald of Salvanieco (Salvagnac)
105	1 June 1164	Gerald, canon of the church of the Holy Sepulchre, gives to John of Tortosa a vineyard, the English cemetery lying to the north-west. In *L'arxiu antic de Santa Anna de Barcelona del 942 al 1200*, ed. Altura i Perucho, no. 371.	Osbert Anglicus and Gilbert Anglicus
106	3 June 1164	Abbot Peter of St. Mary's Valle Laura gives various possessions as fief to Raimundus Cheralt. One is an olive orchard that had been given to the monastery by Gerald of Salveneg (Salvagnac). Another was a vineyard given by the same person. In *El "Llibre Blanch" de Santes Creus*, ed. Udina Martorell, no. 113.	Gerald of Salviniaco (Salvagnac) and Gilbert Anglicus
107	13 June 1164	Berenguer of Avignon and his wife Ramona sells to John, sexton of St. Mary of Tortosa, for 14 morabits an orchard that he had in Bitem. In *Diplomatari de la Catedral de Tortosa*, ed. Virgili, no. 143.	Gilbert Anglicus

Original	First Copy	Second Copy	Third Copy	Fourth Copy
Arxiu Capitular de la S.I. Catedral de Tortosa, Testaments 3, 59 (140.145)				
Arxiu Capitular de la S.I. Catedral de Tortosa, Subtesoreria. 2. 52	Arxiu Capitular de la S.I. Catedral de Tortosa, Cartulary 4, d. 75, fol. 74r			
Lost	Biblioteca Pública de Tarragona, El Llibre Blanch de Santes Creus, cart. no. 168, fol. 115v			
Archivo Historico Nacional, Madrid, Clero secular y regular, c. 2006, fol. 8				
Arxiu Capitular de la S.I. Catedral de Tortosa, Testaments, 1 (without number)	Arxiu Capitular de la S.I. Catedral de Tortosa, Cartulary 6, d. 101, fol. 35			
Lost	Arxiu Capitular de la S.I. Catedral de Tortosa, Extrainventari. Moved on 1171 (195.134)			
Lost	Arxiu Capitular de la S.I. Catedral de Tortosa, Cartulary 2, títol IV, d. VII, fols. 89v–90r			
Archivo Diocesano de Barcelona, Fons de Santa Anna, carp. 2A, perg. 3	Archivo Diocesano de Barcelona, C.D. 1E, no. 12, Lletra B			
Lost	Biblioteca Pública de Tarragona, El Llibre Blanch de Santes Creus, cart. no. 168, fol. 114			
Lost	Arxiu Capitular de la S.I. Catedral de Tortosa, Cartulary 4, d.100, fol. 91v	Arxiu Capitular de la S.I. Catedral de Tortosa, Cartulary 2, Titol IV, d. IX, fol. 93		

No.	Date	Description	Witnesses
108	22 June 1164	King Alfonso II of Aragon gives to Gilbert Anglico a house in Tortosa in gratitude for the help offered by him making a road in the city. In *El "Llibre Blanch" de Santes Creus*, ed. Udina Martorell, no. 114.	Gerald of Silviniacho (Salvagnac)
109	12 September 1164	Controversy between the bishop of Tortosa and the canons on one side and the brothers of the Hospital on the other, for the honours that Martin Gòlia and Sibil had possessed; the curia established that the bishop and the canons possess the urban area and the Order the rural area. In *Diplomatari de la Catedral de Tortosa*, ed. Virgil, no. 147.	Gilbert Anglicus
110	2 January 1165	Peter Stephen and his wife Guia donate, for the salavtion of their souls to God, St Mary's of Tortosa, Bishop Ponz and the canons an orchard that they had close to the wall of the city on the side of the English cemetery, and receive in exchange for their charity 100 morabitis lupins. In *Diplomatari de la Catedral de Tortosa*, ed. Virgili, no. 157.	Gilbert Anglicus and Gerald of Salvingac (Salvagnac)
111	28 April 1165	Ponz makes a donation to Ramon and his wife Maria of houses, which he received from the count of Barcelona inside the walls of Tortosa in the parish of St. James. An annual tribute is established of one good morabit of gold to St. Michael, and the donor retains the right to stay whenever he travels to Tortosa. In *Diplomatari de la Catedral de Tortosa*, ed. Virgili, no. 152.	Peter Galec (Welsh?)
112	27 May 1165	Robert of Cotenes and his wife Guia sell to Eneg Sanc, Master of the House of Tortosa, and the brothers of the Order, an orchard that they have in Palomera by the Ebro. In Pagarolas, *La comanda del Temple de Tortosa: primer periode*, no. 23.	Gerald of Salvanieco (Salvagnac), Gilbert (Anglicus?)
113	21 June 1165	Ponz, scribe, donates to St. Mary's of Tortosa houses that he had in the city of Lleida besides those of the Hospitallers, and other lands and possessions in the same city. In *Diplomatari de la Catedral de Tortosa*, ed. Virgili, no. 153.	Gilbert Anglicus
114	27 March 1166	Peter Mercer sells to John and his wife Merquesa houses that he had in the parish of St. Mary, in the sector of Genova, for 25½ souls in Jaquesa currency. In *Diplomatari de la Catedral de Tortosa*, ed. Virgili, no. 159.	Pagan Angles
115	Before 19 April 1166	Before travelling to Jerusalem, Osbert Angles makes a will. It gives his many possessions to all his relatives and to his wife. It leaves money to the cathedral and to other churches. Gilbert Anglicus, Gerald Salangac, Nicolas Angles (his brother), Joan of Tortosa (his daughter), appear as witnesses and beneficiaries of the will. In *Diplomatari de la Catedral de Tortosa*, ed. Virgili, no. 155.	Osbert Anglicus, Gilbert Anglicus and Gerald of Salvaneg (Salvagnac)
116	19 April 1166	The Jew Haio and his wife Cetona and his son Maimon sell to Osbert Anglicus an orchard which had been originally bought from Peter Stephen in Vilanova, for 55 morabits aiadis and lupins of gold at weight. In *Diplomatari de la Catedral de Tortosa*, ed. Virgili, no. 160.	Joan of Tortosa and Peter Galec (Welsh?)
117	26 October 1166	William of Castellvell gives to St. Mary's of Tortosa, for 6 marks of silver, the honour that he had in Tortosa and his terms from the donation of Count Ramon Berenguer IV. In *Diplomatari de la Catedral de Tortosa*, ed. Virgili, no. 162	Gilbert Anglicus and Gaulas Flamenc (Flemish)

Original	First Copy	Second Copy	Third Copy	Fourth Copy
Lost	Biblioteca Pública de Tarragona, El Llibre Blanch de Santes Creus, cart. no. 168, fol. 115v			
Lost	Arxiu Capitular de la S.I. Catedral de Tortosa, Cartulary 6, 164, fols 62v–63r	Arxiu Capitular de la S.I. Catedral de Tortosa, Cartulary 5, d. 95, fols 47v–48r		
Arxiu Capitular de la S.I. Catedral de Tortosa, Extraventari (264.315)				
Arxiu Capitular de la S.I. Catedral de Tortosa, Remolins, Vilanova (2: Remolins) (280.136)				
Arxiu de la Corona d'Aragó, Barcelona, Sec. 5. arm. 4, v. III, no. 193, fol. 61v				
Lost	Arxiu Capitular de la S.I. Catedral de Tortosa, Extraventari (facsimile)			
Arxiu Capitular de la S.I. Catedral de Tortosa, Santa Maria, Taules Belles (9: Santa Maria) (178.138)				
Arxiu Capitular de la S.I. Catedral de Tortosa, Testaments 3, 23 (275.207)	Arxiu Capitular de la S.I. Catedral de Tortosa, Fabrica, 19, moved			
Arxiu Capitular de la S.I. Catedral de Tortosa, Remolins, Vilanova (3: Vilanova) (275.165)				
Arxiu Capitular de la S.I. Catedral de Tortosa, Tevisola, Anglerola, (1: Anglerola, etc)	Arxiu Capitular de la S.I. Catedral de Tortosa, Cartulary 6, d. 210, fol. 83r			

No.	Date	Description	Witnesses
118	11 November 1166	Bertran of Toulouse and his wife Jordana sell to the monastery of Poblet and Abbot Hugh all the honours which they possess in the territory of Som with all the trees and things within it. In *Cartulari de Poblet*, ed. Pons i Marqués, no. 199.	Gerald of Salvaiaco (Salvagnac)
119	9 December 1166	Cohen and his wife Cethor and his family sell to Petro Iohane of Grenada the rights that they had in Aion over an orchard in Xerta. The orchard was located west of the land of Gerald of Salvanieg (Salvagnac). In *Diplomatari de Santa Maria de Poblet*, ed. Altisent, no. 300.	Gerald of Salvnieg (Salvagnac)
120	30 December 1166	King Alfonso II, with William Ramon and Ramon Montcada, give to Peter Santponç a land in Tortosa, which touches the Ebro and the alfodeo of the men of Narbonne, on the condition that he will build on it. In *Diplomatari de la Catedral de Tortosa*, ed. Virgili, no. 164.	Gilbert Anglicus
121	March 1167x1198	Bertran of Sarlat and his wife Guilelma sell to Raymond Angles houses in the parish of St. Vicent, Lleida. In *Diplomatari de Santa Maria de Poblet*, ed. Altisent, no. 309.	
122	12 July 1167	Guillelm Pucuz and Petro of Tortosa exchange properties. In *Diplomatari de la Catedral de Tortosa*, ed. Virgili, no. 172.	Gerald of Salvanieg (Salvagnac)
123	15 August 1167	William of Caorz and his wife Pelegrina sell for 3 morabits to Guerau, prior of St. Mary's of Tortosa, and to the canons, a quarter of the algecira that had belonged to poor Moferrix Abinalfer, which he had by donation from Count Ramon Berenguer IV between Xerta and Tivenys. In *Diplomatari de la Catedral de Tortosa*, ed. Virgili, no. 174.	Gilbert Anglicus
124	2 September 1167	Gales and his wife Aloys sell a quarter of an algezire and two parts of land which they had at Tibenx to Geraldo prior of St Mary's of Tortosa. In *Diplomatari de la Catedral de Tortosa*, ed. Virgili, no. 177.	Pagan Anglicus and Peter Galeg (Welsh?)
125	19 September 1167	Gerald of Morlans, his daughter Pasxhalia and his brother Brunet sell to Helie and his associate William of Irunda a vineyard and land in Bitem. In *Diplomatari de la Catedral de Tortosa*, ed. Virgili, no. 178.	
126	24 September 1167	Poncius of Montepellier and his wife Maria sell to Poncius, bishop of Tortosa, two orchards that they had in Sum which the count of Barcelona had given to them. One is to the south of the orchard of William of Sivinicho (Salvagnac). In *Diplomatari de la Catedral de Tortosa*, ed. Virgili, no. 179.	William of Sivinicho (Salvagnac)
127	2 October 1167	Gales [Angles?] and his wife Alois bequeath to master Peter of Narbonne and his wife Raimunda and their children the tower located above the farm of Gerald of Salvanieg (Salvagnac). In *El "Llibre Blanch" de Santes Creus*, ed. Udina Martorell, no. 131.	Pagan [Anglicus?], Gerald Salvanieg (Salvagnac) and Gilbert Anglicus

Original	First Copy	Second Copy	Third Copy	Fourth Copy
Lost	Biblioteca Pública de Tarragona, *Cartulari de Poblet*, ms. 241, fols. 131v–132r			
Archivo Historico Nacional, Madrid, Clero secular y regular, c. 2010, fol. 14				
Lost	Arxiu Capitular de la S.I. Catedral de Tortosa, Cartulary 8 (Titòl VIII) d. 87, fol. 141			
Archivo Historico Nacional, Madrid, Clero secular y regular, c. 2011, fol. 7				
Arxiu Capitular de la S.I. Catedral de Tortosa, Extrainventari (140.110)				
Arxiu Capitular de la S.I. Catedral de Tortosa, Remolins, Villanova (6: Xerta) (200,160)				
Arxiu Capitular de la S.I. Catedral de Tortosa, Arenes, Tivenys (7: Tivenys, etc)				
Arxiu Capitular de la S.I. Catedral de Tortosa, Tevizola, Anglerola, (2: Bitem) (211.114)	Arxiu Capitular de la S.I. Catedral de Tortosa, Cartulary 6, d. 166, fol. 63v			
Arxiu Capitular de la Catedral de Tortosa, Cartulary 2, Titol IV, d. XXXIII, fol.1 16				
Lost	Biblioteca Pública de Tarragona, El Llibre Blanch de Santes Creus, cart. no. 168, fol. 113v			

No.	Date	Description	Witnesses
128	15 October 1167	Gauterius of Cassala sells to Osbert Angles olive orchards and lands that he had in Xerta by a comital gift. In *Diplomatari de la Catedral de Tortosa*, ed. Virgili, no. 180.	Pagan Angles
129	24 November 1167	Bernardus Faber and his wife Marchesa and his family sell to God and to Arnaldo of Ture Rubea Master of Spain and to Brother Guillelmeo Berardo commander of the castle of Miravet, land in the territory of Tortosa on the other side of the river. In Pagarolas, *La comanda del Temple de Tortosa: primer periode*, no. 29.	Gerald of Salvanieg (Salvagnac)
130	1 December 1167	Moro and his wife Sibila sell to Gerald, prior of St. Mary's of Tortosa, and to the canons, land that they had as a comital donation in Villa Rubea. In *Diplomatari de la Catedral de Tortosa*, ed. Virgili, no. 182.	Gerald of Silvinac (Salvagnac)
131	31 December 1167	Poncius, scribe, grants to St. Mary's and to its Bishop Poncius houses which he possesses in Lleida. In *Diplomatari de la Catedral de Tortosa*, ed. Virgili, no. 183.	Gerald of Silviniacho (Salvagnac)
132	9 July 1168	Agnes, countess of Tarragona, William of Tarragona, Robert, Berenguer, sons of Agnes, and Sibila, wife of William, for their love of the church and for the remission of their sins donate a house in Tarragona as a place where the brothers of the monastery of Poblet will be able to stay when they come to Tarragona. In *Cartulari de Poblet, ed. Pons i Marqués*, no. 260.	Agnes, William Burdet, Robert Burdet II, Berenguer Burdet, Agnes, wife of William
133	26 July 1168	King Alfonso II of Aragon with the consent of various nobles, including the count of Montpellier, gives the land of Peduls to Gerald de Rivo, Peter de Sancto Martino and Raimund the Charaltir. In *Cartas de población y franquicia de Cataluña*, ed. Font Rius, 1, no. 134.	Gilbert Anglicus
134	6 October 1168	Raimund of Moncada accepts that he is in debt to Gilbert Angles for 120 morabinos. Peter Subiras and Guillelm of Tornamira appear as guarantors to the agreement. In *El "Llibre Blanch" de Santes Creus*, ed. Udina Martorell, no. 139.	
135	19 September 1168	Bernard of Castronovo and Bernard of Espulges make an oath on the altar of St. Felix in the church of the Martyr St. Iusti and Pastoris, and in the presence of Arnau, over the will William (Burdet?) of Tarragona. In *Diplomatari de Santa Maria de Poblet*, ed. Altisent, no. 335.	
136	1 December 1168	Agnes, countess of Tarragona, and her sons Robert and Berenguer, confirm to the monastery of St. Mary's of Poblet the donation of William, son of Agnes, to the monks, for the domain that they have in the area of Rivo de Ulmis known as Metta. In *Diplomatari de Santa Maria de Poblet*, ed. Altisent, no. 342.	Agnes, Robert II and Berenguer
137	1 December 1169	Bernardus of Vic and his wife Emegardis and his family sell to Guillelmus Berardo, master and commander of the Templars in Tortosa and Miravet, a land that used to belong to Pereta the widow of Peter Compang, located on the banks of the Ebro in a place known as Benigello. In Pagarolas, *La comanda del Temple de Tortosa: primer periode*, no. 35.	Viva Anglicus, an English knight

Original	First Copy	Second Copy	Third Copy	Fourth Copy
Arxiu Capitular de la S.I. Catedral de Tortosa, Subtresoreria 2, 97 (260.72)				
Arxiu de la Corona d'Aragó, Barcelona, Sec. 5. arm. 4, v. III, no. 207, fol. 65r				
Arxiu Capitular de la S.I. Catedral de Tortosa, Genova, Vila-roja (9: Vila-roja)				
Lost	Arxiu Capitular de la S.I. Catedral de Tortosa, Cartulary 6, d. 38, fol. 25	Arxiu Capitular de la S.I. Catedral de Tortosa, Prior Major, 2, 7.21		
Archivo Historico Nacional, Madrid, Clero secular y regular, c. 2012, fol. 12	Biblioteca Pública de Tarragona, *Cartulari de Poblet*, ms 241, fs.169r–196v.	Archivo Historico Nacional, Madrid, Clero secular y regular, c. 2012, fol. 13	Archivo Historico Nacional, Madrid, Cod. 992 B, fol. 50r	
Lost	Arxiu de la Corona d'Aragó Cancilleria, perg. de Alfonso I, n, 59	Arxiu de la Corona d'Aragó, Barcelona, Cancilleria, Reg. no. 2. (Varia de Alfonso I no. 2) fol. 10v		
Lost	Biblioteca Pública de Tarragona, El Llibre Blanch de Santes Creus, cart. no. 168, fol. 121			
Archivo Historico Nacional, Madrid, Clero secular y regular, c. 2013, fol. 3				
Archivo Historico Nacional, Madrid, Clero secular y regular, c. 2013, fol. 1	Biblioteca Pública de Tarragona, *Cartulari de Poblet*, ms 241, fs.169v–170r			
Lost	Arxiu de la Corona d'Aragó, Barcelona, Sec. 5. arm. 4, v. III, no. 113, fol. 36r			

No.	Date	Description	Witnesses
138	5 January 1169	Peter, abbot of Santes Creus, gives the honours that used to belong to Guillelm Deztrus and the Saracen Avifora in Bitem and Adusc, to Gerald of Salvanieco and Peter of Guinstario. In *El "Llibre Blanch" de Santes Creus*, ed. Udina Martorell, no. 142.	Gerald of Salvanieco (Salvagnac)
139	15 July 1169	Arnaldus Dolcebal and his family sell to Guillelm Berard, master of the Templars of Tortosa and Miravet, Peter Echeri, Peter Iohannis and other brothers of the Order of the Temple, an orchard in the territory of Tortosa in the place known as Arennis. In Pagarolas, *La comanda del Temple de Tortosa: primer periode*, no. 33.	Gilbert Anglicus
140	1 October 1169	Albertus of Castro Veteri donates to God and to Guillelm, master of the Templars, and to the Order, a land in the territory of Tortosa on the other side of the Ebro, located between the river and the main highway. In *Pagarolas, La comanda del Temple de Tortosa: primer periode*, no. 34.	Gilbert Anglicus
141	7 October 1170	Guillelm of Fontes and his wife Isabel sell to Gilbert Anglicus an orchard in Aldover. In *El "Llibre Blanch" de Santes Creus*, ed. Udina Martorell, no. 148.	Gilbert Anglicus
142	20 December 1170	Guillelm of Copons and his wife Tropina sell to St. Mary's of Tortosa and prior Gerald and the canons, the farm of Antiquos, which was bought from Bertran de Castelet who had received it from the count. In *Diplomatari de la Catedral de Tortosa*, ed. Virgili, no. 210.	Gilbert Anglicus
143	1 January 1171	Ermessend, prior of St. Mary's Valle Laura and St. Felix, with the consent of sister Pelegrina and the entire convent, gives to Iener all their honours in Xerta that they acquired by donation from Peter John. Some conditions are attached to the gift. In *Diplomatari de la Catedral de Tortosa*, ed. Virgili, no. 222.	Gilbert Anglicus
144	30 January 1171	King Alfonso II of Aragon and Ramon Montecatano give to the hospital of church of St. Mary's of Tortosa and to Guillelm the administrator, the vineyard that had been given to Arnau Cavador in Villa Nova. In *Diplomatari de la Catedral de Tortosa*, ed. Virgili, no. 223.	Gilbert Anglicus
145	31 January 1171	King Alfonso II of Aragon together with Guillelm Ramon and Ramon of Montecatano give to Petro of Braia the houses that had been bought from Bernardo Fabro. In *Diplomatari de la Catedral de Tortosa*, ed. Virgili, no. 224.	Gilbert Anglicus
146	31 January 1171	Peter de Braies, with the consent of the brothers of Sanct Genes, sells to St. Mary's of Tortosa and Gerald, prior and the chapter of that church, the houses which he acquired from Bernard, with the later confirmation from King Alfonso II and of Guillemus Raimundo and Raimund of Montecatano. In *Diplomatari de la Catedral de Tortosa*, ed. Virgili, no. 225.	Gilbert Anglicus, Gerald of Salvaneco (Salvagnac)
147	4 March 1171	Bernad of Martorel and his wife Escleria exchange with Ulriguet Nigrapllis and his wife, land that they have in Arrabato on the banks of the Ebro for land in Arenes and 18 morabatinos. In *Diplomatari de la Catedral de Tortosa*, ed. Virgili, no. 227.	William of Salvanieco (Salvagnac) and Gerald of Salvaniecco (Salvagnac)

Original	First Copy	Second Copy	Third Copy	Fourth Copy
Lost	Biblioteca Pública de Tarragona, El Llibre Blanch de Santes Creus, cart. no. 168, fol. 105v			
Lost	Arxiu de la Corona d'Aragó, Barcelona, Sec. 5. arm. 4, v. III, no. 124, fol. 39r			
Lost	Arxiu de la Corona d'Aragó, Barcelona, Sec. 5. arm. 4, v. III, no. 94, fol. 31r			
Lost	Biblioteca Pública de Tarragona, El Llibre Blanch de Santes Creus, cart. no. 168, fol. 116			
Arxiu Capitular de la S.I. Catedral de Tortosa, Grandella, Camarles, 15 (270.280)				
Arxiu Capitular de la S.I. Catedral de Tortosa, Remolins, Vilanova (8: Xerta), ABC				
Arxiu Capitular de la S.I. Catedral de Tortosa, Hospitaller 30				
Arxiu Capitular de la S.I. Catedral de Tortosa, Genova, Vila-roja (1: Genova) (235.140)				
Arxiu Capitular de la S.I. Catedral de Tortosa, Genova, Vila-roja (1: Genova, 42) (210.210).				
Lost	Arxiu Capitular de la S.I. Catedral de Tortosa, Extrainventari, copy of lost ms. from 1/12/1212			

No.	Date	Description	Witnesses
148	23 March 1171	Durandus of Podio and his wife Estephana sell to God and to the Templars of Tortosa and Miravet, land that they had on the other side of the Ebro in the place called Alfarela. In Pagarolas, *La comanda del Temple de Tortosa: primer periode*, no. 39.	Gerald of Salvanec (Salvagnac), William of Salvanec (Salvagnac)
149	13 May 1171	Gerald Rubeus for the salvation of his soul and that of his parents grants land close to Algecira Mazcor to the church of St. Mary's of Tortosa. In *Diplomatari de la Catedral de Tortosa*, ed. Virgili, no. 212.	Gerald of Salvanec (Salvagnac)
150	16 May 1171	Hugh Francigena and his daughter Guillelma, widow of John of Provins, and Peter, her son, sell to Ramon Speleu, with the consent of Ramon Montecatano, some houses which they possess in Tortosa. In *Diplomatari de la Catedral de Tortosa, ed. Virgili*, no. 213.	Gerald of Silvanec (Salvagnac), Peter Galec (Welsh?), John of Tortosa and Gilbert Anglicus
151	15 July 1171	Arnaldus Cavador because of sickness dictates his testament; he leaves many properties to the church of St. Mary's, Tortosa. In *Diplomatari de la Catedral de Tortosa*, ed. Virgili, no. 214.	Pagan Angles and Raymond Angles
152	10 October 1171	Druhet dictates his testament and names Gilbert Angles among others as guarantor. He leaves lands to the church of St. Mary's. In *Diplomatari de la Catedral de Tortosa*, ed. Virgili, no. 218.	Gilbert Anglicus
153	3 November 1171	Robert Otonensis confirms the will made by his brother William Angles in favour of the church of St. Mary's of honours in Xerta, which he had received from the count of Barcelona. In *Diplomatari de la Catedral de Tortosa*, ed. Virgili, no. 220.	Gales Angles, Pagan [Angles?], Jordan [Angles?], Geoffrey [Angles?] and Gerald [Angles?]
154	18 January 1172	Vlugetus Nigra Pelle and his wife Batxera sell to Guillem Berard, master of the Templars, land that they had in the territory of Tortosa on the other side of the river. In Pagarolas, *La comanda del Temple de Tortosa: primer periode*, no. 40.	Petri Galeg (Welsh?)
155	21 January 1172	Theobaldus of Ripol, his son Raymundus Theobald and his wife Ninna sell to Guillelm Berard and theKnights Templar land that they have in the territory of Tortosa by the river. In Pagarolas, *La comanda del Temple de Tortosa: primer periode*, no. 41.	Gilbert Anglicus, Jordan Angles
156	1 June 1172 (Date on Charter is 1162, but it seems to be a mistake according to Udina Martorell)	Gilbert Engles (Anglicus) for the remission of his sins gives properties which he had already granted in his will and his house in Tortosa, to St. Mary's Valle Laura. In *El "Llibre Blanch" de Santes Creus*, ed. Udina Martorell, no. 104.	Gilbert Anglicus
157	8 May 1172	Will of Gilbert Anglicus: he makes his brother Theobald, Gerald of Salviniaco and Jordan Angles among others guarantors of his will. He leaves many lands to the monastery of Santes Creus, his brother, the Templars and the Hospitallers. In *El "Llibre Blanch" de Santes Creus*, ed. Udina Martorell, no. 157.	Gilbert Anglicus, his brother Theobaldo, Gerald of Salviniaco (Salvagnac) and Jordan Angles

Original	First Copy	Second Copy	Third Copy	Fourth Copy
Lost	Arxiu de la Corona d'Aragó, Barcelona, Sec. 5. arm. 4, v. III, no. 212, fol. 66r–v			
Arxiu Capitular de la S.I. Catedral de Tortosa, Donacions i llegats, 7 (270.116)				
Lost	Arxiu Capitular de la S.I. Catedral de Tortosa, Cartulary 2, titol III, d. VI, fols. 55v–57			
Arxiu Capitular de la S.I. Catedral de Tortosa, Extrainventri (310.200)				
Arxiu Capitular de la S.I. Catedral de Tortosa, Testaments 3, 36 (230,156)				
Arxiu Capitular de la S.I. Catedral de Tortosa, Subtesoreria 2, 49.	Arxiu Capitular de la S.I. Catedral de Tortosa, Cartulary 4, d. 70, fols. 69v–70			
Lost	Arxiu de la Corona d'Aragó, Barcelona, Sec. 5. arm. 4, v. III, no. 90, fol. 30r			
Lost	Arxiu de la Corona d'Aragó, Barcelona, Sec. 5. arm. 4, v. III, no.96, fol. 31v			
Lost	Biblioteca Pública de Tarragona, El Llibre Blanch de Santes Creus, cart. no. 168, fol. 104v			
Lost	Biblioteca Pública de Tarragona, El Llibre Blanch de Santes Creus, cart. no. 168, fol. 100			

No.	Date	Description	Witnesses
158	27 September 1172	Arnaldus de Pons donate to Foget the third part of a mill in Aitona on condition of not having another overlord but him. Another part belongs to William Angles. In *Diplomatari de Santa Maria de Poblet*, ed. Altisent, no. 440.	
159	4 November 1172	Stephanus, administrator of the sacristy of the church of St. Mary's of Tortosa, with the consent of Bishop Poncius gives to Geoffrey Anglico and his wife Bernarde the vineyard and olive orchard which the church had received from Gilbert Anglicus in Aldover. When the recipients of the gift are dead the land will return to the church. The recipients are also to pay a rent for the land annually at Candlemas (2 February). The document is signed by Geoffrey Anglico and his wife. In *Diplomatari de la Catedral de Tortosa*, ed. Virgili, no. 234.	Geoffrey Anglico and his wife Bernade, Peter Galleg (Welsh?) and Gerald Salvanieco (Salvagnac).
160	10 November 1172	Bonifacius sell to Guillelm Berard, master of the Templars and the Order, land in the territory of Tortosa in the area called Algizira Mascor. In Pagarolas, *La comanda del Temple de Tortosa: primer periode*, no. 44.	William of Salvenec (Salvagnac)
161	10 November 1172	Ermellina and her son Mallonus sell to Guillelm Berard, master of the Templars and the Order, land that they had in the area called Algizira Mascor in the territory of Tortosa. In Pagarolas, *La comanda del Temple de Tortosa: primer periode*, no. 45.	William of Salvenec (Salvagnac)
162	17 November 1172	William of Salvanec (Salvagnac) and his wife Jordana sell to Gullelm Berard, master of the Templars and the order, land that they had in Tortosa on the other side of the river in a place called Bercat. In Pagarolas, *La comanda del Temple de Tortosa: primer periode*, no. 46.	William of Salvenec (Salvagnac), Jordana wife of William of Salvenec (Salvagnac), Peter Geleg (Welsh?)
163	January 1173	Peter, abbot of Santes Creus, grants to John Angles the monastery's houses in Tortosa that had belonged to Gilbert Anglicus, one in Carrera Antigua and the other in Carrera Maior. In *El "Llibre Blanch" de Santes Creus*, ed. Udina Martorell, no. 177.	Gilbert Anglicus and Theobaldo [Angles?], canon of St. Mary's of Tortosa
164	January 1173	Peter, abbot of Santes Creus, gives to John Angles all the monastery's honours in Xerta. In *El "Llibre Blanch" de Santes Creus*, ed. Udina Martorell, no. 176.	Gilbert Anglicus and Theobald [Anglicus?], canon at St. Mary's of Tortosa
165	5 January 1173	Peter, abbot of Santes Creus, gives to Petro Galeg (Welsh?) and Gerald Ginestar an honour that used to belong to Guillem of Sanct Mainati in the area of Tortosa. In *El "Llibre Blanch" de Santes Creus*, ed. Udina Martorell, no. 179.	Gilbert Anglicus and Canon Theobald [Angles]
166	20 June 1173	Gauceran de Pinos, Guillelm of Acarras and Bernard of Graiana in the presence of the bishop of Urgel publish the last will of Gerald of Graniana; William Anglicus and John Anglicus are left 40 solidos. In *Diplomatari de Santa Maria de Poblet*, ed. Altisent, no. 461.	
167	4 October 1173	Geoffrey Anglicus donates to the monastery of Santes Creus, properties including a plantation with figs and olives, which is south of that of Gilbert [Anglicus?] and other property close to that of Gerald of Selvainec (Salvagnac) in Aldover. In *El "Llibre Blanch" de Santes Creus*, ed. Udina Martorell, no. 172.	Reginald Angles, Galeg [Angles?] and Pagan Angles

Original	First Copy	Second Copy	Third Copy	Fourth Copy
Lost	Archivo Historico Nacional, Madrid, cod. 992B, fol.101v			
Arxiu Capitular de la S.I. Catedral de Tortosa, Subtresoreria 1, 61 (147,250)	Arxiu Capitular de la S.I. Catedral de Tortosa, Cartulary 4, d. 77, fol. 75			
Lost	Arxiu de la Corona d'Aragó, Barcelona, Sec. 5. arm. 4, v. III, no. 222, fols. 68v–69r			
Lost	Arxiu de la Corona d'Aragó, Barcelona, Sec. 5. arm. 4, v. III, no. 224, fol. 69r			
Lost	Arxiu de la Corona d'Aragó, Barcelona, Sec. 5. arm. 4, v. III, no. 186, fol. 60r–v			
Lost	Biblioteca Pública de Tarragona, El Llibre Blanch de Santes Creus, cart. no. 168, fol. 101v			
Lost	Biblioteca Pública de Tarragona, El Llibre Blanch de Santes Creus, cart. no. 168, fol. 120v			
Lost	Biblioteca Pública de Tarragona, El Llibre Blanch de Santes Creus, cart. no. 168, fol. 107			
Lost	Archivo Historico Nacional, Madrid, Clero secular y regular, c. 2019, fol. 12	Archivo Historico Nacional, Madrid, Clero secular y regular, c. 2019, fol. 13		
Lost	Biblioteca Pública de Tarragona, El Llibre Blanch de Santes Creus, cart. no. 168, fol. 107v			

No.	Date	Description	Witnesses
168	5 October 1173	Geoffrey Angles chooses Petro Galeg (Welsh?) and Reginald Angles among others as guarantors of his will. He bequeaths his body to the monastery of Santes Creus and gives the monastery a house in Tortosa and a honour that used to belong to a Saracen. In *El "Llibre Blanch" de Santes Creus*, ed. Udina Martorell, no. 173.	Peter Galeg (Welsh?), Reginald Angles and John Angles
169	19 October 1173	Jordan Anglicus and his brother Osbert Anglicus sell to the church of St. Mary's and to Theobald, administrator of the vestry, 4 olive orchards that used to belong to Avinahal Avingasard. They had been acquired by Osbert from Galterius Cassel. They were in Xerta, east of the land of William of Silviniaco (Salvagnac). In *Diplomatari de la Catedral de Tortosa*, ed. Virgili, no. 249.	
170	20 February 1174	Martinus Formice sells to Guillem Berard, master of the Templar and the order, a vineyard in Bitem which is located in the territory of Tortosa. In Pagarolas, *La comanda del Temple de Tortosa: primer periode*, no. 52.	Gilbert (Anglicus?)
171	27 February 1174	Geoffrey Flamench (Flemish?) and his wife Bernarda sell to St. Mary's of Tortosa and Theobald, the sacristan, two parcels of land, which they had in Aldover by comital donation. In *Diplomatari de la Catedral de Tortosa*, ed. Virgili, no. 263.	Jordan Anglicus, John Anglicus and Pagan Anglicus
172	24 February 1174	Guillelm Berard, master of the Templars, grants Benet, his wife and their successors a vineyard that the Templars had at a place called Lbaris. The Templars reserve the right to recieve a third of the produce, tithes and other privileges. In Pagarolas, *La comanda del Temple de Tortosa: primer periode*, no. 53.	Paetri Galech (Welsh?)
173	23 October 1174	Durandus of Podio and his wife Stephana for the salvation of their souls grant after their death to St. Mary's of Tortosa and its sacristan Theobald an olive orchard which they bought from Berenguer of Cardona which was mixed with that of Gilbert Anglicus in Xerta. In *Diplomatari de la Catedral de Tortosa*, ed. Virgili, no. 259.	
174	9 September 1174	Raymond of Soler gives to Peter of Bagaza and his wife Maria, a piece of land in Fontanet on payment of 6 solidos annually on the the day of St. Michael. The land is beside that of Raymond Angles In *Diplomatari de Santa Maria de Poblet*, ed. Altisent, no. 507.	
175	14 December 1174	Gerald of Silviniacho (Salvagnac) and his wife Raimunda for the redemption of their souls and that of their parents, give to the sacristy of St. Mary's of Tortosa and its titular Theobald, an orchard with trees and olives and all its wealth. The land is east of the honour of Gerald Anglicus in Xerta. In *Diplomatari de la Catedral de Tortosa*, ed. Virgili, no. 260.	Gerald of Silviniacho (Salvagnac) and his wife Raimunda
176	1 June 1175	Examen and his wife Navarra sell to the sacristy of St. Mary's of Tortosa and Theobald a parcel of land that they had in Aldover south of the land of Gilbert Anglicus. In *Diplomatari de la Catedral de Tortosa*, ed. Virgili, no. 264.	Pagan Anglicus
177	12 June 1175	Theobald, brother of Gilbert Anglicus and canon of the church of St. Mary's of Tortosa, gives to the same church for the salvation of his soul and that of his parents land which he acquired from the Saracens together with his brother Gilbert in Aldover and other land in Xerta. In *Diplomatari de la Catedral de Tortosa*, ed. Virgili, no. 265.	Jordan Anglicus and Gilbert Anglicus

Original	First Copy	Second Copy	Third Copy	Fourth Copy
Lost	Biblioteca Pública de Tarragona, El Llibre Blanch de Santes Creus, cart. no. 168, fol. 116v			
Lost	Arxiu Capitular de la S.I. Catedral de Tortosa, Cartulary 4, d. 67, fols. 67v–68r			
Lost	Arxiu de la Corona d'Aragó, Barcelona, Sec. 5. arm. 4, v. III, no. 214, fol. 67r			
Lost	Arxiu Capitular de la S.I. Catedral de Tortosa, Cartulary 4, d. 73, fols. 72v–73r			
Lost	Arxiu de la Corona d'Aragó, Barcelona, Sec. 5. arm. 4, v. III, no. 77, fol. 26r			
Arxiu Capitular de la S.I. Catedral de Tortosa, Subtresoreria 2, 44	Arxiu Capitular de la S.I. Catedral de Tortosa, Cartulary 4, d. 76, fols. 74–75r			
Archivo Historico Nacional, Madrid, Clero secular y regular, c. 2022, fol. 2 (no. 72)				
Arxiu Capitular de la S.I. Catedral de Tortosa, Subtresoreria 2, 53	Arxiu Capitular de la S.I. Catedral de Tortosa, Cartulary 4, d. 68, fols. 68–69r			
Arxiu Capitular de la S.I. Catedral de Tortosa, Subtresoreria 3, 51 (180,150)	Arxiu Capitular de la S.I. Catedral de Tortosa, Cartulary 4, d. 72, fol. 72			
Lost	Arxiu Capitular de la S.I. Catedral de Tortosa, Cartulary 4, d. 74, fol. 73			

No.	Date	Description	Witnesses
178	12 November 1175	Peter, abbot of Santes Creus, gives to Dominic of Aldover and his son Trobad, honours over olive trees and other properties around Tortosa that used to belong to Geoffrey Anglicus. However, there is land which they sold to Gilbert his brother which is not included. In *El "Llibre Blanch" de Santes Creus*, ed. Udina Martorell, no. 189.	Peter Galeg (Welsh?)
179	13 November 1175	Arnaldus of Sancto Petro, his wife Guilia and his son Raymundus sell to the Templars and Arnald of Turre Rubea a vineyard that they had in Tortosa in the area known as Labar. In Pagarolas, *La comanda del Temple de Tortosa: primer periode*, no. 58.	Peter Galeg (Welsh?)
180	February 1176	Peter, abbot of Santes Creus, gives to John Anglico, the houses which the monastery possessed in Tortosa that used to belong Gilbert Anglico. John Anglico promises give his body to the monastery after his death and part of his possessions. In *El "Llibre Blanch" de Santes Creus*, ed. Udina Martorell, no. 195.	Gilbert Anglicus and Peter Galeg (Welsh?)
181	11 February 1176	Gerald of Salvanieco (Salvagnac) and his wife Raimunda for the salvation of their souls donate to St. Mary of Poblet and to Abbot Hugh an orchard in Xerta. In *Diplomatari de Santa Maria de Poblet*, ed. Altisent, no. 551.	Gerald of Salvaieco (Salvagnac), John Anglicus, Peter Galeg.
182	13 February 1176/7	Will of John, chaplain of the church of Aldea. He asks to be accepted as a canon of the church of St Mary's of Tortosa and donates a large amount of his property to it. He also stipulates that his nephews John and Arnaldus will join as canons when they reach the right age. If they have not done so by the time of their deaths, the property will pass to the church. In *Diplomatari de la Catedral de Tortosa*, ed. Virgili, no. 292.	Gerald of Salviniacho (Salvagnac)
183	21 April 1176	Joan de Pinca, for the salvation of his soul, donates to God and to the Virgin Mary and to the Knights Templar, an orchard at Pempin in the territory of Tortosa, contiguous to that of Petro Galeg. In Pagarolas, *La comanda del Temple de Tortosa: primer periode*, no. 61.	Peter Galeg (Welsh?)
184	17 March 1177	Stefanus Clevel and his sons Peter and Stephanus sell to Odes Tremps and his wife Ferreira houses in the parish of St. John, Lleida, contiguous to the land of Raymond Angles. In *Diplomatari de Santa Maria de Poblet*, ed. Altisent, no. 580.	
185	29 October 1177	Accord between Nicholas Anglicus and the canons of the church of St. John and St. Ruffus of Ylerda over an honour which Osbert, brother of Nicholas, had given to Canon Peter. Nicholas would receive 11½ pitchers of olive oil. In *Diplomatari de la Catedral de Tortosa*, ed. Virgili, no. 289.	Nicholas Anglicus
186	9 May 1178	Icobus son of Tabarie sell to Poncius, prior of St. Mary's of Tortosa, two parcels of land in Villa Rubea. In *Diplomatari de la Catedral de Tortosa*, ed. Virgili, no. 294.	Gerald of Salvaniaco (Salvagnac)
187	29 May 1178	Ramon of Zabadia and his wife Maria sell to the church of St. Mary's of Tortosa and to its sacristan, Nicholas, the honour that they had in Tamarit in the area of Tortosa. In *Diplomatari de la Catedral de Tortosa*, ed. Virgili, no. 296.	Gerald of Salvanieco (Salvagnac)

THE CONQUEST AND SETTLEMENT OF TORTOSA, 1148–1180   121

Original	First Copy	Second Copy	Third Copy	Fourth Copy
Lost	Biblioteca Pública de Tarragona, El Llibre Blanch de Santes Creus, cart. no. 168, fol. 117v			
Lost	Arxiu de la Corona d'Aragó, Barcelona, Sec. 5. arm. 4, v. III, no. 258, fol. 78v			
Lost	Biblioteca Pública de Tarragona, El Llibre Blanch de Santes Creus, cart. no. 168, fol. 118			
Archivo Historico Nacional, Madrid, Clero secular y regular, c. 2024 fol. 1	Biblioteca Pública de Tarragona, Cartulari de Poblet, ms. 241, fol. 214r–v	Archivo Historico Nacional, Clero secular y regular, c. 2024 fol. 2.	Archivo Historico Nacional, Clero secular y regular, c. 2024 fol. 3	
Arxiu Capitular de la S.I. Catedral de Tortosa, Testaments 2, 44 (405, 200).				
Lost	Arxiu de la Corona d'Aragó, Barcelona, Sec. 5. arm. 4, v. III, no. 204, fols. 63v–64r			
Archivo Historico Nacional, Clero secular y regular, c. 2025 fol. 14				
Arxiu Capitular de la S.I. Catedral de Tortosa, bishop commune and chapter 41 (220,125)				
Arxiu Capitular de la S.I. Catedral de Tortosa, Genova, Vila-roja (5: Alfondec. La Grassa, 16) (245,180)				
Arxiu Capitular de la S.I. Catedral de Tortosa, Extrainventari	Arxiu Capitular de la S.I. Catedral de Tortosa, Cartulary 4, d. 84, fol. 80			

No.	Date	Description	Witnesses
188	27 January 1179	Ramon of Zaruvira and his wife Ramona sell to Arnald of Arens a land in Arens. In *Diplomatari de la Catedral de Tortosa*, ed. Virgili, no. 305.	Gerald of Salvaniacho (Salvagnac)
189	16 April 1179	William of Salvaniaco and his wife Jordana sell to St. Mary's of Tortosa two orchards of olive trees, one in Xerta and the other in Matrona, which both used to belong to Saracens. In *Diplomatari de la Catedral de Tortosa*, ed. Virgili, no. 307.	William of Salvaniaco (Salavagnac), G[erald] of Salvaniaco (Salvagnac)
190	3 July 1180	Accord achieved between the monastery of Santes Creus and Bertrand, clerk of Tamarit, and Guillelm of Claro Monte about rights over the first fruits of Monte Torne. They agree these will be divided equally between the two parties. In *El "Llibre Blanch" de Santes Creus*, ed. Udina Martorell, no. 231.	Gilbert Anglicus
191	7 March 1181	Ermessenda Buschana and her son Arnald Xicot sell in Lafranch two small parcels of land to Gerald of Silvaniacho. One is to the west of the honour of Gerald Salvaniecho (Salvagnac), the other has on its west the honour of Gerald Salvanc. In *Diplomatari de la Catedral de Tortosa*, ed. Virgili, no. 336.	
192	5 June 1181	Robert Alcaix exchanges with Berengar of Avinionis, master of the Order, and Peter of Auxor, commander of the Order in Tortosa, and the brothers of the Order, land that they had in Algeri Mascor for some owned by the Templars and a sum of money. In Pagarolas, *La comanda del Temple de Tortosa: primer període*, no. 74.	Peter Galeg (Welsh?)
193	30 October 1182	Ramon of Cintillis and his wife Valenza grant to St. Mary's of Tortosa and its head Nicholas two parcels of land in Villa Nova and an orchard and two olive orchards in Xerta. The orchard is east of the honour of Jordan Anglicus. In *Diplomatari de la Catedral de Tortosa*, ed. Virgili, no. 348.	
194	20 March 1183	Ermessind, daughter of Aldeia and wife of Nicholas Anglicus, gives to the sacristy of St. Mary's of Tortosa an honour in Aldover that used to belong to the Saracens. In *Diplomatari de la Catedral de Tortosa*, ed. Virgili, no. 360.	Jordan Anglicus
195	5 June 1183	Johannes Cazafulia sell to St. Mary's of Tortosa a third part of the rights over an olive plantation in Aldover. The other 2 parts belong to the monks of Santas Crues and to Nicholas Anglicus. In *Diplomatari de la Catedral de Tortosa*, ed. Virgili, no. 354.	
196	9 November 1183	Berenguer Garidelli gives to Bernard Alcaide land outside the wall of the city on condition of building a house and paying rent for it. The land is south of that of Ermessend, wife of Jordan Anglicus. In *Diplomatari de la Catedral de Tortosa*, ed. Virgili, no. 357.	
197	January 1184	Alfonso II of Aragon recognizes the rights that the Knights Templar possess in the territory of Tortosa, before donating parts of the city and its territory to them. Among the lands given are two parcels which used to belong to Gilbert Anglicus in Vila Rubeam. In *Liber feudorum maior*, ed. Rosell, 1, no. 477.	

Original	First Copy	Second Copy	Third Copy	Fourth Copy
Arxiu Capitular de la S.I. Catedral de Tortosa, Arenes, Tivenys (2: Arenes) (185,160)				
Lost	Arxiu Capitular de la S.I. Catedral de Tortosa, Cartulary 4, d. 69, fol. 69			
Archivo Historico Nacional, Madrid, Santes Creus, perg. 86	Biblioteca Pública de Tarragona, El Llibre Blanch de Santes Creus, cart. no. 168, fol. 76v			
Arxiu Capitular de la S.I. Catedral de Tortosa, Arenes, Tivenys (4: Arenes)				
Lost	Arxiu de la Corona d'Aragó, Barcelona, Sec. 5. arm. 4, v. III, no. 225, fol. 69v			
Arxiu Capitular de la S.I. Catedral de Tortosa, Subtresoreria 2, 48	Arxiu Capitular de la S.I. Catedral de Tortosa, Cartulary 4, d. 66, fols. 66–67r			
Lost	Arxiu Capitular de la S.I. Catedral de Tortosa, Cartulary 4, d. 78, fols. 75v–76			
Arxiu Capitular de la S.I. Catedral de Tortosa, Cartulary 4, d. 79, fols. 76v–77r				
Arxiu Capitular de la S.I. Catedral de Tortosa, Alfondec, Costa S. Jaume (4: Alfondec, Grassa, 25) (175,185), ABC				
Arxiu de la Corona d'Aragó, Barcelona, perg. Pedro I, no. 277				

No.	Date	Description	Witnesses
198	28 January 1184	William of Salvanec (Salvagnac) and his wife Jordana donate to the Templars an orchard in the territory of Tortosa in the area called Xerta. William promises to pay the Order a pitcher of olive oil every year on Christmas day. In Pagarolas, *La comanda del Temple de Tortosa: primer periode*, no. 82.	William of Salvanec (Salvagnac)
199	26 July 1186	Ramon Adei and his wife Ermengard and his brother Arnaldus owe to Martin of Estorga and his wife Stephanie 6 mazmudines of gold in weight and for this they are supposed to give their houses in Remolins. In *Diplomatari de la Catedral de Tortosa*, ed. Virgili, no. 402.	Jordan Anglicus
200	2 April 1187	Hugh, abbot of Santes Creus, gives to John Anglico and his wife Rosse the monastery's honours in Almonia in the territory of Tortosa which used to belong to Geoffrey Anglico. In *El "Llibre Blanch" de Santes Creus*, ed. Udina Martorell, no. 289.	No clear Anglo-Norman witnesses
201	30 July 1187	Nicholas, sacristan of St. Mary's of Tortosa, with the consent of Poncius, prior, gives Mahomet Alfanec for the duration of his life an orchard that used to belong to Gerald Silvaniaco (Salvagnac) in Xerta. He is to deliver a quarter of its production to the church. The land is to the east of the honour that used to belong to Gilbert Anglicus. In *Diplomatari de la Catedral de Tortosa*, ed. Virgili, no. 414.	
202	1188	Gilbert (Anglicus?) gives lands to the monastery of Poblet. In *Cartulari de Poblet*, ed. Pons i Marqués, no. 181.	John Angles
203	3 May 1188	Poncius, prior of St. Mary's of Tortosa, with the consent of Sancho, of the church of St. John of Campo, gives to Gerald Silvaniaco (Salvagnac) a parcel of land in Arens on the condition of planting a vineyard and giving back to the church a third of the produce. In *Diplomatari de la Catedral de Tortosa*, ed. Virgili, no. 426.	
204	18 June 1189	Berenguer Garidel and his wife Geralda exchange with Poncius, bishop of Tortosa, houses in Tortosa in the borough of Grassas for lands in Ladar. In *Diplomatari de la Catedral de Tortosa*, ed. Virgili, no. 434.	Gerald of Salvaniaco (Salvagnac)
205	7 July 1189	Ermesinda de Provenza and her husband Ramon Vilardel sell to Arnald of Arenis a land south of the land of Gerald Silviniaco (Salvagnac). In *Diplomatari de la Catedral de Tortosa*, ed. Virgili, no. 436.	
206	30 November 1189	John Anglicus and his wife Rossa sell to Hugh, abbot of Santes Creus, an orchard in Aldover. In *El "Llibre Blanch" de Santes Creus*, ed. Udina Martorell, no. 332.	William of Salviniaco (Salvagnac)
207	30 November 1189	Grant to Santes Creus of lands in Xerta is verified by Poncius Aurerius and his wife Dulce. He also promises to enter the monastery as a monk. In *El "Llibre Blanch" de Santes Creus*, ed. Udina Martorell, no. 333.	John Anglicus

THE CONQUEST AND SETTLEMENT OF TORTOSA, 1148–1180 125

Original	First Copy	Second Copy	Third Copy	Fourth Copy
Lost	Arxiu de la Corona d'Aragó, Barcelona, Sec. 5. arm. 4, v. III, no. 255, fol. 78r	Arxiu de la Corona d'Aragó, Barcelona, Sec. 5. arm. 4, v. III, no. 248, fol. 78r		
Arxiu Capitular de la S.I. Catedral de Tortosa, Alfondec, Costa S. Jaume (Costa S. Jaume 1) (162,130)				
Lost	Biblioteca Pública de Tarragona, El Llibre Blanch de Santes Creus, cart. no. 168, fol. 119			
Lost	Arxiu Capitular de la S.I. Catedral de Tortosa, Cartulary 4, d. 14, fol. 14			
Lost	Biblioteca Pública de Tarragona, *Cartulari de Poblet*, ms. 241, no. 181			
Arxiu Capitular de la S.I. Catedral de Tortosa, Arenes, Tivenys (2: Arenes) (180,175), ABC				
Arxiu Capitular de la S.I. Catedral de Tortosa, Tevizola, Anglerola (2: Bitem), ABC				
Arxiu Capitular de la S.I. Catedral de Tortosa, Arenes, Tivenys (1: Arenes) (180,155)				
Lost	Biblioteca Pública de Tarragona, El Llibre Blanch de Santes Creus, cart. no. 168, fol. 106v			
Lost	Biblioteca Pública de Tarragona, El Llibre Blanch de Santes Creus, cart. no. 168, fol. 123			

No.	Date	Description	Witnesses
208	30 November 1189	Raimund of Sentiles and his wife Valencia give to the monastery land in Xerta. In *El "Llibre Blanch" de Santes Creus*, ed. Udina Martorell, no. 334.	John Anglicus
209	1 March 1190	Abbot Hugh of Santes Creus bequeaths vineyards that John Anglico held in Aldover that had belonged to Gilbert Anglicus. In *El "Llibre Blanch" de Santes Creus*, ed. Udina Martorell, no. 338.	No clear Anglo-Normans as witnesses
210	28 April 1191	After many controversies, by deposition of the curia, the important men of Tortosa, including John Anglicus and the canons on one side and the brothers of the Order of the Hospital on the other, reach an agreement over the distribution of tithes over the whole of the territory of Tortosa. In *Diplomatari de la Catedral de Tortosa*, ed. Virgili, no. 456.	
211	25 October 1193	Raimundus Gelegus (Welsh? Galician?) and his people sell to Nicholas, sacristan of the church of Tortosa, two orchards which he had bought from the son (unnamed) of Pagan Anglicus, which are located in Som and in a small land in Avinalop, with the honour of William of Silvaniaco (Salvagnac) on its north west. The other orchard is south of the honour of William Salviniaco (Salvagnac). In *Diplomatari de la Catedral de Tortosa*, ed. Virgili, no. 497.	Ramon Galec (Welsh/Galician?)
212	22 February 1196	Gombadus, bishop of Tortosa, and Poncius, prior with the consent of the chapter, donate to Jacob an orchard that they had in Som, and other properties and rights. In *Diplomatari de la Catedral de Tortosa*, ed. Virgili, no. 535.	William of Salviniaco (Salvagnac)
213	14 October 1196	Peter of Palma gives to Gazone, in gratitude for his services, a house that he had near the church of St. Mary's of Tortosa, in the sector known as Tamarit. In *Diplomatari de la Catedral de Tortosa*, ed. Virgili, no. 551.	John Anglicus
214	13 March 1198	Peter, who was the son of Arnald of Lupricat, sells to Paratge and his wife Guillelma half a vineyard and land in Bitem for which he paid as rent one-fifth of the produce to the bishop of Tortosa. The buyer promises to continue paying the dues to the bishop. In *Diplomatari de la Catedral de Tortosa*, ed. Virgili, no. 568.	William of Salviniaco (Salvagnac)
215	15 January 1199	Peter of Pruneto, prior of St. Rufus of Ylerde, and Bertrandus, canon of the place, exchange with Gombald, bishop of Tortosa, and Poncius, prior of the same church, an orchard that they have in Bitem, which had been owned by Osbert Angles, and the honours that they possess in Xerta which they had acquired from Berenguer Torrogio, for two vineyards the chapter of Tortosa had in Pardinis Ylerde. In *Diplomatari de la Catedral de Tortosa*, ed. Virgili, no. 579.	
216	4 February 1204	Ramona, who was the wife of Berenguer of Torta, sells to Poncius, sacristan of St. Mary's of Tortosa, houses that she had as census from him outside the walls of Tortosa in the place know as Alfondico. The house has on its western side the lands that used to belong to William of Salviniacho (Salvagnac). In *Diplomatari de la Catedral de Tortosa*, ed. Virgili, no. 640.	

THE CONQUEST AND SETTLEMENT OF TORTOSA, 1148–1180   127

Original	First Copy	Second Copy	Third Copy	Fourth Copy
Lost	Biblioteca Pública de Tarragona, El Llibre Blanch de Santes Creus, cart. no. 168, fol. 124			
Lost	Biblioteca Pública de Tarragona, El Llibre Blanch de Santes Creus, cart. no. 168, fol. 124v			
Lost	Arxiu Capitular de la S.I. Catedral de Tortosa, Templars 9, 18/12/1209	Arxiu Capitular de la S.I. Catedral de Tortosa, Cartulary 8, fols. 154–155r	Arxiu Capitular de la S.I. Catedral de Tortosa, Cartulary 6, fol. 13	Arxiu Capitular de la S.I. Catedral de Tortosa, Cartulary 9, fols. 129–130r
Lost	Arxiu Capitular de la S.I. Catedral de Tortosa, Cartulary 4, d. 90, fols. 84–85r			
Arxiu Capitular de la S.I. Catedral de Tortosa, Arenes,Tivenys (6,Tyvenys) (210,165) ABC	Arxiu Capitular de la S.I. Catedral de Tortosa, Cartulary 6, d. 172, fol. 66			
Arxiu Capitular de la S.I. Catedral de Tortosa, Santa Maria, Taules Velles (9: Santa Maria)				
Lost	Arxiu Capitular de la S.I. Catedral de Tortosa, Cartulary 2, titol IV, d. XXIIII, fols. 106v–108r			
Arxiu Capitular de la S.I. Catedral de Tortosa, Tevizola, Anglerola, Bitem (2: Bitem)	Arxiu Capitular de la S.I. Catedral de Tortosa, Cartulary 6, d, 161, fol. 61			
Lost	Arxiu Capitular de la S.I. Catedral de Tortosa, Cartulary 4, d. 120, fols. 109v–110r			

No.	Date	Description	Witnesses
217	4 August 1206	Gombaldus, bishop of Tortosa, and the canons on one side and Brother Martin of Andos, master of the Hospital of Amposta and the brothers on the other, dispute the right to receive tithes from Alde. The Hospitallers claim that after buying the land that they had reached an accord previously with Bishop Poncius. Peter of Tolone and Arnaldus of Tolone are chosen to arbitrate the dispute with the counsel of Pere of Malobosc, master of Vitaler, and Guillelm Gozi. They decide that the cathedral should have the tithes for all that to which it had right and that the Order should have the tithes of everything that they produced from the land from now on. Both parties were to honour the previous accord for the exceptions over the land between the estate of Gerald of Salvanico (Salvagnac) and the caves of Carpaxo and all the way to the sea. In *Diplomatari de la Catedral de Tortosa*, ed. Virgili, no. 672.	
218	4 May 1209	Gog and his wife Basaloni sell to Bernard Bruno and his wife Bernarda a vineyard that she had in the area of Tortosa at the plain of St. John of the Camp. In *Diplomatari de la Catedral de Tortosa*, ed. Virgili, no. 719.	William of Salviniaco (Salvagnac)
219	25 July 1210	Gombaldus, bishop of Tortosa, Poncius, prior, Guillelm of Alos, chamberlain, Bernard, sacristan, Poncius and Peter, priests, give to John, chaplain of St. Mary's of Aldea, the first fruits and tithes of the Christians and Muslims that work in the area of Aldea, and other rights that had been given by Bernardo of Pulcro Loco. In *Diplomatari de la Catedral de Tortosa*, ed. Virgili, no. 734.	John Anglicus
220	No Date	Confirmation of possessions, which Raymond of Copons had through Ramon Puigalt. One orchard in Xerta besides that of William Salvaiec … And another orchard in Assent besides that of Gerald Salvaiec … And also a parcel of land in Bitem between those of Robert Tenes and Reginald Anglicum. In *Cartulari de Poblet*, ed. Pons i Marqués, no. 185.	
221	(31 January 1171)	Peter of Braia with the consent of the brothers of Sanct Genes sells to St. Mary's of Tortosa and to Prior Gerald houses acquired originally from Bernard Fabro and later confirmed by King Alfonso and the Montecatanos. In *Diplomatari de la Catedral de Tortosa*, ed. Virgili, no. 225.	Gilbert Anglicus and Gerald of Salvaneco (Salvagnac)
222	No date	A note about the properties that the monastery of Santes Creus possessed in Xerta. Among them it mentions that there were some that belonged to Gilbert Anglicus who has became a monk at Santes Creus. In *El "Llibre Blanch" de Santes Creus*, ed. Udina Martorell, no. 394.	
223	No date	A note of the properties that the monastery of St. Mary's Valle Laura received in Tortosa, from certain people. Gerald of Salvaniaco (Salvagnac) is mentioned as one of the donors. In *El "Llibre Blanch" de Santes Creus*, ed. Udina Martorell, no. 395.	
224	No date	Note of tributes that a few serfs are expected to give to the monastery of Santes Creus. Gerald Salvanec (Salvagnac), Petro Gelg and John Angles are mentioned. They are to supply olive oil in large quantities for their fiefs. In *El "Llibre Blanch" de Santes Creus*, ed. Udina Martorell, no. 396.	

THE CONQUEST AND SETTLEMENT OF TORTOSA, 1148–1180   129

Original	First Copy	Second Copy	Third Copy	Fourth Copy
Lost	Arxiu Capitular de la S.I. Catedral de Tortosa, Cartulary 3, fols. 28–30r	Arxiu Capitular de la S.I. Catedral de Tortosa, Cartulary 8, titol V, d. IV, no. 55, fols. 93v–94	Arxiu Capitular de la S.I. Catedral de Tortosa, Cartulary 9A, pp. 185–88	Arxiu Capitular de la S.I. Catedral de Tortosa, Rectoria de l'Adea, 54
Arxiu Capitular de la S.I. Catedral de Tortosa, Trevizola, Anglerola (1: Anglerola, etc) (155,175), ABC	Arxiu Capitular de la S.I. Catedral de Tortosa, Trevizola, Anglerola (1: Anglerola, etc) (150,180), ABC. (Original, duplicate)			
Lost		Arxiu Capitular de la S.I. Catedral de Tortosa, Rectoria de l'Aldea, 53 (315,130)	Arxiu Capitular de la S.I. Catedral de Tortosa, Cartulary 8, d. 12, fol. 11v	
Lost		Biblioteca Pública de Tarragona, Cartulari de Poblet, no. 185		
Arxiu Capitular de la S.I. Catedral de Tortosa, Genova, Vila-roja (1: Genova, 42) (210, 210)				
Lost		Biblioteca Pública de Tarragona, El Llibre Blanch de Santes Creus, cart. no. 168, fol. 121v		
Lost		Biblioteca Pública de Tarragona, El Llibre Blanch de Santes Creus, cart. no. 168, fol. 121v		
Lost		Biblioteca Pública de Tarragona, El Llibre Blanch de Santes Creus, cart. no. 168, fol. 122		

Die Kreuzzugsmotivation Friedrichs II.

Volker Caumanns

RWTH Aachen University

In der Reihe der Fürsten, Könige und Kaiser, die in das Heilige Land zogen mit dem Ziel, die christlichen Stätten der muslimischen Herrschaft zu entreißen, sticht einer heraus: Friedrich II. Er tut dies zum einen wegen des Ergebnisses seines Zuges. Nach dem ersten Kreuzzug konnte allein Friedrich II. einen anerkannten Erfolg im Heiligen Land erzielen, und dieser Erfolg wiederum war ungewöhnlich, weil er nicht auf dem Schlachtfeld, sondern am Verhandlungstisch errungen wurde. Zudem war es weniger der Kreuzfahrer Friedrich II., der sich mit dem muslimischen Sultan al-Kāmil vertraglich einigte, sondern wohl eher Friedrich II. als der König Jerusalems.[1] Ungewöhnlich ist auch die lange Zeitspanne zwischen dem Kreuzzugsgelübde und dem Aufbruch ins Heilige Land. Immerhin 13 Jahre dauerte es, bis Friedrich sein erstmals 1215 gegebenes und 1220 erneuertes Versprechen nach mehreren Aufschüben einlöste. Und weil er nicht zum letztlich per Vertrag festgesetzten Zeitpunkt loszog, trat er schließlich die Reise als Exkommunizierter an.

Die Beweggründe, die Friedrich II. zu seinem Kreuzzugsgelübde veranlassten, sind in der Forschung mehrfach erörtert worden, eingehend zuletzt von Wolfgang Stürner und von Bodo Hechelhammer.[2] Beide untersuchen das Kreuzzugsvorhaben des Staufers hinsichtlich der Instrumentalisierung zur Herrschaftssicherung. Stürner verweist dabei zunächst auf zwei generelle Positionen der bisherigen Forschung, in der Friedrichs Kreuznahme im Jahr 1215 hauptsächlich im Hinblick auf Innozenz III. betrachtet wurde, der zwei Jahre zuvor einen neuen Kreuzzug ausgerufen hatte. Die einen, Ernst Kantorowicz folgend, sehen in der Kreuznahme eine gegen päpstliche Pläne gerichtete Übernahme des Führungsanspruchs in der Kreuzzugsbewegung, die anderen widersprechen dieser Auffassung und nehmen das Einverständnis des Papstes oder sogar die päpstliche Förderung der Kreuznahme des jungen Königs an.[3] Stürner selbst kommt nach eingehender

---

Der Beitrag ist die überarbeitete und gekürzte Fassung meiner im Sommersemester 2004 an der RWTH Aachen eingereichten Magisterarbeit.

[1] Rudolf Hiestand, "Friedrich II. und der Kreuzzug," in *Friedrich II. Tagung des Deutschen Historischen Instituts in Rom im Gedenkjahr 1994*, ed. Arnold Esch und Norbert Kamp (Tübingen, 1996), pp. 128–49, hier p. 143.

[2] Wolfgang Stürner, "Kreuzzugsgelübde und Herrschaftssicherung. Friedrich II. und das Papsttum im letzten Pontifikatsjahr Innozenz' III.," in *Papsttum, Kirche und Recht im Mittelalter. Festschrift für Horst Fuhrmann*, ed. Hubert Mordek (Tübingen, 1991), pp. 303–15; Bodo Hechelhammer, *Kreuzzug und Herrschaft unter Friedrich II. Handlungsspielräume von Kreuzzugspolitik (1215–1230)*, Mittelalter-Forschungen 13 (Ostfildern, 2004).

[3] Stürner, "Kreuzzugsgelübde," pp. 303–4; cf. zu dieser Frage auch Hechelhammer, *Kreuzzug*, pp. 40–60.

Analyse der Vorgänge in den Jahren 1212 bis 1216 zu dem Schluss, Friedrich habe sein Kreuzzugsgelübde angetrieben von tief empfundener Dankbarkeit gegenüber Gott abgelegt, durch den er sich auserwählt und zu der nun erlangten Herrschaft geführt glaubte. Der Schwur, einen Kreuzzug unternehmen zu wollen, sei ihm als angemessene Gabe für die empfangene göttliche Gnade erschienen, wissend um die Kreuzzugspläne Innozenz' III. und um die durch die Krönung in Aachen erworbene Würde und Verpflichtung, die sich aus dem Erbe seiner staufischen Vorfahren und der damit verbundenen Nachfolge Karls des Großen ergab, dessen Vorbild als christlicher Herrscher es nachzueifern galt. Dieses Herrschaftsbewusstsein, die staufisch-karolingische Tradition gepaart mit dem Glauben an göttliche Berufung, gilt Stürner als bestimmender Antrieb Friedrichs II. Damit aber war zugleich das Streben verbunden, die von Gott übertragene, das deutsch-römische Kaiserreich und das sizilische Königtum umspannende Herrschaft dauerhaft zu bewahren.[4] Die diesbezüglichen Bemühungen hielten Friedrich II. immer wieder von der Erfüllung seines Kreuzzugsgelübdes ab.[5]

Hechelhammer sieht das 1215 in Aachen gegebene Kreuzzugsversprechen vorrangig motiviert durch die unerfüllten Kreuzzugsgelübde von Friedrichs II. Vater und Großvater, Heinrich VI. und Friedrich I. Barbarossa. Er spricht dabei, ähnlich wie schon Stürner, von dem Bekenntnis Friedrichs "zur staufisch-salisch-karolingischen Tradition und zum programmatischen Erbe" seiner Vorfahren und Vorgänger, also der unter Friedrich Barbarossa ausformulierten Kaiseridee, die die Herrschaftsauffassung Friedrichs II. prägte. Neben dieser aus der verwandtschaftlichen wie institutionellen Tradition erwachsenen Verpflichtung zum Kreuzzug nennt auch Hechelhammer Friedrichs II. Dankbarkeit für die ihm zugekommene göttliche Gnade, Ausdruck der "persönlich empfundenen, religiös-motivierten pietas," als zweites wichtiges Motiv.[6] Friedrichs II. so motiviertes Kreuzzugsgelübde zeigt Hechelhammer als ein in der Folge klug wahrgenommenes und eingesetztes Mittel für die Durchsetzung politischer Ziele.

Die Ergebnisse Stürners und Hechelhammers weisen auf vier Aspekte, die für die Beantwortung der Frage nach der Kreuzzugsmotivation Friedrichs II. ausschlaggebend sind: Religiosität, Tradition, Herrschaftsauffassung und Herrschaftssicherung. Diese Aspekte sind in ihrer Bedeutung für Friedrichs Kreuzzugsgelübde noch nicht zutreffend erfasst und bewertet worden. Deshalb werden sie hier in einem systematischen Zugriff erneut betrachtet. Dazu rücke ich ab von der sich anbietenden und daher üblichen chronologisch geordneten Untersuchung der Vorgeschichte des Kreuzzugs Friedrichs II. und orientiere mich an den genannten vier Aspekten. Diese werden zunächst getrennt voneinander abgehandelt, ihre jeweilige Relevanz für die Kreuznahme diskutiert. Am Ende werden die so gewonnenen Hinweise zu der Kreuzzugsmotivation Friedrichs II. zusammengeführt, die auf eine schon früh

---

[4] Stürner, "Kreuzzugsgelübde," besonders pp. 306 und 315.
[5] Hiestand, "Friedrich II.," pp. 133–35, und Wolfgang Stürner, *Friedrich II.*, 2 Teile (Darmstadt 1992–2000), 1:231–35 und 2:85–139.
[6] Hechelhammer, *Kreuzzug*, pp. 32 und 38–39.

ausgebildete Herrschaftskonzeption hinausläuft, für die das Kreuzzugsgelübde und dessen Umsetzung eine unumgängliche Notwendigkeit darstellte. Die grundsätzliche Problematik bedenkend, die einer auf persönliche Überzeugungen abzielende Untersuchung innewohnt, stütze ich mich im Folgenden auf die in Friedrichs II. Namen erstellten Urkunden, Briefe und Manifeste. Dies sind zwar im strengen Sinn keine Selbstzeugnisse,[7] aber sie entstanden, das denke ich unterstellen zu dürfen, mit dem Willen oder wenigstens dem Einverständnis Friedrichs und können so mindestens Auskunft darüber geben, wie er als Herrscher nach außen erscheinen wollte. Daher werde ich, wie es auch üblich ist, von Äußerungen Friedrichs II. sprechen, wenn ich mich auf die in seinem Namen erstellten Schriften beziehe. Um zu ermitteln, welche Ideen Friedrich bezüglich des Kreuzzugsvorhabens geprägt haben, richtet sich die Aufmerksamkeit auf die zeitgenössische Geschichtsschreibung, aus der auch er sich über seine Vorfahren und die Weltläufe unterrichten konnte und in der wichtige Hinweise für die Auffassung von kaiserlicher Herrschaft enthalten sind, die meines Erachtens das Herrschaftsverständnis Friedrichs II. entscheidend beeinflussten. Diese Zeugnisse werden abgeglichen mit Friedrichs Taten und mit dem ihm zur Verfügung stehenden Handlungsspielraum.[8]

Religiosität

Friedrichs II. persönliche Frömmigkeit ist in der Forschung eine nicht unumstrittene Angelegenheit. Verallgemeinernd kann man sagen, dass in der älteren Forschung seine Religiosität häufig eher zweifelnd betrachtet wurde, vor allem weil man den Staufer aufgrund seiner naturwissenschaftlichen Interessen und seiner Haltung gegenüber den Päpsten für einen den überkommenen mittelalterlichen Vorstellungen entfremdeten Wegbereiter der Neuzeit hielt.[9] Die jüngere Forschung, besonders seit den 1990er Jahren, attestiert Friedrich II. dagegen aufrichtige Gottesfürchtigkeit. Grundlegend dafür ist der eigens diesem Punkt gewidmete Aufsatz Hans Martin

---

[7] Zum Begriff "Selbstzeugnisse" siehe Benigna von Krusenstjern, "Was sind Selbstzeugnisse? Begriffskritische und quellenkundliche Überlegungen anhand von Beispielen aus dem 17. Jahrhundert," *Historische Anthropologie* 2 (1994), pp. 462–71; cf. zu dem teilweise äquivalent gebrauchten Begriff, 'Ego-Dokumente' Rudolf Dekker, "Introduction," in *Egodocuments and History: Autobiographical Writing in its Social Context Since the Middle Ages*, ed. ders., Publicaties van de Faculteit der Historische en Kunstwetenschappen. Maatschappijgeschiedenis 38 (Hilversum, 2002), pp. 7–20, besonders pp. 7–13.

[8] Zum Begriff 'Handlungsspielraum' siehe Alfred Haverkamp, "Einführung," in *Friedrich Barbarossa. Handlungsspielräume und Wirkungsweisen des staufischen Kaisers*, ed. ders., Vorträge und Forschungen 40 (Sigmaringen 1992), pp. 9–47, hier pp. 11–12

[9] Siehe dazu Hans Martin Schaller, "Die Kanzlei Kaiser Friedrichs II. Ihr Personal und ihr Sprachstil," *Archiv für Diplomatik* 4 (1958), pp. 264–327, p. 325, und Marcus Thomsen: *"Ein feuriger Herr des Anfangs ..." – Kaiser Friedrich II. in der Auffassung der Nachwelt*, Kieler Historische Studien 42 (Ostfildern, 2005), pp. 149–210. Programmatisch gegen solche Deutung richtet sich David Abulafia, *Frederick II. A Medieval Emperor* (London, 1988).

Schallers, der erstmals umfassend die verschiedenen greifbaren Äußerungen des religiösen Friedrich darlegt, mit dem Fazit, dass wir mit ihm einen durch und durch frommen Zeitgenossen des 13. Jahrhunderts vor uns haben.[10] Der Grundstock seiner frommen Gesinnung soll bereits in Friedrichs Erziehung gelegt worden sein. Schaller verweist diesbezüglich auf die Vormundschaft des Papstes, die bischöflichen Regenten des Königreichs Sizilien sowie die zahlreichen Geistlichen am Hof in Palermo. Jedoch die überlieferten Aussagen zum Verhalten und zu den Wesenszügen des kindlichen Friedrich klingen nicht nach einem Jungen, der wegen der stetigen Bedrängungen und Bedrohungen, denen seine Person ausgesetzt war,[11] sein Heil in der Zuwendung zu Gott suchte, so dass die Einschätzung des Knaben, er sei "nach Herkunft und Erziehung ein frommer Christ"[12] gewesen, eine zwar keineswegs unwahrscheinliche, jedoch nicht bestätigte Mutmaßung bleiben muss.

Ab der Volljährigkeit und der damit einhergehenden Regierungsübernahme im Jahre 1208 kann sich Schaller auf Aussagen in Friedrichs II. Urkunden und Briefen stützen. Zunächst verweist er auf verschiedene Äußerungen in den Urkunden, die die Dankbarkeit gegen Gott, Gottes Allmacht und seine Barmherzigkeit thematisieren sowie die Erwähnungen der speziell dem christlichen Kaiser obliegenden Aufgaben, wie die Wahrung von Frieden und Gerechtigkeit, die Förderung und Verbreitung des Glaubens, die Bekehrung der Heiden, den Schutz und die Unterstützung von Kirchen und Klöstern, die Bemühungen um die Armenfürsorge und die Armutsbewegung sowie die Förderung diverser geistlicher und ritterlicher Orden. Auch in der Gesetzgebung Friedrichs II. biete sich ein "Bild von Mitleid und Barmherzigkeit," wobei die Ketzergesetze ausdrücklich auszunehmen seien, da sie auf Betreiben der Päpste zurückgingen und der Kaiser als Schutzherr der Kirche deren Erlass nicht habe verweigern können.[13] Die Briefe und Manifeste Friedrichs schließlich befassten sich vornehmlich mit den Themen Armut, Kreuzzug und Endzeit, wobei mehrfach die Verehrung des heiligen Grabes, des Heiligen Kreuzes sowie "des heiligen Nikolaus und Jakobus des Älteren, also der Schutzpatrone der Seefahrer, Pilger, Kreuzfahrer und Heidenbekämpfer" zum Ausdruck komme.[14] Kurz und gut, Schaller bringt eine solche Fülle von Beispielen, die auf Friedrich II.

---

[10] Hans Martin Schaller, "Die Frömmigkeit Kaiser Friedrichs II." *Deutsches Archiv für Erforschung des Mittelalters* (künftig *Deutsches Archiv*) 51 (1995), pp. 493–513; cf. Stürner, *Friedrich II.*, 1:140, 171, 172, 177, 251 und 2:594, und Carlo Fornari, *Federico II un sogno imperiale svanito a Vittoria. Antefatti, cronaca e conseguenze di una sconfitta annunciata* (Parma, 1998), pp. 30–32.

[11] Zu dem Kind Friedrich II. siehe Stürner, *Friedrich II.* 1:105–13 und die Quellenstücke in deutscher Übersetzung in *Kaiser Friedrich II. in Briefen und Berichten seiner Zeit*, ed. und trans. Klaus Joachim Heinisch (Darmstadt, 1977), pp. 15–19.

[12] Schaller, "Frömmigkeit," p. 496.

[13] Ibid., p. 504. Cf. die Bewertung der Ketzergesetzgebung in Kurt-Victor, "Die Ketzerpolitik Friedrichs II.," in *Probleme um Friedrich II.*, ed. Josef Fleckenstein, Vorträge und Forschungen 16 (Sigmaringen, 1974), pp. 309–43, besonders pp. 320–24 (repr. in *Stupor Mundi. Zur Geschichte Friedrich II. von Hohenstaufen*, ed. Gunther G. Wolf, Wege der Forschung 101, 2. Aufl. (Darmstadt, 1982), pp. 449–93).

[14] Schaller, "Frömmigkeit," pp. 507–8.

als frommen christlichen Herrscher hindeuten, dass man einiges zu tun hätte, wollte man ernsthaft dessen Religiosität grundsätzlich anzuweifeln.

Eine kleine Kerbe ist diesem abgerundeten Bild aber zuzufügen. Denn Misstrauen gegenüber einer stets aufrichtig vorgebrachten frommen Haltung Friedrichs ist immerhin nicht ganz unberechtigt, verstand er doch sehr gut, handfeste politische Wünsche und Absichten als durch und durch fromme Ansinnen darzustellen, Frömmigkeit also als Mittel zum Zweck zu gebrauchen, so dass von tiefer Gläubigkeit geprägte Worte manchmal den bitteren Beigeschmack des puren Opportunismus annehmen. Ein Musterbeispiel dafür ist der Brief vom 21. August 1215 an das Generalkapitel der Zisterzienser.[15] Friedrich hebt darin beredt die große Heiligkeit der Mönche und Äbte dieses Ordens und die daher rührende besondere Wirkkraft ihrer Gebete hervor und bittet deshalb, sie mögen ihn in ihre Gebetsgemeinschaft aufnehmen. Eigens erwähnt er noch seine Kreuznahme und erbittet speziell für das Gelingen des anstehenden Unternehmens die Hilfe durch ihre Gebete. Zum Schluss des Briefes aber kommt, so der spontan sich aufdrängende Eindruck bei der Lektüre, das eigentliche Anliegen zur Sprache:

> Adhuc quia recognoscimus, quia omnino ea, que divina clementia circa nos et in nobis misericorditer et miserabiliter operata est, per dominum et patrem nostrum summum pontificem sicut per vicarium et ministrum suum dignata est operari, petimus humiliter et devote, ut quia ad persolvendas debitas gratiarum actiones pro tantis beneficiis nos ipsos iudicamus insufficientes, vos vice et loco nostro hoc apud ipsum velitis piissimis orationibus vestris promereri. Ultimo orationibus vestris nos recommendantes, scire vos volumus, quod omnibus diebus nostris huius sanctissimi ordinis defensores esse volumus et per omnia facta sua tamquam nostra propria promovere.[16]

Bedenkt man, dass dieser Brief knapp zweieinhalb Monate vor dem von Innozenz III. berufenen Laterankonzil abgefasst wurde, kann kein Zweifel über die damit verbundene Absicht bestehen. Es stand zu erwarten, dass neben dem eigentlichen Thema des Konzils, die Vorbereitung und Durchführung eines neuen Kreuzzugs, auch die Herrschaftsfrage im Reich an die Konzilsteilnehmer herangetragen würde.[17] Friedrich musste dafür Vorkehrungen treffen, um nicht am Ende noch von seinem Gegner, dem welfischen Kaiser Otto IV., und dessen Anhängern vor dem Papst ausgestochen zu werden. Es galt deshalb möglichst viele einflussreiche Fürsprecher unter den voraussichtlichen Konzilsteilnehmern zu gewinnen, wie eben die Zisterzienser, die, gerade weil viele Kreuzzugsprediger aus ihren Reihen kamen,[18] wichtige Verbündete sein würden. Friedrichs so fromm anmutender Brief

---

[15] Ibid., p. 501, n. 59 dient dieser Brief als Zeugnis für Friedrichs Hochachtung gegenüber der Heiligkeit des Ordens, ähnlich in Stürner, *Friedrich II*, 1:177–78 mit n. 102.

[16] *Acta Imperii inedita saeculi XIII et XIV. Urkunden und Briefe zur Geschichte des Kaiserreichs und des Königreichs Sizilien*, 2 Bände, ed. Eduard Winkelmann (Innsbruck, 1880; repr. Aalen, 1964), 1, Nr. 131, p. 111, ll. 23–30.

[17] Siehe unten, p. 164.

[18] Zu den Kreuzpredigern siehe Paul B. Pixton, "Die Anwerbung des Heeres Christi: Prediger des Fünften Kreuzzuges in Deutschland," *Deutsches Archiv* 34 (1978), pp. 166–91.

ist also vor allem ein Beleg für politisches Taktieren. Letztlich appelliert Friedrich nicht an die Heiligkeit der Zisterzienseräbte, sondern an ihren weltlichen Verstand, wenn er Gewährung von Schutz und Förderung für die Leistung von diplomatischer Schützenhilfe gelobt.

Mit diesem Beispiel soll (und kann) der grundsätzlichen Frömmigkeit Friedrichs II. nicht widersprochen, sondern lediglich in Erinnerung gebracht werden, dass er sich keineswegs scheute, seine Anliegen und Handlungen zwecks günstigerer Wirkung in christlich-fromme Mäntel zu hüllen, und deshalb nicht hinter jeder der von Schaller angeführten Belegstellen ein lupenreines Zeugnis für die Religiosität des Staufers steckt. Allerdings sind Frömmigkeit und politisches Kalkül nicht grundsätzlich trennbar, sie schließen einander nicht aus. Im Gegenteil sind sie bei Friedrich II. eng miteinander verwoben, denn religiös motivierte Vorstellungen bedingen sein Verhalten als Herrscher. Gemeint ist damit das immer wieder herausgestellte Verständnis, von Gott in besonderer Weise auserwählt und zur Herrschaft bestimmt zu sein.

Sein päpstlicher Vormund Innozenz III. gab Friedrich noch im frühesten Kindesalter zu verstehen, dass er der besonderen göttlichen Liebe und Gunst gewiss sein könne.[19] Dieser als Trost gemeinte Zuspruch sollte sich für den jungen König bei seinem ersten Aufenthalt in Deutschland bewahrheiten. Auf Wunsch Innozenz' III. brach Friedrich II. im März 1212 Richtung Norden auf, um jenseits der Alpen für sein staufisches Erbe zu kämpfen gegen den erst 1209 zum Kaiser gekrönten Welfen Otto IV., der wegen seines unvorhergesehen aufkeimenden, allzu großen Interesses für Sizilien beim Papst in Ungnade gefallen war. Friedrichs Reise verlief insgesamt überaus glücklich, so dass er bereits am 9. Dezember 1212 in Mainz durch den dortigen Erzbischof Siegfried zum König der Römer gekrönt werden konnte. Mit wachsender Unterstützung gelang es dem jungen Friedrich zunächst, sich in den süddeutschen Kernlanden seiner staufischen Vorfahren festzusetzen. Die Schlacht von Bouvines am 27. Juli 1214, in der Friedrichs Verbündeter Philipp II. August von Frankreich trotz ungünstiger Vorzeichen über Otto IV. und dessen Mitstreiter triumphierte, brachte die endgültige Wende zugunsten des Staufers. Als er dann, nach wiederum überraschendem Zusammenbruch der antistaufischen Partei in Aachen, kampflos in die Krönungsstadt einziehen konnte, hatte Friedrich II. allen Grund, einen von Gott selbst geebneten Weg hinter sich zu glauben. Die Kreuznahme am 25. Juli 1215 in der Aachener Marienkirche, unmittelbar nach seiner Weihe und Krönung zum König,[20] als Ausdruck frommer Dankbarkeit zu werten für die in den drei vorangegangenen Jahren erwiesene göttliche Gnade, ist naheliegend. In diesem Sinne äußerte sich Friedrich zweimal rückblickend über seine Kreuznahme. Im Jahre 1224 schrieb er an Papst Honorius III., dessen ungenügende Kreuzzugswerbung beklagend und zugleich seinen eigenen Einsatz betonend:

---

[19] *Die Register Innozenz' III.*, 1, ed. Othmar Hageneder und Anton Haidacher (Graz, Köln, 1964), Nr. 559, p. 816, ll. 9–15; cf. Stürner, *Friedrich II.*, 1:98.

[20] So etwa die Annalen Reiners von Lüttich, MGH SS 16:673, ll. 27–32.

... divino munere cognoscamus, assumpti beneficii non ingrati, nescientes quid exsolveremus altissimo pro omnibus, que contulit et retribuit ipse nobis, cum bonis nostris non egeat, a quo procedit bonorum omnium plenitudo, in holocaustum tamen gratitudinis obsequio sancte crucis obtulimus nosmet ipsos, personam, substantiam et quas ipse concessit opes et regna sibi et terre sancte ministerio deputantes.[21]

Und in seinem Manifest, das 1227 gegen die von Gregor IX. wegen der abgebrochenen Überfahrt zum Heiligen Land ausgesprochene Exkommunikation gerichtet war, heißt es:

Nos autem quid retribueremus Domino pro tot beneficiis, que retribuit ipse nobis, devoto animo metientes, quam cito imperii diadema recepimus Aquisgrani, licet non sit equa facture retributio ad factorem, personam et posse nostrum non in sacrificium, set in holocaustum humiliter obtulimus Domino puro et sincero animo, crucis signaculo nostros humeros decorantes, ut ad recuperationem Terre Sancte votivis et debitis studiis efficaciter intendere deberemus.[22]

Diese beiden Selbsteinschätzungen werden besonders in der neueren Forschung als ernstzunehmende Zeugnisse für die religiöse Motivation der Kreuzzugsplanung Friedrichs II. angeführt.[23] Allerdings ist gegenüber den beiden Aussagen Skepsis angebracht. Mit dem Schreiben von 1224 führte Friedrich Beschwerde bei Honorius III. über den mangelnden Anklang, den die Werbung für den für 1225 geplanten kaiserlichen Kreuzzug fand. Friedrich warf dem Papst vor, unfähige und mit unzureichenden Vollmachten ausgestattete Kreuzprediger entsandt zu haben und insgesamt zu geringes Engagement zu zeigen. Um diesen Vorwurf zuzuspitzen hielt der Kaiser seine eigenen Bemühungen den Taten des Papstes entgegen. Die Erwähnung seines *holocaustum* hat in dem Schreiben also einen konkreten Zweck. Ähnlich ist es bei dem Schreiben von 1227. Friedrich wollte darin den Vorwurf entkräften, sich nicht in versprochenem Maße für das Heilige Land eingesetzt zu haben. So bot er alle nur möglichen Argumente auf, eben auch jenes, er hätte mit seiner Kreuznahme in Aachen ein ihn selbst und seinen Besitz aufzehrendes Dankopfer an Gott geleistet, und zwar in frommer Dankbarkeit für die ihm gewährte göttliche Gnade. Dies heißt letztlich nichts anderes, als dass der Papst mit der Exkommunikation die Erfüllung dieses Gott zu erbringenden Dankopfers zu verhindern drohte. In beiden Fällen also ist die Bezeichnung der Kreuznahme als *holocaustum* durchaus zielgerichtete Rhetorik, die dazu dient, die eigene Leistung hervorzuheben und als einen Gottesdienst zu stilisieren, dessen Behinderung gerade einem Papst nicht einfallen sollte. Lässt schon diese Beobachtung Zweifel an der

---

[21] Schreiben Friedrichs an Honorius III. vom 5. März 1224, *Acta Imperii*, 1, Nr. 261, p. 237, ll. 29–34.
[22] Manifest Friedrichs vom 6. Dezember 1227, MGH Const. 2, Nr. 116, p. 150, ll. 13–18.
[23] So beispielsweise Hiestand, "Friedrich II.," pp. 130–31, Stürner, *Friedrich II.* 1:117 und auch schon Ernst H. Kantorowicz, *Kaiser Friedrich der Zweite. Haupt- und Ergänzungsband* (Düsseldorf, München, 1963, Nachdruck der Ausgabe Berlin, 1927–31), p. 71, jedoch nur mit Verweis auf das Manifest von 1227.

Wahrhaftigkeit der rückblickenden Charakterisierungen der Aachener Kreuznahme aufkeimen, so kommt noch der Zeitfaktor hinzu. Denn, wenn Friedrich II. 1215 in wahrhafter Ergriffenheit den Kreuzzug vor allem anderen schwor, um Gott seine Dankbarkeit zu zeigen, dann muss man sich sehr wundern, dass er – bei allen nachvollziehbaren politischen Begründungen für die vielen Aufschübe – sich so lange mit der Erfüllung seines Gelübdes Zeit ließ. Von einem von tiefer Dankbarkeit erfüllten König würde man doch eine andere Priorisierung erwarten als Friedrich sie an den Tag legte. Nichts hätte etwa dagegen gesprochen zuerst den Kreuzzug zu unternehmen und erst danach die Kaiserkrone zu empfangen (es sei hier an Konrad III. erinnert), zumal mangels Teilnahmeabsichten anderer Könige mögliche Rangstreitigkeiten, wie man sie von früheren Kreuzzügen kannte, nicht zu erwarten waren. Noch weniger hätte dagegen gesprochen, unmittelbar nach der Kaiserkrönung der tiefen Dankbarkeit vollends Ausdruck zu verleihen, so wie bei dieser Gelegenheit erneut versprochen. Aber Friedrich setzte – durchaus einleuchtend, wenn man den Aspekt der Dankbarkeit nicht als vordringlich einstuft – andere Prioritäten. Diese stehen im Zusammenhang mit einer religiösen Empfindung, die Friedrich II. an dem Tag seiner Aachener Kreuznahme nähergelegen haben dürfte, nämlich die schon erwähnte Gewissheit der göttlichen Auserwähltheit.[24] Sie demonstriert Friedrich am deutlichsten bei dem seinen Kreuzzug abschließenden Besuch Jerusalems.

Am 7. September 1228 war Friedrich II. endlich in Akkon angelandet. Fünf Monate später hatte er, ohne nennenswerten Schwertstreich, mit seinem Kreuzzug ein, wenn auch nicht optimales, doch zunächst zufriedenstellendes Ergebnis erzielt. Der mit dem Sultan Ägyptens, Malik al-Kāmil, am 18. Februar 1229 geschlossene Vertrag gab den Christen unter anderem die Kontrolle über die Stadt Jerusalem zurück, mit einem durch einige in christlichen Besitz gegebene Dörfer gebildeten Landkorridor nach Bethlehem und zu der Hafenstadt Jaffa, sowie den Ort Nazareth, mit einem eben solchen Korridor nach Akkon. Zusammen mit dem auf zehn Jahre vereinbarten Waffenstillstand war für die Christen, zumindest für einige Jahre, der sichere Zugang zu den wichtigsten Stätten im Heiligen Land erreicht. Einen weiteren Monat später, am 17. März, zog der Kaiser mit etlichen Kreuzfahrern und Pilgern in Jerusalem ein. Am folgenden Tag zeigte er sich in der Grabeskirche dem versammelten Volk, den Kreuzfahrern und Pilgern als Herrscher des Königreichs Jerusalem, indem er dort die Krone trug.[25] Friedrich II. berichtet über die Ereignisse in einem Rundschreiben, das noch am Tage seines Triumphes in Jerusalem,

---

[24] Cf. Wolfgang Stürner, "Kaiser Friedrich II." in *Kunst im Reich Kaiser Friedrichs II. von Hohenstaufen*, ed. Kai Kappel, Dorothee Kemper, Alexander Knaak (München, Berlin, 1996), pp. 11–20, besonders pp. 14–15, und den Hinweis auf Friedrichs Privileg für Erzbischof Berard von Palermo vom 2. April 1215 in Stürner, *Friedrich II.*, 1:171.

[25] Zum Vertrag siehe Helmuth Kluger, *Hochmeister Hermann von Salza und Kaiser Friedrich II.*, Quellen und Studien zur Geschichte des Deutschen Ordens 37 (Marburg, 1987), pp. 87–91. Zum Tragen der Krone in der Grabeskirche siehe ibid., pp. 95–111 und Hans Eberhard Mayer, "Das Pontifikale von Tyrus und die Krönung der lateinischen Könige von Jerusalem," *Dumbarton Oaks Papers* 21 (1967), pp. 200–10.

am 18. März 1229, abgesandt wurde.[26] Der Grundtenor dieses so genannten Jerusalem-Manifests lautet, das gesamte Unternehmen war begleitet von göttlicher Barmherzigkeit, der errungene Erfolg ein Wunder und die damit einhergehende Erhöhung Friedrichs ein wunderbares Zeichen göttlicher Gnade. Denn schließlich habe, nach langen Verhandlungen mit dem Sultan, in einer für das christliche Heer überaus bedrohliche Lage, Jesus Christus selbst die Rückgabe Jerusalems bewirkt.

Bezüglich der Einschätzung des Manifestes ist der Brief des Deutschordensmeisters Hermann von Salza von Bedeutung, den dieser einige Tage vor dem Einzug in Jerusalem an Gregor IX. schrieb.[27] Das Jerusalem-Manifest und Hermanns Brief weisen starke inhaltliche Ähnlichkeiten auf. Sie haben zu dem Schluss geführt, dass der Ordensmeister an dem Entwurf des kaiserlichen Manifests beteiligt war.[28] In diesem Zusammenhang hat Helmuth Kluger auf die Beschwörung der Gnade Gottes in beiden Schreiben hingewiesen und dies als Zeichen für die im Umkreis des Kaisers verbreitete Bereitschaft gewertet, den erlangten Erfolg angesichts der Widrigkeiten als wunderbare Fügung anzuerkennen. Ausdrücklich gegen die Deutung Kantorowicz', Friedrich II. habe in dem Manifest mit der Berufung auf die göttliche Protektion seines Unternehmens vor allem die eigene kaiserliche Würde hervorheben wollen, nimmt Kluger die sehr ähnliche Tendenz des Schreibens Hermanns von Salza zum Anlass, das in beiden Briefen anklingende religiöse Moment ernst zu nehmen, da man dem Ordensmeister kaum unterstellen könne, sein Bericht sei allein im Sinne der Glorifizierung Friedrichs verfasst. Friedrichs II. Äußerungen im Jerusalem-Manifest sind demnach als wahrhafter Ausdruck frommer Gesinnung anzuerkennen.[29] Unmissverständlich wird den Adressaten des Manifests die Auserwähltheit und Gottunmittelbarkeit des Kaisers vorgestellt. Dies hat natürlich auch einen konkreten Zweck. Der Welt, zuvorderst dem Papst, sollte vorgeführt werden, dass die Exkommunikation Friedrichs zu unrecht erfolgt war. Denn Gott ließ den Gebannten in mehrfacher Weise seiner Gnade teilhaftig werden, das päpstliche Urteil wurde also durch Gott selbst negiert. So heißt es denn im Manifest:

> Ecce nunc quidem dies illa salutaris advenit, in qua veri christicole salutare suum accipiunt a domino Deo suo, ut cognoscat et intelligat orbis terre, quia ipse est et non alius, qui servorum suorum salutem quando vult et quomodo vult operatur.[30]

Der irrende Gregor IX. hatte, so die Intention des kaiserlichen Rundschreibens, die über Friedrich verhängte Strafe aufzuheben. Mit dieser Auffassung stand Friedrich

---

[26] MGH Const. 2, Nr. 122, pp. 162–67.
[27] Ibid., Nr. 121, pp. 161–62.
[28] Otto Vehse, *Die amtliche Propaganda in der Staatskunst Kaiser Friedrichs II* (München, 1929), pp. 33–34; cf. Kluger, *Hochmeister*, pp. 117–19.
[29] Kluger, *Hochmeister*, p. 94 gegen Kantorowicz, *Kaiser*, p. 185. Cf. auch Vehse, *Propaganda*, pp. 29–30, Hiestand, "Friedrich II.," p. 145, und Stürner, *Friedrich II.*, 2:162–63.
[30] MGH Const. 2, Nr. 122, p. 163, ll. 35–38.

nicht allein. So lesen wir in den Akkon-Sprüchen des mit Friedrichs Zug ins Heilige Land gereisten Dichters Freidank:

> got und der keiser hânt erlôst | ein grap, deist aller Kristen trôst. | Sit er daz beste hât getân, | sô sol man in ûz banne lân.[31]

Und in einem zweiten Brief, an einen unbekannten Adressaten aus dem Umkreis der Kurie gerichtet, schrieb Hermann von Salza:

> Consultum etiam fuit ei a multis, ut ibidem sibi faceret divinum officium celebrari, ex quo terram illam de manibus liberaverat Sarracenorum, propter quam excommunicationis erat vinculis innodatus. Nos vero ... restitimus consilio memorato, quia nec ecclesie neque sibi vidimus expedire. Et sic in hoc nostris consiliis aquiescens, non audivit divina, tamen coronam simpliciter sine consecratione de altari accepit et in sedem, sicut est consuetum, portavit.[32]

Hermann bezeugt hier, dass die in Freidanks Akkon-Sprüchen geäußerte Auffassung zumindest in Friedrichs Umgebung von vielen vertreten wurde. Bemerkenswerterweise scheint auch Hermann selbst bezüglich der Auffassung, Friedrich sei als erfolgreicher Kreuzfahrer nicht mehr als exkommuniziert zu betrachten, keine Bedenken gehabt zu haben. Aber auch dieser Brief Hermanns entbehrt nicht eines Zwecks. Dem Deutschordensmeister ist daran gelegen, den auch im Jerusalem-Manifest mitgeteilten Akt des Tragens der Krone – der, wie er betont, *sicut est consuetum* vollzogen wurde – von dem Verdacht frei zu halten, Friedrich habe damit die päpstliche Autorität untergraben. Trotz also des verbreiteten Konsenses, der Bann über Friedrich sei durch Gott selbst als gegenstandslos erwiesen, sollte doch die päpstliche Binde- und Lösegewalt nicht unterlaufen werden. Ob des Kaisers Verzicht auf das Hören einer Messe jedoch allein auf Hermanns Rat zurückzuführen ist, scheint fraglich. Wenn ja, dann wäre der zu unterstellende Wunsch Friedrichs seinen Kreuzzug mit einer Messe in der Grabeskirche zu beenden nur ein weiterer Beleg seiner Frömmigkeit.[33] Die Tendenz allerdings, Gregor IX. nicht vor den Kopf stoßen und ihn nicht durch das Schaffen von Tatsachen überflüssig machen zu wollen, zeigt sich auch im Jerusalem-Manifest, zunächst dadurch, dass das Schreiben vollkommen frei ist von jeglichen Anwürfen gegen den Papst. Zudem wird die einzige religiöse Handlung Friedrichs, von der in dem Manifest berichtet wird, nämlich sein Gebet in der Grabeskirche unmittelbar nach der Ankunft in Jerusalem, in der Ausfertigung für Gregor vorsichtshalber

---

[31] *Freidanks Bescheidenheit. Auswahl, mittelhochdeutsch – neuhochdeutsch*, v. 160, 16–19, ed. Wolfgang Spiewok (Leipzig, 1985), p. 200. Freidank hielt den Bann offenbar von vornherein für ungerechtfertigt und daher nicht für bindend (ibid., v. 157, 17–22, p. 196). Cf. auch Kluger, *Hochmeister*, p. 102 mit n. 88.

[32] MGH Const. 2, Nr. 123, p. 167, ll. 22–28.

[33] Siehe dagegen Mayer, *Pontifikale*, p. 200.

verschwiegen,³⁴ obwohl an einem frommen Gebet doch kaum etwas auszusetzen war.

Zunächst kann bezüglich Friedrichs II. Religiosität bei aller Vorsicht festgehalten werden, dass die am deutlichsten im Jerusalem-Manifest zur Schau getragene Auffassung, Friedrich sei ein Auserwählter Gottes, durchaus grundlegend für sein herrscherliches Selbstbewusstsein gewesen sein kann. Anlass, sich der besonderen göttlichen Protektion teilhaftig zu fühlen, boten die Tage in Aachen im Jahr 1215 und jene in Jerusalem 13 Jahre später genug.

Tradition

In Hinblick auf mögliche Vorbilder seines Engagements für das Heilige Land sind das imperiale und das familiäre Erbe Friedrichs II. zu betrachten. Das imperiale Erbe setzt sich aus zwei Elementen zusammen: einerseits die Rückbesinnung auf das antike, römische Cäsarentum, andererseits die Instrumentalisierung Karls des Großen als Begründer des aus jenem hervorgehenden fränkischen Kaisertums. Beides wurde unter Friedrichs II. Großvater, Friedrich I. Barbarossa, ideologisch ausgebaut. Beide Elemente kehren bei Friedrich II. wieder. Allerdings fällt die Bezugnahme auf das römische Cäsarentum weitestgehend aus dem hier betrachteten Rahmen, da fast alle Verweise darauf, seien es die berühmten Augustalen, das Brückentor von Capua und die sonstigen bildlichen Darstellungen mit antik-imperialem Charakter sowie der weit überwiegende Teil der schriftlichen Belege eines Aufgreifens des Cäsarentums erst ab 1231 greifbar sind.³⁵ Lediglich zwei Hinweise auf die Anknüpfung an die antiken Kaiser vor 1230 sind mir bekannt: Der Befehl, einige unmittelbar nach der Kaiserkrönung 1220 in Rom erlassene Gesetze in den *Corpus iuris civilis* aufzunehmen,³⁶ und Friedrichs II. Kreuzzugsaufruf vom 11. Februar 1221 an die Fürsten des Reiches, indem er darin erinnert "qualiter

---

³⁴ MGH Const. 2, Nr. 122, p. 166, ll. 17–21. Zu den beiden Versionen des Manifests siehe Max Kerner, "Letentur in Domino et exultent omnes recti corde," in *Inquirens subtilia diversa. Dietrich Lohrmann zum 65. Geburtstag*, ed. Horst Kranz und Ludwig Falkenstein (Aachen, 2002), pp. 149–72, besonders p. 154.

³⁵ Zur Cäsaren-Nachfolge der Staufer siehe Walther Kienast, *Deutschland und Frankreich in der Kaiserzeit (900–1270)*, Monographien zur Geschichte des Mittelalters 9 (Stuttgart, 1974), pp. 270–82. Zur Karlsverehrung unter Friedrich Barbarossa siehe *Die Aachener "Vita Karoli Magni" des 12. Jahrhunderts*, ed. Helmut Deutz und Ilse Deutz (Siegburg, 2002), pp. 1–23. Zu den Augustalen siehe Stürner, *Friedrich II.*, 2:250–52, zum Brückentor Tanja Michalsky, "'De ponte Capuano, de turribus eius, et de ymagine Frederici ...'," in *Kunst im Reich Kaiser Friedrichs II.*, ed. Kappel, Kemper, Knaak, pp. 137–51, zu den bildlichen Darstellungen Friedrichs allgemein Peter Cornelius Claussen, "Die Erschaffung und Zerstörung des Bildes Friedrichs II. durch die Kunstgeschichte," in ibid., pp. 195–209.

³⁶ Hans Martin Schaller, "Die Kaiseridee Friedrichs II.," in *Probleme um Friedrich II.*, ed. Fleckenstein, pp. 109–34, hier p. 117 (repr. in *Stupor Mundi*, ed. Wolf, 2. Aufl. (Darmstadt, 1982), pp. 494–526 und in Hans Martin Schaller, *Stauferzeit: Ausgewählte Aufsätze*, MGH Schriften 38 (Hannover, 1993), pp. 53–83).

a diebus antiquis et generationibus seculorum imperatores Romani mundum universum sue subdiderint ditioni auxilio suorum fidelium, qui cum eis usque ad effusionem sanguinis laborarunt".[37] Das andere Element, die Bezugnahme auf Karl den Großen, spielt dagegen gleich zu Beginn des hier betrachteten Zeitraums eine Rolle. Es ist zu klären, ob und inwieweit das Vorbild des Frankenkaisers Friedrich II., der im Zuge seiner Krönung 1215 zweifellos auf dessen steinernen Thron Platz nahm und zwei Tage darauf dessen endgültige Überführung in den eigens dazu gefertigten goldenen Schrein mitvollzog, zu seiner Kreuznahme animierte. Dazu muss der Blick zunächst zurückgewandt werden zu Friedrichs II. staufischem Großvater.

Richtungweisend für die Bedeutung, die Karl der Große unter der Herrschaft Friedrichs I. Barbarossa zuteil wurde, war die Beschreibung der *translatio imperii* seines Onkels Otto von Freising. In seiner noch unter Konrad III. verfassten *Chronica* benennt Otto Karl den Großen und Otto I. als Überträger des römischen Kaisertitels auf das fränkische beziehungsweise das ostfränkisch-deutsche Königtum und macht sie damit zu den Begründern eines neuen fränkisch-römischen Kaisertums.[38] Karl der Große wurde so eine Schlüsselfigur für die Legitimation kaiserlicher Herrschaft. In dem zweiten Werk Ottos von Freising, das nach dessen Tod 1158 der Freisinger Kanoniker Rahewin fortsetzte, den *Gesta Friderici*, formte in besonderem Maße letzterer ein an Einhards Beschreibung des Frankenkaisers Karl orientiertes Herrscherbild Friedrich Barbarossas.[39] Und der im Umfeld des staufischen Hofes tätige so genannte Archipoeta spricht in seinem um 1163 entstandenen Kaiserhymnus *Salve mundi domini* Friedrich I. direkt als Karl an.[40] Des Weiteren wurde Karl der Große 1158 erstmals als *sanctissimus* bezeichnet und im gleichen Jahr begegnet erstmals der Begriff des *sacrum* oder gar *sacratissimum imperium*. Die Stilisierung des Frankenkaisers als Neubegründer des Kaiserreichs und vorbildlicher Herrscher gipfelte in dessen Kanonisation am 29. Dezember 1165, dem Tag des biblischen Idealkönigs David.[41] Dem *sacrum imperium* war mit diesem Akt ein heiliger Reichsgründer beschert, der die Macht durch seine eigene Kraft und Tüchtigkeit an sich gerissen hatte. Die Nachfolger dieses heiligen

---

[37] MGH Const. 2, Nr. 92, p. 116, ll. 9–11.
[38] MGH SS rer. Germ. in us. sch. 45, c. V, 32, p. 257. Cf. dazu Hans-Werner Goetz, *Das Geschichtsbild Ottos von Freising*, Beihefte zum Archiv für Kulturgeschichte 19 (Köln, Wien, 1984), pp. 148–61.
[39] *Ottonis et Rahewini Gesta Friderici I. imperatoris rectius Cronica*, c. IV, 86, ed. Franz-Josef Schmale, Ausgewählte Quellen zur deutschen Geschichte des Mittelalters 17 (Darmstadt, 1965), pp. 708–12.
[40] *Die Gedichte des Archipoeta*, v. 16, ed. Heinrich Watenphul und Heinrich Krefeld (Heidelberg, 1958), p. 70.
[41] Zu den Begriffen *sacrum* und *sacritissimum imperium* siehe Jörg Schwarz, *Herrscher- und Reichstitel bei Kaisertum und Papsttum im 12. und 13. Jahrhundert*, Beihefte zu J. F. Böhmer, Regesta Imperii 22 (Köln, Weimar, Wien, 2003), pp. 86–110 und 199–212. Zum David-Königtum siehe Kantorowicz, *Kaiser, Ergänzungsband*, pp. 73–74, und Aryeh Graboïs, "Un mythe fondamental de l'histoire de France au Moyen Age: Le 'roi David', précurseur du 'roi très chrétien,'" *Revue historique* 187,1, n. 581 (1992), pp. 11–31, hier pp. 13–22.

Karl mussten demnach niemanden um die Kaiserkrone bitten, sie stand ihnen zu. Dem Papst fiel danach die Rolle des Koronators des Kaisers zu, der den krönen musste, der in Aachen den Karlsthron besessen hatte; die Krönung in Aachen designierte den Kaiser. Diese Vorstellung bestätigte Friedrich Barbarossa in einer vom 8. Januar 1166 auf der Grundlage eines vom Aachener Marienstift vorgelegten, gefälschten Privilegs Karls des Großen. In dem inserierten Karlsprivileg berichtet Pseudo-Karl, er habe auf einer Versammlung, der neben zahlreichen Großen des Reiches Papst Leo III. beiwohnte, die Zustimmung erreicht, dass "in ipsa sede [die Aachener Marienkirche, VC] reges, successores et heredes regni, initiarentur et sic initiati iure dehinc imperatoriam maiestatem Rome sine ulla interdictione planius assequerentur".[42] Die Heiligkeit des Stifters unabhängiger, kaiserlicher Macht wird in der kurz vor 1180 entstandenen Aachener Karlsvita begründet. Entscheidende Passagen entnahm der Autor jener Vita der *Historia Turpini*, die Karls des Großen im Auftrag des heiligen Jakobus durchgeführten Kämpfe gegen die in Spanien sitzenden Sarazenen schildert.[43] Die in der *Historia Turpini* erzählten Taten Karls waren für dessen Heiligkeit so bedeutend, dass einige Szenen aus diesem Text auf fünf der acht Dachreliefs des Aachener Karlsschreins abgebildet sind.[44] Doch der unter Friedrich Barbarossa kreierte Karlskult wurde schon von diesem selbst bald nicht mehr wahrgenommen[45] und spielte auch unter Heinrich VI. gegenüber der Rückbesinnung auf die Cäsaren allenfalls eine Nebenrolle, und während des Thronstreites zwischen Philipp von Schwaben und Otto IV. war die Bedeutung des heiligen Karl weitgehend geschwunden.[46] Ein neuer Impuls kam von Otto IV. nach der Überwindung Philipps. Zur Festigung seiner Position plante er an das staufische Erbe anzuknüpfen und auch den Karlskult wieder zu beleben. Im Zuge dessen soll er maßgeblichen Einfluss auf das Bildprogramm des seit den späten 1180er Jahren in Arbeit befindlichen Karlsschreins genommen haben. Die Auswahl der 16 an den Langseiten des Schreins dargestellten Könige und Kaiser sowie die Szenen der Dachreliefs sollen auf die Wünsche des Welfen zurückgehen.[47] Nur

---

[42] MGH DD Karolin. 1, Nr. 295, p. 442, ll. 29–31.
[43] Zu den Aspekten der Heiligkeit Karls siehe *Die Aachener Vita*, ed. Deutz und Deutz, pp. 45–54, ibid., pp. 55–276 auch ein Abdruck der *Vita* nach der Edition *Die Legende Karls des Großen im 11. und 12. Jahrhundert*, ed. Gerhard Rauschen (Leipzig, 1890). Zur *Historia Turpini* siehe *Die Chronik von Karl dem Großen und Roland*, ed. Hans-Wilhelm Klein (München, 1986) und demnächst Volker Caumanns, *Pseudo-Turpin und der heilige Karl – Die Anfänge einer neuen Karlstradition im 12. Jahrhundert* (Diss., Aachen, in Vorbereitung).
[44] Dies sind das Erscheinen des heiligen Jakobus und der Sternenstraße in Karls Traum (*Historia Turpini*, Kap. I), die Eroberung Pamplonas (Kap. II), das Wunder der blühenden Lanzen (Kap. VIII und X) und das Wunder der Kreuzzeichen (zwei Reliefs, Kap. XVI). Abbildungen finden sich z. B. in Ann Münchow und Herta Lepie, "Der konservierte Karlsschrein. Eine Bilddokumentation in Detailaufnahmen," in *Karl der Große und sein Schrein in Aachen*, ed. Hans Müllejans (Aachen, Mönchengladbach, 1988), pp. 56–123.
[45] Dazu demnächst Caumanns, *Pseudo-Turpin*.
[46] Siehe Robert Folz, *Le Souvenir et la légende de Charlemagne dans l'empire germanique médiévale* (Paris, 1950, repr. Geneva, 1973), pp. 251–72
[47] Bernd Ulrich Hucker, *Kaiser Otto IV.*, MGH Schriften 34 (Hannover, 1990), pp. 573–75, dagegen Stürner, *Friedrich II.*, 1:173, n. 96, Anm. 96

aufgrund dieser Initiative Ottos IV. habe dann Friedrich II. 1215 überhaupt aktiv an der Schreinschließung teilgenommen, weil er sich genötigt fühlte zur endgültigen Verdrängung des Kaisers den Karlsschrein samt dem ‚welfischen' Programm zu übernehmen, um sich so "auch auf ideeller Ebene wirksam gegen Otto IV. [zu] stellen".[48] Die Deutung des Bildprogramms am Karlsschrein als welfisch beeinflusst kann jedoch nicht überzeugen. Viel wahrscheinlicher ist, dass bei der Auswahl der dargestellten Herrscher die Aachener Stiftskanoniker federführend waren.[49] Davon unberührt bleibt, Otto IV. habe den Karlskult zu neuer Blüte führen wollen, um den Heiligen, wie es offenbar ursprünglich unter Barbarossa beabsichtigt war, zur Legitimierung eines von allen irdischen Einflüssen unabhängigen Kaisertums zu nutzen. Er mag daher tatsächlich die ins Stocken geratene Fertigstellung des Karlsschreins neu angetrieben haben.

Wie steht es aber mit Friedrich II.? Zweifellos war die auf Karl den Großen zurückgeführte Krönungstradition, die unabhängig von der Verehrung des heiligen Karl Bestand hatte, die entscheidende Motivation nach Aachen zu gehen.[50] Denn, obwohl er bereits seit 1212 *rex Romanorum* war, immerhin gekrönt vom Mainzer Erzbischof, also von einem der beiden traditionellen Koronatoren, konnte sich der junge Staufer nur nach einer Krönung in der Marienkirche Karls des Großen als rechtmäßiger Träger dieses Titels fühlen. Erst die Krönung in Aachen markierte seinen endgültigen Triumph in Deutschland und ebnete den Weg für das Weitere, die Krönung zum römischen Kaiser.[51] In Anbetracht dessen erscheint es als logische Ergänzung, wenn Friedrich II. mit der Schließung des goldenen Schreins des heiligen Kaisers zwei Tage nach seiner Krönung den unter seinem Großvater aufgebauten Karlskult übernahm und somit gleichsam vollendete, was dieser einst begonnen hatte.[52] Man kann dabei leicht in Karl dem Großen eine Vorbildfigur

---

[48] Hucker, *Kaiser*, p. 575.

[49] Zur Deutung der Herrscherfiguren am Karlsschrein siehe Max Kerner, *Karl der Große. Entschleierung eines Mythos* (Köln, Weimar, Wien, 2001), pp. 129–30 mit Literaturhinweisen pp. 137–38 und Kerstin Wiese, "Der Aachener Karlsschrein – Zeugnis lokalkirchlicher Selbstdarstellung," in *Karl der Große und das Erbe der Kulturen*, ed. Franz-Reiner Erkens (Berlin, 2001), pp. 257–67. Cf. auch Hermann Fillitz, "Die kunsthistorische Stellung des Karlsschreins," in *Der Schrein Karls des Großen*, ed. Domkapitel Aachen (Aachen, 1998), pp. 11–27, Hucker, *Kaiser*, pp. 573–76, und Jürgen Petersohn, "Kaisertum und Kultakt in der Stauferzeit," in *Politik und Heiligenverehrung im Hochmittelalter*, ed. ders., Vorträge und Forschungen 42 (Sigmaringen, 1994), pp. 101–46, hier p. 135, n. 162.

[50] Zur Bedeutung der Aachener Krönungstradition siehe Nikolaus Gussone, "Ritus, Recht und Geschichtsbewusstsein. Thron und Krone in der Tradition Karls des Großen," in *Krönungen. Könige in Aachen – Geschichte und Mythos. Katalog der Ausstellung*, 2 Bände, ed. Mario Kramp (Mainz, 2000), 1:35–47.

[51] Cf. die zeitgenössische Aussage bei Guillaume le Breton, *Gesta Philippi Augusti*, in *Oeuvres de Rigord et de Guillaume le Breton, historiens de Philippe Auguste*, 1, ed. Henri-François Delaborde (Paris, 1882), pp. 301–2, dazu auch Stürner, *Friedrich II*, 1:172.

[52] In diesem Sinne Schaller, "Kaiseridee," p. 117, Stürner, *Friedrich II*, 1:172–73, ders., "Kreuzzugsgelübde," p. 306, Klaus van Eickels, Tania Brüsch, *Kaiser Friedrich II. – Leben und Persönlichkeit in Quellen des Mittelalters* (Düsseldorf, Zürich, 2000), p. 85, und Hechelhammer, *Kreuzzug*, p. 32.

für Friedrich II. sehen, denn die Heiligkeit Karls wird in der Aachener Vita mit dessen göttlicher Auserwähltheit, die ihn zu einem Werkzeug Gottes machte, seiner Gerechtigkeit und Barmherzigkeit, seiner Großzügigkeit gegenüber den Armen, seiner Sorge um die Kirche und seinem Wirken in der Ausbreitung des Christentums begründet. Ähnlich sah sich Friedrich II. als von Gott geführt und in seine Herrschaft eingesetzt, auch er war engagiert in der Armenfürsorge und mit seiner Kreuznahme bekundete er, so könnte man sagen, auch bei der Verbreitung des christlichen Glaubens und der Heidenbekämpfung Karl nachahmen zu wollen. Die Vermutung drängt sich auf, der Staufer habe entscheidende Impulse für sein herrscherliches Handeln aus der Aachener Karlsvita und/oder der *Historia Turpini* geschöpft. Ob er allerdings einen der beiden Texte kannte, ist nicht erschließbar. Mit großer Wahrscheinlichkeit wurden ihm aber die für die Kanonisation wichtigsten Elemente von den Aachener Stiftsklerikern vermittelt. Jedenfalls ist es keine weit hergeholte Mutmaßung zu unterstellen, dass dem König der Charakter des Heiligen nahegebracht wurde, bevor er sich darangab, persönlich an der Schließung des Schreins mitzuwirken. Dies konnte auch ohne die entsprechenden Texte anhand des Bildprogramms der Dachreliefs geschehen, dessen Bezug zur *Historia Turpini*, und damit auf den vorbildlichen Heidenbekämpfer Karl, eindeutig ist.[53] Setzte sich Friedrich also durch die Hammerschläge, mit denen er den Karlsschrein schloss, und die Kreuznahme zwei Tage zuvor in diese Tradition? Dies muss man wohl eher verneinen, denn dieser Akt hatte anscheinend keinerlei Nachwirkung, weder für Aachen noch für Friedrich.[54] Die Erhebung der Gebeine an jenem Tag blieb die einzige ideologisch deutbare Bezugnahme Friedrichs II. auf Karl den Großen,[55] von einer auf die Herrschaft nachwirkenden Anknüpfung an einen Traditionsstrang kann demnach kaum die Rede sein.

Die Karlstradition lebte dagegen seit dem Ende des 12. Jahrhunderts in gewandelter Form in Frankreich unter König Philipp II. August auf. Durch seine Heirat mit Elisabeth von Hennegau 1180 war wieder karolingisches Blut in das französische Königshaus gekommen. Schon 1196 entwickelte der Mönch Andreas von Marchiennes auf der Grundlage genealogischer Arbeiten zu den Grafen von Hennegau und Flandern die Theorie vom *Reditus regni Francorum ad stirpem*

---

[53] Zweifel, ob die Dachreliefs des Schreins 1215 bereits fertig waren, äußert Renate Kroos, "Zum Aachener Karlsschrein. 'Abbild staufischen Kaisertums' oder 'fundatores ac dotatores'?" in *Karl der Große als vielberufener Vorfahr*, ed. Lieselotte E. Saurma-Jeltsch, Schriften des Historischen Museums 19 (Sigmaringen, 1994), pp. 49–61. Sie deutet an, die Reliefs könnten erst im Auftrag Friedrichs entstanden sein (ibid., pp. 56–57). Zur Datierung der Dachplatten siehe auch Fillitz, "Stellung," p. 22.

[54] Zu Aachen siehe Rauschen, *Legende*, p. 135, und Albert Sieger, "Probleme um die Kanonisierung Karls des Großen," *Zeitschrift des Aachener Geschichtsvereins* 104/105 (2002/2003), pp. 637–72, besonders pp. 650–51, dagegen August Brecher, "Die kirchliche Verehrung Karls des Großen," in *Karl der Große*, ed. Müllejans, pp. 151–66, hier p. 153. Zur Bedeutung der Schreinschließung für Friedrich Folz, *Souvenir*, pp. 284–86 und Kienast, *Deutschland*, p. 523.

[55] Giuseppe Ligato, "La crociata di Federico II e le chiavi di Gerusalemme," in *Il paese di cortesia: omaggio a Federico II nell'ottavo centenario della nascita* (Genua, 1994), pp. 46–61, besonders pp. 47–49, sieht in der Übergabe der Schlüssel der Stadt Jerusalem an Friedrich II. 1229 eine auf Karl den Großen zurückweisende Symbolhandlung.

Karoli, die darauf hinausläuft, dass mit Philipps und Elisabeths Sohn Ludwig VIII. nach sieben Kapetingern wieder ein Karolinger den Thron Frankreichs besteigen würde. Um 1200 legte dann der Kanoniker Aegidius von Paris dem jungen Ludwig VIII. unter dem Titel *Karolinus* einen Fürstenspiegel vor, in dem auch Philipps II. durch dessen Mutter Adele von Champagne ererbte karolingische Abstammung eigens betont wurde. Die so begründete Karlsnachfolge der französischen Könige fand bereits 1204 Anerkennung von höchster Stelle, als Innozenz III. in einem Schreiben an die Bischöfe Frankreichs Philipp II. einen König aus dem Geschlecht Karls des Großen nannte.[56] Beim Herrschaftsantritt Friedrichs II. 1212 im deutsch-römischen Reich war, modern gesprochen, aus Karl dem Großen bereits Charlemagne geworden; das französische Königtum beanspruchte das Karolingertum für sich. Freilich gedachte man auch im deutschsprachigen Raum weiterhin des großen Frankenkaisers. In der Dichtung war Karl in Friedrichs II. Tagen durchaus lebendig. Hier sind besonders der *Willehalm* Wolframs von Eschenbach und der *Karl* des Strickers zu nennen. Bei letzterem hat es seitens der Forschung sogar Versuche gegeben, ihn mit Friedrich II. in Verbindung zu setzen. Allerdings ist der Karl der deutschen Dichtung des 13. Jahrhunderts in der Regel ein Franzose.[57] Vielleicht also scheute Friedrich vor einer allzu deutlichen Anknüpfung an die Karlsverehrung seines Großvaters zurück, weil Philipp II. von Frankreich sich nun auf den Frankenkaiser als Urahn berief.[58] Der frisch gekrönte staufische König der Römer mochte fürchten, in eine ideelle Konkurrenzsituation mit seinem wichtigen französischen Verbündeten zu geraten. Eine solche Konkurrenzsituation zu riskieren, wäre aus Friedrichs II. Sicht vollkommen überflüssig gewesen, stand ihm doch eine viel ältere Legitimationsmöglichkeit offen, die die Berufung auf die Karolinger in den Schatten stellte, nämlich die Rückbesinnung auf die

---

[56] Zur karolingischen Tradition und der Bedeutung Karls des Großen unter Philipp II. August siehe Folz, *Souvenir*, pp. 277–79, Joachim Ehlers, "Kontinuität und Tradition als Grundlage mittelalterlicher Nationsbildung in Frankreich," in *Beiträge zur Bildung der französischen Nation im Früh- und Hochmittelalter*, ed. Helmut Beumann, Nationes 4 (Sigmaringen, 1983), pp. 15–47, hier pp. 27–32, und Robert Morrissey, *L'empereur à la barbe fleurie. Charlemagne dans la mythologie et l'histoire de France* (Paris, 1997; engl.: *Charlemagne and France* (Notre Dame, IN, 2003)), pp. 116–23. Zur Reditus-Theorie siehe Gabrielle M. Spiegel, "The reditus regni ad stirpem Karoli magni: a new look," *French Historical Studies* 7 (1971), pp. 145–74. Das Schreiben Innozenz' III. ist abgedruckt in *Die Register Innocenz' III.*, 7, unter Leitung von Othmar Hageneder bearbeitet von Andrea Sommerlechner (Wien, 1997), Nr. 43 (42), pp. 72–76, hier p. 73, ll. 30–31.

[57] Dazu Gerhart Lohse, "Das Nachleben Karls des Großen in der deutschen Literatur des Mittelalters," in *Karl der Große Lebenswerk und Nachleben*, 4, ed. Wolfgang Braunfels (Düsseldorf, 1967), pp. 337–47, hier pp. 340–43, und Karl-Ernst Geith, *Carolus Magnus. Studien zur Darstellung Karls des Großen in der deutschen Literatur des 12. und 13. Jahrhunderts*, Bibliotheca Germanica 19 (München, 1977), pp. 147–92.

[58] Einen Hinweis auf ein entsprechend vorhandenes Bewusstsein enthält der wohl zwischen 1217 und 1220 entstandene *Karl* des staufernahen Stricker; siehe Rüdiger Schnell, "Strickers 'Karl der Große'. Literarische Tradition und politische Wirklichkeit," *Zeitschrift für deutsche Philologie* 93 (1974), pp. 50–80 (repr. in *Die Reichsidee in der deutschen Literatur des Mittelalters*, ed. ders. (Darmstadt, 1983), pp. 315–53, hier p. 336).

antiken römischen Kaiser. Doch wie begründet sich dann seine aktive, persönliche Teilnahme an der Schließung des Karlsschreins?

Hier könnte man die Aachener Stiftskleriker ins Spiel bringen. Ihnen konnte die persönliche Teilnahme des neuen Königs an der Schreinschließung nur gelegen sein. Der Kult um den heiligen Karl war, wie schon angemerkt, zu Beginn des 13. Jahrhunderts nicht gerade prominent. Von der mit königlicher Beteiligung abgehaltenen Zeremonie in Anwesenheit zahlreicher Großer des Reiches mochten sich die Aachener Hoffnung auf eine weitere Verbreitung der Karlsverehrung machen. Daraus ließe sich folgern, dass Friedrich weniger an eine staufisch-karolingische Tradition anknüpfen wollte, als er den Schrein verschloss, sondern damit als Dank für die ihm letztlich erwiesene Treue auf einen speziellen Wunsch der Aachener reagierte. Gegen eine solche Interpretation spricht jedoch der Zeitpunkt der Schreinschließung. Wohl ohne sehr eingehende Vorbereitung als letzte von drei bedeutenden Handlungen an einem aus liturgischer Sicht banalen Montag vorgenommen, war der Akt nicht gerade herausragend terminiert. Den Aachenern hätte ein eigens angesetzter Festakt an einem Feiertag, optimalerweise am 29. Dezember, dem Tag der Heiligsprechung Karls des Großen, oder am 28. Januar, seinem Todestag, besser erscheinen müssen. Möglich bleibt dennoch, dass die Kanoniker des Marienstifts Friedrich II. erst auf den Karlskult und den diesen materiell zum Ausdruck bringenden, wenn nicht vollständig, so doch zumindest weitestgehend fertiggestellten Karlsschrein aufmerksam machten. Unwahrscheinlich ist dagegen, dass die Aachener für die feierliche Translation des heiligen Kaisers Montag, den 27. Juli, im Sinn hatten und vorschlugen. Dieser Termin geht auf Friedrich II. zurück.

Wie oben referiert, trieb Otto IV. wahrscheinlich die Fertigstellung des Karlsschreins voran, weil er sich den Kult des Frankenkaisers für seine Herrschaftslegitimation zu Nutze machen wollte. Um dies wirksam werden zu lassen, bedurfte es einer Aufsehen erregenden Inszenierung, die die Bindung des Kaisers an den heiligen Vorgänger aller Welt vor Augen geführt hätte. Hier ist der Gedanke sehr reizvoll, "daß an eine Reliquienerhebung am fünfzigsten Jahrestag der Kanonisation, Elevation und Translation von 1165, also am 29. Dezember 1215, gedacht war".[59] Mit der aktiven Teilnahme an der, dieser Deutung folgend, auf den 27. Juli vorgezogenen Schreinschließung hätte Friedrich II. demnach des Kaisers Platz eingenommen bei einem Akt, den der Welfe, von langer Hand geplant, als Demonstration der Rechtmäßigkeit seiner Herrschaft gedacht hatte. Und durch den Termin, den Jahrestag der militärischen Niederlage Ottos IV. bei Bouvines, verlieh Friedrich der Sache noch eine besondere Spitze. In diesem Licht besehen, wird aus Friedrichs II. "demütig-ehrerbietigem Bekenntnis zur staufisch-karolingischen

---

[59] Bernd Ulrich Hucker, "Otto IV., der kaiserliche Sohn Heinrichs des Löwen," in *Heinrich der Löwe und seine Zeit. Katalog der Ausstellung im Herzog Anton-Ulrich-Museum, Braunschweig 1995*, 2, ed. Jochen Luckhardt und Franz Niehoff (München, 1995), p. 364, in Anlehnung an Petersohn, "Kaisertum," pp. 134–35.

Vergangenheit"⁶⁰ die Demonstration seines persönlichen Sieges über Otto IV.⁶¹ Das Vorbild Karls des Großen, des Vorgängers aus ferner Vergangenheit, spielte also für die Kreuznahme Friedrichs II. keine Rolle.⁶² Wie aber steht es mit den jüngeren Vorbildern?

Einen Kreuzzug zu geloben gehörte zu Friedrichs II. Zeiten bereits zum Usus der deutsch-römischen Könige und Kaiser. Schon Heinrich IV. hatte um 1102/3 einen Kreuzzug gelobt (das Gelübde allerdings nicht eingelöst); Konrad III. war, bevor er König wurde, als Pilger in Jerusalem und führte gemeinsam mit dem Kapetinger Ludwig VII. den Kreuzzug von 1147–49; Friedrich I. zog zweimal, 1147 und 1190, gegen die Muslime im Osten, wobei er jedoch beim zweiten Mal bereits auf dem Hinweg tödlich verunglückte; Heinrich VI. starb kurz vor seinem Aufbruch ins Heilige Land; und auch Philipp von Schwaben hatte erste Schritte für einen Kreuzzug eingeleitet.⁶³ Es ist also naheliegend anzunehmen, dass Friedrich II. sich in der Pflicht sah, ebenso wie alle seine staufischen Vorfahren, einen Kreuzzug zu geloben. Eine solche Pflicht soll sich besonders aus dem gegebenen, aber wegen des plötzlichen Todes nicht eingelösten Kreuzzugsversprechen von Friedrichs II. Vater ergeben haben, weil "Kreuzzugsgelübde in die Erbmasse gehörten und Söhnen, Brüdern, Enkeln die moralische Pflicht auferlegten, sie aufzunehmen." Ersichtlich werde dies am Beispiel Ludwigs VII., der mit seinem Kreuzzug das unerfüllt gebliebene Gelübde seines Bruders Philipp einlösen wollte.⁶⁴ Neben dem nicht eingelösten Kreuzzugsgelübde Philipps, das Otto von Freising angibt, liegen im Falle Ludwigs VII. jedoch noch zwei andere mögliche Gründe für seine Kreuznahme vor: Sigebert von Gembloux und die *Historia Francorum* nennen die Sühne für die Zerstörung der Kirche in Vitry im Jahre 1143, bei der 1300 Menschen getötet worden sein sollen, die darin Zuflucht gesucht hatten, und verschiedene Zeitgenossen wissen von der tiefen Religiosität des Königs zu berichten, die ihn antrieb, auf den Fall der Grafschaft Edessa im Jahr 1144 zu reagieren.⁶⁵ Man muss freilich zugestehen, dass das in den *Gesta Friderici* berichtete Motiv vom nicht erfüllten brüderlichen Gelübde am ehesten Friedrich II. bekannt gewesen sein konnte. Fragwürdig bleibt dennoch, aus diesem, meines Wissens singulären Beispiel, eine Regel abzuleiten. Ebenso fragwürdig ist, ob Friedrich II. sich ausgerechnet von dem Handeln Ludwigs VII., angenommen es war ihm bekannt,

---

⁶⁰ Stürner, *Friedrich II.*, 1:173.

⁶¹ Hier wäre einzuwenden, Otto IV. hätte konsequenterweise vom Schrein entfernt werden müssen, was jedoch nicht geschah. Die Erklärung dafür liefern die Inschriftbögen mit den Herrschernamen. Sie entstammen alle derselben Herstellung, der Bogen mit dem Namen Friedrichs II. ist keine spätere Zufügung (Fillitz, "Stellung," p. 14). Die Inschriftbögen wurden also wahrscheinlich erst nach Friedrichs II. Aufenthalt in Aachen angebracht, so dass er an dem noch nicht erkennbaren Otto IV. gar keinen Anstoß nehmen konnte.

⁶² So auch Hiestand, "Friedrich II.," p. 130, dagegen etwa Abulafia, *Frederick*, pp. 120–21.

⁶³ Hiestand, "Friedrich II.," p. 129, und Hechelhammer, *Kreuzzug*, pp. 33–36.

⁶⁴ Hiestand, "Friedrich II.," pp.132–33.

⁶⁵ Siehe dazu Michael Horn, *Studien zur Geschichte Papst Eugens III. (1145–1153)*, Europäische Hochschulschriften, Reihe III, 508 (Frankfurt a. M., 1992), p. 106 mit n. 422 und n. 423 sowie *Historia francorum*, in RHGF, 12:116.

derart beeinflussen ließ. Aber auch wenn der Kapetinger als Vorbild ausfällt, steht weiterhin offen, der junge König habe, angesichts der oben erwähnten Reihe von Heinrich IV. bis Philipp von Schwaben, mit seinem Aachener Gelübde in die Fußstapfen seiner Ahnen treten wollen, glaubend dies würde sich für den Spross eines Geschlechts kreuzfahrender Herrscher ziemen. Einen dahingehenden Ansatz vertretend spricht Bodo Hechelhammer bezüglich Friedrichs II. Kreuznahme von einer "verpflichtenden Handlung im Angedenken." Damit wird ausdrücklich das Bewusstsein der betreffenden Herrscher unterstellt, eine mit Heinrich IV. beginnende Tradition aufzunehmen. Für ein solches Bewusstsein liegen jedoch keine Belege vor.[66]

Gegen die Annahme, die Kreuznahme sei für Friedrich II. die Erfüllung einer verwandtschaftlichen Verpflichtung gewesen, spricht auch der Befund, dass in seinen Briefen und Manifesten sich nie ein Bezug auf seine Vorfahren findet, wenn vom Kreuzzug die Rede ist. Die beiden einzigen mir bekannten Hinweise auf eines der Vorbilder bezüglich des Kreuzzugs stammen von dem norditalienischen Moralisten Thomasin von Zirclaria und von Papst Honorius III. Thomasin erinnert in seinem 1215/16 entstandenen ethischen Lehrgedicht *Der Welsche Gast* an Friedrich Barbarossa und Heinrich VI., die beide ihre Kreuzzugsgelübde nicht zu vollenden vermochten, und äußert die Überzeugung, der dritte Staufer, Friedrich II., werde das von seinen beiden Vorgängern begonnene zu Ende führen:

> Ich weiz ir zwên ûz dîner slaht | die da vurn mit grôzer maht. | einer was der kaiser Friderich, | der ander der was sicherlîch | dîn veter: du solt der drite | wesen der in volge mite. | der keiser von ungeschiht | volkom über mer niht, | dîn veter volkom dar | und moht ez niht voltuon gar. | du bist der dritte und solt volkomen | und voltuon. ich hân vernomen | daz an der dritten zal ist | ervollunge zaller vrist.[67]

Honorius III. äußerte sich über drei Jahre später in sehr ähnlicher Weise als er am 1. Oktober 1219 mahnend an Friedrich schrieb:

> Certe clare memorie avus tuus Fredericus ad id se viribus totis accinxit, et quis scit, si et tu Fredericus, nepos ipsius, illius memoriam non solum presentibus renovabis in nomine, sed etiam ad posteros prorogabis in opere, si quod ille ferventer in affectu assumpserat, tu salubriter produxeris ad effectum.[68]

Diese beiden Äußerungen zeigen zwar, dass die Erinnerung an Friedrich Barbarossa wach war und mancher vielleicht in dem neuen Träger des Namens tatsächlich

---

[66] Hechelhammer, *Kreuzzug*, pp. 33–36. Er nennt lediglich die einzelnen Kreuznahmen in ihrer Abfolge. Die gewünschten Belege finden sich auch nicht in dem ibid, n. 66 angeführten Aufsatz von Rudolf Hiestand.

[67] *Der Wälsche Gast des Thomasin von Zirclaria*, v. 11797–810, ed. Heinrich Rückert (Leipzig, 1852; repr. Berlin, 1965). Cf. dazu Elizabeth Siberry, *Criticism of Crusading, 1095–1274* (Oxford, 1985), p. 65.

[68] MGH Epist. saec. XIII, 1, Nr. 106, p. 76, ll. 13–17.

einen Fortsetzer, Vollender oder Erneuerer der insgesamt erfolgreichen Herrschaft Friedrichs I. sah. Eine Anspielung auf eine gleichsam rechtliche Verpflichtung lässt sich jedoch weder bei Thomasin herauslesen – er zielt ja eindeutig auf die Erfüllung auf Grund der Dreizahl ab – noch bei Honorius, der es wohl kaum unterlassen hätte, eine sich aus dem unerfüllten Gelübde des Großvaters ableitende Verpflichtung zu erwähnen.[69] Friedrich II. haben solcherlei Anspielungen auf seinen Vorfahr, zumindest die des Papstes war ihm ja bekannt, anscheinend unbeeindruckt gelassen, denn er gedenkt nirgendwo der Einsätze seiner Ahnen für das Heilige Land.[70] So fällt es schwer zu glauben, er habe eine verwandtschaftliche Verpflichtung zum Kreuzzug empfunden.

Was vielmehr als Erbe von staufischer Seite von Friedrich II. übernommen worden scheint, ist die – über das persönlich-verwandtschaftliche Verhältnis hinausreichende – Vorstellung seines Vaters von der Universalität der kaiserlichen Herrschaft, die dieser offenbar anstrebte und aufgrund seines frühen Todes nicht verwirklichen konnte.[71] Dazu fügen sich sehr passend die Ambitionen von Friedrichs normannischen Vorfahren, die ebenfalls bestrebt waren, ihrer Herrschaft einen größeren Radius zu verleihen. Roger II. gelang es in Nordafrika Fuß zu fassen und er versuchte, jedoch mit weniger Erfolg, auch im östlichen Mittelmeerraum seinen Einfluss auf Kosten von Byzanz zu erweitern. Letzteres setzte Wilhelm II., nach dem Verlust der nordafrikanischen Kolonien, unter modifizierten Vorzeichen fort. Anders als sein Vater empfahl sich Wilhelm II. als guter christlicher Herrscher, indem er sich in der Rolle eines Beschützers der Christen im Nahen Osten übte. Nach der Niederlage des christlichen Heeres bei Hattin und der Eroberung Jerusalems 1187 durch Saladin reagierte Wilhelm II. als erster aus dem Westen auf die Hilferufe zur Unterstützung der bedrängten Kreuzfahrerstaaten.[72] Wollte er mit seiner raschen Reaktion die Chance nutzen, sich beim Papst als wichtige Kraft

---

[69] Ein Vorbild dafür hätte die Aufforderung Innozenz' III. an den Bruder des ungarischen Königs sein können, das von seinem Vater ererbte Kreuzzugsgelübde zu erfüllen. Siehe dazu Ursula Schwerin, *Die Aufrufe der Päpste zur Befreiung des Heiligen Landes von den Anfängen bis zum Ausgang Innozenz IV.*, Historische Studien 301 (Berlin, 1937; repr. Vaduz, 1965), p. 94.

[70] Die Äußerung Friedrichs II. in dessen Brief an Honorius III. vom Januar 1219, seine Kreuznahme sei Ausdruck der Dankbarkeit für die göttliche Barmherzigkeit, die ihn "*ad avitum nos regnum et imperium ... sublimavit*" (*Historia diplomatica Friderici secundi sive constitutiones, privilegia, mandata, instrumenta quae supersunt istius imperatoris et filiorum ejus. Accedunt epistolae paparum et documenta varia*, 6 Bände, ed. Jean Louis Alphonse Huillard-Bréholles (Paris, 1852), 1:585), als Beleg für das Aufgreifen der Kreuzzugspläne des Großvaters zu interpretieren (so Hechelhammer, *Kreuzzug*, p. 39, n. 90) scheint mir übertragen (cf. Hiestand, "Friedrich II.," pp. 130–31 mit n. 11).

[71] Zur Vorstellung der Universalität des Kaisertums siehe Hermann Jakobs, "Weltherrschaft oder Endkaiser? – Ziele staufischer Politik im ausgehenden 12. Jahrhundert," in *Die Staufer im Süden*, ed. Theo Kölzer (Sigmaringen, 1996), pp. 13–28, hier pp. 23–26. Auch Hechelhammer, *Kreuzzug*, p. 33 verweist auf die sich "weiterentwickelnde Kaiseridee," die jedoch als rein verwoben mit dem Aspekt der "Handlung im Angedenken" ansieht.

[72] Zu den Aktivitäten der Hauteville im Mittelmeerraum siehe Helene Wieruszowski, "The Norman Kingdom of Sicily and the Crusades," in Setton, *Crusades*, 2:2–43, besonders pp. 7–15 und 33–40. Zur "Mittelmeerpolitik" Rogers II. siehe Hubert Houben, *Roger II. von Sizilien* (Darmstadt, 1997; engl.: Cambridge, 2002), pp. 80–91.

für das Heilige Land zu empfehlen, um aus dieser Position besser gegen Byzanz vorgehen zu können? Hatte er gar, eingedenk der einst verabredeten Nachfolge Rogers II. als König von Jerusalem, die Hoffnung gehegt sich durch seine tatkräftige Hilfe den Baronen Outremers als neuer König zu empfehlen? Steht Friedrichs II. Kreuzzugsgelübde in dieser normannischen Tradition des Engagements im Osten? Eine bessere Grundlage als seine normannischen Vorfahren hatte er, da ihm als Kaiser die Könige von Zypern sowie die Fürstentümer Armenien und Antiochia, letzteres zusammen mit der Grafschaft Tripolis, lehnspflichtig waren.[73] Vielleicht war deshalb die Kaiserkrönung Voraussetzung für den Aufbruch ins Heilige Land. Denn nur als Kaiser konnte Friedrich die Angelegenheiten auf Zypern in seinem Sinne ordnen.

Unter dem Aspekt familiärer Tradition gesehen ist also Friedrichs II. Kreuznahme die Erneuerung des Anspruchs seiner staufischen wie normannischen Vorfahren auf Einfluss im östlichen Mittelmeerraum. Allerdings spielt das familiäre, dynastische Erbe dabei eher eine untergeordnete Rolle, denn dieser Anspruch wird vor allem getragen durch die überkommenen Elemente der so genannten ‚staufischen Kaiseridee', die unter Friedrich II. in eigener Weise ausgeformt wurde.

Herrschaftsauffassung

Hans Martin Schaller fasst die Kaiseridee Friedrichs II. in zwölf Artikeln zusammen. Darin tauchen drei Elemente der schon unter dessen Großvater und Vater ausgebildeten Kaiseridee leicht abgewandelt wieder auf: der Anspruch auf Führerschaft der Christenheit und auf universale Herrschaft sowie der unter Heinrich VI. hinzugekommene "eschatologisch gefärbte Weltkaiser-Gedanke".[74] Allerdings sind sie großenteils aus der Zeit nach der Rückkehr Friedrichs II. aus dem Heiligen Land nachgewiesen. Das bedeutet, es ist noch zu prüfen, ob sie schon vor 1229 für Friedrich relevant waren, und inwieweit dies sein Kreuzzugsengagement beeinflusst haben könnte.

Den Krönungsordines des 13. Jahrhunderts folgend, hatte Friedrich II. bei seiner Kaiserkrönung im November 1220 zu schwören, als *protector* und *defensor* Besitz, Ehre und Rechte von Papst und Kirche in all ihren Belangen zu schützen und zu bewahren.[75] Die Äußerungen in seinen Briefen über die mit dem 'Kaiseramt' verbundenen kirchlichen Pflichten zeigen, dass Friedrich diese Rolle durchaus auszufüllen gedachte.[76] Des Öfteren bezeichnete er sich als Verteidiger der Kirche. Neben den Bezeichnungen *defensor* und *protector* ist dabei der Begriff *advocatus Romanae ecclesiae* oder auch *advocatus apostolica sedes* von Bedeutung. Von Seiten

---

[73] Hiestand, "Friedrich II.," p. 140.
[74] Schaller, "Kaiseridee," pp. 112–14.
[75] MGH fontes iuris N.S., 9, Nr. XVII, p. 63, ll. 3–6 und ibid., Nr. XVIII, p. 73, ll. 11–14.
[76] Siehe beispielsweise die verschiedenen Auszüge in den Anmerkungen in Vehse, *Propaganda*, pp. 6–7.

der Päpste wurde damit traditionell eine dienende Funktion, eine Verpflichtung des Kaisers gegenüber der Kirche verbunden. In diesem Sinne äußerte sich Innozenz III. mit weitreichender Wirkung in der Dekretale *Venerabilem*.[77] Entsprechend dieser kurialen Deutung sind Belege für den Verweis auf die *advocatia* auf kaiserlicher Seite vor Friedrich II. rar. Erst er begann die *advocatia* für seine Zwecke fruchtbar zu machen, indem er sie als Argument benutzte, um vom Papst und aus dem *patrimonium Petri* Unterstützung zu fordern. Denn er könne seinen Pflichten als *advocatus* nur nachkommen, wenn ihm auch die päpstlichen Mittel zur Verfügung stünden.[78] Die *advocatia* beinhaltete also aus Friedrichs Sicht nicht nur Verpflichtungen des Kaisers gegenüber der Kirche, sondern auch solche des Papstes gegenüber dem Kaiser. Daher fühlte sich Friedrich auch berechtigt Honorius III. zu tadeln, dieser sei seinen Verpflichtungen in der Kreuzzugswerbung nicht in ausreichendem Maße nachgekommen.[79] Anhand der Ketzerbekämpfung Friedrichs II. zwischen 1220 und 1225 in Norditalien lässt sich gut beobachten, wie er seine Pflichten als *defensor ecclesiae* einsetzt, um den Reichsrechten gegenüber den lombardischen Städten wieder Geltung zu verschaffen, indem er die kirchlichen Machtmittel für kaiserliche Interessen nutzbar macht.[80] Dies war für Friedrich insofern gerechtfertigt, als Papst und Kaiser eine Einheit an der Spitze der Christenheit bildeten und zu gemeinsamem Handeln bestimmt waren, und deshalb eben auch der Kaiser ein Recht auf die päpstliche Unterstützung hatte. Eine solche Einheit der beiden obersten Gewalten der Christenheit konnte Friedrich im Werk Ottos von Freising kennengelernt haben. Dieser entwickelte die Anschauung einer *civitas permixta*, in der *regnum* und *sacerdotium* als eine Einheit die *ecclesia Dei* bilden.[81] Wenn Friedrich II. nicht schon als Heranwachsender in Sizilien die Schriften seines Urgroßonkels gelesen hatte, so werden sie ihm spätestens im Zuge seines Aufenthaltes in Deutschland bekannt geworden sein. Denn sowohl Ottos Chronik als auch die *Gesta Friderici* waren höchst wahrscheinlich in der Bibliothek der Pfalz Hagenau vorhanden.[82] Damit stand für Friedrich II. spätestens seit 1213 die Gelegenheit offen, diese Werke wahrzunehmen. Es ist jedenfalls keineswegs unwahrscheinlich, dass schon 1215 Friedrich die Auslegung der Zwei-Gewalten-

---

[77] *Regestum Innocentii III papae super negotio Romani imperii* (künftig *RNI*), ed. Friedrich Kempf (Rome, 1947), Nr. 62, p. 172, ll. 13–16. Cf. dazu Werner Goez, "Imperator advocatus Romanae ecclesiae," in *Aus Kirche und Reich. Festschrift für Friedrich Kempf*, ed. Hubert Mordek (Sigmaringen, 1983), pp. 314–28, hier pp. 325–26.

[78] Goez, "Imperator," pp. 323–27.

[79] Brief Friedrichs II. an Honorius III. vom 5. März 1224 in *Acta Imperii*, 1, Nr. 261, hier p. 239, ll. 10–16.

[80] Selge, "Ketzerpolitik," pp. 319–24.

[81] Goetz, *Geschichtsbild*, pp. 204–5, 249–50, 254–64 und 285, sowie Walter Lammers, "Ein universales Geschichtsbild der Stauferzeit in Miniaturen. Der Bilderkreis zur Chronik Ottos von Freising im Jenenser Codex Bose q. 6," in *Alteuropa und die moderne Gesellschaft. Festschrift für Otto Brunner*, ed. Historisches Seminar der Universität Hamburg (Göttingen, 1963), pp. 170–214, hier pp. 212–13.

[82] Franz-Josef Schmale, "Die Gesta Friderici I. imperatoris Ottos von Freising und Rahewins," *Deutsches Archiv* 19 (1963), pp. 168–214, hier pp. 175–76.

Lehre Ottos von Freising im Sinne der *civitas permixta* bekannt und das sich im Laufe seiner Herrschaft zeigende Verständnis seiner *advocatia* vorhanden war. Die Kreuznahme wäre somit eine demonstrative Bekundung der bewussten Übernahme quasi amtlicher Pflichten, nämlich als *rex Romanorum* – oder, wie der Papst ihn nannte, *Romanorum imperator electus*[83] – Schutzherr aller Christen zu sein, und zugleich die Wahrnehmung seiner Rolle als weltlicher Arm innerhalb der Einheit der *civitas permixta*, als der er das von seinem geistlichen Konterpart ausgerufene Unternehmen im Sinne der *concordia* selbstverständlich mit zu tragen hatte.[84]

Diese Rolle konnte nur voll ausgefüllt werden, wenn der kaiserliche Arm eine entsprechende Reichweite hatte. So war mit dem Kaisertum der Gedanke der universalen und hegemonialen Herrschaft verknüpft, der bedeutete, die oberste weltliche Führerschaft innerhalb der *christianitas* inne zu haben.[85] Auf der Grundlage der Bemühungen Konrads III. und Friedrichs I. konnte Heinrich VI. dieses Ideal auf einen neuen Höhepunkt führen. Er vermochte den Anspruch seines Vaters, der bedeutendste unter den christlichen Herrschern zu sein, auszubauen, insbesondere durch die Vereinigung des Reiches mit Sizilien und der lehnsrechtlichen Unterwerfung Zyperns und Armeniens. Wie es mit der Machtausbreitung Heinrichs VI. weiter gegangen wäre, wenn der Tod ihn nicht bereits in jungen Jahren ereilt hätte, lässt sich freilich nicht sagen. Aber mancher Historiker neigt dazu, ihm eine große Zukunft zuzuschreiben, wäre seine Gesundheit besser gewesen.[86] Der hoffnungsvolle Zustand, den Heinrich VI. um 1196 erreicht hatte, wurde in eindrucksvoller Weise literarisch überhöht durch den Kleriker Petrus von Eboli, der 1195/97 den so genannten *Liber ad honorem Augusti* zu Ehren Heinrichs VI. und der Kaiserin Konstanze verfasste. In den ersten beiden Büchern schildert Petrus die Geschichte des Königreichs Sizilien unter Roger II. und dessen Tochter Konstanze bis zur Geburt Friedrichs II. Dabei ist neben Konstanze die zweite Hauptfigur ihr Gatte Kaiser Heinrich VI., von dem die Kaiserkrönung, die Gefangennahme des englischen Königs Richard Löwenherz sowie vor allem die Inbesitznahme des sizilischen Königreiches geschildert werden. Diesen beiden Büchern wurde ein drittes hinzugefügt, wohl auf Betreiben des Kanzlers Heinrichs VI., Konrad

---

[83] Zu diesen Titeln siehe Gerhard Baaken, *Ius imperii ad regnum. Königreich Sizilien, Imperium Romanum und Römisches Papsttum vom Tode Kaiser Heinrichs VI. bis zu den Verzichterklärungen Rudolfs von Habsburg*, Forschungen zur Kaiser- und Papstgeschichte 11 (Köln, Weimar, Wien, 1993), p. 207.

[84] Ein solches Verständnis zeigt sich z. B. in Friedrichs Brief an Gregor IX vom 3. Dezember 1232 (*Historia diplomatica*, 4:409).

[85] Othmar Hageneder, "Weltherrschaft im Mittelalter," *Mitteilungen des Instituts für österreichische Geschichtsforschung* 93 (1985), pp. 257–78; cf. Hans Joachim Kirfel, *Weltherrschaftsidee und Bündnispolitik*, Bonner historische Forschungen 12 (Bonn, 1959), pp. 82–86. Zum *christianitas*-Begriff siehe Jakobs, "Weltherrschaft," p. 14, und Helmut Roscher, *Papst Innozenz III. und die Kreuzzüge* (Göttingen, 1969), pp. 20–27.

[86] So etwa Steven Runciman, *A History of the Crusades*, 3 vols. (Cambridge, 1951–54), 3:108–9, und Stürner, *Friedrich II*, 1:65–66. Eine entsprechende zeitgenössische Äusserung findet sich in der Chronik Ottos von Sankt Blasien, MGH SS rer. Germ. in us. sch. 47, p. 71, ll. 3–6 und 11–13.

von Querfurt, das vornehmlich ein Panegyrikus auf den Kaiser, aber auch auf dessen unlängst geborenen Sohn Friedrich ist.[87] Die mit zahlreichen Abbildungen illustrierte Handschrift – das einzige, aber wahrscheinlich originale Exemplar des Werks – blieb nach dem Tode Heinrichs VI. möglicherweise im Besitz Friedrichs II. Gerade wegen der Bebilderung wäre das Buch für die Erzieher in Palermo gut geeignet gewesen, um dem kleinen Friedrich die Geschichte seiner Eltern zu vermitteln. Dass dieser das Werk kannte, legt Petrus von Eboli in der Widmung seines für Friedrich verfassten Gedichts über die Bäder von Pozzuoli nahe.[88]

Für den hier betrachteten Zusammenhang sind die Lobeshymnen auf Heinrich VI. und seinen Sohn im dritten Buch des *Liber ad honorem Augusti* entscheidend, die an die Herrschaft Friedrichs hohe Erwartungen knüpfen. Ähnlich wie die Friedensherrschaft des antiken Oktavian Augustus in der christlichen Ausdeutung das Erscheinen Christi vorbereitete,[89] wird mit dem gerade geborenen Friedrich II. das Kommen eines neuen Friedensreiches gesehen.[90] Petrus feiert den kleinen Friedrich als künftigen Herrscher einer neuen Ära des Friedens und setzt die Erwartung seiner Geburt parallel zu der Erwartung der Wiederkunft Christi. Den Grundstein für diese Friedensherrschaft würde Heinrich VI. legen, dessen Lebensleistungen – die schon vollbrachten, wie die noch erwarteten – in der Auslegung seines Namens programmatisch festgehalten werden:

Cumque triumphator nudis iam parceret armis, | Nascitur Augusto, qui regat arma, puer. | Felix namque pater, set erit felicior infans: | Hic puer ex omni parte beatus erit. | Nam pater ad totum victrici cuspide partes | Ducet et inperium stare, quod ante dabit. | … O votive puer, renovandi temporis etas, | Exhinc Rogerius, hinc Fredericus eris, | Major habendus avis, fato meliore creatus, | Qui bene vix natus cum patre vincis avos! | Pax oritur tecum, quia, te nascente, creamur; | Te nascente, sumus, quod pia vota petunt; …

*H*ic princeps, ut habet Danielis nobile scriptum, | *E*xaltabit avos, subigens sibi victor Egyptum. | *N*omen in herede patria virtute quiescet. | *R*omani iuris duplici rogus igne calescet. | *I*mperii formam templique reducetad hastra. | *C*um non hostis erit, sua ponet cum Iove castra. | *V*icerit ut mundum, Syon, David arce, reduempta, | *S*iciliam repetens, Rome reget aurea sceptra.[91]

---

[87] Marlis Stähli, "Liber ad honorem Augusti sive de rebus Siculis – die Bilderchronik des Petrus von Ebulo, Cod. 120 II der Burgerbibliothek Bern, als Spiegel der Unio regni ad imperium," in *Die Staufer im Süden*, ed. Kölzer, pp. 211–20.

[88] Petrus de Ebulo, *Liber ad honorem Augusti sive de rebus Siculis*, ed. Theo Kölzer und Marlis Stähli (Sigmaringen, 1994), p. 266, der Text ist abgedruckt in Michael Hanly, "An Edition of Richart Eude's French Translation of Pietro da Eboli's *De balneis puteolanis*," *Traditio* 51 (1996) pp. 232–54, hier p. 252, ll. 2–9.

[89] Jürgen Strothmann, "Christus, Augustus und der mittelalterliche römische Kaiser in der staufischen Herrschaftstheologie," *Archiv für Kulturgeschichte* 84 (2002), pp. 41–65, hier pp. 43–46 und 51–52.

[90] Dies ist eine bemerkenswerte Parallele zu den *Gesta Friderici* Ottos von Freising, der mit Friedrich Barbarossa eine neue, bessere Zeit heraufbrechen sah, cf. Goetz, *Geschichtsbild*, pp. 275–77.

[91] Zitate in Petrus de Ebulo, *Liber*, p. 205, ll. 1369–74, 1377–82 und p. 217, ll. 1463–70 (jeweils mit deutscher Übersetzung), dazu Strothmann, "Christus," p. 55. Die deutsche Übersetzung der Stelle "*Cumque … dabit*" und deren Interpretation durch Strothmann, Heinrich hatte die Waffen bei Geburt

Die Erwartungen an Heinrich VI. konnten aufgrund seines frühen Todes nicht erfüllt werden, der Sieg über "Ägypten" und die volle Wiederherstellung des alten römischen Reichs blieben aus. Darüber hinaus wurde die schon gelungene Vereinigung des Kaiserreichs mit Sizilien im Zuge des Thronstreits zwischen Otto IV. und Philipp von Schwaben wieder aufgehoben. Mit der von Papst Innozenz III. unterstützten Wahl Friedrichs II. zum *rex Romanorum* jedoch dürfte bei manchem Anhänger der Staufer Hoffnung auf eine Erneuerung der von Heinrich VI. erreichten Machtfülle aufgekeimt sein. Und auch in Friedrich selbst mag schon dies die Ahnung, wenn nicht gar die Überzeugung geweckt haben, zur Wiederherstellung und Vervollkommnung der alten Kaisermacht berufen zu sein. Durchaus kann Friedrichs II. Handeln vor dem Hintergrund der Verheißungen im *Liber ad honorem Augusti* so gedeutet werden, dass er zunächst die Grundlage für das ihm durch Petrus von Eboli prophezeite Friedensreich wiederherstellen, also das deutsch-römische Reich zurückgewinnen und es wieder mit Sizilien verbinden, die Kaiserwürde erlangen und schließlich "Ägypten" besiegen, sprich das Heilige Land vollständig in christliche Hände bringen wollte, um dann tatsächlich jene neue Ära des Friedens unter seiner, dem antiken Augustus gleichen, universalen Herrschaft einzuleiten.[92] Und tatsächlich begann ab 1230, die genannten Ziele waren nun (weitgehend) erreicht, eine Art Konsolidierungsphase für Friedrich II., besiegelt durch den Friedensschluss mit Papst Gregor IX., eingeleitet aber durch den Erfolg des Kreuzzugs.[93] Dessen abschließenden Höhepunkt bildete das "Gehen unter der Krone" in der Jerusalemer Grabeskirche. Mit diesem Akt demonstrierte Friedrich seine Herrschaft über die zentrale Stätte der Christenheit und wähnte nun, seinem Bericht an König Heinrich III. von England zufolge, eine neue Zeit des Heils nahe:

… sequenti die coronam portavimus, quam Dominus omnipotens de throno maiestatis sue nos habendam previdens … . Et cum miserationes eius super omnia opera sint eiusdem, cognoscant orthodoxe fidei cultores de cetero et enarrent longe lateque per orbem, quod

---

Friedrichs bereits abgelegt und sollte Friedrich sie aufnehmen, um mit Hilfe des die Lanze führenden *pater*, nach Strothmann Gottvater, die Eroberungen zu vollenden, widersprechen dem Konzept des Textes. Denn Friedrich soll ein Friedensherrscher sein. Zudem ist Heinrichs Sieg über "Ägypten" eine Zukunftserwartung, sein Kreuzzug war erst in Vorbereitung. Petrus widerspräche sich, behauptete er, Heinrich habe bereits die Waffen endgültig abgelegt. Das konjunktivische *parceret* ist also als Konjunktiv zu lesen und *qui regat arma* auf *Augusto* statt auf *puer* zu beziehen. Es ist der *pater* Heinrich, der "mit siegreicher Lanze" das römische Reich erneuern wird.

[92] Ein literarischer Widerschein einer entsprechenden Planung scheint im *Karl* des Strickers vorzuliegen, wo eine solche Abfolge den Eroberungen Karls des Großen zugeschrieben wird, siehe *Karl der Große von dem Stricker*, v. 332–37, 355–58, 450–53 und 469–70, ed. Karl Bartsch (Berlin, 1965), cf. dazu Schnell, "Stricker," pp. 329–30.

[93] Von einem Wendepunkt spricht im Zusammenhang mit dem Kreuzzug schon Kantorowicz, *Friedrich II.*, p. 195. Dem stimmt sogar Albert Brackmann, "Kaiser Friedrich II. in 'mythischer Schau'," *Historische Zeitschrift* 140 (1929), pp. 534–49 (repr. in *Stupor Mundi*, ed. Wolf, 1. Aufl. (Darmstadt, 1966), pp. 5–22, hier p. 7) zu. Ähnlich äußert sich auch Stürner, "Kaiser," p. 17.

ille qui est benedictus in secula visitavit et fecit redemptionem plebi sue et erexit nobis cornu salutis in domo David pueri sui.[94]

Wohlgemerkt ist Friedrich II. damit nicht als neuer David bezeichnet,[95] sondern als Wegbereiter Christi, wie Johannes der Täufer oder eben Oktavian Augustus.[96] Allerdings haben Friedrichs Zeitgenossen ihn und die Staufer insgesamt in eine David-Nachfolge gestellt. Das wahrscheinlich Ende August 1229 vollendete Kanzelrelief in der Kathedrale von Bitonto[97] könnte der bildliche Ausdruck dafür sein, dass die von Friedrich geforderte Verkündung der Aufrichtung des Horns des Heils tatsächlich erfolgte, interpretiert allerdings im Sinne der David-Nachfolge. Das Relief zeigt vier Figuren,[98] links ein König auf einem Thron sitzend, mit einer Krone auf dem Kopf und einem Zepter in der Hand, der drei rechts von ihm stehenden Männern zugewandt ist. Der Erste der drei, nicht bekrönt, deutet mit seiner Hand auf den sitzenden König.[99] Der zweite Stehende ist durch seine insgesamt etwas aufwendiger gestaltete Kleidung und besonders durch eine prächtige Krone von den anderen abgehoben. Der dritte ist in seinem Aussehen ähnlich dem ersten Stehenden dargestellt, nur mit dem Unterschied, dass er eine Kappenkrone trägt. Der Sitzende ist König David, der auf seine jüngsten Nachfolger blickt, nämlich Friedrich II., umgeben von seinen beiden Söhnen; links von ihm, auf David zeigend, Konrad IV., der seinem Vater als König von Jerusalem nachfolgen wird, und rechts von ihm Heinrich (VII.), der Erbe der Kaiserkrone und des Königreichs Sizilien.[100]

---

[94] MGH Const. 2, Nr. 122, p. 166, ll. 21–36. Zu der nicht ganz zweifelsfreien Überlieferung der englischen Version des Jerusalem-Manifests, der das Zitat entstammt, siehe Kluger, *Hochmeister*, pp. 119–21.

[95] So die Deutung beispielsweise in Abulafia, *Frederick*, p. 188, und Schaller, "Kaiseridee," p. 118.

[96] Die Stelle "*visitavit ... sui*" ist bekanntermaßen ein Zitat der Weissagung des Zacharias zum Werdegang seines Sohnes, Johannes des Täufers (Luk. 1.68–69), wo es weiter heißt: "praeibis enim ante faciem Domini parare vias eius, ad dandam scientiam salutis plebi eius" (Luk. 1.76–77). Die Übersetzung der Stelle in *Kaiser*, ed. und trans. Heinisch, p. 178 (wiederabgedruckt in van Eickels, Brüsch, *Kaiser*, p. 193): "... und Uns als Horn des Heils im Hause seines Vaters David errichtet hat [Hervorhebung von mir]," ist abwegig und irreführend.

[97] Zur Datierung des Reliefs siehe Roswitha Neu-Kock, "Das Kanzelrelief in der Kathedrale von Bitonto," *Archiv für Kulturgeschichte* 60 (1978), pp. 253–67, besonders p. 257. Die Datierung auf 1229 setzt voraus, dass das Relief von Beginn an Bestandteil der Kanzel war. Eine spätere Zufügung des Reliefs ist jedoch nicht vollkommen auszuschließen, cf. Stürner, *Friedrich II.*, 2:178, n. 19.

[98] Ich folge der Beschreibung und der Deutung in Neu-Kock, "Kanzelrelief," bes. pp. 254–55 und 262–63.

[99] Hans Martin Schaller, "Das Relief an der Kanzel der Kathedrale von Bitonto," *Archiv für Kulturgeschichte* 45 (1963), pp. 295–12 (repr. in *Stupor Mundi*, ed. Wolf, 1. Aufl. (Darmstadt, 1966), pp. 591–616, in ibid., 2. Aufl. (Darmstadt, 1982), pp. 299–324, und in Schaller, *Stauferzeit*, 1–23) hier p. 305 deutet die offene Hand als Übernahme des Szepters von dem sitzenden König. Dagegen wendet sich Neu-Kock, "Kanzelrelief," p. 261, sie deutet die offene Hand als Huldigungsgestus (ibid., p. 263).

[100] Zur Tradition der Darstellung des Herrschers mit seinen beiden Söhnen oder Mitherrschern siehe die Verweise auf spätantike Beispiele in Frank Kolb, *Herrscherideologie in der Spätantike* (Berlin, 2001), pp. 200–201 und 220–49, und die mittelalterlichen Beispiele in Neu-Kock, "Kanzelrelief," p. 262.

Das Relief könnte in Zusammenhang mit einer Predigt stehen, die der Abt und Diakon Nikolaus von Bari zum Lobpreis Friedrichs II. verfasste. Denn Nikolaus identifiziert die Staufer mit dem Haus Davids und spricht Friedrich II. zweimal als David an.[101] Wenn allerdings ein solcher Zusammenhang besteht, dann nicht in Form einer Illustration,[102] sondern einer Inspirierung des Textes durch das Relief, denn die Predigt des Nikolaus von Bari entstand erst nach 1235.[103] Möglich wäre freilich noch, dass beide unabhängig voneinander auf andere Quellen zurückgehen. Ich denke hier vor allem an den *Liber ad honorem Augusti*. Darin findet sich eine Beschreibung von Wandgemälden, die sich im kaiserlichen Palast in Palermo befunden haben sollen. Diese Wandgemälde sollen sechs Weltalter gezeigt haben, entsprechend der von Augustinus in *De civitate dei* entwickelten Geschichtsauffassung, mit den Staufern an prominenter Stelle. Denn sie, hier Friedrich I. Barbarossa und seine beiden Söhne, folgen dem biblischen König David nach und repräsentieren das sechste, das letzte Zeitalter.[104] Auf folio 143r der einzigen bekannten Handschrift des *Liber ad honorem Augusti* zeigt die Illustration zu dieser Textstelle eine Bildfolge, in der folgend auf König David im fünften Haus, das sechste mit den Staufern, in gegenüber den fünf vorhergehenden Häusern beträchtlich größerer Darstellung, in die Bildmitte gesetzt ist. Das Bild dominiert Friedrich Barbarossa, der, die Kaiserkrone auf dem Kopf, in der Mitte thront und seinen beiden Söhnen, Heinrich, ebenfalls bekrönt, und Philipp, seine Hände auf die Köpfe legt. Petrus und sein Illustrator setzten so Friedrich I. und seine Nachkommen in die Nachfolge Davids und wiesen ihnen als Beherrscher des

---

[101] Die Predigt ist abgedruckt in Rudolf M. Kloos, "Nikolaus von Bari," *Deutsches Archiv* 11 (1954), pp. 166–90 (repr. in *Stupor Mundi*, ed. Wolf, 1. Aufl. (Darmstadt, 1966), pp. 365–95, und ibid., 2. Aufl. (Darmstadt, 1982), pp. 130–60). Ibid., p. 184 finden sich die Angaben zu Nikolaus Person; die David-Bezüge, ibid., § 8, p. 171 sowie §13, p. 174 und § 20, pp. 176–77.

[102] So Schaller, "Relief," pp. 300–305. Demnach seien Friedrich I. (sitzend), Heinrich VI., Friedrich II. und Konrad IV. dargestellt. Heinrich (VII.) sei nicht dargestellt, weil er in der Predigt nicht vorkommt. Während Kloos, "Nikolaus," pp. 184–85 deshalb die Predigt in die Zeit nach der Absetzung Heinrichs (VII.) im Jahr 1235 datiert, meint Schaller, Heinrich fehle in der Predigt, weil er als deutscher König nicht in deren Konzeption passe, die allein das Kaisertum sowie die Königswürden von Sizilien und Jerusalem einbezieht. Heinrich aber war seit 1222 *Romanorum rex et semper augustus* (cf. Stürner, *Friedrich II.*, 2:118, Abb. 3) und auch der Nachfolger Friedrichs im Regnum (ibid., p. 177). Des Weiteren seien auf dem Relief lediglich Friedrich I. und Friedrich II. bekrönt, weil in der Predigt nur von zwei Kronen gesprochen wird. Schaller aber verweist selbst auf eine dritte, die Kappenkrone der dritten stehenden Figur. Zudem gibt er keine überzeugende Erklärung, wieso ausgerechnet Kaiser Heinrich VI. barhäuptig sein soll. Die Darstellung des 1229 noch ungekrönten Konrad IV. ohne Krone ist dagegen einleuchtend. Weitere Deutungen des Kanzelreliefs bietet Peter Cornelius Claussen, "Bitonto und Capua," in *Staufisches Apulien*, Schriften zur staufischen Geschichte und Kunst 13 (Göppingen, 1993), pp. 77–124, hier pp. 77–85. Er sieht in der sitzenden Figur eine Frau, die Personifikation Jerusalems oder Isabelle von Brienne, und verweist dazu auf einen "Indizienbeweis" Heinrich Thelens, den ich, anders als Claussen, nicht für zwingend halte.

[103] So auch Stürner, *Friedrich II.*, 2:177, mit einer Präzisierung auf 1237.

[104] Petrus de Ebulo, *Liber*, p. 233, ll. 1580–82, cf. dazu Particula 46, ibid, p. 217, ll. 1453–54, wo Heinrich VI. bereits entsprechend eingeordnet wird. Petrus' Beschreibung des Palastes muss wohl als fiktiv angesehen werden, siehe den Bildkommentar von Theo Kölzer in Petrus de Ebulo, *Liber*, p. 230. Cf. zu der Bildfolge auch Kölzer, "Liber," p. 44.

sechsten und letzten Zeitalters eine heilsgeschichtliche Rolle zu. Vielleicht taten sie dies in Anlehnung an die David-Nachfolge Karls des Großen, der kaum zufällig am Davids-Tag geheiligt wurde.[105] Die heilsgeschichtliche Einordnung Friedrichs I. und seiner beiden Söhne im Werk des Petrus von Eboli, wäre eine sehr passende Vorlage für das Kanzelrelief. Die oben referierte Deutung des Reliefs zugrunde gelegt, könnte es tatsächlich eine Aktualisierung jenes Motivs sein, indem nun die jüngsten Vertreter des staufischen Hauses, nämlich Friedrich II. und seine Söhne, als David-Nachfolger gezeigt werden. Ebenso könnte die Predigt des Nikolaus von Bari als Ausformulierung des bei Petrus nur knapp angedeuteten Gedankens von der Nachfolge der Staufer des Hauses David und ihrer bis zum Ende der Zeiten reichenden Herrschaft sein.[106]

Es gibt aber noch eine andere mögliche Vorlage für Nikolaus Predigt. Eine allgemeiner gehaltene Konzeption von Herrschaftstradition und bis zum Ende der Zeiten währender Herrschaftsdauer ergibt sich aus der Verknüpfung zweier Werke Gottfrieds von Viterbo, dem *Speculum regum* und dem *Pantheon*.[107] In dem ersten Werk bettet Gottfried die Staufer in eine von den Trojanern abgeleitete *imperialis prosapia* ein.[108] In dem zweiten Werk, dem *Pantheon*, verbindet Gottfried dieses Kaisertum mit den zu seiner Zeit umlaufenden Endzeitvorstellungen, indem er die in der tiburtinischen Sibylle genannten Kürzel von Herrschernamen durch die Anfangsbuchstaben der Kaiser der jüngsten Geschichte bis zu seiner eigenen Gegenwart ersetzt.[109] Beides zusammen gesehen, die *imperialis prosapia* im *Speculum regum* und die Einbindung der deutsch-römischen Kaiser in eine der meist verbreiteten eschatologischen Weissagungen im *Pantheon*, macht die Staufer zu Angehörigen eines Kaisergeschlechts, das seit frühester Zeit herrscht und dies bis zu ihrem Ende weiter tun wird.[110] Zwar fehlt bei Gottfried der Bezug auf David, aber die grundsätzliche Ausrichtung ist dieselbe wie bei Petrus von Eboli, Nikolaus von Bari und dem Kanzelrelief von Bitonto. Ohne hier eine gegenseitige Beeinflussung stichhaltig nachweisen zu können, bleibt festzuhalten, dass auf dem Kanzelrelief und in der Predigt des Nikolaus von Bari während der Blüte der Herrschaft Friedrichs II. Motive auftauchen, die bereits unter dessen Vater Heinrich VI. durch Gottfried von Viterbo auf die römischen Kaiser im allgemeinen und Petrus

---

[105] So Hans Martin Schaller, "Der heilige Tag als Termin mittelalterlicher Staatsakte," *Deutsches Archiv* 30 (1974), pp. 1–24, hier p. 20.

[106] Kloos, "Nikolaus," § 11, p. 172–73, cf. Schaller, "Kaiseridee," p. 119.

[107] Zu Gottfried und seinem Werk siehe Maria E. Dorninger, *Gottfried von Viterbo. Ein Autor in der Umgebung der frühen Staufer*, Stuttgarter Arbeiten zur Germanistik 345 (Stuttgart, 1997).

[108] MGH SS 22: 21–22.

[109] Ibid., pp. 145–46. Zur Sibylle von Tibur siehe Hannes Möhring, *Der Weltkaiser der Endzeit. Entstehung, Wandel und Wirkung einer tausendjährigen Weissagung*, Mittelalter-Forschungen 3 (Stuttgart, 2000), pp. 17–53, zu Gottfrieds Bearbeitung im *Pantheon* ibid., pp. 350 und 356.

[110] Hans Martin Schaller, "Endzeit-Erwartung und Antichrist-Vorstellungen in der Politik des 13. Jahrhunderts," in *Festschrift für Hermann Heimpel zum 70. Geburtstag am 19. September 1971*, 2, Veröffentlichungen des Max-Planck-Instituts für Geschichte 36/II (Göttingen, 1972), pp. 924–47 (repr. in *Stupor mundi*, ed. Wolf, 2. Aufl. (Darmstadt, 1982), pp. 418–48, und in Schaller, *Stauferzeit*, pp. 25–52), hier p. 930, und Jakobs, "Weltherrschaft," pp. 20–21.

von Eboli unmittelbar auf Heinrich und seinen Sohn Friedrich gemünzt waren. Das in den 90er Jahren des 12. Jahrhunderts entwickelte Ideengut blieb offenbar über 30 Jahre lebendig.[111]

Als Herrscher des letzten Zeitalters und Fortführer der das römische Reich beherrschenden *imperialis prosapia* sind die Staufer in den genannten Werken in den göttlichen Heilsplan eingebunden. Der Endzeitkaiser, nach den eschatologischen Prophetien der letzte irdische Herrscher vor dem Erscheinen des Antichristen, würde folglich ein Staufer sein.[112] Die Vorstellung eines Endzeitkaisers leitet sich ab aus dem zweiten Thessalonicherbrief des Apostels Paulus, demzufolge der sich bereits regende Frevler, der Satan, durch eine Macht zurückgehalten werde, die erst wegfallen muss, bevor dieser offen erscheinen könne (2. Thess. 2.6–7). Die bei Paulus noch unbestimmte Macht bekommt durch die Kirchenväter ein Gesicht, sie identifizieren mit ihr das römische Reich.[113] Die im frühen Mittelalter entwickelten eschatologischen Prophetien, angefangen bei der Sibylle von Tibur, über die syrisch-christliche Weissagung des Pseudo-Methodios und den Traktat über den Antichrist des Adso von Montier-en-Der, bringen die Vorstellung eines Endzeitkaisers ein, der die Weltherrschaft, also die Herrschaft über die gesamte *christianitas*, inne haben wird. Erst wenn dieser Endzeitkaiser an einer der heiligen Stätten der Christenheit seine Insignien niederlegt, wird der Antichrist die christliche Welt ins Chaos stürzen.[114] Bei Adso, der mit seinem Traktat konkret auf das fränkisch-römische Reich anspielt, fällt der bei Paulus als Grund für das Auftreten des Antichristen genannte Abfall vom Glauben (2. Thess. 2.3) mit der *discessio* der einzelnen Teilreiche von dem weltumspannenden Reich nach der Abdankung des letzten Herrschers zusammen. Diese Verknüpfung ergibt sich aus der dem römischen Kaiser auferlegten Aufgabe, die Kirche in allen Belangen zu verteidigen und zu schützen.[115] Fällt die durch ihn gegebene Garantie der Ordnung weg, zerfällt das *dominium mundi* und damit die *christianitas*.

Weltherrschaft, im Sinne der Beherrschung der gesamten Christenheit, war also eschatologisch aufgeladen. Doch ist das Streben Friedrichs I. und seines Sohnes Heinrich VI. nach universaler Herrschaft nicht mit dem Wunsch nach dem Endkaisertum und der Erfüllung der Zeiten zu verwechseln. Bezogen auf Heinrich VI. kommt Hermann Jakobs zu dem Schluss, dieser habe vielmehr mit dem Ausbau und der Festigung des Reiches den Willen bekundet, dieses als *katéchon*

---

[111] Auch bei Petrus von Vinea findet sich dieses Gedankengut, siehe Kirfel, *Weltherrschaftsidee*, p. 99.

[112] Zu den Endzeitprophetien allgemein Claude Carozzi, *Weltuntergang und Seelenheil* (Frankfurt a. M., 1996), Bernard McGinn, *Visions of the End. Apocalyptic Traditions in the Middle Ages* (New York, 1999) und Möhring, *Weltkaiser*.

[113] Dazu Jakobs, "Weltherrschaft," p. 18; cf. auch Möhring, *Weltkaiser*, p. 17. Zum Fortleben dieser Vorstellungen siehe Kirfel, *Weltherrschaftsidee*, pp. 85–86.

[114] Zu den genannten Prophetien siehe Möhring, *Weltkaiser*, pp. 28–49, 58–104, 136–43 und 144–48, die Texte sind in englischer Übersetzung abgedruckt in McGinn, *Visions*, pp. 49–50, 75–76 und 82–87.

[115] Carozzi, *Weltuntergang*, pp. 24–27.

zu erhalten und demgemäß die *discessio* zu verhindern. Gerade die Vorausschau, der Kaiser würde durch seinen Machtverzicht das Auftreten des Antichristen herbeiführen, stachelte zum Machterhalt an. Aus der eschatologischen Deutung des Endkaisers erwachse ein gleichsam antieschatologisches Herrscherverhalten. Jakobs verdeutlicht dies am *Ludus de Antichristo*, einem Schauspiel aus dem letzten Viertel des 12. Jahrhunderts.[116] Darin unterwirft der Kaiser die Könige der Griechen, von Jerusalem und von Frankreich, als die prominentesten Vertreter der *christianitas*, und schlägt den heidnischen König von Babylon, der Jerusalem bedroht, in die Flucht. Danach legt er in Jerusalem seine Insignien nieder und leitet so, gemäß den damals umlaufenden Prophetien, die Herrschaft des Antichristen ein. Der König von Jerusalem macht dem Kaiser seinen Verzicht zum Vorwurf: "Romani culminis dum esses advocatus, | sub honore viguit ecclesie status. | Nunc tue patens est malum discessionis."[117]

Der Vorwurf zeigt, was die Menschen vom Kaiser erwarteten, nämlich durch seinen Machterhalt das Kommen des Antichristen hinauszuschieben.[118] Ähnlich sind endzeitliche Äußerungen in der Chronistik des 12. Jahrhunderts als Mahnungen zu verstehen, denen die Hoffnung zu Grunde liegt, das als nahend beschriebene Ende der Zeit könne durch Reformen aufgehalten werden.[119] Da der Kaiser aber hierbei in den göttlichen Heilsplan eingebunden ist, steht es nicht in seiner Entscheidung, wann die Endzeit gekommen sein wird.[120] Die Unmöglichkeit sich selbst zum Endkaiser zu machen, stachelt daher die römischen Kaiser des Mittelalters an, das Reich immer wieder zu erneuern und dessen Macht auszubauen.[121] Dazu gehörte, die Kaiserkrone im eigenen Geschlecht zu halten, als Garantie unverbrüchlicher Herrschaft. Diese auf Heinrich VI. bezogene Deutung ist ohne weiteres auf Friedrich II. übertragbar. Konsequent zu Ende gedacht, hieße dies, Friedrichs II. Aufnahme der Krone vom Altar der Grabeskirche in Jerusalem auch als antieschatologische Demonstration zu deuten.[122]

Die gegen Ende des 12. und Anfang des 13. Jahrhunderts gesteigerte Antichrist-Erwartung spiegelt sich in der zunehmenden Überlieferungsdichte und der

---

[116] Jakobs, "Weltherrschaft," pp. 13 und 28. Zum *Ludus de Antichristo* cf. auch Möhring, *Weltkaiser*, pp. 176–84.

[117] *Ludus de Antichristo. Das Spiel vom Antichrist. Lateinisch, Deutsch*, ed. und trans. Rolf Engelsing (Stuttgart, 1985), p. 24.

[118] Jakobs, "Weltherrschaft," p. 28.

[119] Hans-Werner Goetz, "Endzeiterwartung und Endzeitvorstellung im Rahmen des Geschichtsbildes des früheren 12. Jahrhunderts," in *The Use and Abuse of Eschatology in the Middle Ages*, ed. Werner Verbeke, Daniel Verhelst und Andries Welkenhuysen, Mediaevalia Lovaniensia, Series I, Studia XV (Leuven, 1988), pp. 306–32, hier p. 331 sowie Horst Dieter Rauh, "Eschatology und Geschichte im 12. Jahrhundert. Antichrist-Typologie als Medium der Gegenwartskritik," in ibid., pp. 333–58.

[120] Möhring, *Weltkaiser*, p. 180.

[121] Jakobs, "Weltherrschaft," p. 28.

[122] Cf. Bodo Hechelhammer, "Zur Verwendung eschatologischer Motive in der politischen Korrespondenz Kaiser Friedrichs II. zur Zeit seines Kreuzzuges," in *Ende und Vollendung. Eschatologische Perspektiven im Mittelalter*, ed. Jan A. Aertsen und Martin Pickavé, Miscellanea Mediaevalia 29 (Berlin, New York, 2002), pp. 239–49, hier p. 248.

wachsenden Rezeption des Antichrist-Traktats Adsos von Montier-en-Der.[123] Das Thema war zu Zeiten Heinrichs VI. und seines Sohnes Friedrich also durchaus aktuell. Und Anlass, sich Gedanken um die herausragende eschatologische Rolle des im eigenen Geschlecht vererbten Kaisertums und damit über dessen Bedeutung innerhalb der Heilsgeschichte zu machen, gab es auch. Denn Ende des 12. Jahrhunderts waren Weissagungen im Umlauf, die den französischen König Philipp II. August als Endkaiser erscheinen ließen.[124] Bereits in Adsos Antichrist-Traktat sind es ausdrücklich die westfränkischen *reges Francorum*, und das heißt die Karolinger, die das römische Reich bis zum Ende der Zeiten fortführen und demgemäß den Endzeitkaiser stellen.[125] Und gerade mit Philipps II. Sohn Ludwig VIII. sah man wieder einen Karolinger den französischen Thron besteigen. Daraus ergibt sich eine auf karolingische Tradition gestützte Konkurrenz bezüglich des Endzeitkaisertums. Dabei konnte es für Friedrich II., Philipp II. und dessen Sohn Ludwig VIII. kaum um die Frage gehen, wer nun von ihnen der Endzeitkaiser sei, sondern vielmehr darum, aus wessen Geschlecht dieser letzte Herrscher einst hervorgehen würde, dem kaiserlich-staufischen oder dem französisch-karolingischen. Möglicherweise wollte Friedrich II. mit der Rückbesinnung auf die ältere antik-römische Kaisertradition auch in dieser Hinsicht seinen Vorrang vor den "karolingischen" Königen Frankreichs bewahren.

Zu den bisher referierten, denkbaren Einflüssen auf Friedrichs II. Herrschaftsauffassung lassen sich einige wesentliche Elemente der Lehre des Joachim von Fiore fügen. Dies sind die Einteilung der Weltgeschichte in drei *status*, die Stellung und der Zustand der Kirche Ende des 12. Jahrhunderts und das Verhältnis zwischen der römischen Kirche, mit dem Papsttum als Spitze, und den Königen und Kaisern. Joachim suchte den Lauf der Geschichte durch die Aufdeckung von Analogien im Alten und Neuen Testament sowie dem aus der Historiographie bekannten Geschichtsverlauf bis zu seiner eigenen Zeit zu entschlüsseln. Da die zeitliche Dimension des Alten Testament, das Buch für den ersten *status*, 42 Generationen umfasst musste entsprechend auch der zweite *status*, die Zeit des Gottessohnes und der Geschichte der römischen Kirche, 42 Generationen dauern. Nach dieser Berechnung befand man sich um das Jahr 1200 am Ende der 40. Generation des zweiten *status*. Bis zum Übergang zum dritten *status*, dem des heiligen Geistes, würden demnach noch zwei Generationen vergehen. Da Joachim eine Generation mit 30 Jahren angab, konnte das Ende des mit Christi Geburt begonnenen zweiten *status* und der Beginn einer neuen Zeit in der Heilsgeschichte um das Jahr 1260 erwartet werden.[126] In den verbleibenden beiden Generationen des zweiten *status* sollten entscheidende Veränderungen der Zustände anstehen,

---

[123] Möhring, *Weltkaiser*, p. 169.
[124] Ibid., pp. 174–75, 293–94 und 354.
[125] Ibid., pp. 146–46; cf. Kienast, *Deutschland*, pp. 481–86.
[126] Möhring, *Weltkaiser*, p. 206. Zu Joachims Lehren insgesamt siehe Matthias Riedl, *Joachim von Fiore. Denker der vollendeten Menschlichkeit*, Würzburger Wissenschaftliche Schriften, Reihe Philosophie 361 (Würzburg, 2004).

denn der Übergang zu einem neuen *status* war fließend, so dass die kommenden Jahrzehnte, von Joachims Warte aus gesehen, bereits der Vorbereitung des dritten *status* dienen würden. Gerade die Kirche hatte sich noch zu wandeln, denn sie war in Joachims Augen für den Wechsel zu einer höheren Stufe, die die Zeit des Heiligen Geistes gegenüber der des Sohnes darstellte, schlecht aufgestellt. Sie hatte sich seit der Konstantinischen Schenkung gegen ihre eigentliche Bestimmung zunehmend in weltliche Händel verstrickt. Zwar war für Joachim die Konstantinische Schenkung die der Kirche zustehende Erhöhung, mit der ihr und dem Papsttum die gebührende *summa regni*, die alleinige geistliche wie weltliche Führerschaft der Christenheit verliehen wurde.[127] Aber die Päpste ließen sich hinreißen, die ihnen übertragene weltliche Macht selbst auszuüben, statt sie an die Könige beziehungsweise die Kaiser zu delegieren. Letzteren komme nämlich zu, als treue Diener die weltlichen Angelegenheiten der Kirche in deren Sinn und Auftrag zu übernehmen. Dieses Verhältnis zwischen Kirche auf der einen und Kaisertum auf der anderen Seite – eine *civitas permixta* wie Otto von Freising sie als Ideal ansah, widersprach der von Joachim aufgedeckten Analogie zum Geschichtsverlauf im Alten Testament[128] – beschreibt Joachim bündig in der Schrift *Intelligentia super Catathis ad Abbatem Gaufridum*:

> Pro eo namque quod ecclesiasticus ordo cruenta iudicia vitat et ad tuendos a barbarorum rabie Christianorum fines eidem arma sumere et pugnare non licet, etsi pontifex romanus regni summam susceperit, utpote qui vero regi et vero pontifici successisse in patribus videbatur, oportebat tamen personam laicam vicem eius supplere, que rex nichilominus diceretur et tam in tuendo christiano populo et faciendo iudicio quam in misteriis quoque adimplendis claritatem haberet.[129]

Das an sich positive Verhältnis zwischen Papstkirche und Kaisertum hatte sich jedoch analog zum Verlauf des ersten *status* gewandelt, denn in den Staufern erkannte Joachim die neuen Chaldäer, im Reich das neue Babylon. Den Kaisern des endenden zweiten *status* kam also die Rolle der Verfolger der Kirche zu.[130]

Friedrich II. dürfte Joachims Lehre zumindest in groben Zügen gekannt haben. Sowohl Heinrich VI. und Konstanze als auch Friedrich selbst waren Förderer von Joachims Klostergründung in Fiore. Friedrich ist dem Abt möglicherweise als Fünfjähriger begegnet, als jener sich im März 1200 nach Palermo begab, um die florenser Klöster unter den Schutz des nun elternlosen Thronfolgers zu stellen.[131]

---

[127] Herbert Grundmann, "Kirchenfreiheit und Kaisermacht um 1190 in der Sicht Joachims von Fiore," in ders., *Ausgewählte Aufsätze*, MGH Schriften 25,2 (Stuttgart, 1977), pp. 361–402, hier p. 372, und Riedl, *Joachim*, pp. 143, 145 und 149

[128] Riedl, *Joachim*, pp. 185–87.

[129] Zitiert nach Grundmann, "Kirchenfreiheit," 2:372, n. 20. Cf. Riedl, *Joachim*, p. 189.

[130] Grundmann, "Kirchenfreiheit," 2:384 und Riedl, *Joachim*, pp. 147–48.

[131] Herbert Grundmann, "Zur Biographie Joachims von Fiore und Rainers von Ponza," in ders., *Ausgewählte Aufsätze*, 2:255–360, hier pp. 318–19. Zur Förderung der florenser Klöster durch Friedrich II. siehe Walther Holtzmann, "Papst-, Kaiser- und Normannenurkunden aus Unteritalien. II. S. Giovanni di Fiore," *Quellen und Forschungen aus italienischen Archiven und Bibliotheken* 36 (1956),

Anklänge an Joachims Lehre sind in einer Urkunde Friedrichs von 1213 und in den 1231 erlassenen Konstitutionen von Melfi zu finden.[132] Im Proömium der Konstitutionen von Melfi heißt es, Gott habe die Fürsten eingesetzt,

> ut sacrosanctam ecclesiam, Christiane religionis matrem, detractorum fidei maculari clandestinis perfidiis non permittant et ut ipsam ab hostium publicorum incursibus gladii materialis potentia tueantur atque pacem populis eisdemque pacificatis iustitiam [...] pro posse conservent.[133]

In einer solchen Rolle obliegt es dem Kaiser die Voraussetzungen für das Eintreten der sich nähernden neuen Epoche zu schaffen, zumal der von Joachim erwartete Zustand der *libertas* im dritten *status* wohl ohne eine geistliche und weltliche Führerschaft auskommen sollte.[134] Joachims negative Besetzung des Kaisertums mag – wenn diese Friedrich zur Kenntnis gekommen ist – ein zusätzlicher Ansporn gewesen sein, sich als treuer – jedoch gleichgestellter und keineswegs untergeordneter – Diener der Kirche zu erweisen und eben das erwartete Bild eines babylonischen Verfolgers nicht zu erfüllen. Entscheidend ist, dass man in der ersten Hälfte des 13. Jahrhunderts, auf Joachim vertrauend, das Heraufkommen eines neuen, besseren Zustands der Christenheit erwarten durfte. Für Friedrich II. bedeutete das, er konnte sich mit zunehmendem Alter einer Zeitenwende näher fühlen, die es in seiner Funktion als Kaiser vorzubereiten galt.[135]

In der Geschichtsdeutung Joachims von Fiore mochte Friedrich insgesamt eine Bestätigung der überschwänglichen Voraussagen des Petrus von Eboli gefunden haben[136], die zudem mit dem Geschichtsverlauf, wie ihn Otto von Freising beschrieben hatte, in Einklang stand, insofern als, ähnlich wie mit Friedrich I., nun mit Friedrich II. nach einer Zeit der Wirren, eine Zeit neuen Friedens und

---

pp. 1–21, Klaus Höflinger, Joachim Spiegel: Ungedruckte Stauferurkunden für S. Giovanni in Fiore.- *Deutsches Archiv* 49 (1993), pp. 75–11, und dies., "Ungedruckte Urkunden Kaiser Friedrichs II. für das Florenserkloster Fonte Laurato," *Archiv für Diplomatik* 40 (1994), pp. 105–22.

[132] Zu Friedrichs Urkunde vom Dezember 1213 (in *Historia diplomatica*, 1:283–84) siehe Schaller, "Frömmigkeit," p. 502. Zu der möglichen Selbstdeutung Friedrichs als endzeitlicher *novus dux* oder *novus rex* im Sinne Joachims in den Konstitutionen von Melfi siehe Möhring, *Weltkaiser*, p. 214; cf. auch Enrico Pispisa, *Medioevo fridericiano e altri scritti*, Collana di testi e studi storici 9 (Messina, 1999, ohne Angaben zu Erstveröffentlichungen), pp. 15 und 79.

[133] Wolfgang Stürner, "Rerum necessitas und divina provisio. Zur Interpretation des Prooemiums der Konstitutionen von Melfi (1231)," *Deutsches Archiv* 39 (1983), pp. 467–554, hier, pp. 551–52., ll. 31–36.

[134] Jürgen Miethke, "Zukunftshoffnung, Zukunftserwartung, Zukunftsbeschreibung im 12. Und 13. Jahrhundert," in *Ende und Vollendung*, ed. Aertsen und Pickavé, pp. 504–24, hier p. 518.

[135] In Friedrichs Manifest vom 6. Dezember 1227 heißt es: "*Forte nos Sumus, ad quos devenerunt seculorum fines*" (MGH Const. 2, Nr. 116, p. 148, l. 37). Hechelhammer, "Verwendung," pp. 245–49 verweist auf die Variante in den Ausfertigungen für die italienischen Kommunen, wo es heißt: "*Summus nos ad quos devenerunt seculorum fines*" (*Historia diplomatica*, 3:37), aber wertet beide Aussagen als politische Rhetorik. Einen Hinweis aus dem Jahr 1249 auf eine mögliche Endzeiterwartung Friedrichs gibt Schaller, "Endzeit-Erwartung," p. 30; cf. dazu auch Möhring, *Weltkaiser*, p. 212.

[136] Die Bedeutung der Werke der beiden Autoren für Friedrichs II. Herrschaftsauffassung betont bereits Pispisa, *Medioevo*, pp. 71–84.

neuer Ordnung anbrechen würde. Und die Voraussicht des Wechsels zum dritten und letzten *status* machte wahrscheinlich, die Erwartung, die Staufer würden das letzte Geschlecht kaiserlicher Herrscher sein, sei zutreffend. Und mit Blick auf die verschiedenen Endzeitprophetien musste der Einflussbereich der noch kommenden Kaiser unbedingt Jerusalem beinhalten. So betrachtet war Friedrichs Kreuzzug Teil einer eschatologisch motivierten Politik.[137]

Herrschaftssicherung

Wenn nun schließlich Friedrichs II. Kreuzzugsgelübde als Instrument der Sicherung seiner Herrschaft betrachtet wird, geschieht dies vor dem Hintergrund der beschriebenen Herrschaftsauffassung, die als Leitmotiv dem Handeln des Staufers zugrunde lag. Dabei wird nicht erörtert, inwieweit Friedrich II. das einmal abgelegte Gelübde instrumentalisierte,[138] sondern es werden die Hinweise zusammengetragen, die zeigen, dass die Kreuznahme von vornherein auch als Herrschaft sichernde Maßnahme gedacht war.

Als Friedrich II. am 24. Juli 1215 in Aachen einzog, vermochte er bereits auf eine Reihe von Erfolgen zurückzublicken. Ihm strömten mehr und mehr Anhänger zu, während die Zahl der welfischen Parteigänger schrumpfte. Otto IV. und die Seinen waren seit dem Debakel von Bouvines militärisch am Boden. Und Friedrich würde nun am rechten Ort, der Tradition gemäß, zum *rex Romanorum* gekrönt. Jedoch, er blieb weiterhin ein Gegenkönig und ihm fehlte im Gegensatz zu seinem Gegner die Kaiserkrone. Und bei aller Glücklosigkeit Ottos IV., er lebte und er hatte noch immer Anhänger. Friedrich konnte sich daher auch nach der Aachener Krönung noch nicht endgültig als der neue Herrscher des Reiches sehen, obwohl damit ein weiterer wichtiger Schritt getan sein würde. Die nächste Bewährungsprobe nahte mit dem für den November 1215 anberaumten päpstlichen Konzil. Denn es stand durchaus zu fürchten, dass es Otto IV. gelingen könnte, sich mit Innozenz III. auszusöhnen und von ihm die Lösung der Exkommunikation zu erreichen.[139] Eine Appellation Ottos IV. an das Konzil war wohl bereits 1214 publizistisch vorbereitet worden, wie die *Disputatio inter Romam et papam de Ottone IV. imperatore* vermuten lässt.[140] Die *Roma* argumentiert in der *Disputatio* erfolgreich gegen den Papst für die Lösung des über Otto verhängten Banns und die Absetzung Friedrichs. Der Papst weiß letztlich nicht anders zu antworten, als die *Roma* ebenfalls mit dem Bann zu bedrohen. Daraufhin appelliert diese an das Laterankonzil, das sich in ihrem Sinne

---

[137] Dies nimmt Schaller, "Kaiseridee," p. 114, bereits für Heinrich VI. an. Cf. auch die – allerdings von eschatologischen Bezugnahmen freie – Einschätzung von Friedrichs Selbstsicht als "prince of peace" usw. in Abulafia, *Frederick*, p. 5.

[138] Dazu unfassend Hechelhammer, *Kreuzzug*.

[139] Hucker, "Otto IV.," p. 366, cf. Stürner, "Kreuzzugsgelübde," p. 308.

[140] *Scriptorum Brunsvicensia illustrantium*, 2, ed. Gottfried Wilhelm Leibniz (Hannover, 1710), pp. 525–32. Siehe zu dem Text Eduard Winkelmann, *Philipp von Schwaben und Otto IV. von Braunschweig*, 2 Bände (Leipzig, 1873–78; repr. Darmstadt, 1963), 1:422, n. 1.

zu Gunsten des Kaisers und gegen Friedrich äußert. Das Hauptargument der *Roma* gegen Friedrich ist seine Kleinwüchsigkeit. Friedrich sei entweder auf Grund seiner Jugend oder eines körperlichen Makels nicht zum Herrscher geeignet.[141] Dabei deute die Kleinwüchsigkeit zugleich auf eine gemeine, schwache Persönlichkeit Friedrichs, während Otto trotz geringerer Herkunft das Format eines Königs besitze. Der wie ein Knabe oder Zwerg wirkende, schwache Friedrich könne kaum die Lasten der Herrschaft tragen, vielmehr bedürfe es eines körperlich wie sittlich aufrechten und gereiften Mannes wie Otto:

> Dicetur rex, immo puer; non Oto Tyrannus, | Immo rex. Sed enim Ducis hic est filius, ille | Induperatoris; jus hic colit, ille lacessit; | Subjectis humilem se praebat hic, illo superbum. ...
> Sed in Frederico | Replico. Nemo negat, quin ille brevissimus: ergo | Aut puer aut nanus. ...
> Tumidus humili, Fredericus Otoni, | Exanimis vivo, succedere nititur: ergo | Vult onus Alcidae Thersites ferre, gigantis | Nanus, Teutonici Pygmaeus ... .[142]

Diese Art von Schmähungen gegen Friedrich II. haben die Anhänger Ottos IV. wohl fleißig in Umlauf gebracht. Das legt jedenfalls einer der Sprüche des um 1214/15 von Otto zu Friedrich übergewechselten Walther von der Vogelweide nahe, der sich wie eine direkte Erwiderung auf die Argumente der *Roma* liest:

> Ich wolt hêrn Otten milte nâch der lenge mezzen: | dô hât ich mich an der mâze ein teil vergezzen: | wær er sô milt als lanc, er hete tugende vil besezzen. | Vil schiere maz ich abe den lîp nâch sîner êre: | dô wart er vil gar ze kurz als ein verschrôten werc, | miltes muotes minre vil dan ein getwerc; | und ist doch von den jâren daz er niht entwahsen mêre. | Dô ich dem künege brâhte daz mez wie er ûf schôz! | sîn junger lîp wart beide michel unde grôz. | nû seht waz er noch wahse: erst ieze ûbr in wol risen genôz.[143]

Mit der Doppeldeutigkeit des Begriffs *mâze* spielend – der Maßstab, aber zugleich das sittliche Maß als Grundtugend[144] – entkräftet Walther die Argumentation in der *Disputatio*, indem er die moralische Größe als das entscheidende Maß nennt, an dem ein Herrscher zu messen sei, während die körperliche Größe nichts besage.

Es wäre übertrieben aufgrund der beiden genannten Texte auf einen großen publizistischen Schlagabtausch im Vorfeld des Laterankonzils zu schließen. Sie lassen aber durchaus erkennen, dass von welfisch gesinnter Seite ernstzunehmende Bemühungen ausgingen, ihren jugendlichen Gegner zu verunglimpfen und als der

---

[141] Möglicherweise ist dies eine Anspielung auf die *Deliberatio de tribus electis* Innozenz' III. von 1200/01 (*RNI*, Nr. 29, p. 78, l. 26–p. 79, l. 4).

[142] *Scriptorum Brunsvicensia*, 2, ed. Leibniz, pp. 526 und 529.

[143] Walther von der Vogelweide, *Gedichte*, ausgewählt und übersetzt von Peter Wapnewski (Frankfurt a. M., 1998), p. 170. Siehe dazu Matthias Nix, *Untersuchungen zur Funktion der politischen Spruchdichtung Walthers von der Vogelweide*, Göppinger Arbeiten zur Germanistik 592 (Göppingen, 1993), pp. 254–58

[144] Otfrid Ehrismann, *Ehre und Mut, Âventiure und Minne* (München, 1995), pp. 128–29.

Herrschaft unwürdig erscheinen zu lassen. Daher musste Friedrich darauf bedacht sein, seinem welfischen Widersacher nicht nachzustehen, ihn möglichst in jeder Hinsicht zu übertrumpfen, um so die eigene Position zu festigen und zugleich jene Ottos IV. zu negieren. Die Schließung des Karlsschreins zwei Tage nach Friedrichs Krönung in Aachen wurde bereits in diesem Sinn gedeutet. Ebenso kann die Kreuznahme Friedrichs begründet werden. Denn Otto IV. war seit seiner Kaiserkrönung 1209 mit dem Kreuz bezeichnet. Er legte zwar sein Gelübde im Geheimen vor dem Bischof von Cambrai ab, doch hatte Friedrich wahrscheinlich davon erfahren und zog am Tag seiner Krönung, also in einem höchst feierlichen, öffentlichen Rahmen nicht nur mit Otto gleich, sondern überflügelte ihn, von dessen Gelübde wohl nur sehr wenige wussten, als vorbildlicher, christlicher Herrscher.[145] Dieser Schritt war zugleich mit Blick auf Friedrichs päpstlichen Förderer wichtig. Immerhin hatte Innozenz III. in seiner Kreuzzugsbulle *Quia major nunc* von 1213 den Kreuzfahrern besonderen apostolischen Schutz zugesichert.[146] Dieser Schutz stand freilich auch dem mit dem Kreuz bezeichneten Kaiser zu. Gerade das Kreuzzugsversprechen wäre ein guter Grund gewesen, den gegen ihn verhängten Bann zu lösen, zumal auf einem den Vorbereitungen des neuen Kreuzzugs gewidmeten Konzil. Eine Aussöhnung zwischen Papst und Kaiser hätte Friedrichs Aufstieg ziemlich abrupt beendet. Er konnte sich auf keinen Fall leisten, die Unterstützung seines päpstlichen Vormundes zu verlieren, zumindest solange es Otto IV. gab. Für Friedrich musste es deshalb mit Blick auf die unvorhersehbaren Verhandlungen des Laterankonzils unverzichtbar sein, ebenfalls das Kreuzzeichen zu tragen, um hier nicht zurückzustehen. Dabei mochte zusätzlich das Beispiel des englischen Königs Johann Ohneland in Friedrich II. die Hoffnung geweckt haben, mit der Kreuznahme die besondere Protektion des Papstes zu sichern.[147] Der von seinen Baronen bedrängte Johann hatte am 4. März 1215 das Kreuz genommen. Zwischen Ende März und Anfang Juli gingen mehrere Briefe Innozenz III. nach England, in denen er die dortigen Bischöfe aufforderte, den König zu unterstützen, und die englischen Barone mahnte, die Feindseligkeiten gegen den König sofort zu beenden, um die Kreuzfahrt Johanns nicht zu gefährden.[148]

Neben der Hoffnung auf päpstliche Gunst, konnte Friedrich damit rechnen, durch seine Kreuznahme auch in unmittelbarer Umgebung Unterstützer seiner Herrschaft im Reich zu gewinnen. Schon 1213 bemühte er sich um den Deutschen Orden, was natürlich mit der traditionellen staufischen Förderung dieser frommen Ritter erklärbar ist, was aber ebenso handfeste politische Gründe gehabt haben

---

[145] Hucker, *Kaiser*, p. 575, sieht die Kreuznahme Friedrichs als notwendige Übernahme der Pläne Ottos IV. Dagegen verweist Stürner, *Friedrich II.*, 1:174, n. 97, auf die geheime Kreuznahme des Welfen, ihm folgen Hiestand, "Friedrich II.," p. 132, n. 16, und Hechelhammer, *Kreuzzug*, p. 27. Dass Friedrich über die Kreuznahme Ottos durchaus unterrichtet gewesen sein mochte, zeigt hingegen schon Winkelmann, *Philipp*, p. 392, n. 3 und p. 394, sowie ders., *Kaiser Friedrich II.*, 1 (Leipzig, 1889–97; repr. Darmstadt, 1963), p. 61.

[146] Roscher, *Papst*, p. 144. Die Bulle ist abgedruckt in PL 216, Sp. 817–22.

[147] Stürner, *Friedrich II.*, 1:180, Hechelhammer, *Kreuzzug*, pp. 27–28.

[148] Zu Johanns Kreuznahme siehe Roscher, *Papst*, pp. 156–57.

wird. Wieder ging es dabei direkt gegen Otto IV., der noch 1212 durch Privilegien versuchte den Orden auf seiner Seite zu halten.[149] Eine zweite wichtige Gruppe waren die für Deutschland bestellten Kreuzprediger. Seit Friedrich 1212 deutschen Boden betreten hatte, begegnete er ihnen immer wieder und ab 1214 tauchten sie nahezu regelmäßig in seiner Umgebung auf.[150] Deren Netzwerk und die ihnen kraft päpstlicher Beauftragung anhaftende Autorität in einer der eigenen Sache gegenüber günstigen Stimmung zu wissen, musste ein großer Anreiz für den jungen König gewesen sein. Und wie waren diese Männer besser zu gewinnen als durch eine persönliche Teilnahme am Kreuzzug? Einen Teil der Prediger stellten, dies schon traditionell, die Zisterzienser.[151] Die Kreuznahme mochte versprechen, auch die Fürsprache dieses in weltlichen und geistlichen Kreisen in hohem Ansehen stehenden Mönchsordens zu erlangen. Das Schreiben vom August 1215 an die Zisterzienseräbte, mit dem Friedrich sie unter Hinweis auf seinen ins Auge gefassten Kreuzzug für sich zu gewinnen versucht, wurde bereits besprochen.[152]

Schließlich konnte Friedrich II. auf die Frieden stiftende Dynamik seiner Kreuznahme spekulieren. Die Schlichtung von Konflikten bildete eine wichtige Voraussetzung für die allgemeine Kreuzzugsbereitschaft. Streitende Parteien waren durch ein abgegebenes Versprechen am Kreuzzug teilnehmen zu wollen, besonders bemüht, eine Einigung herbeizuführen, um ihre Gelübde erfüllen zu können. Andererseits waren die zur Kreuzpredigt ausgesandten päpstlichen Legaten in allen Ländern vor allem mit Friedensmaßnahmen beschäftigt, um möglichst vielen Kämpfern Sicherheit für einen Aufbruch ins Heilige Land zu geben. Bezüglich des deutschen Kontingents verweist James M. Powell darauf, dass sich hier sowohl Anhänger Friedrichs II. als auch Ottos IV. zusammenfanden. Darin sieht er durchaus "a result of the process of pacification in Germany," der auch auf Betreiben des päpstlichen Subdiakons Nikolas und des Kreuzpredigers Konrad von Regensburg zurückzuführen sei.[153] Damit stünde Friedrichs Kreuznahme zugleich im Einklang mit den päpstlichen Absichten, da er durch sein Beispiel einen wichtigen Beitrag zur Befriedung und zur allgemeinen Kreuzzugsbereitschaft leistete. Abgesehen davon, musste diese Frieden stiftende Wirkung natürlich ganz im Sinne des frisch gekrönten Königs sein.

Ein heikler Punkt in dem Verhältnis zum Papst war jedoch die Frage der beiden Reiche, dem Kaiserreich und dem sizilischen Regnum. Innozenz III. hatte schon in seiner *Deliberatio de tribus electis* 1200/01 die Herrschaft Friedrichs als Kaiser auch mit der Begründung abgelehnt, er, der ja schon König Siziliens war, dürfe

---

[149] Kluger, *Hochmeister*, p. 6. Kluger nimmt auch an, Hermann von Salza könnte sich bereits während des Laterankonzils als ein den Anliegen Friedrichs nützlicher Diplomat erwiesen haben (ibid., p. 8).
[150] Pixton, "Anwerbung," pp. 178–80.
[151] Ibid., p. 167.
[152] Siehe oben, p. 135.
[153] James M. Powell, *Anatomy of a Crusade* (Philadelphia PA, 1986), pp. 67–87, Zitat pp. 75–76. Cf. Hechelhammer, *Kreuzzug*, pp. 49–58 und 199–211, und Pixton, "Anwerbung," pp. 180–82, der Johannes von Xanten und Konrad von Speyer als die rührigsten Kreuzprediger in Aachen nennt.

nicht Herrscher beider Reiche sein, weil dies deren Vereinigung bedeute und damit die Kirche in Unruhe versetzt werde.[154] Furcht vor einem Engagement Friedrichs II. nördlich der Alpen zeigte Innozenz III. erneut deutlich im Jahr 1208 mit der verfrühten Entlassung des vierzehnjährigen Friedrichs in die Volljährigkeit und der damit verbundenen Herrschaftsübergabe in Sizilien an ihn. Nach sizilischem Recht wäre Friedrichs Volljährigkeit erst mit Vollendung des 18. Lebensjahres eingetreten. Die verfrühte Freigabe in die Mündigkeit im Juli/August des Jahres 1208 war für Innozenz als Papst wie als Regent, besonders mit Blick auf die Kirchenpolitik im sizilischen Reich, alles andere als vorteilhaft.[155] Aber nach der Ermordung von Friedrichs Onkel, Philipp von Schwaben, im Juni 1208 hielt es Innozenz III. offenbar für dringend geboten den jungen Staufer fester an Sizilien zu binden und somit als möglichen Opponenten gegen Otto IV. im deutsch-römischen Reich auszuschalten. Anfang Juli hatte der Papst Otto IV. seiner Unterstützung versichert, unter Hinweis auf Philipps gegnerischen Neffen, den jungen Friedrich.[156] Wenige Jahre später bekam Friedrich II. einen weiteren, diesmal für ihn ganz offensichtlichen Beweis der Unerbittlichkeit Innozenz' III. in der Frage der Vereinigung Siziliens mit dem Kaiserreich. Schließlich verdankte der Staufer seine deutsche Krone letztlich dem Fehler Ottos IV. im Anschluss an seine Kaiserkrönung im Oktober 1209, seine nur sechs Monate zuvor in Speyer gegebenen Zusicherungen verwerfend, nach der sizilischen Königswürde greifen zu wollen. Nach solch schlechter Erfahrung wird Innozenz seinen staufischen Zögling Friedrich mit entsprechend gemischten Gefühlen gegen den aufmüpfigen Kaiser aktiviert haben, denn wer mochte vorhersehen, wie er sich an Ottos Stelle verhalten würde. So forderte Innozenz von seinem Schützling, wohl in der Sorge, dieser könnte die ihm erwiesene päpstliche Unterstützung vergessen wollen, sobald Otto überwunden wäre, die volle Anerkennung der päpstlichen Lehnshoheit über Sizilien. Noch vor seinem Aufbruch leistete Friedrich gegenüber einem päpstlichen Legaten den Treueid und bei seinem Aufenthalt in Rom im April 1212 schwor er dem Papst als Lehnsherrn Siziliens persönlich das Hominium.[157]

Nach der Anerkennung von Friedrichs Wahl und Krönung zum römisch-deutschen König auf dem Laterankonzil 1215 war die Vereinigung der Herrschaft in Reich und Regnum in der Hand Friedrichs in beträchtliche Nähe gerückt; zur Vollendung fehlte allerdings noch dessen Kaiserkrönung. Umso wichtiger war das goldbesiegelte Versprechen Friedrichs, das dieser am 1. Juli 1216 in Straßburg zu Pergament bringen ließ. Nach seiner Krönung zum Kaiser wollte Friedrich sich zu Gunsten seines Sohnes Heinrich, der bereits zum Nachfolger in Sizilien ernannt war, von der Herrschaft über Sizilien zurückziehen, um nicht den Eindruck entstehen zu lassen, es käme zu einer Verbindung mit dem Kaiserreich, indem er, Friedrich, neben

---

[154] *RNI*, p. 79, ll. 5–9.
[155] Baaken, *Ius*, pp. 173–77.
[156] Hucker, *Kaiser*, pp. 98–99.
[157] Stürner, *Friedrich II.*, 1:141 und 143 sowie Baaken, *Ius*, pp. 203–4.

der Kaiserwürde auch die Krone Siziliens innehätte.[158] Das sehr genau formulierte, die Vereinigung der beiden Reiche scheinbar absolut ausschließende Versprechen, lässt eine entscheidende Lücke, deren Nutzung sich bereits in der Umsetzung befand, ehe das Siegelwachs ausgehärtet war. Zwischen Ende Dezember 1215 und April 1216 hatte Friedrich II. den Grafen Albert von Everstein mit der Order nach Sizilien gesandt, seine Gattin Konstanze und seinen Sohn Heinrich nach Deutschland zu holen. Die beiden traten ihre Reise höchstwahrscheinlich Ende Juni/Anfang Juli 1216 an, also wohl noch vor dem plötzlichen Tod Innozenz III. am 16. Juli und während Friedrich in Straßburg mit dem päpstlichen Legaten bezüglich der Bedingungen für seine Kaiserkrönung die Verständigung erreichte, zu der jenes mit Goldbulle besiegelte Versprechen gehörte.[159] Die Reise Konstanzes und Heinrichs hatte, Stürner zufolge, keinen anderen Anlass als den Plan, den bereits 1212 zum sizilischen König gekrönten Knaben auch im Reich zum König erheben zu lassen. Folgerichtig ist in dem Versprechen gegenüber Innozenz nur die Vereinigung von Kaisertum und sizilischem Regnum in Friedrichs Hand ausgeschlossen, nicht aber eine solche unter Heinrichs Herrschaft. Zwei andere Lücken in der *Promissio*, auf die Gerhard Baaken aufmerksam macht, sind die alleinige Nennung Innozenz' III. als Empfänger, so dass mit dessen Ableben die Übereinkunft streng genommen hinfällig wurde, und die Kopplung der Versprechungen Friedrichs an die Kaiserkrönung, womit dieser den Zeitpunkt der Umsetzung nahezu beliebig rausschieben konnte. Den so für sich bewahrten zeitlichen Spielraum nutzte Friedrich, um die Verhältnisse zu seinen Gunsten zu ändern. Baaken verweist darauf, dass Heinrich (VII.) in einer Urkunde vom 13. Februar 1217 das letzte Mal den Titel des Königs von Sizilien führte und auch Konstanze spätestens seit Januar 1218 nur noch als *consors regni* und nicht mehr als *regina Siciliae* genannt wurde. Friedrich hatte also im Laufe des Jahres 1217 seinem Sohn und seiner Gattin die Herrschaftsrechte in Sizilien entzogen, um diese fortan allein inne zu haben.[160] Er verwarf also den vermutlich ursprünglichen Plan, die Herrschaft über beide Reiche für seinen Sohn zu sichern, indem er, als Reaktion auf den plötzlich Tod des Adressaten seines Straßburger Versprechens, nun die Doppelherrschaft in aller Deutlichkeit für sich selbst beanspruchte.[161]

Freilich musste Friedrich auf den möglichen Widerstand des Papstes gegen das listig formulierte Straßburger Versprechen gefasst sein. Auch wird ihm klar gewesen sein, dass es ein großes Wagnis bedeutete, den sizilischen Thronfolger ins Reich bringen zu lassen. Allein wegen seines Aufenthalts dort war größtes Misstrauen des Papstes vorhersehbar und mit dessen hartnäckigem Widerstand

---

[158] MGH Const. 2, Nr. 58, p. 72, ll. 21–33.
[159] Baaken, *Ius*, pp. 217–20 und Stürner, "Kreuzzugsgelübde," pp. 312–13 (genauso Stürner, *Friedrich II.*, 1:189–90).
[160] Baaken, *Ius*, pp. 223 und 226–28.
[161] Die für Friedrich selbstverständliche Zusammengehörigkeit der beiden Reiche zeigt sich auch in einem Diplom für den Deutschen Orden vom Dezember 1216 (Kluger, *Hochmeister*, p. 9). Die in Abulafia, *Frederick*, p. 437, geäußerte Auffassung, Friedrich habe zwischenzeitlich mit dem Gedanken gespielt, die beiden Reiche gemäß päpstlichen Wunsch getrennt zu vererben, halte ich für abwegig.

gegen eine Verbindung beider Königreiche in Heinrichs Händen war allemal zu rechnen. Daher ist es keineswegs unwahrscheinlich, dass die Kreuznahme auch der Besänftigung des Papstes dienen sollte. Vielleicht hatte Friedrich sogar von Anfang an seine künftige Abwesenheit auf dem Kreuzzug als Argument für die zur Sicherung seines Erbes notwendige Krönung seines Sohnes im Blick. Vorbild dafür könnte Friedrichs eigene Wahl zum deutschen König von 1196 gewesen sein, zu deren Durchsetzung Heinrich VI. sein Kreuzzugversprechen in die Waagschale geworfen hatte, wenn auch dies letztlich nicht ausschlaggebend für den Erfolg gewesen war.[162]

Die Kreuzzugsmotivation Friedrichs II.

Die verschiedenen Hinweise zu den behandelten Aspekten zusammenfassend, lässt sich ein schlüssiges Bild von der Kreuzzugsmotivation Friedrichs II. gewinnen. Friedrich hatte vielleicht schon als Kind durch den *Liber ad honorem Augusti* die Idee eingepflanzt bekommen, zur Aufrichtung eines universalen Friedensreiches auserkoren zu sein. Ein entsprechendes Bewusstsein der eigenen Besonderheit konnte er durch die Wirren seiner Kindheit erlangen, in denen er erleben musste, wie scheinbar alle Welt hartnäckig um seine Person kämpfte. Es bedurfte freilich eines deutlichen Impulses, der aus einer den überschwänglichen Zukunftshoffnungen eines Panegyrikers erwachsenen Idee einen konkreten Gedanken, ja eine Überzeugung machte. Der Impuls kam mit der durch Innozenz III. unterstützten Wahl Friedrichs zum *Romanorum imperator* 1211/12. Spätestens die glücklichen Wendungen, die Friedrichs Rückgewinnung seines staufischen Erbes und seinen Griff nach der deutschen Königskrone begleiteten, weckten in ihm die Gewissheit, von Gott selbst berufen zu sein, um tatsächlich jenes von Petrus von Eboli beschworene Friedensreich zu errichten.[163] Die Kenntnis der Werke Ottos von Freising und vielleicht auch derer Gottfrieds von Viterbo sowie einiger Grundzüge der Lehren Joachims von Fiore konnte solcher Überzeugung zusätzlich Nahrung geben und Friedrich II. den Blick auf die mögliche eigene Rolle im göttlichen Heilsplan eröffnen, der durchaus eine eschatologische Dimension anhaftete, indem er nämlich glauben konnte, als römischer Kaiser aus dem letzten Geschlecht, dem diese Würde zukommen sollte, ein Wegbereiter der Wiederkunft Christi und eines neuen Zeitalters zu sein. Als der weltliche Arm der *ecclesia Dei*, im Sinne Ottos von Freising, war Friedrich dabei verantwortlich für die Wahrung von Recht und Ordnung innerhalb der *christianitas*, und dazu musste es sein Bestreben sein, seiner Macht eine alle Christen und alle wichtigen christlichen Stätten einbeziehende Reichweite zu verleihen, also universale kaiserliche Herrschaft zu etablieren. Nach Osten, ins Heilige Land, konnte Friedrich seinen Einfluss allein durch einen

---

[162] Siehe Ulrich Schmidt, *Königswahl und Thronfolge im 12. Jahrhundert*, Beihefte zu J. F. Böhmer, Regesta Imperii 7 (Köln, Wien, 1987), pp. 227–29 und 247–48.
[163] Ähnlich, ohne Verweis auf Petrus, Abulafia, *Frederick*, p. 117.

Kreuzzug tragen. Die spätere Ehelichung Isabellas von Brienne war dabei ein Glücksfall, der die Durchsetzung des kaiserlichen Anspruchs auf die Oberherrschaft auch über das Königreich Jerusalem deutlich erleichterte.

War also das Kreuzzugsgelübde integraler Bestandteil eines religiös durchtränkten und aus tradierten Idealvorstellungen über das Kaisertum gespeisten Herrschaftsprogramms, so erklärt sich die frühe Kreuznahme schon im Jahr 1215 zum einen aus dem Amtsverständnis des designierten Kaisers und zum anderen aus der politischen Lage. Bei Otto von Freising konnte Friedrich das Ideal der *civitas permixta* kennenlernen, das ein einvernehmliches Handeln von Papst und Kaiser zum Wohle der Christenheit beinhaltete. Trotz der vehementen Verfolgung seiner eigenen, den päpstlichen Vorstellungen widerstrebenden Herrschaftsziele und den daraus erwachsenden, heftigen Konflikten kann man bei Friedrich II. das stete Bemühen um Frieden mit dem Papst feststellen, wenn auch nicht um jeden Preis. Daher war der 1213 in die Welt gesandte Aufruf Innozenz' III. zu einem neuen Kreuzzug sicher ein Anlass für Friedrich, bereits am Beginn seiner neuen Herrschaft die Teilnahme an dem vom Papst ausgerufenen Unternehmen zu geloben. Der andere damit unmittelbar verknüpfte Grund für den frühen Zeitpunkt der Kreuznahme war Friedrichs Wissen, dass seine angestrebte erste Zielsetzung, die Vereinigung von Reich und Regnum in einer Hand, der eigenen oder der seines Sohnes Heinrich, das Einvernehmen mit dem Papst gefährden würde. Deshalb diente das Kreuzzugsgelübde auch dazu, dieses Einvernehmen auf einer anderen, mit Blick auf die Bedeutung für die Christenheit zugleich höheren Ebene zu demonstrieren. Und Friedrich brauchte dieses Einvernehmen mit dem Papst, um seinen Konkurrenten im Reich, Otto IV., überwinden zu können.

Es wurde dargelegt, dass der Ablauf des Herrschaftsausbaus, wie er im *Liber ad honorem Augusti* beschrieben ist, dem Agieren Friedrichs gleicht und daher dieser Ablauf als Grundlage für Friedrichs II. Herrschaftsprogramm gedeutet wird. Für eine solche Deutung spricht auch der 1225 geschlossene Vertrag von San Germano. Honorius III. war damals offenbar nicht gewillt, zum wiederholten Male den schon beinahe üblichen Aufschub für den Aufbruch Friedrichs ins Heilige Land zu gewähren. Der festzulegende neue Termin sollte diesmal unwiderruflich sein. In San Germano trafen sich päpstliche Legaten mit Friedrich, um einen Vertrag aufzusetzen, der die Leistungen des Kaisers zur Voranbringung des Kreuzzugs im Einzelnen aufführt und natürlich auch einen neuen Aufbruchstermin bestimmt. Dabei wurde von vornherein jede Abweichung von den Vereinbarungen des Vertrags unter die Strafe der Exkommunikation gestellt.[164] Erst nachdem Friedrich diesen Vertrag besiegelt hatte, lösten ihn die Legaten von der Zusage, die Fahrt im Sommer 1225 anzutreten. Friedrich scheint selbst fest entschlossen und zuversichtlich gewesen zu sein, was die fristgerechte Umsetzung des Vertrags betrifft. Denn er verzichtete darauf, bezüglich des Aufbruchtermins und der zu stellenden Truppen irgendwelche Einschränkungen oder Ausnahmeregelungen für die drohende Exkommunikation

---

[164] MGH Const. 2, p. 130, ll. 41–44.

in den Text einfließen zu lassen.[165] Diese Entschlossenheit auf Seiten des Kaisers erklärt sich am besten daraus, dass die Zeit für seinen Kreuzzug nun gekommen war. Denn seine Herrschaft über Reich und Regnum war 1225 gefestigt, die Nachfolge in beiden Reichen geklärt und die letzten Aufständischen, die sizilischen Sarazenen, waren, zumindest vorerst, gebändigt. Allein die Lombardenfrage, das heißt die Wiederherstellung der vollen Reichsgewalt über Norditalien, war noch offen, doch konnte Friedrich 1225 mit Zuversicht gen Norden blicken.[166] Und Friedrich eröffnete sich mit der Ehelichung Isabellas von Brienne die Möglichkeit, über den hegemonial begründeten kaiserlichen Einfluss hinaus, in Jerusalem zu herrschen.

Der Zug ins heilige Land verlief dann nicht in dem gewünschten Rahmen. Die Umstände erforderten das Erreichen eines möglichst raschen und Kräfte schonenden Erfolgs. Dass dies gelang, dürfte Friedrich tatsächlich eine erneute Bestätigung seiner besonderen Teilhaftigkeit an der Gnade Gottes gewesen sein. Insofern war der Vertrag mit al-Kāmil für Friedrich ein echter Erfolg. Aber er war nicht die endgültige Erfüllung seiner Zielsetzung, sondern nur die erste notwendige Voraussetzung dafür. Das zeigt das weitere Engagement Friedrichs für das Heilige Land.[167] Es ist ein einleuchtender, konsequenter Schluss, wenn Friedrich 1246 anbot, erneut einen Kreuzzug zu unternehmen und fortan im Osten zu bleiben.[168] Denn ohne den echten Einfluss in und auf Jerusalem war die kaiserliche Macht unvollkommen und die heilsgeschichtliche Rolle der kaiserlichen Staufer nicht ausfüllbar. Friedrich II. griff mit seinem Kreuzzugsengagement schon früh auf antik-römische Wurzeln zurück, weil er, wie ein neuer Oktavian Augustus, ein Wegbereiter der Wiederkunft des Herrn zu sein gedachte.

---

[165] Hechelhammer, *Kreuzzug*, p. 168 bezieht den Artikel 9 (MGH Const. 2, p. 131, ll. 1–7) auf alle Vereinbarungen des Vertrags. Der Zusammenhang – die Nennung derjenigen als Zeugen für den Ausgleich eines Säumnisses, die stellvertretend die zugesagten Geldsummen entgegen nehmen sollen – weist eindeutig darauf hin, dass die dort erwähnten "termini solutione" Zahlungstermine sind, sich die Möglichkeit einer Wiedergutmachung also allein auf eventuelle Zahlungssäumnisse bezieht.

[166] Zur vorläufigen Unterwerfung der Sarazenen und zum Stand der Lombardenfrage 1225/26 siehe Stürner, *Friedrich II.*, 2:69, und pp. 99–104.

[167] Zu den gemeinsamen Bemühungen Friedrichs II. und Gregors IX. um einen neuen Kreuzzug siehe Björn Weiler, "Gregory IX, Frederick II, and the Liberation of the Holy Land, 1230–9," in *The Holy Land, Holy Lands, and Christian History. Papers read at the 1998 Summer Meeting and the 1999 Winter Meeting of the Ecclesiastical History Society*, ed. Robert N. Swanson, Studies in Church History 36 (Woodbridge, 2000), pp. 192–206.

[168] Stürner, *Friedrich II.*, 2:167–69.

A Neglected Quarrel over a House in Cyprus in 1299: The Nicosia Franciscans vs. the Chapter of Nicosia Cathedral

Chris Schabel

University of Cyprus

A general sketch of the history of Frankish Cyprus has been drawn, but to evaluate this sketch and to complete the portrait in all its details we must broaden our palette and increase the number and type of brushes at our disposal. The time has come in the modern historiography of Frankish Cyprus to embark on an ambitious program to gather systematically all sources for the period, whether published or unpublished, known or hitherto unknown, and put them in a more usable form, while at the same time compiling a prosopographical database that will assist in the future development of the field.

In 1917, the great historian of the Franciscans in the East, Girolamo Golubovich, published five documents concerning a nasty dispute between the Friars Minor of Nicosia and the chapter of Nicosia Cathedral that took place in 1299.[1] The five *instrumenta* are rare examples of original charters from Frankish Cyprus, constituting parchments 47–49 of S. Francesco al Prato in the Archivio di Stato di Perugia. As noted by the editors of the journal that printed the texts, *Archivum Franciscanum Historicum*, Golubovich's brief article was an addition to what he had incorporated in the relevant first two volumes of his monumental five-volume *Biblioteca bio-bibliografica della Terra Santa e dell'Oriente francescano*.[2] Their absence from those volumes perhaps explains why the documents have not only been neglected in the main historiography on the Latin Church of Cyprus, but also overlooked in works on the Syrian community and on the French language on the island in the early Frankish period, for they contain an important early reference to a raïs of the Syrians and, although the charters are in Latin, they include allegedly verbatim French speeches read out in Famagusta and Nicosia Cathedrals.[3] Golubovich's

---

I would like to thank Neslihan Şenocak of Columbia University for drawing my attention to the documents and for other assistance, Laura Minervini of the Università di Napoli for improving my transcription of the French material, and Daniele Baglioni, Angel Konnari, and Michalis Olympios for helpful comments.

[1] Girolamo Golubovich, "Cipro francescana," *Archivum Franciscanum Historicum* 10 (1917), pp. 357–66.

[2] Girolamo Golubovich, *Biblioteca bio-bibliografica della Terra Santa e dell'Oriente francescano*, 5 vols. (Quaracchi, 1906–27). See note (a) of "Cipro francescana," p. 357.

[3] For example, the events are not discussed in Nicholas Coureas, *The Latin Church in Cyprus, 1195–1312* (Aldershot, 1997); Silvain Beraud, "Terre sainte de Chypre: l'ordre des Frères Mineurs; églises et couvents (1217–1987)," *Κυπριακαί Σπουδαί* 50 (1986), pp. 135–53; Jean Richard, "La cour des Syriens de Famagouste d'après un texte de 1448," *Byzantinische Forschungen* 12 (1987), pp.

Latin transcriptions exhibit few errors of consequence, but the shortcomings in his French text along with the apparent obscurity of the publication more than justify a new edition accompanied by an up-to-date apparatus.[4] In this introduction I shall relate what the documents tell us about the events themselves and what additional information they provide about Cyprus in 1299.

Following Richard the Lionheart's conquest of Cyprus in 1191 and its sale to Guy de Lusignan the following year, Guy's brother Aimery succeeded in creating the kingdom of Cyprus and establishing a Latin ecclesiastical hierarchy on the island in 1196.[5] Nicosia became a Latin metropolitan see with suffragan bishoprics in Paphos, Limassol, and Famagusta. By the 1250s the Cathedral of Holy Wisdom of Nicosia was served by a chapter of sixteen members, including twelve canons and four officers: the dean, archdeacon, treasurer, and cantor. The foundation of the Order of Friars Minor, or Franciscans, postdates the coming of the Latin Church to Cyprus. Francis of Assisi himself may have visited the capital during his stay in Cyprus sometime in 1219–20 during the course of the Fifth Crusade, and the sixteenth-century Cypriot Dominican author Etienne de Lusignan asserts that the Franciscans arrived in Cyprus around the same time as the Dominicans (ca. 1226). By 1244, at least, the Franciscans were in possession of their first Nicosia convent west of the present Paphos Gate in the sixteenth-century Venetian walls of the city, close to the first Dominican convent and the Cistercian nunnery of St. Theodore.[6]

With the growth of the power of these begging or mendicant orders (as the Dominicans and Franciscans were termed), a struggle arose all over Europe concerning the relationship between, on the one hand, the traditional secular clergy running the parish churches and cathedrals and, on the other, the mendicants, who competed with the priests and bishops for donations and fees for all sorts of religious services. Nicosia was no exception, and the local Franciscans and Dominicans did not always get along with the archbishop and chapter of the city's

---

383–98; or in the many linguistic works of Laura Minervini, for example, "Outremer," in *Lo spazio letterario del Medioevo. 2. Il Medioevo volgare*, ed. Piero Boitani, Mario Mancini, and Alberto Varvaro (Rome, 2001), pp. 611–48.

[4] Although the French passages amount to only about fifty lines of text, Golubovich committed about fifty errors (or, sometimes, "corrections"), thus rendering the material much less useful to linguists. Among the Latin errors there is an omission *per homoioteleuton*, along with ten or so errors in the spelling of proper names. In the French, I have italicized the letters I have added in expanding abbreviations.

[5] For the political and ecclesiastical history of Cyprus down to the fourteenth century, see Peter W. Edbury, *The Kingdom of Cyprus and the Crusades 1191–1374* (Cambridge, 1991) and Coureas, *The Latin Church in Cyprus*.

[6] *The Cartulary of the Cathedral of Holy Wisdom of Nicosia*, ed. Nicholas Coureas and Chris Schabel, Texts and Studies in the History of Cyprus 25 (Nicosia, 1997), no. 63; Etienne de Lusignan, *Chorograffia e breve historia universale dell'isola de Cipro principiando al tempo di Noè per il fino al 1572* (Bologna, 1573; repr. Famagusta, 1973; repr. Nicosia, 2004), f. 32v.

Cathedral of Holy Wisdom.[7] For example, it was in the face of strong opposition from the archbishop of Nicosia, Hugh of Fagiano (1250–67), that the Franciscans sold the property on which their first Nicosia convent lay to the Cistercians in the early 1250s, moving their base to a more convenient location within the city.[8] In contrast to their battles with the archbishop, and partly as a cause of those disputes, the Nicosia Franciscans enjoyed the patronage of the crown and nobles early on, as is indicated by the many significant burials in their new site during the reign of King Henry II (1285–1324), who favored the Order.[9] His successor, however, King Hugh IV (1324–59), switched the crown's allegiances to the Dominicans, even persecuting the Franciscans.[10] Nevertheless, the convent continued to flourish despite being displaced by the Dominicans in the hearts of the Lusignans.

The Franciscans eventually founded convents in all four episcopal cities of Cyprus – Nicosia, Paphos, Limassol, and Famagusta – but the first and most important was the Nicosia house. It is particularly interesting to note that its school was so successful that, in 1374, it was a *studium generale*.[11] Travellers' descriptions and perhaps some fragments of sculpture and inscriptions are all that survives of this Franciscan monastery.[12] It possessed two cloisters at the end of the fourteenth century and it was still attractive in 1483.[13] It continued to function after the Venetians annexed the Lusignan kingdom in 1489, surviving down to the Ottoman conquest in 1570.

It was during the monastery's heyday in the reign of King Henry II, then, that the dispute with the cathedral chapter took place. Parchment 47 carries three separate documents that give the background, all acts by or for the bishop of Famagusta, Guy of Trento (1298–1308),[14] drawn up by the cleric Andrew of Vercelli, notary public by imperial authority, who in 1301 and 1302 would be termed the bishop's scribe.[15] The dean of Nicosia Cathedral, Nicholas de Camulio, was living in a

---

[7] See *Cartulary*, nos. 38–39 (1254).

[8] See Chris Schabel, "Frankish Pyrgos and the Cistercians," *Report of the Department of Antiquities (Cyprus)* (2000), pp. 349–60, at pp. 353–54, and the literature cited there.

[9] See various references in Wipertus H. Rudt de Collenberg, "Les Ibelin aux XIIIe et XIVe siècles," Επετηρίδα του Κέντρου Επιστημονικών Ερευνών (hereafter *EKEE*) 9 (1979), pp. 117–265; idem, "Les Lusignan de Chypre," *EKEE* 10 (1980), pp. 85–319; Brunhilde Imhaus, "La mort dans la société franque de Chypre," *EKEE* 24 (1998), pp. 1–75.

[10] Louis de Mas Latrie, *Histoire de l'île de Chypre sous le règne des princes de la maison de Lusignan*, 2 (Paris, 1852), pp. 195–96, 200, 202; Chris Schabel, "Hugh the Just: The Further Rehabilitation of King Hugh IV Lusignan of Cyprus," *EKEE* 30 (2004), pp. 123–52, at pp. 148–50.

[11] *Chartularium Universitatis Parisiensis*, ed. Heinrich Denifle and Émile Châtelain, 3 (Paris, 1894), no. 1394.

[12] For these and the general history, see Golubovich, *Biblioteca bio-bibliografica*, 2:382–387.

[13] Claude Delaval Cobham, *Excerpta Cypria: Materials for a History of Cyprus* (Cambridge, 1908), pp. 26 and 44.

[14] On Guy, see Schabel, "The Latin Bishops of Cyprus,1255–1313, with a Note on Bishop Neophytos of Solea," *EKEE* 29 (2004), pp. 75–111, at pp. 108–9, and the literature cited there.

[15] Andrew is mentioned in various Genoese notarial documents from the summer of 1299 to May 1302: *Notai Genovesi in Oltremare. Atti rogati a Cipro da Lamberto di Sambuceto (3 luglio 1300 – 3 agosto 1301)*, ed. Valeria Polonio, Collana storica di fonti e studi (hereafter CSFS) 31 (Genoa, 1982), nos.

house belonging to the cathedral chapter that abutted the sacristy of the Franciscan convent. The friars wished to obtain the house and, likely after a failed attempt to deal directly with the chapter, at some point before the end of 1298 at the latest, the Franciscans sent their warden (probably the Guido of Bologna named in Document 5)[16] to the papal curia to get the support of Pope Boniface VIII (1295–1303). According to Document 1, the custodian was able to secure a papal letter ordering the sale or exchange of the house to the Minorites and assigning Bishop Guy of Famagusta as executor. Thus, on 20 March 1299, Bishop Guy went to "the place where the chapter of the church of Nicosia is held" and told the members that he would make sure that they received a good price for the house or another house equally good or better in exchange.

The vague way in which the location is described reinforces the impression that the chapter of Nicosia had no special chapterhouse, but met at various places in and around the cathedral precinct.[17] Of the chapter, which consisted of some twelve canons and the officials of the cathedral, the dean and five canons were present, as were many witnesses, including two who acted in that official capacity, Master James of Ulisengo, a surgeon of the Asti diocese,[18] and William de Monchuc of the diocese of Torino. At least four of the members of the chapter who were present are known from other documents. Dean Nicholas himself, a Genoese, is first attested in that capacity in May 1297 and he was probably still dean in January 1324.[19] Canon Baldwin of Cyprus – usually "Master Baldwin," as in Document 3 – was already a member of the chapter by early 1292, although he was also canon of Tortosa in June 1298 and participating in the election of Bishop Guy of Famagusta, which had been

---

112 and 295; *Notai Genovesi in Oltremare. Atti rogati a Cipro da Lamberto di Sambuceto (6 luglio – 17 ottobre 1301)*, ed. Romeo Pavoni, CSFS 32 (Genoa, 1982), no. 155 (25 September 1301: "scribe of the lord bishop of Famagusta"); *Notai Genovesi in Oltremare. Atti rogati a Cipro da Lamberto di Sambuceto (gennaio – agosto 1302)*, ed. Romeo Pavoni, CSFS 49 (Genoa, 1987), nos. 202 (3 May 1302: "bishop's scribe") and 204.

[16] Golubovich, "Cipro francescana," p. 357, suggests that this may be the Guido who was the convent's custodian in 1306.

[17] On the location of the chapter meetings, see Chris Schabel, "Ecclesiastical Monuments and Topography," part of Nicholas Coureas, Gilles Grivaud, and Chris Schabel, "The Capital of the Sweet Land of Cyprus: Frankish and Venetian Nicosia," in *Nicosia: The First 2000 Years*, ed. D. Michaelides (Forthcoming: Nicosia, 2009).

[18] The surgeon Master James of Asti is attested in a document of 1301: CSFS 32, no. 125 (15 September 1301).

[19] *Cartulary*, no. 90; "Actes passés à Famagouste de 1299 à 1301 par devant le notaire génois Lamberto di Sambuceto," ed. Cornelio Desimoni, *AOL* 2 (Paris, 1884), pp. 3–120, no. 96 (brother of Ambroxius of Camulio); *The Synodicum Nicosiense and Other Documents of the Latin Church of Cyprus, 1196–1373*, ed. Chris Schabel, Texts and Studies in the History of Cyprus 39 (Nicosia, 2001), no. J.VIIIb. On 1 September 1296, Boniface VIII wrote a letter to "Nicolino de Camilla canonico Ambianensis [ecclesie], capellano nostro." It is possible that this is the same as Nicholas de Camulio, who would then have been appointed dean of Nicosia in the following months; see *Bullarium Cyprium II: Papal Letters Concerning Cyprus 1262–1314*, ed. Chris Schabel (forthcoming: Nicosia, 2009), no. o-23. For his being Genoese, Golubovich, "Cipro francescana," p. 358 and n. 1, cites a document from 1300.

united with Tortosa. Baldwin was still canon of Nicosia in May 1309, but a year later he himself was bishop of Famagusta. Also known as Baldwin Lambert, he remained bishop of Famagusta until his death in 1328. Peter of Brie was still canon of Nicosia in 1311 when he was serving as administrator of the cathedral.[20] John of Port was already canon of Nicosia in early 1292,[21] while Canon James Bruno would be cantor of Nicosia Cathedral by 1308.[22] One other canon of Nicosia was also present: Peter, the exiled dean of Tyre Cathedral.

The Franciscans had purchased a house from the archbishop in 1292, probably trying to consolidate their holdings around their convent.[23] We do not know the background of that transaction, but it appears that papal involvement in the forced sale or trade of property on Cyprus was not unusual. In a letter of 21 May 1304, Pope Benedict XI (1303–1304) told Bishop Peter Erlant of Limassol to assist the master and Knights Hospitaller in acquiring an oratory or chapel of the Greeks that abutted the Hospitaller headquarters in Limassol and made access awkward. The Greeks did not wish to make another arrangement concerning their oratory or chapel, so Pope Benedict ordered Bishop Peter to force the Greeks to sell or exchange the property.[24]

The Greeks of Limassol probably gave in, but the chapter of Nicosia Cathedral refused to obey the papal directive. According to Document 2, Bishop Guy therefore promulgated a sentence of suspension against them, for fifteen days later, on Saturday 4 April – during Mass in the old Famagusta Cathedral – the master chaplain of the cathedral, Robert Turchetus of Beirut, on the orders of Bishop Guy, read out in public the sentence in French. Turchetus – which Golubovich read as "Giuchetus" – was a priest who apparently knew Arabic, since he is called a "drogumanus ad predicta" in a 1299 document concerning refugees from the mainland.[25] Turchetus would become canon of Nicosia by 1323 and he is obviously the canon of Nicosia "Bibertus Turquetus" mentioned in a document of 1327, the "Bi" no doubt being a scribal error.[26] On the authority of Pope Boniface, Bishop Guy suspended from the divine offices Dean Nicholas, the treasurer Jean de Nores, the chapter, and every rebellious member of the chapter of Nicosia Cathedral. Jean de Nores was a member of the famous Cypriot de Nores family that outlasted the Latin period to survive in

---

[20] *Cartulary*, nos. 65 (10 January 1292, already master) and 90; *Bullarium Cyprium II*, nos. o-30, o-33, q-50 and q-78; the last, from 8 June 1310, specifies that Bishop Baldwin had been sent an earlier letter while he was canon, which letter (q-50) refers to "Baldwin of Cyprus." There were apparently other Baldwins of Cyprus, for in 1311 Peter of Brie was ordered to promote Baldwin of Cyprus to subdeacon: *Registrum Clementis Papae V* (Rome, 1885–92), no. 10497 (there is a typographical error in Schabel, "The Latin Bishops of Cyprus," p. 96, n. 52, with "10447").

[21] *Cartulary*, no. 65.
[22] *Bullarium Cyprium II*, no. q-30.
[23] *Cartulary*, no. 52.
[24] *Bullarium Cyprium II*, no. p-7.
[25] *Notai Genovesi in Oltremare. Atti rogati a Cipro da Lamberto di Sambuceto (11 ottobre 1296 – 23 giugno 1299)*, ed. Michel Balard, CSFS 39 (Genoa, 1983), no. 121 (2 April 1299).
[26] *Synodicum Nicosiense*, no. J.Vb; *Cartulary*, no. 109.

exile in Italy.²⁷ Five men were called to witness the event: Peter Marbre²⁸ of Acre, the cleric Nicolinus of Tripoli, the Genoese Rufinus of Ast,²⁹ and two bootmakers, Obertus of Tripoli and the Genoese Richebonus of Brescia.³⁰

The chapter stood firm. Document 3 informs us that at Sunday Mass on 23 August, again in Famagusta Cathedral, the priest Leo of Tripoli, master chaplain³¹ of the cathedral (perhaps Robert Turchetus had already been promoted to canon of Nicosia) and possesser of an "assize" or minor benefice, announced on behalf of Bishop Guy, in French and before a great multitude of clerics and laypeople, that Dean Nicholas and Jean de Nores the treasurer as well as six canons of Nicosia Cathedral were excommunicates for refusing to sell or exchange their house that abutted the Franciscans' sacristy in Nicosia. It is significant that Leo referred to the "vicaires" of Archbishop Gerard of Nicosia. The word "vicaires" is somewhat vague, for in Old French it could be a singular subject with an "s" ending, whereas later it would be read as plural.³² Certainly the treasurer, Jean de Nores, is the archbishop's vicar, but it is possible that Dean Nicholas was also vicar. Document 5 will refer to "vicarios" plural, but in the famous case of the disputed election of the bishop of Solea around the same time, the three Greek candidates took their claims to the "vicar" of the archbishop, which would appear to refer to Jean de Nores alone. In any case, the fact that no vicar is mentioned in Document 2 suggests that Gerard of Langres, the archbishop, had left Cyprus between 4 April and 23 August 1299, the dates of Documents 2 and 3. He is first attested on the island on 1 May 1297, so the data affirms the assertion of the later *Chronicle of Amadi* that Archbishop Gerard had stayed only two years in Cyprus.³³ That the archdeacon of

---

²⁷ Probably the same Jean de Nores who is listed as canon of Paphos in 1307–10 in Wipertus H. Rudt de Collenberg's table I/1 in Ἱστορία τῆς Κύπρου, V, Μεσαιωνικὸν βασίλειον – Ἐνετοκρατία, part 2, ed. Theodoros Papadopoullos (Nicosia, 1996). On the de Nores family, see Angel Nicolaou-Konnari, "L'identité en diaspora: vies et œuvres de Pierre de Nores (avant 1570? – après 1646) et Georges de Nores (1619–1638)," in *Identités croisées en un milieu méditerranéen: le cas de Chypre (Antiquité – Moyen Age)*, ed. Sabine Fourrier and Gilles Grivaud (Rouen, 2006), pp. 329–53, and the literature cited there.

²⁸ Also cited in Famagusta in October 1300: CSFS 31, nos. 43–45, 69. He is perhaps related to Anthony Marbre, canon of Nicosia in 1339 and 1340: *Cartulary*, no. 109a; *Synodicum Nicosiense*, no. L.14.

²⁹ Rufinus witnessed charters in Famagusta down to 1307: CSFS 31, nos. 26, 55, 61, 74, 163; CSFS 43, nos. 47, 82.

³⁰ Richebonus witnessed numerous charters in Famagusta from 1296 to 1302: CSFS 39, nos. 12, 151; CSFS 31, nos. 275, 280, 366; CSFS 49, nos. 32, 60, 168, 200, 235.

³¹ Not "master and chaplain," as Golubovich, "Cipro francescana," p. 359, writes, placing also a comma in the Latin, p. 362: "magister, capellanus."

³² According to Laura Minervini (personal communication), "vicaires" could be "a residue of an Old French 'cas sujet': -s marks the singular subject. The system declines in the 13th c., but there are scattered residues in many later texts (and Joinville still uses it consistently)."

³³ *Cartulary*, no. 90; *Synodicum Nicosiense*, no. X.33; *Bullarium Cyprium II*, no. o-50; Amadi, *Chroniques d'Amadi et de Strambaldi*, ed. René de Mas Latrie, 1 (Paris, 1891; repr. Nicosia, 1999), p. 233. This would confirm that Gerard's stay in Cyprus was in 1297–99; Coureas, *The Latin Church in Cyprus*, pp. 64 and 73, has him leaving in 1298.

the cathedral and chancellor of Cyprus, Henry of Gibelet, is not mentioned among the excommunicates is due to his absence in Rome at the time.[34]

Canons John of Port, Peter of Brie, Baldwin of Cyprus, and Peter, dean of Tyre, we have already met, but two other canons are listed among the rebels: Gerard of Antioch and James, prior of Saint-Etienne. In 1292 Canon Gerard sold a house in Nicosia to Archbishop John of Ancona. Mentioned again in a document of 1297, he was dead by 1322.[35] Besides the many people attending Mass, there were four official witnesses in addition to many others present: Peter de Rosis, with a minor benefice in Famagusta Cathedral, the cleric Symion of Beirut, Manuel of Savona,[36] and Bartholomew of Naples.

Perhaps owing to the lack of pressure from their absent archbishop and archdeacon, the chapter did not acquiesce. Thus Bishop Guy of Famagusta took the affair to the center of the controversy – Nicosia – beginning the following Sunday. The last two of the five *instrumenta*, each on a separate parchment, were drawn up in the capital by a citizen of that city, Simon "of the Archbishop," notary public by papal authority. Document 4 was executed in Nicosia Cathedral itself during and just after the events described, as in the case of the previous documents. Abbot Henry Chappe of Cistercian Beaulieu Abbey had received his orders via a letter patent from Bishop Guy, sealed with Guy's seal, explaining what was in "a certain papal letter strengthened with a papal bull suspended with a hemp string." Beaulieu, a few hundred meters to the west of the Franciscan convent, was one of the three wealthiest and most powerful monasteries on Cyprus, and Henry, a member of a well-known Cypriot family, was still abbot when he died in Armenia in June 1309 on a mission for the governor, Amaury de Lusignan, lord of Tyre, who had usurped power from his brother, King Henry II, in 1306.[37] When he became abbot is unknown, but he was probably the "abbot of Beaulieu" whom Boniface VIII employed for an assignment in June 1298.[38] At sermon hour during Sunday Mass on 30 August 1299, between Prime and Tierce, when "a great number of people" both men and women were attending the service in the cathedral, Abbot Henry, having summoned the notary for the occasion, entered the cathedral to denounce the excommunicates on the orders of Bishop Guy of Famagusta. Here the document merits translation:

> When the clerics saw the abbot, the clerics Peter Blanchard, a priest and assized of the Church of Nicosia,[39] John of Raoul Fraperius, Stephenotus, assized in said Church of

---

[34] On Henry, see Schabel, "The Latin Bishops of Cyprus," pp. 87–95.

[35] *Cartulary*, nos. 52 (1292, with a rubric of 1322 refering to him as the "late") and 90.

[36] Genoese documents of the time record a Manuel Ricius de Sagona and the Genoese Manuel Scarlata de Sagona. See the indices to CSFS 31 and 32.

[37] Amadi, p. 299. On Beaulieu, see Schabel, "Ecclesiastical Monuments and Topography," and the literature cited there.

[38] *Bullarium Cyprium II*, nos. o-28 and o-29.

[39] Probably the "presbitero Petro magistro capellano Nicosiensis ecclesie" mentioned in a document of 1292: *Cartulary*, no. 52.

Nicosia, Philip, Guiliotus, son of George David, and Geoffrey of Bonafre ascended the stairs of the pulpit of the church and stood atop the stairs defending them. But the abbot went to the stairs and wanted to ascend to the pulpit. Peter Blanchard and the rest of the aforementioned clerics extended their hands with open palms against the chest of the abbot, not allowing him to ascend. But the abbot, seeing that he was unable to ascend to the pulpit, since the clerics and the priest were blocking him, stood up on a certain stool that is at the base of the stairs, showed the papal letter, and began to speak and proclaim to the people. And as soon as he had begun talking, Peter Blanchard, John of Raoul, and Stephenotus angrily ordered the altar boys (*clericuli*) that they had brought with them in a great number to shout and ordered those who were in the choir to pound on the table and stalls and make noise. Complying with these orders, they made and uttered such clamor, sounds, and noise that no one was able to hear or understand the abbot or anyone else – rather the altar boys, with respect to and having grasped the anger and wrath of the aforementioned ministers and with their trust, were insulting the abbot by calling him excommunicated, irregular, and a bad monk. And Stephenotus, John, and Guiliotus, standing beside the abbot on his right and left, were pushing him and threatening him. But the abbot, seeing that he could not be heard by the people because of the loud clamor, sounds, and noise, asked the witnesses written below to come closer to him so that they could hear him. When they had come so close to him that they were touching him, he narrated, said, and announced in French as follows.

Abbot Henry was only able to say a few words and, when he showed the papal letter to the crowd, "Guiliotus reached out his hands in order to destroy the letter, but the abbot was holding it tightly and Guiliotus backed off, although he tried to do this twice and he positioned himself between the abbot and the wall and pushed the abbot down off the stool." Yet the abbot continued and was able to complete his speech, denouncing on behalf of Bishop Guy five members of the chapter as excommunicates – Dean Nicholas, Jean de Nores the treasurer and vicar of the archbishop, and three canons, Gerard of Antioch, Peter of Brie, and John of Port – for not obeying the command of the bishop of Famagusta and, indeed, that of the pope himself. Apparently, Canon James, prior of Saint-Etienne, had changed his mind since the week before and had agreed to obey.

This time there were numerous witnesses, but many could only see and not hear, because of the noise. Abbot Henry had called eight to hear his words: Nicholas of Acre, one of Henry's Cistercian monks at Beaulieu; noble men and lords Matthew of Gibelet, Simon "Arras," and George Jocelin, knights; lords Martin de Nefin,[40] John de Camino, and John the Venetian, a goldsmith; and the most interesting of all, the nobleman and knight "Thomas of Finion, the reeys of the Syrians, which is to say the viscount of the Syrians in Cyprus or in the city of Nicosia." This is, in fact, the earliest clear mention of a raïs of the Court of the Syrians, although it has been neglected in studies on the Syrians of Cyprus. The wording suggests that in 1299 Thomas presided in Nicosia but had authority throughout Cyprus, but by 1355 a

---

[40] Perhaps the Martin de Nefin mentioned in *RRH*, nos. 1364 and 1400, as being in Acre in 1269 and somewhere on the mainland in 1274.

raïs of the Syrians is attested in Famagusta as well.[41] Among the many who could see but not hear were lords Peter de Gloria,[42] John "of the Archbishop," James de Cassas, and James Litardi.

A few weeks after the uproar in the Cathedral of Holy Wisdom, on the evening of Friday 25 September, the scribe Simon and three witnesses, John "Soueque," Gerard of Nicosia, and Little James (*Jaquetto*) the Englishman, were summoned to the Franciscan convent in Nicosia. The warden of the Nicosia Franciscans and the friars gathered in the customary way by the sound of the bell, probably, as in the case of the local Dominicans, in the chapterhouse.[43] Apparently the cathedral chapter had decided to launch an appeal against the papal decision. Thus, according to the fifth *instrumentum*, a very carefully worded legal document, the friars chose two Franciscans as their general and special proctors and nuncios, both of them historically important. The first, Martin, is described as "lector" of the convent, attesting to the functioning of the school; the second, Fulk, was the Franciscans' provincial minister of the Holy Land, or Syria.[44] They both agreed to work together or separately if necessary on the case in the papal curia, and they were given a broad range of powers. It is notable that the "vicars and chapter" had appealed to Bishop Guy, who is now termed "judge delegate" of Pope Boniface rather than merely "executor" of the papal mandate.

Unless there is an *instrumentum* in the Vatican that has not come to light, the story ends here. Nevertheless, there are several lessons to be learned. First, while historians have often drawn attention to the two episodes of violence between Latins and Greeks in and around Nicosia Cathedral in the fourteenth century,[45] such episodes among the Latin secular and regular clergy of the capital were in fact not infrequent.[46] Second, the local Latin clergy on Cyprus was by no means united

---

[41] There is a vague reference to a "raicius" of the Syrians in 1210, but perhaps he was just a bailli. On this topic, although not mentioning the present source, see Richard, "La cour des Syriens." The *RRH* mentions a Thomas of Fignon in Acre in 1260 (no. 1286) and a Thomas of Fenion in Tyre in 1269 (no. 1366).

[42] *RRH* has a Peter de Gloria in Acre in 1277 (no. 1413). Perhaps he was a relative of Balian de Gloria: see Christina Kaoulla and Chris Schabel, "The Inquisition against Peter de Castro, Vicar of the Dominican Province of the Holy Land, in Nicosia, Cyprus, 1330," *Archivum Fratrum Praedicatorum* 77 (2007), pp. 121–98, at p. 155.

[43] Kaoulla and Schabel, "The Inquisition against Peter de Castro," pp. 160, 163, 170, 180, 188.

[44] Early that year, on 10 June, Boniface had given Fulk an important assignment: *Bullarium Cyprium II*, no. o-38.

[45] Those of 1313 and 1360, which are often exaggerated or misinterpreted. The sources are gathered in Chris Schabel, "The Status of the Greek Clergy in Early Frankish Cyprus," in *"Sweet Land ..." Lectures on the History and Culture of Cyprus*, ed. Julian Chrysostomides and Charalambos Dendrinos (Camberley, 2006), pp. 165–208, at pp. 202–7.

[46] Besides the events of 1299, there was the scandalous imprisonment of a papal legate in the Dominican convent in 1329–30: Kaoulla and Schabel, "The Inquisition against Peter de Castro"; the expulsion of the archbishop in the 1280s: Schabel, "The Latin Bishops of Cyprus," pp. 82–83; and various other incidents.

but was fragmented into a great number of factions, sometimes within a single convent or cathedral administration. Names and titles indicate that refugee clerics from the Syrian mainland joined and further reinforced these factions, perhaps upsetting the balance in some cases. Third, and related to this, although in the bull *Unam Sanctam*, which was issued just three years after the events described above, Pope Boniface VIII would "declare, state, define and pronounce that it is altogether necessary to salvation for every human creature to be subject to the Roman Pontiff,"[47] this did not deter even his own secular clergy from openly defying his commands and enduring excommunication. This is another indication that the frequent use of excommunication for affairs like property disputes was weakening its efficacy. This is already well known, but it is important to remind ourselves of the complexities of the Roman Church when dealing with the ecclesiastical history of Frankish Cyprus.

---

[47] B. Tierney, *The Middle Ages: Volume 1: Sources of Medieval History* (New York, 1970), p. 316.

Dramatis personae

The numbers indicate in which Document(s) individuals are mentioned.

Andrew of Vercelli, notary public on imperial authority: 1, 2, 3
Baldwin of Cyprus, canon of Nicosia, master: 1, 3
Bartholomew of Naples: 3
Boniface VIII, pope: 1, 2, 3, 4, 5
Fulk, OFM provincial: 5
Geoffrey of Bonafre, cleric of Nicosia: 4
George Jocelin, knight: 4
Gerard of Antioch, canon of Nicosia: 3, 4
Gerard of Langres, archbishop of Nicosia: 3, 4
Gerard of Nicosia: 5
Guido of Bologna, OFM, custodian of Nicosia convent: 1, 2, 5
Guiliotus, son of George David, cleric of Nicosia: 4
Guy of Trento, bishop of Famagusta and Tortosa: 1, 2, 3, 4, 5
Henry Chappe, abbot of Beaulieu, OCist: 4
James, prior of Saint-Etienne, canon of Nicosia: 3
James Bruno, canon of Nicosia: 1
James de Cassas: 4
James (*Jaquetto*) the Englishman: 5
James Litardi: 4
James of Ulisengo, master, a surgeon of the Asti diocese: 1
Jean de Nores, treasurer of Nicosia, vicar of archbishop: 2, 3, 4
John "of the Archbishop": 4
John de Camino: 4
John of Port, canon of Nicosia: 1, 3, 4
John of Raoul Fraperius, cleric of Nicosia: 4
John "Soueque": 5
John the Venetian, goldsmith: 4
Leo of Tripoli, master chaplain of Famagusta: 3
Manuel of Savona: 3
Martin, OFM, "lector" of Nicosia convent: 5
Martin de Nefin: 4
Matthew of Gibelet, knight: 4
Nicholas of Acre, monk of Beaulieu, OCist: 4
Nicholas de Camulio, dean of Nicosia: 1, 2, 3, 4, 5
Nicolinus of Tripoli, cleric: 2
Obertus of Tripoli, bootmaker: 2
Peter, the dean of Tyre, canon of Nicosia: 1, 3
Peter Blanchard, priest, assized in Nicosia: 4
Peter of Brie, canon of Nicosia: 1, 3, 4
Peter de Gloria: 4
Peter Marbre of Acre: 2
Peter de Rosis, assized in Famagusta: 3
Philip, cleric of Nicosia: 4
Richebonus of Brescia, bootmaker: 2
Robert Turchetus of Beirut, master chaplain of Famagusta: 2
Rufinus of Ast: 2
Simon "Arras," knight: 4
Simon "of the Archbishop," notary public by papal authority: 4
Stephenotus, assized in Nicosia: 4
Symion of Beirut, cleric: 3
Thomas of Finion, rays of the Syrians: 4
William de Monchuc of the diocese of Torino: 1

Document 1

Nicosia, place where Cathedral Chapter meets   20 March 1299

Manuscript: Perugia, Archivio di Stato di Perugia, S. Francesco al Prato, Pergamene 47 (486 × 207 mm).
Summary: Paola Monacchia, *Regesti delle pergamene di S. Francesco al Prato di Perugia (1245–1777)* (Santa Maria degli Angeli, 1984), no. 47A.
Edition: Girolamo Golubovich, "Cipro francescana," *Archivum Franciscanum Historicum* 10 (1917), pp. 360–61 (= G).

In nomine Domini, Amen. Per presens publicum instrumentum pateat universis presentibus et futuris quod hac presenti die, in presentia mei, Andree de Vercellis, publici notarii, et testium infrascriptorum, reverendus pater dominus Guido, divina gratia Famagustanus et Anteradensis episcopus, executor datus per sanctissimum patrem dominum Bonifatium papam VIII, super litteris impetratis per guardianum et conventum Fratrum Minorum Nicossiensium[a] pro habenda domo Nicossiensis capituli que inheret sacristie dictorum fratrum, quam dominus Nicolaus decanus ecclesie Nicossiensis inhabitat, pro precio competenti vel per permutationem alterius, optulit se paratum capitulo Nicossiensi facere dari precium ipsis de capitulo quod exstimata esset domus que est iuxta sacristiam Fratrum Minorum in Nicossia, vel aliam domum eque bonam vel meliorem. Ad quod capitulum interfuerunt venerabiles viri domini Nicolaus de Camulio decanus, Bauduinus de Cipro, Petrus de Bria, Petrus decanus Tirensis, Iohannes de Portu, et Iacobus Brunus, canonici Nicossiensis ecclesie.

Actum Nicossie, in loco ubi tenetur capitulum ecclesie Nicossiensis, anno a Nativitate Domini M°CC°LXXXXIX, Indictione XII, mensis Martii die XX, presentibus testibus ad hoc specialiter vocatis et rogatis discretis viris Magistro Iacobo cirurgico de Ulisengo, Astensis diocesis, et Guillelmo de Monchuc,[b] Taurinensis diocesis, et pluribus aliis.

Et ego, Andreas supradictus de Vercellis, clericus, publicus auctoritate imperiali notarius, predictis interfui et ea rogatus scripti et in hanc publicam formam redegi et meo consueto signo signavi.

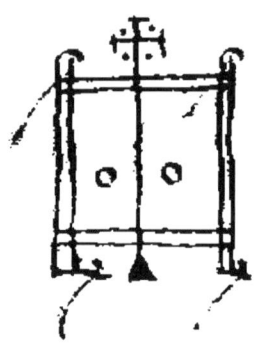

Fig. 1   Notarial sign of Andrew of Vercelli

---

a) Nicossiensium] Nicossiensis G   b) Monchuc] Monçhue G

Document 2

Famagusta Cathedral   4 April 1299

Manuscript: Perugia, Archivio di Stato di Perugia, S. Francesco al Prato, Pergamene 47 (= P).
Summary: Monacchia, *Regesti*, no. 47B.
Edition: Golubovich, "Cipro francescana," pp. 361–62 (= G).

In nomine Domini, Amen. Universis huius publici instrumenti seriem inspecturis pateat evidenter quod in presentia mei, Andree de Vercellis, publici notarii, et testium infrascriptorum, discretus vir dominus Robertus Turchetus[a] de Berito,[b] magister capellanus Famagustane ecclesie, de mandato reverendi patris domini G<uidonis>, divina gratia Famagustani et Anteradensis episcopi, executoris dati per sanctissimum patrem dominum Bonifatium papam VIII, super litteris impetratis per guardianum et conventum Fratrum Minorum Nicossiensium[c] pro habenda domo Nicossiensis ecclesie quam dominus Nicolaus decanus inhabitat, legit et publicavit in ecclesia Famagustana, hora misse, quandam suspensionis sententiam latam per dominum episcopum, executorem predictum, in hunc modum:

> "Nos denuntions de la part do reverend pere en Crist monseignor Guy, par la grace de Deu evesque de Famagoste et de Tortose, par la auctorité que il a da nostre seignor Boniface papa VIII, par suspendus de divine choses messire Nicola deain et messire Iohan de Nores tresorer de l'iglise de Nicossie, et le chapitle de la dite iglise, et chascun do dit capitle reveus et contrarie as amonitions et as commandemans de monsegnor l'evesque desus dit, fait à eus par la chaison de une meison la quel a l'eglise de Nicossie enprès la sacrestie de Frere Menor de Nicossie, que le dit capitle la deient vendre au desus dit Frere Menor ou chanjer en une autre ausi bone o mellior, si comme il e contenu el comma<n>dement do pape."

Actum Famaguste, in ecclesia Famagustana, anno a Nativitate Domini M°CCLXXXXIX,[d] Indictione XII, mensis Aprilis die IIII°, presentibus testibus ad hoc vocatis specialiter et rogatis discretis viris domino Petro Marbre de Accone,[e] Nicolino de Tripolis, clerico, Rufino de Ast, Oberto calegario de Tripolis, et domino Richebono de Brixia calegario, et quampluribus aliis.

Et ego, Andreas qui supra de Vercellis, clericus, publicus auctoritate <imperiali>[f] notarius, predictis interfui et ea rogatus scripsi et in hanc publicam formam redegi et meo consueto signo signavi.

---

[a] Turchetus] Giuchetus G   [b] Berito] mao *add*. P; maior *add*. G
[c] Nicossiensium] Nicossiensis G   [d] M°CCLXXXXIX] M°CC°LXXXXIX G
[e] Accone] Accon G   [f] <imperiali>] imperiali G

Document 3

Famagusta Cathedral					23 August 1299

Manuscript: Perugia, Archivio di Stato di Perugia, S. Francesco al Prato, Pergamene 47.
Summary: Monacchia, *Regesti*, no. 47C.
Edition: Golubovich, "Cipro francescana," p. 362 (= G).

In nomine Domini, Amen. Omnibus hoc publicum instrumentum visuris et audituris pateat manifeste quod in presentia mei, Andree de Vercellis, publici notarii, et testium infrascriptorum, discretus vir dominus Leo de Tripoli, presbiter, magister capellanus et assisius ecclesie Famagustane, hora misse, in dicta ecclesia Famagustana, presente clerici et populi multitudine copiosa, de mandato reverendi patris domini Guidonis, divina gratia Famagustani et Anteradensis episcopi, executoris dati per sanctissimum patrem dominum Bonifatium papam VIII, super litteris impetratis per guardianum et conventum Fratrum Minorum de Nicossia,[a] denuntiavit[b] pro excommunicatis infrascriptos de capitulo Nicossiensi[c] in hunc modum:

"Nos denu*n*tions p*a*r excom*m*uniés de la part do rev*er*end pere en Crist mo*n*seignor Gui, p*a*r la grace de Deu evesq*ue* de Famagoste et de Tortose, p*a*r la auctorité que il a de mo*n*seignor Boniface papa VIII, mess*ire* Nicola dean et mess*ire* Iohan de Nores tresorer de l'iglise de Nicossie et vicaires do reverend pere en Crist mo*n*seignor Gerard, p*a*r la grace de Deu archivesq*ue* de Nicossie, sire Girard de Antioche, sire Ioha*n* de Port, sir*e* Pier*e* de Bria, maistre Bauduin, et sire Piere, dean de Sur, et sire Iaq*ue*, prior de Saint Estiene, canoines de la desus dite iglise de Nicossie, p*a*r ce q*ue* il n'ont volu obeir as coma*n*dema*n*s et as amonitions del desus dit mo*n*seignor l'evesq*ue*, p*a*r la auctorité q*ue* il a do papa, qui ont e*s*té p*a*r le fait de changer une meison q*ue* le capitle de Nicossie a de costé la sac*r*estie de Frere Menor de Nicossie, o de vendre la, p*a*r co*n*venable pris, au guardia*n* et au covent de Freres Menor desus dit."

Actum Famaguste, in ecclesia Famagustana, anno a Nativitate Domini M°CC°LXXXXIX, Indictione XII[a], mensis Augusti die XXIII, presentibus testibus ad hoc specialiter vocatis et rogatis discretis viris Petro de Rosis,[d] assisio Famagustano, Symione[e] de Berito, clerico, Manuello de Saona, Bartholomeo de Neapoli, et pluribus aliis.

Et ego, Andreas supradictus de Vercellis, clericus, publicus imperiali auctoritate notarius, predictis interfui et ea rogatus scripsi et in hanc publicam formam redegi et signo meo consueto signavi.

[a)] Nicossia] Nicosia G   [b)] denuntiavit] denunciavit G   [c)] Nicossiensi] Nicosiensi G
[d)] Rosis] Bosis G   [e)] Symione] Symone G

Document 4

Nicosia Cathedral   Sermon hour, between Prime and Tierce,
                                                Sunday 30 August 1299

Manuscript: Perugia, Archivio di Stato di Perugia, S. Francesco al Prato, pergamene 48 (403 × 274 mm) (= P).
Summary: Monacchia, *Regesti*, no. 48.
Edition: Golubovich, "Cipro francescana," pp. 362–65 (= G).

In nomine Domini, Amen. Noverint universi presens publicum instrumentum inspecturi[a] et etiam audituri[b] quod in presentia mei, notarii publici infrascripti, et testium subscriptorum ad hoc specialiter vocatorum et rogatorum, et populi ibidem existentis in magna quantitate utriusque sexus, religiosus vir Frater Henricus, abbas monasterii Belli Loci, Cisterciensis Ordinis, Nicossiensis diocesis, intravit[c] ecclesiam Nicossiensem[d] maiorem ad infrascriptam denunciationem faciendam, de mandato reverendi patris[e] domini G<uidonis>, Famagustani et Anteradensis episcopi, prout constat per quasdam litteras patentes sigillatas sigillo dicti episcopi, predicto abbati transmissas ex parte sepedicti episcopi a domino summo pontifice Fratribus Minoribus ad infrascripta executoris deputati, prout constat per quasdam litteras papales munitas bulla papali pendenti cum filo canapis. Et dicto abbate a clericis viso, incontinenti Petrus Blanchardi presbiter et assisius ecclesie Nicossiensis, Johannes Raouli Fraperii,[f] Stephenotus assisius dicte ecclesie Nicossiensis, Philipus, Guiliotus[g] filius Georgii David,[h] et Gofredus de Bonafre, clerici, ascenderunt super scalam pulpiti sepedicte ecclesie et super dictam scalam eam munientes steterunt. Predictus vero abbas accessit ad dictam scalam et voluit ascendere super pulpitum predictum. Qui predictus Petrus Blanchardi et reliqui clerici prenominati extenderunt manus suas palmis apertis contra pectus abbatis predicti, non permittentes eum ascendere. Predictus autem[i] abbas, videns quod non poterat ascendere ad dictum pulpitum, clericis predictis et sacerdote obstantibus, stetit super quoddam sedile quod est in pedibus dicte scale, et ostendit predictas litteras papales, et cepit dicere et denunciare populo. Et statim cum incepisset loqui, predicti P<etrus> Blanchardi et J<ohannes> Raouli et Stephenotus irato animo preceperunt clericulis quos secum duxerant in magna quantitate ut vociferarent, et illis qui in coro erant ut tabulas et stalla percuterent et strepitum facerent. Qui mandatis illorum obtemperantes tantum clamorem, sonum, et strepitum fecerunt et emiserunt quod nullus poterat predictum abbatem nec aliquem alium audire vel intelligere, immo pocius predicti clericuli, respectu et intuitu ire ac iracundie predictorum ministrorum et eorum confiducia, iniuriabantur predicto abbati vocando eum excommunicatum, irregularem, et malum monacum. Et predicti Stephenotus

---

[a] inspecturi] inspecturis G   [b] audituri] audituris G   [c] intravit] intravit *exp.* P
[d] Nicossiensem] Nicosien. G   [e] reverendi patris] reverendissimi G   [f] Fraperii] Fraperii G
[g] Guiliotus] Guilotus G   [h] Georgii David] Georgii, David G   [i] autem] vero G

et Johannes et Guiliotus, stantes iuxta abbatem a dextris et a sinistris, collafisabant eum comminando ei. Predictus vero abbas, videns quod non poterat a populo audiri propter validos clamores, strepitum, et sonum predictos, rogavit testes infrascriptos ut magis prope eum accederent ut eum possent audire. Qui, cum accessissent iuxta eum tali modo quod ei inherebant, narravit, dixit, et denunciavit gallicis verbis ut infra:

> "Bones gens, il est ensi que nostre seignor le pape, à la requeste et à la preere dou gardien et des Freres Menors de Nicossie, a mandé coumandant par ses letres à l'evesque de Famagouste – et veés cy les letres de nostre seignor le pape – ..."

Et hiis dictis predictisque litteris papalibus ostensis per eum, predictus Guiliotus ingessit manus suas ad tollendum dictas litteras papales. Sed abbas tenebat eas fortiter, et dictus G<uiliotus> destitit. Tamen bis temptavit hoc facere, et inseruit se inter abbatem et murum, et impulsit abbatem de dicto sedili inferius, dictusque[j] abbas continuavit dictum suum in hunc modum:

> "... que le dit evesque dee commander au chapitle de l'iglise de Nicossie et destreindre les que il deent douner as Freres Menors la maison où le deen de Nicossie herberge, la quel maison est de la dite iglise de Nicossie, en eschange d'une autre itel ou de vendre leur por couvenable pris. De quei l'evesque les amonesta plusors fes et aucuns d'eaus ont obei. Et ceaus qui ne vorent obeir, il leur entredist l'entree de l'iglise et les souspendi des devins. Si que après, leur contumace cressant et la justise amonestant, il les a escoumeniés et denuncier les a fait por escoumeniés par toute Famagouste. Sur ce il nous a mandé comandant par l'autorité qu'il a de nostre seignor le pape en ce fait, et en vertu de la sainte obedience, et soute peine d'escoumenacion par ses letres – et veés cy les letres – que nous deussens en ceste yglise denuncier por escoumeniés de par lui sire Nicolose le deen, sire Johan de Nores, tresorier de l'iglise de Nicossie et vicaires de l'arcevesque de Nicossie, et sire Gerart de Antioche, sire Pierre de Bries, et sire Johan dou Port, chanoines de ceste yglise, por la cause dessusdite. Por la quel chose nous, cum fis d'obedience, veullians le dit comandement de l'evesque – mais plus vraiement apostoliel – acomplir, si cum nous devons et soumes tenus, et doutans la peine de l'escomenacion, soumes nous ores venus yci por acomplir le dit comandement <de l'evesque> – mais plus vraiement apostoliel – et denuncions por escoumeniés de par le dit evesque, por la cause dessus dite, les devant noumés sire Nicolose, deen, sire Johan de Nores, tresorier de ceste yglise et vicaires de l'arcevesque dessus dit, sire Gerart de Antioche, sire Pierre de Brie, et sire Johan dou Port, chanoines de ceste yglise."

Acta sunt Nicossie, in loco prenominato,[k] anno a Nativitate Domini M° ducentesimo nonagessimo nono, Indictione duodecima, die Dominica tricesima mensis Augusti, hora sermonis, videlicet inter Primam et Terciam,[l] presentibus Fratre Nicolao de

---

[j)] dictusque] dictus quidem G   [k)] prenominato] prnominato *a.c.* P   [l)] Terciam] Tertiam G

Accone,[m] monaco monasterii Belli Loci predicti, et nobilibus viris dominis Thoma de Finion, reeys Siriorum (quod est dictu vicecomes Siriorum in Cipro seu civitate Nicossie), Mateo[n] de Biblio, Simone dicto Arras, et Georgio Iocelini, militibus; et dominis Martino de Nefin, Johanne de Camino, et Johanne Venetico, aurifabro, testibus ad hoc specialiter vocatis et rogatis, et pluribus aliis ex populo in magna quantitate, ex quibus aliqui sunt dominus Petrus de Gloria, dominus Johannes dictus de Archiepiscopo, dominus Jacobus de Cassas, dominus Jacobus Litardi, et plures alii predicta omnia videntes, sed non audientes propter clamores validos, sonum, et strepitum predictos.

Et ego, Simon, dictus de Archiepiscopo, civis Nicossiensis, Sacrosancte Apostolice Sedis auctoritate publicus notarius, predictis omnibus interfui et ea rogatus scripsi et in hanc publicam formam reddegi meoque[o] signo consueto signavi et roboravi.

Fig. 2   Notarial sign of Simon "of the Archbishop"

Document 5

Nicosia, Franciscan Convent　　　　　　　Vespers, Friday 25 September 1299

Manuscript: Perugia, Archivio di Stato di Perugia, S. Francesco al Prato, Pergamene 49 (335 × 223 mm) (= P).
Summary: Monacchia, *Regesti*, no. 49.
Edition: Golubovich, "Cipro francescana," pp. 365–66 (= G).

In nomine Domini, Amen. Noverint universi presens publicum instrumentum inspecturi et etiam audituri quod in presentia mei, notarii publici infrascripti, et testium subscriptorum ad hoc specialiter vocatorum et rogatorum, religiosus vir Frater Guido de Bononia, gardianus Fratrum Minorum Nicossiensis civitatis, totusque conventus eiusdem loci ibidem ad hoc sono campane congregatus more solito, fecerunt, constituerunt, et ordinaverunt suos procuratores legitimos generales et speciales ac certos nuncios Fratrem Martinum, lectorem dicti conventus, et Fratrem Fulconem,[a] provincialem eiusdem ordinis, ibidem presentes et mandatum sponte suscipientes, ambos insimul et quemlibet eorum in solidum, ita tamen quod non sit melior condicio occupantis et quod unus incepit, alter perficere valeat, in

---

[m)] Accone] Accon G   [n)] Mateo] Matteo G   [o)] meoque] meo quoque G
[a)] Fulconem] Falconem G

curia Romana, ad impetrandum et contradicendum litteras tam simplices[b] quam legendas gratiam et iusticiam continentes, iudices et loca eligendum, conveniendum, recusandum, et auditorem petendum generaliter contra quoscumque,[c] et specialiter in causa apellationis[d] seu apellationum interpositarum[e] per vicarios et capitulum Nicossiense seu eorum procuratores coram reverendo patre domino G<uidone>, permissione divina Famagustano[f] et Anteradensi episcopo ac iudice delegato a domino nostro B<onifatio> summo pontifice, gardiano et conventui predictis concesso, ad tradendum vel tradi faciendum predictis fratribus quandam domum ecclesie Nicossiensis quam inhabitat decanus ecclesie[g] predicte, in permutatione[h] alterius domus eque bone vel venditione extimationis iusti precii,[i] et ad ipsam totam causam prosequendum, deducendum, ac ventilandum,[j] si eis visum fuerit necece,[k] et ius dicte cause examinandum et fine debito terminandum in dicta curia coram quolibet iudice competenti, uno vel pluribus, ad agendum, defendendum, opponendum, et positionibus[l] respondendum, excipiendum, replicandum, litem contestandum, de calumpnia et veritate dicenda iurandum ac exibendum, in animam eorum et cuiuslibet etiam[m] alterius generis ius iurandum,[n] sententiam petendum et audiendum, apellandum, suplicandum, apellationem prosequendum, et omnia et singula exercendum ac faciendum que merita dicte cause exigunt ac requirunt et que de iure mandatum exigit speciale, et ad alium vel alios procuratores substituendum loco sui et revocandum quando et quociens[o] sibi visum fuerit expedire, et ad omnia et singula faciendum circa predicta vel quodlibet predictorum que dicti gardianus[p] et conventus facere possent, si ibidem adessent, promittentes se ratum et firmum perpetuo habituros quicquid per predictos suos procuratores et nuncios, aut alterum eorum et ab eis substitutos, circa predicta vel quodlibet predictorum fuerit actum, factum, seu procuratum.

Actum Nicossie,[q] in domo Fratrum Minorum predictorum, anno a Nativitate Domini M° decentesimo nonagesimo nono, Indictione duodecima, die Veneris vicessima quinta mensis Septembris, in Vesperis, presentibus domino Johanne dicto Soueque, Gerardo de Nicossia,[r] et Jaquetto Anglico, testibus ad hoc specialiter vocatis et rogatis.

Et ego, Simon, dictus de Archiepiscopo, civis Nicossiensis, Sacrosancte Apostolice Sedis auctoritate publicus notarius, predictis omnibus interfui et ea[s] rogatus scripsi et in hanc publicam formam redegi meoque signo consueto signavi et roboravi.

[b)] simplices] supplices G   [c)] contra quoscumque *inv. a.c.* P   [d)] apellationis] apelationis G
[e)] interpositarum *mg. infra* P   [f)] Famagustano] Famagostano G   [g)] Nicossiensis quam inhabitat decanus ecclesie *om. per homoioteleuton* G   [h)] permutatione] permutationem G   [i)] precii] pretii G   [j)] deducendum, ac ventilandum *om.* G   [k)] necece] necesse G (*lege*)   [l)] positionibus] positoribus G   [m)] etiam] et G   [n)] ius iurandum] iusiurandum G   [o)] quociens] quoties G
[p)] gardianus] guardianus G   [q)] Nicossie] Nicosie G   [r)] Nicossia] Nicosia G   [s)] ea *om.* G

Animal Bones from an Industrial Quarter at Malbork, Poland: Towards an Ecology of a Castle Built in Prussia by the Teutonic Order

Mark Maltby (School of Conservation Sciences,
University of Bournemouth),
Aleks Pluskowski (Department of Archaeology, University of Reading)
and *Krish Seetah* (Department of Archaeology, University of Cambridge)

Introduction

The castle at Malbork began to be constructed by the Teutonic Order as the fortified monastery of Marienburg from the 1270s; between 1309 and 1457 it was the headquarters of the Order in Prussia. During this time the castle expanded significantly and became sub-divided into three sectors, covering an area of around 20 hectares. Subsequent phases of Polish, Prussian and German occupation modified and restored various elements of the structure. From 1945 its restoration was supervised by Polish conservators and in 1997 it was added to the UNESCO list of world heritage sites. Today, the castle is preserved as the most important example of the Teutonic Order's distinctive architecture in Eastern Europe, and remains a major focus of historical, archaeological, architectural and art-historical research, as well as a showcase for the evolution of modern approaches to conservation and restoration. The maintenance of a castle the size of Malbork – the largest fortified brick structure in the world – required significant and complex provisioning networks. Written sources from the fourteenth and fifteenth centuries illustrate the sheer diversity of animal management and animal-related products which were processed for and within the castle.[1] However, the long-term impact of the castle's construction and expansion on the animal resources of its hinterland is also a question with a fundamental archaeological perspective.

Excavations within the bounds of the castle are carefully managed by the archaeology department of the castle museum, and are both rescue- and research-led. Since 2001, Dr. Maria Dąbrowska,[2] in collaboration with Dr. Zbigniew Sawicki and the castle museum, has directed annual excavations in the outer bailey, exploring its complex sequence of changing occupation from the early medieval period through to the nineteenth century. In the last decade, excavators have recognized the potential value of recovering environmental data from archaeological contexts within the castle, and retained all hand-collected animal bones (although no sieving was carried

---

[1] See Erich Joachim, *Das Marienburger Tresslerbuch der Jahre 1399–1409*, 2nd ed. (Bremerhaven, 1973).

[2] Institute of Archaeology and Ethnology, Polish Academy of Sciences, Warsaw.

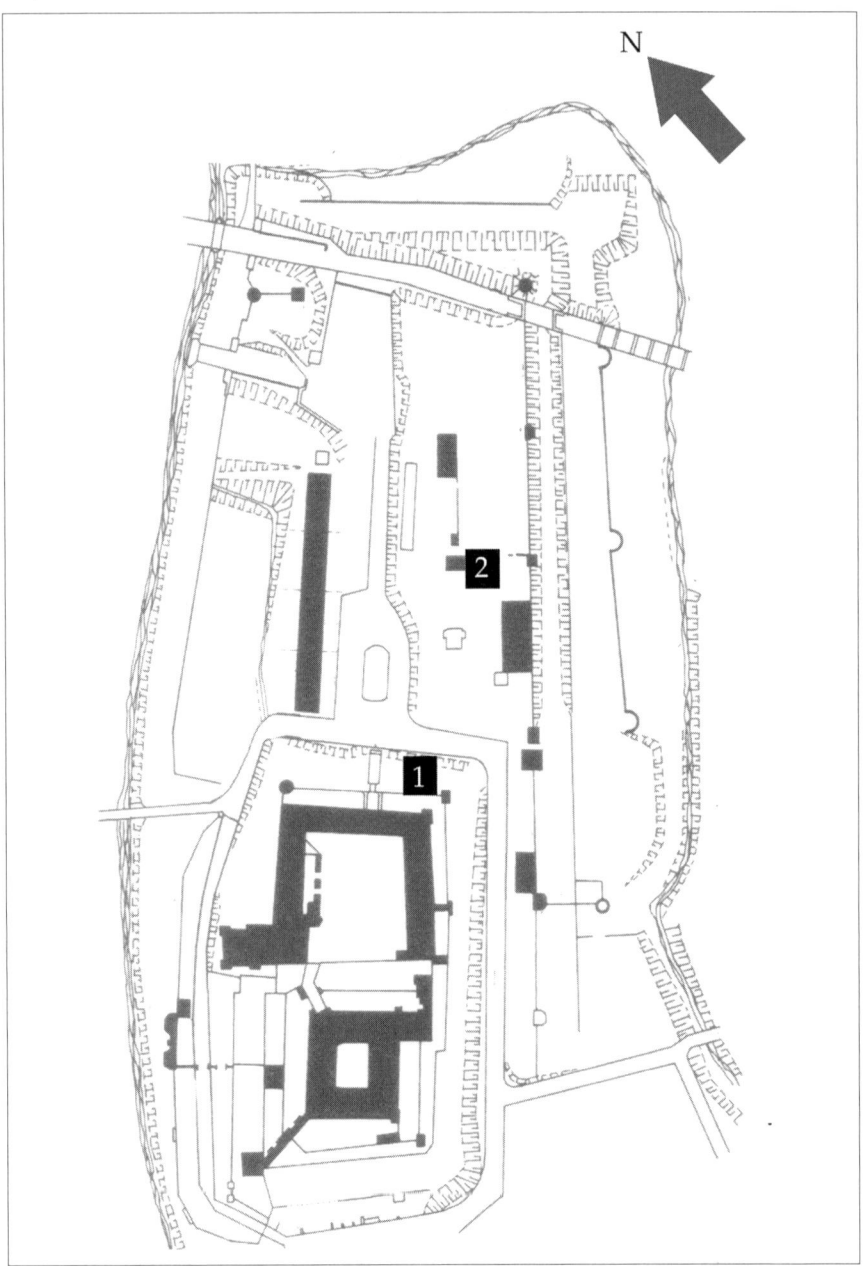

Fig. 1 Excavations in Malbork where animal bones have been recovered
1 = Location of the trench opened across the moat separating the middle and low castles
2 = Location of excavations in the low castle area carried out between 2001 and 2003

out) as well as a number of soil samples for future palaeoenvironmental analysis. In 2005 and 2006, analysis of this faunal assemblage began with the aim of evaluating the potential for exploring the "biological signature" of the site. This paper represents the findings of that evaluation. Despite the modest size of the dataset, this forms an important foundation for exploring the "ecological role" of the Teutonic Order – and other crusading institutions – in the Baltic. In anticipation of future excavations, it is hoped that Malbork will become a case study of international significance for understanding the environmental impact of discrete, highly organized, colonizing groups within the context of endemic warfare and religious conversion.[3]

Methods of Analysis

To date, faunal remains have been recovered from three sets of excavations within the castle at Malbork (see Fig. 1). Firstly, 41 fragments have been stored in the castle museum from excavations conducted by German archaeologists in the 1930s. They have no contextual information and have not been included in this report. Secondly, 84 fragments were recovered from a trench opened across the moat separating the middle and low castles (Fig. 1.1). Thirdly, 5,040 bones were recovered from excavations in the low castle area between 2001 and 2003 (Fig. 1.2). The total assemblage consisted of 5,125 animal bone fragments from 233 contexts, of which 2,856 (56 per cent) were identified to species or species group (Table 1). The largest sample (2,964 fragments) was obtained from early post-medieval deposits. Assemblages from other periods totalled fewer than 700 fragments. The majority of bones made available for analysis were identified and recorded by the authors during September 2005 at Malbork Castle. A few bones were subsequently sent to England to confirm provisional identification against reference material and Sheila Hamilton-Dyer assisted in the identification of some of the bird and fish bones. All animal bones from the various excavations were recorded onto a database which forms part of the site archive.

The assemblages have been divided into various phases based on spot-dating of the ceramic assemblage and coin finds. These periods are as follows:

- Early medieval: these cover various cultural phases between the ninth and thirteenth centuries.
- Medieval: fourteenth and fifteenth centuries. This includes the period of occupation by the Teutonic Order.
- Early post-medieval: sixteenth to eighteenth centuries.
- Modern: nineteenth century onwards.
- Mixed: contexts where ceramics are from a variety of periods.

---

[3] Aleks Pluskowski, "The Ecology of Medieval Crusading: Reflections on a New Research Agenda," in preparation, to be submitted to *Medieval Archaeology*.

Table 1 Animal bones from Malbork Castle

	Period						
	EM	Med	EPM	Modern	Mixed	Unphased	Total
Cattle	14	111	618	106	166	76	1091
Sheep/Goat	56	102	237	47	46	37	525
Pig	20	114	429	58	59	45	725
Horse	3	35	78	13	31	13	173
Dog		4	13	5	6	3	31
Cat			8	6	1		15
Red Deer		1	5	1			7
Roe Deer	2	2	6	1	3	1	15
Hare			12	1	2	1	16
Polecat			3				3
Otter						1	1
Domestic Fowl		6	65	14	6	1	92
Mallard		1	12	4	2	1	20
Other Duck		1	2	1			4
Goose	1	5	74	17	7	2	106
Capercaillie			7	2			9
Turkey				1			1
Partridge			1				1
Pigeon			1				1
Eagle			1				1
Corvid			9			1	10
Cod			1				1
Sturgeon			1	1			2
Pike			2				2
Cyprinid	1	1	1		1		4
Total Identified	*97*	*383*	*1586*	*278*	*330*	*182*	*2856*
Unid. Large Mammal	16	136	929	122	196	95	1494
Unid. Medium Mammal	38	64	264	48	38	27	479
Unid. Small Mammal			1				1
Unid. Mammal	8	29	116	12	10	14	189
Unid. Bird	1	11	67	13	9	4	105
Unid Fish			1				1
Total Undentified	*63*	*240*	*1378*	*195*	*253*	*140*	*2269*
Total	160	623	2964	473	583	322	5125

Note: Counts are of numbers of individual specimens (NISP)
EM = early medieval; Med = late medieval: EPM = early post-medieval; Modern = post-1800

These subdivisions are fairly crude but are adequate for an assessment of the potential value of the faunal data.

Context

The majority of animal bones included in this report were recovered from excavations in the northern part of the forecastle (*predzamcza*), used by the Teutonic Order from the mid-fourteenth century (see Fig. 2). Since no twentieth-century buildings had been constructed in this area, it was particularly suitable for a detailed programme of archaeological research which began in 1997.[4] Written sources from the late-fourteenth and fifteenth centuries indicate this part of the castle was used for the storage of building materials, such as bricks, stones and roof tiles; there are also imprecise references to stables. During the wars of the seventeenth and subsequent centuries the buildings were destroyed.[5] The aim of the programme of excavations, entitled "*Zaplecze rzemieślniczo-gospodarcze na Przedzamczu Północnym Zamku Malborskiego*" ("The back of the industrial site in the northern forecastle of Malbork Castle") was to clarify the use of this specific area of the castle, especially the post-Teutonic phases which are most represented in the archaeology.

Period Representation

Early Medieval

Only 97 identified fragments were recovered, which limits any detailed analysis of species representation, particularly as the material includes bones associated with different cultural groups occupying the site over several hundred years. In a sample of 95 mammal fragments, sheep/goat (59 per cent) are the most common, followed by pig (21 per cent), cattle (15 per cent) and horse (3 per cent). Although the sample is very small, there is a significantly larger percentage of sheep/goat in this assemblage compared with those from later periods. Their counts are swollen slightly by the inclusion of five vertebrae from a neonatal animal and the presence of substantial numbers of lamb bones in some layers in Trench 33. Although more than a single individual was represented and there is no record that any of them were articulated, it is possible that many of these belonged to one animal. Roe deer (*Capreolus capreolus*) (2 per cent) is the only wild mammal species identified,

---

[4] See Maria Dąbrowska, "Malbork – zamek, woj. Pomorskie. Opracowanie wyników badań archeologiczno-architektonicznych prowadzonych na Przedzamczu Północnym w V–VIII 2001 roku," Unpublished Report (2001); Maria Dąbrowska, "Malbork – zamek. Sprawozdanie z badań archeologiczno-architektonicznych przeprowadzonych na tereniePrzedzamcza Północnym wlipcu I sierpnia 2003 roku," Unpublished Report (2003).
[5] Ibid.

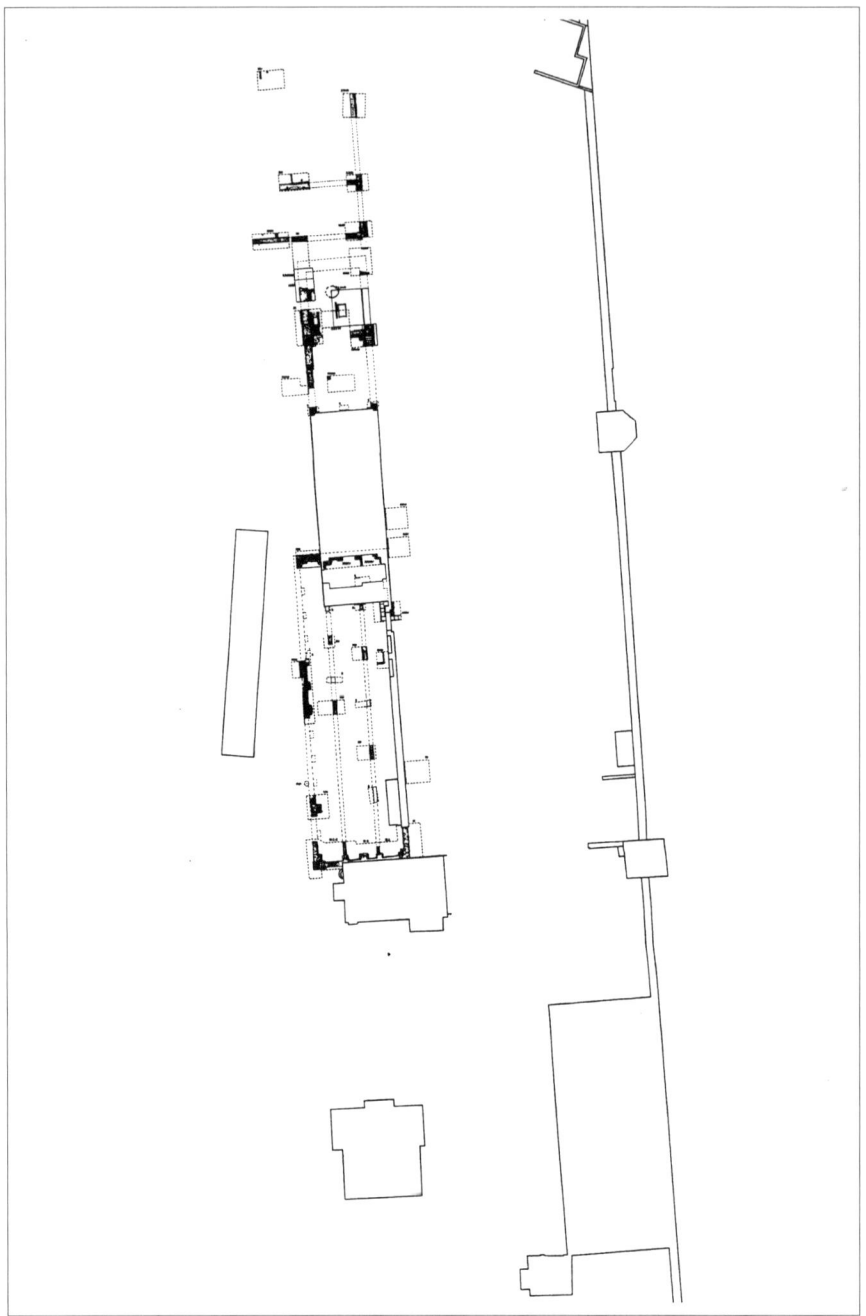

Fig. 2 Trenches opened in the northern part of the forecastle (*predzamcza*); an area used by the Teutonic Order from the mid-fourteenth century and subsequently into the modern era

although a fragment of pig scapula is from a very large animal, which could conceivably have belonged to a wild boar (*Sus scrofa*). There is a single bone each of goose (*Anser* sp.) and cyprinid (carp family).

Medieval

The sample from this period is disappointingly small. However, 383 fragments were identified including 369 from mammal species. Horse included nine bones from a vertebral column, which have been excluded from the following calculations of mammal species percentages. There is a fairly even representation of pig (32 per cent), cattle (31 per cent) and sheep/goat (28 per cent), which contrasts with the early medieval assemblage, as sheep/goat elements were dominant. Even excluding the associated bones, horse elements occur more frequently (7 per cent) and there are also small numbers of dog (1 per cent), roe deer (0.6 per cent) and red deer (*Cervus elaphus*) (0.3 per cent) elements. Two of the pig bones are large enough to be considered to have been from wild boar. 13 bones from at least four species of bird were recorded. Domestic fowl, domestic goose (*Anser anser*) and two species of duck including mallard/domestic duck (*Anas platyrhynchos*) are present (see Table 1). A single cyprinid bone is however the only species of fish identified. Nevertheless, there is an increase in species diversity evident in this sample. The Simpson's Diversity Index increased from 1.58 for the early medieval sample to 1.99.[6]

Early Post-Medieval

This produced by far the largest assemblage with 1,586 identified fragments. These include 50 bones from a pig burial and 11 bones from a vertebral column of a horse. Excluding these associated bone groups, 1,348 elements of mammal were identified. Cattle (46 per cent) are by some margin the most common species represented followed by pig (28 per cent) and sheep/goat (18 per cent). The relative abundance of sheep/goat therefore continues to decline whereas cattle elements are significantly more abundant than in samples from earlier periods. Horse (5 per cent) continues to be fairly well represented. Domestic dog (1 per cent) and cat (0.6 per cent) are also present in small numbers. Elements of wild species form 2 per cent of the mammalian assemblage with hare (*Lepus* sp.) (0.9 per cent), roe deer (0.4 per cent), red deer (0.4 per cent) and polecat (*Mustela putorius*) (0.2 per cent) being identified. Bird bones form a significant part of the identified assemblage providing 11 per cent of the identified material excluding bones in associated groups. Goose and domestic fowl continue to be the most common species identified, and smaller numbers of duck, corvids, capercaillie (*Tetrao urogallus*), partridge (*Perdix perdix*), woodpigeon (*Columba plaumbus*) and eagle (cf. *Haliaeetus albicilla*) are

---

[6] Edward H. Simpson, "Measurement of Diversity," *Nature* 163 (1949), p. 688.

also present. Seven of the eight corvid bones are of a size of large rooks (*Corvus frugilegus*). There is also a bone of a small species, the size of a jackdaw (*Corvus monedula*). Only five fish bones were identified including those of pike (*Esox lucius*), cyprinid, cod (*Gadus morhua*) and sturgeon (*Acipenser sturio*). The Simpson's Diversity Index of 1.98 is almost identical to that of the medieval assemblage.

Modern

A sample of 278 identified fragments was obtained, of which 238 belong to mammals. Cattle (45 per cent) continue to be best represented followed by pig (24 per cent) and sheep/goat (20 per cent). Horse (5 per cent), cat (3 per cent), dog (2 per cent), red deer, roe deer and hare (each 0.4 per cent) are also present. The relative abundance of the mammalian species is therefore very similar to that encountered in the early post-medieval sample. Thirty-nine bird bones were identified forming 14 per cent of the identified material. These derive from at least six species with domestic fowl and goose again the most commonly represented. Small numbers of bones of ducks, capercaillie and turkey (*Meleagris gallopavo*) are also present. The only identified fish bone belonged to a sturgeon.

Mixed and Unphased

A significant proportion of the assemblage examined could not be assigned to a specific period. Counts of these are included in Table 1. A total of 512 identified elements were recorded. Generally, species representation is similar to the samples assigned to the early post-medieval and modern periods, which would support the impression that most of the mixed and unphased material derived from these later periods. The only species identified that was not also found amongst the phased material is the otter (*Lutra lutra*).

Species Representation

Cattle

Although the early post-medieval assemblage is the only one large enough for detailed assessment, it does not appear to differ greatly from the smaller medieval and modern samples. There is no great bias towards particular parts of the body. The presence of significant numbers of foot and cranial elements suggests that much of the processing was carried out within or in the vicinity of the castle. However, elements of little food value such as metacarpals, metatarsals and mandibles are as well represented as most of the major meat-bearing limb bones. Horncores are also generally well represented. There are, however, small concentrations of these; most particularly in several seventeenth-century layers from Trench 9, which indicate this was at one time an area where hornworking waste was deposited perhaps from a workshop nearby. Similarly, four worked metapodials were found in a sixteenth-century deposit in Trench 17, suggesting small-scale boneworking.

Regarding the mortality profiles of cattle at the site, three neonatal or juvenile calves are represented but nearly all of the others have fully developed tooth rows and belong to adult animals, some of which were quite elderly. The more abundant epiphyseal fusion data, although again mostly derived from the early post-medieval assemblage, also shows the survival of relatively few unfused bones in the early-fusing category, supporting the tooth eruption evidence that few cattle under a year old are represented. However, 9 per cent of the cattle elements were recorded as porous indicating that bones of young calves were recovered. This implies that veal was consumed fairly regularly and by implication dairy production was of importance in cattle husbandry.

There is evidence for a modest kill-off of immature cattle for meat in their second and third years. Although only one mandible is from an animal of that age, about 30 per cent of the later-fusing epiphyses are unfused and belonged to animals under about 36 months of age. If, as discussed above, about 10 per cent of these are from calves under a year old, it implies that about 20 per cent of the cattle represented were slaughtered between one and three years old. However, over half of the latest-fusing epiphyses have fused and belonged to cattle over three years of age, indicating an emphasis on the slaughter of prime beef cattle as well as more mature individuals probably utilized for breeding, milk and traction before culling. The culling of immature males and the keeping of the majority of females into adulthood for breeding, and sometimes milking purposes, is the norm for most domestic mammal husbandry regimes. Degenerative joint diseases are widely reported in the zooarchaeological literature on livestock, and incidences of eburnation (a hardening of the bone at articular surfaces which become stripped of cartilage as a result of wear) and exostoses noted on cattle here (as well as sheep and pig) were not unexpected. All these conditions are more likely to occur in older animals.[7]

Sheep/Goat

There is also little variation in the relative representation of sheep/goat elements in different periods. Although all parts of the body are represented, there is a slight bias towards upper limb bones, particularly in the early post-medieval deposits. Since metapodials are as well represented, this suggests a bias towards leg joints in the assemblage, although whole carcasses were also being processed and discarded at the castle. All five of the detached horncores belonged to goats, suggesting that these were brought to the site for working. All of these belonged to males,

---

[7] László Bartosiewicz, Wim Van Neer and An Lentacker, *Draught Cattle: Their Osteological Identification and History*, Annalen Zoölogische Wetenshappen 281 (Tervuren, 1997).

indicating a preference for the acquisition of their larger horns for the manufacture of horn artefacts.

No neonatal mortalities are represented and probably only two mandibles belonged to lambs of under a year old. The more abundant epiphyseal fusion data provided no evidence that lambs or kids under 8–12 months old are represented in the early post-medieval assemblage. Even allowing for poor preservation of unfused epiphyses, it does seem that few sheep and goats were slaughtered until at least their second year. Second year mortalities are more commonly represented in the mandible sample with probably six of the mandibles from all periods belonging to animals of that age. In the early post-medieval sample, only 56 per cent of the distal tibia and distal metapodial epiphyses have fused, implying that many sheep were slaughtered at an age where they were nearing full size. Curiously, 56 per cent of the surviving latest-fusing epiphyses in the same sample have fused, indicating that few of the sheep and goats represented were killed between two and four years of age. However, several mandibles probably belonged to sheep/goats killed at that age. It ought to be borne in mind that unfused specimens are more likely to have been destroyed by gnawing and that there is likely to be a bias towards fused bones. Older sheep brought to the castle are likely to have included breeding stock and animals kept for their wool. It is noted, however, that no very old sheep/goats are represented in the mandibles with toothwear evidence. The early medieval sample includes a number of porous bones of lambs, indicating the slaughter of a greater proportion of younger animals than encountered in the later periods. It is not clear from this limited sample whether this was a general trend.

Pig

Once again, analysis of element representation relies heavily on the large sample from the early post-medieval deposits. As in the sheep/goat assemblage, pig upper limb bones are well represented; it is unusual for the femur to be so well represented, yet here it provides the second highest NISP and MNE counts.[8] Although the smaller metapodials have less chance of being retrieved, their low numbers could imply that many of the pig limb bones were brought to the castle as part of fresh or preserved joints, having previously had their feet removed. Although mandible and skull fragments are common, they do not dominate the samples which contrast to other assemblages where pigs have formed an important part of the analysed material. Again, this suggests that there is a bias towards ham joints.

Nineteen pig mandibles provided tooth ageing evidence. Six (32 per cent) of these belonged to pigs under a year old. One of these was from a neonatal mortality. Its presence along with the discovery of the partial skeleton of the young pig suggests that some pigs at certain times may have been kept at the castle. Most of these six

---

[8] NISP = number of identified specimens (that is, individual bone fragments); MNE = minimum number of elements (that is, a measure of skeletal abundance).

mandibles, however, are likely to have belonged to pigs slaughtered between 6 and 12 months. The fusion evidence provides less evidence for the slaughter of pigs under a year old, with only 17 per cent of the early-fusing epiphyses (omitting the bones from the skeleton) being unfused. Again, this probably reflects the poorer survival of unfused specimens. Although there are only, at most, two mandibles from pigs killed between 12–24 months of age, the fusion evidence shows that only 46 per cent of the surviving later-fusing epiphyses are fused. There may be some discrepancy in the accuracy of estimating ages from the two methods. However, it would appear that a substantial proportion of pigs represented by the limb bones were slaughtered during their second year. Seven mandibles belonged to fully mature pigs probably over two years of age. However only 12 per cent of the late-fusing epiphyses are fused indicating that the great majority of the surviving limb bones are from pigs under three years old. Six pig mandibles with surviving canines or their alveoli belonged to males and only two to females. Eleven out of 12 loose mandibular canines belonged to males but recovery bias against the smaller female teeth needs to be taken into consideration here. However, there may have been some preference towards the acquisition of male pigs for slaughter as found in a number of British medieval urban assemblages.[9]

Horse

There is no evidence that any of the horse bones were butchered although it is clear that their carcasses became disarticulated after deposition. Indeed only two groups of articulated bones were found; from a late medieval context (Trench 29, context 15) and from an eighteenth-century deposit (Trench 16, context 6). In both cases several of the associated bones were pathologically fused, denying them the opportunity to disarticulate (see below). The fragmentary nature of the horse assemblage is demonstrated by the recovery of substantial numbers of loose teeth, which form a higher percentage of the counts than in other major mammals. Whilst partly a consequence of the greater size of many horse teeth, which are less likely to have been overlooked during excavation, their presence indicates that elements of most horse carcasses became very dispersed. In addition, only two of the horse bones recovered showed any sign of gnawing damage. This suggests that there has been a lot of disturbance of buried animals and confirms that much of the faunal material generally has been subjected to secondary deposition. There are no biases in the surviving bones that cannot be explained by factors of differential recovery and fragility of the elements.

The pair of mandibles recovered from a medieval deposit had heavy wear on all the teeth and belonged to an old animal. The crown height of the third molar measured only 21.5mm, indicating it was very likely to have been over 15 years

---

[9] Umberto Albarella, "Meat Production and Consumption in Town and Country," in *Town and Country in the Middle Ages: Contrasts, Contacts and Interconnections, 1100–1500*, ed. Kate Giles and Christopher Dyer (London, 2005), pp. 131–47.

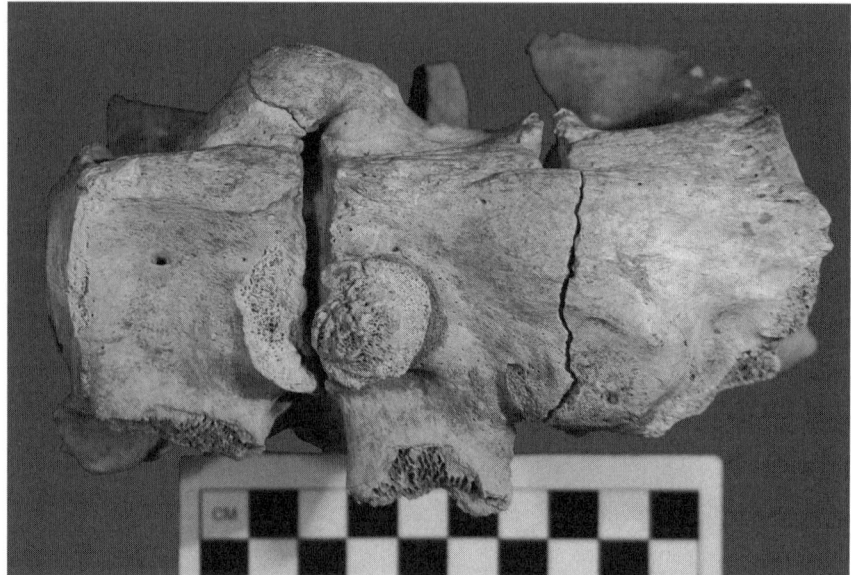

Fig. 3 A pathological horse spine from an eighteenth-century context

old.[10] A group of four maxillary teeth from an early post-medieval deposit also belonged to a mature individual. Epiphyseal fusion data in general showed that very few limb bones were unfused indicating that most horses would have lived to maturity in their role as working animals.

Evidence for Warhorses?

Two pathological horse spines provided more detailed insights into the use of these animals at the castle. The first example was from an eighteenth-century context (16006; dated by association with a coin of 1736). The partial spine, fused, fragmented and found together with non-pathological vertebrae, consisted of 3 thoracic (out of the usual 18), 6 lumbar (a full set) and 1 sacral vertebrae (out of the usual 5). Of these, 3 thoracic and 4 lumbar were ankylosed (pathologically fused) (see Fig. 3). The second pathological horse spine, also from an adult animal, was from a medieval context (29015) and consisted of 3 thoracic vertebrae (VT 16–18) and 6 lumbar vertebrae (VL 1–6), all of which displayed signs of severe exostosis. On the thoracic vertebrae this had resulted in fusion of all the articular processes; on the lumbar fusion had occurred between two sets of transverse processes and the ventral crests (see Fig. 4).

---

[10] Marsh Levine, "The Use of Crown Height Measurements and Eruption-wear Sequences to Age Horse Teeth," in *Ageing and Sexing Animal Bones from Archaeological Sites*, ed. Bob Wilson, Caroline Grigson and Sebastian Payne, BAR British Series 109 (Oxford, 1982), pp. 223–50.

Fig. 4   A pathological horse spine from a medieval context

Load-bearing as a result of riding is perhaps the most likely explanation. Improper saddling is a potential contributor to vertebral disorders, and the affected vertebrae in this case are located in the central-lower part of the animal's back.[11] However, it may also be suggested that a rider wearing heavy plate armour, weighing several dozen kilograms on the basis of surviving examples, would have contributed a significantly higher load than an unarmoured or lightly armoured rider. From the latter half of the fourteenth century warhorses were in some cases also furnished with armour.[12] Indeed, changes in late-medieval armour design, which saw an increase in the density and surface area of plate armour, necessitated the breeding of stronger warhorses capable of carrying an increased load.[13] Later cavalry armour became

---

[11] Cyril Ambros and Hans-Hermann Müller, *Frühgeschichtliche Pferdeskelettfunde aus dem Gebiet der Tschechoslowakei* (Bratislava, 1980), p. 80; Marsha Levine, Geoff Bailey, Katherine Whitwell and Leo Jeffcott, "Palaeopathology and Horse Domestication: The Case of Some Iron Age Horses from the Altai Mountains, Siberia," in *Human Ecodynamics. Symposia of the Association for Environmental Archaeology* (19), ed. G. N. Bailey, R. Charles and N. Winder (Oxford, 2000), pp. 123–33, at p. 13.

[12] Andrzej Nowakowski, *Arms and Armour in the Medieval Teutonic Order's State in Prussia*, Studies on the History of Ancient and Medieval Art of Warfare 2 (Lódz, 1994), p. 105.

[13] Zdzisław Zygulski (jun.), *Broń w dawnej Polsce: na tle uzbrojenia Europy i Bliskiego Wschodu* (Warsaw, 1975), p. 113.

lighter, particularly in Poland where Turkish and Persian equestrian equipment was both used and copied.[14] The life expectancy of warhorses was variable and many would have been killed in battle although some may have lived to an old age; there is no evidence for the type of culling seen in modern veterinary practice.[15] The castle at Malbork was the site of sieges by the Polish army in 1410, by the Swedes in 1626 and the Prussians in 1772; however, for obvious reasons the discovery of fragmentary horse remains within the outer bailey (or lower castle) should not be seen as representative of a battlefield deposition.

A plausible interpretation of the pathology described above is that the animals acquired this condition as a result of functioning as heavy cavalry for the Order and the later royal Polish (or perhaps late-eighteenth century Prussian) garrison. Although the Order systematically bred the smaller, indigenous *Sweik* horse as a pack animal (even though it was used by local Prussian tribes as light cavalry),[16] the warhorse hypothesis is lent further credence by the presence of robust and comparatively large horse bones in similar contexts – particularly hooves – as well as the presence of significant stables for warhorses in the outer bailey.[17] The documents of the Teutonic Order indicate that high investment was consistently put into the management of warhorses for military service; breeding was carefully controlled on the Order's estates in late-medieval Prussia where mares were typically kept in farms and studs were separately stabled at castles. Routine gelding of colts (young male horses) at the age of three years designated them for military service as *mönchpferde* or "monk horses," although occasionally ungelded warhorses were also used in the Order's army. A large and reliable supply of warhorses was fundamental to the success of the Order's military campaigns in the Baltic.[18]

Inter-vertebral fusion is variably reported on the remains of medieval horses. In this respect, the discovery of fused horse spines at Malbork Castle is not surprising. Whilst the presence of this pathological lesion may be the result of ordinary "wear and tear" developing in older animals, the preference for keeping warhorses at castle sites and breeding mares on farms, combined with the robust size of the extant remains point towards a military function for at least the medieval horse. Out of a total of 39 horse vertebrae identified in the assemblage, belonging to at least three (but potentially more) animals, less than half displayed any signs of pathology. The prevalence of this condition at the site in the various phases of occupation is impossible to estimate on the basis of two horse spines. It will be interesting to compare these data with other horse remains recovered from Teutonic

---

[14] Jerzy Petrus, Maria Piątkiewicz-Dereniowa and Magdalena Piwocka, *Wschód w zbiorach wawelskich. Przewodnik* (Cracow, 1988).

[15] László Bartosiewicz and Gábor Bartosiewicz, "'Bamboo Spine' in a Migration Period Horse from Hungary," *Journal of Archaeological Science* 29 (2002), pp. 819–30, at p. 819.

[16] Sven Ekdahl, "Horses and Crossbows: Two Important Warfare Advantages of the Teutonic Order in Prussia," in: *MO, 2*, pp. 119–52.

[17] See the index in Joachim, *Das Marienburger Tresslerbuch* for specific references to horses in Malbork at the end of the fourteenth century.

[18] Ekdahl, "Horses and Crossbows."

Order castle and farm sites, but also battlefields where more complete specimens may be available. This will enable any vertebral pathology to be readily compared with the health of extravertebral bones – something that was impossible to do in this instance.[19]

Other Mammals

Most of the dog elements represented belonged to adults with 14 out of 15 limb bone epiphyses having fused. A radius recovered from the moat did, however, belong to a neonatal puppy. As in the case of horse, there is no evidence that dog carcasses were utilized for meat or other products; yet none of the 31 bones formed associated groups. This again indicates the extent of disturbance that has taken place in the formation of the bone assemblages. Five of the 15 cat bones are mandibles, two of which from Trench 9, context 17 (later seventeenth century), form a pair. Apart from these, none of the cat bones form associated groups, although there is no evidence for skinning or other disarticulation marks. The cat assemblage includes a pair of mandibles from a kitten and two from adult animals. Amongst the surviving limb bones, two belong to kittens and one to an older but still immature cat. Five limb bones are fully fused and belonged to adults.

Roe deer are the most common of the wild species represented. Metatarsal fragments were the most commonly identified, most of them surviving as small portions of shaft. Metapodials may have been utilized for boneworking, although there is no evidence for this on any of these specimens. The presence of upper limb bones indicate the presence of meat joints and butchery marks were observed on a scapula and pelvis. Three of the seven red deer elements, all from early post-medieval contexts, consist of small sections of worked antler, confirming that antler was brought to the castle as raw material for processing. A proximal portion of a metatarsal from the same period also has evidence of working. Two tibiae show evidence for the introduction of joints of meat.

Most of the 16 bones identified as hare are from the hindlimbs, although three humeri were also found. A pair of humeri and the skull of an adult polecat were found in Trench 14, context 7 (early post-medieval). These are probably all from the same adult animal, whose body may have been brought to the castle for skinning, although there is no butchery evidence to confirm this. The humerus of an adult otter was found in an unphased context (Trench 27, context 4).

Birds

Differential retrieval is likely to be one of the major causes of bias in the representation of bird bones; the most common bones (tibiotarsus, humerus, ulna and femur) are also amongst the largest bones in the skeleton. Similarly, most of

---

[19] Bartosiewicz and Bartosiewicz, "Bamboo Spine," p. 825.

the domestic duck/mallard assemblage is derived from the larger wing bones. The goose element representation demonstrates a more equal distribution, although even here, smaller bones such as the radius and scapula are under-represented. The samples of the rarer species are too small for detailed interpretation (see Table 2), although the capercaillie bones include two coracoids and a sternum probably from the same bird in Trench 9, contexts 12–13 (early post-medieval).

Small porous bones from immature birds are more likely to be overlooked during excavation and are also less likely to survive. However, 14 (20 per cent) out of 69 domestic fowl bones with surviving articular surfaces were porous, indicating that culling of some young chickens was taking place and that some birds were probably kept by the inhabitants of the castle. Three tarsometatarsi have no spurs indicating they belonged to hens; there were no specimens of tarsometatarsi with spurs (usually indicative of cockerels). 93 per cent of the goose bones, all mallard/domestic duck bones and the single turkey tibiotarsus with surviving articular surfaces are from adults.

Evidence of Butchery and Boneworking

The bone assemblage from Malbork Castle offered an important opportunity to evaluate the range of tools, techniques and methods employed to process animal carcasses on the site. Cut marks were recorded on 483 bones, accounting for 9.4 per cent of the total fragment count and 17 per cent of the identifiable portion of the assemblage. Although in the majority of cases only one mark was evident per bone, this was by no means the situation in all cases, and in total 779 distinct implements marks were noted from the assemblage as a whole.

The evidence points to a mode of butchery that depended heavily on use of the cleaver (see Table 3). Of the total number of implement marks recorded, 425 (54 per cent) were made with this tool. As noted in the main discussion above, cattle were the most abundantly recorded species (and also most likely to survive in the archaeological record); it is therefore no surprise that the majority of cut marks were also noted on this species. The dependence on the cleaver becomes more prevalent during historic periods in Europe. This is arguably due to developments and advances in tool manufacture, as well as a shift towards increased size of cattle.[20] In the case of the Romano-British period for example, the shift towards use of the cleaver is focused on urban or military sites and is noted to occur in conjunction with a systematic and regimented mode of butchery.[21] However, there is little

---

[20] Umberto Albarella, "Size, Power, Wool and Veal: Zooarchaeological Evidence for Late Medieval Innovations," in *Environment and Subsistence in Medieval Europe*, ed. Guy De Boe and Frans Verhaeghe (Bruge, 1997), pp. 19–30.

[21] Mark Maltby, "Iron Age, Romano-British and Anglo-Saxon Animal Husbandry," in *The Environment of Man, the Iron Age to Anglo-Saxon Period*, ed. Geoffrey Dimbleby and Martin Jones, BAR British Series 37 (Oxford, 1981), pp. 155–204.

Table 2 Bird skeletal element counts (NISP) from Malbork Castle

	Fowl	Mallard	Other Duck	Goose	Caper.	Turkey	Part.	Pigeon	Eagle	Corvid
Skull	1			1						
Mandible				2						
Coracoid	6	2		8	2				1	2
Furcula	1			6						
Sternum	3	3		6	2					
Scapula	2	1	1	4	1					
Humerus	15	2	2	15	1					1
Radius	1	4		5						
Ulna	13	3		12						1
Carpometacarpus	4	3		10						2
Pelvis	2			1						
Synsacrum	4			2						
Femur	10		1	4	1			1		
Tibiotarsus	22	1		16		1	1			4
Fibula				2						
Tarsometatarsus	8	1		12	2					
Total	92	20	4	106	9	1	1	1	1	10

Note: Caper. = Capercaillie; Part. = Partridge

evidence for this same approach in later historic periods and this would appear to be the case for the assemblage at Malbork. Whilst there is clear evidence in the tool signatures themselves for the presence of a range of tools, some probably with steel edges, their mode of employment revolves around smaller tools for disarticulation with cleavers used to process bone. Cleavers were rarely used for disarticulation.

The second most prevalently recorded implement signature is that of "fine blade" marks. This tool would be used for the initial tasks of skinning, some aspects of disarticulation and for meat removal. While indications of chopping marks can be assigned with some confidence to the cleaver, fine blade marks have the potential to be derived from a range of tools which would be employed for multiple parts of the butchery process. However, the presence of this tool signature would seem to indicate the occurrence of blades that had well-honed edges, probably with the inclusion of steel into the cutting portion.

There is evidence for butchery activity on wild mammals such as red and roe deer, focused primarily on bone working, and on hare. Butchery marks on wild birds such as the capercaille represent preparation for consumption, as the cuts indicate the removal of the large portions of flesh that form the pectoral muscles. There is further tenuous evidence for the consumption of cats in the medieval period; the only butchery mark recorded on this species is associated with meat

Table 3 Summary of butchery marks observed on the animal bone assemblage

a Proportions of recorded implement marks

Implement type	Σ Implement marks	% Implement marks (Σ = 779)
Cleaver	425	54
Blade	67	8.6
Large blade	32	4.1
Fine blade	167	21
Saw	23	2.9
Blade + cleaver	8	1
Fine blade + cleaver	32	4.1
Undetermined	25	3.2

b Proportions of butchery per species

Species	Σ Bones with cuts	% of butchered bone (Σ – 484)
Anser sp.	8	1.6
Felis cattus (cat)	1	0.2
Bos taurus (cow)	313	65
Cervus elaphus (red deer)	3	0.6
Capreolus capreolus (roe deer)	2	0.4
Ovicaprid (sheep/goat)	28	6
Sus scrofa (pig)	69	14
Lepus sp.	1	0.2
Tetrao urogallus (capercaillie)	2	0.4
Unidentified fish	1	0.2
Unidentified large mammal	34	7
Unidentified medium mammal	22	4

c **Butchery "function"**

Activity recorded	Σ Function	% Implement marks (Σ = 779)
Skinning	38	4.8
Disarticulation	161	20
Meat removal	97	12
Bone breaking	82	10
Pot sizing*	209	27
Marrow extraction*	25	3.2
Disarticulation + other	19	2.4
Meat removal + other	27	3.4
Undetermined	121	15

* These two functions effectively involve "bone breaking" but were recorded separately where the *specific* activity was evident.

removal from the humerus. One might anticipate skinning of cats but this activity does not explain the presence of a cut mark on the humerus, an area that would not be involved in the skinning process. Cut marks, observed on several cat humeri from a thirteenth-century well in Cambridge, England, have been interpreted as evidence of dismemberment for food.[22] It is possible the example from Malbork may also hint at provisioning inadequacies resulting in starvation and opportunistic consumption of any available meat, perhaps as the result of a siege.

Regarding bone/horn working, a total of 26 separate working marks were recorded on 25 bones. Of these, 20 (80 per cent) were recorded on cattle bones, 3 (12 per cent) on red deer and 1 (4 per cent) on sheep-goat; 22 (85 per cent) of the individual marks were identified as saw marks. Not surprisingly, all bone working marks were created after gross disarticulation had occurred. With one exception, an unidentified large mammal shaft fragment, all indications of bone working occurred either on the horn core (bovid) / antlers (cervid) or metapodials. From this limited sample it is clear that a specific and systematic approach was taken towards the processing of bone/horn for working, with certain carcass portions clearly favoured for particular qualities.

The combined evidence indicates a range of animals was disarticulated with variations in technique according to species and portion of the carcass being processed. Variety in tool type is also evident, with indications that the metallurgic techniques employed involved the steeling of the cutting edge, a method commonly found in the medieval and post-medieval period.[23] There was evidently a network

---

[22] Rosemary Luff and Marta Moreno-García, "Killing Cats in the Medieval Period: An Unusual Episode in the History of Cambridge, England," *Archaeofauna* 4 (1995), pp. 93–114, at p. 107.

[23] Ronald Tylecote, *The Early History of Metallurgy in Europe* (London, 1987).

of diverse trades dependent on butchers to provide specific carcass parts following the processing of animal bodies. In one sense this may suggest that the castle itself was relatively self-contained, able to provision various craft specialists. There is also evidence for the exploitation of wild resources, particularly of cervids, which would have provided an arguably more prestigious commodity; yet it remains unclear just how important wild resources would have been. Aside from butchers, other trades were present and these include artisans working with bone and fur; it is possible that different quarters of the castle served different animal processing functions. All these issues will be key points to address in future excavations.

Discussion of the Animal Bones Assessment Programme: Towards a Biological Signature

The identification and recording of this faunal assemblage was intended to ascertain the potential of the studies of this material in any future excavations at Malbork Castle. The assessment has demonstrated that animal bones generally survive quite well at the site, with fairly low percentages of eroded and weathered bones. Bones buried in waterlogged deposits and in cess pits are likely to survive very well. The major problems encountered concern the effects of carnivore scavenging with large numbers of bones damaged by gnawing, as well as evidence for substantial movement of bones through secondary deposition. The large number of contexts containing residual material is testament to this problem.

Because most of the bones are from the early modern period, it has not been possible to make many comparisons with assemblages from earlier periods. In particular, there are as yet only small amounts of material than can be confidently assigned to the period of occupation by the Teutonic Order. Similarly, the bones from the early medieval period derive from deposits that span several hundred years and belong to more than one cultural group. One of the priorities for future work would be to target well-dated assemblages from these earlier periods. Similarly, nearly all of the excavation trenches that have provided material for this survey are from the outer areas of the castle complex. It would be essential to obtain well-dated assemblages from deposits in the more prestigious central areas, such as the high castle.

The assessment has demonstrated that most of the animal bones deposited in all periods belong to domestic mammals. There are hints that there may have been changes in the importance of the major species in different periods with sheep/goat being best represented in the early medieval period. Further metrical data (that is, measurable bones) are required to establish whether there was a significant bias amongst the adult cattle towards cows, which may in turn be linked to significant dairy production. Analysis of skeletal elements has suggested that some of the cattle, sheep and pig bones were from joints of meat brought to the castle. There are indications that veal calves were quite commonly eaten. Initial results suggest that this may have been a practice that had a long history and it will be interesting to test this against larger samples. It remains to be seen whether such evidence becomes more marked in the central areas of the castle where a greater quantity of table and kitchen waste may have been deposited. However, even with the limited evidence recovered to date, it is possible to suggest that at least pigs and chickens were kept in some areas of the castle. The low numbers of articulated bones of non-food species such as dog, cat and horse indicate that a high degree of disturbance and secondary deposition has taken place, although it is interesting to note that horses in particular could be buried within the lower castle. There has as yet been no evidence for large deposits of waste bones that one would expect to encounter in areas where butchers commonly operated. It could well be that such waste was removed and deposited away from the castle, if indeed such butchery took place there. Clearly, more archaeological and documentary research is required to investigate this further. What has been discovered, however, are small groups of horn-working, bone-working and antler-working waste. It will be interesting to discover whether there are any larger concentrations of such material, which may help to pinpoint the locations of such activities.

Bones of game animals are relatively poorly represented. Most of the red deer elements are refuse from industrial processes rather than food remains. However, small numbers of roe deer, red deer and hare bones represent evidence for the exploitation of wild mammals for food. Again, it will be interesting to observe whether assemblages from central areas of the castle produce evidence for greater numbers of such bones. Several of the pig bones are of sufficiently large size to suggest that they were from wild boar. Although there is no evidence for fur working, the presence of polecat and otter may indicate the remains of animals exploited for their fur. Whilst pathological horse spines can be plausibly linked to the presence of "warhorses" at the site, further metrical analysis of horse remains is required to establish whether the two types of horses recognised in documentary sources are also represented in the archaeological material.[24]

The bird assemblage is almost certainly biased towards the larger bones of the larger species. It is clear, however, that domestic fowl and goose were commonly eaten in the later periods of occupation. This is likely to have been the case in earlier periods too, but more material is required to confirm this. There is evidence that several other species of bird were also exploited for their meat. These include a number of duck species (including domestic), capercaillie, partridge and woodpigeon. There is even evidence of a domestic turkey bone in the modern period. The bones of rooks and small corvids are likely to be from the carcasses of birds resident in the vicinity of the castle. The presence of white-tailed eagle is not easily explained, although it could have been a bird exploited for its meat, or perhaps for its plumage. Sieving of deposits is needed to gain a better understanding

---

[24] Ekdahl, "Horses and Crossbows."

of the relative importance of birds to the diet and it is highly unlikely that anything like the full range of bird species exploited has been encountered.

This is certainly the case with regards to the fish bones. Sieving programmes carried out on many Polish medieval sites have produced abundant evidence of these species.[25] The few bones recovered by hand are all from species that have been commonly encountered on Teutonic Order sites such as the castle at Mała Nieszawka.[26] They include both freshwater species (pike; cyprinids) perhaps caught locally and marine species (sturgeon; cod) probably imported as salted and/or smoked fish. As yet, there is no archaeological evidence for the consumption of fish at Malbork in the medieval periods, and this needs to be addressed. Documentary sources on the other hand point to the fundamental importance of fish at the site, including references to multiple species as well as offices associated with their management, such as a *Fischmeister* and *Fischerknecht*.[27]

There is no doubt that analyses of further samples of carefully excavated and reliably dated animal bones from Malbork Castle will provide significant insights into how animals were exploited at the site during its long history. The opportunity to compare this evidence with the exceptional documentary sources available is one that could provide important new insights not only into human-animal relationships at Malbork itself, but also a much greater appreciation of the "ecological role" of crusading institutions in the Baltic and the other frontiers of Christendom.

Acknowledgements

The authors would like to thank Dr Maria Dąbrowska, Dr. Zbigniew Sawicki, Dr. Janusz Trupinda and Dr. Mariusz Mierzwiński for facilitating access to the faunal assemblages, for providing work space and accommodation, for their patience and continuing support and for their generous hospitality. We would also like to thank Sheila Hamilton-Dyer for her assistance in clarifying the identity of bird and fish remains, and Laszlo Bartosiewicz for his help and advice in the preparation of this report. Finally, we would like to thank the McDonald Institute for Archaeological Research, The Society for Medieval Archaeology, The Society of Antiquaries of London, and Clare College, Cambridge, for funding this research.

---

[25] Daniel Makowiecki, *Historia ryb i rybołówstwa w holocenie na Niżu Polskim w świetle badań archeoichtiologicznych* (Poznań, 2003).

[26] Ibid., p. 126.

[27] See the index in Joachim, *Das Marienburger Tresslerbuch*, for specific references to varieties of fish and fish management at the castle.

REVIEWS

Elena Bellomo, *The Templar Order in North-West Italy (1142–c.1330)* (The Medieval Mediterranean, 72) Leiden and Boston: Brill, 2008. Pp. xii, 464. ISBN 978 90 04 16364 5.

This extraordinary monograph is the fruit of the author's doctoral research and thesis completed at the Catholic University of the Sacred Heart in Milan, and later at the University of Padua. Bellomo consulted at least sixteen archives in Italy, including the Archivio Segreto Vaticano, as well as libraries there, in France, Spain, and in Germany. Her bibliography runs to almost forty pages, and is in itself, a marvellous resource to virtually all primary and secondary sources on the Order of the Militia of the Temple in north-west Italy, and to a large degree, on Italian Templars throughout Italy.

The "Introduction" stresses the unfortunate fact that few scholarly studies have been written on the Military Orders in Italy and that many of those which have been written are not based on solid verifiable evidence (pp. 1–2). Happily, Bellomo lists works written on this area and discusses the reliability of many of them in the copious footnotes. I am not convinced, nevertheless, that all the secondary works used here are totally reliable. I would advise the reader to check further on the evidentiary basis used in some Italian secondary works. Her discussion of how she carried out her research and found many hitherto unused source documents is fascinating (pp. 3–7). Her links between local noble families and the Hospitallers or Templars is one of the most useful elements in this study. Alarmingly, and perhaps because of the enormous interest in the Templars created by several works of fiction published recently, some documents consulted as recently as 1993 have vanished from the archive concerned (p. 7).

The book is divided into two parts: the first, "The Templar Order in North-West Italy: a General Picture" (pp. 13–215), discusses the beginnings and growth of the order during the period under discussion from 1142 through the thirteenth century. It describes the relations between the Lombard Templars and the papacy, secular powers, and other religious orders, and concludes with the sea-going activities of the order, particularly the Ligurian houses. Much information here helps us to understand choices made by the Templars in the founding of their properties: "there was a recurring pattern to how the Templars established their settlements: the houses were located outside the city walls, or in any case way from inhabited zones" (p. 61); "there was a network of houses that covered the whole of the zone in question" (p. 68). It would be fascinating to compare this statement with evidence from France or other areas.

The section "Charitable and hospital activities" (pp. 68–73) causes a potential misunderstanding. Discussing Templar "hospitals" implies that the order ran healing establishments. As the vast preponderance of testimony everywhere indicated,

Templars did not operate hospitals as medical establishments but rather, in most places, hostels: places where good men could stay for a short time. Bellomo refers to this sort of place as a "hospice" on p. 186 and elsewhere, but on pp. 148–50, the terms "hospitals" and "hospices" both occur. Information on the crops grown by members of the order and the other sources of their income is very useful in our assessment of their properties. She mentions "cereal crops and wine production ... vegetable crops, cheese production and horse and pig rearing" (p. 77). A large number of these houses also had as many as 150 tenants paying rent (ibid.)

Chapter III of Part I is entitled "Hierarchical Organisation". It elucidates the geographical separation of parts of Italy into provinces but stresses that the terms used changed to reflect different areas over time (p. 84). A very useful section (pp. 90–108) lists the masters of Lombardy and Italy, and their delegates, chronologically when the information exists. This portion is followed by a description of the various categories of professed and lay persons in the order. Chapter IV, one of the most useful, describes the interactions between the order, the nobility, and ecclesiastical and communal institutions (pp. 129–74). Given the difficulty scholars experience in tracking local Italian politics, noble families or religious orders, this chapter is essential for anyone working in any of these areas. Quite a few statements are mere guesses or hypotheses (see p. 173, for example), but they are clearly identified as such. Chapter V, "From the Early Fourteenth Century to the End of the Order" (pp. 175–214) covers a period when more documentary evidence is available. A considerable amount of very useful data occurs here in the form of references to inquisitorial records, hearings, and inventories. M. Barber, A. Demurger, R. Caravita, and published trial records are understandably widely used in notes. The "Conclusion" (p. 215), informs us that during the 200 years under review here "the Temple's influence in Northwest Italy was by no means negligible." These houses were placed on "the main East–West routes" (ibid.). As happened elsewhere, particularly during the thirteenth century, "sharp conflict [arose] between the Order and local institutions" (p. 216).

Part II, "The Templar Houses in North-West Italy" (pp. 223–357), is divided into those known to exist and others whose existence cannot be confirmed. They are listed in chronological order of their founding. Where possible, the precise location of the holding is listed as well as mention of the few still-standing buildings which belonged to the order. Dates when the holding was taken over by the Order of St. John of Jerusalem are also given. Since primary source evidence – wills, deeds, mentions in contracts of purchase or sale, or disputes – appears wherever possible, this section provides what would be needed to undertake studies of local properties.

Appendix I is a list of houses which definitely existed, ordered by date of attestation and including type, usually *domus* or *mansio*, and church plus dedication. Appendix II lists all known Templar masters of Lombardy and of Italy in chronological order, with footnotes identifying the sources of these data. Appendix III provides a list of Templar and lay brethren including rank, and name of their house if they originated from north-west Italy or if documents attested to this fact. It means that many, often important, members of the order will appear in the previous appendix but not in this one: Bianco da Pigazzano and Giacomo da Montecucco, for example. Part 3 of this portion includes those members or lay associates whose credentials cannot be verified.

Four figures show parts of facades of Templar buildings, many of which look heavily restored. The "Bibliography", is extraordinary in its depth and reference to almost every conceivable article or monograph published in Italy, plus many others. The "Index" (pp. 431–64) is very complete.

I have to disagree on a few points in this imposing work. Bellomo suggests that the Templars "were never involved in this [charitable] kind of action" (p. 47). As the testimony of more than 900 Templars in the various hearings stipulated, charity was carried on weekly in all the various properties as stated by Brother Dennis from Vienne: "they undertook charity as they should and each week made offerings of bread and of money and sometimes of meats, sometimes of cloaks, and clothing" (*The Trial of the Templars in Cyprus*, ed. Anne Gilmour-Bryson, 1988, p. 180, and *passim*). Virtually all Templars in the Paris and Pontifical hearings discussed bread and other food given out once or twice weekly, gifts of money, and of other items. Bellomo herself states (p. 73) that "charity work was by then a well-established practice in the Milan Templar house".

I found about twenty instances of what I believe is infelicitous translation from the original Italian. I see no reason for so many sentences, some of them long, remaining in Latin when none of the words in the citation are significant linguistically. The inclusion of a glossary for some relatively unfamiliar Latin or Latino-Italian words in the text would improve the readability. I was unable to ascertain what the extremely frequent footnote references to *Carte*, I/ 2, doc. 336, p. 541 (p. 45, note 172 and *passim*) meant. The bibliography contains nineteen items beginning *Le carte* and three beginning *Carte*. According to Dr. Bellomo the myriad *Carte* references with no further word attached refer to *Carte in Appendice ai monumenti revennati del conte Marco Fantuzzi*, ed. A. Tarlazzi, 2 vols (Ravenna, 1875).

This monumental work on the Templars in north-west Italy is by far the most useful, well researched, and complete book on the topic. Every serious library and every scholar interested in the Military Orders in Italy at this time must obtain access to this work. One may only hope that the author or others will provide equally detailed studies of the Order of the Knighthood of the Temple in other parts of Italy.

ANNE GILMOUR-BRYSON
UNIVERSITY OF MELBOURNE

Jochen Burgtorf, *The Central Convent of Hospitallers and Templars: History Organization, and Personnel (1099/1120–1310)* (History of Warfare, 50). Leiden and Boston: Brill, 2008. Pp. xxvii, 761. ISBN 978 90 04 16660 8.

The history of the Military Orders is a hot topic and this is one of the best of the high-quality research studies that have been published in the last few years. Dr. Burgtorf writes the history of the officers and their relations with the masters in the convents (or communities of brothers) in the headquarters of the Hospital and the Temple in Jerusalem, Acre and Cyprus, before examining their standing and individual and collective responsibilities, their careers and personalities. He concludes with a valuable and detailed list – over 230 pages long – of the individuals who can be identified as holding these offices, together with material on their careers. His tables are very informative and he demonstrates convincingly that I was wrong to see a different pattern in the career development of Templar and Hospitaller officials, particularly with respect to the stage at which they held senior posts in Europe. He is revealing on the evolution of the posts of grand commander and marshal, although he seems to underplay the importance of the conventual priors in terms of their relationship with the orders' clergy worldwide and he misses the point of the odd career patterns of the hospitallers, for reasons on which I will touch below.

Dr. Burgtorf is very reluctant to concede that the Templars were in difficulties by 1300. He argues that the Hospitallers or the Teutonic Knights could well have suffered the same fate, had they been subject to similar external pressures after 1307. One could answer that they were not accused, as were the Templars, of having a rite of passage that involved the grossest blasphemy. If there was some truth in this charge – and I am not the only historian to believe that there was – it is reasonable to question the management of the Temple and the efficiency of its chains of command. Dr. Burgtorf does not agree that there were important structural differences between the two orders. He explains the sparse and abbreviated form of Templar legislation, compared with that issued by the Hospitallers, with the argument that because the Temple developed a military machine early it needed only "fine tuning" thereafter, whereas the Hospitallers had to transform their institution into a military order over a much longer period. This is not very convincing. Other religious institutions of the central Middle Ages regulated themselves enthusiastically on all sorts of issues. The surviving legislation of the Temple, moreover, has little to do with military affairs (only 17 per cent of the code that followed the Rule) and that of the Hospital has even less (only 9.4 per cent of the statutes, *esgarts* and *usances*).

Dr. Burgtorf tries to counter the argument that the Templar chapters-general in the East were not representative by arguing that the great Western officials could have attended them, in spite of the fact that there is no reference to them doing so, unlike their Hospitaller counterparts. Necessary to his argument is the conviction that Templar chapters-general met each year. It is true that an agreement of 1258 between the Military Orders was supposed to be recited annually in the orders' general chapters, but this could simply have been a pious wish, because there is no other evidence that Templar or Hospitaller chapters-general met regularly, let alone annually.

At no stage does one get the impression that Dr. Burgtorf has come to terms with the fact that the Templar and Hospitaller brothers were professed religious, living devotional lives in communities shaped by the traditions of the Church. He does not take enough account of those members of the convents who were not in government, although they would have had considerable influence behind the scenes. The orders are treated as if they were secular institutions and for comparisons Dr. Burgtorf does not look to other religious orders but to the temporal world. A theme, for example, is that the orders aped "princely courts" in their choice of titles for conventual officers and for those in their entourages, and in their use of the word *palatium/ palais* for their conventual headquarters. He may well be right with respect to the Templars, but the early use by the Hospitallers of such titles surely stemmed from their conception of themselves as serfs and slaves of their lords the poor and the sick. Dr. Burgtorf redates an inscription to a Templar brother to the twelfth century on the grounds that there was a reference to his humility, appearing to assume that humility was no longer seen as a desirable attribute a century later, in spite of the fact that the word was regularly used in the protocols of the grand masters. He states that the Hospitaller use of servants was related to a situation in which the brothers could not themselves fulfil all the duties, but he does not recognize that the Templar use of professed brother sergeants on a very large scale, which probably reflected Cistercian influence, was abnormal. In the same way he points out that the title of hospitaller in the Hospital was "dead end" until late in the thirteenth century, but he does not seem to have considered that the nursing side of the order's activities may well have constituted a career in itself. And he fails to see the point of the dispute – fundamentally over the relationship between nursing and warfare – within the Hospitaller convent that ended the mastership of Gilbert of Assailly around 1170. Because he treats it in administrative terms he does not notice that two letters from Pope Alexander III in the late 1170s demonstrate that it was still rumbling on.

The issues I have raised are for debate and in no way diminish the admiration I have for Dr. Burgtorf's achievement. His book is a very valuable one and is a must for every serious historian's library.

JONATHAN RILEY-SMITH
EMMANUEL COLLEGE, CAMBRIDGE

Griechische Briefe und Urkunden aus dem Zypern der Kreuzfahrerzeit: Die Formularsammlung eines königlichen Sekretärs im Vaticanus Palatinus graecus 367, ed. and trans. Alexander Beihammer (Cyprus Research Centre: Texts and Studies in the History of Cyprus, 57). Nicosia: Cyprus Research Centre, 2007. Pp. 434. ISBN 978 9963 0 8107 3.

The Vaticanus Palatinus graecus 367 comprises a compilation of texts and documents assembled by a senior member of the Greek bureaucracy in Cyprus around the year 1320. Among other things, the contents include theology, mathematical problems, a Passion cycle, poetry, letters, and legal and diplomatic documents, the earliest of which date from as far back the 1210s. There is also a scatter of annalistic materials. The compiler, who in the past has been wrongly identified as Konstantinos Anagnostes, belonged in a group of orthodox families that held an essential role in both royal government and in the orthodox church. Their expertise in the law and in drafting documents for both church and state ensured them key positions within the framework of Frankish rule. The compiler may have put this anthology together for the benefit of a younger relative who aspired to a similar career, and a number of the documents would appear to been drafted by the compiler himself or relate to members of his own family. He would appear to have added to the collection over a number of years, utilizing items that he himself evidently found interesting.

The manuscript therefore offers an eclectic assemblage that is, strictly speaking, neither a letter collection nor a chancery manual; it does, however, give a unique insight into the world of the legally-trained Greek bureaucrat in Lusignan Cyprus. It is a veritable treasure house, illustrating both the abiding importance of Byzantine legal tradition well over a century after the advent of Lusignan rule and the effects of the changed circumstances brought about by the Frankish conquest. The compiler clearly served both as an official in the royal *secrète* and as a notary for the orthodox bishops of Amathus-Limassol. Invaluable as it is for the history of Cyprus and in particular the world of the upper echelons of the Greek community under Frankish rule, the collection is important too both for Byzantine studies in general and for linguistic research.

Dr. Beihammer has chosen to leave aside the literary works and has produced a new edition with a translation into German of the letters, legal materials and annals. He has provided a detailed and comprehensive introduction in which he discusses the significance of the manuscript and its contents, and what can be known of its compiler and his *milieu*. The manuscript has long been known, and most of the material has appeared in print before. However, in the past scholars tended to pick out the documents they regarded worthy of attention rather than consider the collection as a whole. As a result, the published versions of the texts have until now been dispersed in a number of places, and it has not been possible to gain much sense of the scope and diversity of the material. The commentary is most helpful. Beihammer (p. 371) rightly takes the present reviewer to task for his failure to take the evidence furnished by this manuscript when considering the date of the death of King Henry I (18/10/1253 as given by the Vat. Palat. gr. 367 is more likely than 18/01/1254), but he might have pointed out (pp. 367–68) that Roland de la Baume, *grand bailli* of the royal *secrète*, is likely to have been identical to the senior knight of that name who appears in the *Chronique d'Amadi's* narrative of the years 1308 and 1310. In short, there is much here to excite further interest and open further lines of research. To give just one example: in 1287 we find the bishop of Amathus-Limassol agreeing to permit a certain Bishop Athanasios of Joppa to consecrate a priest within his diocese, an all-too-rare insight into church affairs in Palestine in the immediate aftermath of Frankish rule.

Alexander Beihammer has produced an excellent edition of a manuscript that is of fundamental importance, and through his translation and commentary has made it much more readily available to scholars. He is to be congratulated.

PETER EDBURY
CARDIFF UNIVERSITY

Byzantines and Crusaders in Non-Greek Sources, 1025–1204, ed. Mary Whitby (Proceedings of the British Academy, 132). Oxford: Oxford University Press, 2007. Pp. xxvii, 428. ISBN 978 0 19 726378 5.

This volume is the product of a colloquium of the *Prosopography of the Byzantine World* (PBW) project held in 2002, and comprises fourteen essays on prosopography: "the study of a defined group of people as individuals and members of families", as the first essay, by Michael Jeffreys, explains. Lest this sound too specialized, it should be stressed that many of the contributors have produced wider-ranging studies and bibliographies than the definition suggests.

After Jeffreys' introductory chapter the rest of the essays are organized by language and geography, each consisting of a short introductory survey written by an expert in the field, and a bibliography of sources, with details of editions and translations. The first five discuss sources mainly written in Latin, beginning with Jonathan Riley-Smith, "Pilgrims and Crusaders in Western Latin Sources". This contribution holds considerable interest for crusade historians, firstly because it contains some reflections on Professor Riley-Smith's own prosopographical survey, *The First Crusaders* (1997): for example, in relation to charter evidence he points out that a charter tells only of an individual's intention to go on crusade, and in the absence of corroborating evidence we cannot know whether or not he left home. Secondly, Riley-Smith has suggestions for prosopographical research earlier in the eleventh century and through the twelfth. His bibliography is divided into library (narrative) sources, focusing particularly on eye-witness accounts, and archival (diplomatic) material. The latter is so numerous and diverse that each sub-section is headed by suggestions of registers, handlists and catalogues as a first stage to locating sources. I would add to the "charters" section the comprehensive bibliography to Riley-Smith's *First Crusaders*. In "Crusader Sources from the Near East" Peter Edbury follows a similar pattern, perhaps with more regard for the "Byzantine" in the PBW: as he points out, the sources throw little light on Byzantine individuals, but they do illuminate Latin attitudes to Byzantium. His bibliography offers within each sub-section editions, translations and secondary literature. The archives of Genoa, Venice, Pisa and Barcelona are covered in two chapters by Michel Balard and Michael Angold; the secondary sources probably outnumber the primary in these. Vera von Falkenhausen has contributed an essay on the south Italian sources, which confines its attention to primary sources.

For many the book will be of considerable interest for the chapters about sources in unfamiliar languages. Krijnie Ciggaar's is entitled "Visitors from North-Western Europe to Byzantium. Vernacular Sources: Problems and Perspectives". It deals mainly with Scandinavian sources and has a very thorough bibliography which includes runic inscriptions as well as sagas, and has details of translations. Following the route of the Varangians, Simon Franklin's chapter on Slavonic sources is next; he points out that much prosopographical analysis has been done on these texts already, which may be just as well, as a large number have not yet been translated into a western European language. The same difficulty attends the following three contributions: by Stephen H. Rapp Jr. on Georgian sources; Tim Greenwood on Armenian; and Witold Witakowski on Syriac. Optimistically, Rapp has included a section in his bibliography on "Dictionaries and Linguistic Aids", but I fear most of us will remain dependent on the erudition of these scholars. It is, however, encouraging to see the wealth of material that is extant, over and above the well known Matthew of Edessa, BarEbroyo (erroneously known to many of us as Bar-Hebraeus) and Michael the Elder ("the Syrian").

The last three chapters are on non-Christian sources. Carole Hillenbrand has tackled the biggest challenge in the book, to discuss "Sources in Arabic". As she points out: "Given the daunting vastness of the medieval Muslim world, stretching from Spain to India, this survey, and its accompanying bibliography, cannot hope to be comprehensive." Hillenbrand has therefore restricted her discussion to the "heartlands of medieval Islam", leaving aside Spain, India and Berber north Africa. The territories she covers are also those neighbouring Byzantium (Anatolia, however, having little contribution to make), but within these limitations she mentions Christians who wrote in Arabic, and also historians writing in Persian. Hillenbrand has further focused closely on examples of works which will be of particular use to the PBW. In her historiographical survey she draws attention to the Muslim tradition of writing biographical dictionaries, biographies and autobiographies, which, however, rarely mention Byzantine individuals, and only slightly more often Franks. For more general purposes the better known genres – city chronicles, universal histories and dynastic histories – are likely to yield more of interest to Byzantinists and crusade historians. Hillenbrand ends her introductory essay with a plea, which we echo, for translations of Arabic texts which have not previously been translated. The bibliography which follows includes a critical commentary on each of the primary sources listed, with editions and translations, as well as comprehensive lists of secondary and reference works. It makes engrossing and enlightening reading.

Rounding off the volume, Jeremy Johns has contributed "Arabic Sources for Sicily", a smaller landscape, but mirroring Hillenbrand's panorama in its critical detail, and Nicholas de Lange has written on Jewish sources relating to the Byzantine Jewish community, many of them preserved in the Cairo Genizah. Again the bibliography, by Joshua Holo, whets the appetite for more translations of these sources. The book contains an excellent index and ten useful maps. At first acquaintance this volume, despite its striking dustjacket, might seem destined to gather dust on the library's reference shelves. Open the covers, however, and it is a treasure trove of insights and perspectives on the world of the Byzantines and crusaders. It is highly recommended to experienced scholars, and even more highly to anyone embarking on historical research in this area.

SUSAN B. EDGINGTON
QUEEN MARY, UNIVERSITY OF LONDON

Simonetta Cerrini, *La révolution des Templiers: Une histoire perdue du XIIe siècle.* Paris: Perrin, 2007. Pp. 319. ISBN 978 2 262 01923 5.

Books on the Templars abound, and somewhat sensational titles are not rare in this context. The Templars do not mark a revolution in the development of the Western church, as its militarization was a long process which had its decisive turning-points during the eleventh century when the peace-movements of Southern France turned militant and were accepted by the reformed Roman papacy. And the foundation of the Templars is definitely not a forgotten history of the twelfth century, as its importance for the history of the crusades has always been noticed. Yet it would be absolutely inappropriate to judge the present publication from its title. Its author Simonetta Cerrini is a meticulous scholar, thoroughly acquainted with biblical language and liturgical practice. Her PhD thesis, "Une expérience neuve au sein de la spiritualité médiévale: l'ordre du Temple, 1120–1314. Etude et édition des règles latine et française", presented at the Sorbonne in 1998 contains as its first part an edition that will be published by Brepols in the Corpus Christianorum Continuatio Medievalis. The present book contains most of the second part and the whole third part of the PhD-thesis. It outlines the main results of Simonetta Cerrini's research on Hugues de Païens, the founder and first Master of the Templars, who died in May 1136 or 1137. The nine chapters are somewhat artificially arranged according to the nine extant manuscripts with the Templar rule in Latin or French and additional texts concerning the order in Nîmes, London, Paris, Bruges, Prague, Munich, Rome, Baltimore and again Paris. But the book is much more than merely a description of manuscripts and a detective story, although it inevitably includes some lines on Laurent Dailliez, "une sorte d'agent 007 à la recherche de manuscrits" (p. 39), who was killed by a car accident in 1990.

The latest research on the origins of the Templars by Alain Demurger, Cristina Dondi, Alan Forey, Anthony Luttrell and others is aptly presented. In the Holy Land a group of devout fighters offering protection for Christian pilgrims was recognized at the council of Nablus in 1120 and received lodgings near the Temple of Salomon from King Baldwin II. Hugues de Païens is just a spelling convention; the founder's place of origin in Champagne, Burgundy or Italy remains obscure. The founder of the order is, however, identified with a certain "Hugo peccator" whose letter is extant only in the Nîmes manuscript where the rubric ascribes it to the theologian Hugues of St Victor; Hugues de Païens sent the letter to his comrades in Jerusalem from the West while advertising for his militia and obtaining ecclesiastical recognition at the council of Troyes in 1129. The precise legal status of the new community gave rise to discussions. Traditionally this has been seen as reflecting the problems contemporary churchmen had to accept fighting as a truly meritorious task, because it involves bloodshed. Simonetta Cerrini broadens this perspective. In her view medieval society was theoretically composed of three estates, *oratores*, *bellatores* and *laboratores*; the Templars as lay fighters desired recognition and prestige for a group that the educated and high clergy had so far despised. According to Simonetta Cerrini Hugues de Païens can be compared to St Francis of Assisi who also desired recognition and prestige for humble people (pp. 66f.). But as the *bellatores* were often noblemen and recognized as such by ecclesiastical rites, this is probably an exaggeration aimed at modern critics who might denounce fighting monks as an un-Christian innovation of the medieval Western church. It is true that the Templars were primarily lay religious, although the order included non-fighting priests. But during the eleventh, twelfth and thirteenth centuries many religious communities were formed which devoted themselves to caring for the sick and to running hospitals, services that were performed by lay members. So the Templars cannot be called revolutionary simply because fighting, their sole task, was performed by laymen whom the church held in lower esteem than ordained clergy. Nor can this be the main reason why the Templars were finally suppressed by Pope Clement V in 1312 (pp. 67f.), especially as other military-religious orders such as the Hospitallers and the Teutonic Knights continued to flourish.

On the whole, the book is based on a close reading of all relevant sources, including the treatise "De laude nove militie" by Bernard of Clairvaux; it offers ample commentaries on biblical, liturgical and ecclesiastical quotations. The Rule of St Benedict and not the so-called Rule of St Augustine is singled out as the most important example on which the rule of the Templars was modelled. The aims of Hugues de Païens are described as anti-ascetic and anti-heroic, because physical fitness ruled out excessive fasting and because martial glory had to be curbed by Christian humility. The book ends with Usamah ibn Munqidh, one of the rare Muslim contemporaries who praised the Templars for the respect of Islamic worship. This fits well with the apparent intention to draw a basically favourable picture of the Templars vis-à-vis modern criticism of holy wars. It should be noted, however, that at the time the Templars were never confronted with such criticism, which was made possible only after the European enlightenment tried to render obsolete the medieval Christian (and Muslim) conviction of being God's chosen people.

KARL BORCHARDT
UNIVERSITÄT WÜRZBURG AND MONUMENTA GERMANIAE HISTORICA

Paul M. Cobb, *Usama ibn Munqidh: Warrior-Poet of the Age of Crusades* (Makers of the Muslim World). Oxford: Oneworld Publications, 2005. Pp. xxiv, 136. ISBN 1 85168 403 4.

Usama ibn Munqidh (d. 1188) needs almost no introduction. Few students and scholars who work on the crusading period have not heard of this dashing Muslim emir and his *Kitab al-I'tibar* (Book of Learning by Example), in which he provides anecdotes about the strange and unsavoury practices of the Franks, including barbaric medical practices, bloody judicial trials and punishments, and bizarre sexual habits. Yet to summarize the text thus only pays attention to ten pages of Usama's work (out of 255 in the standard translation by Philip K. Hitti), and more recently a number of scholars have sought to explore Usama's life and activities in a more balanced manner, both reconsidering the *Kitab al-I'tibar* with a deeper awareness of its literary artifice and taking account of his other works. In the light of this perceived need to reconsider Usama's life and writings, Paul Cobb's biography of him is a timely and vital contribution to "Usama studies" in particular and crusade studies in general. While much shorter than the last biography of Usama to be written, Hartwig Derenbourg's 731-page *Vie d'Ousâma* (published in 1889), it is still a thoughtful consideration of the emir and his activities, and its brevity and engaging style also make it ideal for use with students in classes on the crusades. In addition, Cobb has been able to make use of works by Usama and others that were unavailable to Derenbourg, making his study more comprehensive in its use of sources.

After a brief introductory preface, Cobb's study opens with an introduction to the historical setting in which Usama lived. Even before the arrival of the crusaders, the Levant was a complex mosaic of mostly Muslim states engaged in a shifting web of political alliances and inhabited by a diverse mixture of peoples of different ethnicities and religions. Cobb lays out this landscape with care, emphasizing both the diversity of the region and the common cultural threads, primarily epitomized in patriarchy, belief in one god and esteem for skill in warfare, literary talents and gentility, that helped to unify at least the elite classes of the region. In doing so he provides a text that on its own would be ideal for use in the classroom to introduce students to the Muslim world on the eve of the crusades.

The meat of Cobb's study is broadly divided into three sections. In Chapters 1–3 he provides a full biography of Usama, while Chapters 4 and 5 discuss, respectively, Usama's worldview and his interactions with the Franks. In the first section Cobb traces Usama's life from birth to death, using as his witnesses both Usama and other sources. We are provided with a meticulous chronology that gives an ordered context to the anecdotes that are transmitted in a rather jumbled fashion in the *Kitab al-I'tibar*, and Cobb also tells us much about what Usama carefully omits in his work, particularly with regard to the political entanglements in which he became involved. In addition, Cobb contextualizes and surveys Usama's literary output, considering both the various works that have survived and those lost works that we only know of through mentions in other sources. In his biography Cobb emphasizes in particular Usama's attachment to his home town of Shayzar, both in terms of his hopes to return there after he was exiled by his uncle in 1131, and his grief and nostalgia after the destruction of the town and most of his family in an earthquake in 1157. These sentiments appear in both his prose writings and his poetry.

The over-arching theme of Chapter 4 is Usama's preoccupation with order, which he saw as being the result of creatures living in accordance with God's laws and established social hierarchies. When these were neglected, chaos would result. Cobb highlights a number of topical foci in Usama's works where such concerns are made evident, including his religious fatalism, his thoughts on miracles and holy figures, his attitudes towards women's and men's honour, and his contemplation of the activities of animals. He also gives consideration to Usama's own practice of Islam, which seems to have been broadly Sunni but with Shi'ite tendencies, though ultimately it remains obscure. Whatever the truth of this, what is clear is that Usama saw the world as being ultimately subject to divine decree, with some of the stranger incidents that he witnessed being evidence of this.

Chapter 5, as noted earlier, deals specifically with Usama's attitudes towards the Franks, a necessary element for a complete discussion despite the attention that such anecdotes have received in the past. Cobb maintains a healthy awareness of the factors that were likely to have influenced Usama's presentations of the Franks, taking account of the author's prejudices, both apparent and unstated, and what seem to have been misunderstandings or expressions of ignorance on Usama's part. In addition to considering well-known anecdotes about the Franks from the *Kitab al-I'tibar*, Cobb also makes use of other works by both Usama and other Muslim and Frankish writers, giving his study a breadth of viewpoint that helps to strengthen his argument for a rather mixed attitude towards the Franks held by Usama.

Cobb closes his work with a brief afterword considering Usama's place in Islamic history and a number of useful addenda, including a short guide to further reading, a bibliography, a list of principal characters and dynastic tables.

Any criticisms that this reviewer might make of Cobb's work are minor and reflect editing issues rather than major problems. At times, in the second part of the book, he introduces anecdotes that he has already cited earlier in a manner that seems to suggest that he is unaware that he has used them previously, which leaves one feeling that we almost have two or more works that have not been fully integrated. More unfortunate is a running typo in Cobb's introduction to his work: Cobb explains the concept of the *iqta'*, a form of land administration used among the elites of the Muslim world that was analogous to the European fief, but each time that the word is used it is rendered as *iatq*. One hopes that this will be corrected in any subsequent reprinting of the text. However, these issues in no way detract from the overall value of Cobb's work.

In conclusion, *Usama ibn Munqidh: Warrior-Poet of the Age of Crusades* provides a clear and thoughtful biography of Usama that helps the reader both to navigate the rather chaotic layout of the *Kitab al-I'tibar* and to gain an insight into the mind and historical experiences of the emir. Cobb's careful treatment, complemented by his appealing writing style, make this a book that will be of interest to lay readers, students and scholars, both old friends and new acquaintances of Usama's.

NIALL CHRISTIE
UNIVERSITY OF BRITISH COLUMBIA AND CORPUS CHRISTI COLLEGE,
VANCOUVER, CANADA.

Gary Dickson, *The Children's Crusade: Medieval History, Modern Mythistory.* Basingstoke and New York: Palgrave Macmillan, 2008. Pp. xvii, 246. ISBN 978 1 4039 9989 4.

The so-called Children's Crusade of 1212 is easily the most mystifying episode of the medieval crusade movement. It certainly is the crusade that has engendered more historiographical myths than any other one. This mainly is due to the fact that, although the event attracted the attention of many contemporaries, the Children's Crusade was not deemed worthy of spilling much ink by those recording it. Even though the procession of a great number of youths from France and Germany across the Alps into Italy was noted by many, most thirteenth-century writers only mentioned the Children's Crusade in passing, taking a hostile attitude towards its participants, their behaviour and objectives. For the modern historian, therefore, the task of reconstructing the events is as difficult as assessing the motivations and aims of the participants. These difficulties go a long way towards explaining why Gary Dickson's book is the first single-author modern scholarly monograph on the Children's Crusade. Into it the author has distilled many years of research which have made him the foremost authority on the topic.

The book's subtitle is very appropriate but might also be misleading. As Dickson himself rightly points out, the process of producing mythistory of the Children's Crusade is by no means a "modern" phenomenon but one which started back in the thirteenth century when people first wrote about the event. Mythologizing the events of 1212 was part and parcel of committing them to memory from the very start: "Disengaged from linear events, liberated by mythic motifs, the medieval runaways, now equipped for time travel, hurtled through the centuries" (p. 6), to quote Dickson himself and to give a fine example of the engaging and pleasant style in which he writes. Dickson makes a conscious and valuable effort to disentangle history from mythistory and establish the course and development of historical memory. Considering the Children's Crusade within the history of the early thirteenth century, Dickson approaches the event from two angles. First of all he presents it as belonging to the crusade movement which was fundamentally reshaped by Pope Innocent III in the years leading up to 1212, in particular by the intensification of crusade propaganda and liturgy on behalf of the Albigensian Crusade and the crusade in Spain prior to Las Navas de Tolosa and the plans for a new crusade to the Holy Land. It is from this context that the Children's Crusade took its main impetus and direction. Dickson's hypothesis that the Children's Crusade was born in the Île-de-France in the context of the liturgical back-up of the crusade propaganda for the Spanish crusade, as was expressly suggested only by a fourteenth-century chronicler, can ultimately not be proven. But Dickson's fine research makes a convincing case that this is the most likely origin of the Children's Crusade.

Secondly, Dickson demonstrates that much of the underlying motivation and the dynamics of the event must be understood in terms of religious revivalism, which was a recurring phenomenon of medieval religion and which the religious developments of the early decades of the thirteenth century strongly favoured. It is thus not surprising that a revivalist movements, such as the Children's Crusade, made up of what Dickson calls "medieval Pentecostalists", arose at a time when lay religion was becoming a major focus of church development led primarily by the budding mendicant orders. This is also where the crusade movement met religious lay enthusiasm by trying to extend the fight against enemies of the church to society at large. Dickson rightly refuses to try to resolve the much debated question of the age of the *pueri*. Clearly dominated by youths, the movement probably included a fairly wide age range. More significant, according to Dickson, is the social origin of the movement within a largely rural agrarian underclass. This indicates that the Children's Crusade was not a unique phenomenon but one which needs to be considered as the first instance of a number of late medieval crusades that were unofficial, in the sense that they were not sanctioned by the papacy, and bore traits of social revolt, such as the Shepherds' Crusades of 1251 and 1320 and the Hungarian Peasants' Crusade of 1514 to name some of the most prominent examples.

It is Dickson's great achievement to firmly couch the Children's Crusade in these political, social and religious contexts and thus anchor the historiographical debates surrounding the event in a modern academic discourse, as far as the scant sources make it possible. In the later chapters of the book, Dickson turns to mythistory and the way in which the Children's Crusade was remembered and mythologized throughout history from the "Eminent Mythistorians" of the thirteenth century (Alberic of Trois-Fontaines, Matthew Paris and Vincent of Beauvais) to twentieth-century novelists such as Kurt Vonnegut who presents his hero Billy Pilgrim in *Slaughterhouse Five* as a modern-day child crusader. The survey Dickson offers is both interesting and necessary in order to appreciate just how difficult writing about the Children's Crusade is, given the complexity of the historical memory. The events of 1212 triggered people's imagination for all sorts of reasons and pushed their fantasies in all sorts of directions. Dickson deftly guides the reader through a mass of writings, including academic works, explaining the motives which shaped the process of committing the Children's Crusade to memory. Fascinating as it is, this section has the feel of being a little too encyclopaedic at times. To fully understand how writers included and used the Children's Crusade in their works, a much more thorough examination of the literary works in question would be necessary. But this was not Dickson's aim.

Gary Dickson has written an important book on a difficult topic. We must be grateful to him for doing what others have shunned or failed at, namely producing a comprehensive modern history of the Children's Crusade which will become a standard work and will help us all better to sort history from myth.

CHRISTOPH T. MAIER
UNIVERSITÄT ZÜRICH

George Akropolites, *The History*, trans. with an introduction and commentary by Ruth Macrides (Oxford Studies in Byzantium). Oxford: Oxford University Press, 2007. Pp. xxi, 440. ISBN 978 0 19 921067 1.

Historians of the First, and indeed Second, Crusade with little Greek have long made use of the translations of Anna Comnena's *Alexiad*, in the elegant and accurate English version by Georgina Buckler, and the less satisfying but approachable Penguin paperback by E. R. A. Sewter. For the later years of the twelfth century, and the events of 1204, Nicetas Choniates is the principal Greek voice, rendered into English more than two decades ago by Harry Magoulias. Now George Akropolites has found his Buckler, and all non-Hellenists, and many with Greek, must be grateful, indeed relieved. Ruth Macrides had produced an accurate and readable translation, which precedes her edition of the text for the *Corpus Fontium Historiae Byzantinae*. There is an extensive commentary and a thorough 100-page introduction.

This is a work of mature scholarship, stitching together insights gained and tested over three decades of engagement with Akropolites' work, and indeed with every other pertinent Greek text of the eleventh, twelfth and thirteenth centuries. Consequently, it serves as a wonderful introduction more generally to thirteenth-century historiography in Greek. Theodore Skoutariotes and George Pachymeres receive careful scrutiny in the introduction, and there are frequent cross references in the commentary. Crusade historians are encouraged to recall the provocative argument of Peter Charanis, drawing from Skoutariotes, that Alexios I was largely responsible for calling the First Crusade. They may be disappointed to learn that we still cannot say for certain whether Skoutariotes was the author of the pertinent chronicle, although Macrides adduces another reason, besides those advanced by A. Kazhdan, that he may not have been.

Akropolites' history covers the years 1204–61, with explanations of important events leading up to 1204, stopping abruptly and in such a manner as to suggest some part of the text has been lost. However, as Macrides shows, this was likely not substantial, and the work was completed probably in 1267, while the author still held high administrative office. It is certainly to be dated to the reign of Michael VIII Palaiologos (1259–82), whose recapture of Constantinople from the Latins forms the denouement. Akropolites appears frequently in his text at appropriate junctures, "the historian in the history" – a Macrides article of 1996, and a theme in her other works – who demonstrates his access to power and his role in shaping affairs. Contrary to received opinion, but in a manner beyond refutation, Macrides shows that her author is hostile to his greatest patron, the emperor Theodore II Laskaris, who elevated Akropolites to his lofty position as *megas logothetes*, imperial private secretary and sometime ambassador plenipotentiary. Theodore Laskaris is Akropolites' most developed character; far more so than his ultimate patron, Michael Palaiologos, whose family is introduced early in the narrative and is praised throughout, in contrast to the Laskarides.

Crusade historians may be disappointed by Akropolites' abbreviated account of the events of 1204 – "to relate all that happened to the city would be a matter of long discussion and not in accord with the present subject" – but they will be fascinated by the extended study of Alexios III and his actions subsequent to his expulsion from Constantinople. As Macrides notes, Alexios acted always as if he had not lost the imperial dignity, and with an intention to recover the throne and his capital. He married his third daughter Eudokia to Leo Sgouros, who was fighting the Latins effectively around Corinth, and turned against his son-in-law Theodore I Laskaris (married to Alexios' second daugher Anna), when he was declared emperor in Nicaea. Akropolites shows Alexios, however, to be a pawn of the Sultan of Iconium in his own designs to seize Byzantine lands, starting at Antioch-on-the-Maeander. There, Theodore triumphed personally in a duel with the sultan, although "neither the emperor nor any of those with [him] knew by whom" the sultan was decapitated. Alexios III also suffered by Theodore's success, banished to the monastery of Hyakinthos where he would die. But all did not go Theodore's way, for in that battle he lost most of the 800 "Italians" who fought for him. Theodore had evidently paid more handsomely than Henry of Flanders (Latin Emperor 1206–16), who is said to have feared Theodore's "Italians", and henceforth was far more successful in fighting against him. There are many more such compelling set pieces.

In his work of classicizing history, Akropolites uses speeches largely to introduce and explain the reasons for military encounters, but also to indicate his own opinions. Several speeches relating to wars with the Bulgarians will interest military historians, including the first speech, within an account of John III's campaign of September to December 1246 (which follows the only large gap in the narrative, omitting coverage of the years 1243–46). Akropolites accompanied the emperor on this campaign, but he cannot be held to provide an accurate account of what was advised by the prescient speaker, one Andronikos Palaiologos, father of Akropolites' patron Michael VIII.

This is a work of profound scholarship, and well produced. One cavil might be that the translation of each chapter and its commentary are presented together, in the same font and size, separated only by a brief description (chapter heading) in italics. The tired eye cannot easily discern where one ends and the other begins. If this is a fault, it must be attributed to the press, not to Macrides, thanks to whom the thirteenth century no longer is an outlier to Byzantinists in the Anglo-American academy. If placed on a reading list beside M. Angold's classic *A Byzantine Government in Exile*, and the far more recent work by D. Angelov, *Political Thought and Imperial Power in Late Byzantium*, students have a solid English-language foundation for further study. And readers of this journal now have no excuse for neglecting to consider the actions and interests of the Byzantines after the Fourth Crusade.

PAUL STEPHENSON
UNIVERSITY OF DURHAM

Norman Housley, *Fighting for the Cross: Crusading to the Holy Land*. New Haven and London: Yale University Press, 2008. Pp. xvii, 357. ISBN 978 0 300 11888 9.

Competing Voices from the Crusades, ed. Andrew Holt and James Muldoon (Fighting Words). Oxford and Westport, CT: Greenwood World Publishing, 2008. Pp. xxxiv, 333. ISBN 978 1 84645 011 2.

I confess that I thought the crusades had been well covered from every perspective, and I am therefore the more enthusiastic about Norman Housley's *Fighting for the Cross*. This is a comprehensively researched and detailed exploration of "the lived experience of crusading", which also makes absorbing and stimulating reading. The scope of the book is clearly defined from the start: geographically it covers crusading to the East, and chronologically the period 1095–1291. Further, it deals only with "proper" crusaders, that is, those who took the cross and travelled to the East on official expeditions, excluding thereby pilgrims, settlers and members of the military orders. This focus is maintained throughout, and it allows the account to be structured chronologically – not from First Crusade to Seventh and beyond, but according to the internal logic of a crusade from preaching to remembrance.

There is, though, a preliminary chapter outlining "Crusading in the East" to set the scene. Its sole reference recommends fuller, conventional narrative accounts of the crusading movement, and the outline is augmented by a list of "Important dates" among the end matter. Having briskly disposed of this necessary context, Housley then embarks on his enterprise, beginning with "The call to crusade" and an examination of motivation which encompasses popular religion, with some graphic images of purgatory and hell, and the spiritual importance of Jerusalem. He is careful to point out that crusading was always a minority activity, using this to adduce reasons why some people chose to take the cross. "Signed with the Cross" is about the preparations for departure, some of them practical – there is an insightful section on the importance of credit – some spiritual, others emotional. The journey overland, "Eastward bound", includes a balanced account of the attacks on the Jews, and identifies the problem of desertion. Going by sea carried its own hazards, such as crowding, poor nutrition, and illness, as well as the more urgent fire and shipwreck.

On arrival in the East, the preoccupation is "Crusading warfare": this chapter starts with some background on the Seljuq Turks' conquest of Asia Minor and an assessment of their strengths and weaknesses as an enemy. The roles of non-combatants in the army are described first, as is numerically justified. In this regard, Housley dismisses the idea that crusading armies became "leaner and fitter" as they progressed: he argues that the "the weak were culled by privation and disease: the ranks of the feeble were all too easily replenished" (p. 118). Cavalry, infantry and naval forces are given due weight, and then there are case studies of sieges (from Antioch to Damietta) and of battles (Antioch to Mansurah), ending with a "military balance sheet".

Fighting was only a part of the crusading experience, though, and the chapter in which Housley looks at "The needs of the flesh" – every aspect of daily life from food and famine to gambling, prostitution and homesickness – is fascinating. As Housley observes (p. 148): "As a synthesis of warfare and pilgrimage, crusading brought together the privations and dangers involved in both. Death, wounds and capture were in grim alliance with exhaustion, hunger and disease." The needs of the spirit follow, in a chapter entitled "Storming Heaven" which discusses the crusade as "penitential theatre" and covers every aspect of religious belief and behaviour. Housley concludes from this that the "monk at war" was a synthesis that ultimately did not work, and that the crusaders ultimately shared their religious beliefs with those who stayed at home. Attitudes to the enemy are investigated in "Saracens", a chapter containing fewer surprises and unexpected pleasures. "Brave New World", which follows, explores the crusaders' knowledge, and cultural aspects of their experience in the East. Housley gauges their prior assumptions, and points out the scriptural "lens" which filtered their vision, which was further distorted by their fascination by the fantastic, and restricted by their interest in biblical lands, not those beyond. Their reaction to the splendour of eastern cities leads, via Constantinople, to an account of relations with the Byzantines. This again draws on the most recent scholarship and is decently nuanced, as are descriptions of reactions to the eastern churches and the Mongols. "Brave New World" works as a chapter title in an ironic way; "Remembrance of Things Past", the final chapter, is a cliché too far (what else would one remember?). The content, however, brings the book to a very satisfactory conclusion. Apart from a short excursus on the journey home, wherein we take leave of Joinville whose narrative has been such a good source of anecdote, the theme is commemoration, which Housley concludes was less important to the papacy than using earlier crusades as material for exhortation. He comments judiciously on the histories engendered by the movement, a conflation of truth, inaccuracy and legend, but in keeping with his carefully maintained contemporary focus he does not stray into more modern historiography, which he covered in his excellent *Contesting the Crusades* (2006).

True to his purpose, Housley has brought the experience of crusading vividly to life. He has done this by weaving together short quotations and paraphrases from primary sources to make a seamless narrative: there are no more than a handful of extended quotations which require indentation. The enormous range of sources is fully referenced in nearly 1,400 endnotes, and there is a bibliography of works cited. The index has useful sub-entries rather than a bald list of page numbers. Only one aspect of the printed matter mildly irritated me, which was the frequent use of abbreviations such as "who'd", "they'd", and "couldn't". What hope of persuading students to write in formal register when Professor Housley has embraced the demotic? Other than this, the book is a handsome production. There is a section of eighteen colour plates, including several less usual ones; nine useful maps; and fifty-two black-and-white illustrations. These include rather a lot of buildings, which are not very informative, and it would have been handy if the dating of manuscripts had been included consistently, but overall the quality of the book's production values does credit to Yale, as its great originality and readability do to the author.

Andrew Holt and James Muldoon, *Competing Voices from the Crusades* is in a series called "Fighting Words". In fourteen chapters the editors bring together primary sources: "side-by-side extracts from Christian, Muslim and Byzantine participants in the Crusades." The scope of the volume is similar to Housley's: although the Timeline in the endmatter runs from 610 to 1699, the chapters are concerned with crusading to the East between the preaching of the First Crusade in 1095 and the capture of Acre in 1291. An introduction sets the scene by reviewing popular perceptions of the crusades and contrasting them with the scholarly debate, and provides a historiographical overview which leads into some background history.

The First Crusade is covered in three chapters, and a study of these reveals the editors' approach, with some of its strengths and weaknesses. Each chapter begins by providing the historical context and then discusses the sources. The documents follow, each with a short introduction. For "Pope Urban II's Calling of the First Crusade, 1095" the sources are Alexios' letter to Robert of Flanders, and four versions of Urban's sermon. For "Attacks on the Jews during the First Crusade, 1096" they are Albert of Aachen, Ekkehard of Aura and Solomon bar Simson, then three documents related to St Bernard's preaching of the Second Crusade. "Crusader massacre of the inhabitants of Jerusalem, 1099" uses *Gesta Francorum*, Raymond of Aguilers, Ibn al-Qalanisi, Ibn al-Athir, and a letter of Archbishop Manasses of Reims. In each case the historiographical commentary in the text and notes reveals that the editors are conversant with the most recent literature (though Chapter 3 would have benefited from knowledge of Kedar's article on the massacre [*Crusades* 3, 2004]), but the translations are taken from much older editions – many of them over a hundred years old. This is less worrying than the choice of these three episodes to represent the First Crusade. As Housley finds room to observe in his historical overview (p. 3): "The siege of Antioch was the pivotal event in the First Crusade." An account of the crusade which ignores the sieges and battle of Antioch is a grave distortion, and hard to understand: the sources exist in quantity, including Anna Komnene, who is not quoted anywhere in the volume, and Antioch is surely more central to crusading than the attacks on the Rhineland Jews? There are two chapters on the Second Crusade: one presents accounts of the siege of Damascus; the second offers contemporary explanations for the failure of the crusade. These are light on "competing voices" – only Ibn al-Qalanisi represents the Muslims – and the siege of Lisbon is not so much as mentioned in passing. However, the Third Crusade is not discussed at all: there are chapters on the battle of Hattin and on Saladin's capture of Jerusalem, but on the siege of Acre or the crusade of Richard I – nothing. The four chapters that follow cover the sack of Constantinople in 1204, using Latin and Greek sources; the crusade of Frederick II, 1228–29; the crusade of Louis IX, 1248–49, including rather a lot of the fifteenth-century al-Makrisi in a translation of 1848; and the fall of Acre, 1291.

The eleven chronological chapters are followed by three thematic ones. The first, "Life on a crusade, 1095–1270", offers the most direct comparison with Housley's book. It has extracts on physical conditions (mostly hunger and thirst), and spiritual concerns. The latter include *Gesta Francorum* on the discovery of the Holy Lance, an episode which is difficult to appreciate without the historical context, and Ibn al-Athir on the True Cross. The greatest number of extracts relates to prisoners of war and has the best balance of Christian and Muslim sources, and there is also a section on women which (reflecting the sources) struggles to find any positive images. "Life in the Crusader States" mixes the usual overused quotations from Usama with the less well-known Burchard of Mount Sion on Muslims, and Syrian and Greek Christians. An extract from Imad ad-Din returns to the subject of prostitution. Thus far, all the translated sources have been taken from previous translations and collections. Finally in Chapter 14, on canon law, "some sources never before translated into English" are to be found, translated by Muldoon, co-editor of the collection. These do offer a new and interesting perspective. The endmatter comprises the timeline; two outline maps; a chapter-by-chapter list of sources and copyright holders; a bibliography which does not separate primary and secondary sources (and eccentrically but disarmingly lists Albert of Aachen, duly among the As, but led by his editor's surname); notes, which include quite a lot of commentary; and a useful index.

It does *Competing Voices* no favours to review it alongside Housley's excellent book. Nonetheless, it does offer fourteen documented case studies which could be useful in the classroom. For individual crusades, there are better collections: for example, Edward Peters' *The First Crusade* (2nd ed., 1998) includes substantial extracts from Arabic and Hebrew sources as well as Latin and Greek ones. The claim to be "uniquely multi-perspective" is ambitious: E. Hallam (ed.), *Chronicles of the Crusades* (1989), which is intermittently reprinted and widely available secondhand, could make the same claim, and offers more comprehensive coverage of the subject, as well as lavish illustrations. There are good things in *Competing Voices*, but it does not have the originality and sheer inspiration of *Fighting for the Cross*.

SUSAN B. EDGINGTON
QUEEN MARY, UNIVERSITY OF LONDON

International Mobility in the Military Orders (Twelfth to Fifteenth Centuries): Travelling on Christ's Business, ed. Jochen Burgtorf and Helen Nicholson (Religion and Culture in the Middle Ages). Cardiff: University of Wales Press, 2006. Pp. xxi, 218. ISBN 0 7083 1907 6.

This is a useful and high-quality little volume, a collection of seventeen essays by military order historians from Israel to America and in between. The widely different specialties of the authors are tied together in a masterful introduction by Alan J. Forey, with a useful conclusion by Forey and the two editors, which lays out paths for profitable future research. (NB: In the interests of full disclosure, this reviewer must confess that he is currently engaged in editing a similar type of volume with the two editors of the work under consideration here.)

The subject of this volume – mobility in the military orders – is defined as geographical mobility, not social or hierarchical mobility. The papers are based on sessions held at the Leeds Medieval Congress in 2002, with five additional contributions from authors who did not present at those sessions. The primary focus is on the twelfth and thirteenth centuries, though several of the contributions either emphasize the later period, or include it. The editors note that more work needs to be done on mobility in the military orders in the fourteenth and fifteenth centuries, for which much more evidence survives than for earlier centuries. This is the case generally for military order research. One hopes that, in the future, military order historians will avail themselves of the opportunities provided by the rich array of sources for the late Middle Ages and early modern periods – one thinks, for example, of the extensive microfilmed and digitized archives of the Hospitallers, relatively easily accessible to North American researchers at the Malta Study Center of the Hill Museum and Manuscript Library in St John's University, Minnesota – and that we may begin to fill the gaps in our knowledge of the military orders after the loss of the Holy Land in 1291, and before the dispersion of the Hospitallars by Napoleon in 1798. Military order studies are often viewed as an area of medieval history, but this is not exclusively or necessarily the case; the Hospitallers, for example, functioned as a military order almost as long after 1500 (nearly three centuries) as they did before (nearly four centuries). At any rate, as the editors note, there is plenty of work left to do on the subject of military order mobility, despite the admirable start made here.

The volume is divided into two main sections. The first section includes articles of a more general scope: Jochen Burgtorf on the high officers of the Templars and Hospitallers, Judith Bronstein on the mobilization of Hospitaller manpower, Theresa Vann on the exchange of information and financial resources between Hospitaller Rhodes and the West, Jürgen Sarnowsky on Hospitaller brethren on Rhodes, Kay Peter Jankrift on mobility in the Order of St Lazarus, Alain Demurger on the various travels of the Spanish Templar Berenguer of Cardona, and Axel Ehlers on the fascinating Teutonic priest John Malkaw. The second section, simply titled "Regional Studies", includes contributions by Helen Nicholson on the tension between the needs of the various governments in the British Isles and the Orders of the Temple and the Hospital, Elena Bellomo in an article which makes the most of the limited sources available on the Templars in northwestern Italy, Christian Vogel on Provençal Templars, Jean-Marie Allard on Templars from Limoges (drawing on trial records), Zsolt Hunyadi on Hungarian and Slavonian Hospitallers, Pierre Bonneaud on Catalan Hospitallers on Rhodes, Klaus van Eickels on the Rheno-Flemish bailiwick of the Teutonic Knights, David Marcombe on the English elements of the Order of St Lazarus, and Maria Cristina Cunha on the Order of Avis.

There are some surprising conclusions: for example, that even before the loss of the Holy Land, there was relatively little movement "outside their home areas" by military order brethren ("Conclusion," p. 203). The image of the military orders as organizations constantly transferring large numbers of men from one location to another is not supported by the sources. Less surprising, perhaps, is the observation that those who travelled were generally of higher status than those who did not (p. 203).

The volume itself is of a high material standard – reassuring to see at a time when some publishers are cutting corners for economic reasons. Alas, the footnotes are placed at the end of each essay: all-too-typical and all-too-annoying. This is an unapologetically serious and scholarly book, and its natural readers would not have been frightened by spotting footnotes at the bottom of the page where they belong, and where, in this age of sophisticated computer typesetting software, there is no excuse for not putting them. (As most people know, however, this is a decision that is generally beyond the control of editors – but publishers, please take notice!)

The weaknesses of this volume are those common to all enterprises of this type – the necessarily scattershot approach means that there is a certain unevenness of quality at times, and that some areas receive more treatment while others receive less, not necessarily because they deserve it, but because no single author has tried to cover the entire ground (with the exception, of course, of the "Introduction" and "Conclusion," but even there, the opportunities are somewhat limited by space).

The strength of this particular book lies in the generally high quality of the contributions, and in the work which Alan Forey and the editors have done to tie the volume together. All in all, it provides a good introduction to an under-explored field. The best summary for this review, perhaps, is the next to last sentence in the book itself: "The studies in this volume do not conclude research in the area of international mobility within the military religious orders, but ... serve to open it up and reveal possibilities for future research" (p. 206). And this it does very well.

PAUL F. CRAWFORD
CALIFORNIA UNIVERSITY OF PENNSYLVANIA

Conor Kostick, *The Social Structure of the First Crusade* (The Medieval Mediterranean, 76). Leiden and Boston: Brill, 2008. Pp. xii, 324. ISBN 978 90 04 16665 3.

This book, in which a crusade is interpreted intelligently in the context of Historical Materialism, is a welcome contribution to crusade historiography. Dr. Kostick looks closely at eight well-known narrative accounts of the First Crusade, four by eyewitnesses and four by contemporaries who wrote soon after the fall of Jerusalem. He analyzes their treatment of different categories of crusaders in the first two chapters. Thereafter, the part the crusaders played is treated thematically, with two chapters on the poor, two on the knights, two on the leaders and one on women. In the conclusion he turns to broader questions, including that of motivation.

Dr. Kostick uses his material to divide the crusaders into two "classes", of *nobiles* and *pauperes*, which he then subdivides into social groupings. He refers to economic status when defining class and he seems to employ other forms of categorization – birth, legal status – to establish subordinate social groups, although he is much less concerned with those elements, like kinship and clientage, that transcended them. He does not define his terms very precisely: for example, the words "vassal" and "aristocrat", are used either inappropriately or without any explanation of what he means by them. This is not, I am sure, because he is unaware of the importance of clear and accurate definitions – he criticizes previous historians, including myself, for using loose language at times – but sharper distinctions would be inappropriate to an analysis which is dependent on bundling up a heterogeneous body of men and women from different parts of western Europe into his two classes, the actions and inter-reactions of which, he believes, determined the course of the crusade. Perhaps for the same reason he treats the language used by his authors – particularly those writing after the crusade had triumphed – almost as literally as an evangelical Christian would Holy Writ. At times he seems to forget that Robert the Monk, Baldric of Bourgueil and Guibert of Nogent were writing literary and theological treatises-cum-histories. Dr. Kostick draws, for example, on rhetorical flourishes, such as Baldric of Bourgueil's account of a speech made by Bohemond of Taranto, to justify his contention that the term *nobilis* was already being used of knights in general. This is necessary to the case he makes for the knights being subsumed into the ranks of the nobility much earlier than has been hitherto supposed, especially as much of the rest of his evidence confirms, rather than challenges, the prevailing view that the association of knighthood with nobility was a development of the late twelfth century.

He also maintains that the crusade ended with the conversion of the poor who settled in the East into free tenant farmers. This was certainly the case with some of them, but most of the evidence to which he draws attention dates from later in the twelfth century and relates to the *villeneuves* which were being established in the Palestinian countryside. These seem to have been populated by more recent immigrants from Europe, who had never been crusaders.

His identification of a group of *juvenes* or *tyrones* within the arms-bearers, noted not so much for their age as for their bravery, is a real contribution to the history of the First Crusade. I had hoped that looking at the crusaders through new lenses might well reveal other unusual things about them, but although the chapters on the crusade itself are interesting and will provide a reader who is not au fait with recent research with an idea of conditions on the march, much of what Dr. Kostick writes – on the active and influential role of the poor, the seriousness with which we should consider the reports of the visionaries, the dependence of the knights on their horses, the significance of the households of the magnates, the running of the crusade by committee – has been considered by others in the last thirty years. His methodology may have constrained, rather than liberated, his imagination.

In his conclusion, Dr. Kostick writes a few pages in defence of Materialism. It would be possible, even against the background of his categorization of the crusaders into two classes, to treat ideological motivation as a symptom of each individual's social existence – he himself maintains that most women on the crusade were "on pilgrimage" – but his conception of the role of the poor seems to have persuaded him to confront one of the prevailing opinions on the reasons why men and women took the cross. This is caricatured by him as the view that motivation was "primarily spiritual". It would be more accurate to portray the supporters of this interpretation as believing that the forces that moved many people were an amalgam of beliefs, senses, emotions, prejudices and predispositions, which were rooted in society as well as in religion. Dr. Kostick does not draw attention to the most telling aspect of their case, which is the near absence of evidence for the profit motive and the large number of references which confirm the importance of ideas in the recruitment of crusaders. It is true, of course, that evidence rarely gives the whole picture and Dr. Kostick is right to stress that the charter material tells us next to nothing about the motivation of the poor; but neither do the narrative sources. It is surely more convincing and methodologically more fruitful to work on the basis of the evidence that is available to us, however imperfect that may be.

Dr. Kostick can produce little by way of serious counter-argument to what he calls "the 'act of love' contention". Even when he brings in the aspirations of the Italian merchants, he cannot find much evidence to support his case other than the fact that in the end the maritime cities gained trading privileges. So desperate does he appear to become that he drags in the invasion of Iraq in 2003. Otherwise, he deploys the usual mélange of assumptions, and isolated and irrelevant cases. These include the pledging of Normandy, which he describes as a mortgage, which it was not. It was a vifgage, as a result of which a lender occupied the property that was being pledged. The money raised by William II of England was, of course, used for the crusade, but it was screwed out of England to enable William to get his hands on Normandy. Dr. Kostick also resurrects the family of Hongre in Burgundy, for which he refers to Hans Mayer as an authority. Mayer was simply repeating an assertion, made by Georges Duby in his book on the Maconnais, which rested on sources that, as was unfortunately often the case with Duby, turn out to have been so sketchy as to be almost non-existent.

Nevertheless, it must be recognized that Dr. Kostick has written a pioneering work of Historical Materialism. He should also be respected for trying to put forward an alternative and materialist explanation of motivation.

JONATHAN RILEY-SMITH
EMMANUEL COLLEGE, CAMBRIDGE

Christopher MacEvitt, *The Crusades and the Christian World of the East: Rough Tolerance* (The Middle Ages Series). Philadelphia: University of Pennsylvania Press, 2008. Pp. viii, 272. ISBN 978 0 8122 4050 4

This is a clever, thought-provoking and fluently-written book that tackles a relatively neglected subject – relations between the Franks and the indigenous Christians of the Levant down to *c*.1187. As the author points out, much of the academic work on the medieval Eastern Mediterranean has concentrated, understandably, on the struggle between Christianity and Islam. Given, however, Pope Urban's stated concerns to help "Eastern Christians", along with the substantial Christian population in some parts of the lands conquered by the Franks, particularly Edessa, this is an issue well worth addressing. As Fulcher of Chartres wrote, the First Crusaders themselves were unsure as to how to treat the local Christians – should they view them as heretics, potential allies, or just inferior subject peoples? The answer posited by MacEvitt was "rough tolerance", a concept that encompasses power, conflict and oppression, yet also allows multiple religious communities to exist in a religiously charged land. The primary focus of this book – and indeed, its strongest elements – concern northern Syria from the mid-eleventh to the mid-twelfth centuries. MacEvitt offers an excellent overview of the variety of Christian groups present in the region and quite splendidly demonstrates just what a turbulent society existed there. People were accustomed to frequent changes of ruler, experiencing regimes that ranged from the Seljuk Malikshah (who showed a "fatherly affection for all the inhabitants of his lands" according to the Armenian writer Matthew of Edessa), to local Byzantine warlords and then, in 1097–98, the crusaders.

Given this context, it was not surprising that the Franks were believed to be Byzantine mercenaries and, initially at least, they were treated as such, rather than as religious colonists or holy warriors. This worked to the crusaders' advantage as they exploited the patchwork of local affiliations and soon took power for themselves. MacEvitt neatly demonstrates that at this early stage the main threat to Frankish rule in Edessa was not the Muslims but rival Armenian nobles. He also shows the considerable limitations of Count Baldwin I and II's authority. Yet through the adoption of indigenous customs, such as the veneration of local saints, by resisting the temptation to institute sweeping legal changes, plus through the practice of intermarriage, the Franks were able to consolidate their position. Struggles between the locals and the newcomers were specific and personal: they were not set in terms of Catholic against Armenian. Thus the latter never felt oppressed or persecuted as a group and this was another important factor in the Franks' survival. Count Baldwin II of Edessa married an Armenian and on his accession to the throne of Jerusalem in 1118, and with the subsequent rule of Queen Melisende, both alongside her husband King Fulk and on behalf of the young Baldwin III, Armenian blood arrived in the royal house; MacEvitt shows royal patronage of the indigenous churches to good effect.

A couple of aspects in the study are less effective, however. The suggestion that crusading historiography still adheres to a segregationalist model is to largely ignore, or seriously undervalue, Ronnie Ellenblum's *Frankish Rural Settlement in the Latin Kingdom of Jerusalem* (1998). In fact, the levels of interaction shown by Ellenblum could have acted as a basis for MacEvitt to take his arguments further forwards, rather than spending time tilting at older ideas. The author also claims that a lack of evidence in the Frankish sources regarding the affairs of the indigenous Christians reveals an attitude of indifference – and indifference forms one feature of rough tolerance. Fulcher of Chartres and William of Tyre are mentioned by name, but surely it is pertinent to indicate that their concerns were the deeds of the heroic, crusading Franks – not to offer a comprehensive picture of the polyglot society of the Levant. In other words, their agendas did not prioritize the locals and their silence does not necessarily equate with indifference.

Towards the end of the book, MacEvitt indicates the Eastern Christians became drawn towards the Greek Orthodox Church. The 1160s and 1170s are usually seen as the time when Manuel Comnenus and the Franks formed close ties as the latter sought outside help against the rising strength of Islam. The author shows that the emperor also sought to use this situation to draw the Eastern Churches towards reunion with Byzantium and this, coupled with internal political tensions within the Armenian and Jacobite Churches, caused these groups to define their beliefs more sharply and to help bring about the end of rough tolerance. While this may well have been the case, MacEvitt's neglect of the contemporary position of the Catholic Church – rigorously defining its boundaries at, for example, the Third Lateran Council (1179) – is a little odd.

In conclusion, I remain unsure as to whether the phrase "rough tolerance" fits the author's findings, especially for northern Syria. It seems to place too strong an emphasis on the violence at the start of the conquest – surely a pretty inevitable bedfellow of such a process anyway. This "rough" phase passed fairly rapidly and from then on "tolerance" predominated. This looks more like a *modus vivendi* with, obviously, the Franks as the primary political force, but the "rough" aspect largely dispensed with. In Edessa at least, this bears some resemblance to the earlier situation under the Muslims and the Byzantines, although there is a feel of far greater integration with the Franks. To me, the label does not convey the primary achievement of this work – the substantial level of daily interaction between the Franks and the local Christians in northern Syria. Caveats aside, the author is to be congratulated on a fascinating and significant contribution to the ever-expanding historiography of relations between the crusaders and the peoples of the Levant.

JONATHAN PHILLIPS
ROYAL HOLLOWAY UNIVERSITY OF LONDON

Hannes Möhring, *Saladin: The Sultan and his Times, 1138–1193*, trans. David. S. Bachrach with an introduction by Paul M. Cobb. Baltimore: The Johns Hopkins University Press, 2008. Pp. xxviii, 113. ISBN 978 0 8018 8992 9.

Hans Möhring has been writing about Saladin and his Ayyubid dynasty since his 1977 dissertation, published in 1980 as *Saladin und der Dritte Kreuzzug: aiyubidische Strategie und Diplomatie im Vergleich vornehmlich der arabischen mit den lateinischen Quellen.* He knows the principal sources well and is a reliable guide to the politics of the twelfth-century Near East and to the struggle between Saladin and the Latin kingdom of Jerusalem.

This book, published in German in 2005, Möhring presents as the first biography of Saladin in German; in English it is not the first, but it certainly will be the most approachable and readable for students of the crusades. This is not a work of original scholarship, but rather a clear, readable biography with no footnotes. The introduction, by Paul Cobb, does a fine job of presenting the context for Saladin's life and rule for the novice reader to whom terms like "Fatimid" and "atabeg" are unfamiliar. Cobb opens with an evocation of Saladin's tomb at the Umayyad mosque of Damascus, where he has two sarcophagi: his original simple wooden casket (now encased in glass) and the elaborate baroque tomb carved in marble at the behest of Kaiser Wilhelm II in 1903. This sets up nicely the dialogue between the historical sultan and the romantic Western myth surrounding him, which made him into the paragon of knightly and princely virtues. A myth subsequently reappropriated by various Arab rulers, including the Syrian Bath dynasty in the twentieth century, as we see in the modern bronze statue of the sultan on horseback adjacent to the citadel of Damascus.

This is very much a crusader historian's biography, and readers interested in other aspects of his rule (economic, cultural, religious) may come away disappointed. Yet to those interested primarily in the crusades, Möhring proves a sure-footed and reliable guide. He starts (Chapter 1) with an introduction to the crusader East: the irruption of the crusaders in a late tenth-century Near East where the Fatimids confront the Seljuks and their heirs, the establishment of the crusader states, and the place of Muslim subjects in the Latin states. The second chapter, "Crusade and Jihad", traces the reactions of Syrian Muslim rulers and authors to the presence of *Ifranj* ("Franks") in Palestine, focusing on the growing evocation of Jihad in the mid-twelfth century, evocation used deftly by Nur al-Din to consolidate his power. The following chapters trace Saladin's rise and his viziership of Egypt under the putative authority of Nur al-Din (Chapter 3), his fight to assert himself as Nur al-Din's heir in Syria (Chapter 4), his victory at Hattin in 1187 and the subsequent conquest of Jerusalem (Chapter 5), and his struggle against the troops of the Third Crusade (Chapter 6). A final chapter takes a brief look at some of the European portrayals of the sultan.

Specialists will take issue with some of Möhring's assertions, for example, that Saladin "appears to have dreamed of carrying the jihad to Europe, in order to conquer Constantinople and Rome, following the destruction of the Crusader states" (p. 79). This claim seems to be based on a passage in Baha al-Din's biography of Saladin, in which the sultan gazed out to sea and mused about pursuing the war against the Franks to Europe: to say that this was his "dream" is to give far too much credence to this passage. A more fundamental flaw is the narrow focus on dynastic and military history: the reader comes away with little sense of the bases of power and prestige in the twelfth-century Near East: the use of *iqta* land grants to the military elite, the patronage of the scholarly elite, the riches gleaned from Egypt's flourishing trade.

There is little of interest here for scholars of either the twelfth-century Near East or the crusades, who will be better off reading Anne-Marie Eddé's much more ambitious and scholarly *Saladin* (Paris: Flammarion, 2008). Eddé gives a much richer more rounded portrait of the sultan and his times, delving into the cultural, social and economic aspects of his reign. Möhring's work will be of interest primarily to teachers of courses on the crusades and their students.

JOHN V. TOLAN
UNIVERSITÉ DE NANTES

Gli ordini ospedalieri tra centro e periferia. Giornata di studio Roma, Istituto Storico Germanico, 16 giugno 2005, ed. Anna Esposito and Andreas Rehberg (Ricerche dell'Istituto Storico Germanico di Roma, 3). Roma: Viella, 2007. Pp. 331. ISBN 978 88 8334 261 5.

Conferences and their proceedings mushroom these days, as do Festschriften. There is no doubt that such volumes can be valuable if the collected papers summarize recent research, offer new interpretations, or publish hitherto unknown sources. On the other hand, editing these volumes consumes time and money. Certainly it is fine to have a book with twelve papers – eleven in Italian and one in English – on important ecclesiastical orders connected with hospitals. And that the book is published only two years after the conference means that the papers are up to date. The introduction by Andreas Rehberg ("Una categoria di ordini religiosi poco studiata: gli ordini ospedalieri. Prime osservazioni e piste di ricerca sul tema 'Centro e periferia,'" pp. 15–70) enumerates several institutions based on important hospitals or caring for Christians with special needs – the Holy Sepulchre in Jerusalem (later in Perugia), St. John in Jerusalem (later on Rhodes), St. Mary in Jerusalem (later in Prussia), St. Thomas in Acre (later in London), St. Mary in Bethlehem (later in Clamecy, Burgundy), St. Mary in Nazareth (later in Barletta), the Lazarites (later in Boigny near Orléans), the Mercedarians of Barcelona, the Trinitarians of Cerfroid (near Paris), the Antonines of Saint-Antoine (near Vienne), the Order of S. Spirito with its two centres at Montpellier and Rome, the three groups of *Cruciferi* in Bologna, Prague and Huy (near Liège), the congregations of Altopascio (in Tuscany), Mortara (in Lombardy), the Great St Bernard, Aubrac (north of Toulouse), Roncesvalles (in the Pyrenees) and Arrouaise (between Flanders and Vermandois). Rehberg then goes on to explain some questions for comparative research: the fate of the archives, the purposes ("spirituality"), the papal recognition, the central convent, the administration of remote possessions, the economic activities and alms-raising. One might add further questions such as the recruitment of members, the careers of officers, the provincial and general chapters. Traditional distinctions between "monks" and "canons" with and without the rule of St Benedict or between "orders" and "congregations" with and without solemn vows are not sufficient to describe and explain the functions of and the lifestyle in these organizations. Contrary to what its title says, Rehberg's paper proves that there have been some studies, but much more remains to be done.

Two summaries of international research concerning the Hospitallers are offered by Roberto Greci ("L'ordine di S. Giovanni di Gerusalemme tra centro e periferia," pp. 73–99) and by Giuliana Albini ("La ricchezza dell'ordine di S. Giovanni [secoli XII–XIV]," pp. 101–36). Marina Gazzini ("L'ordine di S. Giovanni e la società locale tra religiosità e assistenza. Italia centrosettentrionale, secoli XII–XIV," pp. 137–57) tries a similar survey for northern and central Italy. Kay Peter Jankrift ("Una rete a maglie larghe. Sull'organizzazione dell'ordine di S. Lazzaro di Gerusalemme nel XIII e XIV secolo," pp. 159–66) draws on his great book *Leprose als Streiter Gottes* (Münster, 1996) and his essay in *International Mobility in the Military Orders* (reviewed above).

Non-military hospitaller orders were apparently very keen on alms-raising. At least this issue figures prominently in their sources. Robert N. Swanson ("Marginal or mainstream? The hospitaller orders and their indulgences in late medieval England", pp. 169–94) reviews it for England; he publishes a letter of 1380 by which the proctor of Altopascio in England and Wales grants spiritual merits to a married couple, a similar printed letter of 1520 issued by the proctor of S. Spirito in Sassia, and two advertisements with spiritual privileges written in English and offered to benefactors of S. Spirito in Sassia from about 1513–21. Andreas Meyer ("Altopascio, Lucca e la questua organizzata nel XIII secolo", pp. 195–209) sums up his contribution in *Hospitäler in Mittelalter und Früher Neuzeit* (ed. Gisela

Drossbach, Munich, 2007, pp. 55–105); he adds three documents of 1243/44 edited already in his earlier paper which relate to alms-raising for which in this case local Templars offered their protection. Raffaela Villamena ("I Cerretani come intermediari degli Antoniani [a proposito di due documenti del 1315 e del 1492]," pp. 211–30) is about the people from Cerreto di Spoleto and surrounding places who specialized in alms-raising. She also discusses two as yet unpublished statutes about alms-raising issued by the abbot of the Antonines in 1315 and in 1492; only the latter document is edited here.

The final part of the volume is devoted to the Order of S. Spirito, formed by Pope Innocent III and based on the two hospitals of S. Spirito in Sassia near the Vatican in Rome and of Saint Esprit in Montpellier: Mario Sensi ("L'espansione dell'ordine di S. Spirito in Umbria e nelle Marche," pp. 233–50) discusses, among other things, again the *questuarii* from Cerreto, for whom in 1484/86 a *Speculum Cerretanorum* was composed by Tesco Pini, vicar general of the bishop of Spoleto (ed. Pietro Camporesi, Torino, 1973). Anna Esposito ("L'ospedale di S. Spirito di Roma e la confraternita veneziana dello Santo Spirito alla fine del '400," pp. 251–72) explains and edits a very detailed agreement of 1492 between S. Spirito in Rome and a local confraternity. Françoise Durand ("L'hôpital du Saint-Esprit *in Saxia* et ses filiales de Besançon et Dijon (XIIIe–XVe siècles)", pp. 273–88) is an interesting example of how provincial loyalties wavered between the two central houses at Montpellier and Rome. Giscla Drossbach ("L'ordine di S. Spirito nei territori del Sacro Romano Impero. Dagli inizi sino alla metà del XV secolo," pp. 289–300) draws on her great book *Christliche* caritas *als Rechtsinstitut. Hospital und Orden von S. Spirito in Sassia* (Paderborn, 2005).

Some of the papers will be consulted for some time to come, either because they outline questions for future research or because they study and sometimes publish important sources. So time and money have not been wasted. Moreover, the conference proceedings could and should encourage more fundamental studies about administrative rules and practices, relations with local people including the so-called "semi-religious," and relations with charitable institutions founded by kings, princes or towns. Charity was big business in the Middle Ages. The competition between the institutions active in this field deserves further scholarly attention.

KARL BORCHARDT
UNIVERSITÄT WÜRZBURG AND MONUMENTA GERMANIAE HISTORICA

Jacques Paviot, *Les ducs de Bourgogne, la croisade et l'Orient (fin XIVe siècle–XVe siècle)* (Cultures et civilisations médiévales). Paris: Presses de l'Université de Paris-Sorbonne, 2003. Pp. 392. ISBN 2 84050 316 6.

Die ältere Forschung hielt die Ära der Kreuzzüge mit dem Fall Akkons im Jahre 1291 für abgeschlossen. Da alle späteren Unternehmungen, die auf eine Rückeroberung des Heiligens Landes zielten, letztlich scheiterten, galten sie als Projekte von Phantasten. Seit längerem gilt diese Haltung für überholt, zumal es eine Reihe von "later crusades" (N. Housley) gab, die nicht mehr primär die Rückeroberung des Heiligen Landes verfolgten, aber die Idee des Heiligen Krieges im Zeichen des Kreuzes weiterhin verfochten. In diesen historiographischen Kontext gehört die vorliegende Studie von Jacques Paviot. Der Autor lässt durchblicken, dass er der "pluralistischen" Ausrichtung der Kreuzzugshistoriographie verpflichtet (S. 12; S. 294) ist, und er setzt sich zum Ziel, die fortwährende Präsenz des Kreuzzugsthemas am burgundischen Hof nachzuweisen.

Das Werk ist in zwei Teile gegliedert: "Les ducs de Bourgogne et la croisade" und "L'Orient à la cour de Bourgogne"; eine Edition wichtiger Dokumente sowie ein Orts- und Personenverzeichnis runden es ab.

Der erste Abschnitt dokumentiert die vielfältigen Pläne, Botschaften und Veranstaltungen am burgundischen Hof, die um das Thema einer "croisade" kreisen. Dabei lassen sich bei den vier Valois-Herzögen verschiedene Einstellungen gegenüber Kreuzzugsplänen nachweisen: Philippe le Hardi und Jean sans Peur sehen anfänglich in einem Kreuzzug die Gelegenheit, sich gegenüber dem französischen Königtum – dem bisherigen Träger des Kreuzzuggedankens – in Szene zu setzen. Die Katastrophe von Nikopolis führt bei beiden zu einer kühleren und realistischeren Einschätzung, was den Krieg gegen die Ungläubigen betrifft. Bei Philippe le Bon unterscheidet der Autor zwei Phasen: Der Kreuzzug als "affaire privée et ancrée dans la réalité" und – nach dem Fall von Konstantinopel – "une affaire publique et ancrée dans l'imaginaire" (S. 63); später spricht Paviot auch von einem "rêve chevaleresque" (S. 238). Am Ende seiner Regierungszeit muss Philippe le Bon sich öffentlichen Spott über seine "projets fumeux" gefallen lassen, wie ein bissiges Spottlied über den Kreuzzug, den Philippe le Bon zu Hause vor seinem Kamin durchführt, belegt (S. 175f.). Charles le Téméraire erbt vom Vater die Kreuzzugspläne, aber sein fehlendes Engagement und seine unberechenbare Rastlosigkeit führen dazu, dass er in den Augen der Zeitgenossen das vom Vater erworbene "capital symbolique fondé sur la croisade" verspielt (S. 293; vgl. auch S. 195: "il aurait finalement dilapidé l'héritage de la croisade de la maison de Bourgogne en s'en servant comme un prétexte").

Der zweite Abschnitt geht der Anwesenheit des Orient-Themas am burgundischen Hofe nach; es handelt sich teilweise um die erweiterte Version älterer Artikel (S. 239, Anm. 1; S. 257, Anm. 1). Die Bücher der herzoglichen Bibliothek, die Kontakte mit Zypern und Rhodos, die Anwesenheit von (christianisierten) Türken und Mauren lassen den burgundischen Hof im 15. Jahrhundert zu einem herausragenden Informationspunkt betreffend Orient werden (S. 199; S. 271); griechische Flüchtlinge aus Konstantinopel sind am burgundischen Hofe hingegen nur als zeitweilige Besucher nachweisbar.

Die Ergebnisse von Paviots Forschungen erklären somit ein Paradoxon der "later crusades": Seit dem ersten Kreuzzug, vor allem seit Philippe Auguste und Saint Louis gilt das französische Königtum als Träger des Kreuzzugsgedankens *par excellence*.

Im 15. Jahrhundert wird diese Aufgabe aber von den "rois très chrétiens" nicht mehr wahrgenommen. Es sind die burgundischen Herzöge, die gemäss Paviot während der Krise des Hundertjährigen Krieges in die Bresche springen und sich auch auf diese Weise aus ihrer nachgeordneten Stellung als Lehensleute des französischen König zu befreien versuchen. Indem sie in die Fussstapfen ihrer Oberherren treten, können sie die herausragende Stellung des burgundischen Herzogtums europaweit dokumentieren.

CLAUDIUS SIEBER-LEHMANN
UNIVERSITÄT BASEL

Philippe de Mézières, *Une epistre lamentable et consolatoire adressée en 1397 à Philippe le Hardi, duc de Bourgogne, sur la défaite de Nicopolis (1396)*, ed. Philippe Contamine and Jacques Paviot, with the collaboration of Céline Van Hoorebeeck (Société de l'histoire de France). Paris: Société de l'histoire de France, 2008. Pp. 270. ISBN 978 2 35407 116 5.

This new edition of Philippe de Mézières's epistolary response to the disaster at Nicopolis derives from its sole manuscript, Brussels Bibliothèque royale MS. 10486. The full text is given, preceded by a substantial introduction in which the editors address questions of authorship, origins, thematic content and manuscript transmission. The text is clearly laid out and equipped with explanatory footnotes. It can be precisely dated to 1397, after news reached France of events at Nicopolis, but before Philip the Bold set in motion the ransom payments for the prisoners, who included his son and heir John of Nevers. So it constitutes a comprehensive reaction to the fourteenth century's greatest crusading defeat, written by that period's most fervent and prolific crusading enthusiast. From that point of view it is an important text and this scholarly and accessible edition is very welcome.

Anybody looking for originality in the *Epistre* will be disappointed. Mézières was probably over 70 when he wrote it and he had set out his ideas at exhaustive length just a few years previously in his masterpiece, *Le Songe du Vieil Pelerin* (ed. G. W. Coopland, Cambridge, 1969). A few more years spent "en ma povre sellette" in the Celestine convent at Paris did not equip him with anything new to say. Once Mézières has finished lamenting what has happened he asks what should be done about the captured Christians. Either they can be ransomed (as of course they were) or they can be rescued. Naturally Mézières favours the latter course of action, and this launches him on a lengthy regurgitation of the whole process of moral and military reform, centred on the formation of a new chivalric order, that by this point had been his life's supreme goal for half a century. Three great armies should be recruited which would all make their way eastwards to rescue the captives and crush Turkish power. Nobody needed to worry about how these massive hosts would be funded: the same knights who would rush to join Mézières's Order of the Passion would also queue up to hand over thousands of florins from their patrimonies for the crusading cause. And all this in the wake of Nicopolis! One almost expects a fourth army, one made up of flying pigs.

Setting aside the crusading prescription as pure fantasy, we are bound to ask what can be gained from this example of late Mézières (he would die early in 1405). The answer, I suggest, is two-fold. First, it contributes to our own assessment of what actually happened at Nicopolis, and it illuminates the lively debate conducted by contemporaries about who was to blame. Mézières offers two culprits. The first is the undisciplined French chivalry. Their faults lead him to reiterate well-worn themes about the need for order (*règle*), discipline, obedience and justice in any army, not just a crusading one. This places Mézières firmly within the lobby for French military reform whose most fervent representative, in terms of Nicopolis apologetics, was the hypercritical Religious of S. Denis. Christ, "le vray patron et souverain chevetaine de l'ost," had indignantly abandoned the Christian army, leaving it to its just deserts. The other culprit is the Balkan schismatics, the so-called allies of the Westerners, rotten apples as Mézières terms them, who hate the Catholics so much that they prefer Turkish to Hungarian rule.

The other value of this text, as so often with Mézières, lies in what one can pick up not from his argument, all too often repetitive, turgid and weighed down by allegory, but from passing anecdotes and reminiscences about his own past. There is nothing here as fascinating as the famous passage in *Le Songe du Vieil Pelerin* about the annual herring catch in the Sound, which makes that text suddenly burst into life. But there are interesting passages, like those reflecting on the First Crusade, the Hattin campaign, the siege of Acre during the Third Crusade, and recent Cypriot history. The *Epistre* reminds us how deep Mézières's own perspective on events was by this stage in his life. His memories stretched back almost as far as Joinville's at the point when he composed the final text of his *Vie de saint Louis*. Particularly instructive is his final section, in which he gives a short but revealing account of the Turkish emirates of Aydin, Karaman and Germiyan during the time when he was chancellor of Cyprus.

The publication of this new edition of the *Epistre* prompts one to reflect that a re-evaluation of its author is long overdue. Ideally, there is more editorial work to be done first. It is astonishing that to consult a printed version of Mézières's most important statements on his Order of the Passion, Paris Bibliothèque Mazarine MS. 1943, one has to locate a copy of A. H. Hamdy's edition, published in the *Bulletin of the Faculty of Arts of Alexandria University* in 1964. We require a systematic analysis of Mézières's ideas, their sources and development, together with an objective attempt at evaluating his genuine influence, as opposed to his asserted one. The conclusion may be that he deserves his reputation as the oft-consulted repository of wisdom about crusading to the east throughout the second half of the fourteenth century. Or perhaps his status will be whittled down to that of a marginally important, though highly opinionated, eccentric. Certainly, as he himself complained, the dismal fate of the Nicopolis expedition is proof that people were not listening to him. And there is no sign that this *Epistre* fell on anything but deaf ears.

NORMAN HOUSLEY
UNIVERSITY OF LEICESTER

Jonathan Phillips, *The Second Crusade: Extending the Frontiers of Christendom*. New Haven and London: Yale University Press, 2007. Pp. xxix, 364. ISBN 978 0 300 11274 0.

Publishers' blurbs and reviewers' quotations on book jackets often exaggerate, but their praise rings true for *The Second Crusade*. Jonathan Phillips's work fills many needs, and it does so very well. Phillips ably captures the crusade's complexity as well as its drama in the Levant, the Baltic, and the Iberian peninsula. He augments the narrative with insightful analysis drawing together the best research – including his own – from many areas of crusades studies. Finally, he explores historiographical debates and demonstrates careful research techniques without detracting from the narrative, so that even a non-specialist can understand the limitations of historical sources. The result is a book that beginning students can read without difficulty, thanks to the clear narrative and supporting apparatus, and that more established scholars can rely upon for authoritative synthesis. Finally, researchers will find many promising new lines of enquiry emerging from the points Phillips makes.

The book opens with Zengi's attack on Edessa in 1144, which Phillips sees as a necessary, not sufficient, cause for the crusade. He argues that Zengi's success fanned the flames of Catholic expansionist ideology, which had burned brighter after the First Crusade. Eugenius III and Bernard of Clairvaux then seized upon the opportunity to call for an official campaign, with the pope playing a central role. Both men also responded to local situations in the Iberian peninsula and the Baltic, covering military endeavors in these regions with the same spiritual umbrella that applied to the Jerusalem crusade. Yet their approval does not correspond, in Phillips's formulation, to an overarching plan; instead, they reacted to a groundswell of popular support. Clerical and lay contemporaries often wrote about all these campaigns as ways to expand Christendom (a fact that Phillips uses to support current pluralist definitions of crusading). Lay enthusiasm for holy war also explained the success of recruiting efforts, especially at the highest levels of secular society. It is no wonder, then, that the failure in Jerusalem tended to overshadow successes elsewhere, both in medieval writings and in modern historiography. Phillips concludes that the Second Crusade merits further study because it reveals a crucial and early stage in the larger crusading movement.

To that end, Phillips connects many strands of this complicated story in novel ways. Instead of providing a cursory background chapter and then treating the Second Crusade as a self-contained endeavor, he places mid-twelfth century events into context – specifically, European Catholics' growing interest in holy war after

1099. Two important chapters on the period between 1100 and 1146 incorporate a compelling variety of sources (chronicles, charters, letters, *chansons de geste*, artwork, and songs) that intertwined memories of the First Crusade with new appeals to piety and honor, especially family honor. As European pilgrims and warriors continued traveling to the Crusader States, they brought home relics and stories that inspired more zeal. Thus, by the time Eugenius issued *Quantum praedecessores*, he could tap into a longstanding and highly effective tradition to recruit new crusaders. Moreover, the papal curia's monastic connections across western Europe could capitalize on both the papal bull and vivid memories of crusading and pilgrimage. St. Bernard's letters and sermons employed the same emotionally laden imagery of spiritual benefit and social prestige that could be won by someone who fought for the Holy Sepulcher. Phillips's compelling discussion credits many cooperating elites, lay and clerical, for launching the crusade.

Yet these leaders could not retain total control. Once Louis VII and French nobles took the cross, unofficial preachers stirred up anti-Semitic violence. Bernard's efforts to rein them in may have led him to the Holy Roman Empire, where emperor-elect Conrad vowed to crusade. Phillips portrays Conrad as the senior partner in the Jerusalem campaign, arguing against older interpretations that downplayed imperial leadership. He continues this theme in several chapters on crusade preparations in France and the Empire, carefully working through chroniclers' varied authorial purposes and other source limitations to rehabilitate Conrad's reputation. Chapters 6 and 7 are especially valuable in their coverage of personal motivations, finances, logistics, and diplomatic considerations vis-à-vis Sicily and Byzantium.

At this point, Phillips turns to the Lisbon expedition, examining England and Iberia at length for the first time. He brings in his own research to good effect, showing how the Portuguese and the crusaders derived mutual advantage from cooperating. His careful analysis of Raol's *De expugnatione lyxbonensi* indicates how crusading ideology could encompass fighting anywhere on behalf of Christendom. Phillips then resumes his description of the crusade to Jerusalem with separate chapters on Conrad's and Louis's marches. He preserves the chronicles' dramatic stories without taking them at face value in discussing several key battles. Here, too, his treatment of international relations is most illuminating, for Phillips pays careful attention to all concerned parties: the Seljuks, the Greek emperor Manuel, and Raymond of Antioch, as well as the European crusaders. This multi-faceted discussion greatly clarifies various points; for example, the crusaders' strategic mistakes at Damascus make more sense when one considers Muslim and Frankish sources alongside the European ones.

Phillips then turns to other holy wars in the Baltic and eastern Iberia. His command of the primary and secondary literature is exemplary, drawing upon the best studies available. Both chapters beautifully support his argument that the Church reacted to regional conditions instead of imposing a top-down program, for in each place local holy warriors ultimately pursued their own goals of assimilation rather than conquest. Yet like the Lisbon chapter, these two chapters seemed out of place chronologically and thematically, since their events often preceded those at Jerusalem. Narrative flow might have been stronger if Phillips had treated Iberia, Lisbon, and then the Baltic prior to Conrad's and Louis's marches and the Damascus siege. Such an organizational scheme would also have driven home the point that failure in the Levant all but crushed crusading enthusiasm after 1148, the subject of the final chapter. Both the papacy and the laity moved much more cautiously, and diplomatic realignments between Constantinople, Germany, Sicily, and France made further campaigns to Jerusalem much less palatable.

Phillips set ambitious goals in this book, simultaneously planning to narrate several complex operations, set them into a geopolitical and ideological context, explore historiographical debates, and propound arguments of his own. He largely fulfilled these goals, not only through his scholarship and excellent writing, but through his own innovative research. Phillips shows remarkable dexterity at synthesizing narratives, assessing relevant scholarship, and gently steering readers toward a nuanced understanding of the issues, as for example debates over defining the *Reconquista* as a crusade in Chapter 13.

Phillips also offers explicit and implicit lessons in methodology, since he drew upon so many source genres. Narrative sources, which offer connected stories about cause and effect, often overshadow other types of information. But these stories can all too easily seduce historians who do not constantly consider authorial purpose and rhetorical devices. Phillips balances chronicles with other information, and he shows readers how he uses different source genres.

Yet background material on the most important sources is sprinkled throughout the book. A chapter on primary sources or an introductory essay in the bibliography would be very useful, especially for readers less familiar with the Second Crusade. It would also allow Phillips to explore the strengths of different genres and weigh different texts or artifacts within the same genre. Here Phillips needed to pay more attention to his audience: crusades historians are more likely than other readers to realize that William of Tyre wrote long after the crusade ended, but this is not mentioned. Sometimes Phillips draws on a source extensively before putting it into context; for example, he uses Odo of Deuil's text many times before covering it in depth in Chapter 10. Nor does Phillips discuss the lack of sources available for the kingdom of Jerusalem at this time, in contrast to Odo's wealth of information on Antioch.

Insufficient attention to the overall landscape of source materials comprises the only major weak spot of the book. Jonathan Phillips has produced a very important work that fulfils my personal ideal for a historical work: rather than answering every question one could imagine, he opens the door to new possibilities. Readers will find this journey very stimulating as they follow the Second Crusaders across Europe and the Mediterranean.

DEBORAH GERISH
EMPORIA STATE UNIVERSITY

Religiones Militares. Contributi alla storia degli Ordini religiosi-militari nel medioevo, ed. Anthony Luttrell and Francesco Tommasi (Biblioteca di Militia sacra, 2). Città di Castello, 2008. Pp. 277. ISBN 978 88 901124 2 5.

This volume, published to commemorate the arrest of the Templars in 1307, is a sequel to the very successful *Acri 1291*, which appeared in 1996. The standing of the editors has ensured that the papers, attached to several of which are editions of unpublished documents, are of a consistently high standard. In "The Hospitaller Background of the Teutonic Order," Anthony Luttrell argues cogently that the Teutonic Knights owed their independence to Hospitaller mismanagement and, in "L'ordinamento geografico-amministrativo dell'Ospedale in Italia (secc.XII–XIV)," Francesco Tommasi unravels authoritively the complicated history of the Italian Hospitallers. The two editors also combine in "Una falso donazione per l'Ordine dell'Ospedale (1120)." Karl Borchardt ("Die Johanniter in den Supplikenregistern von Papst Innozenz VI. 1352–1362") draws attention to an interesting and valuable source. Rafaël Hyacinthe ("L'Ordre de Saint-Lazare de Jérusalem dans le contexte spirituel des croisades: une réévaluation") provides by far the best treatment to date of St. Lazarus in the Latin East and gives the first convincing account of that order's militarization. Helen Nicholson, who is preparing an edition of the English enquiries into the Templars, describes in interesting detail (in "The Trial of the Templars in the British Isles") the source material for her topic and the state of research on it. Kristjan Toomaspoeg, who has made the subject of the military orders in Sicily very much his own, publishes (in "Le fine dei Templari in Sicilia [1305–1327]") materials on the suppression of the Temple on the island. Damien Carraz, already responsible for the best regional history of the military orders, makes (in "L'affiliation des laics aux commanderies templières et hospitalières de la basse vallée du Rhône [XIIe–XIIIe siècles]") an important contribution to the debate on the meaning of confraternity and other forms of association. Robert Vinas ("Les personnels de la commanderie du Masdéu en 1307 et après") reveals the individuals attached to the Templar commandery in Roussillon and their subsequent histories. Mariarosaria Salerno ("Templari e Ospedalieri di San Giovanni in Calabria in età medievale: risultati ed ipotesi") gives an account of the military orders in an important south Italian region. And Joan Fuguet Sans ("Pinturas, miniaturas y graffiti de los Templarios en la Corona de Aragón") shows how much survives of wall paintings, miniatures and graffiti associated with the order of the Temple in north-eastern Iberia. The collection is a good example of the quality and range of modern research on the military orders.

JONATHAN RILEY-SMITH
EMMANUEL COLLEGE, CAMBRIDGE

Jonathan Riley-Smith, *The Crusades, Christianity, and Islam*. New York: Columbia University Press, 2008. Pp. 144. ISBN 978 0 231 51794 2.

Jonathan Riley-Smith has joined a distinguished group, those who have delivered the Bampton Lectures in America since Arnold Toynbee spoke in 1940. Columbia University has thus recognized not only a leading scholar but the field of crusade studies, to which he has contributed so much. These lectures are not a recital of the crusade narrative, but the reflections of one who has thought much about the meaning of crusading and the changes that have occurred in its development over the last 800 years. More than anyone else Riley-Smith has been responsible for expanding the chronological and geographical parameters of crusade, while providing a very specific definition: The war must be holy, it must be authorized by the pope, and its members were vowed to its purpose. He maintains that the crusade sprang from essential elements in medieval religion. He does not, however, discuss the calls for assistance from the Byzantine Empire or some Eastern Christians, which were directed to the papacy.

The four lectures examine the concept of crusading beginning with its inception in the late eleventh century and its penitential character as pilgrimage, the linking of imperialism and crusade in the nineteenth century and its resurrection by Islamist and Nationalist movements in the twentieth century. Having bitten off such a large chunk, the author shows that he has not merely thought about the crusades in these contexts but has also been conscious of contemporary controversies. He is not, however, content to provide a textbook discussion. Rather, he opens his mind to us in a way that reveals how a historian approaches the most complex topics. He reminds us that some in the medieval period had doubts whether Christians could participate in war without sinning. He cites the example of St. Louis, the only crusade leader to be canonized, not, however, as a martyr but as a confessor. His discussion of the place of the crusade in the Church's thinking about penance provides a very interesting discussion of the military orders. His third lecture is devoted to a neglected aspect of the work of Cardinal Lavigerie, namely, his opposition to slavery in Algeria and his effort to found a military order to protect emancipated slaves. The final lecture dwells extensively on the modern resurgence of crusade terminology in the Islamic World.

Riley-Smith reminds us that the crusade has undergone many changes and made many different associations in its long history. It would be easy to find omissions or to quarrel with details, but this is not that kind of book. A more significant issue is his handling of the contemporary scene in the Muslim world. His views seem to me be closer to those of Bernard Lewis than Carole Hillenbrand. Lewis puts his emphasis on the impact of jihadism on the West, with the interests of Israel in the mix, whereas Hillenbrand puts more emphasis on internal developments. As recently as thirty years ago, the major concerns in the Muslim World, aside from the Palestinian-Israeli conflict, were focused on internal development. I believe that changed, not because new elements were introduced, but because the major powers increasingly carried their conflicts into the Islamic World. It became more and more difficult to maintain the status quo after the Iranian Revolution. Some Western leaders fell into the trap of broadening conflicts rather than trying to isolate them. This opened the door further for the kinds of reaction that Riley Smith and others describe. The appeal of many Muslims to crusade ideology represents an ahistorical cry of frustration that resonates only slightly against the concerns for oil and national power that move some Westerners, but stirred the feelings of victimization that are very common in the Near and Mid-East in the post-imperialist world.

JAMES M. POWELL
EMERITUS, SYRACUSE UNIVERSITY

Alexios G. C. Savvides, *Byzantino-Normannica: The Norman Capture of Italy and the First Two Norman Invasions in Byzantium (A.D. 1081–1085 and 1107–1108)* (Orientalia Lovanensia Analecta, 165). Louvain: Peeters, 2007, Pp. 96. ISBN 978 90 429 1911 2.

Das Buch enthält eine faktenorientierte Übersicht folgender Ereignisse: der Aufstieg Robert Guiskards in Unteritalien zwischen etwa 1060 und 1080, der normannische Angriff auf Byzanz unter demselben Anführer 1081–1085 und der Angriff Bohemunds von 1107/8. Von den insgesamt 96 Seiten entfallen 29 auf Einleitung, Herrscherlisten und Literaturverzeichnis, 55 Seiten enthalten Text und Anmerkungen. Der Rest wird von einer Karte und dem Index beansprucht. Es ist klar, daß bei einem solchen Umfang keine neuen Erkenntnisse und auch keine vertiefte Diskussion des behandelten Themas erwartet werden können. Savvides beschränkt sich denn auch auf eine rein positivistische Darstellung der Fakten, zu denen er in den Anmerkungen Quellen und Literaturangaben aufzählt, ohne aber in irgendeiner Weise zwischen den verschiedenen Angaben und Auffassungen innerhalb der Forschung zu unterscheiden oder die Unterschiede überhaupt als solche zu kennzeichnen. Trotz des Umfangs der Literaturliste weist die Aufzählung einige Lücken auf.

Methodisch bedenklich sind die unterschiedslosen Zitate aus Quellen und Sekundärliteratur, mit denen Savvides die Dastellung aufzulockern sucht. Eine Diskussion findet nicht statt, Zitate aus der Sekundärliteratur wecken manchmal den Eindruck, mehr aufgrund ihrer Prägnanz als wegen ihrer wissenschaftlichen Relevanz ausgesucht worden zu sein. Eher aus dem populärwissenschaftlichen Bereich kommen – niemals argumentativ belegte – Behauptungen wie etwa diejenige, daß Bohemund der wohl schlimmste Gegner der gesamten byzantinischen Geschichte gewesen sei: "probably the worst enemy Byzantium ever encountered" (p. 32). Da hat Byzanz ja doch wohl erheblich gefährlichere Feinde gehabt, wie selbst ein oberflächlicher Blick auf die Geschichte dieses Reiches zeigt! Auf den ersten Blick lustig, aber doch Anzeichen für eine schlampige Redaktion ist die Feststellung, daß Robert Guiskard "piece [*sic*] proposals" (p. 52) an Kaiser Alexios geschickt habe. Schlimmer ist, daß Savvides den Mitteilungen seiner Quellen, vor allem Anna Komnene und Wilhelm von Apulien, völlig kritiklos folgt, ohne nach dem Hintergrund und nach den Motiven zu fragen, die ihren Darstellungen zugrundeliegen.

Fazit: Das Buch enthält nichts Neues. Für eine populärwissenschaftliche Darstellung ist es zu überfrachtet mit Anmerkungen, Zitaten und – häufig unnötigen – Hinweisen auf Arbeiten einzelner Forscher. Für eine wissenschaftliche Arbeit ist es methodisch zu unsauber und zu unkritisch gegenüber den Quellen und der Sekundärliteratur. Für eine Forschungsübersicht schließlich fehlt die Diskussion der unterschiedlichen Meinungen, Ansätze und Methoden.

RALPH-JOHANNES LILIE
BERLIN-BRANDENBURGISCHE AKADEMIE DER WISSENSCHAFTEN, BERLIN

The Seventh Crusade, 1244–1254: Sources and Documents, ed. and trans. Peter Jackson (Crusade Texts in Translation, 16). Aldershot and Burlington, VT: Ashgate, 2007. Pp. xvi, 256. ISBN 978 0 7546 5722 4.

Most students learn about King Louis IX of France's crusade to Egypt in 1248 from Jean de Joinville's *Vie de Saint Louis*, which has long been available in English translation. Joinville's all too human reactions to fear, danger, and loss, his intimacy with a legendary king, and his curiosity about the world beyond the borders of Christianity (and even Islam) make him essential reading for first-time students of the crusades. But for all his curiosity and wide-ranging (not to say rambling) style, Joinville actually left a lot out of his memoir. We hear little from him about the political negotiations that preceded the campaign, the competition for recruits and money among the various theaters of crusading activity, the wildly complex politics of the Ayyubid domains in the mid-thirteenth century, and the passionate reaction to the crusade's failure back home. These are important historical issues, but they are difficult to study because the sources that might shed light on them – contemporary letters, charters, contracts, and chronicles – are scattered and, unlike Joinville's text, mainly un-translated. By gathering these sources together in a single volume of English translations, Professor Jackson has performed a great service to students, teachers, and scholars of the crusades.

Several discoveries await those who know about the crusade primarily through Joinville. A rich selection of imperial and papal letters reveals the ambivalent attitudes of Frederick II and Innocent IV toward Louis's crusading plans. Locked in conflict with each other, the two leading powers of Christendom both worried, but for different reasons, about the upcoming campaign. Frederick, who claimed the kingdom of Jerusalem for his son Conrad, feared that the crusade might bring comfort to his many enemies there. Innocent feared that Louis's preparations might siphon resources away from other papal crusading priorities: the war in the Baltic; the defense of eastern Europe against the Mongols; and, most of all, his own campaign against Frederick, which was then being waged on the pope's behalf by the anti-king William of Holland. As a result of these concerns, Louis did not receive as much support from church and empire as he may have wished.

More revelations come in the section on the "crusade" of the *Pastoureaux*, a series of popular uprisings that swept the French countryside in the wake of Louis's defeat and capture in the Nile Delta. A wide range of contemporary chronicle accounts shows how a movement that began as an effort to rescue the king quickly took on anti-clerical and anti-Jewish overtones. This chapter provides an excellent opportunity for students to explore the wider social ramifications of crusading in the European heartland.

Best of all, readers will encounter at first hand in this collection the fascinating politics of the Muslim Middle East in the mid-thirteenth century, the period that witnessed the violent ascent of the Mamluks. The two most frequently cited Muslim sources for this era are the late medieval compilations of Ibn al-Furat and al-Maqrizi. Professor Jackson brings us much closer to the action with generous excerpts from Ibn Wasil, a well-connected author who spent much of the crusade in Cairo and some of it in the sultan's camp at Mansura, and from the Sibt Ibn al-Jawzi, who wrote from Damascus but had access to the lost memoirs of an Egyptian grandee. The Sibt offers a damning portrait of al-Muʿazzam Turan Shah, the briefly-reigning sultan whose assassination at the hands of his father's Mamluk guard would effectively end Ayyubid rule in Egypt. "When he was drunk," the Sibt tells us, "he gathered candles and would slash at the heads [of the candles] with his sword and lop them off, saying 'Thus shall I do with the Bahriyya,' and he would mention his father's mamluks by name" (p. 161). With the help of the Sibt, we can now appreciate just how unready Turan Shah was to rule.

The decision to focus on contemporary letters and documents gives the volume a thematic focus. The sources address the crusade as a military expedition to the East: its recruitment and funding; its diplomatic foundations; its disastrous course in Egypt; and the aftermath in Syria and France. Those who, following in the footsteps of W. C. Jordan, wish to study the transformations in Capetian government that Louis's preparations for the crusade initiated, will want to look elsewhere for source material. By concentrating on the campaign, Professor Jackson allows himself the space for a superb scholarly apparatus and the inclusion of invaluable Arabic sources. The volume thus makes it possible to teach the crusade from both Muslim and Christian perspectives – an often articulated but seldom achieved goal of crusades pedagogy. This is an exemplary primary source reader that, having once been the preserve only of fortunate undergraduates at Keele University, is now available to students throughout the English-speaking world.

MICHAEL LOWER
UNIVERSITY OF MINNESOTA

Alessandro Vanoli, *La Spagna delle tre culture. Ebrei, cristiani e musulmani tra storia e mito* (La storia. Temi, 1). Roma, Viella, 2006. Pp. 317. ISBN: 88 8334 202 X,

The title of this book by an Italian hispanist and political scientist might be slightly misleading, for it may conjure images of chess-playing Muslims and Christians from the "Cantigas de Santa Maria", letting readers expect yet another narrative on Iberian *convivencia*. In reality, however, this study is both more ambitious and more restricted than its title suggests. On the one hand, its scope is far more ample than a mere depiction of Christian-Muslim-Jewish cohabitation in mediaeval Iberia, for the author understands interfaith relations in a very wide sense: He aims at showing both peaceful and antagonistic (including military) relations between the adherents to the three major religions, and thus goes further than a traditional description of *convivencia* on the Iberian Peninsula. His objective is "una storia della tre culture dal punto di vista della loro comunicazione" (p. 12). In fact, Vanoli's aim is wider still: the study is no less than a cultural, political and military history of the Iberian Peninsula from the eighth century up to the present day. The author leaves no doubt as to his position in the controversy between Claudio Sánchez Albornoz, who postulated the existence of a perpetual *homo ibericus*, who maintained his freedom during a secular struggle against the Muslim invasion, and Americo Castro, who saw Iberian culture as a product of interfaith relations: "si chiudeva allora, in modo drasticamente triste, quel lungo periodo di quasi novecento anni, cha aveva visto l'Islam fare parte, nel bene o nel male, della storia spagnola" (p. 214). But Vanoli, though closer to Castro's views than to those of Sánchez Albornoz, is in no way uncritical and at one point even casts doubt on the title of his own study: "Se mai vi fu qualcosa come la 'Spagna delle tre culture' (e per alcuni versi mi sembla licito dubitarne), ora davvero giunto alla fine" (p. 157).

At the same time, Vanoli also delimits his field of research. Following the lines laid out by Maurice Halbwachs, Jan Assmann and others, he is particularly interested in the history of cultural memory, that is, in the *Erinnerungsgeschichte* of interfaith relations on the Iberian Peninsula. This interest accounts for the book's structure. It is divided into two parts – "La Spagna delle tre culture," which offers a chronological synthesis of Iberian history with special emphasis on interfaith relations (pp. 17–190), and "La Spagna delle tre culture, dalla storia al mito," which presents an overview of the positions Spaniards took towards interfaith relations from the sixteenth to twenty-first centuries (pp. 193–312). Both the wider definition of interfaith relations and the specific question which Vanoli attempts to answer are important and to be welcomed. However, in his attempt to present a general survey of Iberian history, the author sometimes overshoots the mark by including passages with little relation to interfaith interaction. Adhering closer to his field of research would have allowed the author to follow his objective in more detail. The second part in particular would have benefited greatly from an in-depth treatment of historical memory instead of presenting a wide overview of Spanish history.

Historians of the Crusades will find basic information on the so-called "Reconquest" in the stricter sense, as the book summarizes the major campaigns and shifts in power. Vanoli also deals with the relation between the crusading idea and the *Reconquista* (pp. 121–27). Quite in line with recent scholarship, he postulates that from the beginning of the twelfth century onwards events in the Levant influenced older Iberian notions of territorial reconquest. More importantly, Vanoli discerns a shift in the way Christians depicted Muslims in the course of the thirteenth century: prior to that, individual Muslims had been portrayed in a stereotypically negative fashion, usually in order to enhance the position of the ruling monarchs. The giant leap the reconquest made in the first half of the thirteenth century coincided with a new vision of Christian–Muslim conflict: the latter was now seen as part of a wider antagonism not so much between individuals, but between Christianity and Islam (pp. 124–26). Later chapters deal with the concept of Reconquista in modern historiography and its development over time (pp. 250–54, 288–90, 293–95). The author not only shows the importance of interfaith relations for collective identity in modern Spain, but also the role this issue played for the image that the West created of the Iberian Peninsula (pp. 254–62). Not surprisingly, considering the immense field the author covers, some recent studies and shifts in research have been overlooked. There are even passages which are definitely inexact or even incorrect: The Spanish military orders for example are dealt with in a short paragraph which contains a number of mistakes (p. 134: not all Iberian Orders were tied to the Cistercians, "Giuliano del Pero" is not a valid translation for "San Julián de Pereiro", and there is no order officially titled "Militia sancti Benedicti cisterciensis ordinis"). But in general the study presents a reliable synthesis.

Thus, in spite of some criticism of individual points and the deficiencies such wide syntheses tend to show, this book is recommendable reading for historians interested in Crusader Spain. First, it offers a general backdrop to the campaigns between Muslims and Christians. Second, it sets antagonistic relations in due perspective by including descriptions of the non-violent forms of interfaith interaction on the Iberian Peninsula. Third, it draws attention to the history of research in the field, offering an important contribution to the *Erinnerungsgeschichte* of mediaeval Iberia, a memory that has not only led to the "return of the Jews" (pp. 270–74), but also to present-day aspirations of recovering Muslim Al-Andalus (pp. 302–9). A translation of this intelligently written book into other languages would thus be welcome.

Nikolas Jaspert
Ruhr-Universität Bochum

Short Notices

Diplomatics in the Eastern Mediterranean 1000–1500: Aspects of Cross-Cultural Communication, ed. Alexander D. Beihammer, Maria G. Parani and Christopher D. Schabel (The Medieval Mediterranean, 74). Leiden and Boston: Brill, 2008. Pp. xvi, 467. ISBN 978 90 04 16547 2.

This volume publishes the proceedings of a conference held at Nicosia, Cyprus, in April 2006. After an introduction by Alexander D. Beihammer ("Eastern Mediteranean Diplomatics: The Present State of Research") the papers are grouped in three parts. *Part I: Archival Sources for the Latin East:* "Multilingualism and Institutional Patterns of Communication in Latin Romania (Thirteenth–Fourteenth Centuries)" by David Jacoby, "*Casastica Feudorum Crete*: Land Ownership and Political Changes in Medieval Crete (13th–15th Centuries)" by Charalambos Gasparis, "The Status of the Patriarch of Constantinople after the Fourth Crusade" by William O. Duba, "Antelm the Nasty, First Latin Archbishop of Patras" by Chris Schabel, "Intercultural Communication: The Teutonic Knights in Palestine, Armenia, and Cyprus" by Hubert Houben, "Documents from the Hospitaller Registers on Rhodes Concerning Cyprus, 1409–1459: Form and Contents" by Karl Borchardt, "A Matter of Great Confusion: King Richard I and Syria's *Vetus de Monte*" by Brenda Bolton. *Part II: Chancery Traditions in Medieval Cyprus:* "Aspects du notariat public à Chypre sous les Lusignans" by Jean Richard, "The Structure and Content of the Notarial Deeds of Lamberto di Sambuceto and Giovanni da Rocha, 1296–1310" by Nicholas Coureas, "La *Massaria* génoise de Famagouste" by Michel Balard, "La registre de la *curia* du capitaine génois de Famagouste au milieu du XVe siècle: une source pour l'étude d'une société multiculturelle" by Catherine Otten-Froux, "Diplomatic Relations between Cyprus and Genoa in the Light of the Genoese Juridical Documents: ASG, Diversorum Communis Ianue, 1375–1480" by Svetlana V. Bliznyuk, "Diplomatics and Historiography: The Use of Documents in the *Chronicle* of Leontios Makhairas" by Angel Nicolaou-Konnari. *Part III: Diplomatics and Diplomacy among Byzantium, Islam and the West*: "The First Ottoman Occupation of Macedonia (ca. 1383–ca.1403): Some Remarks on Land Ownership, Property Transactions and Justice" by Kostis Smyrlis, "Intercultural Exchange in the Field of Material Culture in the Eastern Mediterranean: The Evidence of Byzantine Legal Documents (11th to 15th Centuries)" by Maria G. Parani, "Documents in Intercultural Communication in Mamluk Jerusalem: The Georgians under Sultan an-Nasir Hasan in 759 (1358)" by Johannes Pahlitzsch, "Das vergessene Zypern? Das byzantinische Reich und Zypern unter den Lysignan" by Peter Schreiner, "Religion in Catholic–Muslim Correspondence and Treaties" by Benjamin Z. Kedar, "Élites byzantines, latines et musulmanes: Quelques examples de diplomacie personnalisée (Xe–XVe siècles)" by Michel Balivet.

The Fourth Crusade: Event, Aftermath, and Perceptions: Papers from the Sixth Conference of the Society for the Study of the Crusades and the Latin East, Istanbul, Turkey, 25–29 August 2004, ed. Thomas F. Madden (Crusades – Subsidia, 2). Aldershot and Burlington, VT: Ashgate, 2008. Pp. xxiii, 184. ISBN 978 0 7546 6319 5.

This book unites eleven papers given at the sixth conference of the SSCLE at Constantinople on the theme of the Fourth Crusade. The papers are divided into three groups: *Event:* "Richard I and the Early Evolution of the Fourth Crusade" by Vincent Ryan, "Venise et son arrière-pays au temps de la Quatrième Croisade" by Pierre Racine, "The 'Four Crusades' of 1204" by Marco Meschini. *Aftermath:* "The Latin Empire of Constantinople's Fractured Foundation: The Rift between Boniface of Montferrat and Baldwin of Flanders" by Thomas F. Madden, "The Greeks of Constantinople under Latin Rule" by David Jacoby; "The Effects of the Fourth Crusade on European Gold Coinage" by Robert D. Leonhard Jr. *Perceptions:* "The *Translatio Symonensis* and the Seven Thieves: A Venetian Fourth Crusade *Furta Sacra* Narrative and the Looting of Constantinople" by David M. Perry, "Between Justification and Glory: The Venetian Chronicles' View of the Fourth Crusade" by Serban Marin, "Per Innocenzo III i Cristiani Latini 'peggiori degli altri:' l'anno 1204. Un sintomo di nuova cultura" by Giulio Cipollone, "Aux sources de la chronique en prose française: entre déculturation et acculturation" by Cyril Aslanov, "Arab Perspectives on the Fourth Crusade" by William J. Hamblin.

The Military Orders. Volume 3: History and Heritage, ed. Victor Mallia-Milanes. Aldershot and Burlington, VT: Ashgate, 2008. Pp. xxii, 306. ISBN 978 0 7546 6290 7.

In this volume thirty papers given at the third military orders conference at St John's Gate, London, in September 2000 are collected. The papers are divided into four parts: *Part I: Historiography*: "Hospitaller Historiography: Heritages and Heresies" by Anthony T. Luttrell, "A Survey of Research on the History of the Military Orders in Poland in the Middle Ages" by Maria Starnawska, "Historiopgraphy and History: Medieval Studies on the Military Orders in Spain since 1975" by Luis Garcia-Guijarro Ramos, "The Knights Templar between Theatre and History: Raynouard's works on the Templars (1805–1813)" by Alain Demurger. *Part II: Liturgy and Fiction, Heraldry and Piety*: "Sad Stories of the Death of Kings: Last Illnesses and Funerary Rites of the Grand Masters of the Order of St John from Aubusson to the Cotoners" by Ann Williams, "The Liturgical Policies of the Hospitallers between the Invention of Printing and the Council of Trent: The Evidence of the Early Printed Breviaries and Missals" by Cristina Dondi, "Hospitallers, Mysticism, and Reform in Late-Medieval Strasbourg" by Karl Borchardt, "Heraldry in Medieval Rhodes: Hospitallers and Others" by Anna-Maria Kasdagli, "The Fictional Hospitaller: Images and Stories of the Knights of Malta in Count Jan Potocki's *Manuscript*

Found in Saragossa" by Yuri Stoyanov. *Part III: Templars, Teutonic Knights, and Other Military Orders*: "The Templar Order in North-West Italy: A General Picture (1142–1312)" by Elena Bellomo, "The Templar James of Garrigans: Illuminator and Deserter" by Alan Forey, "The University of Paris and the Trial of the Templars" by Paul F. Crawford, "A Look Through the Keyhole: Templars in Italy from the Trial Testimony" by Anne Gilmour-Bryson, "Teutonic Castles in Cilician Armenia: A Reappraisal" by Kristian Molin, "The Use of Indulgences by the Teutonic Order in the Middle Ages" by Axel Ehlers, "Innocent III and the Origin of the Sword Brothers" by Barbara Bombi, "The Military Orders and Papal Crusading Propaganda" by Rudolf Hiestand, "The Hospitaller and Templar Houses of Périgord: Some Observations" by David Bryson, "The Battle of Tannenberg-Grunwald-Zalgiris (1410) as Reflected in Twentieth-Century Monuments" by Sven Ekdahl. *Part IV: Hospitallers*: "The Decree of 1262: A Glimpse into the Economic Decision-Making of the Hospitallers" by Judith Bronstein, "The Hospitallers Order in Acre and Manueth: The Ceramic Evidence" by Edna J. Stern, "Bioarchaeological Analysis of the Latrine Soil from the Thirteenth-Century Hospital of St John at Acre, Israel" by Pierce D. Mitchell, Jacqui P. Huntley, and Eliezer Stern, "The Hospitallers and the 'Peasants' Revolt' of 1381 Revisited" by Helen J. Nicholson, "The Hospitallers and the Kings of Castile in the Fourteenth and Fifteenth Centuries" by Carlos Barquero Goñi, "The Visit of the Emperor Mauel II Palaeologus at the Priory of St John in 1401" by Julian Chrysostomides, "John Kaye, the 'Dead Turk', and the Siege of Rhodes" by Theresa M. Vann, "The Hospitaller Fraternity of St John at SS Johan and Cordula in Cologne" by Klaus Militzer, "Hospitaller Commanderies in the Kingdom of Hungary (*c*.1150–*c*.1330)" by Zsolt Hunyadi, "Frisians and Foreigners in the Hospitaller House of Sneek: Origins and Careers" by Johannes Adriaan Mol, "Hospitaller Baroque Culture: The Order of St John's Legacy to Early Modern Malta" by Victor Mallia-Milanes.

The Military Orders. Volume 4: On Land and by Sea, ed. Judi Upton-Ward. Aldershot and Burlington, VT: Ashgate, 2008. Pp. xvii 292. ISBN 978 0 7546 6287 7.

In this volume twenty-seven papers given at the fourth military orders conference at St John's Gate, London, in September 2005 are collected. The papers are divided into two sections: *Part I: General Issues*: "*Milites ad terminum* in the Military Orders during the Twelfth and Thirteenth Centuries" by Alan Forey, "Recent Issues in Polish Historiography of the Crusades" by Darius von Güttner Sporzynski, "A Comparison of Health at a Village and Castle in the Kingdom of Jerusalem during the Twelfth Century" by Piers Mitchell, "Competition between the Military-Religious Orders in Central Europe, *c*.1140–*c*.1270" by Karl Borchardt, "The Military Orders and the *Chronicle of Morea*" by Kristian Molin, "The Military Orders and their Navies" by Jürgen Sarnowsky, "A New Chronology for the Scandinavian Branches of the Military Orders" by Christer Carlsson, "The Portuguese Military Orders and the Oceanic Navigations: From Piracy to Empire (Fifteenth to Early Sixteenth

Centuries)" by Luís Adão da Fonseca. *Part II: Specific Issues*: "Ecclesiastical Reform and the Origins of the Military Orders: New Perspectives on Hugh of Payn's Letter" by Luis Garcia-Guijarro Ramos, "The Hospital of St John, the Bedroom of *Caritas*" by Myra Bom, "The Layout of the Jerusalem Hospital in the Twelfth Century: Further Thoughts and Suggestions" by Denys Pringle, "The Reputation of Gerard of Ridefort" by Malcolm Barber, "The London and Paris Temples: A Comparative Analysis of Their Financial Services for the Kings during the Thirteenth Century" by Ignacio de la Torre, "Murder in the Preceptory? The Strange Case of Peter of Valbéon, Preceptor of the Hospitaller House of St Naixent (Dordogne), 1277–1304" by David Bryson, "The Teutonic Knights during the Ibelin–Lombard Conflict" by Nicholas Morton, "Hospitaller Estate Management in the Medieval Kingdom of Hungary (Thirteenth to Fourteenth Centuries)" by Zsolt Hunyadi, "Apects of Non-Noble Family Involvement in the Order of the Temple" by Jochen Schenk, "Templar Trial Testimony: Voices from 1307–1311" by Anne Gilmour-Bryson, "Funerary Monuments of Hospitaller Rhodes: An Overview" by Anna-Maria Kasdagli, "The Search for the Defensive System of the Knights in Southern Rhodes" by Michael Heslop, "Regulations concerning the Reception of Hospitaller *Milites* in the First Half of the Fifteenth Century" by Pierre Bonneaud, "The Hospitallers and the Catholic Kings of Spain, 1474–1516" by Carlos Barquero Goñi, "The Fifteenth-Century Maritime Operations of the Knights of Rhodes" by Theresa M. Vann, "The Priory of Vrana: The Order of St John in Croatia" by H. J. A. Sire, "Encounters with the 'Other': Hospitallers and Maltese before the Great Siege of 1565" by Emanuel Buttigieg, "Building Biographies: Graffiti, Architecture and People at the Hospitaller Preceptory at Ambel (Zaragoza), Spain" by Christopher Gerrard and Robert Dauber, "A Man with a Mission: A Venetian Hospitaller on Eighteeth-Century Malta" by Victor Mallia-Milanes.

Jonathan Riley-Smith, *Crusaders and Settlers in the Latin East* (Variorum collected studies series, 912). Aldershot and Burlingon, VT: Ashgate, 2007. Pp. xii, 364. ISBN 978 0 7546 5967 9.

This collection comprises twenty-one articles previously published elsewhere between 1972 and 2005. They are grouped into four thematic sections which are preceded by an introductory article and a preface and followed by an index: "Present and past" (1993); *Crusading:* "Casualties and the number of knights on the First Crusade" (2002); "Early crusaders to the East and the cost of crusading 1095–1130" (1995); "Family traditions and the participation in the Second Crusade (1992); "Toward an understanding of the Fourth Crusade as an institution" (2005); "Crusading as an act of love" (1980); "Christian violence and the crusades" (2002); "The politics of war: France and the Holy Land" (2002); *The Latin East*: "Families, crusades and settlement in the Latin East, 1102–1131" (1997); "Some lesser officials in Latin Syria" (1972); "Government in Latin Syria and the commercial privileges of foreign merchants" (1973); "King Fulk of Jerusalem and 'the Sultan of Babylon'" (1997); "Government and the indigenous in the Latin kingdom of Jerusalem" (2002); "The Crown of France and Acre, 1254–1291" (2004); *The Military Orders in the Central Middle Ages*: "The origins of the commandery in the Temple and the Hospital" (2002); "Guy of Lusignan, the Hospitallers and the gates of Acre" (2001); "Further thoughts on the layout of the Hospital in Acre" (2004); "Were the Templars guilty?" (2004); "The structures of the Orders of the Temple and the Hospital in *c*.1291" (2004); *The Shadow of Crusading*: "The Order of St John in England, 1827–1858" (1994); "Islam and the crusades in history and imagination, 8 November 1898–11 September 2001" (2003).

SOCIETY FOR THE STUDY OF THE CRUSADES AND THE LATIN EAST

BULLETIN No. 29, 2009

Editorial

Année après année, ce *Bulletin* tisse un lien essentiel à la vie de notre Société: il rassemble les adresses des membres, leurs données bibliographiques les plus récentes, travaux en cours, thèmes de recherche, projets, informations variées sur les événements scientifiques, les colloques, les expositions, présentations multiples de l'histoire plurielle des croisades et de l'Orient latin. Cet axe fécond – on oserait dire central – permet d'appréhender l'histoire de l'Orient comme de l'Occident médiéval au plus profond de leur ensemble.

Ce bulletin est donc un irremplaçable outil de travail. Il est aussi un instrument privilégié des relations humaines entre des chercheurs du monde entier. Il entend favoriser les échanges directs entre chacun, un meilleur accès à la production scientifique par un contact qui peut aussi être personnel grâce à notre annuaire. Les thèses soutenues depuis peu, ou encore en cours montrent le dynamisme de notre domaine: leur signalement vise à encourager les plus jeunes, nombreux à adhérer et à participer aux Congrès de la Société, comme à Avignon en 2008. Ce bulletin n'existerait donc pas sans votre apport: celui des informations que vous transmettez; celui de votre soutien financier par vos cotisations et abonnements.

N'hésitez pas à user et à abuser! Votre fidélité et l'arrivée de nouveaux membres de tous les continents sont pour notre Comité (le "vôtre") une vive stimulation: la satisfaction de servir, bien sûr de façon toujours perfectible. Après l'admirable travail accompli par le Prof. Karl Borchardt qu'il faut chaleureusement remercier pour son excellence et sa disponibilité, la tâche me revient de regrouper et de présenter vos indications. J'ai tenté d'harmoniser leur forme avec celle de notre revue *Crusades*. Compte-tenu du volume de vos apports, mais aussi de leur diversité et des mises à jour propres à chacun, des erreurs se sont peut-être glissées lors de la rédaction finale du *Bulletin*: je vous en adresse par avance mes excuses et la promesse des rectifications nécessaires. Toute suggestion ou aide de votre part sera bienvenue.

Au moment de "boucler" cette nouvelle édition du *Bulletin* no. 29, 2009, à l'instant où la photographie de notre Société se révèle dans son ensemble à travers les contributions de chacun, permettez-moi une confidence: quelle richesse!

La découvrir en primeur est une belle récompense. Je vous invite à la partager.

François-Olivier Touati

Message from the President

Dear Fellow Members,

First, I should like to express my own thanks and those of the Society to our former President, Michel Balard, and also to our former secretary, Sophia Menache, and our former Bulletin editor, Karl Borchardt, all of whom retired last year, for all the work which they have done on our behalf, and which culminated in the highly successful and enjoyable conference held at Avignon last August.

Preparations are already being made for the next main conference, which will meet at Caceres in Spain during the last week of June in 2012. The Committee has been to inspect the site of that conference, which has been organized by our conference secretary, Manuel Rojas. It is a very fine former Franciscan monastery, dating from the late Middle Ages and early Renaissance, which has been converted into a modern conference centre. We were all very favourably impressed by this location. Our thanks are due to Manuel for his efforts on our behalf.

The Committee is concerned about the needs of our many postgraduate members who are seeking financial support and academic employment in the present bleak economic climate. We have appointed Professor Jonathan Phillips, of Royal Holloway University of London, to be the Society's Officer for Postgraduate Members. He will co-ordinate initiatives on their behalf. By the time the Bulletin is published you will have been circularized with details of the projected postgraduate programme.

In the coming year membership renewal forms will contain an additional section, asking supervisors to list their postgraduate students working in the field of Crusades studies, together with their thesis topics. Not all such postgraduates belong to the Society, so in this way we hope to make a wider range of information about postgraduate work in progress available to our members.

You will also receive a request to let Zsolt Hunyadi, who is in charge of the Society's website, know about forthcoming conferences of interest to members. Details of these will continue to be published in the Bulletin, but it is hoped that members will find it helpful when planning personal timetables to have advance notice of such conferences.

My good wishes to you all for the coming year.

Bernard Hamilton

Practical Information

Our treasurer, **Prof. James D. Ryan, 100 West 94th Street, Apartment 26M, New York NY 10025, USA, james.d.ryan@verizon.net** has again (as ever) been successful in recruiting new members. We should thank him warmly for all his efforts. If you have any queries concerning your subscriptions and payments, please contact him at the above address.

The *Bulletin* editor would like to remind you that, in order to avoid delays, he needs to have information for the Bulletin each year at an early date, usually in January or February. My address is: **Prof. François-Olivier Touati, La Croix Saint-Jérôme, 11 allée Émile Bouchut, 77123 Noisy-sur-École, France;** email: francoistouati@aol.com

I want to thank all members who provide me with bibliographical data. In order to make the *Bulletin* more useful for you, it would be helpful if those members who edit proceedings or essay volumes could let me know not only about their own papers but also on the other papers in such volumes. You are encouraged to supply any information via email.

Dr Zsolt Hunyadi is webmaster for our official website: **http://www.sscle.org**. There you can find news about the SSCLE and its publications as well as bibliographical data and links to related sites.

Our journal entitled *Crusades*, now Volume 8, 2009, allows the Society to publish articles and texts; encourages research in neglected subfields; invites a number of authors to deal with a specific problem within a comparative framework; initiates and reports on joint programmes; and offers reviews of books and articles. Editors: Benjamin Z. Kedar, Jonathan Phillips and Jonathan Riley-Smith; associate editor: William Purkis; reviews editor: Christoph Maier; archaeology editor: Denys R. Pringle.

Colleagues may submit papers for consideration to either of the editors, Professor Benjamin Z. Kedar and Professor Jonathan Phillips. A copy of the style sheet is to be found in the back of this booklet.

The journal includes a section of book reviews. In order to facilitate the reviews editor's work, could members please ask their publishers to send copies to: **PD Dr Christoph T. Maier, Reviews editor, *Crusades*, Sommergasse 20, 4056 Basel, Switzerland**; ctmaier@hist.uzh.ch or ctmaier@tele2.ch. Please note that *Crusades* reviews books concerned with any aspect(s) of the history of the crusades and the crusade movement, the military orders and the Latin settlements in the Eastern Mediterranean, but not books which fall outside this range.

The cost of the journal to individual members is £25, $46 or €32; the cost to institutions and non-members is £65, US$130 or €93. **Cheques in these currencies should be made payable to SSCLE. For information on other forms of payment contact the treasurer.**

Members may opt to receive the *Bulletin* alone at the current membership price (single £10, $20 or €15; student £6, $12 or €9; joint £15, $30 or €21). Those members who do not subscribe to the journal will receive the Bulletin from the Bulletin editor.

François-Olivier Touati

Contents

	List of abbreviations	266
1.	Recent publications	267
2.	Recently completed theses	280
3.	Papers read by members of the Society and others	281
4.	Forthcoming publications	292
5.	Work in progress	302
6.	Theses in progress	306
7.	Fieldwork planned or undertaken recently	308
8.	News of interest to members:	
	a) Conferences and seminars	308
	b) Other news	309
9.	Members' queries	309
10.	Officers of the Society and accounts	309
11.	Income and expenditure for the SSCLE	310
12.	List of members and their addresses	312
	Institutions subscribing to the SSCLE	331

List of abbreviations

ArCr: *Archaeology and the Crusades: Proceedings of the Round Table, Nicosia, 1 February 2005*, ed. Peter Edbury and Sophia Kalopissi-Verti (Athens: Pierides Foundation, 2007), xviii+209pp.

Avignon SSCLE: La Papauté et les Croisades, *The Papacy and the Crusades*, VIIe Congrès international de la SSCLE, 7th Quadrennial Conference of the SSCLE, Avignon, 27–31 August 2008.

DEM: *Diplomatics in the Eastern Mediterranean, 1000–1500: Aspects of Cross-Cultural Communication, Proceedings of the Conference, Univ. of Cyprus, Nicosia, 7–9 April 2006*, ed. Alexander D. Beihammer, Maria G. Parani, Christopher D. Schabel, The Medieval Mediterranean 74 (Leiden: Brill, 2008).

DOMMA: *Dictionnaire des ordres militaires au Moyen Âge*, ed. Nicole Bériou and Philippe Josserand (Paris: Fayard, 2008).

EHR: *English Historical Review*.

EncycCru: *The Crusades: An Encyclopedia*, 4 vols., ed. Alan V. Murray (Santa Barbara, CA: ABC-CLIO, 2006).

FF: *Fighting for the Faith during Renaissance and Reformation: Late Medieval and Early Modern Crusading*, Univ. of Southern Denmark, Odense, 12–13 November 2007.

Fourth Crusade: *The Fourth Crusade Revisited. Papers of an International Conference on the Fourth Crusade (1204), Andros, 27–30 May 2004)*, ed. Otto Pierantonio Piatti, Pontificio Comitato di Scienze Storiche, Atti e Documenti, vol. 25, Città del Vaticano: Libreria Editrice Vaticana, 2008.

Fourth Crusade, Istanbul: *The Fourth Crusade: Events, Aftermaths, and Perceptions. Papers from the Sixth Conference of the Society for the Study of the Crusades and the Latin East, Istanbul, Turkey, 25–29 August 2004*, ed. Th. MADDEN, Ashgate, Aldershot, 2008.

HES: International colloquium on the History of Egypt and Syria in the Fatimid, Ayyubid and Mamluk Eras, Katholieke Universiteit Leuven.

HME: The *Hospitallers, the Mediterranean and Europe, Festschrift for Anthony Luttrell*, ed. Karl Borchardt, Nikolas Jaspert, Helen Nicholson, Aldershot: Ashgate, 2007, xiv+321pp.

HWPP: *Holy War in Past and Present: The Crusader Phenomenon and its Relevance Today in the Conflict Between East and West*, Research Conference organised by Sophia Menache, Judith Bronstein, and Adrian Boas, The Institute for Advanced Studies at the Hebrew University of Jerusalem and the Israel Science Foundation, Jerusalem, 1–6 June 2008.

ILH: *In Laudem Hierosolymitani: Studies in Crusades and Medieval Culture in Honour of Benjamin Z. Kedar*, ed. Iris Shagrir, Ronnie Ellenblum, Jonathan Riley-Smith (Aldershot: Ashgate, 2007), xxiii+468pp.

IMC: International Medieval Congress, Kalamazoo or Leeds.

Knighthoods of Christ: *Knighthoods of Christ: Essays on the History of the Crusades and the Knights Templar Presented to Malcolm Barber on his 65th Birthday*, ed. Norman Housley, Ashgate: Aldershot, 2007.

Mercenaries: *Mercenaries and Paid Men. The Mercenary Identity in the Middle Ages*, Proceedings of the Conference held at University of Wales, Swansea, 5–8 July 2005, ed. John France, *History of Warfare*, 47, Leiden-Boston: Brill, 2008.

MO3: *The Military Orders*, vol. 3: *Their History and Heritage*, ed. Victor Mallia-Milanes Aldershot: Ashgate, 2008.

MO4: *The Military Orders*, vol. 4: *The Military Orders on Land and by Sea*, ed. Judith Upton-Ward, Aldershot: Ashgate, 2008.

MO5: *The Military Orders: Politics and Power*, 5th conference on the Military Orders, Cardiff University, 3–6 September 2009.

OM14: *Die Ritterorden als Träger der Herrschaft: Territorien, Grundbesitz und Kirche*, ed. Roman Czaja and Jürgen Sarnowsky, Ordines Militares, 14, Toruń, 2007, 300pp.

RM: *Religiones militares: Contributi alla storia degli Ordini religioso-militari nel medioevo*, ed. Anthony Luttrell and Francesco Tommasi, Biblioteca di Sacra Militia, 2, Città di Castello, 2008.

1. Recent publications

ANCKAER, Jan, "Thierry of Alsace, count of Flanders", in *The Crusades. An Encyclopedia*, Santa Barbara: ABC Clio, 2006, IV, p. 1174; "Philip of Alsace, count of Flanders", *ibid.*, III, pp. 953–54; "Robert II, count of Flanders", *ibid.*, IV, pp. 1039–40; "The Low Countries and the Crusades", *ibid.*, III, pp. 758–62.

ANDREI, Filippo, "Il Salterio glossato di San Romualdo", *Benedictina*, 49, 2002, pp. 23–52; "Un frammento delle 'Enarrationes in Psalmos' di Agostino alla Biblioteca Marucelliana di Firenze", *Scriptorium*, 56, 2002, pp. 316–20; "Frammenti di un codice del Canzoniere di Petrarca alla Biblioteca degli Intronati di Siena", *Filologia e critica*, 31, 2006, pp. 118–28.

ANTAKI MASSON, Patricia, "The Crusader castle of Beirut", ARAM, 13–14, 2001–2002, pp. 323–53.

BALARD, Michel, *Les Latins en Orient, XIe–XVe siècle*, Paris, PUF, coll. Nouvelle Clio, 2006, 455pp.; *La Méditerranée médiévale. Espaces, itinéraires, comptoirs*, coll. Les Médiévistes français, Paris, Picard, Paris 2006, 200pp.; *Les marchands italiens à Chypre*, Centre de Recherche Scientifique. Recueil de travaux II, Nicosie 2007, 254pp.; Compte-rendu de l'ouvrage de Claude Reignier Conder *The Latin Kingdom of Jerusalem*, in *Medieval Encounters*, t. 14/1, pp.141–43.; "La *Massaria* génoise de Famagouste", in DEM, pp. 235–49; "L'empire génois au Moyen Age", in F. Hurlet, ed., *Les Empires. Antiquité et Moyen Age. Analyse comparée*, Rennes 2008, pp. 181–97; "Les épices au Moyen Âge", *Revue de la Société d'Histoire de Montmorency*, t. 25 (2007), pp. 92–108; "Bilan de la Quatrième Croisade", *Nichifutsu Bunka. Revue de collaboration culturelle franco-japonaise*, t. 72, mars 2006, pp. 107–22.

BALLETTO, Laura, "Doria Filippo", in *Dizionario Biografico dei Liguri dalle origini ai nostri giorni*, VI, Genova, 2007, pp. 657–74; "Antonio di Ponzò e Bernabò di Carpena: due notai lunigianesi fra Genova e il Vicino Oriente nel secolo XIV", *Memorie della Accademia Lunigianese di Scienze Giovanni Capellini*, LXXVII, La Spezia, 2007, pp. 17–58; "Echi genovesi della caduta di Costantinopoli", in *La prise de Constantinople: l'événement, sa portée et ses échos (1453–2003). Actes de Colloque (Tunis, 11–12–13 décembre 2003)*, ed. M. T. Mansouri, Tunis, 2008, pp. 27–70.

BARBER, Malcolm, "The Reputation of Gerard of Ridefort", in MO4, pp. 111–19; "Was the Holy Land betrayed in 1291?", in *Medieval Historical Discourses. Essays in Honour of Professor Peter S. Noble*, ed. M. J. Ailes, A. Lawrence-Mathers, and F. Le Saux, *Reading Medieval Studies*, 34, 2008, pp. 35–52.

BELLOMO Elena, *The Templar Order in North-west Italy (1142–c.1330)*, The Medieval Mediterranean, 72, Leiden: Brill, 2008, xiv+ 466pp.

BIRD, Jessalyn, "The Crusades: Eschatological Lemmings, Younger Sons, pala Hegemony and Colonialism" in *Misconceptions about the Middle Ages*, ed. Stephen J. Harris and Bryon L.

Grisby, Routlege, 2008, pp. 85–89; "Crusaders' Rights Revisited: the Use and Abuse of Crusade Privileges in Early Thirteenth Century France", in *Law and the Illicit in Medieval Society*, ed. R.M. Karras, J. Kaye and E.A. Matter, University of Pennsylvania Press, 2008.

BISAHA, Nancy, "Discourses of Power and Desires: The Letters of Aeneas Silvius Piccolomini (1453)", in *Florence and Beyond*, ed. David Peterson and Daniel Bornstein, University of Toronto Press, 2008; reviewed for *Crusades*: *The Crusade of Varna, 1443–1445*, trans. C. Imber, Crusade Texts in Translation, 14, Aldershot: Ashgate, 2006.

BOMBI, Barbara, "The *Dialogus miraculorum* of Caesarius of Heisterbach as a Source for the Livonian Crusade", in *Aspects of Power and Authority in the Middle Ages*, ed. B. Bolton and C. M. Meek, Turnhout: Brepols, 2007, pp. 305–26; "Innocent III and the Origin of the Sword Brethren", in MO3, pp. 147–53; "La disputa tra l'arcivescovo Federico di Riga e l'Ordine Teutonico ad Avignone", in *L'Ordine Teutonico tra Mediterraneo e Baltico: incontri e scontri tra religioni, popoli e culture*, Atti del Convegno della Commissione Storica Internazionale per le ricerche sull'Ordine Teutonico (Bari-Lecce-Brindisi, 14–16 settembre 2006), Galatina 2008 (Acta Theutonica, 4), pp. 125–51 [in Italian with German translation].

BONNEAUD, Pierre, *Els Hospitalers catalans a la fi de l'Edat Mitjana, L'orde de l'Hospital a Catalunya I a la Mediterrània, 1396–1472*, Lleida: Pagès editors, 2008, 447pp.; "Regulations concerning the Reception of Hospitaler *Milites* in the First Half of the Fifteenth Century", in MO4, pp. 201–6; "La règle de l'*ancianitas* dans l'ordre de l'Hôpital, le prieuré de Catalogne et la *Castellania de Amposta* aux XIVe et XVe siècles", in *The Hospitallers, the Mediterranean and Europe, Festricht for Anthony Luttrell*, ed. Karl Borchardt, Nikolas Jaspert and Helen J.Nicholson, Aldershot: Ashgate, 2007, pp. 221–32.

BORCHARDT, Karl, "Hospitallers, Mysticism, and Reform in Late-Medieval Strasbourg", in MO3, pp. 73–78; "Etappen der Tätigkeit des Johanniterordens in Deutschland", in *Zur Geschichte des Johanniterordens im friesischen Küstenraum und anschließenden Binnenland*, Beiträge des Johanniter-Symposiums vom 11. bis 12. Mai 2007 in Cloppenburg-Stapelfeld, hg. Heimatbund für das Oldenburger Münsterland, red. Hajo van Lengen. Beiträge zur Geschichte des Oldenburger Münsterlandes, Die 'Blaue Reihe', Heft 15, Cloppenburg, 2008, pp. 21–31; "Documents from the Hospitaller Registers on Rhodes Concerning Cyprus, 1409–1459: Form and Contents", in DEM, 2008, pp. 159–69; "Die deutschen Johanniter zwischen Ministerialität und Meliorat, Ritteradel und Patrizia", in *Städtische Gesellschaft und Kirche im Spätmittelalter*, Kolloquium Dhaun 2004, ed. Sigrid Schmitt and Sabine Klapp, Geschichtliche Landeskunde, 62, Stuttgart, 2008, pp. 67–74; "Competition between the Military-Religious Orders in Central Europe, c.1140–c.1270", in MO4, pp. 29–34; "Die Johanniter in den Supplikenregistern von Papst Innozenz VI. 1352–1362", in RM, pp. 9–25.

BRATU, Cristian, *Herméneutiques*, Iasi (Romania): Junimea Publishing House, 2000; "L'esthétique des chroniqueurs de la quatrième croisade et l'épistémè gothico-scolastique", in *The Medieval Chronicle*, Amsterdam: Rodopi, 5, 2007, pp. 61–76; "The Aesthetics of the Chroniclers of the Fourth Crusade and the Gothic-Scholastic Episteme", *Reading Medieval Studies*, Reading: University of Reading, 31, 2005, pp. 3–26; "Le métathéâtre en tant que métaphore de l'aliénation. Les sources et les mécanismes de l'angoisse", *Limbaje si Comunicare/Languages and Communication*, Suceava University Press, 4, 1999, pp. 429–50.

BRUNDAGE, James A., *Medieval Origins of the Legal Profession: Canonists, Civilians, and Courts*, Chicago: University of Chicago Press, 2008, xvii, 607pp.; "The Teaching and Study of Canon Law in the Law Schools", in *The History of Medieval Canon Law in the Classical Period, 1140–1234: From Gratian to the Decretals of Pope Gregory IX*, ed. Wilfried Hartmann and Kenneth Pennington, Washington: Catholic University of America Press, 2008, pp. 98–120; "Legal Ethics: A Medieval Ghost Story", in *Law and the Illicit in Medieval Europe*, ed. Ruth Mazo Karras, Joel Kaye, and E. Ann Matter, Philadelphia: University of Pennsylvania Press, 2008, pp. 47–56.

BRYSON, David, "The Hospitaller and Templar Houses of Perigord: Some Observations," in MO3, pp. 167–73; "Murder in the Preceptory? The Strange Case of Peter of Valbeon...", in MO4.

BURGTORF, Jochen, *The Central Convent of Hospitallers and Templars: History, Organization, and Personnel (1099/1120–1310)*, History of Warfare, vol. 50, Leiden: Brill, 2008, xxviii–761pp.

BUTTIGIEG, Emanuel, "Childhood and adolescence in early modern Malta (1565–1632)", *Journal of Family History*, 33:2, April 2008, pp. 139–55; "Encounters with the 'Other': Hospitallers and Maltese before the Great Siege of 1565", in MO4, pp. 229–34.

CARLSSON, Christer, "A New Chronology for the Scandinavian Branches of the Military Orders", in MO4; *Kronobäcks klosterkyrkoruin. Arkeologisk undersökning. Mönsterås socken. Småland. Sweden*, ed. with Emma Angelin-Holmén and Cecilia Ring, Kalmar länsmuseum, Kalmar, 2008 [An archaeological report over a research-excavation in Kronobäck Hospitaller Commandery in Sweden]; *Utgraving i toppen av murverket på Værne klosterruin, Rygge kommune*, ed. with Mona Beate Buckholm, Östfold museum, Sarpsborg. Norway, 2008. [An archaeological report over a research-excavation in Værne Hospitaller Commandery in Norway].

CARR, Annemarie Weyl, "Dumbarton Oaks and the Legacy of Byzantine Cyprus", *Near East Archaeology*, 71:1–2, 2008, pp. 95–103; "The Face Relics of John the Baptist in Byzantium and the West", *Gesta* 47, 2008, pp. 159–77; "Perspectives on Visual Culture in Early Lusignan Cyprus: Balancing Art and Archaeology", in ArCr, pp. 83–110.

CARRAZ, Damien, "De nouvelles Amazones ? Les femmes aux croisades", *Histoire et images médiévales*, 13, mai–juin–juillet 2008, pp. 54–61; "Archéologie des commanderies de l'Hôpital et du Temple en France (1977–2007)", *Cahiers de Recherches Médiévales*, 15, 2008, pp. 175–202; "L'affiliation des laïcs aux commanderies templières et hospitalières de la basse vallée du Rhône (XIIe–XIIIe siècles)", in RM, pp. 171–90.

CARRIER, Marc, "L'image d'Alexis Ier Comnène selon le chroniqueur Albert d'Aix", *Byzantion. Revue internationale d'études byzantines*, 78, 2008, pp. 1–32; "Pour en finir avec les *Gesta Francorum*: une réflexion historiographique sur l'état des rapports entre Grecs et Latins au début du XIIe siècle et sur l'apport nouveau d'Albert d'Aix", *Crusades*, 7, 2008, pp. 13–34; "Ordéric Vital sur les rapports entre Grecs et Latins à la veille de la deuxième croisade", *Memini. Travaux et documents*, 11, 2007, pp. 131–50.

CASSIDY-WELCH, Megan, "The Crusades: experience, memory and history", *Agora*, 43: 3, 2008, pp. 19–22; with Peter Sherlock, ed., *Practices of Gender in Late Medieval and Early Modern Europe*, Turnhout: Brepols, 2008: "Introduction", *ibid.*, pp. 1–6, and "Creating and reflecting gender in late-medieval and early modern Europe", *ibid.*, pp. 319–28; "Grief and Memory after the Battle of Agincourt" in *The Hundred Years War II: Different Vistas*, ed. Andrew Villalon and Donald Kagay, Leiden: Brill, 2008, pp. 133–50.

CHRISTIE, Niall G. F., "Motivating Listeners in the Kitab al-Jihad of ʿAli ibn Tahir al-Sulami (d. 1106)", *Crusades*, 6, 2007, pp. 1–14; "A Rental Document from 8th/14th Century Egypt", *Journal of the American Research Center in Egypt*, 41, 2004, released 2007, pp. 161–72.

COBB, Paul M., Usama ibn Munqidh, *The Book of Contemplation: Islam and the Crusades*.

Translated and annotated by Paul M. Cobb, London: Penguin Classics, 2008; "Introduction: The World of Saladin", in Hannes Möhring, *Saladin: The Sultan and His Time, 1138–1193*, trans. David S. Bachrach, Baltimore: Johns Hopkins University Press, 2008, pp. ix–xxiii.

CONNELL, Charles W., "Reading the Middle Ages: The 'Post-Modern' Medievalism of C. S. Lewis", in *Sehnsucht: The C. S. Lewis Journal*, 2007, pp. 19–28.

COUREAS, Nicholas S., "The Role of Cyprus in provisioning the Latin Churches of the Holy Land in the Thirteenth and Early Fourteenth Centuries", in *Egypt and Syria in the Fatimid, Ayyubid and Mamluk Eras*, 5, Proceedings of the 11th, 12th and 13th HES, ed. U. Vermeulen and K. D'hulster, Leuven, Peeters, 2007, pp. 407–18; "Trade between Cyprus and the Mamluk Lands in the Fifteenth Century, with Special Reference to Nicosia and Famagusta", *ibid*., pp. 419–38; "The Coptic Presence in Cyprus during the Fifteenth and Sixteenth centuries", *ibid.*, pp. 439–50; "Mamluks in the Cypriot Chronicle of George Boustronios and their Place within a Wider Context", in *Continuity and Change within the Realms of Islam, Studies in honour of Prof. Urbain Vermeulen*, ed, K. D'hulster and J. van Steenbergen, Leuven, Peeters, 2008, pp. 135–49; "Papal Judge-Conservators among the Greek Clergy in Lusignan Cyprus, Southern Italy and Sicily in the Fourteenth Century", in *Sacri Canones Servandi Sunt*, ed. P. Krafl, Prague, 2008, pp. 313–23; "The Structure and Content of the Notarial Deeds of Lamberto di Sambuceto and Giovanni da Rocha", in DEM, pp. 223–34; "Codex Palatinus Graecus 367: A Thirteenth Century Method of Determining Vessel Burden?" (with M. Harpster), *The Mariner's Mirror*, vol. 94:1, 2008, pp. 8–20; "Commercial Relations between Cyprus and Constantinople during the Fourteenth Century", [*Epeteris*] *Cyprus Research Centre Review*, 34, 2008, pp. 121–36; "Entertainment in Lusignan and Venetian Cyprus" [in Greek], in: *En Chordais kai Organois: Entertainment in Cyprus from Antiquity to the Present*, ed. M. Vryonidou, Nicosia, 2008, pp. 84–121; "Genoese Merchants and their Activities in Nicosia from March to October 1297", *Kypriakai Spoudai*, 69, 2008, pp. 41–56.

CRAWFORD, Paul F., "The Trial of the Templars and the University of Paris" in MO3, pp. 115–22; "The Military Orders and the Last Decade of the Thirteenth Century", [*Epeteris*] *Cyprus Research Centre Review*, 33, 2007, pp. 77–97.

CUSHING, Dana, Book Review: D. Nicolle et al., *The Baltic Crusades*, Osprey, 2007, in deremilitary.org, August 2008.

DEVRIES, Kelly, *Medieval Weapons: An Illustrated History of their Impact* (with Robert Douglas Smith), Santa Barbara: ABC-CLIO, 2007; *Battles of the Crusades, 1097–1444: From Dorylaeum to Varna* (with M. Dougherty *et al.*), London: Amber Books, 2007; "The introduction and use of the Pavise in the Hundred Years War", *Arms and Armour*, 4, 2007, pp. 93–100; "Medieval Mercenaries: Methodology, Definitions and Problems", in *Mercenaries*, pp. 43–60; *A Cumulative Bibliography of Medieval Military History and Technology Update 2003–2006*, History of Warfare, 46, Leiden: Brill, 2008; *Battles that changed Warfare: 1457 BC–AD 1991* (with M. Dougherty, C. Jorgensen, C. Mann and C. McNab), London: Amber Books, 2008; "Invasion v. Conquest: Comparative Destruction in the Warfare of the Mongols and Ottomans" in *The Archaeology of Destruction*, ed. Lila Rakoczy, Cambridge Scholars Group, 2008, pp. 287–302; "An Adventure in Persistence, or Finding the Ravenna Gun", *The ICOMAM Magazine*, 1, Sept. 2008, pp. 32–34; "The Hundred Years Wars: Not One but Many", in *The Hundred Years Wars*, part II: *A Wider Focus*, ed. L.J. Andrew Villalon and Donald J. Kagay, Leiden: Brill, 2008, pp. 3–34; "The Sea as a Defense for the British Isles from 55 BCE to 1066 CE", in *L'acqua nell'Alto Medioevo*, LVa Settimana di Studi, Spoleto: Centro Italiano di Studi sull'Alto Medioevo, 2008, I, pp. 319–56.

DICKSON, Gary, *The Children's Crusade: Medieval History, Modern Mythohistory*,

Basingstoke-New York: Palgrave-MacMillan, 2008, 246pp.; "Dante, Boniface VIII, and the Jubilee", in *Dante and the Church: Literary and Historical Essays*, ed. Paolo Acquaviva and Jennifer Petrie, Dublin: Four Court Press, 2007, pp. 11–24 [includes Dante and Boniface Crusades]; "Massacre of the Innocents ? Sacral Violence and the Paradox of the Children's Crusade" in *Under Fire: Childhood in the Shadow of Wars*, ed. E. Goodenough and A. Immel, Detroit MI: Wayne State University Press, 2008, pp. 29–38.

DORAN, John, "Authority and Care. The Significance of Rome in Twelfth-Century Chester", in *Roma Felix: Formation and Reflections of Medieval Rome*, ed. E. O'Carragain and C. Neuman de Vegvar, Aldershot: Ashgate, 2008; "Innocent III and the uses of spiritual marriage", in *Pope, Church and City*, ed. Frances Andrews, Christoph Egger and Constance Rousseau, Leiden: Brill, 2004, pp. 101–14; "Rites and wrongs: the Latin mission to Nicaea, 1234", *Studies in Church History*, 32, 1996, pp. 131–144; "Oblation or obligation? A canonical ambiguity", *Studies in Church History*, 31, 1995, pp. 127–141.

DOUROU-ELIOPOULOU, Maria, "Allusions of the Fourth crusade in latin sources of the 13th and the 14th century", in *Fourth crusade*, pp. 237–43; "Organization of the Fourth Crusade", *Anniversary volume for the Fourth Crusade and the Greek world*, Institute of Byzantine Studies, National Research Foundation, Athens, 2008, pp. 115–129; "The presence of the Aragonese in Romania based on 14th-century aragonese documents", *Eoa kai Esperia*, 7, 2007, pp. 47–55; "The contribution of Antoni Rubio I Lluch in the study of the Catalans in Greece during the 14th century", *ibid.*, pp. 129–35; "Aragonese, Angevins and Venetians in the eve of the fall of Constantinople", in *Constantinopla, 550 anos de su caida*, Centro de Estudios Bizantinos, Neogriegos y Chipriotas, Universidad de Granada, Granada, 2006, II, pp. 29–34; "Western institution in the principality of Athens", in *Proceedings of the International Congress for the Peloponnese after the 4th crusade*, Athens-Mystras, 2007, pp. 437–45.

EDBURY, Peter, "1191 μ.Χ.: Κατακτηση, συνεχεια και αλλαγη" ["1191: Conquest, Continuity and Change"], in *Κυπρος*, ed. A. Marangou *et al.*, Athens, 2007, pp. 282–95; *British historiography on the Crusades and Military Orders: from Barker and Smail to contemporary historians*, Cardiff Historical Papers, 3, 2007, p. 22 (electronic version: http://www.cardiff.ac.uk/hisar/research/projectreports/historicalpapers/index.html; "Celestine III, the Crusade and the Latin East", in *Pope Celestine III (1191–1198): a Diplomat on the papal throne*, ed. John Doran and Damian J. Smith, Aldershot: Ashgate, 2008, pp. 133–47.

EHLERS, Axel, "The Use of Indulgences by the Teutonic Order in the Middle Ages", in MO3, pp. 139–45.

EKDAHL, Sven, "The Siege Machines during the Baltic Crusades", in *Envahisseurs et leurs armes*, ed. Tadeusz Poklewski-Koziell, Fasciculi Archaeologiae Historicae, 20, Łódź: Instytut Archeologii et Etnologii PAN, Warszawa and Polska Akademia Nauk, Oddzial w Łodzi, 2008, pp. 29–51; "The Teutonic Order's Mercenaries during the 'Great War' with Poland-Lithuania (1409–11)", in *Mercenaries*, pp. 345–61; "St Birgitta of Sweden, the Battle of Tannenberg (Grunwald) and the Foundation of the Monastery *Triumphus Mariae* un Lublin", in *Między Śląskiem a Wiedniem* [Book in honour of Professor Krzysztof A. Kuczyński], ed. Aleksander Kosłowski, Małgorzata Znyk, Płock: Państwowa Wyższa Szkoła Zawodowa w Płocku, 2008, pp. 287–301; "The Battle of Tannenberg-Grunwald-Žalgiris (1410) as reflected in Twentieth-Century Monuments", in MO3, pp. 175–94.

FAVREAU-LILIE, Marie-Luise, "Die Wahrnehmung des Vierten Kreuzzuges ausserhalb Venedigs. Perspektiven der Geschichtsschreibung im 13. Jahrhundert", in *Fourth Crusade*, pp. 215–36.

FLORI, Jean, "Éthique chevaleresque et idéologie de croisade", in *1105. Cruïlla de civilitzacions*, ed. Flocel Sabaté, Balaguer, Lleida, 2007, pp. 25–52; *L'islam et la fin des Temps. L'interprétation prophétique des invasions musulmanes dans la chrétienté médiévale*, Paris: Seuil, 2007, 444pp.; "De l'Anonyme normand à Tudebode et aux Gesta Francorum. L'impact de la propagande de Bohémond sur la critique textuelle des sources de la première croisade", *Revue d'Histoire Ecclésiastique*, 2007, 3/4, pp. 717–46; *Bohémond d'Antioche, chevalier d'Aventure*, Paris: Payot, 2007, 380pp.; "Le rôle de la reconquête dans la formation de l'idée de Guerre sainte", in *Les Français en Espagne du VIIIe au XIIIe siècle*, Actes Congrès Transpyrénalia, 21–25 mai 2007, pp. 35–43; *La Fin du Monde au Moyen Age*, Paris, Gisserot, 2008, 128pp.

FOLDA, Jaroslav, *Crusader Art: The Art of the Crusaders in the Holy Land, 1099–1291*, London and Williston, VT: Lund Humphries/Ashgate, 2008, 176pp., 95 colour illustrations, 13 maps.

FOREY, Alan J., "The Templar James of Garrigans: Illuminator and 'Deserter'", MO3, pp. 107–14; "Henry II's crusading Penances for Becket's murder", *Crusades*, 7, 2008, pp. 153–64; "*Milites ad terminum* in the Military Orders during the Twelfth and Thirteenth Centuries", in MO4, pp. 5–11.

GABRIELE, Matthew, ed. (with Jace Stuckey), *The Legend of Charlemagne in the Middle Ages: Power, Faith, and Crusade*, New York: Palgrave Macmillan, 2008, 200pp.

GAPOSCHKIN, M. Cecilia, "Louis IX, Crusade, and the Promise of Joshua in the Holy Land", *Journal of Medieval History*, 33:1, 2008; *The Making of Saint Louis: Kingship, Sanctity, and Crusade in the Later Middle Ages*, Ithaca: Cornell University Press, 2008.

GARCÍA-GUIJARRO, Luis, "The Aragonese Hospitaller Monastery of Sigena: its Early Stages, 1188–ca.1210", in *Hospitaller Women in the Middle Ages*, ed. Anthony Luttrell and Helen Nicholson, Ashgate, Aldershot, 2006, pp. 113–51; "The Growth of the Order of the Temple in the Northern Area of the Kingdom of Valencia at the Close of the Thirteenth Century: A Puzzling Development?", in *Knighthoods of Christ*, pp. 165–81; "The Valencian Bailiwick of Cervera in Hospitaller and Early Montesian Times, ca. 1230?–ca. 1330", in *Essays Presented to Anthony Luttrell on his 75th Birthday*, ed. H. Nicholson, K. Borchardt and N. Jaspert, Ashgate: Aldershot, 2007, pp. 205–20; "Historiography and History: Medieval Studies on the Military Orders in Spain since 1975", in MO3, pp. 23–43; "Ecclesiastical Reform and the Origins of the Military Orders: New Perspectives on Hugh of Payns' Letter" in MO4, pp. 77–83.

GEORGIOU, Stavros G., "Some Remarks on the Title of Despotes in the Era of the Komnenoi and the Angeloi", *Byzantina*, 27, 2007 [= Afieroma ste mneme tes Elles Pelekanidou], pp. 153–64 [Greek with English summary]; "A Short Reference on the History of the Bishopric of Tamassos", *Epeterida Kentrou Meleton Hieras Mones Kykkou*, 8, 2008, pp. 59–72 [Greek].

GILLINGHAM, John, "The Kidnapped King: Richard I in Germany, 1192–1194", *German Historical Institute London Bulletin*, 30, May 2008, pp. 5–34.

GILMOUR-BRYSON, Anne, "A look through the Keyhole: Templars in Italy from the Trial Testimony", in MO3, pp. 123–30; "Italian Templar Trials: Truth or Falsehood," in *Knighthoods of Christ*, pp. 209–28; "Templar Trial Testimony: Voices from 1307–1311", in MO4, pp. 163–74.

GOURDIN, Philippe, "Les pays du Maghreb et la rivalité entre Catalans et Italiens pour dominer les routes commerciales de Méditerranée occidentale (fin XIVe–début XVe siècle)", in *Relazioni economiche tra Europa e mondo islamico. Secc. XIII–XVIII*, Atti della Trentottesima Settimana di Studi, Prato, 1–5 maggio 2006, ed. Simonetta Cavaciocchi,

Florence, Istituto Internazionale di Storia Economica "F. Datini", serie II, 38, 2007, pp. 595–601; *Tabarka. Histoire et archéologie d'un préside espagnol et d'un comptoir génois en terre africaine (XVe–XVIIIe siècle)*, Rome–Tunis, 2008, 626pp. (Collection de l'Ecole française de Rome, 401).

VON GUETTNER, Darius, "Recent Issues in Polish Historiography of the Crusades", in MO4, pp. 13–21.

HAMILTON, Bernard, "The Templars, the Syrian Assassins and King Amalric of Jerusalem", in HME, pp. 13–24; "Pope John X (914–928) and the antecedents of the First Crusade", in ILH, pp. 309–18.

HARRIS, Jonathan, *Constantinople: Capital of Byzantium*, London: Hambledon Continuum, 2007, xviii + 289pp.

HARSCHEIDT, Michael, "Rhodes, Rule, Regularity, van kosmopolitisme tot imperialisme, het geheim van de 'Basic Principles'", *Trigonum Coronatum*, 7, Antwerp, 1999, pp. 165–88.

HESLOP, Michael, "The search for the Byzantine Defensive System in Southern Rhodes", *Byzantinos Domos*, 16, Thessaloniki, April 2008, pp. 69–81; "The search for the Defensive System of the Knights in Southern Rhodes », in MO4.

HODGSON, Natasha, *Women, Crusading and the Holy Land*, Woodbridge, Boydell, 2007; "Reinventing Normans as crusaders ? The Gesta Tancredi of Raoul of Caen", *Anglo-Norman Studies*, 30, 2008.

HOUSLEY, Norman, *Fighting for the Cross. Crusading to the Holy Land*, Yale University Press, 2008, xvii+357pp.; "Recent scholarship on crusading and medieval warfare, 1095–1291: convergence and divergence", in *War, Government and Aristocracy in the British Isles, c.1150–1500; Festschrift for Michael Prestwich*, London, Boydell, 2008, pp. 197–213.

HUNT, Lucy Anne, "Door panels from the Church of the Virgin, al-Mu^{c}allaqa, Old Cairo", in *Byzantium 330–1453, Catalogue of the Exhibition*, ed. Robin Cormack and Maria Vassilaki, London, Royal Academy of Arts, 25 October 2008–22 March 2009, p. 458, no. 307.

HUNYADI, Zsolt, "(Self)Representation: Hospitaller seals in the Hungarian-Slavonian Priory up to c.1400", in *Selbstbild und Selbstverständnis der geistlichen Ritterorden*. Ordines Militares – Colloquia Torunensia Historica XIII, Hrsg. Roman Czaja und Jürgen Sarnowsky, Toruń: Uniwersytet Mikołaja Kopernika, 2005, pp. 199–212; "The Hospitallers in the Medieval Kingdom of Hungary, c.1150–1387. Theses of doctoral dissertation", *Chronica*, 5, 2005), pp. 156–60; "A johanniták Magyarországon a XIV. század végéig" [Hospitallers in Hungary up to the end of the 14th century], in *Magyarország és a keresztes háborúk. Lovagrendek és emlékeik*, Szerk. ed. Laszlovszky József, Majorossy Judit, Zsengellér József, Máriabesnyő-Gödöllő: Attraktor, 2006, pp. 195–208; "A keresztes háborúk." [Crusades] In *Középkori egyetemes történelem (Térképvázlatok gyűjteménye)*. ed. Richárd Szántó, Szeged-Miskolc: JATEPress, 2007, pp. 206–17; "Hospitaller Commanderies in the Kingdom of Hungary (c.1150–c.1330)", in MO3, pp. 257–68; "The Teutonic Order in Burzenland (1211–1225): new re-considerations", in *L'Ordine Teutonico tra Mediterraneo e Baltico: incontri e scontri tra religioni, popoli e culture*. Acta Teutonica 5, ed. Hubert Houben, and Kristjan Toomaspoeg, Galatino: Mario Congedo, 2008, pp.151–70; "Estate management of the Hospitallers in the medieval Kingdom of Hungary (13th–14th centuries)", in MO4, pp. 145–53; ed. with József Laszlovszky, *The Crusades and the Military Orders: Expanding the Frontiers of Medieval Latin Christianity*, 2nd revised ed., CEU Medievalia 9, Budapest: CEU Department of Medieval Studies-CEU Press, 2008, 517pp. (with CD-ROM).

JACOBY, David, "The Jews in Byzantium and the Eastern Mediterranean: Economic Activities from the Thirteenth to the Mid-Fifteenth Century", in *Wirtschaftsgeschichte der mittelalterlichen Juden: Fragen und Einschätzungen*, ed. Michael Toch und Elisabeth Müller-Luckner, München, 2008, pp. 25–48; "Marino Sanudo Torsello on Trade Routes, Commodities, and Taxation", in *Philanagnostes. Studi in onore di Marino Zorzi*, ed. Chryssa Maltezou and Peter Schreiner, Istituto Ellenico di Studi Bizantini and Postbizantini, Bibliotheca, Venezia, 2008, pp. 185–97; "Die Kreuzfahrerstadt Akko", in Burgen und Städte der Kreuzzugszeit, ed. Mathias Piana, Petersberg: Michael Imhof Verlag, 2008, pp. 242–51; "Multilingualism and Institutional Patterns of Communication in Latin Romania (Thirteenth-Fourteenth Centuries)", in DEM, pp. 27–48; "Byzantium, the Italian Maritime Powers, and the Black Sea before 1204", *Byzantinische Zeitschrift*, 100, 2007, pp. 677–99; "Silk Production", in *The Oxford Handbook of Byzantine Studies*, ed. Elizabeth Jeffreys with John Haldon and Robin Cormack, Oxford, 2008, pp. 421–28; "The Greeks of Constantinople under Latin Rule, 1204–1261", in *Fourth Crusade, Istambul*, pp. 53–73; "After the Fourth Crusade", in *The Cambridge History of the Byzantine Empire, c.500–1492*, ed. Jonathan Shepard, Cambridge, 2008, pp. 731–58; "Caviar Trading in Byzantium", in Rustam Shukurov, ed., *MARE ET LITORA. Essays presented to Sergei Karpov for his 60th Birthday*, Moscow, 2009, pp. 349–64.

JASPERT, Nikolas, "Peregrinos gallegos a Palestina y las relaciones entre los cabildos de Compostela y Jerusalén en el siglo XII", *Potestas*, 1, 2008, pp. 149–69; "Interreligiöse Diplomatie im Mittelmeerraum. Die Krone Aragón und die islamische Welt im 13. und 14. Jahrhundert", in *Aus der Frühzeit europäischer Diplomatie. Zum geistlichen und weltlichen Gesandtschaftswesen vom 12. bis zum 15. Jahrhundert*, ed. Claudia Zey, Claudia Märtl, Zürich 2008, pp. 151–90; *Die Kreuzzüge*, 4. rev. ed., Darmstadt 2008; "Carlomagno y Santiago en la memoria histórica catalana", in *El camí de Sant Jaume i Catalunya. Actes del congrés internacional celebrat a Barcelona, Cervera i Lleida, els dies 16, 17 i 18 d'octubre de 2003*, ed. Maria Teresa Ferrer i Mallol, Pere Verdés, Montserrat 2008, pp. 91–105; "Transmediterrane Wechselwirkungen im 12. Jahrhundert. Der Ritterorden von Montjoie und der Templerorden", in MO4, pp. 257–78; *The Hospitallers, the Mediterranean and Europe. Festschrift für Anthony Luttrell*, [HME], ed. with Karl Borchardt and Helen J. Nicholson; "Die Wahrnehmung der Muslime im lateinischen Europa der späten Salierzeit", in *Salisches Kaisertum und neues Europa. Die Zeit Heinrichs IV. und Heinrichs V.*, ed. Bernd Schneidmüller, Stefan Weinfurter, Darmstadt 2007, pp. 307–40.

JENSEN, Janus Møller, *Denmark and the Crusades, 1400–1650*, The Northern World, 30, Leiden: Brill, 2007, 399pp.; "Denmark and the First Crusades. The Impact of Crusade Ideology in Denmark in the First Half of the Twelfth Century", *Nordic Historical Review*, 4, 2007, pp. 82–100; "The Forgotten Crusades: Greenland and the Crusades, 1400–1523", *Crusades*, 7, 2008, pp. 199–215; "Humanister, korstog og kortlægningen af det yderste nord i Renæssancen [Humanists, crusade and the mapping of the far north during the Reniassance]", in *Renæssancen i svøb. Dansk renæssance i europæisk belysning 1450–1550* [The Renaissance in Denmark in a European perspective], ed. Lars Bisgaard, Jacob Isager and Janus Møller Jensen, Odense: University Press of Southern Denmark, 2008.

JENSEN, Kurt Villads, "Danmarks krigshistorie før 1600," in *Danmarks Krigshistorie*, ed. Ole Frantzen og Knud J.V. Jespersen, København: Gad 2008, bd. 1, 20–155. [History of War in Denmark, until 1600, in *History of War in Denmark*].

JOSSERAND, Philippe, articles "Order of Alcántara", "Order of Avis", "Order of Santiago", "Santiago de Compostela", in EncycCru; " En quête de suffrages: le lignage Manuel et l'ordre de Santiago aux XIIIe et XIVe siècles", in *Actas del Congreso Tierra del Quijote, Tierra de Órdenes Militares*, ed. Ricardo Izquierdo Benito, Tolède, 2007, pp. 177–93; "État de fait, état de droit: un document inédit sur l'ingérence royale dans l'élection du maître de

Santiago au temps de Pierre Ier de Castille", in *Le prince, l'argent, les hommes au Moyen Âge. Mélanges offerts à Jean Kerhervé*, ed. Jean-Christophe Cassard, Yves Coativy, Alain Gallicé et Dominique Le Page, Rennes, 2008, pp. 161–70; "*Et succurere Terre sancte pro posse:* les Templiers castillans et la défense de l'Orient latin au tournant des XIIIe et XIVe siècles", *Cahiers de Recherches Médiévales. A Journal of Medieval Studies*, 15, 2008, pp. 217–35 (to be also published in *V Encontro sobre ordens militares*, Palmela 2006, ed. Isabel Cristina Ferreira Fernandes).

JOTISCHKY, Andrew, ed., *The Crusades. Critical Concepts in Historical Studies*, London: Routledge, 2008, 4 vols; "The Christians of Jerusalem, the Holy Sepulchre and the Origins of the First Crusade", *Crusades*, 7, 2008, pp. 35–57.

KALOPISSI-VERTI, Sophia, "Representations of the Virgin in Lusignan Cyprus", in M. Vassilkaki, ed., *Images of the Mother of God. Perceptions of the Theotokos in Byzantium*, Ashgate, Aldershot 2005, pp. 305–19; "The Impact of the Fourth Crusade on Monumental Painting in the Peloponnese and Eastern Central Greece up to the End of the Thirteenth Century", in *Byzantine Art in the Aftermath of the Fourth Crusade. The Fourth Crusade and its Consequences. International Congress March 9–12, 2004*, ed. Panayotis L. Vocotopoulos, Academy of Athens, Research Centre for Byzantine and Post-Byzantine Art, Athens 2007, pp. 63–104.

KEDAR, Benjamin Z., "Religion in Catholic-Muslim Correspondence and Treaties", in DEM, pp. 407–21; "Ramleh during the Crusader Period and at the End of the Ottoman Period – the Evidence of Aerial Photographs", *Qadmoniot*, 41, 2008, pp. 69–74 [in Hebrew]; "Rashi's Map of the Land of Canaan, ca. 1100, and Its Cartographic Background", in *Cartography in Antiquity and the Middle Ages*, ed. Richard J.A. Talbert and Richard W. Unger, Leiden, 2008, pp. 155–68.

KOSTICK, Conor, *The Social Structure of the First Crusade*, Leiden: Brill.

KRÄMER, Thomas, "Der Deutsche Orden in Frankreich – Ein Beitrag zur Ordensgeschichte im Königreich Frankreich und im Midi", in *L'ordine Teutonico nel Mediterraneo. Atti del Convegno internazionale di studio Torre Alemanna (Cerignola) – Mesagne – Lecce 16–18 ottobre 2003*, a cura di Hubert Houben, Galatina, 2004, pp. 237–76.

LAPINA, Elizabeth, "*Nec signis nec testis creditur*: the Problem of Eyewitnesses in the Chronicles of the First Crusade", *Viator: Medieval and Renaissance Studies*, 38, 2007, pp. 111–39.

LOUD, Graham A., "New evidence for the workings of the royal administration in mainland Southern Italy during the later twelfth century", in *Puer Apuliae. Mélanges offerts à Jean-Marie Martin*, ed. E. Cuozzo, V. Déroche, A. Peters-Custot and V. Prigent, Paris: Centre de récherche d'Histoire et Civilisation de Byzance, 2008, pp. 161–83.

LUCHITSKAYA, Svetlana, "Krestovie pochodi", in *Istoricheskaia enziklopedia* ("Crusades", in *Historical encyclopaedia*), Moscow: Interprax, 2007, pp. 710–21 [in Russian].

LUTTRELL, Anthony, ed. with F. Tommasi, *Religiones Militares: Contributi alla storia degli Ordini religioso-militari nel Medioevo*, Città di Castello, 2008, 277pp., [RM] includes following contributions: "The Hospitaller Background of the Teutonic Order", pp. 27–41 and, with F. Tommasi, "Una falsa donazione per l'Ordine dell'Ospedale (1120)", pp. 265–77; "Die späteren Kreuzzüge", in *Kreuzritter. Pilger, Krieger, Abenteurer*, ed. M. Pfaffenbichler, Schallaburg, 2007, pp. 106–13; "Hospitaller Historiography: Heritages and Heresies", in MO3, pp. 3–11; "Introduzione generale" in M. Salerno-K. Toomaspoeg, *L'Inchiesta pontificia del 1373 sugli Ospedalieri di San Giovanni di Gerusalemme nel Mezzogiorno d'Italia*, Bari, 2008, pp. 7–30; "Licences for Hospitaller Sisters at Pamiers and Morlaas:

1371", *Bulletin de la Société de l'Histoire et du Patrimoine de l'Ordre de Malte*, XX, 2008, pp. 68–69.

MACK, Merav,"The Italian quarters of Frankish Tyre: mapping a medieval town", *Journal of Medieval History*, 33, 2007, pp. 147–65.

MADDEN, Thomas F., ed., *The Fourth Crusade: Event, Aftermath, and Perceptions*, Brookfield, Ashgate Publishers, 2008 [abb.: *Fourth Crusade, Istambul*]; "The Latin Empire of Constantinople's Fractured Foundation: The Rift Between Boniface of Montferrat and Baldwin of Flanders", *Ibidem*, pp. 45–52.

MARVIN, Laurence W., *The Occitan War: A Military and Political History of the Albigensian Crusade, 1209–1218*, Cambridge University Press, 2008, xxvi+328pp.

MASÈ, Federica, *Patrimoines immobiliers ecclésiastiques dans la Venise médiévale (XIe-XVe siècles). Une lecture de la ville*, Collection École française de Rome, 358, Rome, 2006, 295pp.; "*Promissiones et refutations*: engagement de preneurs à bail et fidélisation ratée de paroissiens à Venise au XIIIe siècle", in *Serment, promesse et engagement: rituels et modalités au Moyen Age*, VIe Colloque du CRISIMA, Montpellier, 2001, Presses universitaires de la Méditerranée, 2008, pp. 447–54; "Il patrimonio immobiliare del patriarca di Grado e lo sviluppo del quartiere dei veneziani a Costantinopoli (XI–XIII secolo)", in *Patrimoni e trasformazioni urbane II Congresso dell'Associazione Italiana di Storia Urbana*, Rome, 24–26 juin 2004; "Modèles de colonisation vénitienne: acquisition et gestion du territoire urbain en Méditerranée orientale (XIe –XIIIe siècles), in *L'expansion occidentale (XIe-XVe siècles). Formes et conséquences*, XXXIIIe Congrès de la Société des Historiens Médiévistes de l'Enseignement Supérieur, Madrid 2002, Paris: Publications de la Sorbonne, 2003, pp. 133–42.

MAYER, Hans Eberhard, "Krondienst rund ums Mittelmeer. Die Laufbahn des Pierre d'Etampes", *Archiv für Diplomatik*, 53, 1007, pp. 309–21; *Historia wypraw krzyzowych*, transl. by Tadeusz Zatorski, Cracovia, 2008, 461pp.; *Zwei deutsche Kreuzzugsgeschichten in Züricher Sicht. Eine Replik*, Kiel, 2008 (privately printed); "Ein Bischof geht einkaufen. Heinrich von Linköping im Hl. Land", *Zeitschrift des Deutschen Palästina-Vereins*, 124, 2008, pp. 51–60.

MENACHE, Sophia, "When Jesus met Mohammed in the Holy Land: Attitudes Toward the 'Other' in the Crusader Period", *Medieval Encounters*, 14, 2008, pp. 218–37; "Israeli Historians of the Crusades and Their Main Areas of Research, 1946–2008", *Storia della Storiografia*, 53, 2008, pp. 3–24; "Medieval States and Military Orders: The Order of Calatrava in the Late Middle Ages" in ILH, pp. 457–68; "Jacques de Molay, the Last Master of the Temple", in *Knighthood of Christ*, pp. 229–40.

MESCHINI, Marco, "The '4 Crusades' of 1204", in *Fourth Crusade, Istambul*, pp. 27–42; "Il tempo dei crociati", in *Tempus mundi umbra aevi: tempo e cultura del tempo tra Medioevo e età moderna. Atti del convegno (Brescia, 29–30 marzo 2007)*, ed. G. ARCHETTI, A. BARONIO, Fondazione civiltà bresciana, Brescia 2008, pp. 165–82.

MICHAUDEL, Benjamin, "Aiyubidische und mamlukische Befestigungen in syrischen Küstengebiet zur Zeit der Kreuzzüge" and "Burzaih", in *Burgen und Städte der Kreuzzugszeit*, ed. Mathias Piana, Petersberg: Michael Imhof Verlag, 2008, pp. 102–9 et 178–87; "La fortification comme sceptre des Ayyoubides et des Mamelouks dans le Bilad al-Sham et en Egypte à l'époque des Croisades", *Bulletin d'Etudes Orientales*, Supplément au volume LVII (2006–2007), 2008, pp. 51–64; "Armes et techniques militaires en Islam", in *Qantara – Patrimoine méditerranéen*, 2008, www.qantara-med.org; "The use of fortification as a political instrument by the Ayyubids and the Mamluks in Bilad al-Sham and in Egypt (12th–13th centuries)", in *Mamluk Studies Review*, vol. 11/1, 2007, pp. 55–67; "La fortification islamique dans l'Orient des Croisades: la Syrie" et "Le château de Saône/Qal'at Salāh al-Dīn", in *Un patrimoine commun: forteresses de l'époque des Croisades* (ICOMOS), 2007, www.patrimoinecommun.org.; articles "Crac des Chevaliers, 'Qal'at Salāh al-Dīn' Qal'a Shayzar" in *Museum With No Frontiers – Discover Islamic Art*, 2006, www.discoverislamicart.org; "The Development of Islamic Military Architecture during the Ayyubid and Mamluk Reconquests of Frankish Syria", in *Muslim Military Architecture in Greater Syria*, ed. H. Kennedy, Brill, 2006, pp. 106–21.

MILITZER, Klaus,"Die Hospitaltätigkeit des Deutschen Ordens", in *Institutions de l'Assistance sociale en Lotharingie médiévale*, ed. Michel Pauly, Luxembourg, Publications de la Section historique de l'Institut Grand-Ducal, 121-CLUDEM, 19, 2008, pp. 421–36; "The Hospitaller Fraternity of St John at SS Johan and Cordula in Cologne", in MO3, pp. 253–56.

MITCHELL, Piers D., (with Eliezer Stern, Eliezer, and Yotam Tepper, "Dysentery in the crusader kingdom of Jerusalem: an ELISA analysis of two medieval latrines in the city of Acre (Israel)", *Journal of Archaeological Science*, 35:7, 2008, pp. 1849–1853 [reported in the news section of *Science* magazine, 30 May 2008, 320, p. 1139]; "Contrasts in the standard of health in different communities in the medieval Kingdom of Jerusalem", in MO4, pp. 23–28; "Combining palaeopathological and historical evidence for health in the crusades", in *Proceedings of the 8th Annual Conference of the British Association for Biological Anthropology and Osteoarchaeology*, ed. Martin Smith and Megan Brickley, Oxford: Archaeopress 2008, pp. 9–16; (with Jacqui Huntley and Eliezer Sterns), "Bioarchaeological analysis of the 13th century latrines of the crusader hospital of St. John at Acre, Israel", in MO3, pp. 213–23.

MOL, Johannes, "Die friesischen Johanniterklöster im Mittelalter", in H. van Lengen, ed., *Zur Geschichte des Johanniter-Ordens im friesischen Küstenraum und anschliessenden Binnenland*, Beiträge zur Geschichte des Oldenburger Münsterlandes, 15, Cloppenburg: Heimatbund für das Oldenburger Münsterland, 2008, pp. 42–65; "Frisians and Foreigners in the Hospitaller House of Sneek: Origins and Careers", in MO3, pp. 269–78.

MURRAY, Alan V., "Kingship, Identity and Name-Giving in the Family of Baldwin of Bourcq", in *Knighthoods of Christ*, pp. 27–38; "Baltic Crusades", Microsoft Encarta Reference Library [CD and DVD], Microsoft Corporation, 2007; "The Origin of Money-Fiefs in the Latin Kingdom of Jerusalem", in *Mercenaries;* "Finance and Logistics of the Crusade of Frederick Barbarossa", in ILH.

NICHOLSON, Helen J., "The Hospitallers and the 'Peasants Revolt' of 1381 revisited", in MO3, pp. 225–33; "Crusades", in *The Oxford Encyclopedia of Women in World History*, ed. Bonnie G. Smith, New York: Oxford University Press, 2008.

NICOLAOU-KONNARI, Angel, ed., *"La Serenissima" and "La Nobilissima": Venice in Cyprus and Cyprus in Venice*, Acts of the Conference, Nicosia, 21 October 2006, Nicosia: Bank of Cyprus Cultural Foundation, 2008; Review of "George Boustronios, *A Narrative of the Chronicle of Cyprus 1456–1489*, translated from the Greek by Nicholas Coureas together with an anthology of Greek texts of the fourteenth and fifteenth centuries relating to Cyprus and translated by Hans Pohlsander, Cyprus Research Centre, Texts and Studies in the History of Cyprus, 51, The Greece and Cyprus Research Center, Albany N.Y., Sources for the History of Cyprus, 13, Nicosia, 2005. p. 252", *Crusades*, 7, 2008, pp. 226–29; "Diplomatics and Historiography: The Use of Documents in the *Chronicle* of Leontios Makhairas", in DEM, pp. 293–323.

NICOLLE, David, *Normannyi*, co-authored with C. Gravett, Moscow: Eksmo, 2007, 256pp.; *Knights of Jerusalem: The Crusading Order of Hospitallers 1100–1565*, Oxford: Osprey,

2008, 223pp.; *Poitiers AD 732*, Oxford: Osprey, 2007, 96pp.; *Medieval Polish Armies 966–1500*, co-authored with W. Sarnecki, Oxford: Osprey, 2007, 48pp.; *Saracen Strongholds AD 630–1050: The Middle East and Central Asia*, Oxford: Osprey, 2008, 64pp.; *The Ottomans, Empire of Faith, illustrated historical Atlas*, Ludlow: Thalamus, 2008, 192pp.; "Trésors oubliés: Dépôts d'armes et d'armures médiévales en Syrie", *Histoires et Images Médiévales*: Thématiques, 14, August–October 2008, pp. 26–33; "Introduction", for J. Braconnier *et al.*, eds, *The Life of a Knight, 1171–1252, From Philip Augustus to Saint Louis*, Paris: Histoire et Collecions, 2008; "A Medieval Islamic Arms Cache from Syria", *Journal of the Arms & Armour Society*, 19, 2008, pp. 152–63; *Crusader Castles in the Holy Land: An Illustrated History of the Crusader Fortifications of the Middle East and Mediterranean*, Oxford, 2008, 240pp.; *The Second Crusade: Disaster outside Damascus*, Oxford: Osprey, 2008, 96pp.

PAUL, Nicholas L., "Crusade, Memory and Regional Politics in Twelfth-Century Amboise", *Journal of Medieval History*, 2005, pp. 127–41; "The Chronicle of Fulk le Réchin: a Reassessment", *Haskins Society Journal*, 2006, pp. 19–35; "Arsūf, Battle of", in EI, third edition, 2008; Review of "J. Pryor, ed., *Logistics and warfare in the age of the crusades* in *Al-Masaq: Islam and the medieval Mediterranean*, 2008".

PAVIOT, Jacques, (with Philippe Contamine, and coll. Céline Van Hoorebeeck), ed., Philippe de Mézières, *Une Epistre lamentable et consolatoire, adressée en 1397 à Philippe le Hardi, duc de Bourgogne, sur la défaite de Nicopolis (1396)*, Paris: Société de l'histoire de France, 2008, 269pp.; cf. www.shfrance.org; éd. *Projets de croisade (v. 1290 – v. 1330)*, Paris: Académie des inscriptions et Belles-Lettres, Collection de documents inédits sur l'histoire des croisades, XX, 2008, 416pp.; cf. www.aibl.fr

PERRA, Photeine V., "The transition from Hospitaller to Ottoman Rhodes: A note on the information by Piri Reis and Ewliya Chelebi", *Domus Byzantinus*, 16, 2007 [Greek]; "Relations between the Knight Hospitallers of Rhodes and Venice during the First Venetian-Ottoman war (1463–1479)", *Byzantiaka*, 27, 2008 [Greek]; "Review essay a propos of a new Prosopographical Lexicon of Byzantine History and Civilization", *Byzantion*, 78, 2008.

PHILLIPS, Jonathan, Contributions on "Bohemond of Taranto", "Frederick Barbarossa" and "Baibars" for: *The Art of War, Volume 1: Great Commanders of the Ancient and Medieval World*, ed. Andrew Roberts, London: Quercus Books, 2008.

PHILLIPS, Simon D., *The Prior of the Knights Hospitaller in Late Medieval England*, Woodbridge, Boydell, 2009.

PIANA, Mathias, ed., *Burgen und Städte der Kreuzzugszeit*, Studien zur internationalen Architektur- und Kunstgeschichte, 65, Petersberg: Michael Imhof Verlag, 2008, 496pp.; "Die Erforschung von Burgen und Städten der Kreuzzugszeit – eine Standortbestimmung", *Ibidem*, pp. 10–30; (with Adrian Boas), "Die Kreuzfahrerstadt Ascalon", *ibid.*, 263–73; "Die Templerburg Chastel Blanc", *ibid.*, pp. 293–301; "Die Deutschordensburg Montfort (Qal'at al-Qur'ain)", *ibid.*, pp. 343–55; "Die Kreuzfahrerstadt Sidon (Sagette, flaidfl)", *ibid.*, pp. 367–83; "Die Kreuzfahrerburg Toron (Qal'at Tibnin)", *ibid.*, pp. 396–407; "Die Kreuzfahrerstadt Tortosa", *ibid.*, pp. 408–21; "Die Kreuzfahrerstadt Tripoli", *ibid.*, pp. 422–37; (with Michael Losse) "Kreuzfahrerburgen auf der Peloponnes und im übrigen Griechenland", *ibid.*, pp. 456–66.

POWER, Amanda, "In the last days at the end of the world: Roger Bacon and the reform of Christendom" in *Acts of the Franciscan History Conference held at the Franciscan International Study Centre on 9th September 2006*, ed. J. Rohrkasten and M. Robson, Canterbury Studies in Franciscan History, 1, Canterbury, 2008, pp. 135–51; "Franciscan Advice to the Papacy in the Middle Ages", *History Compass*, 5.5, 2007, pp. 1550–75;

"A mirror for every age: the reputation of Roger Bacon", *EHR*, 121, no. 492, 2006, pp. 657–92.

PRYOR, John H., "A view from a masthead: the First Crusade from the Sea," *Crusades*, 7, 2008, pp. 87–152; "Shipping and seafaring", in *The Oxford handbook of Byzantine studies*, ed. Elizabeth M. Jeffreys, Oxford, 2008, ch. II.8.9, pp. 482–91.

PURKIS, William J., *Crusading Spirituality in the Holy Land and Iberia, c.1095–c.1187*, Woodbridge: The Boydell Press, 2008, xii+215pp.; "Religious Symbols and Practices: Monastic Spirituality, Pilgrimage and Crusade", in *European Religious Cultures: Essays Offered to Christopher Brooke on the Occasion of His Eightieth Birthday*, ed. M. Rubin London: Institute of Historical Research, 2008, pp. 69–88.

RACINE, Pierre, "Did Frederic Barberousse have a Mediterranean Policy?", in *Imago Temporis Medium Aevum*, 1, 2007, pp. 87–104; "A proposito di *Les Latins en Orient*", *Nuova Rivista Storica*, XCII, 2008, pp.173–92.

RICHARD, Jean, "La Toison d'Or et la croisade sous Philippe le Bon", in *L'Ordre de la Toison d'Or, Mémoires de l'Académie de Dijon*, 142 bis, 2007, pp. 65–69.

RYAN, Vincent, "Richard I and the early evolution of the Fourth Crusade", in *Fourth crusade, Istambul*, pp. 3–13.

ROLL, Israel, "The Encounter of Crusaders and Muslims at Apollonia-Arsuf as Reflected in the Archaeological Finds and Historical Sources", in *The Encounter of Crusaders and Muslims in Palestine as Reflected in Arsuf, Sayyiduna ʿAli and other Coastal Sites*, I. Roll, ed. O. Tal and M. Winter, Tel Aviv, 2007, pp. 9–103 [Hebrew]; "Apollonia-Arsuf", *NEAEHL*, 5, 2008, pp. 1568–71; "Der fruehislamische Basar und die Kreuzfahrerburg in Apollonia-Arsuf", in *Burgen und Staedete der Kreuzzugszeit*, ed. M. Piana, Petersberg, 2008, pp. 252–62.

RUBENSTEIN, Jay, "Cannibals and Crusaders", *French Historical Studies*, 31, 2008, pp. 325–52; "Godfrey of Bouillon vs Raymond of Saint-Gilles: How Carolingian Kingship trumped Millenarianism at the End of the First crusade", in *The Legend of Charlemagne in the Middle Ages. Power, Faith and Crusade*, ed. M. Gabriele and J. Stuckey, Palgrave, 2008.

SCHRYVER, James G., "Nabataean Landscape & power: Evidence from the Petra Garden & Pool Complex" (with L.-A. Bedal), in *Crossing Jordan – North American Contributions to the Archaeology of Jordan*, ed. Thomas E. Levy, P. M. Michèle Daviau, Randall W. Younker and May Shaer, London: Equinox Publishing Ltd., 2007, pp. 375–83; (with Leigh-Ann Bedal and Kathryn L. Gleason), "The Petra Garden and Pool Complex, 2003–2005", *ADAJ* [*Annual of the Department of Antiquities of Jordan*], 51, 2007, pp. 151–76; "Gamle fund i nyt lys" [New Light on Old Finds], *Nyt fra Nationalmuseet*, 119, June–July–August 2008, pp. 34–35 [in Danish, translated by John Lund of the National Museum]; "Cyprus at the Crossroads: Understanding the Paths taken in the Art and Architecture of Frankish Cyprus," in *POCA 2005: Postgraduate Cypriot Archaeology*, ed. G. Papantoniou, A. Fitzgerald, and S. Hargis, pp. 13–23, BAR International Series 1803, Oxford: Archaeopress, 2008.

Iris SHAGRIR, ed. with Ronnie Ellenblum and Jonathan Riley-Smith, *In Laudem Hierosolymitani: Studies in Crusades and Medieval Culture in Honour of Benjamin Z. Kedar*, Aldershot: Ashgate, 2007 [=ILH].

SHAWCROSS, Teresa, "'Do Thou Nothing without Counsel': Political Assemblies and the Ideal of Good Government in the Thought of Theodore Palaeologus and Theodore Metochites", *Al-Masaq*, 20, 2008, pp. 89–118; "In the Name of the True Emperor: Politics of Resistance after the Palaiologan Usurpation", *Byzantinoslavica*, 66, 2008, pp. 203–27; *Review* of George Boustronios, *A Narrative of the Chronicle of Cyprus, 1456–1489*, translated from the Greek by Nicholas Coureas together with an Anthology of Greek Texts of the Fourteenth and

Fifteenth Centuries relating to Cyprus and Translated by Hans Pohlsander, Cyprus Research Centre, Texts and Studies in the History of Cyprus LI – Sources for the History of Cyprus XIII, Nicosia, Cyprus Research Centre 2005, *Jahrbuch der Oesterreichischen Byzantinistik*, 58, 2008, pp. 225–27.

SMITH, Caroline, Joinville and Villehardouin, *Chronicles of the Crusades*, translated with and introduction and notes, London: Penguin Classics, 2008, 384pp.; *Crusading in the Age of Joinville*, Aldershot: Ashgate, 2006, 216pp.; "Martryrdom and crusading in the thirteenth century: remembering the dead of Louis IX's crusades', *Al-Masaq: Islam and the medieval Mediterranean*, 15, 2003, pp. 189–96.

TOUATI, François-Olivier, *Vocabulaire historique du Moyen Âge (Occident, Byzance, Islam)*, Paris: La Boutique de l'Histoire, 2007 [4th enlarged edn].

TYERMAN, Christopher J., *God's War: A New History of the Crusades*, Harvard U.P., 2008 (transl. in Spanish and Bulgarian); "Principes et populus: Civil Society and the First Crusade", in *Cross, Crescent and Conversion*, ed. S. Barton and P. Linehan, Leiden: Brill, 2008.

UPTON-WARD, Judi, ed., *The Military Orders*, vol. 4: *On Land and by Sea*, Aledershot: Ashgate, 2008, xviii–292pp. [=MO4].

VILLEGAS-ARISTIZABAL, Lucas, "Algunas notas sobre la participación de Rogelio de Tosny en la Reconquista Ibérica", *Estudios Humanísticos de la Universidad de Leon*, III, 2004, pp. 263–74; "Roger of Tosny's adventures in the County of Barcelona", *Nottingham Medieval Studies*, LII, 2008, pp. 5–16.

WEBER, Benjamin, "Conversion, croisade et oecuménisme à la fin du Moyen-Age. Encore sur la lettre de Pie II à Mehmed II", *Crusades*, 7, 2008, pp.181–97.

WEIDENKOPF, Steven A., *Epic. A Journey through Church History*, Ascension Press, 2009.

2. Recently completed theses

ABD-AL RASHID, Rehab, The Successors Questions in the Kingdom of Jerusalem 1099–1291 PhD, University of Alexandria, supervised by Mahmoud Said Omran.

ANDREI, Filippo, *Le fonti storiche e letterarie della «Chanson de Jérusalem»*, PhD, Univ. di Siena, 2005, supervisor M.L. Meneghetti, University of Milan; foreign supervisors: Ph. Ménard, Univ. de Paris IV-Sorbonne, P. Lorenzo Gradín, Univ. of Santiago de Compostela; *Il Salterio glossato di San Romualdo. Edizione critica (Ps. I-L) e studio delle fonti*, Tesi di Laurea, Firenze, 2001, supervisor S. Cantelli Berarducci.

BALDWIN, Philip B., *Marketing the Crusades: 1095–1229*, M.A. Thesis, Queen's University at Kingston, 2007.

BARTOS, Sebastian, *Negotiations of Power in Medieval Society: Ecclesiastical Authorities and Secular Rulership in Little Poland, 1177–1320*, PhD, CUNY Graduate Center, 2008.

BERNER, Alexander, *Crusaders from the Lower Rheinland*, PhD, Bochum University, supervised by Nikolas Jaspert.

BLEY, Matthias, Purity, *Reform and the Other*, PhD, Bochum University, supervised by Nikolas Jaspert.

BRATU, Cristian, *L'Émergence de l'auteur dans l'historiographie médiévale en prose en langue française* [The Emergence of the Author in French Medieval Historiography], PhD, New York University, 2007.

CHRISSIS, Nikolaos G., *Crusading in Romania: A Study of Byzantine-Western Relations and Attitudes, 1204–1282*, Ph.D, University of London, 2008, supervised by Jonathan Harris.

DORAN, John, *The Legacy of Schism: Relations between the Papacy and the City of Rome, c.1130–c. 1210*, PhD, University of London, 2008.

GURACK, Ditte, *The Devotion to the Virgin Mary in the Military Orders (12th–16th Century)*, PhD, Bochum University, supervised by Nikolas Jaspert.

KAFFA, Elena, *The Greek Church of Cyprus, the Morea and Constantinople during the Frankish Era (1196–1303)*, PhD, Cardiff University, supervised by Peter Edbury.

KHALAWY, Iman, *The Role of Charles Count of Anjou in the Crusades Age in Islamic East and Tunis 1248–1286*, MA, University of Alexandria, supervised by Mahmoud Said Omran.

LAPINA, Elizabeth, *'Things Done in a Foreign Land': Representations of the First Crusade in Texts and Images in the Twelfth Century*, PhD, The Johns Hopkins University, 2007.

MACK, Merav, *The Merchant of Genoa: the Genoese, the Crusades and the Latin East, 1187–1220s*, PhD, University of Cambridge, 2004.

MATZOUKIS, Claire, *Recherches sur le monachisme latin en Terre sainte: Notre-Dame de Josaphat*, MA, Université de Tours, supervised by François-Olivier Touati.

MICHAUDEL, Benjamin, *Ayyubid and Mamluk Fortifications in Coastal Syria between the end of the 12th and the beginning of the 14th century*, Thèse de doctorat d'Archéologie, Université de Paris IV-Sorbonne, 2005.

MILLIMAN, Paul, *Disputing Identity, Territoriality, and Sovereignty: The Place of Pomerania in the Social Memory of the Kingdom of Poland and the Teutonic* Ordensstaat, Cornell University, 2007.

MORRIS, April Jehan, *Balanced on a Blade: Images of Templar Ideology in the Frescoes at Le Dognon, Cressac (Sud-Charente), France*, MA, Art History, Southern Methodist University, Dallas, Texas, USA, 2007.

MORTON, Nicholas, *The Teutonic Knights in the Holy Land, 1190–1291*, 2008.

NIDAM, Nora, *Sagar al-Dur, princesse égyptienne au temps des croisades*, MA, Université de Tours, supervised by François-Olivier Touati, 2007.

PAUL, Nicholas L., *Crusade and family memory before 1225*, PhD, Univ. of Cambridge, 2005.

PYMM, Rachael, *Jacques de Vitry: the attitude of a high-standing western European ecclesiastic to the Latin East and the thiteenth-century crusades to the East*, MA, Royal Holloway, University of London, supervised by Jonathan Phillips.

SMITH, Caroline, *The presentation and practice of crusading according to John of Joinville and his contemporaries*, PhD, University of Cambridge, 2004.

TOLSTOY-MILOSLAVSKY, Dmitri, *Manuel I Komnenos and Italy: Byzantine Foreign Policy, 1135–80*, PhD, University of London, 2008, supervised by Jonathan Harris.

3. Papers read by members of the Society and others

AMOUROUX, Monique, "Louis VII, Innocent II et la seconde croisade", Avignon SSCLE.

BALARD, Michel, "Le commerce génois à Alexandrie (XIIe–XIVe s.)", colloque Alexandrie et le commerce de la Méditerranée médiévale, Alexandrie, avril 2008; "Buondelmonti et la guerre sainte", colloque Holy War: Past and Present. The Crusader Phenomenon and its Relevance Today, Jérusalem, juin 2008; "L'historiographie française de la guerre sainte", conférence introductive à Avignon SSCLE; "Il Regno nell'orizzonte mediterraneo", XVIIIe Giornate normanno-sveve, Bari, octobre 2008; "Population et administration de Famagouste au début du XVe siècle", Table-ronde sur L'histoire de Famagouste, Nicosie, octobre 2008.

BALLETTO, Laura, "Genova e il Mediterraneo Orientale nel tardo medioevo", at: The nautical cities of Italy and Eastern Mediterranean, Atene, 2005; "Chios, un grande caposaldo dell'Impero genovese nel Mediterraneo orientale", at: Genova, Chios, Cristoforo Colombo. Mare e cultura, Salonicco, 17 ottobre 2007; "Economia e commercio a Cipro nel periodo genovese", at: Medieval Famagusta. Workshop in memory of A.H.S. "Peter" Megav, Nicosia, 25–26 ottobre 2008.

BARBER, Malcolm, "Why were the Templars arrested in 1307?", at: California University of Pennsylvania, one-day conference to mark the 700th anniversary of the arrest of the Templars, October, 2007; "Why did the West fail to recover the Holy Land between 1291 and 1320?", at: HWPP; The Challenge of State Building in the Twelfth Century: the Crusader States in Palestine and Syria, The Stenton Lecture, University of Reading, November, 2008.

BELLOMO, Elena, "The *Domus Sancte Marie Montis Gaudii* de Jerusalem in North-West Italy", Avignon SSCLE.

BERKOVICH, Ilya, "The Battle of Forbie (1244)", Avignon SSCLE.

BISAHA, Nancy, "Pope Pius II: Renaissance Patron ?", at: *Renaissance Society of America Annual Conference*, Chicago, April 2008.

BONNEAUD, Pierre, "La papauté et les Hospitaliers de Rhodes aux lendemains de la chute de Constantinople (1453–1467)", Avignon SSCLE.

BORCHARDT, Karl, "Die Johanniter und ihre Balleien in Deutschland während des Mittelalters", at: Regionalität und Transfergeschichte, Ritterordens-Kommenden der Templer und Johanniter im nordöstlichen Deutschland und in Polen seit dem Mittelalter, Potsdam, 22 May 2008; "The Master in his Cave: Fr. Gilbert d'Assailly and the Militarization of the Hospital of St John of Jerusalem during the Twelfth Century", at: HWPP; "Casting out Demons by Beelzebul: Did the Papal Preaching against the Albigensians Ruin the Crusades?", Avignon SSCLE.

BRATU, Cristian, "Cohérence discursive et incohérence politique chez Geoffroy de Villehardouin", at: French and Italian Graduate Students' Conference, University of Texas at Austin, 2004; The Rise of the Medieval Chronicler, at: Yale University, Florilegium: Graduate Student Medieval Studies Conference, 2005; 2005, Columbia University, Graduate Student Conference "How Sweet Are Your Words to My Taste". Eating Food, Imbibing Drink and Devouring Texts in the Middle Ages: "Images of Hunger and Abundance in the Writings of Villon and Rabelais"; 2005, University of Reading (UK), 4th International Medieval Chronicles Conference: "Les Chroniques de la 4e croisade et l'épistémè gothico-scolastique"; 2006, International Medieval Congress, Leeds (UK): "L'économie des émotions chez Philippe de Commynes"; 2006, Cornell University, Entralogos: Romance Studies Graduate Conference: Turns, Returns, Detours: (Hi)story and (Re)presentation: "The Missing Link in the Genealogical Representation of Medieval History"; March 2008, Fordham University, Remembering the Crusades: Myth, Image, and Identity: "Remembering the Crusades, Remembering the Self"; April 2008, University of North Texas, Women in French Conference: "Authorship, Authority, and Gender in the Middle Ages" – presider of sessions VII (Women Authors in the Middle Ages I) and XV (Female Authority in the Late Medieval and Early Modern Period II); September 2008, University of Texas at San Antonio, European Film Conference, "Femmes dans le jardin: Éléments pour une nouvelle interprétation d'Inch'Allah dimanche"; December 2008–MLA Convention, San Francisco: "Hundred Years War Literature: Making and Breaking Boundaries" (panel hosted by Dr. Deborah McGrady, UVA): "Crossing Boundaries in the Third Book of Froissart's Chronicles"; December 2008, Barnard College, Barnard Medieval and Renaissance Conference: The

Shape of Time in the Middle Ages and Renaissance, "Genealogical Time and Its Gaps in Froissart's Chroniques".

BRUNDAGE, James A., "The Managerial Revolution in the English Church, 1175–1250" Pennsylvania State University, Conference on England at the Time of Magna Carta, 28–29 March 2008; "Henry of Livonia: The Chronicler and His Work", Conference on Henry of Livonia, Tallinn University, Center for Medieval Studies and Nordic Centre for Medieval Studies, 22–24 May 2008; "The Case of the Shrinking Client", Thirteenth International Congress of Medieval Canon Law, Esztergom–Budapest, 3–9 August 2008; "Default on the Payment of Legal Fees", Conference on From Causa to Brocard: The Creation of the Ius Commune, University of Edinburgh, 12–13 December 2008; "Law as a Profession in the Middle Ages", Conference on *Utrumque ius*? The Education of a Lawyer. Church, Law and Society in the Middle Ages, University of Cambridge, 18–20 December 2008.

BRYSON, David, "Clement V and the Road to Avignon, 1305–09", Avignon SSCLE.

BURGTORF, Jochen, "The Military Orders in the Latin East: Select Aspects", Summer University: From Holy War to Peaceful Cohabitation: Diversity of Crusading and the Military Orders, Central European University, Budapest, Hungary, July 2008.

BUTTIGIEG, Emanuel, "The Hospitaller Knights of Malta: Serving the Poor and Defending the Faith, 1580–1700", at: Gender, Vocation and Career, Economic History Society Women's Committee 19th Annual Workshop, Institute of Historical Research, London, 1 November 2008.

CARLSSON, Christer, "Kronobäck Hospitaller Commandery – A fieldstudy", Avignon SSCLE.

CARR, Annemarie Weyl, "Famagusta: Fate and Fame of a Crusader Boom Town", at: University of Akron, September 2008; "The Virgin's Church at Asinou, Cyprus: A small Paradise in the Time", at: DePaul University, April 2008; "Iconography and Identity: Syrian Elements in the Art of Crusader Cyprus", at: University of Leiden, December 2008.

CARRAZ, Damien, "Les Lengres, entre négoce, fidélité politique et lutte contre l'infidèle. L'opportunisme d'une famille de marchands marseillais au XIVe siècle", Avignon SSCLE.

CARRIER, Marc, "Effeminate Greeks as Seen by the Chroniclers of the Crusades", at: McGill Medievalists' Sessions, March 2008.

CASSIDY-WELCH, Megan, "Heresy and blood in the Historia Albigensis of Pierre les Vaux-de-Cernay'/'L'Heresie et le sang dans *l'Historia Albigensis* de Pierre des Vaux-de-Cernay", at: Le Sang, International Medieval Society, Université de Paris IV-Sorbonne, 2008; "Images of Incarceration in late-medieval Germany", at: Imagination, Books and Community in Medieval Europe Conference, State Library of Victoria; "Frightful Abodes of Misery: The Medieval Prison", invited public lecture, State Library of Victoria, 2008"; "Remembering home: space, testimony and memory in thirteenth-century France", Australian and New Zealand Association for Medieval and Early Modern Studies conference, University of Tasmania, 2008; "Displacement after the Albigensian Crusade", at: Australian and New Zealand Association for Medieval and Early Modern Studies conference, University of Adelaide, 2007.

CHRISTIE, Niall G. F., "Creating Sacred Identity: Looking Backwards and Forwards with ʿAli ibn Tahir al-Sulami (d. 1106)", at: New England Medieval Conference, Crusade, Jihad and Identity in the Medieval World, Dartmouth College, Hanover, USA, October 2008; "Preaching Crusade and Jihad, 1095–1105", Keynote Speaker, at: Thompson Rivers University Undergraduate Conference in History, Philosophy and Politics, Thompson Rivers University, Kamloops, Canada, January 2008.

CONNELL, Charles W., "War or Peace: The Struggle over Public opinion at the Time of the First Crusade", Avignon SSCLE; "Public Opinion and Peace in the Middle Ages", at: 43rd International Congress on Medieval Studies, Kalamazoo, Mai 2008; "*Quod omnes tangit*: Law and Public Opinion in the Middle Ages", at: ACMRS Annual Conference, February 2008.

COSGROVE, Walker Reid, "The episcopate between the Rhône and the Garonne: Insignificant, Incapable, or Zealous Defenders of the Faith?", at: IMC Kalamazoo, 2008; "Righting the Ship: the Clergy of languedoc on the Eve of Albigensian Crusade", at: The Crusades Studies Forum, Saint-Louis, USA, April, 2008; "No Country for bad Bishop", at: 14th Annual Graduate Student Association Research Symposium, Saint-Louis University, USA, April 2008.

COUREAS, Nicholas S., "Genoese Merchants and the Export of Grain from Cyprus to Cilician Armenia: 1300–1310", at: Culture of Cilician Armenia, International Conference, Antelias, Lebanon, 14–18 January 2008; "Taverns in Medieval Famagusta", at: Medieval Famagusta: An International Workshop for the Advanced Study of History, Art, Architecture and Cultural Management, 4–5 April, Paris, France; "Commercial Relations between Genoese Famagusta and the Mamluk Sultanate, 1374–1464", at: 17th HES, May 2008; "Delegating Powers: The Avignon Papacy and Archbishop Philip of Cyprus", at: IMC Leeds 7–10 July 2008; "From the Middle Ages to the Renaissance: Elements of Transition in the Chronicle of George Boustronios", at: IV Medieval Chronicles Conference, 21–25 July 2008, Belfast, UK; "A Medieval Cypriot Diaspora: Non-noble Cypriot Migration throughout the Mediterranean from the Thirteenth to the Sixteenth Centuries", at: Avignon SSCLE; "The Latin Church and the non-Latin Christians of the City of Famagusta in the Fourteenth Century", at: Workshop on Medieval Famagusta, 25–26 October 2008, Nicosia Cyprus.

CRAWFORD, Paul F., "Before the Military Orders: the Fusion of the Military and Monastic Vocations from Gregory VII to Bernard of Clairvaux", Avignon SSCLE.

DEVRIES, Kelly, "Coins of the Realm? Issues of Coinage by Rebel Governments in the Southern Low Countries during the Late Middle Ages", at: 42nd IMC, Kalamazoo, 2007; "What did Flemish Soldiers Wear at the Battle of Courtrai, 1302 ?", at: 14th IMC Leeds, 2007; "The Ravenna Gun ", at: The XXXIV International Commitee for the History of Technology Symposium, Copenhagen, August 18, 2007; "War and the International State", at: Crossing the Divide: Continuity and Divide in Late Medieval and Early Modern Warfare, University of reading, September 11, 2007; "Trebuchets", at: Echols Scholar Engineering Program, University of Virginia, Charlottesville, April 1, 2008; "Saint Francis on Crusade", at: 35th Annual Sewanee Mediaeval Colloquium, Francis, Dominic, their Orders and their Tradition, The University of the South, Sewanee, Tennessee, April 11, 2008; "Meet the Mongols: Dealing with Mamluk Victory and Mongol Defeat in the Middle East in 1260", at: Society for Military History Meeting, Ogden, Utah, April 18, 2008; "Mary Dupuis and Jacques de Bourbon: Soldier-Eyewitnesses to the Siege of Rhodes in 1480 and 1522", at: 43rd IMC, Kalamazoo, 2008; "Standing up to the Ottoman empire: Civilian Resistance to Turkish Expansionism during the Fifteenth, Sixteenth and Seventeenth Centuries", at: XXXIV International Congress of Military History, Military Conflicts and Civil Population: Total Wars, Limited Wars, Asymmetrical Wars, Trieste, September 2, 2008.

DICKSON, Gary, US University lecture tour on the general theme of "Medieval Childhood and the Children's Crusade as Rite of Passage" at: Binghamton Univ., Washington Univ., St. Louis, St. Louis Univ., Johns Hopkins Univ., Univ. of North Carolina, Chapel Hill, Univ. of Pennsylvania, Philadelphia, Columbia Univ., Univ. of California, Berkeley, Stanford University, September–October 2008.

DOUROU-ELIOPOULOU, Maria, "Athens during the Frankish period (1204–1311)", at: El Dominio latino en Atenas, Encuentro Cientifico, Instituto Cervantes-Museo de la Ciudad de Atenas, Athens, 3 April, 2008; "Archival material for the Latins in Frankish Cyprus", at: IV International Cyprological Congress, 29 April– 3 May 2008.

EDBURY, Peter, "Famagusta and the Tradition of History Writing in Frankish Cyprus", at: a Colloquium on Medieval Famagusta (Paris, 4–5 April 2008); "The Old French Translation of William of Tyre and Templars", CEU Budapest, July 2008; "New Perspectives on the Old French Continuations of William of Tyre", Avignon SSCLE; "Famagusta and the Lusignan Kingdom of Cyprus, 1192–1374", at: Colloquium on Medieval Famagusta, Nicosia, 25–6 October 2008; "Philip of Novara and *Le Livre de Forme de Plait*", Cardiff research seminar, Dec. 2008.

EDGINGTON, Susan B, "Translating the *Chanson d'Antioche*" with Carol Sweetenham, IHR seminar, London, 28 April 2008; "The Concept of Holy War in the *Chanson d'Antioche*", at: HWPP; "Orthodoxy, Heterodoxy and Heresy in the *Historia* of Albert of Aachen (1095–1120)", Avignon SSCLE.

EKDAHL, Sven, "Aufmarsch und Aufstellung der Heere bei Tannenberg/Grunwald (1410). Eine kritische Analyse", Oddział Polskiego Towarzystwa Historycznego w Mrągowie, Mrągowo, 15 May 2008; "Die Söldnerwerbungen des Deutschen Ordens für einen geplanten Angriff auf Polen am 1 Juni 1409. Ein Beitrag zur Vorgeschichte der Schlacht bei Tannenberg", Jahrestagung der Historischen Kommission für ost-und westpreussische Landesforschung, Bütow, 3 October 2008.

FOLDA, Jaroslav, "Byzantine Chrysography and Its Impact in the 13th Century", at: DePaul University, Chicago, November 6, 2008; "Byzantine and Crusader Icons, and the Italian 'Maniera Greca': The Evidence of Chrysography" at: Furman University, Greenville, SC, May 14, 2008; "Writing in Gold: Chrysography and 13th Century Icon Painting, East and West", at: Maryland Institute College of Art, Baltimore, MD, 17 April 2008; "Picturing the First Crusade and Commemorating the Fall of Jerusalem," plenary lecture at: Remembering the Crusades: Myth, Image, and Identity, 28th Annual Conference of the Center for Medieval Studies, Fordham University, New York City, March 29–30, 2008; "The Use of Çintamani as Ornament: A Case Study in the Afterlife of Forms", at: The Afterlife of Forms: A Symposium in Honor of Annemarie Weyl Carr, Southern Methodist University, Dallas, TX, 23–24 February 2008.

FOREY Alan J., "The Papacy and Muslims living under Christian Rule in Spain (12th and 13th Centuries)", Jerusalem, June 2008; "Papal Claims to authority ver lands gained from the Infidel in the Iberian Peninsula and North Africa", Avignon SSCLE.

GABRIELE, Matthew, "Fight the Muslims (Please?): The Rhetoric of the 1010, 1074, and 1095 Papal Calls to Action," at: Global Encounters: Legacies of Exchange and Conflict (1000–1700), Chapel Hill, NC, November 2008; "Being a Frank in the 11th Century: Responding to the Call in 1095," at: Crusade, Jihad and Identity in the Medieval World, Dartmouth, NH, October 2008; "The Carolingians and the First Crusade", at: the Conference of the Medieval Academy of America, Vancouver, Canada, April 2008; "Remembering the Future: Charlemagne, Last Emperor, and the Response to the First Crusade", at: Remembering the Crusades: Myth, Image, and Identity, 28th Annual Conference of the Center for Medieval Studies at Fordham University, New York City, March 2008.

GARCÍA-GUIJARRO, Luis, "Reconquest and Crusade, 11th–13th Centuries: A Historiographical Survey", at: Crusading at the Periphery of Europe: Crusades in the Iberian Peninsula and the Baltic Region, University of Aalborg, Aalborg, Denmark, 14 September 2007; "Las

Cruzadas: mitos y distorsiones?", at: La Edad Media: sesgos y prejuicios historiográfico, University of Extremadura, Cáceres, Spain, 21 April 2008; "Las peregrinaciones al Santo Sepulcro de Jerusalén entre los siglos IV al XI", at: V Jornadas Nacionales de Cofradías Medievales de la Sangre de Cristo, Calatayud, Spain, 26 April 2008; "Crusade Ideology in the Realms of Leon, Castile and Aragon, 11th–13th Centuries", at: HWPP; "Reconquest, the Papacy and the Political Consolidation of the Catalan Counties, c.1060–c.1100", Avignon SSCLE; "Guerra y religión en el contexto hispánico del siglo XIII", at: L'Església en temps de Jaume I, Institut d'Estudis Ilerdencs, Institut d'Estudis Catalans, Lérida, Spain, 18 September 2008; "Idéologie de la guerre et de la conquête chrétienne dans la péninsule ibérique au XIIIe siècle", at: Le XIIIe siècle en Languedoc et dans les possessions de Jacques le Conquérant, IVe Journées historiques à Clermont l'Hérault, Lodève et Montpellier, Prieuré de St Michel de Grandmont, Soumont, 24 October 2008; "Guerra e ideología: la Reconquista en el contexto de la cristiandad latina", at: I Symposium Internacional, La conducción de la guerra (950–1350): Historiografía, University of Extremadura, Cáceres, Spain, 19 November 2008.

GEORGIOU, Stavros G., "The Court Hierarchy under Alexios I Komnenos (1081–1118): The Reform of the System of the Honorofic Titles and the Adoption of New Perceptions in the Administration of Empire", at: Workshop of Byzantine Studies, Interdepartmental Postgraduate Programme in Byzantine Studies, University of Cyprus, Nicosia, 23 January 2008.

Anne GILMOUR-BRYSON, "*Vox in excelso* deconstructed. Exactly what did Clement say?", Avignon SSCLE.

VON GUETTNER, Darius, "The Christianisation of Prussia: politics and war", at: Seventh Biennial International Conference of the Australian and New Zealand Association for Medieval and Early Modern Studies (ANZAMEMS), 2–6 December 2008, University of Tasmania, Hobart, Australia; "Against the Saladinistas, against the enemies of the Holy Faith, against the shameful idolaters" – The twelfth century narrative sources from Poland on crusading along the Baltic littoral, at: Crusading at the periphery of Europe – Crusades on the Iberian Peninsula and in the Baltic region, 12–14 September 2007, Aalborg University, Denmark; "The Ultimate Perversion" – the End of the Crusader State in Prussia (the Treaty of Kraków 1525), at: FF; "Conquest of Prussia before 1230", at: School of Historical Studies Work In Progress Day, 31 May 2007, The University of Melbourne, Australia; "Crusades against pagans in the Baltic", at: The University of Melbourne, Australia, 15 September 2008; "Against the Slavs and other pagans inhabiting the North: Poland and the Papacy", at: Avignon SSCLE; "Pollexianorum cervicosa feritas – The barbarism of the pagan Pollexians in the literary convention of Master Vincentius", at the Conference Ars Scribendi. Art of writing in the medieval Bohemia and Poland, Gniezno, Poland, 15–18 September 2008.

HARRIS, Jonathan, December 2008: "The Fourth Crusade and the Looting of Constantinople 1204", Bournemouth Historical Association; June 2008: "Alexios I and the First Crusade', Teachers' Advisory Group Day, Royal Holloway, University of London; May 2008: 'Manuel II and the Lollards', Workshop on Manuel II Palaiologos's *Dialogue with a Persian*, King's College London; April 2008: "Greeks at the papal curia in the fifteenth century", at conference on Greeks, Latins, and Intellectual History 1204–1500: Debates, Influences, Impressions, Translations, Migrations, University of Cyprus; December 2007: "Constantinople as City State, 1369–1453", Hellenic Studies Workshop, Princeton University; November 2007: "New approaches to Western travellers accounts of Constantinople, 1403–1453", Encounters Seminar Series, Barber Institute of Fine Art, University of Birmingham.

HESLOP, Michael, "The Search for the Defensive System of the Knights in the Dodecanese. Part I: Chalki, Symi, Tilos and Nisyros", Avignon SSCLE.

HODGSON, Natasha, "Reconstructing an honorable hero for a dishonourable crusade – the case of Baldwin IX of Flanders", at: Remembering the Crusades Conference, Fordham University, New York, USA, March 2008; "Lions, Tigers and Bears: Encounters with animals and bestial imagery in crusade sources", at: IMC, Leeds, July 2008, revised for the University of Cardiff research seminar, November 2008; "Honour, Shame and the Fourth Crusade", Avignon SSCLE.

HUNYADI, Zsolt, "The social composition of the military-religious orders in the medieval Kingdom of Hungary", at: V Encontro Sobre Ordens Militares/5th Meeting on the Military Orders – Military orders and Orders of Knighthood: Between Occident and Orient, Palmela, 15–18 February 2006; "The Teutonic Order in Burzenland: recent re-considerations", at: Convegno internazionale – Historische Kommission zur Erforschung des Deutschen Ordens, Lecce–Bari–Brindisi, 13–17 September 2006; "The international mobility of the military-religious orders", at: Borders and Crossings: Inaugural Partnership Conference of the University of Manitoba and University of Szeged, Szeged, 15–16 June 2007; "Hungary and the Third Crusade: a turning point in the attitude towards crusading", at: IMC Leeds, 9–12 July 2007; "Uses of literacy by the Templars and Hospitallers in the Medieval Kingdom of Hungary", at: Colloquia Torunensia, Die Rolle der Schriftlichkeit in den geistlichen Ritterorden des Mittelalters: innere Organisation, Sozialstruktur, Politik, Toruń, 27–30 September 2007; "A lovagrendek kutatása Közép-Európában [State of research on the military-religious orders], Medieval Studies in East-Central Europe: Hungarian-Slovakian Joint Conference, Szeged, 15–16 November 2007.

IRWIN, Robert, "The Mamluk Army of Syria and the Crusader States", Avignon SSCLE.

JENSEN, Janus Møller, "Late Medieval Crusading in Scandinavia 1300–1536. Message and impact in literature, society and politics", at: Central European University, Budapest, July 2008; "Politics and crusade. Scandinavia, the Avignon Papacy and the crusade in the fourteenth century", Avignon SSCLE. For a full list, please visit www.crusades.dk

JENSEN, Kurt Villads, "Physical extermination of physical sin in the Baltic Crusades", at: Alter Orbis, ANZAMEMS 7th biennial conference in Hobart, Tasmania, 25 November–10 December 2008; "Changing Landscapes and Changing Peoples during the Nordic Crusades", at: Avignon SSCLE; "Late Crusades in the North", at: International workshop at Central European University in Budapest on From Holy War to Peaceful Co-habitation – Diversity of Crusading and the Military Orders, July 2008; 6.–10. July: "Sea and Deserts, Storm and Earthquakes: Crusading as Nature's Battle against Evil" at: IMC Leeds, May 2008; "Henry of Livonia on War", at: Congress The Chronicle of Henry of Livonia: Crusading and Chronicle Writing on the Medieval Frontier, Centre for Medieval Studies, Tallinn University; "The Thirteenth-Century Concept of Progress in Religion and in Societies: The Beginning of the Idea of the White Man's Burden?", at: Congress Meeting the Other, The Renvall Institute, Helsinki University, May 2008.

JORDAN, William Chester, "John Peckam on the Crusade", at: IMC Kalamazoo, 10 May 2008.

JOTISCHKY, Andrew, "Migration and Cultural Interaction: the Crusader States", at: Postgraduate Research Training Symposium, University College London, April 2008; "Ethnic and Religious Categories in the Treatment of Jews and Muslims in the Crusader States", at: Antisemitism and Islamophobia in Europe: Comparisons, Contrasts, Connections, University

College London, Goldsmiths College and Edge Hill, June 2008; "Western Pilgrims to Greek Orthodox Monasteries in the Crusader States", Avignon SSCLE.

KEDAR, Benjamin Z., (with Cyril Aslanov), "Problems in the Study of Trans-Cultural Borrowing in the Frankish Levant", at: Integration und Desintegration der Kulturen im europäischen Mittelalter, Haus Villigst/Schwerte, 31 March–2 April 2008; "Latin Christianity and the Holy Land – An Overview", at: Honours Class of the Faculty of Theology, University of Leiden, 16 May 2008; "Some Personal Observations on the Research of the Crusades, 1958–2008", at: HWPP, June 2008; "The Eastern Christians in the Crusading Kingdom of Jerusalem", at: Eastern Christianity, Judaism and Islam between the Death of Muhammad and Tamerlane, Slovak Academy of Sciences, Dolná Krupá, 25–28 June 2008; "The Uses of Aerial Photography for the Study of the Frankish Kingdom of Jerusalem", Tel Aviv University, 14 July 2008; "The Albigensian Crusade in the Historiography of the Crusades", Avignon SSCLE; "The Role of Cultural Institutions in Promoting Culture", at: Indo-Israeli Colloquium on Preserving Cultural Identities in Today's World, New Delhi, 10 September 2008; "Crusade and Jihad as seen by the Adversary: Muslim Perceptions of Crusading", Latin Perceptions of Jihad, at: The New England Medieval Conference on Crusade, Jihad and Identity in the Medieval World, Dartmouth College, 3–4 October 2008; "What's New in the Study of the Crusader Kingdom of Jerusalem?", at: the Oriental Institute, University of Chicago, 6 October 2008.

KOSTICK, Conor, "Myth of the First Crusade in Baldric of Dol's amendment of the Gesta Francorum", at: Remembering the Crusades: Myth, Image and Identity, Fordham University, New York, 29–30 March 2008; "The Economic background to the First Crusade", at: IMC, Leeds, July 2008; "God's Bounty: Providing for Crusaders 1096–1148", Ecclesiastical History Society, University of Galway, 24 July 2008.

LIGATO, Giuseppe, "L'araldica dell'impero latino di Costantinopoli in un brano della biografia dell'imperatore Enrico I scritta da Enrico di Valenciennes", presentato al convegno su Bonifacio di Monferrato, Acqui Terme, 8 settembre 2007; "Rinaldo di Châtillon signore dell'Oltregiordano", at: La Transgiordania nei secoli XII–XIII e le frontiere del Mediterraneo medievale, Convegno internazionale, Firenze, 6–8 novembre 2008; "Gesti e codici cavallereschi fra cristiani e musulmani nelle capitolazioni di città durante le crociate (secc. XI–XIII)", at: Cavalieri e città, Atti del convegno, Volterra, 19–21 giugno 2008.

LAPINA, Elizabeth, "Maccabees and the Battle of Antioch (1098)", at: Conference Dying for the Faith, Killing for the Faith: Old-Testament Faith-Warrior (Maccabees 1 and 2) in Cultural Perspective, Universität Konstanz/Akademie der Diözese Tottenburg-Stuttgart, Weingarten, March 2008; "'A Fire in the Sky coming from the West': References to Cardinal Points in the Chronicles of the First Crusade", Avignon SSCLE.

LOUD, Graham A., "The Papal 'Crusade' against Frederick II in 1228–30", Avignon SSCLE.

LUCHITSKAYA, Svetlana, "*Fides contra idolatria*: representing the Holy War in the Crusader Sources", at: HWPP.

MADDEN, Thomas F., "The Fourth Crusade in Venetian Eyes," at: Crusade, Jihad, and Identity in the Medieval World, The Leslie Center for the Humanities, Dartmouth College, October 4, 2008; "The Excommunication of the Venetians on the Fourth Crusade", at: IMC Kalamazoo, 2008; "The Crusades and Us: Medieval and Modern Perspectives on Christendom's Holy Wars", at: The William J. Davis, S.J., Lecture, Gonzaga University, April 10, 2008; "Memory and the Diversion of the Fourth Crusade," at: 28th Annual Conference of the Center for Medieval Studies, Fordham University, March 29, 2008; "Medieval and Modern Perspectives on the Crusades", at: Year of the Middle East Lecture Series, Reinhardt College, March 12, 2007; "The Crusades: Then and Now," at: The Center for the Humanities, University of Missouri, April 3, 2006.

MARVIN, Laurence W., "The White and Black Fraternities of Toulouse in the Albigensian Crusade", at IMC, Kalamazoo, 11 May 2008; "The Problem of Atrocity and the Albigensian Crusade", at: Georgia Medievalist Group, Waleska, GA, 27 September 2008.

MENACHE, Sophia, "Clement V and the Challenge of Crusade", Avignon SSCLE.

MICHAUDEL, Benjamin, "Muslim Military Architecture in the Near East and in Egypt at the Time of the Crusades", at: International symposium, *Middle East Studies Association*, Washington, November 2008; "Ayyubid and Mamluk Fortifications built upon Crusader Castles along Coastal Syria", Avignon SSCLE; "Fortifications in Coastal Syria under the Military Orders and the Muslims at the Time of the Crusades", at: International workshop From Holy War to Peaceful Co-habitation. Diversity of Crusading and the Military Orders, Central European University, July 2008, Budapest; "Muslim Military Architecture at the time of the Crusades", at: Pazmany Peter Catholic University of Pilicsaba, Hungary, March 2007; "Ayyubid and Mamluk Fortifications in Coastal Syria from the End of the 12th Century to the beginning of the 14th Century", at: International symposium on Castles and Towns of the Crusader Period in the Eastern Mediterranean, January 2006, Braubach, Germany.

MILLIMAN, Paul, "Boundary Narratives and State Formation on the Frontier of Latin Christendom: The Early Fourteenth-Century Disputes between the Kingdom of Poland and the Teutonic *Ordensstaat*", at: Monasteries on the Borders of Medieval Europe: New Perspectives, School of History, University of Leeds, September 2008; "Contentious Memories of the Prussian Crusade in the Fourteenth-Century Kingdom of Poland and Teutonic *Ordensstaat*", at: Remembering the Crusades: Myth, Image and Identity, Center for Medieval Studies, Fordham University, New York, NY, March 2008 (Abstract: http://www.fordham.edu/mvst/conference08/crusades/milliman.html).

MITCHELL, Piers D., "Health in crusader Caesarea", at: HWPP; "A biomedical approach to health in the crusades", at: International Conference on Biomedical Sciences in Archaeology, Crete, 24–26 September 2008; "Migration from medieval Europe to the Middle East with the crusades", at: Conference of the American Association for Physical Anthropology, Columbus, USA, 10–12 March 2008; "Gastrointestinal disease in the crusades", at: Conference on Medieval Disease, Disability, and Medicine, University of Oxford, UK, 5–6 July 2008; "The bioarchaeology of latrines and cesspools of crusader Acre", at: IMC, Leeds, 7–10 July 2008; "Dysentery in the crusades: an ELISA analysis of latrines and cesspools from medieval Acre", at: European Conference of the Palaeopathology Association, Copenhagen, Denmark, 25–7 August 2008; "Attitudes to the cause of disease during the crusades", at: Avignon SSCLE.

MOL, Johannes, "Traitor to Livonia? The Teutonic Order's land marshal Jasper van Munster and his actions at the outset of the Livonian crisis, 1554–1556", at: Conference on the Dutch Baltic relations in a historical perspective, Riga, 2008, April 24; "Das kulturelle Erbe des Deutschen Ordens in den heutigen Niederlanden", at: Konferenz Das kulturelle Erbe des Deutschen Ordens in Europa, Malbork, 2008, September 28.

NICHOLSON, Helen J., "Women in the crusades", at: Herefordshire Historical Association, 22 February 2008; "The Grail and the Templars: contrasting medieval concepts of Chivalry", at: the Institute for Medieval Studies, University of Leeds, 27 February 2008; "Hospitaller Women", at: the St John's Historical Society Study Day, St John's Gate, Clerkenwell, 12 April 2008; "At the Heart of Medieval London: The New Temple in the Middle Ages", at: In Despight of the Devouring Flame: the Temple Church in London, Courtauld Institute,

London, 14 June 2008; "The trial of the Templars in the British Isles, 1308–1311", at: the West Yorkshire Emmaus Society, Leeds, 2 July 2008; "Myths and Reality: the Crusades and the Latin East as presented during the Trial of the Templars in the British Isles, 1308–1311", at: Avignon SSCLE; "The role of women in the Military Orders", at: Congrès "Tempeliers" at Ypres, Belgium, 13 September 2008.

Angel NICOLAOU-KONNARI, "The Crusader Ideology in the Greek Cypriot Chronicle of Leontios Makhairas: Holy War or National War?", at: HWPP.

NICOLLE, David, "Three Hoards from Syria", Avignon SSCLE.

OMRAN, Mahmoud Said, "The Military Order in Portugal in the Middle Ages", at: Symposium in Honor of the late Saad Zaghloul Abd al-Hamead, Faculty of Arts, Alexandria University, 5 April 2008; "The Reconquista of Syria and Omer's mosque in al-Quds", Symposium of Islamic History, Faculty of Arts, Alexandria University, 5 November 2008.

ORDMAN, Jilana, "Creating the Crusader, 1095–1099", Avignon SSCLE.

PAUL, Nicholas L., "*Les livres, les gestes, e les estoires*: the authorship, function, and proliferation of dynastic historical narratives in the twelfth century", at:, Haskins Society Conference, Georgetown University, November 2008; "Ripoll and Jerusalem: Crusade, Identity, and Dynastic Legitimacy in Catalonia", Crusade, Jihad and Identity Conference, Dartmouth University, October 2008; "Lion knights: crusade, memory, and the culture of the European nobility", at: Center for Medieval Studies Lecture Series, Fordham University, January, 2008; "The knight, the hermit, and the pope: some problematic narratives of early crusading piety", at: Patristic, Medieval, and Renaissance Conference, Villanova University, October, 2007; "Dynastic texts and the construction of crusading traditions in twelfth century Catalonia" at: Crusading at the Periphery of Europe: Crusades in the Iberian Peninsula and in the Baltic Region, Lindholm Høje Museum, Aalborg, Denmark, September 2007; "Bohemond's war and words: propaganda, narrative, and the Crusade of 1107", at: IMC Kalamazoo, May 2006; "Constructing an Angevin crusading past in the *Chronica de gestis consulum Andegavorum*", at: Charles Homer Haskins Society Conference, Georgetown University, November 2006; "The presence of the past: crusading memories of the medieval nobility", at: Collective Memory and the Uses of the Past: An Interdisciplinary Conference, University of East Anglia, July 2006; "The disappearance of Baldwin of Mons: crusade memory and dynastic history in late twelfth-century Hainault", at: Conference on Crusades: Medieval Worlds in Conflict, Saint Louis University, February 2006.

PHILLIPS, Jonathan, "Ibn Jubayr and Saladin's 'unified' Near East", at: HWPP; Avignon SSCLE; "Crusader Perceptions of Constantinople", at: *Thyrathen*. A one-day colloquium on the secular world of Byzantium, King's College, London, December 2008.

PHILLIPS, Simon D., "Hospitaller Relations with the Local Communities on Cyprus" at: the Fourth International Congress of Cypriot Studies, Nicosia, April–May 2008.

PIANA, Mathias, "The Castle of Toron (Qal'at Tibnîn) in South Lebanon – New Evidence for an Ayyubid Reconstruction", at: 17th HES, University of Gent, 14–16 May 2008; "The Concentric Crusader Castle, A Reassessment", Avignon SSCLE.

PRYOR, John H., "The First Crusade viewed from the sea: the Genoese experience", at: Conference in honour of Professor Benjamin Z. Kedar on the occasion of the presentation to him of [ILH] *In laudem Hierosolymitani: studies in Crusades and medieval culture in honour of Benjamin Z. Kedar*, Hebrew University of Jerusalem, 25 February, 2008; "The tears of Saladin: the Siege of Acre, 1189–1191", at: Department of History, Hebrew University of Jerusalem, 26 February, 2008; "A view from a masthead: the First Crusade viewed from the sea", at: Workshop in honour of Professor Richard W. Unger on the occasion of his retirement, Department of History, University of British Columbia, Vancouver, Canada, 2–3 April 2008; "A medieval Mediterranean maritime revolution: Crusading by Sea ca 1096–1204", Avignon SSCLE.

PURKIS, William J., "Which way to the Holy Sepulchre? Pilgrimage Goals for Iberian Crusaders, c.1096–c.1140", at: Centre for the Study of the Middle Ages (CeSMA) Seminar, University of Birmingham, 18 February 2008; "Beyond the Flesh: Bernard of Clairvaux and the Contemplative Templar", at: Avignon SSCLE; "Eleventh- and Twelfth-Century Perspectives on State (Re)Building in the Iberian Peninsula", at: The Challenge of State-Building: A Symposium, University of Reading, 20 November 2008.

RICHARD, Jean, "La place de Famagouste dans les institutions du royaume des Lusignans", at: Famagusta Workshop, Nicosia, 2008.

RODRIGUEZ GARCIA, José Manuel, "¿Yendo a las cruzadas de prestado?. Material y personal alquilado, s. XIII", at: *VI jornadas luso-españolas de Historia Medieval. La guerra y Aljubarrota*, Alcobaça, 7 November 2008.

ROLL, Israel, "Architectural Plan of the Crusader Castle at Arsuf", at: HWPP.

RUBENSTEIN, Jay, "The Apocalyptic First Crusade", at: Université Paris IV-Sorbonne-E.P.H.E, March 2008; "The *Liber floridus* as a Source for Crusade Memory", at: Remembering the Crusades, Fordham University Conference, March 2008; "The Apocalypse in Retrospect: Holy War and the First Crusade", at: New England Medieval History Conference, Dartmouth College, October 2008.

RYAN, Vincent, "The New Knighthood and the Idealized Lady: Templar Devotion to the Virgin Mary", at: Crusades Study Forum, St Louis University, December 2008.

SCHRYVER, James G., "The Later Antique and Early Medieval Gardens of the East," at: *XVIIth International Congress of Classical Archaeology*, Rome, 25 September 2008.

SHAGRIR, Iris, "The Fall of Acre as a Mental Crisis: Riccoldo of Monte Croce and Thaddeus of Naples", Avignon SSCLE.

SMITH, Caroline, "John of Joinville in old age: the values and consequences of longevity", at: Medieval Studies Lecture Series, Fordham University, May 2007; "Saints and sinners at sea on the first crusade of Saint Louis", at: Medieval Worlds in Conflict, Saint Louis University Crusades Symposium, February 2006; "Literary production and preservation in the context of the crusades: a new approach to songs in Old French", at: Midwest Medieval History Conference, October 2005; "Why not to take the cross: John of Joinville's decision against joining Louis IX's second crusade", at: IMC, Kalamazoo, May 2005.

TOKO, Hirofumi, "'Plato or Socrates' in Constantinople?: the heretical trial of John Italos (1082)", at: Annual Conference of the Historical Association of Tokai University, Tokai University, Hiratsuka, 28 June 2008; "The abbot's power and the monk's labor of the monastery of Stoudios in the days of Symeon the New Theologian", at: 59th Annual Conference of the Society of Historical Studies of Christianity, Kyushu Lutheran College, Kumamoto, 19 September 2008.

TOUATI, François-Olivier, "La papauté et l'ordre de Saint-Jean de Jérusalem au Moyen Âge", at: Paris, École normale supérieure, 4 avril 2008; "La papauté face aux innovations hospitalières de Terre sainte", at: Avignon SSCLE.

TYERMAN, Christopher J., "Henry of Livonia and the Ideology of the Crusaders", Tallinn Conference on Henry of Livonia, May 2008.

WEBER, Benjamin, "Buying Paradise? The Financial Participation to the Crusades against the Turks ans its Spiritual Reward in the Fifteenth Century Papal Theory", at: IMC, Leeds,

July 2008; "Nouveau mot ou nouvelle réalité? Le terme *cruciata* et son utilisation dans les textes pontificaux du XVe siècle", Avignon SSCLE; "Le soutien de la papauté à Mathias Corvin pour sa lutte contre les Turcs entre désengagement pontifical et stratégie nouvelle", at: International congress *Mathias Corvinus and his Time*, Cluj-Napoca, October 2008.

4. Forthcoming publications

ANDREI, Filippo, ed., Ps.-Romualdus, *Glosula super Psalmos*, in: *Corpus Christianorum Continuatio Mediaevalis*, Turnhout, Brepols; "Alberto di Aachen e la Chanson de Jérusalem", in: *Medioevo romanzo*.

BALLETTO, Laura, "Ricordi genovesi di atti notarili redatti a Famagosta intorno alla metà del Trecento", *Epeterida*; "In memoria di Geo Pistarino", *Nuova Rivista Storica*, 2009; "Brevi note su Pera genovese a metà del XIV secolo", in: *Festschrift for John Pryor*, 2009; "Spigolando tra gli atti notarili genovesi del Quattrocento", in: *Miscellanea in onore di Cesare Scalon*, Udine 2009.

BARBER, Malcolm, ed. and trans., with K. Bate, *Letters from the East in the Twelfth and Thirteenth Centuries*, Crusade Texts in Translation, Aldershot: Ashgate, 2009.

BUTTIGIEG, Emanuel, "Knighthood, Masculinity and the Other: The Hospitaller Knights of Malta in the Sixteenth and Seventeenth Centuries", in: *Masculinity and the Other: Historical Perspectives*, ed. Heather Ellis and Jessica Meyer, Cambridge Scholars Publishing.

BELLOMO, Elena, new Latin ed. and trans. into Italian of Caffaro, *Ystoria captionis Almarie et Turtuose, De liberatione civitatum Orientis Liber* and anonymous *Regni Ierosolimitani brevis hystoria*, in Caffaro, *Opere*, in coll. with Antonio Placanica, Edizione Nazionale dei Testi Mediolatini, Società Internazionale per lo Studio del Medioevo Latino (SISMEL); "The First Crusade and the Latin East seen from Venice: the Account of the *Translatio sancti Nicolai*", in: *Early Medieval Europe;* "Sapere nautico e geografia sacra alle radici dei portolani medievali (secoli XII–XIV)", *Quaderni di Storia religiosa;* "Le tessere ed il mosaico: metodi d'indagine ed indirizzi di ricerca sulla milizia templare in Italia nord-occidentale (1142–1308)", *Rivista di Storia della Chiesa in Italia*; "Rinaldo da Concorezzo, archbishop of Ravenna, and the Trial of the Templars in North Italy", in: *The Trial of The Templars. 1307–2007;* "Scorci di un orizzonte mediterraneo: Genova e l'Oriente latino nella storiografia italiana (1951–2001)", in: *Runciman Conference*; Lombardie, Albenga, Barozio, Fontana, Giacomo da Montecucco, Livorno Ferraris, Milan, Modène, Parme, Plaisance, in: DOMMA; "Da Occidente ad Oriente: il magistero di Barozio, maestro templare di Lombardia e d'Italia (1200–c.1205)"; "A neglected source for the History of the Hospital: The Letter of Master Jobert (1171/72–1177) to the Citizens of Savona".

BIRD, Jessalyn, "James of Vitry's Sermons to Pilgrims (Sermones ad peregrinos): A Recontextualization", in: *Essays in Medieval Studies: Proceedings of the Illinois Medieval Association*, 25, 2009; multiple articles for the *Encyclopedia of Medieval Pilgrimage*, ed. Larissa Raylor *et al.*, Leiden: Brill.

BOMBI, Barbara, "Celestine III and the Conversion of the Heathen on the Baltic Sea", in: *Celestine III: in the Light of Europe*, ed. J. Doran and D. Smith, Aldershot 2008; "An archival Network: the Teutonic Knights in the thirteenth and fourteenth centuries", in: Proceedings of the Anglo-Scandinavian Conference, Studies in Church History, Subsidies; trad.: Oliviero di Colonia, *I Cristiani e il favoloso Egitto. Scontri e incontri durante la V crociata*, Studi di Aldo Angelo Settìa e Barbara Bombi (ed. Marietti 1820), Milano, 2009.

BONNEAUD, Pierre, "Dos encomiendas hospitalarias de la Segarra, Cervera y Granyena a finales de la Edad Media", *Miscellana cerverina*.

BORCHARDT, Karl, ed. with Anthony Luttrell and Ekhard Schöffler, *Documents from the Hospitaller Registers on Rhodes Concerning Cyprus, 1409–1459*, Cyprus Research Centre, 2009.

BRATU, Cristian, "Mirrors for princes" in: *Handbook of Medieval Studies: Concepts, Methods, Historical Developments, and Current Trends in Medieval Studies*, ed. Albrecht Classen. Berlin-New York: De Gruyter, 2009; Entries on the "Chronique Saintongeaise", the "Chronique de Saint-Maixent" (co-authored with Régis Rech), "François Bonivard", "Guido de Bazochis", "Le Canarien", "Jean Creton", "Jean Dardel", "Jean Maupoint", "Jean de Roye", the "Miroir historial abregié de France", in: *Encyclopaedia of the Medieval Chronicle*, Leiden-Boston: Brill, 2009; panel on "Authorship in Medieval Chronicles", IMC Kalamazoo, 2009.

BRUNDAGE, James A., "*E pluribus unum*: Regional Variations in Marriage Formation and the Impact of the Professionalization of Law", in: *Regional Variations in Marriage Formation*, ed. Mia Korpiola, Leiden: Brill, 2009; "My Learned Friend: Professional Etiquette in Medieval Courtrooms", in: *Readers, Texts and Compilers in the Earlier Middle Ages: Studies in Medieval Canon Law in Honour of Linda Fowler-Magerl*, ed. Kathleen G. Cushing and Martin Brett, Aldershot: Ashgate; "Tools of the Trade: Medieval Advocates and Their Libraries", in: *To Collect the Minds of the Law: Rare Law Books, Law Book Collections and Libraries*.

BURGTORF, Jochen, with Paul Crawford and Helen Nicholson, eds, *The Trial of the Templars*, Aldershot: Ashgate, 2009.

CARR, Annemarie Weyl, (with Andreas Nicolaides), *Asinou: The Church and Frescoes of the Panagia Phorbiotissa*, Cambridge MA, Harvard University Press, 2009; "Sinai and Cyprus: Holy Mountain, Holy Isle", in: *Holy Image, hallowed Ground*, Symposium on the exhibition at the J. Paul Getty Museum, Los Angeles; "The 'Holy Sepulchre' of St. John Lampadistes, Kalopanagiotis", in: *Hierotopy. New Jerusalems in Byzantium and Medieval Russia*, ed. Alexei Lidov, Moscow: Indrik, 2008; "Iconography and Identity: Syrian Elements in the Art of Crusader Cyprus", in: *Religious Origins of Nations?* ed. Bas ter Haar Romeny, Leiden: Brill, 2009.

CARRAZ, Damien, entries for DOMMA; (avec Jean-Marc MIGNON), "La maison templière de Richerenches (Vaucluse). Premiers résultats de l'étude architecturale et archéologique", *Archéologie du Midi Médiéval;* "*Causa defendende et extollende christianitatis*. La vocation maritime des ordres militaires en Provence (XIIe–XIIIe siècle)", in: *Les ordres militaires et la mer*, *130e Congrès national des sociétés historiques et scientifiques (La Rochelle, 21 avril 2005)*, Paris, CTHS; "*Christi fideliter militantium in subsidio Terre Sancte*. Les ordres militaires et la première maison d'Anjou (1246–1342)", in: *As Ordens Militares e as Ordens de Cavalaria entre o Occidente e o Oriente, Actas do V Encontro sobre Ordens Militares, Palmela, 15 a 18 de fevereiro 2006*, ed. I.C. Ferreira Fernandes, Lisboa; "Military Orders and the Town (Twelfth to Early Fourteenth Centuries). Urban Commanderies Case in the Rhône River Low Valley", *Chronica. Annual of the Institute of History of the University of Szeged*, 6; "L'ordre du Temple dans la Provence du XIIe siècle: l'ambiguïté d'une nouvelle expérience spirituelle à l'âge des réformes", in: *Monachisme et réformes dans la vallée du Rhône (XIe–XIIIe s.), 7e journée d'études du Centre d'Études d'Histoire religieuse Méridionale (Saint-Michel de Frigolet, 18 novembre 2006)*, *Études Vauclusiennes;* "L'emprise territoriale de la seigneurie monastique. Les commanderies provençales du Temple (XIIe–XIIIe siècle)", in: *Les pouvoirs territoriaux en Italie centrale et dans le Sud de la France. Hiérarchies, institutions et langages (12e–14e siècles): études comparées*, actes de la table-ronde de Chambéry, 4 mai 2007, *Mélanges de l'École française de Rome-Moyen*

Âge; "Pro servitio maiestatis nostre. Templiers et hospitaliers au service de la diplomatie de Charles Ier et Charles II", in: *La Diplomatie des États Angevins aux XIIIe et XIVe siècles*, actes du colloque de Szeged-Budapest, 13–16 septembre 2007; "Les ordres militaires et le fait urbain en France méridionale (XIIe–XIIIe siècle)", in: *Moines et religieux dans la ville (XIIe–XVe siècle), Cahiers de Fanjeaux*, no. 44.

CASSIDY-WELCH, Megan, "Images of Blood in the Historia Albigensis of Pierre of les Vaux-de-Cernay", *Heresis*, 2009; "Images of incarceration in late-medieval art", in: *Imagination, Books and Community in Medieval Europe*, ed. G. Kratzmann, MacMillan Art Publishing/State Library of Victoria, 2009.

CHRISTIE, Niall G. F., "Military Organisation and Warfare," in: *The Islamic World*, ed. Andrew Rippin, Routledge, 2008; *The Book of the Jihad of ʿAli ibn Tahir al-Sulami (d. 1106): Text, Translation and Commentary*, Aldershot: Ashgate, 2009.

CONNELL, Charles W., "From Spiritual Necessity to Instument of Torture: Water in the Middles Ages", in: *Proceedings of the Conference on the Nature and Function of Water*, Leiden: Brill, 2008.

COUREAS, Nicholas S., "Commerce between Mamluk Egypt and Hospitaller Rhodes in the mid-fourteenth Century: The Case of Sidi Galip Ripolli", in: *Egypt and Syria in the Fatimid, Ayyubid and Mamluk Eras*, 6, Proceedings of the 14th and 15th HES, ed. U. Vermeulen and K. D'hulster, Leuven, Peeters, 2009; "The Reception of Arabic Medicine in Lusignan and Venetian Cyprus", in: *ibid.*; "Losing the War but Winning the Peace: Cyprus and Mamluk Egypt in the 15th Century", in: *Egypt and Syria in the Fatimid, Ayyubid and Mamluk Eras*, 7, Proceedings of the 16th and 17th HES, Leuven, Peeters, 2010; "A Political History of Nicosia", in: *A History of Nicosia*, ed. D. Michaelides, Nicosia, 2009; "An Ecclesiastical History of Nicosia", in: *ibid.*; Articles on "Gastria" and "Kolossi", DOMMA; "The Greek Monastery of St Margaret of Agros in Lusignan Cyprus", *Revue des Études Byzantines*, 2009; "Between Latins and Native Tradition, The Armenians in Lusignan Cyprus, 1191–1373", in: Actes du Colloque: *L'Église arménienne entre Grecs et Latins (fin XIe – milieu XVe s.)*, ed. G. Dedeyan and I. Augé, Montpellier, 2009; "The French Element in the Culture of Latin Cyprus: A varied, diachronic and multifaceted relationship" [in Greek], in: *Epeteris tes Kypriakes Istorikes Hetaireias*, Nicosia, 2009; "Stunted growth: The Latin Clergy of Cyprus in the Ottoman Period", in: *The Minorities of Cyprus: Development Patterns and the Identity of the Internal-Exclusion* [book], Cambridge Scholars Publishing, Newcastle, 2009.

CRAWFORD, Paul F., "The Involvement of the University of Paris in the Trials of Marguerite Porete and of the Templars, 1308–1310", in: *The Trial of the Templars (1307–2007)*, ed. Jochen Burgtorf, Paul F. Crawford and Helen J. Nicholson, Aldershot: Ashgate, 2009; Articles on "Crusades," "Hospitallers," "Templars," "Children's Crusade," and "Military Religious Orders", in: *New Westminster Dictionary of Church History*, ed. Christopher Ocker *et al.*, Westminster: John Knox Press.

DANSETTE, Béatrice, éd., Bernard de Breydenbach, *Voyage en Terre sainte et en Égypte*, transcription, traduction et notes sous la direction du Professeur Jean Meyers, collectif.

DOUROU-ELIOPOULOU, Maria, *Latin settlement in the ex-byzantine empire (Romania) during the Crusades (13–15th centuries)*. Book.

DENNIS, George T., *The Tactical Constitutions of Leo VI*, Dumbarton Oaks, Washington D.C., 2009.

DEVRIES, Kelly, "Standing up to the Ottoman empire: Civilian Resistance to Turkish Expansionism during the Fifteenth, Sixteenth and Seventeenth Centuries", in: *Military*

Conflicts and Civil Population: Total Wars, Limited Wars, Asymmetrical Wars, Acta XXXIV International Congress of Military History, Trieste, 2008, Rome, International Commission of Military History, 2009; "Women in Medieval warfare", in: *Brill Companion to Women's Military History*, ed. Barton Hacker and Margaret Vining, Leiden: Brill, 2009; "Warfare and the International State System", *Cambridge History of Warfare*, vol. 3: *Early Modern*, ed. Frank Tallett and David Trim, 2009; "Successfull Defenses against Artillery Sieges during the Fifteenth Century: Orléans, 1428–29 and Neuss, 1474–75", in: *Artillerie et Fortification (XIIIe–XVe siècles)*, Presses de l'Université de Rennes, 2009.

DICKSON, Gary, *Medieval Revivalism in Medieval Christianity*, vol. 4, ed. Daniel E. Borstein, *People's History of Christianity*, gen. ed. Denis R. Janz, Minneapolis: Augsburg Fortress Press, 2008.

DONDI, Cristina, "Missale vetus ad usum Templariorum", in: *Dal 'Messale' templare di Reggio Emilia tracce per la storia dell'ordine d'oltremare in Italia*, ed. Dolores Boretti, Reggio Emilia, Cassa di Risparmio Fondazione Manodori, 2008, 70pp.

EDBURY, Peter, A critical edition of Philip of Novara, 'Livre de forme de plait', Cyprus Research Centre, 2009; "The Arrest of the Templars in Cyprus", in: *The Trial of the Templars (1307–2007)*, ed. Jochen Burgtorf, Paul F. Crawford and Helen J. Nicholson, Aldershot: Ashgate, 2009; "Famagusta and the Tradition of History Writing in Frankish Cyprus", in a collection of essays on Medieval Famagusta, ed. Michael Walsh, Nicholas Coureas and Peter Edbury; "The Old French Translation of William of Tyre and Templars", in: *From Holy War to Peaceful Co-habitation;* "Famagusta and the Lusignan Kingdom of Cyprus, 1192–1374", for a volume on Medieval Famagusta, ed. Chris Schabel, Angel Nicolaou-Konnari, Catherine Otten-Froux and Gilles Grivaud; "Ramla: The Crusader town and lordship (1099–1268)", for a collection of essays on Ramla, ed. Denys Pringle; Articles for DOMMA.

EDGINGTON, Susan B., with Carol Sweetenham, *The Chanson d'Antioche: a translation and commentary*, Ashgate: Crusade Texts in Translation series, 2009; "Pagans and Others in the *Chanson de Jérusalem*", in: *Languages of Love and Hate*, ed. S. Lambert and E. James, Turnhout: Brepols, 2009.

EKDAHL, Sven, "Ein Privatbrief vom Herbst 1410 an Margreth Lucassyne, Witwe des Marienburger Bürgermeisters Lucas, im Haus des Danziger Bürgermeisters Konrad Letzkau", in: *Preussenland*, Marburg: N.G. Elwert, 2009; "Aufmarsch und Aufstellung der Heere bei Tannenberg/Grunwald (1410). Eine kritische Analyse", in: *'Krajobraz grunwaldzki' w dziejach polsko-krzyżackich i polsko-niemieckich na przestrzeni wieków. Wokół mitów i rzeczywistości*, ed. Jan Gancewski, Tradycje kulturowe i historyczne ziem pruskich IV, Mrągowo: Wydział Humanistyczny Uniwersytetu Warmińsko-Mazurskiego w Olsztynie, 2009; "Die Söldnerwerbungen des Deutschen Ordens für einen geplanten Angriff auf Polen am 1. Juni 1410", in: *Militärgeschichte des Preussenlandes*, ed. Bernhard Jähnig, Tagungsberichte der Historischen Kommission für ost- und westpreussische Landesforschung, Marburg: N.G. Elwert, 2010; "Tannenberg (bataille de)", in: DOMMA; *Das Soldbuch des Deutschen Ordens 1410/1411. Die Abrechnungen für die Soldtruppen*, ed. Sven Ekdahl, Teil II: Personengeschichtlicher Kommentar, Verzeichnisse und Register, Veröffentlichungen aus den Archiven Preussischer Kulturbesitz 23/II, Köln-Wien: Bölhau, 2010.

FAVREAU-LILIE, Marie-Luise, "Die Venezianer im Heiligen Land", in: *Venedig im Schnittpunkt der Kulturen. Außen-und Innensichten europäischer Reisender im Vergleich*, ed. Felicitas Schmieder and Klaus Herbers (Studi. Schriften des Deutschen Studienzentrums in Venedig); "Die italienischen Seestädte und die islamische Levante (Ägypten und Syrien) im Zeitalter der Kreuzzüge (12./13.Jh.)", in: *The Eastern Mediterranean between Christian Europe and the Muslim Near East (11th–13th centuries)*, Papers of the international conference Istanbul, 17–20 May 2007, Beirut (Schriften des Deutschen Orient-Instituts Beirut/Istanbul).

FLORI, Jean, *Une introduction aux sources de la Première croisade: chroniqueurs ou propagandistes ?* Genève: Droz, 2009.

FOLDA, Jaroslav, "Byzantine Chrysography in Crusader Art and Maniera Greca Painting," in: *Festschrift in Honor of Thomas F. Mathews*, New York, Metropolitan Museum of Art, 2009; "Picturing the First Crusade and Commemorating the Fall of Jerusalem," in: *Acta of the 28th Annual Conference of the Center for Medieval Studies, Fordham University*, (2008), Leiden: Brill, 2009.

GABRIELE, Matthew, "The Provenance of the *Descriptio qualiter Karolus Magnus*: Remembering the Carolingians at the Court of King Philip I (1060–1108) before the First Crusade," *Viator* 39 (2008).

GEORGIOU, Stavros G., "A Contribution to the Study of the Byzantine Prosopography: The Byzantine Family of Opoi", *Byzantion*, 78, 2008; "Eumathios Philokales as Stratopedarches of Cyprus (ca. 1092)", *Byzantinoslavica*, 66, 2008; "Studies on the Court Hierarchy of the Komnenian Era I: The Attribution of the Title of Sebastocrator to Isaac Komnenos, the Third-Born Son of Alexios I Komnenos (1081–1118)", *Epeteris Hetaireias Byzantinon Spoudon*, 53, 2007–2008 [Greek with English summary]; "Studies on the Court Hierarchy of the Komnenian Era II: The Title of Pansebastohypertatos", *Byzantinos Domos*, 17, 2008–2009 [Greek with English summary].

GOURDIN, Philippe, "Les relations politiques et économiques entre l'Italie tyrrhénienne et le Maghreb au XVe siècle », 2001 (2009 ou 2010, BEFAR, Rome); "Des 'Latins de cour' dans la Tunis hafside du XVe siècle", *Revue de l'Institut des Belles Lettres Arabes de Tunis (IBLA)*, 2009; "Les Génois à Tabarka au XVIe siècle", dans *L'expansion génoise et les îles de Méditerranée au XVIe siècle*, Actes du colloque de Mariana, Corse, (octobre 2007), 2009; "La place laissée aux chrétiens dans les pays musulmans. L'exemple du Maghreb au Moyen Âge", dans *Espaces et rituels: traditions et transgressions*, Actes du colloque de l'Université de Picardie-Jules Verne, Amiens, janvier 2008, à paraître en 2009.

VON GUETTNER, Darius, *Poland and the Crusades in the Twelfth Century: The Idea of Holy War and its Reception in The Piast Monarchy*, Brepols, 2009; Entries in: *The Oxford Dictionary of the Middle Ages*, ed. R. E. Bjork, Oxford University Press; "The twelfth-century narrative sources on crusading in Prussia", in: *The Crusading in Iberia and the Baltic region*, ed. I. Fonnesberg Schmidt and T. K. Nielsen, Brill; "The Ultimate Perversion – the End of the Crusader State in Prussia" in: FF, ed. J. Møller Jensen, University of Southern Denmark; Entries in *The Encyclopedia of Medieval Chronicle*, ed. G. Dunphy, Brill; "The Idea of Crusade and the Piasts during the First and Second Crusades," in: *The Church in the Monarchies of the Přemyslids and the Piasts*, Uniwersytet Adama Mickiewicza; "Poland and the Second Crusade," in: *The Second Crusade in Perspective, II: Eastern Europe and the March towards the Holy Land*, ed. J. T. Roche and J. Møller Jensen, Brepols; "Pollexianorum cervicosa feritas – The barbarism of the pagan Pollexians in the literary convention of Master Vincentius", in: *Ars Scribendi. Art of writing in the medieval Bohemia and Poland*, Uniwersytet Adama Mickiewicza; "*Jerosolima capitur a paganis*: Poland and the Third Crusade," in: *The Third Crusade*, ed. J. Møller Jensen and D. Gerish, Turnhout: Brepols.

HARRIS, Jonathan, *The End of Byzantium*, New Haven and London: Yale University Press, 2011; ed. with Catherine Holmes, *Unities and Disunities in the Late Medieval Eastern Mediterranean World*, Oxford University Press, 2010; "Constantinople as City State, c.1360–1453", *ibidem*; "Greeks at the papal curia in the fifteenth century", in: *Greeks,*

Latins, and Intellectual History 1204–1500: Debates, Influences, Impressions, Translations, Migrations, ed. Martin Hinterberger and Christopher D. Schabel, Leuven: Peeters, 2010; with Dmitri Tolstoy, "Alexander III and Byzantium", in: *Alexander III*, ed. Peter Clarke and Anne Duggan, Aldershot: Ashgate, 2009; "Collusion with the infidel as a pretext for military action against Byzantium", in: *Clash of Cultures: the Languages of Love and Hate*, ed. Sarah Lambert and Liz James, Turnhout: Brepols, 2009; "The problem of supply and the sack of Constantinople", in *Fourth Crusade*; "The Goudelis family in Italy after the Fall of Constantinople", *Byzantine and Modern Greek Studies*, 2009.

HUNT, Lucy Anne, "A Christian Arab Gospel Book: Cairo, Coptic Museum ms Bibl. 90 in its Mamluk Context", *Mamluk Studies Review*, Chicago, 2009.

HUNYADI, Zsolt, *Hospitallers in the Medieval Kingdom of Hungary, c.1150–1387*, CEU Medievalia, METEM Könyvek, Budapest–Szeged, 2009, c.260pp.; *A keresztes háborúk kora* [The age of the Crusades], Debrecen: Tóth & Co, 2009, c.130pp.; with László Pósán, *A lovagrendek a középkorban* [Military-religious orders in the Middle Ages], Debrecen: Tóth & Co, 2009, c.130pp.; "King and Crusaders: Hungary and the Second Crusade", in: *The Second Crusade in Perspective*, ed. Jason T. Roche, and Janus Møller Jensen, Turnhout: Brepols, 2009; "The social composition of the military-religious orders in the medieval Kingdom of Hungary", in: *As Ordens Militares e as Ordens de Cavalaria entre o Ocidente e o Oriente*, ed. Isabel Cristina Ferreira Fernandes, Lisboa: Colibri, 2009; "Uses of literacy by the Templars and Hospitallers in the Medieval Kingdom of Hungary", in: *Die Rolle der Schriftlichkeit in den geistlichen Ritterorden des Mittelalters: innere Organisation, Sozialstruktur, Politik*, Ordines Militares – Colloquia Torunensia Historica XV, Hrsg. Roman Czaja und Jürgen Sarnowsky, Toruń: Uniwersytet Mikołaja Kopernika, 2009.

IRWIN, Robert, *Men of the Sword, Men of the Pen, Collected Studies on Mamluk History and Arabic Literature*, Variorum, 2009.

JASPERT, Nikolas, "Die Kreuzzüge – Motivationen, Mythos und Missverständnisse", in: *Stauferzeit – Zeit der Kreuzzüge*, ed. Karl-Heinz Rueß, Göppingen, 2009; "Reconquista. Interdependenzen und Tragfähigkeit eines wertekategorialen Deutungsmusters", in: *Christlicher Norden – Muslimischer Süden. Die Iberische Halbinsel im Kontext kultureller, religiöser und politischer Veränderungen zwischen dem 11. und 15. Jahrhundert*, ed. Alexander Fidora / Matthias Tischler, Frankfurt am Main, 2009; "The election of Arnau de Torroja as ninth Master of the Knights Templar (1180): An enigmatic decision reconsidered", in: *V Encontro sobre Ordens Militares*, ed. Cristina Ferreira Fernandes, Palmela, 2009; "Der Zisterzienserorden in den iberischen Reichen des Hochmittelalters: Ein Sonderweg?", in: *Norm und Realität: Kontinuität und Wandel der Zisterzienser im Mittelalter*, ed. Franz J. Felten / Werner Rösener, Münster 2009; "Zeichen und Symbole in den christlich-islamischen Beziehungen des Mittelalters", in: *Religiosità e civiltà. Le comunicazioni simboliche (secoli IX–XIII)*, ed. Giancarlo Andenna / Gert Melville, Münster 2009.

JENSEN, Janus Møller, "Holger Danske og dansk identitet. En dansk helt i kamp for troen ca. 1450–1550" [Ogier the Dane and Danish identity. A Danish hero fighting for the faith], in: *Tankar om ursprung* [Perceptions of origins], ed. Lars Hermanson and Samuel Edquist, 2009; A volume of articles on the second crusade (with Jason T. Roche) and a volume on medieval enemy images in the age of the crusades (with Christian Høgel), in preparation. Both will be in English. A volume also in English called *Fighting for the faith. Crusade during Renaissance and Reformation* is in the preliminary stages (*cf.* FF).

JOSSERAND, Philippe, avec Carlos de Ayala Martínez, "La actitud de los freiles de las Órdenes

Militares ante el problema de la muerte en Castilla (siglos XII–XIV)", in: *Dejar los muertos enterrar a los muertos. El difunto entre el aquí y el más alla en Francia y en España (siglos XI–XV)*, éd. Isidro Bango Torviso et Xavier Dectot, colloque réuni à Madrid en décembre 1999; "Las Órdenes Militares y el mar en el contexto de la batalla del Estrecho de Gibraltar (mediados del siglo XIII a mediados del XIV)", in: *III Jornadas Rubicenses*, éd. Oswaldo Brito González, colloque réuni à Yaiza (Canaries) en mai 2002; "Les ordres militaires castillans et la bataille du détroit de Gibraltar sous le règne d'Alphonse X", in: *130ᵉ congrès des sociétés historiques et scientifiques*, La Rochelle, 2005; "Nuestro moro que tiene a Cervera. Un châtelain musulman au service de l'ordre de l'Hôpital au début du XIVᵉ siècle", in: *Minorités et régulation sociale au Moyen Âge*, éd. Stéphane Boissellier, François Clément et John Tolan, colloque réuni à Fontevraud en juin 2007; "Les croisades de Terre sainte et les ordres militaires dans les chroniques royales castillano-léonaises (milieu XIIᵉ–milieu XIIIᵉ siècle)", in: *Christlicher Norden, Muslimischer Süden. Die Iberische Halbinsel im Kontext kultureller, religiöser und politischer Veränderungen zwischen dem 11. und 15. Jahrhundert*, éd. Matthias Tischler et Alexander Fidora, Francfort-sur-le-Main, 2007; "Entre dos frentes: aproximación a las empresas militares de los Templerios del Occidente pensionnaire (siglos XII–XIV)", in: *I Congreso Internacional de Historia Medieval. Identidad, conflictuel y representación de la frontera en la España medieval*, éd. Alejandro Rodríguez de la Peña), Huéscar, 2008; "Vientos de cambio. Las transformaciones de la orden de Calatrava a partir de finales del siglo XIII a través de la normativa cisterciense", in: *I Congreso Internacional. El nacimiento de la orden de Calatrava. Primeros tiempos de expansión (siglos XII y XIII)*, éd. Luis Rafael Villegas Díaz, Almagro, 2008; « Portrait de maître en héros croisé. La chronique perdue de Pelayo Pérez Correa », in: *Mémoires, histoires et images des croisades aux derniers siècles du Moyen Age*, éd. Martin Nejedly et Daniel Baloup, Prague, 2008.

JOTISCHKY, Andrew, with Caroline Hull, *The Penguin Historical Atlas of the Bible Lands*, Harmondsworth: Penguin, 2009; "Eugenius III and the Church in the Crusader States", in B. Bolton and A. Jotischky, ed., *Pope Eugenius III*; "The Spoils of War: Sinai MS Gr 512 and its Fate", *Crusades*, 9, 2010.

JUBB, Margaret, Articles on the "Estoires d'Outremer", "Chronique d'Ernoul", and "Eracles (Guillaume de Tyr)" in: *Encyclopedia of the Medieval Chronicle*, ed. Graeme Dunphy, Leiden, Brill, 2009.

KOSTICK, Conor, "The afterlife of Bishop Adhemar of Le Puy", *Studies in Church History*, 45, July 2009; *The Fall of Jerusalem, 1099*, Hambledon Press, 2009, "A further discussion on the authorship of the Gesta Francorum", *Reading Medieval Studies*, XXXIII, 2009, 11pp.; "*Iuvenes* and the First Crusade (1096–1099): knights in search of glory ?", *Journal of Military History*, 2009, 20pp.

KRÄMER, Thomas, article: "Beauvoir", in: DOMMA; "Terror, Torture and the Truth – The Testimonies of the Templars revisited", in: *The Trial of the Templars (1307–2007)*, ed. Jochen Burgtorf, Paul F. Crawford and Helen J. Nicholson, Aldershot: Ashgate, 2009.

LAPINA, Elizabeth, "La représentation de la bataille d'Antioche (1098) sur les peintures murales de Poncé-sur-le-Loir", *Cahiers de Civilisation Médiévale*, 2009.

LIGATO, Giuseppe, "Cristoforo Buondelmonti e la colonna di Teodosio I a Costantinopoli: retaggi medievali e curiosità antiquarie della prima età umanistica", in: *Oriente e Occidente nel Rinascimento*, atti del convegno, Chianciano-Pienza, 16–19 luglio 2007.

LOUD, Graham A., "The chancery and charters of the kings of Sicily (1130–1212)", *English Historical Review*, 2009; "Byzantium and Southern Italy (876–1000), in: *The Cambridge History of the Byzantine Empire*, ed. Jonathan Shepard, 2009; Translations of 'the sack of

St. Vincent on Volturno', 'the Vatican text of King Roger's assizes', Caffaro's 'Capture of Almeria and Tortosa', and part of the 'Casauria Chronicle' in Medieval Italy: a Documentary Survey, ed. K. Jansen, Frances Andrews and Joanna Drell, University of Pennsylvania Press.

LUCHITSKAYA, Svetlana, *Wie starben die Jerusalemer Könige, Das Individuum und die Seinen. Individualität in der okzidentalen und in der russischen Kultur in Mittelalter und früher Zeit/ Mediävistik*, Berlin-New York: W. de Gruyter.

MACK, Merav, "Genoese perspectives of the Third Crusade".

MADDEN, Thomas F., "Crusades" in: *The Oxford Dictionary of the Middle Ages*, Oxford: Oxford University Press.

MARVIN, Laurence W., "The White and Black Fraternities of Toulouse and the Albigensian Crusade, 1210–1211", *Viator*, 2009.

MASÈ, Federica, "Analyse comparée de chantiers d'urbanisation au cours du Moyen Age: les ecclésiastiques vénitiens à l'œuvre et l'entrée en scène de l'état (XIe–XVIe siècle)", in: *VIIIth International Conference of the European Association of Urban History*, Stockholm, 2006, sous presse à l'Ecole française de Rome; "Le quartier des Vénitiens à Constantinople du XIe au XIIIe siècle: la fin d'un réseau?", sous presse aux Presses universitaires de Strasbourg; "Recours à l'écrit et exploitation de la propriété urbaine", *XXXIXe Congrès de la Société des Historiens Médiévistes de l'Enseignement Supérieur, Le Caire, 2008*, Paris, Publications de la Sorbonne, 2009.

MENACHE, Sophia, "Iglesia y Monarquía en la Edad Media Tardía: Conflictos y Semejanzas", in: *Aragon en la Edad Media*, ed. Luis Garcia Guijarro, Historica et Archaelogica Mediaevalia; "Emotions from the Holy Land – The First Crusader Kingdom", in: *Proceedings of the Huesca Conference, 2007*, ed. Luis Garcia Guijarro; "Self-Image and 'the Other' in the Second Crusader Kingdom: 1187–1291", in: Studies in Medieval Culture in Honour of Aaron Gurevitch [Russian], ed. Svetlana Luchitskaya, Kirill Levinson, *et al.*; "In Pursuit of Peace in a Conflicted Area: The Israeli Contribution to the History of the Crusades", in: *Proceedings of the Teruel Conference*, ed. L.Garcia Guijarro.

MICHAUDEL, Benjamin, "La campagne de Saladin en Syrie côtière à la fin du XIIe siècle", *Annales Islamologiques*, IFAO, Cairo, 2009.

MITCHELL, P. D., "The spread of disease with the crusades", in: *Between Text and Patient: The Medical Enterprise in Medieval and Early Modern Europe*, ed. B. Nance and E. F. Glaze, Florence: Sismel; "Military Medicine", in: *Oxford Dictionary of the Middle Ages*, ed. R. E. Bjork, Oxford: Oxford University Press; "Medical treatment", "Disease", in: *Medieval Warfare and Military Technology: an Encyclopedia*, ed. C. Rogers, Oxford: Oxford University Press; "Medical and nursing care in the military orders", i: W. T. Reich and J. S. C. Riley-Smith, ed., *Chivalry, Honor and Care*, Washington: Georgetown University Press; with D. Syon and D. Stern, "Water installations at Crusader ʿAkko", *ʿAtiqot*.

MORTON, Nicholas, *The Teutonic Knights in the Holy Land, 1190–1291*, Boydell, 2009.

MURRAY, Alan V., "The Capture of Jerusalem in Western Narrative Sources of the First Crusade", in *Jerusalem the Golden: The Conquest of the Dream (From the West to the Holy Land)*, ed. Luis Garcia-Guijarro Ramos; "Henry the Interpreter: Language and Communication in the Thirteenth-Century Livonian Mission", in *Crusading and Chronicle Writing on the Medieval Baltic Frontier: The Chronicle of Henry of Livonia*, ed. Carsten Selch Jensen, Linda Kaljundi and Marek Tamm, Aldershot, 2009.

NAUS, James L., *Crusades: Medieval Worlds in Conflict*, ed. Thomas F. Madden, James Naus and Vince Ryan, Ashgate.

NICHOLSON, Helen J., *The Knights Templar on Trial: the trial of the Templars in the British Isles*, to be published by The History Press in May 2009.

NICOLAOU-KONNARI, Angel, "Apologists or Critics? The Reign of Peter I of Lusignan (1359–1369) viewed by Philippe de Mezières and Leontios Makhairas", International Symposium *The Age of Philippe de Mezières: Fourteenth-Century Piety and Politics between France, Venice, and Cyprus* organised by Renate Blumenfeld-Kosinski, Kiril Petkov, and Chris Schabel (Nicosia, 11–13 June 2009); Review of 'Damien Coulon, Catherine Otten-Froux, Paule Pagès, and Dominique Valérian (ed.), *Chemins d'outre-mer. Études d'histoire sur la Méditerranée médiévale offertes à Michel Balard*, Université Paris I – Panthéon Sorbonne, Byzantina Sorbonensia – 20, Centre de Recherches d'Histoire et de Civilisation Byzantines, Publications de la Sorbonne, Paris 2004, 2 vol., *Jahrbuch der Österreichischen Byzantinistik* (2009); "Genoa: the Formation of the City and its Foreign Policy", in: N. Moschonas, ed., *The Italian Maritime Cities (Amalfi, Pisa, Genoa, Venice) and the Eastern Mediterranean*, National Hellenic Research Foundation, 6th Series of Lectures (Athens 2005), Athens, 2009 [in Greek]; "Anonymous Short Chronicle of Cyprus (Chronica delli Re, et successi del Regno di Cipro di Gallico in Italiano tradutta)", "Boustronios, Georgios", "Machairas, Leontios", in: *Encyclopedia of the Medieval Chronicle*, ed. Graeme Dunphy, Brill, 2009.

NICOLLE, David, *Citadels of Christendom: Crusader Fortifications 1097 to 1573 AD*, Osprey, Oxford 2009; *Late Mamluk & Early Ottoman Military Equipment in the Light of Finds from the Citadel of Damascus*, IFPO, Damascus, 2009; Articles "Équipement", "Armement", "Archers", "Bannière", "Escadron", "Piétons", in DOMMA; Article "Seljuks", in: *Encyclopedia of Medieval Warfare*, New York; *The Arab-Islamic Conquests (7th–8th centuries AD)*, Osprey, Oxford 2009; Articles "Ali al-Rawandi", "Abu Bakr Najm al-Din Muhammad Ibn ʿAbd al-Rahman al-Shayzari", "Mubarakshah, Fakhr-i Mudabbir"; "Abu ʿAli al-Hasan Ibn ʿAli Nizam al-Mulk", "Usama Ibn Munqidh", for *Encyclopedia of Military Philosophy*; *Saracen Strongholds: 2 The Central & Eastern Islamic Lands 12th–16th centuries*, Osprey, Oxford 2009; "Byzantine, Western European, Islamic and Central Asian Influence in the Field of Arms and Armour from the 7th to 14th century AD", in: A. Atasoy, ed., *Crosspolinations*, Cambridge 2009.

O'MALLEY, Gregory, "The Ottomans and the earlier Tudors (1485–1547)", in: *Fighting for the Faith during the Renaissanvce and Reformation*, ed. J. M. Jensen, 2010 [FF].

PERRA, Photeine V., *The Lion against the Crescent: The First Venetian-Ottoman War and the Conquest of the Helladic Lands (1463–1479)*, Athens: Papazisis Publications, 2009 [Greek]; "The Peloponnese in the course of 1460's: The sources testimony", in: *Peloponnesus during Turkish and Venetian Dominion (1460–1821)*, 3rd International Congress of Oriental and African Studies [Greek].

PHILLIPS, Simon D., "Hospitaller Relations with the Local Communities on Cyprus", in: Proceedings of the Fourth International Congress of Cypriot Studies, Society of Cypriot Studies, Nicosia; "The Hospitallers' Acquisition of the Templar Lands in England", in: *The Trial of the Templars (1307–2007)*, ed. Jochen Burgtorf, Paul F. Crawford and Helen J. Nicholson, Aldershot: Ashgate, 2009.

PIANA, Mathias, "From Montpèlerin to ʿarflbulus al-Mustafiaddfl – The Frankish-Mamluk Succession in Old Tripoli", in: *Egypt and Syria in the Fatimid, Ayyubid and Mamluk Eras*, VI, ed. Urbain Vermeulen, Kristof D'hulster, Orientalia Lovaniensia Analecta 183, Leuven: Peeters, 2009.

POWER, Amanda, *Roger Bacon and the Defence of Christendom*, Cambridge University Press, 2010.

PRYOR, John H., "The 'Cargo Manifest' of a Pisan galley, 1281", in: *Festschrift* for Andrew Watson, ed. B. Catlos; "A medieval Mediterranean maritime revolution: Crusading by Sea ca 1096–1204", in: Proceedings of the Symposium, *Tradition and transition: maritime studies in the wake of the Byzantine shipwreck at Yassi Ada, Turkey*, at the Institute of nautical Archaeology, Texas A&M University, College Station, Texas 2–4 November, 2007.

PURKIS, William J., "The Past as a Precedent: Crusade, Reconquest, and Twelfth-Century Memories of a Christian Iberia", in: *Medieval Memories: Case Studies, Definitions, Contexts*, ed. L. Dolezalova, Brill, 2009.

RACINE, Pierre, *Frédéric Barberousse, illusions et désillusions d'un empereur médiéval*, Paris, Perrin, 2009.

RICHARD, Jean, "La correspondance entre le pape Innocent IV et les princes musulmans d'Orient", *Oriente moderno*, t. 88; "Les familles féodales franques dans le comté de Tripoli", *Congrès de Kaslik*, 2002; "Papacy and Cyprus. Introduction historique", *Bullarium Cyprium*, I, 2010.

SCHRYVER, James G., "Towards an Archaeology of Borderlands: Boundary Negotiation in Frankish Cyprus," in: *Boundaries in Depth and in Motion*, I. William Zartman, ed., pp.198–230, University of Georgia Press; "Ruins, Remembrance and Royalty: The O'Conors' use of Ancient Monuments and Landscapes", *Beyond Saints and Scholars: Irish Medieval Studies in the Twenty-First Century*, St. Louis University, St. Louis, MO, October 27, 2008.

SHAGRIR, Iris, "The Visitatio Sepulchri at the Latin Church of the Holy Sepulcher in Jerusalem", *Al-Masaq: Islam & the Medieval Mediterranean*, 2009; "Bynames in the Latin Kingdom of Jerusalem", in: *Anthroponymie et déplacements: migrations, réseaux, métissage*, ed. M. Bourin, Madrid: Publications de la Casa de Velazquez, 2009.

SHAWCROSS, Teresa, *The Chronicle of Morea: Historiography in Crusader Greece*, Oxford: Oxford University Press, 2009; "Greeks and Franks after the Fourth Crusade: Identity in the Chronicle of Morea", in: *Languages of Love and Hate: Conflict, Communication, and Identity in the Medieval Mediterranean*, ed. S. Lambert and L. James, Brepols: Turnhout, 2009; "'Listen, all of you, both Franks and Romans': The Narrator in the Chronicle of Morea", in: *Byzantine History as Literature*, ed. R. Macrides, Aldershot: Ashgate; "The Lost Generation (ca.1204–ca.1222): Political Allegiance and Local Interests in the Crusader Lands", in: *The Eastern Mediterranean in the Thirteenth Century: Identities and Allegiances*, ed. J. Herrin, Aldershot: Ashgate; "The Making of a Byzantine Emperor in Crusader Constantinople (1204–1261): Visual Symbols, Ritual and Titulature", in: *Between Byzantines and Turks: Understanding the Late Medieval Eastern Mediterranean World*, ed. K. Fleet, J. Harris, and C. Holmes, Oxford University Press.

SMITH, Caroline, "Saints and sinners at sea on the first crusade of Saint Louis", in: *Crusades: Medieval worlds in conflict*, proceedings of the Saint Louis University crusade history Symposium (15–18 February 2006), ed. T. Madden, V. Ryan and J. Naus, Aldershot: Ashgate.

STAPEL, Rombert, "'Onder dese ridderen zijn oec papen'. De priesterbroeders in de balije Utrecht van de Duitse Orde, 1350–1600", *Jaarboek voor Middeleeuwse Geschiedenis*, 11, Uitgeverij Verloren, Hilversum 2008 [Prosopographical research on the priest-brethren of the Utrecht bailiwick of the Teutonic Order, 1350–1600].

STOHLER, Patrick, "Wahrnehmung und Traditionsbildung in einem Traktat des 14. Jh."; "Das 18. Jahrhundert und 'der Kreuzzug': Genese und Entwicklung eines Konzepts".

TESSERA, Miriam Rita, *Papato, Chiesa e regno latino di Gerusalemme nel XII secolo*, Milano,

Vita & Pensiero, autumn 2009; "Orientalis Ecclesia: The Papal Schism of 1130 and the Latin Church of the Crusader States", *Crusades*, 8, 2009.

TAMMINEN, Miikka, "Who Deserves the Crown of Martyrdom? Martyrs in the Crusade Ideology of Jacques de Vitry (1160/70–1240)" in: *Coping with Old Age and Death – Passages from Antiquity to the Middle Ages II*, Brepols, 2009; "Enemy Gods and Godless Enemies: the Theme of Pollution in the Crusade Propaganda of Jacques de Vitry and Eudes de Châteauroux", in: *Medieval Images of the Other in Scandinavia, Western Europe and Byzantium*, University of Southern Denmark, Brepols, 2009; "Saracens, Schismatics and Heretics in Jacques de Vitry's *Historia Orientalis*", published by the Finnish Institute at Rome in Acta Instituti Romani Finlandiae (AIRF), 2009.

TOKO, Hirofumi, "The Studite monastic tradition and Symeon the New Theologian", *The Journal of Historical Studies of Christianity*, 63, 2009.

TOUATI, François-Olivier, "'Aime et fais ce que tu veux'. Les chanoines réguliers et l'assistance charitable au Moyen Âge", in: *Les chanoines réguliers, émergence, expansion (XIe–XIIe siècles)*, dir. M. Parisse, Presses de l'Université de Saint-Étienne, 2009; articles "Egypte", "Hôpitaux" "Lèpre, lépreux", "Maccabées", "Médecine", "Saint-Lazare de Jérusalem", in: DOMMA; "Orient latin: nouveaux objets, nouvelle histoire ?", *Médiévales*.

VILLEGAS-ARISTIZABAL, Lucas, "Anglo-Norman involvement in the conquest of Tortosa as part of the Second Crusade", *Crusades*, 8, 2009.

WEBER, Benjamin, "Papes et croisades. XIVe–XVe siècles. Historiographie et perspectives" in: *Les croisades tardives. Historiographie et perspectives de recherche;* "Vain Hope or Insincere Justification? Jerusalem in 15th Century's papal letters", in: *Fighting for the Faith during Renaissance and Reformation*, [FF], ed. J.M. Jensen and J.M. Roche.

5. Work in progress

BALARD, Michel, La Méditerranée au Moyen Age; Les épices au Moyen Âge.

BARBER, Malcolm, *The Crusader States in the Twelfth Century*, Yale University Press [book].

CRAWFORD, Paul F., see *Bulletin*, 27, 2007, p. 49.

BELLOMO, Elena, "Diplomazia e Crociata nel Mediterraneo di inizio Trecento: il Francescano savonese Filippo Brusserio"; "I Sentieri della memoria: crociata e reliquie oltremarine in un'anonima cronaca monferrina medievale" [articles]; The Spanish military Orders in Italy (XIII–XVI centuries).

BIRD, Jessalyn, Women and the Crusades; with Edward Peters and James Powell, *Sourcebook for the Crusades, c.1204–c.1274*, University of Pennsylvania Press.

BISAHA, Nancy, with Robert Brown, translation of Pius II's *De Europa*, and study dealing with Pope Pius II's concept of Europe and Asia.

BRATU, Cristian, Book project on the Emergence of the Author in French Medieval Chronicles/ L'Émergence de l'auteur dans les chroniques médiévales en prose.

BRUNDAGE, James A., "Canon Law in the Medieval Battle of the Disciplines" [article]; "Quaestiones Cantabrigienses", edition of a manuscript collection of *quaestiones disputatae*.

BRYSON, David, A paper for MO5, Cardiff, Sept. 2009 "Power, Region and Identity: the mystery of the Templar Preceptors Raymond del Boisso and Raymond Robert".

CARRAZ, Damien, "Confréries de *milites* et défense de l'orthodoxie (XIe–XIIIe siècles)", *Noblesse et défense de l'orthodoxie (XIIe–XVIIe siècles)*, Journée d'études, Université de

Rennes II, 27 octobre 2007; "Les enquêtes générales de la papauté sur l'ordre de l'Hôpital (1338 et 1373). Analyse comparée dans le prieuré de Saint-Gilles", *Les pratiques politiques de l'enquête princière (Occident, XIIIe–XIVe siècles)*, colloque international d'Aix-en-Provence-Marseille, 19–21 mars 2009; "Aux origines de la commanderie hospitalière de Manosque. Le dossier des comtes de Forcalquier dans les archives de l'ordre", *La mémoire des origines propres chez les ordres religieux militaires au Moyen Âge*, Göttingen, Mission Historique Française en Allemagne, juin 2009; "Ordres militaires et élites constituées. Rapport", *Élites et ordres militaires au Moyen Âge. Hommage à Alain Demurger*, Lyon, octobre 2009.

CASSIDY-WELCH, Megan, "Memories of space in thirteenth-century France: displaced people after the Albigensian crusade", *Parergon: Journal of the Australian and New Zealand Association for Medieval and Early Modern Studies*, 2010; Imprisonment in the Medieval Religious Imagination; The Medieval Refugee: Memory, Space and the Aftermath of War in thirteenth-century France (supported by an Australia Research Council Grant from 2008–2011).

CHRISTIE, Niall G. F., *Preaching Holy War: Crusade and Jihad, 1095–1105*, with Deborah Gerish (to be published by Ashgate in 2010).

COLEMAN, Edward, "Ireland and the Crusades. A survey of the evidence"; "The Italian city communes and the Crusades in the twelfth century" [articles].

CONNELL, Charles W., *Public Opinion in the Middles Ages* [book].

CORRIE, Rebecca W., *Conradin Bible: The Expectation of Hybridity* [book]; Arezzo Choir Manuscripts inthe 13th Century; *Images of the Virgin between East and West* [book].

COUREAS, Nicholas S., The Latin Church in Cyprus, 1313–1378 (Cyprus Research Centre); The Life of Peter Thomas By Philippe de Mézières: A Translation into English (Cyprus Research Centre).

CUSHING, Dana, Identification of crusaders and site visits, ms *De itinere navali* (Accademia delle Scienze, Torino, MM.V.II).

DICKSON, Gary, Rite de Passage ? The Children Crusade and Medieval Childhood.

EDBURY, Peter, Paper on the Ernoul and Eracles mss account of the battle of Cresson (for MO5, Cardiff, Sept. 2009); Paper on Guillaume de Machaut's Prise d'Alexandrie and the tradition of history writing in Cyprus; Paper on cross cultural relations as illustrated by the legal treatises of John of Ibelin and Philip of Novara; *The Third Crusade* [book]; with Elizabeth Walker, *Chronique d'Amadi* (translation); further work on the manuscripts of the Ernoul, Bernard the Treasurer and the Old French Continuation of William of Tyre.

EDGINGTON, Susan B., "Medicine", a chapter in *Conflict and Cohabitation* (provisional title), ed. C. Kostick; Guido da Vigevano's *Regimen sanitatis:* edition, translation and commentary; an update on novels of the First Crusade.

VAN ELST, Toon, From Dover to Damiata: Former *Brabançons* and Flemish mercenaries in the Fifth Crusade.

FAVREAU-LILIE, Marie-Luise, *The Italians in the Latin and Muslim East* (Die Italiener im Heiligen Land, Teil 2).

FOLDA, Jaroslav, Study of the origins and development of Chrysography in Byzantine and Crusader painting.

FOREY, Alan J., The Papacy and the Spanish Reconquest; Western converts to Islam; Paid Troops in the service of the military Orders.

GABRIELE, Matthew, *The Legend of Charlemagne and the Origins of the First Crusade*, under consideration (expected 2010).

GARCÍA-GUIJARRO, Luis, The ideology of War in the Iberian Peninsula in the Central Middle Ages: Reconquista and Crusade; The Catalan counties and Aragón: their relationship with the papacy, 10th–11th centuries.

GILCHRIST, Marianne M., Research on the career and reputation of Conrad of Montferrat.

GILMOUR-BRYSON, Anne, The guilt of the Templars according to the major principal and secondary sources.

VON GUETTNER, Darius, Conquest of Prussia 1147–1230 (research project); History of Prussia before 1400; Translation of a chronicle written by Master Vincentius (so called Wincenty Kadlubek) in 1190–1208: *Magistri Vincentii dicti Kadlubek Chronica Polonorum* into English; The Hospitallers and Templars in the Kingdom of Poland: early settlements; Charters of Polish Dukes for The Hospitallers and Templars; The Piast Dynasty and the Crusading Orders; Henry, Duke of Sandomierz, a Polish Crusader to Jerusalem; Holy War in the Baltic Littoral before 1230; Duchy of Ostrog.

HAMILTON, Bernard, *The Crusades and the Wider World*, Continuum Books, 2009; with Andrew Jotischky, *Latin and Orthodox Monasticism in the Crusader States*, CUP, 2009.

HARRIS, Jonathan, Research into the last 150 years before the fall of Constantinople.

HODGSON, Natasha, Women and the Albigensian Crusade, Leeds IMC.

JOSSERAND, Philippe, éd. avec Nicole Bériou, DOMMA; avec Mathieu Olivier, coordination d'une table-ronde à la Mission Historique Française en Allemagne à Göttingen en juin 2009, *La mémoire des origines propres dans les ordres religieux-militaires au Moyen Age.*

HOUSLEY, Norman, *Regenerating the Crusade: the Catholic Church and the Turkisch Treat, 1453–1505*, Oxford University Press.

IRWIN, Robert, The contribution of 20th century Arabists to the historiography of the Crusades; Orientalism.

JOTISCHKY, Andrew, with Bernard Hamilton, *Latin and Orthodox Monasticism in the Crusader States*, CUP; *The Crusaders and the Peoples of the Crusader States*, London: Continuum.

KEDAR, Benjamin Z., *A cultural history of the Kingdom of Jerusalem* [book]; Inventio patriarcharum – part 2 [article]; The battle of Arsuf, 1191[article].

KOSTICK, Conor, *Social unrest and the Second Crusade* [Post-Doctoral Research sponsored by the Irish Research Council for the Humanities and Social Sciences]; *The Crusades: Conflict and Cohabitation* [sponsorised by the Centre of Mediterranean and Near Eastern Studies at Trinity College Dublin and the Long Room Hub].

LIGATO, Giuseppe, Il mito della crociata nel frammento di mosaico pavimentale recuperato dalla basilica di S. Maria Maggiore a Vercelli.

LOUD, Graham A., *The Crusade of Frederick Barbarossa*, Ashgate: Crusader Texts in Translation series, expected publication 2010.

LUCHITSKAYA, Svetlana, *Daily life in the Latin kingdom of Jerusalem* [book].

MACK, Merav, "Captives, merchants and diplomats in the buffer-zone of the crusades", paper in preparation for the WHA 2009 meeting.

MADDEN, Thomas F., Crusading and the development of Venetian identity.

MASÈ, Federica, Histoire urbaine. Les Vénitiens à l'œuvre en métropole et en Méditerranée orientale: acquisition, urbanisation et gestion publique et/ou privée des quartiers et donc du patrimoine foncier et immobilier (choix politiques, religieux, sociaux et économiques);

"La gestion comptable des patrimonies immobiliers urbains entre Venise et les possessions vénitiennes en Méditerranée orientale (XIIIe–XVe siècle)", 14èmes Journées d'Histoire de la Comptabilité et du Management-Academy of Accounting Historians 2009 Research Conference, 26–27 mars 2009, Université Paris-Sud 11; "Franceschina Bratti, femme indépendante, et sa relation privilégiée avec le monastère de San Giorgio Maggiore à Venise (seconde moitié du XVe siècle)", Colloque en l'honneur d'André Vauchez, Paris, Institut de France, Paris, 30 novembre–2 décembre 2009.

MESCHINI, Marco, *Percezione dell'idea di crociata nella Cristianità dei secoli XI–XIII*. [Progetto di ricerca finanziato dal Consiglio Nazionale delle Ricerche, Roma, 2008–2009].

NICHOLSON, Helen J., *The Trial of the Templars in the British Isles, 1308–1311*, Ashgate [edition with translation of the surviving testimonies]; *The Knights Templars' English Estates, 1308–11*, transcription and analysis of the inventories and accounts of the Templars' properties in England during the trial of the Templars; ed., with Jochen Burgtorf and Paul Crawford, the papers from the sessions 'The Trial of the Templars, 1307–2007' at the IMC Kalamazoo and IMC Leeds, 2007; ed. papers relating to the Military Orders presented at Avignon SSCLE.

MITCHELL, P. D., Bioarchaeological analysis of latrine soil from multiple crusader period cesspools from, Israel; Archaeological study of health in the crusader population of Blanchegarde Castle, Israel.

NICOLAOU-KONNARI, Angel, *History of Limassol*, co-editor with Chris Schabel, Medochemie Series 2, 2009/10; with C. Schabel, "Frankish and Venetian Limassol", *ibidem*; *Two Cypriots of the Diaspora: Works and Days of Pietro and Giorgio de Nores* [Cyprus Research Centre] Nicosia, 2010; *The Encounter of Greeks and Franks in Cyprus in the Late Twelfth and Thirteenth Centuries. Phenomena of Acculturation and Ethnic Awareness*, Birmingham University Press, Ashgate, 2010; *Medieval Famagusta*, co-editor with G. Grivaud, C. Otten-Froux, C. Schabel, and A. Weyl Carr, 2010/11; "Women and Family Life (in Lusignan and Venetian Famagusta)", *ibidem*.

NICOLLE, David, book on the Grand Chevauchee of John of Gaunt in 1373, for the Osprey "Raid" series; book on Medieval Islamic fortification in North Africa and the Iberian Peninsula, for the Osprey 'Fortress' series; general history of the Ottoman conquest of the rump Byzantine Empire and the Balkans from 1300 to 1500, for Pen & Sword publishers.

PAUL, Nicholas L., *Remembering the crusades: myth, image, and identity* [collected essays], co-edited with Suzanne Yeager; Tradition, memory, and identity: the medieval noble family and the crusading past [monograph]; "Boamundus sapientissmus: propaganda, literacy, and a warlord's wisdom" [article]; "Ripoll and Jerusalem: Crusade, identity, and dynastic legitimacy in Catalonia" [article].

PAVIOT, Jacques, "Les croisades tardives (XIVe–XVIe s.): bilan historiographique et état de la recherche: France et Angleterre", in: *Les croisades tardives (XIVe–XVIe s.): bilan historiographique et état de la recherche. Actes du colloque de toulouse, 22–23 mars 2007*, Toulouse, 2009; "Boucicaut et la croisade", in: *La noblesse et la croisade: piété, diplomatie, aventure. Actes du colloque de Prague, 26–27 octobre 2007*, Toulouse, 2009; "Inciter le roi de France à partir à la croisade: Le sermon *Exaltavi lignum humile* de Pierre de La Palud (1332) et le *Discours du voyage d'outre-mer* de Jean Germain (1451)", in: *Croisade et discours de guerre sainte à la fin du Moyen Âge. Légitimation, propagande, prosélytisme. Actes du colloque de Toulouse, 27–28 mars 2008*, Toulouse, 2009; "Des images pour la croisade? À propos de la Flagellation de Piero della Francesca et de Notre-Dame de Grâce de Cambrai, in: *Mémoires, histoires et images des croisades aux derniers siècles du Moyen Âge. Actes du colloque de Prague, 20–21 novembre 2008*, Toulouse, 2009 ou 2010.

PHILLIPS, Jonathan, A long-term research project on Italy and the Crusades (monograph and articles); Ibn Jubayr's travels to the Muslim Near East [article]; Perceptions of crusading in the modern world [article].

PHILLIPS, Simon D., The military orders on Cyprus and Rhodes in the Late Middle Ages; The Hospitaller Priory at Clerkenwell and the local community 1400–1540.

PRYOR, John H., Crusading by sea: the maritime history of the Crusades, 1095–1291 (continuing, previously notified). This is now planned as a two-volume work. The first will be devoted to the maritime technology, the ships and technologies and techniques of navigation and naval warfare; Sea Technologies, in: The Cambridge History of War. Volume two: War and the medieval world, ed. Reuven Amitai, Anne Curry, David Graff; new edition of the *Libellus de expugnatione Terrae Sanctae per Saladinum* with facing translation, commentary, and studies of several themes of the work. [This work is being undertaken together with a group of students, including Keagan Brewer, Deyel Dalziel-Charlier, Jennifer Green, and James Kane].

PURKIS, William J., The Cistercians and the Crusades: Narratives, Texts and Commemorative Traditions.

RICHARD, Jean, *Bullarium Cyprium*, t. III (Jean XXII–Grégoire XI).

RUBENSTEIN, Jay, Holy War and History: The First Crusade at the End of the Time.

SCHRYVER, James G., with Tasha Vorderstrasse, A study of the Port St. Symeon ware from Hama, in the National Museum of Copenhagen.

SHAGRIR, Iris, Creating a Frankish Capital: Jerusalem in the 12th Century.

TESSERA, Miriam Rita, Il sogno di re Amalrico, la reliquia della Vera Croce e la canonizzazione di Bernardo di Clairvaux [article]; Melisenda, regina di Gerusalemme [book].

TOUATI, François-Olivier, *Les actes et documents relatifs à Saint-Lazare de Jérusalem (Orient-Occident)*, édition; "Le récit des origines de Saint-Lazare de Jérusalem: mythe ou réalité(s) ?", *La mémoire des origines dans les ordres religieux militaires au Moyen Âge*, Göttingen, Mission Historique Française en Allemagne, 25–26 juin 2009; "Éléments pour une prosopographie des frères de Saint-Lazare de Jérusalem", *Élites et ordres militaires au Moyen Âge*, Lyon, 21 octobre 2009.

TYERMAN, Christopher J., *Crusade Historiography*, Manchester University Press.

6. Theses in progress

ANTAKI MASSON, Patricia, The topography of Crusader Tyre, Doctorat, Université de Poitiers, France.

BALDWIN, Philip B., Pope Gregory X and the Crusades, PhD, Queen Mary, University of London.

BARBÉ, Hervé, Le château de Safed et son territoire durant la période des croisades, PhD, Hebrew University of Jerusalem, supervised by Benjamin Z. Kedar and Nicolas Faucherre.

BISHOP, Adam, The development of crusader law in the twelfth century, PhD, Centre for Medieval Studies, University of Toronto.

BUTTIGIEG, Emanuel, A study of the Hospitaller Knights of Malta, with reference to nobility, faith and masculinity, 1580–1700, PhD, Peterhouse, University of Cambridge.

CARLSSON, Christer, The Hospitaller Commanderies in Scandinavia: A study of their economic development 1291–1536, PhD, University of Southern Denmark in Odense.

CARR, Michael, Motivations and Response to Crusades in the Aegean: c.1302–1348, PhD, Royal Holloway, University of London, supervised by Jonathan Harris.

COSGROVE, Walker Reid, Clergy and Crusade: the Church of Languedoc during the Albigensian Crusade, PhD, Saint-Louis University, USA

CUSHING, Dana, Critical edition, translation and reconstruction of the Germanic Crusaders' sealift and siege of Almohad Silves (1189–1191) from an eyewitness account.

FROUMIN, Robin, Crusader churches built on the remains of Byzantine Churches in the Holy Land and Pilgrims who visited these Churches, MA, Haifa University, supervised by Adrian Boas.

GOURINARD, Henri, Egypt in medieval itineraries, MA, Hebrew University of Jerusalem, supervised by Benjamin Z. Kedar and Martin Aurell.

IKONOMOPOULOS, Konstantinos, Byzantium and Jerusalem, 9th–13th Centuries, PhD, Royal Holloway, University of London, supervised by Jonathan Harris.

KOOL, Robert, The Circulation and Use of Coins in the Latin kingdom of Jerusalem, 1099–1291, PhD, Hebrew University of Jerusalem, supervised by Benjamin Z. Kedar and Michael Metcalf.

KRÄMER, Thomas, Ritterorden und Klerus in Südfrankreich und Süddeutschland. Studien zu Konflikten und Konfliktbewältigung in Provence/ Languedoc und Bayern/ Baden-Württemberg (Military Orders and clergy in Southern France and Southern Germany. Studies to conflicts und conflict resolution in Provence/ Languedoc and Bavaria/ Baden-Wuerttemberg [Working title].

MORRIS, April Jehan, Imag[in]ing the 'East': The Holy Land as Threat and Desire in the Aquitaine, 1095–1195, PhD, Art History, University of Texas at Austin.

MYLOD, Liz, Pilgrimage in the Holy Land in the Thirteenth Century, PhD, Institute for Medieval Studies, University of Leeds.

NAUS, James L., Crusading and Capetian Dynastic Ideology: 1099–1226, PhD, Saint Louis University.

ORDMAN, Jilana, Feeling like a Crusader: Crusader Affect and Crusade Theology, 1095–1291, PhD, Loyola University, Chicago.

PACKARD, Barbara, Remembering the First Crusade through Narrative History, 1099–c. 1300, PhD, Royal Holloway, University of London.

PARK, Danielle, 'Leaving their spouses and sons behind for the sake of the Lord': Regencies, Lords and Lands – the Impact of the Crusades to the Holy Land on Medieval West, c.1095–1255, PhD, Royal Holloway, University of London.

PARKER, Kenneth Scott, The Impact of the Crusades on the Christian Churches of the Near East, 1291–1402, PhD, Royal Holloway, University of London, supervised by Jonathan Harris.

PERRY, Guy, The Career and Significance of John of Brienne, king of Jerusalem, emperor of Constantinople, PhD, University of Oxford.

PETRE, James, Crusader Castles of Cyprus: The Fortifications of Cyprus under the Lusignans, 1191–1489, PhD, Cardiff University, supervised by Denys Pringle.

RONEN-RUBIN, Jonathan, Intellectual Activities in Acre, 1191–1291, PhD, Hebrew University of Jerusalem, supervised by Benjamin Z. Kedar and Laura Minervini.

RUSSELL, Eugenia, Encomia to St Demetrius in Late Byzantine Thessalonica, PhD, Royal Holloway, University of London, supervised by Jonathan Harris.

RYAN, Vincent, Mary Wills It: The Cult of the Virgin Mary and the Crusading Movement during the High Middle Ages, PhD, Saint Louis University.

SMITH, Thomas, Honorius III and the papal correspondence of the Fifth Crusade, MA, University of Kent, supervised by Barbara Bombi.

STAPEL, Rombert, Cronike van der Duytscher Oirden ["Jüngere Hochmeisterchronik"], PhD, Leiden University/Fryske Akademy.

STOHLER, Patrick, The Making of an Idea: Europe (1096–1291), PhD, University of Basle, C.H.

TAMMINEN, Miikka, Who Deserves the Crown of Martyrdom? Martyrs in the Crusade Propaganda of Jacques de Vitry (1160/70–1240) and Eudes de Châteauroux (c.1190–1273) PhD, University of Tampere, Finland.

WEBER, Benjamin, Lutter contre les Turcs. Les formes nouvelles de la croisade pontificale au XVe siècle, Doctorat, Université de Toulouse, France.

ZELNIK, Joseph, *Silent enim leges inter arma*?: Laws of War in the Latin Kingdom of Jerusalem, PhD, Bar-Ilan University, Israel, supervised by Yvonne Friedman.

7. Fieldwork planned or undertaken recently

ANDREI, Filippo, Italian Literature; Romance Philology; Medieval Latin Literature.

ANTAKI MASSON, Patricia, Archaeological study of the cistercian abbey of Belmont (Lebanon).

BALARD, Michel, A chapter for the *History of Famagusta* (Chypre).

CARLSSON, Christer, Further research-excavations is planned to be carried out in Værne Hospitaller Commandery in Norway in the summer of 2009.

FOLDA, Jaroslav, Study of paintings with Chrysography in collections and exhibitions in Washington, D.C., Baltimore, London, and Cambridge during 2008.

KEDAR, Benjamin Z., coordinating excavations in Acre's Genoese quarter.

MICHAUDEL, Benjamin, June 2009: Syro-French joint archaeological survey in the Nahr al-Kabir al-Shamali region (Coastal Syria) to locate and study the architectural remains of medieval settlements; October–November 2009: 3rd campaign of the Syro-French joint archaeological mission on Saladin/Saône/Sahyun Castle (Syria).

MITCHELL, P.D., Research visit to Blanchegarde castle excavation in Israel to study health in the crusader population there, June 2008.

NICOLLE, David, Permission obtained from the Syrian Ministry of Antiquities to make an in-depth study of a substantial hoard of 13th–14th century Islamic military equipment, found in the Citadel of Damascus.

8. News of interest to members

a) Conferences and seminars

Entre Orient et Occident: nommer les lieux au Moyen Âge. Journée d'étude organisée par François-Olivier Touati, Université de Tours, 13 mars 2009: point de départ d'une plus large enquête sur les interférences toponymiques et la réciprocité des transferts entre Occident et Orient latin.

Les projets de croisade et leurs objectifs. XIIIe–XVIIIe siècles. Colloque international coordonné par Jacques Paviot, Institut de France et Fondation Simone et Cino del Duca, Paris, 12–13 juin 2009.

La Mémoire des Origines dans les Ordres religieux-militaires au Moyen Âge. Colloque international coordonné par Philippe Josserand et Olivier Mathieu, Mission historique française en Allemagne (MHFA), Göttingen, 25–26 juin 2009.

The Military Orders: Politics and Power. Fifth conference on the Military Orders, coord. Helen Nicholson, will have taken place at Cardiff University, 3–6 September 2009.

Cultural Encounters during the Crusades. International congress at the Danish Institute in Damascus, 5–9 October 2009. Programme and registration at: www.damaskus.dk

The Crusades Studies Forum at Saint Louis University is a venue for the presentation of current research, the discussion of recent scholarship, and the exploration of new directions in topics relating to the Crusades. Participants include those local to the Saint Louis region as well as distinguished scholars from across the globe. All are welcome to attend and participate in the forum. During the 2008/2009 academic year, CSF presenters include Gary Dickson (University of Edinburgh), Jay Rubenstein (University of Tennessee), Laurence Marvin (Berry College), and Alan Murray (University of Leeds). For more information see: http://crusades.slu.edu.

A seminar on crusade archaeology in the North is scheduled to take place in Norway in 2009 organized jointly by Christer Carlsson and Janus Møller Jensen. The members of SSCLE will receive further information via the mailing list.

John Pryor is planning a month in North America in February–March 2010, beginning with the Crusades Conference at Saint Louis University on 17–20 February and ending with the meeting of the Medieval Academy of America in New Haven in March. In between he plans to visit several other North American universities.

A new and modern museum is now beeing built on the battlefield of Grunwald (Tannenberg, Žalgiris) in Poland. The inauguration will take place at the 600 anniversary of ther battle in July 2010.

b) Other news

The direction of archaeological excavations at Apollonia-Arsuf is carried out from now on by Dr. Oren Tal, of Tel Aviv University.

An international exhibition dedicated to the History of the Military Orders between the 12th and 16th centuries will be held at the Hôtel-Dieu in Beaune (Burgundy, France) from November 2010 until March 2011.

9. Members' queries

With regard to his new edition and translation of the *Libellus de expugnatione Terrae Sanctae per Saladinum* (see *Work in Progress*), John Pryor knows of only four MSS containing the work: BL Cotton Vespasian DX and Cotton Cleopatra B.I, BndeF MS. Lat. 15076, and London, College of Arms, MS. Arundell II. If any member knows of any other MS. containing the work, he would be very grateful for the reference.

10. Officers of the Society

President: Professor Bernard Hamilton. Honorary Vice-Presidents: Professor Jean Richard, Professor Jonathan Riley-Smith, Professor Benjamin Z. Kedar, Professor Michel Balard.

Secretary: Professor Luis García-Guijarro Ramos. Assistant Secretaries: Dr Adrian Boas, Secretary to the President and to the Officer for Postgraduate Members; Professor Manuel Rojas, Conference Secretary. Editor of the Bulletin: Professor François-Olivier Touati. Treasurer: Professor James D. Ryan. Website: Dr Zsolt Hunyadi.

Committee of the Society: Professor Antonio Carile (Bologna), Professor Robert Huygens (Leiden), Professor Hans Eberhard Mayer (Kiel).

11. Income and expenditure for the SSCLE from 1 October 2007 to 30 September 2008

This report shows SSCLE assets in separate columns, totaling the amount in each of the three currencies in which these funds are held. Whenever notes that follow refer to the total assets or liabilities of the society, these are totaled and reported in sterling followed by the equivalent amount in dollars and in euros. In each case these are computed using the prevailing rates as of 30 September 2008 (i.e.: £1 = $1.78 = €1.27), rounded to the nearest whole unit.

Using these currency equivalencies, on 1 October 2007, the total of SSCLE funds equaled £13,562 (or $24,141 or €17,224). On 30 September 2008 the society's assets totaled £17,694 (or $31,494 or €22,471). 369 subscriptions were paid during this reporting period, the majority of which (274) were for membership with the journal (*Crusades* Vol. 7). Additional funds were received for back issues of the journal. Because the society is billed for the journal only after it is published, and *Crusades* Vol. 7 was published November 2008, the bill for that volume, and for back issues ordered during the fiscal year but unbilled as of 30 September 2008, must be considered as pending charges against SSCLE's assets. These charges, totaling £6,000 (or $10,680 or €7,620), are roughly equal to one-third of the society's funds on deposit as of the close of the reporting period. The expenditure of funds for the journal (£4,560, reported above) was in payment for *Crusades* Vol. 6, for 2007, which was mailed out in December 2007.

Notable expenses this period include funds for the President's travel to Avignon, to finalize plans for the Conference held there in August 2008. The conference was very successful, academically, socially and fiscally. From the fiscal perspective, registration was sufficient to cover all the expenses, and the surplus realized will augment the society's funds. Since the accounts of the conference remain open at the time of this writing, however, and the anticipated surplus will not be paid until the 2008–9 fiscal year, that sum will be included in next year's report.

Notable developments during the past year include the decision, made at the Avignon meeting, to increase the subscription for dues with the journal *Crusades* to £25 (or the equivalent in the other two currencies). This will help insure the fiscal health of the society going forward. In addition, at the request of many members, beginning October 2008, payment for dues can be made for up to three years at one time. Also noteworthy is the significant increase in the number of subscriptions paid in US dollars. This is partly due to the growing use of Paypal, an on-line bank with which the society has an account, through which members can pay their subscriptions using a credit card. This option is particularly attractive to members whose currency is other than sterling, the euro, or the dollar, because they pay lower bank charges when using Paypal.

It is apparent that the society is fiscally stronger than it has been over the past several years. It is hoped that this year's modest increase in dues, coupled with rising subscriptions to the society, will restore the healthy reserve the treasury formerly enjoyed. No further increase in dues is needed or anticipated at this time, but, in the unlikely event that the cost of publishing *Crusades* were to rise, there would be an immediate proportional increase in

U.S. Accounts ($)	U.K. Accounts (£)	Euro Accounts (€)
BALANCES CARRIED FORWARD, 1 OCTOBER 2007		
$15,949.47	**£1,283.06**	**€4,214.73**
INCOME		
$8,529.66 Subs. etc., received	£2,279.50 Subs. etc., received	€3,450.60 Subs. etc.
$43.24 Interest received	£6.64 Interest received	
$8,572.90 Total income	**£2,286.14 Total income**	**€3,450.60 Total income**
EXPENDITURES		
$479.64 Postage, supplies, etc.	£0.00 Postage	€174.40 Postage
$44.16 Bank charges	£0.00 Bank charges	€67.96 Bank charges
	£4,560.00 Expenditures for journal	€165.90 Travel – preparation conference
($523.80) Total expenditures	**(£4,560.00) Total expenditures**	**(€408.26) Total expenditures**
SURPLUS OF INCOME OVER EXPENDITURES		
$8,049.10	**(£2,273.86)**	**€3,042.34**
TRANFER OF FUNDS BETWEEN CURRENCIES		
($8,000.00) Transferred to UK	£3,991.62 FromUS$	(€1,000.00) Transferred to UK£
	£777.91 From €	
BALANCES ON HAND, 30 SEPTEMBER 2008		
US Accounts ($)	UK Accounts (£)	Euro Accounts (€)
$15,998.57	**£3,778.73**	**€6,257.07**

the rate for dues with the journal. As in past years, I remain grateful to the members of the SSCLE for their support, encouragement and unfailing courtesy.

Respectfully submitted,
James D. Ryan, Treasurer

12. List of members and their addresses

(* Recorded as new member)

Prof. Baudouin van den ABEELE, Rue C. Wolles 3, 1030 Bruxelles, BELGIUM; vandenabeele@mage.ucl.ac.be

Dr David S. H. ABULAFIA, Gonville and Caius College, Cambridge CB2 1TA, ENGLAND, UK

Brian ALLISON LEWIS, c/o Sabic, P.O. Box 5101, Riyadh 11422, SAUDI ARABIA

Dr Martín ALVIRA CABRER, Universidad Complutense de Madrid, C/Marañosa, 2, 4° Izquierda, 28053 Madrid, ESPAÑA; martinalvira@yahoo.es

Prof. Reuven AMITAI, The Eliyahu Elath Chair for the History of the Muslim Peoples, Institute of Asian and African Studies, Hebrew Univ., Jerusalem 91905, ISRAEL; r_amitai@mscc.huji.ac.il

Dr Monique AMOUROUX, 2, Avenue de Montchalette, Cassy, 33138 Lanton, FRANCE; monique.amouroux@aliceadsl.fr

*Jan Anckaer, Rue des Fleuristes 5, B-1082 Brussels, Belgium; jananckaer@yahoo.com

Prof. Alfred J. ANDREA, 161 Austin Drive, Apartment 3, Burlington VT 05401, USA; aandrea@uvm.edu

*Dr Filippo ANDREI, 1644 Oxford Street, Apt. 5, Berkeley CA, 94709, USA; filandrei@berkeley.edu

Patricia ANTAKI, Domaine de Gaillat, 8, Chemin de Lasseguette, 64100 Bayonne, FRANCE; patriciaantaki@yahoo.com

Dr Benjamin ARBEL, School of History, Tel-Aviv Univ., Tel-Aviv 69978, ISRAEL; arbel@post.tau.ac.il

Dr Marco AROSIO, Università del Sacro Cuore, Milano, ITALY; marco_arosio@tin.it

Dr Thomas S. ASBRIDGE, Dept. of History, Queen Mary and Westfield College, Univ. of London, Mile End Road, London E1 4NS, ENGLAND, UK; t.s.asbridge@qmul.ac.uk

Prof. Zubaida ATTA, 19 Sphinx Building – Sphinx Square, Apartment 85, Muhandessin, Cairo, EGYPT; prof.zatta@yahoo.com

Dr Hussein M. ATTIYA, 20 Ahmed Sidik Street, Sidi Gaber El-Shiek, Alexandria, EGYPT; husseinattiya@hotmail.com

*Marc J. AYERS, 1029 Mountain Oaks Drive, Birmingham, AL 35226, USA; mayers@baboult.com

Prof. Taef Kamal EL-AZHARI, International Affairs Dept., Qatar Univ., Faculty of Arts, 2713 Doho, QATAR; taef@gega.net

Dr Mohammed AZIZ, P.O. Box 135513, Beirut, LEBANON

Dr Bernard S. BACHRACH, Univ. of Minnesota, Dept. of History, 633 Social Sciences Building, Minneapolis MN 55455, USA; bachr001@tc.umn.edu

Dr Xavier BAECKE, Koningsvarenweg 9, 9031 Gent, BELGIUM; xavierbaecke@hotmail.com

Dr Dan BAHAT, P.O. Box 738, Mevasseret Zion 90805, ISRAEL; danbahat@gmail.com

Archibald BAIN, Dufftown, Banffshire AB55 4AJ, SCOTLAND, UK; ArchieBain@aol.co.uk or gilliesbeag@yahoo.co.uk

Prof. Michel BALARD, 4, rue des Remparts, 94370 Sucy-en-Brie, FRANCE; Michel.Balard@univ-paris1.fr

Prof. Susan BALDERSTONE, Adjunct Professor in Cultural Heritage, Deakin Univ., Melbourne, AUSTRALIA; susan.balderstone@bigpond.com

*Philip B. BALDWIN, RR 2, 5738 County Road 1, Consecon, Ontario, K0K 1T0, CANADA; pipbb@yahoo.com

Laura BALLETTO, Via Orsini 40/B, 16146 Genova, ITALY; Laura.Balletto@lettere.unige.it

Prof. Malcolm BARBER, Dept. of History, Univ. of Reading, P.O. Box 218, Whiteknights, Reading RG6 6AA, ENGLAND, UK; m.c.barber@reading.ac.uk

Dr Michael BARDOT, Dept. Behavioral and Social Sciences, Lincoln Univ., 820 Chestnut Street, Room 310 Founders Hall, Jefferson City MO 65102, USA; Bardotm@lincolnu.edu

Prof. John W. BARKER, 5611 Longford terrace, Madison, WI, 53711 USA; jwbarker@wisc.edu

Dr Sebastian BARTOS, 319 Oak Center Place, Valdosta GA 31602, USA; sebartos@hotmail.com

Dr Bruce BEEBE, 1490 Mars Lakewood OH 44107, USA; lgbeebe@aol.com

Prof. George BEECH, Western Michigan Univ., Dept. of History, Kalamazoo MI 49008-5020, USA; george.beech@wmich.edu

Dr Gregory D. BELL, Duke Univ., History Dept., Durham NC 27708, USA; gdb@duke.edu

Elena BELLOMO, via dei Rospigliosi 1, 20151 Milano, ITALY; elena.bellomo@libero.it

*Colin Bennett, PO Box 0408, United States Military Academy, West Point, NY 10997-0408, USA; colin.bennett@usma.edu

Matthew BENNETT, 58 Mitchell Avenue, Hartley Wintney, Hampshire RG27 8HG, ENGLAND, UK; mattbennett@waitrose.com

Dr Nora BEREND, St Catharine's College, Cambridge CB2 1RL, ENGLAND, UK; nb213@cam.ac.uk

Ilya BERKOVICH, Peterhouse, Cambridge CB2 1RD, ENGLAND, UK; ib275@cam.ac.uk

Steven BIDDLECOMBE, 65 Conybeare Road, Canton, Cardiff CF5 1GB, WALES, UK

Jessalynn BIRD, 1514 Cortland Drive, Naperville IL 60565, USA; jessalynn.bird@iname.com

Prof. Nancy BISAHA, Vassar College, History Department, Box 711, 124 Raymond Avenue, Poughkeepsie NY 12604, USA; nabisaha@vassar.edu

*Adam BISHOP, 3400 Rhonda Valley, #53, Mississauga, Ontario, CANADA, L5A 3L9; adam.bishop@utoronto.ca

Charl BLIGNAUT, P.O. Box 566, Ventersdorp 2710, North-West Province, SOUTH AFRICA; charlblignaut777@yahoo.com

Prof. John R. E. BLIESE, Communication Studies Dept., Texas Tech Univ., Lubbock TX 79409, USA

Dr Adrian J. BOAS, 10 HaRav Berlin Street, Jerusalem, 95503 ISRAEL or Institute of Archaeology, Hebrew Univ. of Jerusalem, Jerusalem 91905, ISRAEL; adrianjboas@yahoo.com

Prof. Mark S. Bocija, Columbus State Community College, 550 E. Spring Street, Columbus OH 43216-1609, USA; mbocija@cscc.edu

Louis Boisset, Université Saint-Joseph de Beyrouth, BP 166 778, Achrafieh, Beirut, LEBANON; lboisset@usj.edu.lb

Brenda M. Bolton, 8 Watling Street, St Albans AL1 2PT, ENGLAND, UK; brenda@bolton.vianw.co.uk

Dr Barbara Bombi, School of History, Rutheford College, Univ. of Kent, Canterbury CT2 7NX, ENGLAND, UK; bb55@kent.ac.uk

Pierre Bonneaud, Chemin des chênes verts, Pont des Charrettes, 30700 Uzès, FRANCE; pierrebonneaud@yahoo.es

Prof. Karl Borchardt, c/o Monumenta Germaniae Historica, Ludwigstraße 16, 80539 München, for letters: Postfach 34 02 23, 80099 München, GERMANY; karl.borchardt@mgh.de

Prof. Charles R. Bowlus, History Dept., Univ. of Arkansas, 8081 Mabelvale Pike, Little Rock AR 722099-1099, USA; Haymannstraße 2A, 85764 Oberschleißheim, GERMANY; crbowlus@ualr.edu

Prof. Charles M. Brand, 180 South 38th Street, Boulder, CO 80305, USA; cmbrand@indra.com

Dr Cristian Bratu, Baylor University, One Bear Place #97392, Waco, TX 76798-7392, USA; Cristian_Bratu@baylor.edu

Dr Michael Brett, School of Oriental and African Studies, Univ. of London, Malet Street, London WC1E 7HP, ENGLAND, UK

Heidi Bridger, The Old Station House, Kedington Road, Sturmer, Essex CB9 7XR, ENGLAND, UK; hbridger@hotmail.com

Robert Brodie, Saint Agnes Lodge, 16 High Saint Agnesgate, Ripon, North Yorkshire HG4 1QR, ENGLAND, UK; robertbrodie@btinternet.com

Dr Judith Bronstein, Ilanot 29/2, Haifa 34324, ISRAEL; Judith_bronstein@hotmail.com

Prof. Elizabeth A. R. Brown, 160 West 86th Street PH4, New York NY 10024, USA; earbrown160@aol.com

Prof. James A. Brundage, 1102 Sunset Drive, Lawrence KS 66044-4548, USA; jabrun@ku.edu

*David Bryson, 1935 Westview Drive, North Vancouver, B.C., Canada V7M3B1; dbryson1935@telus.net

*Andrew Buck, 6a Old Lodge Lane, Purley, Surrey, CR8 4DE, ENGLAND, UK; ledzep_4_ever_69@hotmail

Dr Marcus G. Bull, Dept. of Historical Studies, Univ. of Bristol, 13-15 Woodland Road, Clifton, Bristol BS8 1TB, ENGLAND, UK; m.g.bull@bris.ac.uk

Dr Jochen Burgtorf, California State Univ., Dept. of History, 800 North State College Boulevard, Fullerton CA 92834-6846, USA; jburgtorf@fullerton.edu

Prof. Charles Burnett, The Warburg Institute, Univ. of London, Woburn Square, London WC1H 0AB, ENGLAND, UK; charles.burnett@sas.ac.uk

The Rev. Prof. Robert I. Burns, 300 College Avenue, Los Gatos CA 95030, USA

Dr Peter Burridge, Harmer Mill, Millington, York YO4 2TX, ENGLAND, UK

Emanuel Buttigieg, 'Dar San Anton', 20, Triq l-Imqades tal-Qedem, Hal Tarxien. TXN1463. MALTA; emanuel_buttigieg@yahoo.co.uk

Ane Lise BYSTED, Dept. of History, Univ. of Southern Denmark, Campusvej 55, 5230 Odense M, DENMARK; bysted@hist.sdu.dk

Dr J. P. CANNING, History Dept. Univ. College of North Wales, Bangor, Gwynedd, WALES, UK

Prof. Franco CARDINI, P.O. Box 2358, 50123 Firenze Ferrovia, ITALY

Christer CARLSSON, Litsbyvägen 65, 18746 Täby, SWEDEN; cc_arch75@hotmail.com

Dr Annemarie Weyl CARR, Division of Art History, Southern Methodist Univ., P.O. Box 750356, Dallas TX 75275-0356, USA; during the calendar year 2009: 608 Apple Road, Newark DE 19711, USA; acarr@smu.edu

Michael CARR, 18b Leighton Crescent, Kentish Town, London NW5 2QY, ENGLAND, UK; M.Carr@rhul.ac.uk

Dr Damien CARRAZ, 14, rue François Arago, 84000 Avignon, FRANCE; damien.carraz@wanadoo.fr

Marc CARRIER, 1038 Péladeau, St-Jean-sur-Richelieu, Québec, J3A 2A2, CANADA; marc.t.carrier@umontreal.ca

Dr Megan CASSIDY-WELCH, School of Historical Studies, Univ. of Melbourne, Victoria 3010, AUSTRALIA; mecass@unimelb.edu.au

Prof. Brian A. CATLOS, Dept. of History, Univ. of California Santa Cruz, Stevenson Academic Center, 1156 High Street, Santa Cruz CA 95064-1077, USA; bcatlos@ucsc.edu

Prof. Fred A. CAZEL Jr., 309 Gurleyville Road, Storrs Mansfield CT 06268-1403, USA

Dr Simonetta CERRINI, Via Carducci 68A, 15076 Ovada (Alessandria), ITALY; alloisiocerrini@inwind.it

William CHAPMAN, 68 Carisbrooke Gardens, Yeovil, Somerset BA20 1BY, ENGLAND, UK; bill-chapman@pilgrim-env.co.uk

Dr Martin CHASIN, 1125 Church Hill Road, Fairfield CT 06432-1371, USA; mchasin@att.net

Nikolaos G. CHRISSIS, Flat 16, Victoria House, South Lambeth Road, SW8 1QT, London, UK; N.Chrissis@rhul.ac.uk

Dr Katherine CHRISTENSEN, CPO 1756 Berea College, Berea KY 40404, USA; katherine_christensen@berea.edu

Dr Niall G. F. CHRISTIE, Corpus Christi College, 5935 Iona Drive, Vancouver, BC, V6T 1J7, CANADA; niallchristie@yahoo.com

Ioanna CHRISTOFORAKI, Aristotelous 26, Chalandri, Athens 15234, GREECE; joanna.christoforaki@archaeology.oxford.ac.uk

Prof. Giulio CIPOLLONE, Piazza S. Maria alle Fornaci 30, 00165 Roma, ITALY; cipolloneunigre6009@fastwebnet.it

Dr G. H. M. CLAASSENS, Departement Literatuurwetenschap, Katholieke Universiteit Leuven, Blijde Inkomststraat 21, Postbus 33, 3000 Leuven, BELGIUM

Pierre-Vincent CLAVERIE, 9 rue du Bois-Rondel, 35700 Rennes, FRANCE; pclaverie@ac-rennes.fr

David J. CLOVER, 5460 Ocean View Drive, Oakland CA 94618, USA; rollsroyceggm24@yahoo.com

Paul M. COBB, Dept. of Near Eastern Languages & Civilizations, University of Pennsylvania, Philadelphia, PA 19104, USA; pmcobb@sas.upenn.edu

Dr Penny J. COLE, Trinity College, 6 Hoskin Avenue, Toronto, Ontario M5S 1HB, CANADA; pjcole@trinity.utoronto.ca

*Dr. Edward COLEMAN, Dept. of History and Archives, Faculty of Arts and Celtic Studies, University College Dublin, Belfield, Dublin 4, IRELAND; Email: edward.coleman@ucd.ie

Prof. Eleanor A. CONGDON, Dept. of History, Youngstown State Univ., 1 University Plaza, Youngstown OH 44555, USA; eacongdon@ysu.edu

Prof. Charles W. CONNELL, P.O. Box 6023, History Dept., Northern Arizona Univ., Flagstaff AZ 86011, USA; charles.connell@nau.edu

Prof. Giles CONSTABLE, Institute for Advanced Study, 506 Quaker Road, Princeton NJ 08540, USA

Prof. Olivia Remie CONSTABLE, Dept. of History, Univ. of Notre Dame, Notre Dame IN 46556-0368, USA; constable.1@nd.edu

Prof. Robert F. COOK, French Language and General Linguistics Dept., Univ. of Virginia, 302 Cabell Hall, Charlottesville VA 22903, USA

Barry COOPER, Director of Studies, Loretto School, Linkfield Road, Musselburgh, East Lothian EH21 7RE, SCOTLAND, UK; bcooper@loretto.com

Prof. Rebecca W. CORRIE, Phillips Professor of Art, Bates College, Lewiston ME 04240, USA; rcorrie@bates.edu

Walker Reid COSGROVE, History Dept., Saint Louis Univ., 3800 Lindell Boulevard, Saint Louis MO 63108, USA; cosgrowr@slu.edu

Prof. Ricardo Luiz Silveira da COSTA, Rua Joao Nunes Coelho 264 apto. 203, Ed. Tom Jobim – Bairro Mata da Praia – Vitória   Espírito Santo (ES), CEP 29.065-490, BRAZIL; ricardo@ricardocosta.com

Dr Nicholas S. COUREAS, P.O. Box 26619, Lykarittos, 1640 Nicosia, CYPRUS; ncoureas@moec.gov.cy

The Rev. H. E. J. COWDREY, 19 Church Lane, Old Marston, Oxford 0X3 0NZ, ENGLAND, UK; fax (0)1865 279090

Prof. Paul F. CRAWFORD, 5 Mum Drive, Washington PA 15301, USA; crawford_p@cup.edu

Dana CUSHING, PO Box 187, Grand Island, NY 14072, USA; dana@antimony.biz

Charles DALLI, Dept. of History, Faculty of Arts, Univ. of Malta, Msida MSD06, MALTA; cdalli@arts.um.edu.mt

Philip Louis DANIEL, Archivist, Equestrian Order of the Holy Sepulchre of Jerusalem, 37 Somerset Road, Meadvale, Redhill, Surrey RH1 6LT, ENGLAND, UK; fax 01737-240722

Dr Béatrice DANSETTE, 175, Boulevard Malesherbes, 75017 Paris, FRANCE; beatricedansette@orange.fr

Americo De Santis, 88 East Main Street, Box Number 141, Mendham NJ 07945, USA; ricodesantis@hotmail.com

Prof. Bernhard DEMEL O.T., Leiter des Deutschordenszentralarchivs, Singerstraße 7, 1010 Wien, AUSTRIA; tel. 513 70 14

*John A. DEMPSEY, 218 Edgehill Road, Milton MA 02186-5310, USA; jdempsey@wsc.ma.edu

Dr Alain DEMURGER, 5, rue de l'Abricotier, 95000 Cergy, FRANCE; ademurger@orange.fr

Prof. George T. DENNIS, S.H. Jesuit Center, 300 College Avenue, Los Gatos, CA 95031, USA; gdennis@calprov.org

*Eugene DE RASS, Po Box 35043, Ottawa ON K1Z 1A2, Canada; eugene959@gmail.com

*Kelly DEVRIES, Department of History, Loyola College, 4501 N Charles Street, Bltimore, MD 21210-2699, USA; kdevries@loyola.edu

Dr M. Gary DICKSON, History, School of History, Classics, and Archaeology, Univ. of Edinburgh, Wm. Robertson Building, 50 George Square, Edinburgh EH8 9JY, SCOTLAND, UK; garydickson1212@blueyonder.co.uk

Prof. Richard DIVALL, 301 / 228 The Avenue, Parkville, Melbourne 3052, AUSTRALIA; maestro@spin.net.au

Dr Erica Cruikshank DODD, 4208 Wakefield Place, Victoria, B.C. V8N 6E5, CANADA; edodd@uvic.ca

César DOMÍNGUEZ, Universidad de Santiago de Compostela, Facultad de Filologia, Avda. Castealo s/n, 15704 Santiago (La Coruna), ESPAÑA

Cristina DONDI, 128 Berkeley Court, Glentworth Street, London NW1 5NE, ENGLAND, UK; christina.dondi@history.ox.ac.uk

*Dr John DORAN, Dept of History and Archaeology, University of Chester, Parkgate Road, Chester, CH1 4BJ, ENGLAND, UK; j.doran@chester.ac.uk

Ara DOSTOURIAN, Box 420, Harmony RI 02829, USA

Maria DOUROU-ELIOPOULOU, Kephallenias 24, Althea 19400, Attiki, GREECE; meliop@cc.uoa.gr

John DURANT, 32 Maple Street, P.O. Box 373, West Newbury MA 01985, USA

Dr Valerie EADS, 308 West 97th Street, New York NY 10025, USA

Prof. Richard EALES, School of History, Univ. of Kent, Canterbury CT2 7NX, ENGLAND, UK; r.eales1@btinternet.com

Ana ECHEVARRÍA ARSUAGA, Facultad de Geografía e Historia, Departimento de Historia Medieval, Av. Conde de Aranda 1, 3° E, 28200 San Lorenzo del Escorial (Madrid), ESPAÑA; anaevjosem@hotmail.com

Prof. Peter W. EDBURY, Cardiff School of History and Archaeology, Cardiff Univ., Cardiff CF10 3EU, WALES, UK; edbury@cf.ac.uk

Dr Susan B. EDGINGTON, 3 West Street, Huntingdon, Cambs. PE29 1WT, ENGLAND, UK; s.b.edgington@btinternet.com

Dr Axel EHLERS, Gehägestraße 20 N, 30655 Hannover, GERMANY; aehlers1@gwdg.de

Prof. Sven EKDAHL, Sponholzstraße 38, 12159 Berlin, GERMANY; Sven.Ekdahl@t-online.de

Dr Ronnie ELLENBLUM, 13 Reuven Street, Jerusalem 93510, ISRAEL; msronni@pluto.mscc.huji.ac.il

Prof. Steven A. EPSTEIN, History Dept., Univ. of Kansas, Lawrence KS 66045-7590, USA; sae@ku.edu

Dr Helen C. EVANS, The Medieval Dept., The Metropolitan Museum of Art, 1000 Fifth Avenue, New York NY 10028, USA; helen.evans@metmuseum.org

Michael EVANS, 301 West Broomfield, Kewardin 10-03, Mount Pleasant MI 48858, USA; m_r_evans@hotmail.com

Prof. Theodore EVERGATES, 146 West Main Street, Westminster MD 21157, USA

John C. FARQUHARSON, 19 Long Croft Lane, Cheadle Hulme, Cheadle, Cheshire SK8 6SE, ENGLAND, UK; jc.f@btinternet.com

Nicolas FAUCHERRE, 4, rue de l'Hôtel de Ville, 44000 Nantes, FRANCE; n.faucherre@wanadoo.fr

Prof. Marie-Luise FAVREAU-LILIE, Kaiser-Friedrich-Straße 106, 10585 Berlin, GERMANY; mlfavre@zedat.fu-berlin.de

Gil FISHHOF, Dept. of Art History, Tel Aviv Univ., Tel Aviv 69978, ISRAEL; fishhofg@post.tau.ac.il

Dr Jean FLORI, 69, rue Saint Cornély, 56340 Carnac, FRANCE; flori.jean@wanadoo.fr

Prof. Jaroslav FOLDA, Dept. of Art, Univ. of North Carolina, Chapel Hill NC 27599-3405, USA; jfolda@email.unc.edu

Dr Michelle FOLTZ, M.D., PMB 33, P.O. Box 1226, Columbus MT 59019, USA; mfoltz@imt.net

Dr Iben FONNESBERG SCHMIDT, Dept. of History, Aalborg Univ., Fibgerstraede 5, 9220 Aalborg, DENMARK; imfs@ihis.aau.dk

Luis Adão DA FONSECA, Rua do Revilão 521, 4100-427 Porto, PORTUGAL; luisadaofonseca@netcabo.pt

Harold FORD, P.O. Box 871009, Stone Mountain GA 30087, USA; tsh212511@aol.com

Dr Alan J. FOREY, The Bell House, Church Lane, Kirtlington, Oxon. OX5 3HJ, ENGLAND, UK; foreys@somail.it

Edith FORMAN, 38 Burnham Hill, Westport CT 06880, USA

Barbara FRALE, via A. Gramsci 17, 01028 Orte (VT), ITALY; barbara-frale@libero.it

Dr John FRANCE, History Dept., Univ. of Wales, Swansea SA2 7PP, WALES, UK; j.france@swansea.ac.uk

Daniel Franke, 242 Up Meigs Street, Rochester NY 14607, USA; dfranke@mail.rochester.edu

Prof. Yvonne FRIEDMAN, 3 Ben Zion, Jerusalem 95423, ISRAEL; yfried@mail.biu.ac.il

Robin FROUMIN, P.O. Box 9713, Hadera 38541, ISRAEL; robin_fr@zahav.net.il

Michael and Neathery FULLER, 13530 Clayton Road, St Louis MO 63141, USA

Prof. Matthew GABRIELE, Dept. of Interdisciplinary Studies, Virginia Tech, 342 Lane Hall (0227), Blacksburg VA 24061-0227, USA; mgabriele@vt.edu

Cecilia GAPOSCHKIN, 6201 Wentworth Hall, Room 110, Dartmouth College, Hanover NH 03755, USA; m.c.gaposchkin@dartmouth.edu

Prof. Luis GARCÍA-GUIJARRO, Facultad de Ciencias Humanas, Plaza de la Constitución s/n, 22001 Huesca, SPAIN; luguijar@unizar.es

Sabine GELDSETZER, M.A., Westheide 6, 44892 Bochum, GERMANY; sabine.geldsetzer@ruhr-uni-bochum.de

Dr Stavros G. GEORGIOU, P.O. Box 25729, 1311 Strovolos, CYPRUS; stggeorgiou@yahoo.gr

Dr Ruthy GERTWAGEN, 30 Ranas Street, P.O. Box 117, Qiryat Motzkin 26317, ISRAEL; ruger@macam.ac.il

Dr Marianne M. GILCHRIST, Flat 10, 13 Kelvin Drive, Glasgow G20 8QG, SCOTLAND, UK; docm@silverwhistle.free-online.co.uk

Prof. John B. GILLINGHAM, 49 Old Shoreham Road, Brighton, Sussex BN1 5DQ, ENGLAND, UK; johnbgilli@gmail.com

Prof. Anne GILMOUR-BRYSON, 1935 Westview Drive, North Vancouver, B.C. V7M 3B1, CANADA; annegb@telus.net

Charles R. GLASHEEN, 4300 Yacht Club Road, Jacksonville FL 32210, USA; rglashee@comcast.net

Prof. Dorothy F. GLASS, 11 Riverside Drive, Apartment 6-OW, New York NY 10023, USA; dglass1@att.net

*Prof. Philippe GOURDIN, 11, avenue du général de Gaulle, 91000 Évry, France; philgourdin@yahoo.fr

Michael GRAYER, 192 York Road, Shrewsburg, Shropshire SY1 3QH, ENGLAND, UK; m.grayer@btopenworld.com

Prof. Gilles GRIVAUD, 8, rue de Général de Miribel, 69007 Lyon, FRANCE

The Rev. Joseph J. GROSS, Trinitarian History Studies, P.O. Box 42056, Baltimore MD 21284, USA; jjgross@trinitarianhistory.org

Dr Darius von GUETTNER, School of Historical Studies, Univ. of Melbourne, Victoria 3010, AUSTRALIA; d.guttner@unimelb.edu.au

Prof. Klaus GUTH, Greiffenbergstraße 35, 96052 Bamberg, GERMANY; klaus.guth@uni-bamberg.de

*Martin HALL, 8 Stanhope Place, London, W2 2HB, ENGLAND, UK; martin.allan.hall@gmail.com

Adina HAMILTON, 469 Albert Street, Brunswick, West Victoria 3055, AUSTRALIA or History Dept., Univ. of Melbourne, Parkville, Victoria 3052, AUSTRALIA

Prof. Bernard HAMILTON, 7 Lenton Avenue, The Park, Nottingham NG7 IDX, ENGLAND, UK; bernhamilt@yahoo.com

*Dr Mona HAMMAD, P.O. Box 13726., Dept. of History, Univ. of Jordan, Amman 11942, JORDAN; monahammad@hotmail.com

Peter HARITATOS Jr., 1500 North George Street, Rome NY 13440, USA

Jonathan HARRIS, Dept. of History, Royal Holloway, Univ. of London, Egham, Surrey TW20 0EX, ENGLAND, UK; jonathan.harris@rhul.ac.uk

Kathryn D. HARRIS, 6 Gallows Hill, Saffron Walden, Essex CB11 4DA, ENGLAND, UK; lfiddock@ntlworld.com

*Dr. Michael HARSCHEIDT, Dellbusch 229, D-42279 Wuppertal, GERMANY; office@harscheidt.de

Dr Alan HARVEY, Dept. of Historical and Critical Studies, Univ. of Northumbria, Newcastle-upon-Tyne NE1 8ST, ENGLAND, UK; alan.harvey@unn.ac.uk

Prof. Eva HAVERKAMP, Rice Univ., History Dept. MS 42, for letters P.O. Box 1892, Houston TX 77251-1892 or for packages 6100 Main Street, Houston TX 77005, USA; haver@rice.edu

David HAY, 164 McCaul Street, Apartment 1, Toronto, Ontario M5T 1WA, CANADA

Prof. Thérèse de HEMPTINNE, Universiteit Gent, Faculteit van de Letteren, Vakgroep Middeleeuwse Geschiedenis, Blandijnberg 2, 9000 Gent, BELGIUM

Michael HESLOP, The Old Vicarage, 1 Church Street, Lower Sunbury, Middlesex TW16 6RQ, ENGLAND, UK; michaelheslop@ntlworld.com

Dr Paul HETHERINGTON, 15 Luttrell Avenue, London SW15 6PD, ENGLAND, UK; phetherington@ukonline.co.uk

Prof. Rudolf HIESTAND, Brehmstraße 76, 40239 Düsseldorf, GERMANY

Charles A. HILKEN, P.O. Box 4825, St Mary's College, Moraga CA 94575, USA; chilken@stmarys-ca.edu

James HILL, 2/4 Cassam Place, Valley Heights, New South Wales 2777, AUSTRALIA

Dr George HINTLIAN, Armenian Patriarchate, P.O. Box, Jerusalem 14001, ISRAEL

Dr Martin HOCH, Konrad-Adenauer-Stiftung, Rathausallee 12, 53757 Sankt Augustin, GERMANY; Lobebaer@gmail.com

Dr Natasha HODGSON, Dept. of History, Heritage and Geography, Nottingham Trent Univ., Clifton Campus, Nottingham NG11 8NS, ENGLAND, UK; natasha.hodgson@ntu.ac.uk

Laura H. HOLLENGREEN; Univ. of Arizona, School of Architecture, 1040 North Olive, P.O. Box 210075, Tucson AZ 85721-0075, USA; laurah@u.arizona.edu

Dr Catherine HOLMES, University College, Oxford OX1 4BH, ENGLAND, UK; catherine.holmes@univ.ox.ac.uk

Andrew P. HOLT, 6340 N.W. 216th Street, Starke FL 32091, USA; 904-964-5377; apholt@ufl.edu

Jan HOSTEN, Kaaistraat 12, 8900 Ieper, BELGIUM; jan.hosten@leicon.be

*Dr C. Patrick HOTLE, Culver-Stockton Coll., NO. 1 College Hill, Canton, MO 63435, USA; photle@culver.edu

Prof. Norman J. HOUSLEY, School of Historical Studies, The Univ. of Leicester, Leicester LE1 7RH, ENGLAND, UK; hou@le.ac.uk

Prof. John HOWE, Texas Tech Univ., Dept. of History, Box 41013, Lubbock TX 79409-1013, USA; John.Howe@ttu.edu

Lubos HRADSKY, Svermova 23, 97404 Banska Bystrica, SLOVAK REPUBLIC; lubohradsky@centrum.sk

Prof. Lucy-Anne HUNT, Dept. of History of Art and Design, Righton Building, Cavendish Street, Manchester M15 6BK, ENGLAND, UK; l.a.hunt@mmu.ac.uk

Dr Zsolt HUNYADI, 27 Szekeres u., 6725 Szeged, HUNGARY; hunyadiz@hist.u-szeged.hu

Prof. Robert B. C. HUYGENS, Witte Singel 28, 2311 BH Leiden, THE NETHERLANDS

Sheldon IBBOTSON, P.O. Box 258, Rimbey, Alberta T0C 2JO, CANADA; bronwen@telusplanet.net

Robert IRWIN, 39 Harleyford Road, London SE11 5AX, ENGLAND, UK; irwin960@btinternet.com

John E. ISLES, 10575 Darrel Drive, Hanover MI 49241, USA; jisles@hughes.net

Prof. Peter JACKSON, School of Humanities – History, Univ. of Keele, Keele, Staffs. ST5 5BG, ENGLAND, UK; p.jackson@his.keele.ac.uk

Martin JACOBOWITZ, The Towers of Windsor Park, 3005 Chapel Avenue — 11P, Cherry Hill NJ 08002, USA

Prof. David JACOBY, Dept. of History, The Hebrew Univ., Jerusalem 91905 ISRAEL; jacobgab@mscc.huji.ac.il

Prof. Nikolas JASPERT, Ruhr-Univ. Bochum, Historisches Institut – Lehrstuhl Mittelalter II, Universitätsstraße 150 (GA 4/31), 44801 Bochum, GERMANY; nikolas.jaspert@rub.de

Dr Janus Møller JENSEN, Dept. of History and Civilization, Univ. of Southern Denmark, Campusvej 55, 5230 Odense M, DENMARK; jamj@hist.sdu.dk or: mailto:jamj@hist.sdu.dk

Prof. Kurt Villads JENSEN, Dept. of History and Civilization, Univ. of Southern Denmark, Campusvej 55, 5230 Odense M, DENMARK; kvj@hist.sdu.dk

Prof. William Chester JORDAN, Dept. of History, Princeton Univ., Princeton NJ 08544, USA; wchester@princeton.edu

Philippe JOSSERAND, 3, allée Flesselles, 44000 Nantes, FRANCE; ph.josserand@wanadoo.fr

Dr Andrew JOTISCHKY, Dept. of History, Lancaster Univ., Lancaster LA1 5PE, ENGLAND, UK; a.jotischky@lancaster.ac.uk

Dr Margaret A. JUBB, Dept. of French, Taylor Building, Univ. of Aberdeen, Old Aberdeen, AB15 9NU, SCOTLAND, UK; m.jubb@abdn.ac.uk

Elena KAFFA, 2B Thiron Kaimakli, 1026 Nicosia, CYPRUS; niryida@yahoo.com

*Prof. Sophia KALOPISSI-VERTI, Kronou 30, Palaio Faliro, GR-175 61 Athens, Greece; skalop@arch.uoa.gr

Dr Sini KANGAS, Dept. of History, PL 4 (Porthania 384), 00014 Univ. of Helsinki, FINLAND; shkangas@mappi.helsinki.fi

Dr Fotini KARASSAVA-TSILINGIRI, Th. Kairi 14, Nea Smyrni, Athens 17122, GREECE; ptsiling@teiath.gr

Tatiana KARTSEVA, 73–50 Vavilova Street, Ap. 50, Moscow 117335, RUSSIA; tvkartseva@hotmail.com

Anna-Maria KASDAGLI, 59 Stockholmis Street, 85100 Rhodes, GREECE.

Prof. Benjamin Z. KEDAR, Dept. of History, The Hebrew Univ., Jerusalem 91905, ISRAEL; fax (home) 972-8-970-0802, bzkedar@mscc.huji.ac.il

Alexander KEMPTON, Skøyenveien 30, 0375 Oslo, NORWAY; alexansk@student.hf.uio.no

Prof. Nurith KENAAN-KEDAR, Dept. of Art History, Tel-Aviv Univ., Tel-Aviv 69978, ISRAEL; kenaank@post.tau.ac.il

Dr Hugh KENNEDY, Medieval History Dept., Univ. of St Andrews, 71 South Street, St Andrews, Fife KY16 9AL, SCOTLAND, UK

Dr Andreas KIESEWETTER, Lochiel Street 701, 0043 Pretoria — Faerie Glen, SOUTH AFRICA; kiesewetter@telkomsa.net

Prof. Sharon KINOSHITA, Associate Professor of Literature, Humanities Academic Services, Univ. of California Santa Cruz, Santa Cruz CA 95064, USA; sakinosh@ucsc.edu

Dr Klaus-Peter KIRSTEIN, Frankenstraße 251, 45134 Essen, GERMANY; k.kirstein@r25.de

Dr Michael A. KOEHLER, Hertogenlaan 14, 1970 Wezembeek-Oppem, BELGIUM; koehler.family@pandora.be

Prof. Athina KOLIA-DERMITZAKI, Plateia Kalliga 3, Athens 11253, GREECE; akolia@arch.uoa.gr

Dr Conor KOSTICK, c/o Dept. of Medieval History, Trinity College, Dublin, IRELAND; kosticc@tcd.ie

Thomas KRÄMER, Friedrich-Franz-Straße 18, 12103 Berlin, GERMANY; thomas_kraemer@yahoo.com

Prof. Jürgen KRÜGER, Steinbügelstraße 22, 76228 Karlsruhe, GERMANY; krueger-kunstgeschichte@t-online.de

*Suha KUDSIEH, Box: 19027, 360 A Bloor Street W., Toronto, ON., M5S 3C9 CANADA; suhakudsieh@trentu.ca

Sarah LAMBERT, 35 Cromer Road, London SW17 9JN, ENGLAND, UK; slambert@gold.ac.uk

The Rev. William LANE, Brooke Hall, Charterhouse, Godalming, Surrey GU7 2DX, ENGLAND, UK; wjl@charterhouse.org.uk

Elizabeth LAPINA, Department of History, Queen's University, 49 Bader Lane, Watson Hall, Room 212, Kingston, ON, CANADA, K7L 3N6; ealapina@yahoo.com

Dr Robert A. LAURES, 1434 West Maplewood Court, Milwaukee WI 53221-4348, USA; dr001@voyager.net

Stephen LAY, c/o Dept. of History, Monash Univ., Melbourne, AUSTRALIA

Armelle LECLERCQ, 36, rue de l'Orillen, 75011 Paris, FRANCE; armelle73@yahoo.com

Eric LEGG, PSC 98 Box 36, Apo AE 09830, USA; ericlegg@hotmail.com

Robert D. LEONARD Jr., 1065 Spruce Street, Winnetka IL 60093, USA; rlwinnetka@aol.com

Richard A. LESON, 2720 St Paul Street, Apartment 2FF, Baltimore MD 21218, USA; ral2@jhunix.hef.jhu.edu

Dr Yaacov LEV, P.O. Box 167, Holon 58101, ISRAEL; yglev@actcom.net.il

Dr Christopher G. LIBERTINI, 27 Lombard Lane, Sudbury MA 01776, USA; clibertini@aol.com

*Dr Tom LICENCE, Magdalene College, Cambridge, CB3 0AG, ENGLAN, UK; tol21@cam.ac.uk

Laura S. LIEBER, Dept. of Religion, Middlebury College, Middlebury VT 05753, USA; llieber@middlebury.edu

Dr Giuseppe LIGATO, Viale San Gimignano 18, 20146 Milano, ITALY; giuseppeligato@virgilio.it

Prof. Ralph-Johannes LILIE, Kaiser-Friedrich-Straße 106, 10585 Berlin, GERMANY; liliefavreau@arcor.de

Dr Ora LIMOR, 5b Elroey Street, Jerusalem 92108, ISRAEL; orali@openu.ac.il

Prof. Guy LOBRICHON, 4, Impasse Caillod, 84000 Avignon, FRANCE; guy.lobrichon@univ-avignon.fr

Prof. Peter W. LOCK, 9 Straylands Grove, Stockton Lane, York YO31 1EB, ENGLAND, UK; ptrlock425@googlemail.com

Scott LONEY, 4153 Wendell Road, West Bloomfield MI 48323, USA; scottloney@ameritech.net

Prof. Graham A. LOUD, School of History, Univ. of Leeds, Leeds LS2 9JT, ENGLAND, UK; g.a.loud@leeds.ac.uk

Prof. Michael LOWER, Dept. of History, Univ. of Minnesota, 614 Social Sciences Building, 267 19th Avenue South, Minneapolis MN 55455, USA; mlower@umn.edu

Zoyd R. LUCE, 2441 Creekside Court, Hayward CA 94542, USA; zluce1@earthlink.net

Dr Svetlana LUCHITSKAYA, Institute of General History, Leninski pr. 89-346, Moscow 119313, RUSSIA; svetlana-luchitskaya@yandex.ru

Andrew John LUFF, Flat 3, The Hermitage, St Dunstans Road, Lower Feltham, Middlesex TW13 4HR, ENGLAND, UK; andrew@luffa.freeserve.co.uk

Dr Anthony LUTTRELL, 20 Richmond Place, Bath BA1 5PZ, ENGLAND, UK; margaretluttrell@gmail.com

Christopher MACEVITT, Dumbarton Oaks, 1703 32nd Street NW, Washington DC 20007, USA

Dr James B. MACGREGOR, Assistant Prof. of History, Dept. of History, Philosophy, and Geography, Missouri Western State Univ., 4525 Downs Drive, Saint Joseph MO 64507, USA; macgregor@missouriwestern.edu

Dr Merav MACK, The Van Leer Jerusalem Institute, 43 Jabotinsky Street, P.O. Box 4070, Jerusalem, 91040, ISRAEL; www.vanleer.org.il

Dr Alan D. MACQUARRIE, 173 Queen Victoria Drive, Glasgow G14 7BP, SCOTLAND, UK

[See also Mc]

Prof. Thomas F. MADDEN, Dept. of History, Saint Louis Univ., 3800 Lindell Boulevard, P.O. Box 56907, Saint Louis MO 63108, USA; maddentf@slu.edu

Ben MAHONEY, 131 High Street, Doncaster, Victoria 3181, AUSTRALIA; bmahoney@abl.com.au

PD Dr Christoph T. MAIER, Sommergasse 20, 4056 Basel, SWITZERLAND; ctmaier@hist.uzh.ch or ctmaier@tele2.ch

Chryssa A. MALTEZOU, Istituto Ellenico di Studi Bizantini e Postbizantini di Venezia, Castello 3412, 30122 Venezia, ITALY; info@istitutoellenico.org

Prof. Lucy DER MANUELIAN, 10 Garfield Road, Belmont MA 02478, USA; lucy.manuelian@tufts.edu

Prof. Laurence W. MARVIN, History Dept., Evans School of Humanities, Berry College, Mount Berry GA 30149-5010, USA; lmarvin@berry.edu

*Dr Federica MASÈ, 100 rue de la Roquette, 75011 Paris, FRANCE; f.mase@free.fr

Prof. Hans Eberhard MAYER, Historisches Seminar der Universität Kiel, 24098 Kiel, GERMANY

Robert MAYNARD, The Old Dairy, 95 Church Road, Bishopsworth, Bristol BS13 8JU, ENGLAND, UK; maynard966@btinternet.com

Brian C. MAZUR, 718 W. Webster, Royal Oak MI 48073, USA; bcmazur1066@yahoo.com

Roben MCDONALD MARLOW, 36 Burton Old Road West, Lichfield, Staffordshire WS13 6EN, ENGLAND, UK; roben@mac.com

Patrick MCINTOSH, 3703 Maplecrest Avenue, Parma OH 44134, USA; p.mcintosh@csuohio.edu

Dr Marianne McLeod GILCHRIST: see to Dr Marianne M. GILCHRIST

M. MCNAUGHTON, The Old Rectory, River Street, Pewsey SN9 5DB, ENGLAND, UK; pewsey_books@hotmail.com

Gerald P. MCOSKER, Salve Regina Univ., 100 Ochre Point Avenue, Newport, RI 06240, USA; gerald.mcosker@salve.edu

Prof. Sophia MENACHE, Dept. of History, Univ. of Haifa, Haifa 31905, ISRAEL; menache@research.haifa.ac.il

Marco MESCHINI, Via alle Cascine 37/B, 21100 Varese, ITALY; marco.meschini@unicatt.it

*Dr Benjamin MICHAUDEL, IFPO, P.O.Box 344, Damascus, Syria; benjamin_michaudel@hotmail.com

Prof. Klaus MILITZER, Winckelmannstraße 32, 50825 Köln, GERMANY; klaus.militzer@uni-koeln.de

Greg MILLER, 105 Valley Street, Burlington IA 52601, USA; greg.miller@lpl.com

Jane MILLIKEN, 26 Emmetts Farm Road, Rossmore NSW 2557, AUSTRALIA; jane.milliken@swahs.health.nsw.gov.au

Paul Richard MILLIMAN, Dept. of History, Univ. of Arizona, 3213 E Pima St, Tuscon AZ 85716, USA; prmilliman@gmail.com

Peter John MILLS, 3 Huxley Road, Leyton, London E10 5QT, ENGLAND, UK; petermills@lireone.net

Prof. Laura MINERVINI, Dipartimento di Filologia Moderna, Università di Napoli Federico II, Via Porta Di Massa 1, 80133 Napoli, ITALY; lrminer@unina.it

Dr Piers D. MITCHELL, 112 Queen's Walk, Stamford, Lincolnshire PE9 2QE, ENGLAND, UK; p.mitchell@clara.co.uk

PD Dr Hannes MÖHRING, Wilhelm-Bode-Straße 11, 38104 Braunschweig, GERMANY; hannes_moehring@web.de

Prof. Johannes A. (Hans) MOL, Grote Dijlakker 29, 8701 KW Bolsward, THE NETHERLANDS; hmol@fryske-akademy.nl

Dr Kristian MOLIN, 38 Vessey Terrace, Newcastle-under-Lyme, Staffordshire ST5 1LS, ENGLAND, UK; kristian.molin@nottingham.ac.uk

Dauvergne C. MORGAN, 235 Tooronga Road, Glen Iris, Melbourne, Victoria 3142, AUSTRALIA

Jonathan C. MORGAN, 19 Elia Street, Islington, London N1 8DE, ENGLAND, UK; jonathan.morgan@whb.co.uk

J. Diana MORGAN, 64 Victoria Avenue, Swanage, Dorset BH19 1AR, ENGLAND, UK

Hiroki MORITAKE, Kami-Ono 371, Hiyoshi-mura, Kitauwa-gun, Ehime-ken 798-1503, JAPAN; jerus@hiroshima-u.ac.jp

*April Jehan MORRIS, 1114 Camino La Costa, Apt. 2075, Austin, Texas 78752, USA; ajehanmorris@gmail.com

The Rev. Prof. Colin MORRIS, 12 Bassett Crescent East, Southampton SO16 7PB, ENGLAND, UK; cm5@soton.ac.uk

Dr Rosemary MORRIS, Dept. of History, Univ. of York, York YO10 5DD, ENGLAND, UK; rm22@york.ac.uk

Dr Nicholas MORTON, History Department, Swansea University, SA2 8PP, WALES, UK; mortonnic@hotmail.com

Suleiman Ali MOURAD, Smith College, Dept. of Religion, Wright Hall 114, Northampton MA 01063, USA; smourad@smith.edu

Roger D. MULHOLLEN, Center for Study of Ancient Religious History, 13217 W. Serenade Circle, Sun City West AZ 85375-1707, USA; audrog@aol.com

Prof. M. E. MULLETT, Institute of Byzantine Studies, Queen's Univ. of Belfast, Belfast BT7 1NN, NORTHERN IRELAND, UK; m.mullett@qub.ac.uk

Dr Alan V. MURRAY, International Medieval Institute, The University of Leeds, Parkinson 103, Leeds LS2 9JT, ENGLAND, UK; a.v.murray@leeds.ac.uk

Stephen R. A. MURRAY, Apartment 351, 176 The Esplanade, Toronto, Ontario M5A 4H2, CANADA; sramurray@hotmail.com

Claude MUTAFIAN, 216, rue Saint-Jacques, 75005 Paris, FRANCE; claude.mutafian@wanadoo.fr

Liz MYLOD, Parkinson 4.06, Institute for Medieval Studies, University of Leeds, LEEDS LS2 9JT, UK; mesejm@leeds.ac.uk

Abdollah NASERI, History Group, Theology Faculty, Alzahra Univ., Deh Vanak, Tehran, IRAN; a.naseri@az-history.com

James NAUS, Dept. of History, Saint Louis Univ., 3800 Lindell Boulevard, Saint Louis MO 63108, USA; nausjl@slu.edu

Alan NEILL, 13 Chesham Crescent, Belfast BT6 8GW, NORTHERN IRELAND, UK; neilla@rescueteam.com

Dr Helen J. NICHOLSON, School of History and Archaeology, Cardiff Univ., Humanities Building, Colum Drive, Cardiff CF10 3EU, WALES, UK; nicholsonhj@cardiff.ac.uk

Angel NICOLAOU-KONNARI, P.O. Box 54106, 3721 Limassol, CYPRUS; an.konnaris@cytanet.com.cy

Dr David NICOLLE, 67 Maplewell Road, Woodhouse Eaves, Leicestershire LE12 8RG, ENGLAND, UK; david.c.nicolle@btinternet.com

J. Mark NICOVICH, 119 Short Bay Street, Hattiesburg MS 39401, USA; mark.nicovich@gmail.com

Marie-Adélaïde NIELEN, 254, avenue Daumesnil, 75012 Paris, FRANCE; marie-adelaide.nielen@culture.gouv.fr

Prof. Torben Kjersgaard NIELSEN, Institute for History, International and Social Studies, Aalborg Univ., Fibigerstraede 5, 9220 Aalborg OE, DENMARK; tkn@ihis.aau.dk

Yoav NITZEN, 4 H'Adereth Street, Jerusalem 92343, ISRAEL; raem@bezeqint.net

*Leila NORAKO, 1415 Clover St., Rochester, NY 14610 USA. email: lknorako@gmail.

Dr Randall L. NORSTREM, 28822 Pacific Highway S., Federal Way WA 98003, USA; templariidvm@yahoo.com

Shmuel NUSSBAUM, P.O. Box 2201, Petah-Tiqva 49120, ISRAEL; nshmuel7@netvision.net.il

Elvor Andersen OFTESTAD, Faculty of Theology, Postboks 1023 Blindern, 0315 Oslo, NORWAY; e.a.oftestad@teologi.uio.no

Dr Gregory O'MALLEY, 4 Holly Bank, Hugglescote, Leicestershire LE67 2FR, ENGLAND, UK; gregoryomalley@btinternet.com

Prof. Mahmoud Said OMRAN, History Dept., Faculty of Arts, Univ. of Alexandria, Alexandria, EGYPT; msomran@dataxprs.com.eg; Web Site: www.msomran.com

Col. Erhard (Erik) OPSAHL, 5303 Dennis Drive, McFarland WI 53558, USA; epopsahlw@aol.com

Jilana ORDMAN, 1327 North Maplewood Avenue, Apartment 2, Chicago IL 60622, USA; jordman@luc.edu

Rhiain O'SULLIVAN, Second Floor Flat, 116–117 Saffron Hill, London EC1N 8QS, ENGLAND, UK; rhiainaroundtheworld@hotmail.com

Catherine OTTEN, 9, rue de Londres, 67000 Strasbourg, FRANCE; otten@umb.u-strasbg.fr.

*Marcello PACIFICO, Corso Pisani 274, 90120 Palermo, ITALY; marcellopacifico@unipa.it

Barbara PACKARD, 35 Marnham Crecent, Greenford, Middlesex UB6 9SW, ENGLAND, UK; bcpackard@yahoo.co.uk

Dr Johannes PAHLITZSCH, Parallelstraße 12, 12209 Berlin, GERMANY; pahlitz@zedat.fu-berlin.de

Dr Aphrodite PAPAYIANNI, 40 Inverness Terrace, London W2 3JB, ENGLAND, UK; aphroditepapayianni@hotmail.com

Danielle PARK, 2 Blagrave Rise, Tilehurst, Reading, Berks RG3 14SF, ENGLAND, UK; D.Park@rhul.ac.uk

Kenneth Scott PARKER, History Dept., Royal Holloway, Univ. of London, Egham, Surrey TW20 0EX, ENGLAND, UK; kscottparker@gmail.com

Dr Peter D. PARTNER, Murhill Farmhouse, Murhill, Limpley Stoke, Bath BA2 7FH, ENGLAND, UK; pdp4@aol.com

Aurelio PASTORI RAMOS, Ejido 1365/802, 11100 Montevideo, URUGUAY; apastori@um.edu.uy

Martin PATAIL, 2211 South West First Avenue Unit 102, Portland OR 97210, USA; patailm@pdx.edu

*Dr Nicholas L. PAUL, Department of History, Fordham University, Dealy Hall, 441 E. Fordham Road, Bronx, NY 10458; npaul@fordham.edu

Prof. Jacques PAVIOT, Faculté des Lettres et Sciences humaines, Université de Paris XII – Val de Marne, 61, avenue du Général de Gaulle, F-94010 Créteil Cedex, FRANCE; paviot@univ-paris12.fr

Michael J. PEIXOTO, 168 East 82nd Street, Apartment 5B, New York NY 10028-2214, USA

Peter Shlomo PELEG, 2 Mordhai Street, Kiryat Tivon 36023, ISRAEL; fax 972 4 9931 122; ppeleg@netvision.net.il

*Christopher PERKINS, 137 Adrian Drive, Stockbridge, GA 30281, USA; gop7384@yahoo.com

Photeine V. PERRA, Hexamilia Corinth, Corinth 201 00, GREECE; fperra@hol.gr

Prof. David M. PERRY, Assistant Professor, Dept. of History, Dominican Univ., 7900 Division Street, River Forest IL 60305, USA; dperry@dom.edu

*Guy PERRY, Lincoln College, Oxford, OXI 3DR, England, UK; guy.perry@lincoln.ox.ac.uk

Nicholas J. PERRY, P.O. Box 389, La Mesa NM 88044, USA; nicholasperry@earthlink.net

James PETRE, The Old Barn, 8A Church Road, Stevington, Bedfordshire MK43 7QB, ENGLAND, UK; jamespetre@btinternet.com

Theodore D. PETRO, New England College, 24 Bridge Street, P.O. Box 74, Henniker NH 03242, USA; tpetro@nec.edu

Dr Christopher Matthew PHILLIPS, Social Science Dept., Concordia Univ., 800 N. Columbia Avenue, Seward NE 68434-1556, USA; Matthew.Phillips@cune.edu

Prof. Jonathan P. PHILLIPS, Dept. of History, Royal Holloway Univ. of London, Egham, Surrey TW20 0EX, ENGLAND, UK; j.p.phillips@rhul.ac.uk

Dr Simon D. PHILLIPS, Department of History and Archaeology, University of Cyprus, P.O. Box 20537, 1678 Nicosia,Cyprus; Phillips.Simon@ucy.ac.cy or simphlld@aim.com

Dr Mathias PIANA, Benzstraße 9, 86420 Diedorf, GERMANY; mathias.piana@phil.uni-augsburg.de

Maria Cristina PIMENTA, Rua Costa Cabral, 1791 1°, 4200-228 Porto, PORTUGAL; cristinapimenta@clix.pt

*Marion PINCEMAILLE, 11 rue d'Obermodern, 67330 Zutsendorf, FRANCE; marion.mes.pin@orange.fr or marion.pincemaille@free.fr

Paula Maria de Carvalho PINTO COSTA, Rua Central do Viso, 102, 4250-130 Porto, PORTUGAL; ppinto@letras.up.pt

Clive PORRO, 36 Castle Road, Whitstable, Kent CT5 2DY, ENGLAND, UK; clive.porro@btinternet.com

Dr Jon PORTER, Change and Tradition Program, Butler Univ., 4600 Sunset Avenue, Indianapolis IN 46208, USA; jporter1@butler.edu

*Valentin PORTNYCKH, 2 Pigorov Street, 630090, Novosibirsk, RUSSIA; valport@list.ru

Prof. James M. POWELL, 5100 Highbridge Street, Apartment 18D, Fayetteville NY 13066, USA; mpowell@dreamscape.com

*Dr Amanda POWER, Department of History, University of Sheffield, Sheffield, S 10 2TN, UK; a.power@sheffield.ac.uk

Prof. R. Denys PRINGLE, School of History and Archaeology, Cardiff Univ., P.O. Box 909, Cardiff CF10 3EU, WALES, UK; pringlerd@cardiff.ac.uk

Dragan PROKIC, M.A., Rubensallee 47, 55127 Mainz, GERMANY; dragan.prokic@o2online.de

Prof. John H. PRYOR, Centre for Medieval Studies, Univ. of Sydney, John Wolley Building A20, Sydney, New South Wales 2006, AUSTRALIA; john.pryor@usyd.edu.au

*Emmanuelle PUJEAU, Ca Antica d'En Duras, Chemin de Fregouville, 32200 Maurens, France; emmanuelle.pujeau@wanadoo.fr

Dr William J. PURKIS, School of History and Cultures, Univ. of Birmingham, Edgbaston, Birmingham B15 2TT, ENGLAND, UK; w.j.purkis@bham.ac.uk

Rachael PYMM, 4 Beechtree Avenue, Englefield Green, Egham, Surrey TW20 0SR, ENGLAND, UK; peruvian_explorer@hotmail.com

*Gary RAMSELL, 25 Kings Road, East Sheen, London, SW148PF; gary@ramsell.com

Prof. Pierre RACINE, 8, rue Traversière, 67201 Eckbolsheim, FRANCE; racine.p@evc.net

Yevgeniy / Eugene RASSKAZOV, Worth Avenue Station, P.O. Box 3497, Palm Beach FL 33480-3497, USA; medievaleurope@apexmail.com

Prof. Geoffrey W. RICE, History Dept., Univ. of Canterbury, Private Bag 4800, Christchurch 8041, NEW ZEALAND; geoff.rice@canterbury.ac.nz

Prof. Jean RICHARD, 12, rue Pelletier de Chambure, 21000 Dijon, FRANCE

Maurice RILEY Esq., 2 Swallow Court, Winsford, Cheshire CW7 1SR, ENGLAND, UK; rileymaurice@yahoo.com

Prof. Jonathan S. C. RILEY-SMITH, The Downs, Croxton, St Neots, Cambridgeshire PE19 4SX, ENGLAND, UK; jonathan.rileysmith@btinternet.com

Prof. Louise Buenger ROBBERT, 709 South Skinker Boulevard Apartment 701, St Louis MO 63105, USA; lrobbert@mindspring.com

Jason T. ROCHE, Seaview, Kings Highway, Largoward, Fife KY9 1HX, SCOTLAND, UK; jtr@st-andrews.ac.uk

José Manuel RODRÍGUEZ-GARCÍA, Av. Conde de Aranda 1, 3° E, 28200 San Lorenzo del Escorial (Madrid), ESPAÑA; anaevjosem@hotmail.com

*Jean-Marc ROGER, 14 rue Jean Jaurès, 86000 Poitiers, FRANCE; j-m.roger@wanadoo.fr

*Prof. Manuel ROJAS, Departamento de Historia, Facultad de Filosofia y Lettras, Universidad de Extremadura, 10071- Càceres, SPAIN; mrojas@unex.es

Prof. Israel ROLL, Institut of Archaeology, Tel-Aviv Univ., Ramat Aviv, Tel-Aviv 69978, ISRAEL; rolli@post.tau.ac.il

Prof. Myriam ROSEN-AYALON, Institute of Asian and African Studies, The Hebrew Univ., Jerusalem 91905, ISRAEL

Prof. John ROSSER, Dept. of History, Boston College, Chestnut Hill MA 02467, USA; rosserj@bc.edu

Prof. Jay RUBENSTEIN, Dept. of History, Univ. of Tennessee, 6th Floor, Dunford Hall, Knoxville TN 37996-4065, USA; jrubens1@utk.edu

Jonathan RUBIN-RONEN, Elazar Hamodai 12, Jerusalem 93671, ISRAEL; yonigali@gmail.com

Prof. Frederick H. RUSSELL, Dept. of History, Conklin Hall, Rutgers Univ., Newark NJ 07102, USA; frussell@andromeda.rutgers.edu

Prof. James D. RYAN, 100 West 94th Street, Apartment 26M, New York NY 10025, USA; james.d.ryan@verizon.net

Vincent RYAN, Dept. of History, Saint Louis Univ., 3800 Lindell Boulevard, Saint Louis MO 63108, USA; ryanvt@slu.edu

Dr Andrew J. SARGENT, 33 Coborn Street, Bow, London E3 2AB, ENGLAND, UK; andrewsargent@dfes.gsi.gov.uk

Prof. Jürgen SARNOWSKY, Historisches Seminar, Universität Hamburg, Von-Melle-Park 6, 20146 Hamburg, GERMANY; juergen.sarnowsky@uni-hamburg.de

Christopher J. SAUNDERS OBE, Watery Hey, Springvale Road, Hayfield, High Peak SK22 2LD, ENGLAND, UK; christopher.saunders@savoyim.com

Prof. Alexios G. C. SAVVIDES, Aegean Univ., Dept. of Mediterranean Studies, Rhodes, GREECE; or: 7 Tralleon Street, Nea Smyrne, Athens 17121, GREECE; savvides@rhodes.aegean.gr

Christopher SCHABEL, Dept. of History and Archaeology, Univ. of Cyprus, P.O. Box 20537, 1678 Nicosia, CYPRUS; schabel@ucy.ac.cy

Dr Jochen SCHENK, Emmanuel College, Cambridge CB2 3AP, ENGLAND, UK; or Spardorferstraße 7, 91054 Erlangen, GERMANY; jg.schenk@gmail.com

Prof. Paul Gerhard SCHMIDT, Seminar für lateinische Philologie des Mittelalters, Albert-Ludwigs-Universität Freiburg, Werthmannstrasse 8, 79085 Freiburg i. Br., GERMANY; schmidt@mittelatein.uni-freiburg.de

Dr James G. SCHRYVER, Univ. of Minnesota Morris, HUM 104, 600 East 4th Street, Morris MN 56267, USA; schryver@morris.umn.edu

Dr Beate SCHUSTER, 19, rue Vauban, 67000 Strasbourg, FRANCE; beaschu@compuserve.com

Prof. Rainer C. SCHWINGES, Historisches Institut der Universität Bern, Unitobler – Länggass-Straße 49, 3000 Bern 9, SWITZERLAND; rainer.schwinges@hist.unibe.ch

Per SEESKO, Heden 18, 2., lejl. 10, 5000 Odense C, DENMARK; seesko83@yahoo.com

Einat SEGAL, 20 Neve Rehim Street, Ramat Hasharon, ISRAEL; eisegal@netvision.net.il

Iris SHAGRIR, Dept. of History, The Open Univ. of Israel, P.O. Box 808, Ra'anana 43107, ISRAEL; irissh@openu.ac.il

Prof. Maya SHATZMILLER, Dept. of History, The Univ. of Western Ontario, London, Ontario N6A 5C2, CANADA

*Dr Teresa SHAWCROSS, Trinity Hall, Cambridge CB2 1TJ, ENGLAND, UK; teresa.shawcross@googlemail.com

Dr Jonathan SHEPARD, Box 483, 266 Banbury Road, Oxford OX2 7DL, ENGLAND, UK; nshepard@easynet.co.uk

Vardit SHOTTEN-HALLEL, 12 Dan Street, P.O. Box 1404, Ramat Hasharon 47100, ISRAEL; shotten-hallel@012.net.il

William SHULL, 2707 South Rutherford Boulevard, Apartment 1004A, Murfreesboro TN 37130, USA; wshull@gmail.com

* Warren C. SCHULZ, De Paul Univ., Dept. of History, 2320 Kenmore, Chicago, IL 60614, USA; wschultz@depaul.edu

Dr Elizabeth J. SIBERRY, 28 The Mall, Surbiton, Surrey KT6 4E9, ENGLAND, UK; sibersealyham@totalise.co.uk

Kaare Seeberg SIDSELRUD, Granebakken 9, 1284 Oslo, NORWAY; kss@sidselrud.net

Raitis SIMSONS, Konsula 15A-1, Riga 1007, LATVIA; raitiss@btv.lv

Dr Corliss K. SLACK, Dept. of History, Apartment 1103, Whitworth Univ., Spokane WA 99251, USA; cslack@whitworth.edu

Rima E. SMINE, 25541 Altamont Road, Los Altos Hills CA 94022, USA

*Dr Caroline SMITH, 551, 47th Road, 3L, Long Island City, NY 11101, USA; caroline.a.smith@gmail.com

*Thomas SMITH, F8/F Virginia Woolf College, The Pavilion, Giles Lane, Canterbury, Kent, CT2 7BQ, ENGLAND; thomas.smith.503@gmail.com

Simon SONNAK, 658 Canning Street, North Carlton, 3054 Victoria, AUSTRALIA; ssonnak@bigpond.net.au

Arnold SPAER, 8 King David Street, Jerusalem 94104, ISRAEL; hui@spaersitton.co.il

Brent SPENCER, 3 9701 89 Street, Fort Saskatchewan, Alberta T8L IJ3, CANADA; ktcrusader@yahoo.com

Dr Alan M. STAHL, 11 Fairview Place, Ossining NY 10562, USA; amstahl@optonline.net

*Rombert STAPEL, Fryske Akademy, Postbus 54, 8900AB, Leeuwarden, The Netherlands / home: Koolgracht 33, 2312PD, Leiden, The Netherlands; rstapel@fryske-akademy.nl / r.j.stapel@hum.leidenuniv.nl

Rodney STARK, 170 Camino Rayo del Sol, Corales NM 87048, USA; rs@rodneystark.com

Alan D. STEVENS, Campbell College, Dept. of History, Belmont Road, Belfast BT4 2ND, NORTHERN IRELAND, UK; alan.d.stevens@ntlworld.com

Paula R. STILES, 7772 Fraser Street, Vancouver, B.C. V5X 3X1, CANADA; thesnowleopard@hotmail.com

Patrick STOHLER, Oetlingerstraße 192, 4057 Basel, SWITZERLAND; Patrick.Stohler@unibas.ch

Dr Myra STRUCKMEYER, 171 North Hamilton Road, Chapel Hill NC 27517, USA; struckme@alumni.unc.edu

Jace STUCKEY, Louisiana Tech Univ., History Dept., P.O. Box 8548, Rushton, LA 71272, USA; jace@latech.edu

Miikka TAMMINEN, Kaarina Maununtyttären tie 1142, 36200 Kangasala, FINLAND; miikka.tamminen@uta.fi

Miriam Rita TESSERA, via Moncalvo 16, 20146 Milano, ITALY; monachus_it@yahoo.it

Prof. Peter THORAU, Historisches Institut, Univ. des Saarlandes, for letters Postfach 15 11 50, 66041 Saarbrücken, for packages Im Stadtwald, 66123 Saarbrücken, GERMANY; p.thorau@mx.uni-saarland.de

Dr Steve TIBBLE, Copsewood, Deadhearn Lane, Chalfont St Giles, Buckinghamshire HP8 4HG, ENGLAND, UK; steve.tibble@btinternet.com

Prof. Hirofumi TOKO, 605-3 Kogasaka, Machida, Tokyo 194-0014, JAPAN; htoko@mtd.biglobe.ne.jp

Prof. John Victor TOLAN, Département d'Histoire, Université de Nantes, B.P. 81227, 44312 Nantes, FRANCE, or: 2, rue de la Chevalerie, 44300 Nantes, FRANCE; john.tolan@univ-nantes.fr

Ignacio DE LA TORRE, Saxifraga 9, 28036 Madrid, ESPAÑA; ide@profesor.ie.edu

Prof. François-Olivier TOUATI, La Croix Saint-Jérôme, 11, allée Emile Bouchut, 77123 Noisy-sur-Ecole, FRANCE; francoistouati@aol.com

Catherine B. TURNER, Flat 3, 1055 Christchurch Road, Boscombe East, Bournemouth BH7 6BE, ENGLAND, UK

Dr Christopher J. TYERMAN, Hertford College, Oxford, Catte Street, Oxford OX1 3BW, ENGLAND, UK; christopher.tyerman@hertford.ox.ac.uk

Dr Judith M. UPTON-WARD, 6 Haywood Court, Reading, Berks. RG1 3QF, ENGLAND, UK; juptonward@btopenworld.com

*Toon VAN ELst, Prof. Piccardlaan 32, 2610 Wilrijk, Belgium; toonvanelst@hotmail.com

Theresa M. VANN, Hill Monastic Manuscript Library, St John's Univ., Collegeville MN 56321, USA; tvann@csbsju.edu

Rafael VELÁZQUEZ PAREJO, c/ Villa de Rota, n°2, 4° F, 14005 Córdoba, ESPAÑA; mariceli50@hotmail.com

Dr Lucas VILLEGAS-ARISTIZABAL, 74 Queens Road East, Beeston, Nottingham, Nottinghamshire, NG9 2GS, ENGLAND, UK; lucasvillegasa@gmail.com+

Fiona Weir WALMSLEY, 41 Broomley Street, Kangaroo Point, Queensland 4169, AUSTRALIA; f.walmsley@optusnet.com.au

Dr Marie-Louise VON WARTBURG MAIER, Paphosprojekt der Universität Zürich, Rämistraße 71, 8006 Zürich, SWITZERLAND; paphos@hist.unizh.ch

Benjamin WEBER, 24, rue du Taur, 31000 Toulouse, FRANCE; benji.tigrou@gmail.com

*Steven A. WEIDENKOPF, 6814 Barnack Drive, Springfield UA 22152, USA; the weidenkopfs@verizon.net

Dr Mark WHITTOW, St Peter's College, Oxford OX1 2DL, ENGLAND, UK; mark.whittow@st-peters.oxford.ac.uk

Raymond WIESNER, 1725 Graham Avenue, Apartment 409, St. Paul MN 55116-3280, USA; raymondwiesner@yahoo.com

Timothy WILKES, A. H. Baldwin & Sons Ltd., 11 Adelphi Terrace, London WC2N 6BJ, ENGLAND, UK; timwilkes@baldwin.sh

The Rev. Dr John D. WILKINSON, 7 Tenniel Close, London W2 3LE, ENGLAND, UK; johnwilkinson@globalnet.co.uk

Dr Ann WILLIAMS, 40 Greenwich South Street, London SE10 8UN, ENGLAND, UK; ann.williams@talk21.com

Prof. Steven James WILLIAMS, Dept. of History, New Mexico Highlands Univ., P.O. Box 9000, Las Vegas NM 87701, USA; stevenjameswilliams@yahoo.com

* Ian James WILSON, 1 Freeman Close, Hadleigh, Suffolk, IP7 6HH, England, UK

Peter van WINDEKENS, Kleine Ganzendries 38, 3212 Pellenberg, BELGIUM; Peter. VanWindekens@vlm.be

Prof. Johanna Maria VAN WINTER, Brigittenstraat 20, 3512 KM Utrecht, THE NETHERLANDS; j.m.vanwinter@let.uu.nl

Dr Noah WOLFSON, 13 Avuqa Street, Tel-Aviv 69086, ISRAEL; noah@meteo-tech.co.il

Prof. Shunji YATSUZUKA, 10–22 Matsumoto 2 chome, Otsu-shi, Shiga 520, JAPAN; shunchan@mub.biglobe.ne.jp

William G. ZAJAC, 9 Station Terrace, Pen-y-rheal, Caerphilly CF83 2RH, WALES, UK

Prof. Ossama Zaki ZEID, 189 Abd al-Salam Aref Tharwat, Alexandria, EGYPT; ossama_zeid@hotmail.com

Joseph ZELNIK, 25 Wingate Street, Ra'anana 43587, ISRAEL; jzelnik@galilcol.ac.il

Ann ZIMO, 10209 Loma Drive, Knoxville TN 37922, USA; thezeem@gmail.com

Institutions subscribing to the SSCLE

Bibliothécaire Guy Cobolet, Le Bibliothécaire, École Française d'Athènes, 6, Didotou 10680 Athènes, GREECE

Centre de Recherches d'histoire et civilisation de Byzance et du Proche-Orient Chétien, Université de Paris 1, 17, rue de la Sorbonne, 75231 Paris Cedex, FRANCE

Centre for Byzantine, Ottoman and Modern Greek Studies, Univ. of Birmingham, Edgbaston, Birmingham B15 2TT, ENGLAND, UK

Corpus Christianorum — Brepols Publishers, Sint-Annaconvent, Begijnhof 39, 2300 Turnhout, BELGIUM

Couvent des Dominicains, École Biblique et Archéologique Français, 6 Nablus Road, Jerusalem 91190, ISRAEL

Deutsches Historisches Institut in Rom, Via Aurelia Antica 391, 00165 Roma, ITALY

Deutschordenszentralarchiv (DOZA), Singerstraße 7, 1010 Wien, AUSTRIA

Dumbarton Oaks Research Library, 1703 32nd Street North West, Washington D.C. 20007, USA

Europäisches Burgeninstitut, Schlossstraße 5, 56338 Braubach, GERMANY; ebi@deutsche-burgen.org

Germanisches Nationalmuseum, Bibliothek, Kornmarkt 1, 90402 Nürnberg, GERMANY

History Department, Campbell College, Belfast BT4 2 ND, NORTHERN IRELAND, UK

The Jewish National and University Library, P.O. Box 34165, Jerusalem 91341, ISRAEL

The Library, The Priory of Scotland of the Most Venerable Order of St John, 21 St John Street, Edinburgh EH8 8DG, SCOTLAND, UK

The Stephen Chan Library, Institute of Fine Arts, New York Univ., 1 East 78th Street, New York NY 10021-0102, USA

Metropolitan Museum of Art, Thomas J. Watson Library, Serials Dept., 5th Avenue at 82nd Street, New York NY 10028, USA

Museum and Library of the Order of St John, St John's Gate, Clerkenwell, London EC1M 4DA, ENGLAND, UK

Order of the Christian Knights of the Rose, Brent R. Spencer, Grand Master, P.O. Box 3423, Fort Saskatchewan, Alberta T8L 2T4, CANADA

Order of the Temple of Jerusalem, Priory of England and Wales, c/o Mr. John Reddington, 2 Alberta Gardens, Coggeshall, Coldchester, Essex CO6 1UA, ENGLAND, UK

Serials Department, 11717 Young Research Library, Univ. of California, Box 951575, Los Angeles CA 90095-1575, USA

Sourasky Library, Tel-Aviv Univ., Periodical Dept., P.O. Box 39038, Tel-Aviv, ISRAEL

Teutonic Order Bailiwick of Utrecht, Dr John J. Quarles van Ufford, Secretary of the Bailliwick, Springweg 25, 3511 VJ Utrecht, THE NETHERLANDS

Türk Tarih Kurumu [Turkish Historical Society], Kizilay Sokak No. 1, Sihhiye 06100 Ankara, TURKEY

Eberhard-Karls-Universität Tübingen, Orientalisches Seminar, Münzgasse 30, 72072 Tübingen, GERMANY

University of California Los Angeles Serials Dept. / YRL, 11717 Young Research Library, Box 951575, Los Angeles CA 90095-1575, USA

University of London Library, Periodicals Section, Senate House, Malet Street, London WC1E 7HU, ENGLAND, UK

University of North Carolina, Davis Library CB 3938, Periodicals and Serials Dept., Chapel Hill NC 27514-8890, USA

Universitätsbibliothek Tübingen, Wilhelmstraße 32, Postfach 26 20, 72016 Tübingen, GERMANY

University of Reading, Graduate Centre for Medieval Studies, Whiteknights, P.O. Box 218, Reading, Berks. RG6 6AA, ENGLAND, UK

University of Washington, Libraries, Serials Division, P.O. Box 352900, Seattle WA 98195, USA

University of Western Ontario Library, Acquisitions Dept., Room M1, D. B. Weldon Library, London, Ontario N6A 3K7, CANADA

The Warburg Institute, Univ. of London, Woburn Square, London WC1H 0AB, ENGLAND, UK [John PERKINS, Deputy Librarian, jperkins@a1.sas.ac.uk]

W. F. Albright Institute of Archaeological Research, 26 Salah ed-Din Street, P.O. Box 19096, Jerusalem 91190, ISRAEL.

Guidelines for the Submission of Papers

The editors ask contributors to adhere to the following guidelines. Failure to do so will result in the article being returned to the author for amendment, or may result in its having to be excluded from the volume.

1. Submissions. Submissions should be made on 3.5 inch, high-density IBM compatible disks or on CDs and in two typescripts, double-spaced with wide margins. Please send these to one of the editors. Remember to include your name and address on your paper.

2. Peer Review. All submissions will be peer reviewed. They will be scrutinized by the editors and sent to at least one outside reader before a decision on acceptance is made.

3. Length. Normally, the maximum length of articles should not exceed 6,000 words, not including notes. The editors reserve the right to edit papers that exceed these limits.

4. Notes. Normally, notes should be REFERENCE ONLY and placed at the end of the paper. Number continuously.

5. Style sheet. Please use the most recent *Speculum* style sheet (currently *Speculum* 75 (2000), 547–52). This sets out the format to be used for notes. Please note that this is not necessarily the same format as has been used by other edited volumes on the crusades and/or the Military Orders. Failure to follow the Speculum format will result in accepted articles being returned to the author for amendment. In the main body of the paper you may adhere to either British or American spelling, but it must be consistent throughout the article.

6. Language. Papers will be published in English, French, German, Italian and Spanish.

7. Abbreviations. Please use the abbreviation list on pp. ix–xi of this journal.

8. Diagrams and Maps should be referred to as figures and photographs as plates. Please keep illustrations to the essential minimum, since it will be possible to include only a limited number. All illustrations must be supplied by the contributor in camera-ready copy, and free from all copyright restrictions.

9. Italics. Words to be printed in italics should be italicised if possible. Failing this they should be underlined.

10. Capitals. Please take every care to ensure consistency in your use of capitals and lower case letters. Use initial capitals to distinguish the general from the specific (for example, "the count of Flanders" but "Count Philip of Flanders").

11. Summary of Article. Contributors will be required to provide a 250 word summary of their paper at the start of each article. This will be accompanied by the author's email address. The summary of the paper is to be in English, regardless of the language of the main article.

Editors

Professor Benjamin Z. Kedar
The Institute for Advanced Studies
The Hebrew University of Jerusalem
Jerusalem 91904, Israel
bzkedar@mscc.huji.ac.il

Professor Jonathan Phillips
History Department
Royal Holloway, University of London
Egham
Surrey TW20 0EX
England, U.K.
J.P.Phillips@rhul.ac.uk

SOCIETY FOR THE STUDY OF THE CRUSADES AND THE LATIN EAST MEMBERSHIP INFORMATION

The primary function of the Society for the Study of the Crusades and the Latin East is to enable members to learn about current work being done in the field of crusading history, and to contact members who share research interests through the information in the Society's Bulletin. There are currently 467 members of the SSCLE from 41 countries. The Society also organizes a major international conference every four years, as well as sections on crusading history at other conferences where appropriate.

The committee of the SSCLE consists of:
Prof. Bernard Hamilton, *President*
Prof. Jean Richard, Prof. Jonathan Riley-Smith, Prof. Benjamin Z. Kedar and Prof. Michel Balard, *Honorary Vice-presidents*
Prof. Luis García-Guijarro Ramos, *Secretary*
Dr Adrian Boas and Prof. Manuel Rojas, *Assistant Secretaries*
Prof. James D. Ryan, *Treasurer*
Prof. François-Olivier Touati, *Bulletin Editor*
Dr Zsolt Hunyadi, *Website*

Current subscription fees are as follows:
- Membership and Bulletin of the Society: Single £10, $20 or €15;
- Student £6, $12 or €9;
- Joint membership £15, $30 or €21;
- Membership and the journal *Crusades*, including the Bulletin: £25, $46 or €32.